Lecture Notes in Computer Science 16937

The series Lecture Notes in Computer Science (LNCS), including its subseries Lecture Notes in Artificial Intelligence (LNAI) and Lecture Notes in Bioinformatics (LNBI), has established itself as a medium for the publication of new developments in computer science and information technology research, teaching, and education.

LNCS enjoys close cooperation with the computer science R & D community, the series counts many renowned academics among its volume editors and paper authors, and collaborates with prestigious societies. Its mission is to serve this international community by providing an invaluable service, mainly focused on the publication of conference and workshop proceedings and postproceedings. LNCS commenced publication in 1973.

Genoveva Vargas-Solar · Kostas Stefanidis ·
Themis Palpanas · Patrick Marcel ·
Mirian Halfeld-Ferrari
Editors

Advances in Databases and Information Systems

30th European Conference, ADBIS 2026
Orléans, France, September 28 – October 1, 2026
Proceedings

Springer

Editors
Genoveva Vargas-Solar
CNRS
Cedex, France

Kostas Stefanidis
Tampere University
Tampere, Finland

Themis Palpanas
Université Paris Cité
Paris, France

Patrick Marcel
Université d'Orléans
Cedex, France

Mirian Halfeld-Ferrari
Université d'Orléans
Cedex, France

ISSN 0302-9743 ISSN 1611-3349 (electronic)
Lecture Notes in Computer Science
ISBN 978-3-032-39819-2 ISBN 978-3-032-39820-8 (eBook)
https://doi.org/10.1007/978-3-032-39820-8

This Springer imprint is published by the registered company Springer Nature Switzerland AG
The registered company address is: Gewerbestrasse 11, 6330 Cham, Switzerland

Preface

This LNCS volume contains the main-track papers presented at the 30th European Conference on Advances in Databases and Information Systems (ADBIS 2026), held in Orléans, France, from September 28 to October 1, 2026. Continuing a long-standing tradition, the conference brought together researchers, practitioners, and students to present high-quality results, discuss emerging challenges, and foster exchange across the foundations, technologies, and applications of data management and information systems.

The first ADBIS conference was held in Saint Petersburg, Russia, in 1997. Since then, ADBIS has been organized annually across Europe, most recently in Tampere, Finland (2025); Bayonne, France (2024); Barcelona, Spain (2023); Turin, Italy (2022); Tartu, Estonia (2021); Lyon, France (2020); and Bled, Slovenia (2019). Earlier editions took place in Budapest, Hungary (2018); Nicosia, Cyprus (2017); Prague, Czech Republic (2016); Poitiers, France (2015); Ohrid, North Macedonia (2014); Genoa, Italy (2013); Poznań, Poland (2012); Vienna, Austria (2011); Novi Sad, Serbia (2010); Riga, Latvia (2009); Pori, Finland (2008); Varna, Bulgaria (2007); Thessaloniki, Greece (2006); Tallinn, Estonia (2005); Budapest, Hungary (2004); Dresden, Germany (2003); Bratislava, Slovakia (2002); Vilnius, Lithuania (2001); Prague, Czech Republic (2000); Maribor, Slovenia (1999); and Poznań, Poland (1998). The official ADBIS portal, http://adbis.eu, provides information on the conference series, its publications, and the wider community.

The program of ADBIS 2026 included keynote talks, research papers, tutorials, demos, workshops, a doctoral consortium school (DCS), as well as a diversity, equity, and inclusion (DEI) panel and keynote.

The proceedings of ADBIS 2026 are the outcome of a rigorous review and selection process. The conference received 80 research submissions, of which 22 were accepted as full papers for presentation and publication in this Springer LNCS volume, corresponding to an acceptance rate of 27.5%. Each submission was carefully evaluated by members of the Program Committee and additional reviewers, with at least three single-anonymous reviews informing the discussion and final decision. The broader technical program also included 18 short papers and 5 demonstration papers, published in the companion volume in Springer's Communications in Computer and Information Science (CCIS) series.

The selected papers span a broad spectrum of topics in data management and information systems. To provide a coherent presentation, they were organized into eight thematic sessions: (1) Core database systems and serialization; (2) Similarity, topic modeling, and knowledge graphs; (3) Knowledge graphs, text-to-SQL, and metadata extraction; (4) Data cleaning, semantic discovery, and AutoML; (5) Sustainability, privacy workflows, and clinical analytics; (6) Similarity search, truth discovery, and anomaly detection; (7) Text analysis, graph neural networks, privacy, and Ethereum analytics; and (8) Integration, auditing, diversification, and embeddings. Together, these sessions illustrate both the depth of foundational database research and the growing reach of data-management methods across scientific, industrial, and societal domains.

Following a successful ADBIS tradition, the authors of the best research papers presented at ADBIS 2026 will be invited to submit substantially extended and revised versions to a special issue of Elsevier's Information Systems. Invitations will be issued to top-ranked conference contributions, whose authors will be expected to add new results, deeper evaluations, and significant new material. All invited manuscripts will undergo an independent journal peer-review cycle, and the final set of accepted articles will be determined through that subsequent review process. The Program Committee Chairs gratefully acknowledge the Editors-in-Chief of Information Systems for endorsing and approving this initiative.

Beyond the peer-reviewed contributions, ADBIS 2026 offered an engaging program of keynote talks, tutorials, demonstrations, workshops, and a doctoral consortium school. Four keynote speakers addressed timely scientific and societal directions for the data-management community:

- **Zoi Kaoudi (IT University of Copenhagen, Denmark)** delivered the keynote "Query Optimization in the Wild: From Cross-Platform Data Systems to Multi-Agent Systems." Her talk examined the evolving role of query optimization, from cost-based optimization in cross-platform data systems to emerging generate-and-explore approaches and the challenges of multi-agent systems.
- **Wolfgang Lehner (TU Dresden, Germany)** delivered the keynote "Reproducible Query Optimization Research for Data Systems." His talk explored the challenges of evaluating and comparing query optimization techniques and outlined perspectives for reproducible optimizer research.
- **Maria-Esther Vidal (Leibniz University Hannover and TIB – Leibniz Information Centre for Science and Technology, Germany)** delivered the keynote "From Normal Forms to Knowledge Graph Ecosystems: Foundations for Trustworthy AI." Her talk connected systematic data and knowledge modeling with trustworthy AI, emphasizing knowledge-graph ecosystems, data quality, and biomedical and clinical applications.
- **Tiziana Catarci (Institute of Cognitive Sciences and Technologies, National Research Council, Italy)** delivered the keynote "Gender Gap in ICT: From Missing Women to Missing Data." This DEI keynote addressed gender gaps and stereotypes in ICT, bias in AI systems, and the need to make inclusion technically visible through data modeling, quality, integration, provenance, privacy, fairness, analytics, and information-systems design.

Five tutorials offered in-depth engagement with emerging methods, tools, and application domains:

- "***Deep Learning for Time Series Classification and Regression with aeon***", presented by Ali Ismail-Fawaz and Maxime Devanne (Université de Haute-Alsace, France), Antoine Guillaume (Novahé, France), Anthony Bagnall (University of Southampton, UK), and Germain Forestier (Université de Haute-Alsace, France, and Monash University, Australia).

- "***Navigating the Vector Search Landscape: ANN Indexes for Modern AI Systems***", presented by Ilias Azizi and Themis Palpanas (Université Paris Cité, France) and Vassilis Christophides (ETIS, CNRS, ENSEA, France).
- "***Towards Optimized Big Satellite Data Management in Agricultural Monitoring through Causal-Based xAI: A Tutorial from the EDEM***", presented by Michele Linardi (CYU, ENSEA, CNRS, Cergy, France) and Claudia Paris (University of Twente, The Netherlands).
- "***Digital Tourism - From Tripadvisor Circulation Graphs to Behavior Extraction and Characterization***", presented by Nicolas Travers (De Vinci Research Center, France).
- "***A Survey on Multisided Fairness in Recommender Systems***", presented by Reza Shafiloo, Maria Stratigi, and Kostas Stefanidis (Tampere University, Finland).

ADBIS 2026 also hosted four affiliated workshops:

- 8th Workshop on Modern Approaches in Data Engineering and Information System Design (MADEISD),
- 2nd International Workshop on Entity Resolution and Graph Alignment (ERGA),
- 2nd International Workshop on Fairness Exploration in Heterogeneous Data and Algorithms (FEHDA), and
- Diversity, Equity and Inclusion for Teaching Advanced Databases and Information Systems workshop (DEI4Teach).

All four workshops addressed cutting-edge topics that call for extensive research from both a foundational and an application perspective to progress the state of the art. Overall, MADEISD, ERGA, and FEHDA received 23 submissions, of which 12 were selected for presentation and publication. The acceptance rate for each workshop did not exceed 50%. DEI4Teach contributed one paper summarizing the main topics discussed in the workshop. The accepted workshop papers appear in the companion CCIS proceedings volume.

The conference participated in the Database Diversity, Equity and Inclusion initiative, encouraging authors and participants to adopt DEI-aware communication practices in papers and presentations. In addition to the dedicated keynote by Tiziana Catarci, the DEI4Teach workshop was organized as an interactive World Café. The workshop fostered collaborative reflection and the exchange of experiences on integrating diversity, equity, and inclusion into the teaching of advanced database and information systems topics. A dedicated plenary session later presented the principal insights, shared vision, and recommendations emerging from the workshop discussions. These activities reaffirmed the conference's commitment to a more inclusive, equitable, and representative research community.

We warmly thank everyone whose dedication made ADBIS 2026 possible:

- the authors, whose research and commitment formed the foundation of the conference;
- the keynote speakers and tutorial presenters for sharing their expertise and perspectives;
- the members of the Program Committee and the external reviewers for their careful evaluations, constructive comments, and thoughtful discussions;
- the members of the ADBIS Steering Committee for their trust, guidance, and support;

- the workshop, tutorial, demonstration, doctoral consortium school, DEI, sponsorship, and organizing teams for developing the scientific program and attending to the many practical details of the event;
- the CMT staff for supporting submission, reviewing, discussion, and final-material collection; and
- the Springer staff for enabling publication of the ADBIS 2026 proceedings in the LNCS and CCIS series.

We are also grateful to the sponsors of ADBIS 2026: ACM, Région Centre Val de Loire, Université d'Orléans, UFR Sciences et Techniques, Springer, ICVL (Fédération Informatique Val de Loire), Technopole Orléans, Mairie d'Orléans, and LIFO (Laboratoire d'Informatique Fondamentale d'Orléans). Their support contributed substantially to the success of the conference.

We hope that these proceedings will serve both as a valuable record of the research presented at ADBIS 2026 and as a source of inspiration for future work in data management, information systems, and their evolving applications.

September 2026

Genoveva Vargas-Solar
Kostas Stefanidis
Themis Palpanas
Patrick Marcel
Mirian Halfeld-Ferrari

Organization

General Chairs

Patrick Marcel	Université d'Orléans, France
Mirian Halfeld-Ferrari	Université d'Orléans, France

Program Chairs

Genoveva Vargas Solar	CNRS, France
Kostas Stefanidis	Tampere University, Finland
Themis Palpanas	Université Paris Cité, France

Workshop Chairs

Panos Vassiliadis	University of Ioannina, Greece
Tatjana Welzer	University of Maribor, Slovenia

Doctoral School Chairs

Enrico Gallinucci	University of Bologna, Italy
Verónika Peralta	Université de Tours, France

Tutorial Chairs

Matteo Francia	Università di Bologna, Italy
Nicolas Labroche	Université de Tours, France

Proceedings Chairs

Silvia Chiusano	Politecnico di Torino, Italy
Cristina Dutra de Aguiar	Universidade de São Paulo, Brazil

Test of Time Award Chairs

Yannis Manolopoulos	University of York, Europe Campus, Greece
Mirjana Ivanovic	University of Novi Sad, Serbia

Diversity and Inclusion Chairs

Barbara Catania	University of Genoa, Italy
Cécile Favre	Lumière University Lyon 2, France

Special Issues Chairs

Oscar Romero	Universitat Politècnica de Catalunya, Spain
Julien Aligon	Université Toulouse Capitole, France

Demonstration Chairs

Alexandre Chanson	Université de Tours, France
Madhulika Mohanty	Inria Saclay, France

Sponsorship Chairs

Francesca Bugiotti	CentraleSupélec, France
Johann Gamper	University of Bozen-Bolzano, Italy

Community Chair

Nicolas Travers	École Supérieure d'Ingénieurs Léonard de Vinci, France

Publicity Chairs

Lorena Etcheverry	Universidad de la República, Uruguay
Robert Wrembel	Poznań University of Technology, Poland
Carlos Ordoñez	University of Houston, USA
Ladjel Bellatreche	National Engineering School for Mechanics and Aerotechnics, France

Website Chairs

Nicolas Hiot	Université d'Orléans, France
Lingchen Wang	Université d'Orléans, France
Yousif Elias	Université d'Orléans, France

Research Track Program Committee

Alberto Abelló	Universitat Politècnica de Catalunya, Spain
Maribel Acosta	Technische Universität München, Germany
Cristina D. Aguiar	Universidade de São Paulo, Brazil
Rocio A Aldeco-Pérez	Universidad Nacional Autónoma de México, Mexico
Bernd Amann	Sorbonne University, CNRS, France
Witold Andrzejewski	Poznań University of Technology, Poland
Sylvio Barbon Junior	University of Trieste, Italy
Nelly Barret	INSA Lyon & LIRIS, France
Andreas Behrend	Technical University of Cologne, Germany
Ladjel Bellatreche	ISAE-ENSMA, France
Nadia Bennani	INSA Lyon, France
Fadila Bentayeb	Université Lumière Lyon 2, France
Sandro Bimonte	INRAE, France
Paweł Boiński	Poznań University of Technology, Poland
Drazen R. Brdjanin	University of Banja Luka, Bosnia and Herzegovina
Francesca Bugiotti	CentraleSupélec, France
Barbara Catania	University of Genoa, Italy
Mónica Caniupán	Universidad del Bío-Bío, Chile
Silvia Chiusano	Politecnico di Torino, Italy
Antonio Corral	University of Almería, Spain
Jerome Darmont	Université Lumière Lyon 2, France
Christos Doulkeridis	University of Piraeus, Greece
Stefania Dumbrava	ENSIIE INRIA IRIF, France
Johann Eder	Universität Klagenfurt, Austria
Markus Endres	Technische Universität München, Germany
Javier A. Espinosa-Oviedo	University of Lyon 1 Claude Bernard, France
Lorena Etcheverry	Universidad de la República, Uruguay
Georgios Evangelidis	University of Macedonia, Greece
Johann Gamper	Free University of Bozen-Bolzano, Italy
Mirian Halfeld-Ferrari	Université d'Orléans, France
Herodotos Herodotou	Cyprus University of Technology, Cyprus

Mirjana Ivanovic	University of Novi Sad, Serbia
Alexandros Karakasidis	University of Macedonia, Greece
Eleftheria Katsiri	Democritus University of Thrace, Greece
Zoubida Kedad	University of Versailles Saint-Quentin-en-Yvelines, France
Georgia Koloniari	University of Macedonia, Greece
Yannis Manolopoulos	University of York, Europe Campus, Greece
Maude Manouvrier	Université Paris Dauphine-PSL, France
Patrick Marcel	Université d'Orléans, France
Jose-Norberto Mazon	Universidad de Alicante, Spain
Maria Medina	Universidad Politécnica de Puebla, Mexico
Sara Migliorini	University of Verona, Italy
Alex Mircoli	Università Politecnica delle Marche, Italy
Simona Nisticò	University of Calabria, Italy
Boris Novikov	Unaffiliated, Finland
George Pallis	University of Cyprus, Cyprus
George Papastefanatos	Athena Research Center, Greece
Veronika Peralta	University of Tours, France
Edelmira Pasarella	Universitat Politècnica de Catalunya, Spain
Giuseppe Polese	University of Salerno, Italy
Anna Queralt	Universitat Politècnica de Catalunya, Spain
Elisa Quintarelli	Università degli Studi di Verona, Italy
Franck Ravat	Institut de Recherche en Informatique de Toulouse, France
Sonja Ristić	University of Novi Sad, Serbia
Gunter Saake	University of Magdeburg, Germany
Ingo Schmitt	Brandenburg University of Technology, Germany
Sana Sellami	Université d'Aix-Marseille, France
Sergey A. Stupnikov	Russian Academy of Sciences, Russia
Panos Vassiliadis	University of Ioannina, Greece
Yannis Velegrakis	Utrecht University, Netherlands
Goran Velinov	Ss. Cyril and Methodius University in Skopje, North Macedonia
Maria-Esther Vidal	Leibniz University of Hannover and TIB-Leibniz Information Centre for Science and Technology, Germany
Szymon Wilk	Poznań University of Technology, Poland
Robert Wrembel	Poznań University of Technology, Poland
Tetiana Yemelianenko	Université Lumière Lyon 2 CNRS LIRIS, France
Demetrios Zeinalipour-Yazti	University of Cyprus, Cyprus
Zheying Zhang	Tampere University, Finland
Ester Zumpano	University of Calabria, Italy

Demonstration Track Program Committee

Alberto Abelló	Universitat Politècnica de Catalunya, Spain
Julien Aligon	Université Toulouse Capitole, France
Nelly Barret	INSA Lyon & LIRIS, France
Drazen R. Brdjanin	University of Banja Luka, Bosnia and Herzegovina
Javier A. Espinosa-Oviedo	University of Lyon 1 Claude Bernard, France
Johann Gamper	Free University of Bozen-Bolzano, Italy
Moncef Garouani	Université Toulouse Capitole, France
Tomáš Horváth	Edinburgh Napier University, UK
Alexandros Karakasidis	University of Macedonia, Greece
Zoubida Kedad	University of Versailles, France
Maude Manouvrier	Université Paris Dauphine-PSL, France
Sara Migliorini	University of Verona, Italy
Boris Novikov	Unaffiliated, Finland
Sergey A. Stupnikov	Russian Academy of Sciences, Russia
Robert Wrembel	Poznań University of Technology, Poland

Steering Committee Chair

Yannis Manolopoulos	University of York, Europe Campus, Greece

Steering Committee

Andreas Behrend	TH Köln, Germany
Ladjel Bellatreche	ENSMA Poitiers, France
Maria Bielikova	Kempelen Institute of Intelligent Technologies, Slovakia
Barbara Catania	University of Genoa, Italy
Tania Cerquitelli	Politecnico di Torino, Italy
Richard Chbeir	IUT de Bayonne et du Pays Basque, France
Silvia Chiusano	Politecnico di Torino, Italy
Jérôme Darmont	Lumière University Lyon 2, France
Johann Eder	Alpen-Adria-Universität Klagenfurt, Austria
Johann Gamper	Free University of Bozen-Bolzano, Italy
Tomáš Horváth	Pavol Jozef Šafárik University, Slovakia
Mirjana Ivanović	University of Novi Sad, Serbia
Manuk Manukyan	Yerevan State University, Armenia

Kjetil Nørvåg	Norwegian University of Science and Technology, Norway
Boris Novikov	Unaffiliated, Finland
George Papadopoulos	University of Cyprus, Cyprus
Jaroslav Pokorny	Charles University in Prague, Czech Republic
Oscar Romero	Universitat Politècnica de Catalunya - BarcelonaTech, Spain
Kostas Stefanidis	Tampere University, Finland
Sergey Stupnikov	Russian Academy of Sciences, Russia
Bernhard Thalheim	Christian Albrechts University of Kiel, Germany
Goce Trajcevski	Iowa State University, USA
Valentino Vranić	Pan-European University, Slovakia
Tatjana Welzer	University of Maribor, Slovenia
Genoveva Vargas-Solar	CNRS, France
Robert Wrembel	Poznań University of Technology, Poland
Ester Zumpano	University of Calabria, Italy

Contents

Data Cleaning, Semantic Discovery and AutoML

Text, GNNs, Privacy and Ethereum Analytics

Keynote Talks

From Normal Forms to Knowledge Graph Ecosystems: Foundations for Trustworthy AI

Maria-Esther Vidal[1,2,3](✉), Yashrajsinh Chudasama[1,2], Enrique Iglesias[2,3], and Disha Purohit[2,3]

[1] TIB-Leibniz Information Centre for Science and Technology, Hannover, Germany
[2] Leibniz University Hannover, Hannover, Germany
[3] L3S Research Center Germany, Hannover, Germany
vidal@l3s.de

Abstract. Knowledge Graph Ecosystems (KGEs) integrate heterogeneous data to support reasoning, analytics, and artificial intelligence. Structural anomalies introduced during KG creation or in the materialized graph negatively affect construction efficiency, graph quality, and downstream learning tasks. This paper presents a unified view of normalization as a quality-management mechanism spanning the KGE life cycle. We integrate normalization theories for Data Integration Systems (DISs) and Knowledge Graphs (KGs), showing how they eliminate structural anomalies before and after KG creation while preserving semantic equivalence. Experimental results show that DIS normalization reduces the computational cost of KG creation, whereas KG normalization produces structurally cleaner graphs that consistently improve the predictive performance of KG Embedding models. These findings establish normalization as a fundamental design principle for scalable KGEs.

1 Introduction

KGs have become a fundamental data structures for integrating heterogeneous data and supporting reasoning, analytics, and AI in domains such as science, medicine, and industry. In practice, however, KGs are not developed in isolation. They are created, validated, enriched, queried, and continuously evolved within KGEs, which comprise heterogeneous data sources, ontologies, mappings, constraints, and the processes required to manage them throughout their life cycle. Consequently, structural deficiencies introduced in one component may propagate across the ecosystem, affecting both the efficiency of KG creation and the quality of downstream analytical tasks.

The main problem addressed in this paper is that existing normalization approaches consider DISs and KGs independently, despite the fact that both constitute complementary components of the same KGE. As a consequence, there is currently no unified understanding of normalization as a quality-management mechanism spanning the KGE life cycle.

G. Vargas-Solar et al. (Eds.): ADBIS 2026, LNCS 16937, pp. 3–12, 2027.
https://doi.org/10.1007/978-3-032-39820-8_1

The main idea of this paper is to view normalization as a cross-cutting mechanism that operates at two complementary stages of the KGE life cycle. Before KG materialization, DIS normalization restructures data sources and mapping assertions to eliminate redundancy and costly joins while preserving the generated KG. After materialization, KG normalization restructures the graph itself to eliminate representational and semantic anomalies, producing structurally consistent graphs that better support querying, reasoning, and machine learning.

The main contributions (Cs) of this paper are: **(C1)** We present a unified perspective that positions DIS normalization and KG normalization within the life cycle of KGEs. **(C2)** We characterize the structural anomalies addressed by each normalization theory and explain their complementary roles in improving ecosystem quality. **(C3)** We empirically evaluate both normalization theories. The results show that DIS normalization significantly improves the efficiency of KG creation by reducing execution time and memory consumption, while KG normalization consistently improves the structural quality of KGs and the predictive performance of Knowledge Graph Embedding models.

2 Preliminaries

Knowledge Graph Ecosystems. A KGE comprises the resources and processes required to create, maintain, and exploit a Knowledge Graph (KG) throughout its life cycle [5]. Formally, a KGE is represented as $\mathcal{E} = (D, O, M, C, G, L)$, where D denotes heterogeneous data sources, O an ontology, M a set of mapping assertions, C integrity constraints, G the materialized KG, and L provenance and execution logs. A KGE evolves through a life-cycle $LC = (LCS, R)$ where LCS is a sequence of life-cycle steps and R is a precedence relation of the steps; each step transforms one or more ecosystem components. Among these steps, KG creation is central. It is defined by the data integration system $\mathcal{I}_{\mathcal{E}} = (O, D, M)$ [9], whose execution materializes the KG. Mappings are typically expressed in declarative languages such as R2RML or RML [3]. They associate logical sources with RDF subjects and predicate-object maps that generate entities, attributes, and relationships. Multi-source mappings require join conditions, whose number largely determines the complexity of KG creation. Let $R(A_1, \ldots, A_n)$ denote the schema of a relational source. A functional dependency $X \rightarrow Y$ holds whenever two tuples that agree on X also agree on Y. Functional dependencies constitute the basis for the normalization of data integration systems.

Knowledge Graphs. A KG is a $G = (V, E, P)$, where V is a set of entities, P a set of predicates, and $E \subseteq V \times P \times V$ a set of RDF triples. In this paper, graph size and connectivity are characterized using the numbers of entities, predicates, and triples, together with the average in-degree and out-degree of graph nodes.

Normalization. Normalization is a semantics-preserving transformation that eliminates structural anomalies while preserving the represented knowledge. This paper considers two complementary normalization theories. Data Integration System normalization restructures data sources and mapping assertions before KG materialization, whereas Knowledge Graph normalization restructures the materialized graph through progressively stronger graph normal forms.

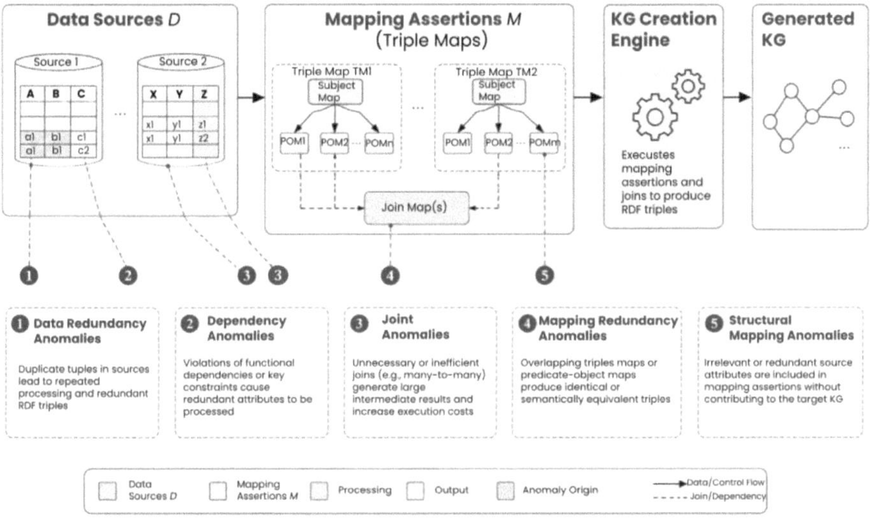

Fig. 1. Structural anomalies addressed by DIS normalization. Data redundancy, join, mapping redundancy, dependency, and structural mapping anomalies increase the complexity of KG creation. DIS normalization eliminates these anomalies through schema decomposition and mapping restructuring.

3 Normalization as a Life-Cycle Mechanism in KGEs

3.1 Normalization of Data Integration Systems

Normalization of Data Integration Systems (DISs) extends the principles of relational normalization to the declarative components involved in KG creation. Rather than considering only relational schemas, it jointly analyzes the data sources and the mapping assertions defining the transformation into RDF, yielding a semantics-preserving transformation of the complete data integration system $\mathcal{I}_{\mathcal{E}} = (O, D, M)$ [7]. Guided by the functional dependencies defined over the source schemas, DIS normalization eliminates the structural anomalies illustrated in Fig. 1. Data redundancy anomalies arise from duplicate tuples and redundant attributes that increase storage and processing costs during KG materialization. Join anomalies originate from unnecessary joins between logical sources, producing expensive intermediate results and increasing execution time and memory consumption. Mapping redundancy anomalies correspond to overlapping triples maps or predicate-object maps that generate identical or semantically equivalent RDF triples. Dependency anomalies occur when mapping assertions include attributes that are functionally determined by others, whereas structural mapping anomalies arise from source attributes that do not contribute to the generation of entities, properties, or relationships. Together, these anomalies unnecessarily increase the computational complexity of KG creation without affecting the semantics of the generated KG [7]. The normalization process decomposes source relations into higher normal forms while preserving functional dependencies and guaranteeing lossless reconstruction. The corresponding mapping assertions are automatically rewritten over the normalized sources, removing redundant mapping constructs, unnecessary joins, and non-essential source attributes while generating exactly the same KG as the original DIS [7]. Formally, let $\mathcal{I}_{\mathcal{E}} = (O, D, M)$ be a data integration system and let $\mathcal{I}'_{\mathcal{E}} = (O, D', M')$ denote its normalized counterpart. DIS normalization guarantees: **i) Semantic preservation:** both systems generate the same KG; **ii) Dependency preservation:** functional dependencies remain valid after decomposition; **iii) Lossless decomposition:** normalized relations preserve all information contained in the original sources; and **iv) Reduced structural complexity:** redundant attributes, joins, and mapping constructs are eliminated. Previous experimental studies demonstrated that these transformations substantially reduce execution time, memory consumption, and the overall computational cost of KG creation while preserving semantic [7].

3.2 Normalization of Knowledge Graphs

Whereas DIS normalization restructures the declarative components before KG materialization, KG normalization operates directly on the generated graph. Its objective is to eliminate representational and semantic anomalies while preserving the intended meaning of the represented knowledge. KG normalization is founded on a hierarchy of four KG NFs (KG-NFs) proposed by Purohit et al. [11], each eliminating one of the anomaly classes illustrated in Fig. 2. Missing grounding anomalies occur when entities are represented as anonymous resources rather than globally identifiable IRIs, preventing explicit identification and graph integration. Relation ambiguity anomalies arise when predicates are overloaded with multiple semantic interpretations or incompatible domains and ranges, reducing semantic precision. Type inconsistency anomalies correspond to violations of domain, range, or cardinality constraints, whereas constraint violation anomalies represent facts that contradict the integrity constraints defined by the ontology or shape schema. These anomalies reduce graph quality and negatively affect querying, reasoning, graph analytics, and downstream machine learning [11]. The four KG normal forms progressively eliminate these anomalies. The first NF (1KG-NF) replaces anonymous resources with explicit identifiers. The second NF (2KG-NF) assigns unique semantic interpretations to predicates with well-defined domains and ranges. The third NF (3KG-NF) enforces structurally consistent typing and property assignments, eliminating inconsistencies arising from conflicting domain, range, or cardinality constraints. Finally, the fourth NF (4KG-NF) validates every asserted fact against the integrity constraints defined by the ontology or shape schema, ensuring semantic consistency [11]. Normalization is performed through semantics-preserving graph transformation rules that rewrite the graph into an equivalent representation satisfying progressively stronger structural and semantic constraints while preserving entity identities, information content, and logical entailments. Formally, let $G = (V, E, P)$ be a KG and let G' denote its normalized representation. KG normalization guarantees: **i) Semantic equivalence:** both graphs represent the same domain knowledge; **ii) Information preservation:** no valid facts are lost during normalization; **iii) Constraint satisfaction:** normalized graphs satisfy the corresponding KG normal forms; and **iv) Improved structural quality:** representational ambiguity and semantic inconsistencies are eliminated. As demonstrated in [11], enforcing the four KG normal forms produces structurally cleaner graphs that facilitate querying, reasoning, graph analytics, and machine learning while preserving the represented knowledge.

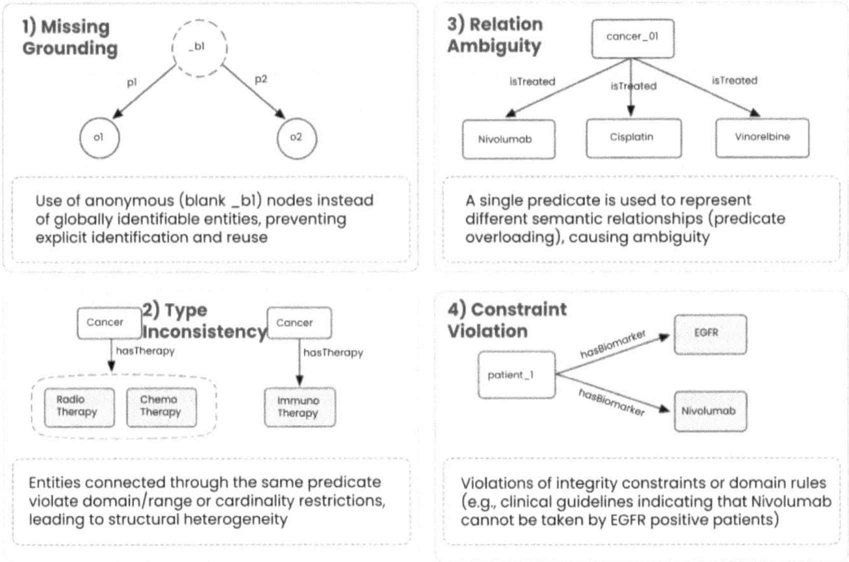

Fig. 2. Structural anomalies addressed by KG normalization. The four KG Normal Forms progressively eliminate missing grounding, relation ambiguity, type inconsistency, and constraint violation anomalies while preserving the semantics.

3.3 A Unified View of Normalization Across the KGE Life Cycle

Although DIS normalization and KG normalization were proposed independently, they address complementary stages of the same Knowledge Graph Ecosystem life cycle. DIS normalization operates before KG materialization by restructuring data sources and mapping assertions, thereby preventing structural anomalies from propagating into the generated graph. KG normalization subsequently restructures the materialized KG by eliminating the remaining representational and semantic anomalies that affect its quality and usability. Together, these complementary normalization theories establish a continuous quality-management mechanism spanning multiple life-cycle steps. DIS normalization improves the efficiency and scalability of KG creation [7], whereas KG normalization improves the structural quality and semantic consistency of the generated graph [11]. This unified perspective extends normalization beyond its traditional role as a preprocessing technique and positions it as a fundamental design principle for building scalable, maintainable, and trustworthy KGEs.

4 Experimental Evaluation

4.1 Experimental Setup

The experimental evaluation assesses normalization at two stages of the KGE life cycle: (i) DIS normalization during KG creation and (ii) KG normalization after materialization. The first study evaluates the impact of DIS normalization on the structural complexity and execution efficiency of KG creation, whereas the second study evaluates the impact of KG normalization on graph quality and downstream link prediction. For DIS normalization, we use the KROWN benchmark [14]. The evaluated DIS comprises one synthetic relational source containing 10 million tuples with 20 attributes, together with two triples maps, two concept mapping assertions, twenty attribute mapping assertions, and five multi-source role mapping assertions. The original and normalized DISs are compared in terms of structural complexity, execution time, and peak memory consumption during KG materialization. For KG normalization, we use three benchmark KGs: YAGO3-10 [10], DB100K [4], and French Royalty [6]. Original and normalized KGs are evaluated using TransE [2], TransH [16], TransD [8], RotatE [12], ComplEx [13], TuckER [1], and CompGCN [15]. Predictive performance is measured using Hits@1, Hits@3, Hits@5, Hits@10, and MRR.

4.2 Impact on Data Sources and Mapping Assertions

Figure 3 summarizes the structural changes introduced by the normalization of the Data Integration System and their impact on the efficiency of KG creation. The normalization process decomposes the original denormalized data source into sixteen normalized relations according to the functional dependencies identified in the source schema (Fig. 3b). Although the number of data sources increases, each relation becomes substantially smaller, reducing the average number of records from 10 million to approximately 71 thousand. The largest relation contains only 670 thousand records, while the smallest contains 10 thousand records. This decomposition removes data redundancy while preserving all information required for KG materialization. The mapping specification is automatically restructured to reflect the normalized schema (Fig. 3a). Consequently, the number of triples maps increases from two to sixteen, while all join mappings are eliminated. Attribute mapping assertions remain unchanged, whereas the number of relationship mapping assertions increases slightly to preserve the semantics of the generated KG. Despite the larger number of mapping assertions, the resulting specification is structurally simpler because it no longer requires costly join operations. These structural changes directly improve the efficiency of KG creation. As illustrated in Fig. 3c, all evaluated KG creation engines exhibit lower execution times and reduced peak memory consumption after normalization. The elimination of join mappings and the reduction of data redundancy decrease the computational effort required during materialization while generating a KG that is semantically equivalent to that produced by the original DIS.

Property	Orig.	Norm.
#DataSources	1	16
#TripleMaps	2	16
#JoinMaps	5	0
#POM-Attrib	10	10
#POM-Rel	10	15

(a) DIS properties.

Property	Orig.	Norm.
Avg. records	10M	71K
Max. records	10M	670K
Min. records	10M	10K

(b) Data sources

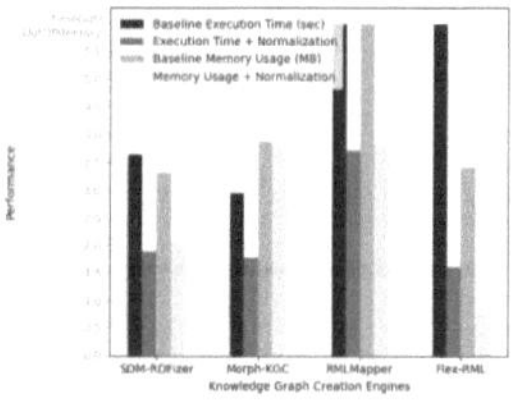

(c) Execution time and peak memory.

Fig. 3. DIS normalization on KG creation. (a) Structural changes introduced by normalization in the mapping specification. (b) Structural characteristics of the normalized data sources after schema decomposition. (c) Execution time and memory consumption of KG creation engines before and after normalization. Normalization eliminates join mappings, reduces data redundancy, and substantially improves the efficiency of engines while preserving semantics of generated KG.

4.3 Impact on Knowledge Graph Structure and Link Prediction

Table 1 summarizes the structural changes produced by KG normalization across the three benchmark knowledge graphs. Normalization consistently increases the number of triples and predicates by replacing ambiguous or overloaded relationships with semantically explicit representations and by materializing additional structural information required to satisfy the proposed normal forms. Consequently, the normalized KGs exhibit more balanced connectivity, reflected

Table 1. Structural statistics of the original and normalized benchmark knowledge graphs. The table investigates and compare the in-degree and out-degree of original and normalized KGs across a range of benchmarks.

Category	Benchmark	Configuration	#Triples	#Predicates	Avg. In-degree	Avg. Out-degree
Real-world KGs	French Royalty	Original	12265	13	10659	4744
		Normalized	15850	5309	15850	5309
	YAGO3-10	Original	1202021	38	420953	86018
		Normalized	1347063	92979	1346913	93020
	DB100K	Original	787933	471	439682	147325
		Normalized	876181	1610	516792	169334

by higher average in-degree and out-degree values across all benchmarks. These changes indicate that normalization produces structurally more consistent graph representations while preserving the intended semantics of the original knowledge.

Fig. 4 evaluates the impact of these structural changes on downstream numerical inductive learning. Across all benchmarks, the normalized KGs consis-

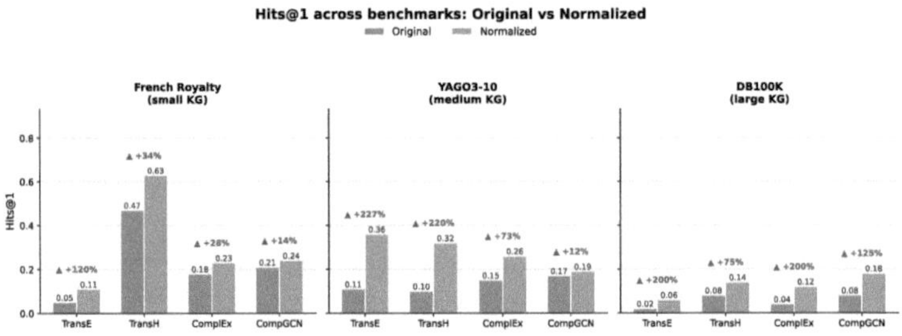

(a) Hits@1 analysis for KGE models (Original vs. Normalized), for the real-world KGs. The percentage change for each model is also included.

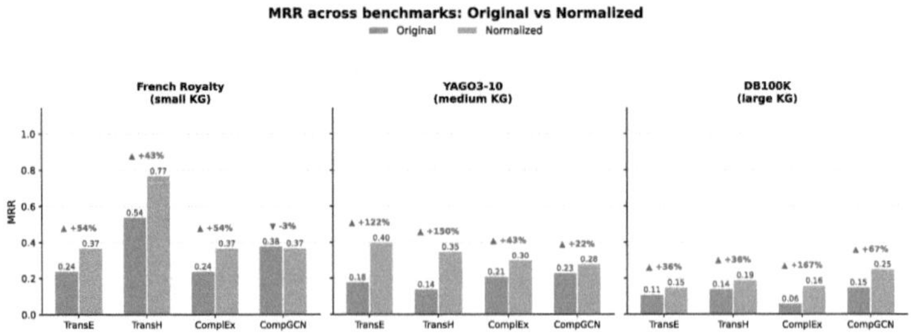

(b) MRR analysis for KGE models (Original vs. Normalized), for the real-world KGs. The percentage change for each model is also included.

Fig. 4. Impact of KG Normalization on Numerical Inductive Learning. The plot illustrates the performance via Hits@1 and MRR comparison for four KGE models under Original vs. Normalized KG across all benchmarks; Normalization improves both metrics, most pronounced on YAGO3-10.

tently outperform their original counterparts in terms of Hits@1 and MRR. The largest improvements are observed for YAGO3-10, whose original graph contains a substantial number of ambiguous and structurally inconsistent relationships that are eliminated during normalization. Similar, albeit smaller, improvements are obtained for the French Royalty and DB100K benchmarks. The observed improvements are consistent across all evaluated Knowledge Graph Embedding models, demonstrating that the benefits of normalization are largely independent of the underlying embedding architecture. By replacing ambiguous graph structures with semantically explicit representations, KG normalization provides cleaner learning signals that facilitate the optimization of embedding models and improve their ability to predict missing links. Overall, these results indicate that KG normalization not only improves the structural quality of knowledge graphs but also enhances the effectiveness of downstream machine learning tasks. This complements the results obtained for DIS normalization, where normalization improves the efficiency of KG creation, demonstrating that normalization acts as a quality-management mechanism throughout the KGE life cycle.

5 Conclusions and Future Directions

This paper presented a unified perspective on normalization as a quality-management mechanism. We showed that normalization operates at two complementary levels: DIS normalization improves the efficiency of KG creation by restructuring data sources and mapping assertions, whereas KG normalization improves the structural quality of the materialized graph by eliminating representational and semantic anomalies. The experimental evaluation demonstrated that DIS normalization reduces execution time and memory consumption during KG creation, while KG normalization consistently improves the predictive performance of KG Embedding models. These results establish normalization as a fundamental design principle for building scalable, maintainable, and trustworthy KGEs.

Future work will investigate normalization techniques for additional KGE components, including ontologies, integrity constraints, and provenance metadata, as well as methods for automatically detecting and repairing structural anomalies throughout the ecosystem life cycle. We also plan to study the impact of normalization on emerging AI paradigms, including Retrieval-Augmented Generation, Knowledge-Augmented Generation, and neuro-symbolic systems.

References

1. Ivana Balazevic, Carl Allen, and Timothy M. Hospedales. Tucker: tensor factorization for knowledge graph completion. CoRR **abs/1901.09590** (2019)
2. Antoine Bordes, Nicolas Usunier, Alberto Garcia-Durán, Jason Weston, and Oksana Yakhnenko. Translating embeddings for modeling multi-relational data. NIPS'13, pp. 2787–2795, Red Hook, NY, USA. Curran Associates Inc (2013)

3. Anastasia Dimou, Miel Vander Sande, Pieter Colpaert, Ruben Verborgh, Erik Mannens, and Rik Van de Walle. RML: a generic language for integrated RDF mappings of heterogeneous data. In Christian Bizer, Tom Heath, Sören Auer, and Tim Berners-Lee, editors, Proceedings of the Workshop on Linked Data on the Web co-located with the 23rd International World Wide Web Conference (WWW 2014), Seoul, Korea, vol. 1184, 08 Apr 2014 , CEUR Workshop Proceedings. CEUR-WS.org (2014)
4. Boyang Ding, Quan Wang, Bin Wang, and Li Guo.: Improving knowledge graph embedding using simple constraints. CoRR, abs/1805.02408 (2018)
5. Geisler, S., et al.: From genesis to maturity: managing knowledge graph ecosystems through life cycles. Proc. VLDB Endow. **18**(5), 1390–1397 (2025)
6. Halliwell, N., Gandon, F., Lecue, F.: User Scored Evaluation of Non-Unique Explanations for Relational Graph Convolutional Network Link Prediction on Knowledge Graphs. ACM, In K-CAP (2021)
7. Iglesias, E., Chaves-Fraga, D., Auer, S., Vidal, M.-E.: Normalization-driven optimization of knowledge graph creation for semantically grounded information fusion. Inf. Fusion **134**, 104337 (2026)
8. Guoliang Ji, Shizhu He, Liheng Xu, Kang Liu, and Jun Zhao. Knowledge graph embedding via dynamic mapping matrix. In: Proceedings of the 53rd Annual Meeting of the Association for Computational Linguistics and the 7th International Joint Conference on Natural Language Processing, vol. 1, pp. 687–696 (2015)
9. Maurizio Lenzerini. Data integration: a theoretical perspective. In: ACM Symposium on Principles of Database Systems (2002)
10. Farzaneh Mahdisoltani, Joanna Biega, and Fabian M. Suchanek. YAGO3: A knowledge base from multilingual wikipedias. In: CIDR (2015)
11. Purohit, D., Chudasama, Y., Vidal, M.-E.: VANILLA: validated knowledge graph completion - a normalization-based framework for integrity, link prediction, and logical accuracy. Knowl. Based Syst. **325**, 113939 (2025)
12. Zhiqing Sun, Zhi-Hong Deng, Jian-Yun Nie, and Jian Tang. Rotate: Knowledge graph embedding by relational rotation in complex space. In: 7th International Conference on Learning Representations ICLR 2019, New Orleans, LA, USA. OpenReview.net (2019)
13. Théo Trouillon, Johannes Welbl, Sebastian Riedel, Éric Gaussier, and Guillaume Bouchard. Complex embeddings for simple link prediction. CoRR, abs/1606.06357 (2016)
14. Van Assche, D., Chaves-Fraga, D., Anastasia Dimou.: KROWN: a Benchmark for RDF Graph Materialization (2024)
15. Shikhar Vashishth, Soumya Sanyal, Vikram Nitin, and Partha P. Talukdar. Composition-based multi-relational graph convolutional networks. CoRR, abs/1911.03082 (2019)
16. Zhen Wang, Jianwen Zhang, Jianlin Feng, and Zheng Chen. Knowledge graph embedding by translating on hyperplanes. In: Proceedings of the AAAI Conference on Artificial Intelligence, **28**(1) (2014)

Reproducible Query Optimization Research for Data Systems

Wolfgang Lehner(✉)

Department of Computer Science, TUD Dresden University of Technology, 01062 Dresden, Germany
wolfgang.lehner@tu-dresden.de
https://lehner.db-tu-dresden.de/

Abstract. Query optimization remains an unsolved challenge in database research, driven by workload complexity, large data volumes, and an explosion in the design space of execution alternatives. Despite consensus on evaluation metrics such as q-error and throughput/latency measures, standardized, easy-to-use benchmarking remains scarce, limiting reproducibility and fair comparison. This extended abstract introduces PostBound, a lightweight modular framework for prototyping query optimization strategies, offering individual optimization hooks and fully composable optimization pipelines to (a) inspect existing system behavior in a semi-automated fashion and (b) rapidly prototype novel optimization schemes to be evaluated in an end-to-end scenario. The abstract outlines the overall motivation of optimizer research, the state of the current methodology, core concepts and goals of PostBound, and two use cases facilitated by PostBound.

Keywords: data systems · query optimization · repeatability

1 Query Optimization Research: Are We Polishing a Round Ball?

The discipline of query optimization, often referred to as a "black art", has its origins in the early phases of relational database research. One of the pioneering systems, Systems R, introduced almost 50 years ago, already featured fully functional query optimizer components. The foundational principles of query optimization were documented in a seminal paper by Pat Selinger and colleagues [13,14], devising core principles such as logical rewrite rules and the use of "magic numbers" to handle missing information on predicate selectivity–concepts that remain relevant in modern state-of-the-art database systems.

At first glance, the problem of query optimization might appear straightforward. It involves converting a descriptive specification of the desired result set into a tree-structured data flow graph, where base tables serve as leaf nodes, internal nodes represent physical operators, and the connections denote data

G. Vargas-Solar et al. (Eds.): ADBIS 2026, LNCS 16937, pp. 13–20, 2027.
https://doi.org/10.1007/978-3-032-39820-8_2

flow. This might seem like a simple problem, given the finite set of tables and physical operators to choose from.

However, as many researchers and practitioners are well aware, the real complexity of query optimization arises from the incomplete knowledge of data characteristics and subsequently the "hard-to-predict" nature of operations like grouping and filtering. These factors make it challenging to accurately estimate cardinalities as the main driver of query execution costs.

As a result, query optimization remains an active area of research, with a vibrant community continuously striving to advance the field [12]. While the goals of query optimization have evolved over timeshifting from finding the "optimal" plan to identifying a "good enough" plan that is robust against unanticipated data characteristics, the significance of query plan quality persists. A poorly chosen plan can lead to severe performance degradation and, in some cases, even prevent a query from executing successfully.

Main Drivers for Query Optimization Research

Two primary drivers motivate the need for query optimization methods in modern database systems. First, database engines are increasingly deployed as execution platforms that allow application logic to be pushed closer to the data, for example, by constructing large SQL statements composed of multiple interconnected SQL blocks, frequently using nested WITH clauses. Such queries may reference hundreds of tables and deploy hundreds of operators, resulting in highly complex query execution plans that are challenging to optimize.

Second, database engines extend well beyond managing simple table structures. Modern systems offer multi-model capabilities encompassing XML, JSON, graph, and vector extensions. In addition, the relational world expands to include more complex objects, such as multi-level partitioned tables, materialized views, and support for Open Table Format (OTF) standards like Apache Iceberg. The cumulative effect of this functional breadth and structural complexity is reflected in the scale of real-world deployments, where a single system may govern upwards of 100.000 distinct objects. Together, these factors underscore the necessity of efficient, effective, and especially robust query optimization strategies (Fig. 1).

Methodology in Query Optimization Research

Investigating the literature of the last few years, we can see many publications addressing sub-problems of plan enumeration, cardinality estimation (usually after joins), or, more generally, novel approaches to cost models [1,4–6,9–11]. This activity is partly driven by the rise of learned models targeting specific scenarios, most notably learned cardinality estimators. At the evaluation level, the community has informally converged on standardized quality metrics such as Q-error to assess the accuracy of proposed methods in an analytical context. Experimental evaluations predominantly rely on PostgreSQL as *the* standard execution platform. There are mainly two reasons for this procedure: PostgreSQL is widely used and thus a perfect place to demonstrate the comparability and

Fig. 1. Visualization of the complexity of an State-of-the-Art Query Plan

practical impact of a novel idea. It also provides an open source environment, which allows multiple options to extend and modify the behavior of individual components.

Despite this de facto consensus within the data management community, the approach exhibits significant limitations in practice. Research prototypes are typically developed as isolated implementations centered on a specific technique, with little focus on portability or reproducibility, for example, across version changes. Benchmark environments are similarly individualized: evaluations are commonly built around specific workloads—such as JOB, STATS, or TPC variants—without standardizing physical database design, system parameters, or runtime conditions such as buffer pool prewarming.

In summary, while the community has reached broad agreement on analytical quality metrics, experimental comparability remains constrained by the absence of a unified evaluation methodology. PostgreSQL seems to be a common ground; the surrounding evaluation procedures, however, are neither consistently fair nor reliably reproducible, resulting in substantial implementation overhead when developing and comparing novel query optimization schemes.

2 PostBound: A Framework for Query Optimization Research

PostBound [3] is a lightweight framework developed to address two central challenges in query optimization research: the efficient prototyping of novel optimization methods and the consistent, reproducible benchmarking of these methods. By abstracting routine aspects of query optimization—such as query parsing and join graph construction—PostBound enables researchers to concentrate on the core technical aspects of their work. The framework achieves this through flexible optimization hooks that enable seamless integration of custom modifications into the optimization process. Furthermore, PostBound includes a repository of predefined hooks and re-implementations of established optimization approaches, thereby supporting direct empirical comparisons within a unified experimental environment.

A central concept in PostBound is the definition of optimization pipelines, which are applied on a join graph of a query. These pipelines are designed to be extensible, allowing researchers to modify existing workflows or develop entirely new optimization strategies by implementing custom hooks. This modularity allows users to isolate and investigate specific subproblems—such as cardinality estimation or join ordering—while leveraging the broader infrastructure for experimental control. The user-controlled experimental workflow, which runs on top of existing system backends, ensures that the impact of novel optimization techniques can be rigorously evaluated in a reproducible, systematic manner.

To support robust and reproducible benchmarking, PostBound incorporates a comprehensive benchmark support suite. This suite governs system behavior by managing tasks such as query preparation and cache prewarming, and provides tooling for a range of widely used datasets and benchmarks. The objective is to create a consistent execution environment that reflects the behavior of real-world database systems, thereby enabling evaluations that extend beyond traditional metrics such as q-error. Currently, PostBound supports both PostgreSQL and DuckDB as backend systems. The execution of query plans generated within the framework is mediated by a hinting interface. For PostgreSQL, this is implemented via the pg_hint_plan or pg_lab extension, both of which provide mechanisms to instruct the optimizer at a fine-grained level. For DuckDB, a dedicated patch is required to enable a comparable hinting mechanism.

Use Case I: Understanding Systems

Although PostBound was originally devised for the rapid development and comparison of query optimization approaches, it has proven equally effective as an analytical tool for investigating the behavior of existing systems [2]. To illustrate this, a systematic experimental evaluation–referred to as the Distortion Experiment–was conducted on the PostgreSQL query optimizer to assess plan stability.

The experiment first computes the true cardinalities of all intermediate results for a given query, then applies controlled distortion factors to simulate varying degrees of cardinality under- and overestimation, thereby exposing optimizer sensitivity across a wide spectrum of potential misestimation.

Experiments were carried out using the Join Order Benchmark (JOB). The results indicate that only 10% of queries exhibit stable plan selection across the full distortion range. A majority–70%–show gradual plan evolution as distortion increases, yet these structural changes do not consistently correlate with observable runtime differences. The remaining 20% of queries display near-random plan selection behavior. For example, JOB query 8c (Fig. 2a) generated six distinct plans, with the minimum execution time observed under substantial overestimation of cardinalities. In contrast, JOB query 6e (Fig. 2b) exemplifies the unstable regime, where the optimizer oscillates between plans with different performance characteristics; in this case, even marginal changes in cardinality estimates can trigger plan switches that result in significant performance degradation. These findings underscore the practical utility of PostBound as a diagnostic framework for evaluating optimizer robustness.

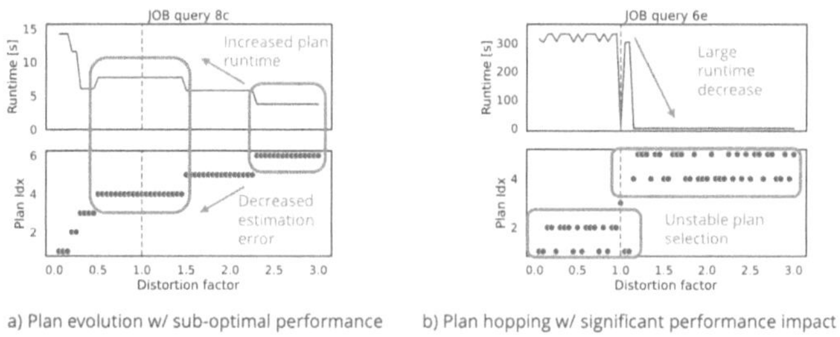

Fig. 2. Query plan stability in case of under-/overestimation of cardinalities.

Use Case II: Improving Systems

The concept of an optimizer "playground" enables the systematic development and evaluation of novel query optimization strategies. One such approach, the Upper-bound Enumeration Strategy (UES), replaces point estimates for intermediate result cardinalities with upper bounds [7], resulting in a prioritization of "safer" joins. UES determines these upper bounds by taking the maximum frequency moment of the join columns across the participating relations, yielding a simple, albeit conservative, estimate.

As shown in Fig. 3b, applying UES across all JOB benchmark queries yields execution times that, while mostly slower than those produced by traditional optimistic join ordering 3a, are notably more consistent. The traditional approach, however, occasionally results in long-running outliers, whereas UES effectively reduces such tail latencies through its conservative cardinality estimates.

Further comparative analysis is provided in Fig. 3c, which contrasts the runtimes of UES with those of TONIC after applying UES, a strategy that incrementally builds a knowledge base of effective physical operator choices [8]. TONIC maintains a synopsis of query execution plans, recording join paths, selected physical operators, and their associated costs from previously executed queries. This accumulated information enables the system to recall and refine operator selection decisions for subsequent queries.

The development and experimental evaluation of both UES and TONIC were facilitated by the PostBound infrastructure, which allowed the researcher to "play" with different optimization methods and parameter configurations, thereby supporting the exploration and assessment of these approaches within a controlled research setting.

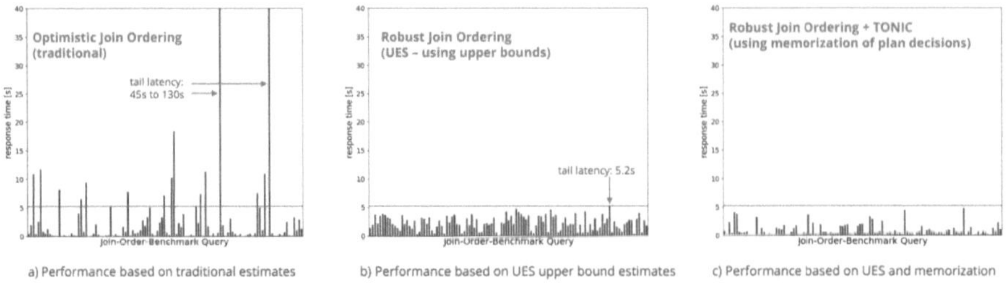

Fig. 3. Performance evaluations of JOB queries comparing the traditional approach with UES upper bounds without/with use of memorization of previous optimizer decisions.

3 Summary

Although query optimization has a long research tradition, it remains a very active evolving field, with a substantial number of publications addressing specific sub-problems such as plan enumeration and cardinality estimation. However, query optimization is still considered a"black art" based on complex algorithmic patterns and cost models deeply embedded in the internals of query engines. This opacity presents a significant barrier to reproducibility and hinders systematic comparison of novel approaches against existing state-of-the-art methods. To address these challenges, we present PostBound, a framework that aims to shed light on query optimization research by making it more transparent and consistently reproducible. PostBound also facilitates the design of novel research directions by providing a framework that allows us to focus on the critical parts of the optimizer. Beyond its role as a research infrastructure, the development of PostBound is guided by a set of non-functional design goals, including ease of use, powerful abstractions, high customizability, and rapid onboarding facilitated by pre-packaged optimization algorithms. Comprehensive documentation lowers the initial entry barrier for researchers who wish to build upon or extend its capabilities. It is our hope that PostBound can serve as a useful reference point for the community and help make query optimization research more open and comparable.

Acknowledgments. This work was partly funded by (1) by the German Research Foundation (DFG) under a Reinhart Koselleck-Project grant (LE-1416/28-1) and (2) the European Union's Horizon research and innovation program under grant agreement no. 101189551. Views and opinions expressed are, however, those of the author(s) only and do not necessarily reflect those of the European Union or the European Health and Digital Executive Agency. Neither the European Union nor the granting authority can be held responsible for them.

This work is the result of a group effort. The following team members of the Dresden Database Technology Research group shall be explicitly thanked for their contribution:

Rico Bergmann, Dirk Habich, Alexander Krause, Johannes Pietrzyk, and many more. This work was subject to the use of you.com for language polishing and grammar correction of this manuscript.

References

1. Anneser, C., et al.: Autosteer: learned query optimization for any SQL database. Proc. VLDB Endow. **16**(12), 3515–3527 (2023). https://doi.org/10.14778/3611540.3611544, https://www.vldb.org/pvldb/vol16/p3515-anneser.pdf
2. Bergmann, R., Hartmann, C., Habich, D., Lehner, W.: An elephant under the microscope: analyzing the interaction of optimizer components in postgresql. Proc. ACM Manag. Data **3**(1), 9:1–9:28 (2025).https://doi.org/10.1145/3709659
3. Bergmann, R., Hertzschuch, A., Hartmann, C., Habich, D., Lehner, W.: PostBOUND: PostgreSQL with upper bound SPJ query optimization. In: König-Ries, B., Scherzinger, S., Lehner, W., Vossen, G. (eds.) Datenbanksysteme für Business, Technologie und Web (BTW 2023), 20. Fachtagung des GI-Fachbereichs ,,Datenbanken und Informationssysteme" (DBIS), 06.-10, März 2023, Dresden, Germany, Proceedings. LNI, vol. P-331, pp. 283–304. Gesellschaft für Informatik e.V. (2023).https://doi.org/10.18420/BTW2023-14
4. Deeds, K.B., Suciu, D., Balazinska, M.: SafeBound: a practical system for generating cardinality bounds. Proc. ACM Manag. Data **1**(1), 53:1–53:26 (2023). https://doi.org/10.1145/3588907
5. Doshi, L., et al.: Kepler: Robust learning for parametric query optimization. Proc. ACM Manag. Data **1**(1), 109:1–109:25 (2023).https://doi.org/10.1145/3588963
6. Haffner, I., Dittrich, J.: Efficiently computing join orders with heuristic search. Proc. ACM Manag. Data **1**(1), 73:1–73:26 (2023).https://doi.org/10.1145/3588927
7. Hertzschuch, A., Hartmann, C., Habich, D., Lehner, W.: Simplicity done right for join ordering. In: 11th Conference on Innovative Data Systems Research, CIDR 2021, Virtual Event, 11-15 Jan 2021, Online Proceedings (2021). www.cidrdb.org, https://vldb.org/cidrdb/2021/simplicity-done-right-for-join-ordering.html
8. Hertzschuch, A., Hartmann, C., Habich, D., Lehner, W.: Turbo-charging SPJ query plans with learned physical join operator selections. Proc. VLDB Endow. **15**(11), 2706–2718 (2022). https://doi.org/10.14778/3551793.3551825, https://www.vldb.org/pvldb/vol15/p2706-hertzschuch.pdf
9. Hilprecht, B., Schmidt, A., Kulessa, M., Molina, A., Kersting, K., Binnig, C.: DeepDB: learn from data, not from queries! Proc. VLDB Endow. **13**(7), 992–1005 (2020). https://doi.org/10.14778/3384345.3384349, http://www.vldb.org/pvldb/vol13/p992-hilprecht.pdf
10. Khamis, M.A., Deeds, K., Olteanu, D., Suciu, D.: Pessimistic cardinality estimation. SIGMOD Rec. **53**(4), 1–17 (2024). https://doi.org/10.1145/3712311.3712313
11. Kipf, A., Kipf, T., Radke, B., Leis, V., Boncz, P., Kemper, A.: Learned cardinalities: estimating correlated joins with deep learning. In: 9th Biennial Conference on Innovative Data Systems Research, CIDR 2019, Asilomar, CA, USA, 13-16 Jan 2019, Online Proceedings (2019). www.cidrdb.org , https://vldb.org/cidrdb/2019/learned-cardinalities-estimating-correlated-joins-with-deep-learning.html
12. Leis, V., Gubichev, A., Mirchev, A., Boncz, P., Kemper, A., Neumann, T.: Still asking: how good are query optimizers, really? Proc. VLDB Endow. **18**(12), 5531–5536 (2025). https://doi.org/10.14778/3750601.3760521, https://www.vldb.org/pvldb/vol18/p5531-viktor.pdf

13. Selinger, P.G., Adiba, M.E.: Access path selection in distributed database management systems. In: Deen, S.M., Hammersley, P. (eds.) Proceedings International Conference on Data Bases, ICOD 1980, University of Aberdeen, UK, 1980. pp. 204–215. Heyden and Son (1980)
14. Selinger, P.G., Astrahan, M.M., Chamberlin, D.D., Lorie, R.A., Price, T.G.: Access path selection in a relational database management system. In: Bernstein, P.A. (ed.) Proceedings of the 1979 ACM SIGMOD International Conference on Management of Data, Boston, Massachusetts, USA. pp. 23–34. ACM (1979). https://doi.org/10.1145/582095.582099

Query Optimization in the Wild: From Cross-platform Data Systems to Multi-agent Systems

Zoi Kaoudi(✉)

IT University of Copenhagen, Copenhagen, Denmark
zoi@itu.dk

Abstract. For decades the query optimizer has been the intellectual center of data management: the component that decides, on our behalf, how a declarative request should be executed. This talk traces a personal research path in which that same ideaseparating what we want computed from how it is computed, and searching a large space of alternatives for a good plankeeps resurfacing in new and larger guises. My journey passes through cross-platform data processing, where Apache Wayang made the execution engine the new unit of choice, moves on through the shift from hand-crafted to learned cost models and optimizers, and reaches today's frontier: the optimization of multi-agent data pipelines, where the optimizer must jointly choose pipeline topology, language models, and execution engines under genuinely multi-objective, Pareto trade-offs. Along the way a new objective has become impossible to ignore: energy. Treating energy as a first-class optimization goal, alongside latency, monetary cost, and accuracy, is both a scientific opportunity for our community and a societal necessity.

Keywords: Query optimization · Cross-platform data processing · Learned optimizers · Multi-agent data pipelines · Sustainable computing

1 Query Optimization as a Way of Thinking

The founding promise of data management is a declarative one: say *what* you want computed, not *how* to compute it, and let the system find a good way to do it. The query optimizer is what makes that promise real. It takes as input an abstract (non-specific) query[1] representation (a.k.a. logical plan) and outputs a concrete specification of how such a query should be executed (a.k.a. execution or physical plan). It is easy to treat the query optimizer as an implementation detail (i.e., a box between the parser and the executor) but we have come to see it as one of the most durable ideas in data systems: the separation of intent from execution, coupled with a principled search over a space of alternative plans.

[1] The query here can be an SQL query, a dataflow job, an ML/AI pipeline, or any other user input.

G. Vargas-Solar et al. (Eds.): ADBIS 2026, LNCS 16937, pp. 21–28, 2027.
https://doi.org/10.1007/978-3-032-39820-8_3

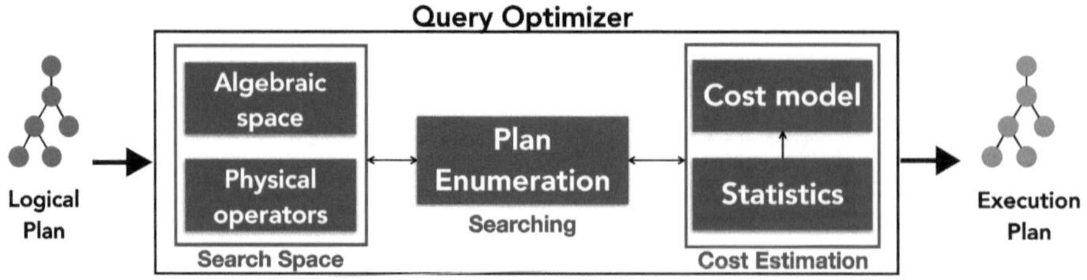

Fig. 1. Main components of a traditional relational query optimizer (adapted from [9])

Ioannidis abstracted the relational query optimizer's components in 1996 [9]. As shown in Fig. 1, a relational query optimizer requires three main components: a *search space* of candidate plans that are equivalent in result but not in cost; *cost estimation* that predicts how expensive each candidate will be; and *plan enumeration*, the strategy that searches this space for a good plan. Interestingly, whatever the era or setting, the same components remain valid well beyond the relational setting. What to choose among (search space), how to score the choices (cost estimation), and how to search among them (plan enumeration) can vary.

The thesis of this talk is that the idea of query optimization is remarkably portable. Every time our computational substrate or data has grown more heterogeneous, the optimizer question has returned, only bigger. When data took shapes the relational model was not built for (e.g., XML, RDF), the question was how to optimize over a different data model. When data outgrew a single machine, the question became *how to distribute*. When it outgrew a single system, the question became *which engine*. And now, as we build data pipelines out of stochastic AI agents, the question is returning in its most open-ended form yet. My aim here is to trace that arc through my own work, and to argue that the optimizer, properly reimagined, is the right lens for building AI systems that are not only efficient but also sustainable.

2 One Query, Many Engines

It is well-known that no single system is best at everything. Relational engines, dataflow systems, graph processors, streaming platforms, and specialized stores each dominate some region of the workload space. Recent data analytics tasks have become increasingly complex, often spanning several of these at once. *Cross-platform data processing* takes this heterogeneity as a first class design assumption rather than an inconvenience: a single analytical task should be free to span multiple engines, with each sub-computation running wherever it is cheapest or fastest.

This has been the central concern of Apache Wayang[2] [2], which started as a research prototype called Rheem [1].[3] In Wayang, a task is expressed as

[2] https://wayang.apache.org/.

[3] Rheem was donated to the Apache Software Foundation and renamed Wayang.

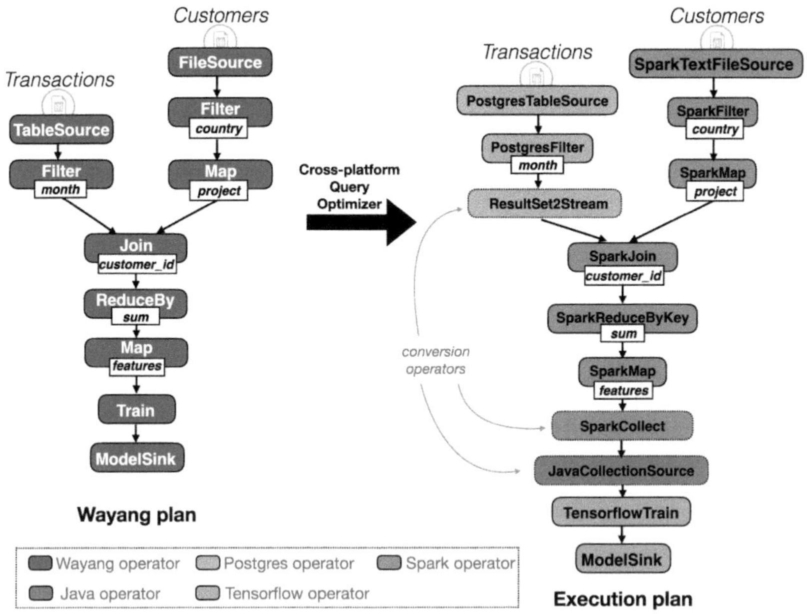

Fig. 2. An example cross-platform optimization task in Apache Wayang. *Left:* the platform-agnostic Wayang plan, which joins transactions with customers, aggregates per customer, extracts features, and trains a model. *Right:* one execution plan chosen by the cross-platform optimizer, which pushes the transaction filter down to Postgres, runs the join and aggregation on Spark, and trains on TensorFlow, inserting conversion operators (e.g., `ResultSet2Stream`, `SparkCollect`) to move data across engines.

a platform-agnostic plan and its optimizer outputs a platform-specific plan. Figure 2 shows an example analytical task that trains a machine learning model over two datasets (a *Transactions* table and a *Customers* file) to predict customer churn. The platform-agnostic Wayang plan (left) filters transactions by month, filters and projects customers by country, joins the two on `customer_id`, sums the amount spent per customer, extracts features, and trains a model. None of these operators names a concrete engine; deciding where each one runs is the cross-platform query optimizer's job. The execution plan on the right is one such choice: the transaction filter is pushed down to Postgres, where that table already resides; the customer processing, join, and aggregation run on Spark; and training runs on TensorFlow. Because consecutive operators may land on different engines, the optimizer additionally inserts *conversion operators* (e.g., `ResultSet2Stream`, `SparkCollect`) that move data across platform boundaries. This single task thus spans four systems.

We have built a cost-based optimizer that uses cost formulas, with profiling to tune the coefficients of these formulas, a novel plan enumeration algorithm, and a lossless pruning approach to navigate the search space [12]. Crucially, data movement is not modeled as file-based intermediate data exchange, which can be very costly, nor as a fixed one-to-one link between each pair of platforms, which scales poorly, but as a channel conversion graph: a graph whose paths capture the many possible ways and intermediate data representations by which data can be moved from one platform to another. A dedicated data movement optimization process then selects the least costly path through this graph [13].

3 From Hand-crafted to Learned Optimizers

An optimizer is only as good as its model of the environment it operates on. The cost model is that model, and hand-tuned cost models do not scale gracefully to a landscape of constantly changing, heterogeneous engines. This is what motivated us to replace the mathematical cost models of Wayang with a machine learning model. In [11], we show how a cross-platform query optimizer can make more informed decisions with less effort by utilizing a regression model and a vector-based plan enumeration algorithm.

Since then, learned query optimization has become a very active area, at least in academia, spanning the whole optimizer pipeline [5,6,18]. One line replaces individual estimators, learning cardinalities [19,21] or predicting operator and query costs directly, increasingly with models designed to transfer across databases and workloads in a zero-shot fashion [7,23]. A second line goes end-to-end, learning the plan-selection policy itself, as in Neo [17], Bao [16], and Balsa [22].[4] Even in this learned setting, the structure of Fig. 1 still holds. What changes is only what fills each box: cost estimation is now performed by a learned model rather than analytical formulas, its statistics are replaced by training data, and plan enumeration may be driven by reinforcement learning rather than a symbolic search.

The deeper shift, though, is not just replacing each component with a learned counterpart but rethinking the problem and the search. Starting from the relational setting, note that the optimizer never truly needs the cost of a plan; it needs only to know which plan is better. This means that instead of estimating cost, it suffices to estimate *rank*. We can thus reframe query optimization as a learning-to-rank problem [3], using a listwise learning-to-rank model together with an adaptive dynamic-programming enumeration algorithm that, at each level of the plan lattice, prunes the candidate set down to an adaptively chosen number of plans.

The second rethinking concerns enumeration itself. If enumeration is the bottleneck, why enumerate at all? A promising direction is to treat cross-platform query optimization not as a search problem but as a prediction to be learned, mapping a platform-agnostic plan directly to a good execution plan and reserving explicit search for offline refinement. Whether this can outperform classical enumeration across the full cross-platform space is one of the open questions that remain to be answered.

---

[4] The above list of references is by no means exhaustive.

4 The New Frontier: Multi-agent Data Pipelines

Large language models have quietly introduced a new execution substrate. We now build *multi-agent data pipelines*: systems in which several agents, backed by different models and tools, collaborate to solve complex data tasks. Yet today's pipelines are largely ad hoc: hand-wired topologies, a single pre-chosen model, and a single execution engine behind the tools. The result is fragmented, redundant, and often startlingly expensive.

Seen through the optimizer's lens, this is the same problem again, generalized along three axes and against three objectives. The optimizer must choose the pipeline topology (which agents exist and how they connect), the model for each step (which LLM at which accuracy–cost point), and the execution engine for each operation. This calls for a new direction, which we term *data systems for agents*: systems in which the multi-agent pipeline itself is the object of optimization, analogous to earlier efforts that brought database principles to bear on machine learning pipelines [14]. This is the vision behind NOMA [10], a next-generation class of query optimizers for multi-agent systems that co-optimizes topology, model, and engine. The optimizer's task, moreover, is now inevitably multi-objective: a classical optimizer largely minimizes latency, while an optimizer for agentic workflows must balance three objectives, i.e., latency, accuracy, and monetary cost, navigating a Pareto frontier rather than optimizing a scalar.

Three things make this genuinely new. First, the space of operations is effectively unbounded: agents are not confined to a fixed algebra like relational operators, so the optimizer needs a far more open and extensible design. Second, the operators are stochastic: the same agent, on the same input, varies in latency, token usage, and output accuracy, so a point cost is not enough—the optimizer must reason about calibrated distributions over each objective. Third, the environment drifts: model prices, capabilities, and availability change week to week, so optimization must be continuous rather than one-shot. The prize for getting this right is large. In real multi-agent pipelines we have observed a cost gap of up to 153× between naive and well-optimized configurations.

There is, however, a deeper break. Through every stage of this talk, the structure of Fig. 1 held: optimization ran to completion and handed a finished plan to execution, cleanly separated. In the agentic setting, for the first time, that separation may have to go. Because an agent's output determines what the pipeline does next, the topology is data-dependent and cannot be fully fixed in advance; and because a step's cost and accuracy are revealed only once it has run, the estimates that drive optimization become available only during execution. Optimization can therefore no longer cleanly precede execution: the two must be interleaved, with the optimizer acting less as a compiler that emits a plan and more as a runtime controller.

5 Energy as a First-Class Optimization Objective

There is another objective that our field has either not paid attention to or has treated as an afterthought: energy. It can no longer be one. AI workloads are projected to push data center's electricity demand to around 945 TWh by 2030, comparable to the entire current electricity consumption of Japan [8]. When a single pipeline can differ by two orders of magnitude in energy depending on how it is configured, the choice of plan is no longer only a performance or economic question but also an environmental one.

Energy is not entirely new to our field: the database community raised energy-aware query optimization over a decade ago [4,15,20]. Even then, the picture was mixed. Some work showed that response time could be traded for energy, batching or slowing execution to reach more efficient points [15]; other work found that, within a single server, the fastest plan is typically also the most energy-efficient, leaving little room for a separate energy-aware optimizer [20]. Perhaps because of this ambiguity or because of the limited benefits, these ideas were never adopted in practice. The line of work largely went quiet. We can no longer afford that. In today's heterogeneous landscape, the question our community set aside is open and pressing again.

The encouraging news is that our community is unusually well-equipped to take this on. We already think natively in terms of cost models, search over alternatives, and multi-objective trade-offs; extending the objective vector to include Joules, and treating latency, monetary cost, accuracy, and energy as axes of a single *Pareto frontier*, is a natural continuation of what optimizers have always done. What it requires is deliberate: energy-aware cost primitives that generalize across engines, models, and hardware; optimization procedures that navigate a multi-objective frontier under user-defined budgets and quality constraints; and, not least, benchmarks that measure energy as seriously as we measure runtime. From this perspective, Green AI need not be a separate agenda from query optimization, but query optimization that accounts for all of its costs, energy included.

6 Outlook

The idea of query optimization—keep the query's intent separate from its execution and let an optimizer search the space of possible plans for a good one—has now stretched from a single machine to heterogeneous engines to fleets of stochastic agents. At each step the community was tempted to declare the optimizer a solved or secondary problem, and at each step the substrate changed underneath us and the problem returned, larger and more consequential. I expect this to continue. The open challenges I find most pressing are a scalable multi-objective optimizer for agentic pipelines; optimization that is robust to stochasticity and drift; and theory and benchmarks that treat energy as a first-class citizen. None of these is niche: together they describe how data analytics can remain not only powerful, but affordable and sustainable, in the age of AI. I look forward to working on them with this community.

Acknowledgments. The research described in this talk is the product of many collaborations. I am deeply grateful to the students, postdocs, and colleagues who shaped it. In particular, I would like to thank Juri Petersen and Mads Sejer Pedersen for their ongoing work on cross-platform optimization, Xiao Li for ongoing work on learning-to-rank query optimization, and my collaborator Ioana Giurgiu for the work and fruitful discussions that gave life to this new line of research on multi-agent systems. This work was partially supported by the Carlsberg Foundation (CF-23-0836).

References

1. Agrawal, D., et al.: RHEEM: enabling cross-platform data processing - may the big data be with you! Proc. VLDB Endow. **11**(11), 1414–1427 (2018)
2. Beedkar, K., et al.: Apache Wayang: a unified data analytics framework. SIGMOD Rec. **52**(3), 30–35 (2023)
3. Behr, H., Markl, V., Kaoudi, Z.: Learn what really matters: A learning-to-rank approach for ML-based query optimization. In: Datenbanksysteme für Business, Technologie und Web (BTW). LNI, vol. 331, pp. 535–554 (2023)
4. Harizopoulos, S., Shah, M.A., Meza, J., Ranganathan, P.: Energy efficiency: the new holy grail of data management systems research. In: CIDR (2009)
5. Heinrich, R., Li, X., Luthra, M., Kaoudi, Z.: Learned Cost Models for Query Optimization: from Batch to Streaming Systems. Proc. VLDB Endow. **18**(12), 5482–5487 (2025)
6. Heinrich, R., Luthra, M., Wehrstein, J., Kornmayer, H., Binnig, C.: How good are learned cost models, really? insights from query optimization tasks. Proc. ACM Manag. Data **3**(3), 172:1–172:27 (2025)
7. Hilprecht, B., Binnig, C.: Zero-shot cost models for out-of-the-box learned cost prediction. Proc. VLDB Endow. **15**(11), 2361–2374 (2022)
8. International Energy Agency: Energy and AI. Tech. rep., IEA, Paris (2025). https://www.iea.org/reports/energy-and-ai
9. Ioannidis, Y.E.: Query optimization. ACM Comput. Surv. **28**(1), 121–123 (1996)
10. Kaoudi, Z., Giurgiu, I.: Rethinking query optimization for multi-agent systems. Proc. VLDB Endow. **20**(1), 46–52 (2026). https://doi.org/10.14778/3845598.3845602
11. Kaoudi, Z., et al.: Ml-based cross-platform query optimization. In: ICDE, pp. 1489–1500 (2020)
12. Kruse, S., et al.: RHEEMix in the data jungle: a cost-based optimizer for cross-platform systems. VLDB J. **29**(6), 1287–1310 (2020)
13. Kruse, S., Kaoudi, Z., Quiané-Ruiz, J., Chawla, S., Naumann, F., Contreras-Rojas, B.: Optimizing cross-platform data movement. In: 35th IEEE International Conference on Data Engineering, ICDE. pp. 1642–1645 (2019) https://doi.org/10.1109/ICDE.2019.00162
14. Kumar, A., Boehm, M., Yang, J.: Data management in machine learning: Challenges, techniques, and systems. In: SIGMOD, pp. 1717–1722 (2017)
15. Lang, W., Patel, J.M.: Towards eco-friendly database management systems. In: CIDR (2009)
16. Marcus, R., Negi, P., Mao, H., Tatbul, N., Alizadeh, M., Kraska, T.: Bao: Making learned query optimization practical. In: SIGMOD, pp. 1275–1288 (2021)
17. Neo: a learned query optimizer. Proc. VLDB Endow. **12**(11), 1705–1718 (2019)

18. Mparmparousis, K., Tsapelas, C., Koutrika, G.: What drives learned optimizer performance? A systematic evaluation. In: EDBT, pp. 605–618 (2026)
19. Sun, J., Zhang, J., Sun, Z., Li, G., Tang, N.: Learned cardinality estimation: a design space exploration and a comparative evaluation. Proc. VLDB Endow. **15**(1), 85–97 (2021)
20. Tsirogiannis, D., Harizopoulos, S., Shah, M.A.: Analyzing the energy efficiency of a database server. In: SIGMOD, pp. 231–242. ACM, New York, NY, USA (2010)
21. Wang, X., Qu, C., Wu, W., Wang, J., Zhou, Q.: Are we ready for learned cardinality estimation? Proc. VLDB Endow. **14**(9), 1640–1654 (2021)
22. Yang, Z., Chiang, W., Luan, S., Mittal, G., Luo, M., Stoica, I.: Balsa: Learning a query optimizer without expert demonstrations. In: SIGMOD, pp. 931–944 (2022)
23. Zhang, Q., Xie, S., Sabek, I.: LIMAO: a framework for lifelong modular learned query optimization. Proc. VLDB Endow. **18**(11), 4546–4559 (2025)

Core Database Systems and Serialization

SYCLDB: A Cross-Vendor Heterogeneous Analytical DBMS

Ivan Donchev Kabadzhov(✉), Eugenio Marinelli, and Raja Appuswamy

EURECOM, Biot, France
ivan.kabadzhov@eurecom.fr

Abstract. The rapid growth of AI and analytical workloads has increased the need for fast, interactive analytical data processing. This, in turn, has led to a surge of interest in designing accelerated analytical database engines that can exploit modern GPUs to scale computation. While GPUs provide the massive data-parallelism required by modern analytics, the software landscape remains dominated by closed-source, vendor-locked programming models, like CUDA, limiting portability across multi-vendor GPUs. In this work, we present SYCLDB, an end-to-end analytical database engine built upon the SYCL open standard, designed to enable efficient, hardware-agnostic execution across a wide range of accelerators using a single codebase. By implementing core relational operators as modular SYCL kernels, integrating them with a SQL frontend based on Apache Calcite and Apache Thrift, and supporting Apache Arrow for efficient columnar ingestion, SYCLDB reduces dependence on vendor-specific GPU programming stacks by enabling a single SYCL codebase to execute analytical query pipelines across Intel, AMD, and NVIDIA GPUs.

Keywords: Analytical Databases · SYCL · Heterogeneous Computing · GPU Acceleration · Cross-Vendor Portability

1 Introduction

The growing popularity of AI and analytics in virtually all application domains has led to a rapid increase in the amount of data gathered by enterprises and scientific institutions alike, with the global datasphere being projected to reach 250ZB by the year 2025 [13]. Modern analytical workloads demand fast, interactive query processing over massive scalar, vector, matrix datasets, which heavily relies on core relational operations like filtering, star-schema joins, and aggregations. Thus, the traditional workhorse of the computing industry, the general-purpose CPU, cannot be optimized to meet the diverse requirements of such heterogeneous workloads. This shortcoming of CPUs, in combination with the cessation of Dennard scaling [6], has led to a growing interest in the adoption of GPU-accelerated database engines. However, most state-of-the-art systems today are developed to target primarily NVIDIA GPUs, and hence build on the

G. Vargas-Solar et al. (Eds.): ADBIS 2026, LNCS 16937, pp. 31–47, 2027.
https://doi.org/10.1007/978-3-032-39820-8_4

proprietary CUDA software stack that hinders their portability to GPUs and accelerators from other vendors [7,15,19]. Thus, there is a need for developing open, standards-based, cross-vendor approach to hardware acceleration.

Over the past few years, SYCL [14] has emerged as a high-level, open-standard programming model integrating data-parallel acceleration into C_{++}. Expressing data-parallel computations in SYCL provides two key advantages over other competing programming models. First, SYCL builds on a portable high-level programming language by implementing an open standard in contrast to other data-parallel languages that are proprietary (CUDA) or low level in nature (OpenCL [17]). Second, SYCL is a single-source by nature as it allows host and device code to co-exist in a single file. While recent research has investigated the performance–portability trade-offs of using SYCL for accelerating key HPC applications [4] and isolated primitives [3,5,8], its application to database engine design remains limited. Prior work (XJoin [10]) was restricted to kernel-level performance benchmarking of isolated projection and join operators. To understand the utility of an open standard for database design, two open questions must be studied: (i) it is necessary to implement a full-fledged query executor that can interpret complex query plans from application benchmarks and compare the design with state-of-the-art CUDA counterparts [7,15,19]; (ii) it is necessary to investigate the integration of SYCL toolchains with pluggable SQL front-ends to demonstrate fully-interpreted, end-to-end SQL query execution.

In this work, we present *SYCLDB*–a cross-architecture, performance-portable, query execution engine that can accelerate SQL query execution using not just NVIDIA GPUs, but also GPUs from other vendors (like Intel Flex, AMD Instinct, etc.) using a single code base. *SYCLDB* implements key relational operators as a sequence of highly tuned, independent kernels in SYCL. To drive SYCL kernels from SQL frontend, *SYCLDB* integrates Apache Calcite [2] and Apache Thrift [16] to build a composable query parsing/optimization front end that can transform SQL queries into a directed acyclic graph of SYCL kernels.

Using *SYCLDB*, we perform a rigorous multi-platform evaluation on NVIDIA, AMD, and Intel hardware, demonstrating that: (i) in end-to-end query execution, *SYCLDB* outperforms state-of-the-art GPU database systems (achieving up to 1.22× speedup on average over HeavyDB and up to 4.72× over SiriusDB) as well as the leading in-memory CPU database DuckDB by 4.7× to 10.7× (6.37× on average); and (ii) *SYCLDB* is fully portable across multi-vendor GPUs, enabling end-to-end SQL query execution on all evaluated platforms and demonstrating both the high performance portability of SYCL and its readiness to integrate with standard SQL front-ends. Crucially, *SYCLDB* does not represent a final design point; rather, it serves as a highly performant, open-source prototype that establishes an actionable engineering trajectory for future compilation research in cross-architecture database design. We make *SYCLDB* publicly available[1] for further research on standards-based analytics acceleration.

[1] https://gitlab.eurecom.fr/dislab/sycldb.

2 Design

This section details the physical implementation of *SYCLDB*, highlighting the specific features of the SYCL programming model that guide its implementation.

2.1 Memory Management

SYCLDB is optimized for high-throughput analytical workloads. Thus, similar to state-of-the-art GPU database engines [7,15,19], it adopts a columnar storage architecture where each table attribute is maintained as a separate, contiguous array. *SYCLDB* supports data stored in Apache Arrow-compatible columnar buffers to enable direct data ingestion from external sources. *SYCLDB* is also presently designed to work only in the scenario where all data is resident in GPU memory similar to other GPU database engines. As our goal is to be portable across multi-vendor GPUs, we do not assume the existence of high-performance interconnect like NVLink, but rather only low-bandwidth PCIe links connecting the host CPU and GPU. In such scenarios, it is well known [15] that PCIe data transfers become a bottleneck in query execution. To avoid this, similar to other GPU engines, *SYCLDB* reads all input columns during the startup phase and moves them to GPU memory. CUDA-based database engines rely on explicit functions for allocating and transferring memory between host (CPU) and device (GPU) memory, such as `cudaMalloc` and `cudaMemcpy`. Additionally, CUDA offers pinned memory, which ensures that data transfers between host and device are more efficient. In SYCL, similar functionalities are available via the Unified Shared Memory (USM) model [14] which we use to migrate data from host memory to GPU device memory.

2.2 *SYCLDB* Primitives

At its core, *SYCLDB* is organized as a library of relational primitives that are used as building blocks for implementing higher-level relational operators. There are four fundamental primitives, namely, selection, projection, build, and probe.

Selection and Projection. In order to support selection and projection relational operations, *SYCLDB* supports a generic per-element selection primitive that evaluates a boolean predicate. *SYCLDB* currently targets fixed-width numeric columns, where selection predicates are expressed as binary comparisons between an input column and a constant reference value. To support multiple comparison operations, we implement selections as basic switch statements of functionals, deciding the binary operation. Listing 1a shows a basic selection primitive that operates on a single element (`col`). It compares `col` with the value `v` using the comparison type `comp` and sets the resulting boolean value.

```
template <typename T, typename Compare>
bool selection_primitive(const T& col, const T& v) {
    Compare comp{};
    return comp(col, v);
}
```

(a) Generic selection primitive acting on one element

```
// Pass 1: First selection predicate
bool *flags = sycl::malloc_device<bool>(F.len, q);

q.parallel_for(sycl::range<1>(F.len), [=](sycl::id<1> idx) {
    size_t i = idx[0];
    flags[i] = selection_primitive<int, sycl::less<>>(F.A[i], 100);
});
```

(b) Invoking a selection primitive from a SYCL kernel

```
// Pass 1: First selection predicate
bool *flags = sycl::malloc_device<bool>(F.len, q);

q.parallel_for(sycl::range<1>(F.len), [=](sycl::id<1> idx) {
    size_t i = idx[0];
    flags[i] = selection_primitive<int, sycl::less<>>(F.A[i], 100);
});

// Pass 2: Second selection predicate
q.parallel_for(sycl::range<1>(F.len), [=](sycl::id<1> idx) {
    size_t i = idx[0];
    flags[i] &= selection_primitive<int, sycl::less<>>(F.B[i], 50);
});
```

(c) Kernel-at-a-time execution strategy

Listing 1: *SYCLDB* primitive and operator execution strategy

Build and Probe. To support the relational hash join operator, *SYCLDB* implements two core primitives: *build* and *probe*. The design targets hash-based equi-joins over fixed-width key columns, matching the join patterns commonly found in star-schema workloads like the Star Schema Benchmark (SSB) [11]. We utilize a pointer-free, array-based hash table with linear probing and simple remainder hashing. The *build* primitive populates the hash table from the build relation, while the *probe* primitive evaluates matches from the probe relation.

2.3 Relational Operators

SYCLDB uses these primitives to implement higher-level relational operators that process input relations in a massively parallel fashion across different GPU backends. In SYCL, data-parallel *kernels* are coordinated from the host and submitted asynchronously to a device *queue* via work requests. Control returns immediately to the host code once the kernel is queued for execution on the associated accelerator device. Unlike CUDA which requires kernel dimensions to be explicitly specified, SYCL allows developers to specify a 1D-range that spans a given input array. This design delegates physical thread-block partitioning and warp scheduling entirely to the underlying driver runtime, which automatically maps the work across the hardware's streaming multiprocessors. *SYCLDB* uses this functionality to simplify the implementation of relational operator kernels.

Selection Operator. Each selection condition has to apply a binary operation between a column and a fixed reference value (that is `SELECT` x `FROM` R `WHERE` $x < v$). Multiple such conditions can appear in the same query. To enable efficient, materialization-free condition evaluation, *SYCLDB* keeps track of selection flag vectors for each relation similar to other analytical engines. These vectors encode whether each tuple remains active after the predicates evaluated so far. For conjunctive predicates, each new predicate result is combined with the previous flag value, so a tuple remains active only if it satisfies all conditions processed up to that point.

The code in Listing 1 shows the code corresponding to a selection operator with two conditions. The code contains several key variables: a queue (`q`) representing the device context, the input relation (`F`) to be processed, a selection flags array (`sf`) to store the results of the comparison operation, and the cardinality of the relation (`F.len`). Additionally, it includes comparison operator (`sycl::less`), as well as a constant value (`100`/`50` for first/second conditions) against which the column (`A`/`B`'s entries for first/second conditions) are compared. In Listing 1, the selection primitive evaluates a single predicate and returns its boolean result. Predicate composition is handled by the operator kernel. The first pass initializes the flag vector, while subsequent passes update each flag by combining the previous value with the newly evaluated predicate. The kernel's body employs a simple parallel-for loop over a 1D-range of size `F.len`. Inside the loop, the selection primitive is called with the appropriate arguments for each element at index `i`. This design keeps each predicate pass compact and allows the frontend to compose arbitrary conjunctions of supported predicates while preserving a portable kernel-at-a-time execution model. At present, *SYCLDB* supports fixed-width numeric attributes and simple comparison predicates, such as $=$, $<$, $>$, $\leq$, and $\geq$, which are executed directly inside SYCL kernels.

Join Operator. The join operator is implemented by two separate kernel invocations, each mapping the build and probe primitives respectively. The current operator supports equi-joins over fixed-width keys, which are sufficient to express the Star Schema Benchmark (SSB) join patterns used in our evaluation. The hash table produced by the build primitive is materialized and made available to the probe kernel via GPU global memory. The probe kernel also materializes its result vector of joined values in GPU global memory for consumption by downstream operators (like aggregation).

Aggregation Operator. Global aggregation is essential for executing SQL operators such as `SUM`, `COUNT`, and `MIN/MAX`. *SYCLDB* currently supports these aggregations over fixed-width numeric columns, where the aggregation operation is associative and commutative. State-of-the-art GPU implementations of global aggregation, like Crystal [15], often explicitly orchestrate a multi-level hierarchy: using sub-group shuffles for intra-warp communication, local memory for inter-warp synchronization, and global atomics for inter-group finalization. For instance, Fig. 1 illustrates a `SUM` reduction. Each work-item in step zero loops internally to stream data from global memory into a local register accumulator (`Acc`). This strategy ensures perfectly coalesced memory accesses and hides instruction latency through deep pipelining. Once the streaming phase is complete, the runtime automatically transitions to Step 1 and Step 2, performing an efficient tree-based reduction within *local memory*. As a result, the final inter-group reduction involves a minimal number of partial results, which drastically reduces contention on global atomic units.

While this approach provides high performance, it has the limitation that it is hardware specific and requires complex fine tuning corresponding to the underlying device. With SYCL, we can express this entire high-performance pipeline in a single line of code that leverages a key enhancement introduced in the SYCL 2020 revision [14]: the *reducer* class–equipped with built-in support for common aggregation functions, such as sum, product, minimum, and maximum. Listing 2 shows an example reduction that performs an entire associative-commutative reduction over `data[0..N)` into the scalar location `*sum` in a single kernel call, leaving the choice of in-kernel reduction strategy (work-group tree reduction, subgroup shuffle, final atomic merge) to the SYCL runtime.

Reading the call left to right, we can see that the code submits a single, 1-D range kernel to the queue `q`. The second argument, `sycl::reduction(sum, sycl::plus<>())`, is a *reduction descriptor* that declares that there is a scalar accumulator at the address `sum`, to be combined using `sycl::plus<>()`. This is followed by a lambda whose parameter `sum` deliberately shadows the outer pointer of the same name. Inside the kernel, `sum` is no longer a pointer to memory but a *reducer* object supplied by the runtime. The reducer accumulates thread-local (or `work-item`-local in SYCL) partials, the runtime combines partials across the threadblock (or `work-group` in SYCL) using whatever shared-memory primitive the target backend exposes, and a small number of threadblocks perform the final atomic update against the underlying location. This unified abstraction delegates the structural arrangement of the multi-stage aggregation pipeline to the underlying SYCL compiler toolchain, which automatically optimizes execution for each respective hardware backend.

GROUP BY Operator. State-of-the-art GPU implementations of the `GROUP BY` operation would either sort the input by group key and run a segmented reduction, or build per-block partial histograms in shared memory and then merge them globally. Both alternatives trade off more memory traffic and more kernel launches for reduced contention with atomics. More recently, based on the fact that modern GPUs are much better at handling warp and block-level atomics, Crystal [15] proposed a tiled implementation. Each thread block builds a *private* hash table in shared memory, aggregates its own tile against that local table using atomics (`atomicCAS` and `atomicAdd` on `__shared__` locations), synchronizes once with `__syncthreads()`, and then merges the local table into the global result with one `atomicAdd` per occupied slot. This implementation assumes that the number of groups in a `GROUP BY` is small enough to fit in shared memory. When this is not the case, Crystal falls back to direct global atomics with `atomicAdd`. The downside of this approach is that it is hardware specific, as it relies on three different CUDA synchronization mechanisms–warp shuffles and shared-memory atomics internally, a block-wide barrier between phases, and the fact that NVCC compiler lowers the `atomicAdd` it to a PTX `atom.relaxed.gpu.add.u64` instruction, which provides relaxed memory ordering semantics. Relaxed memory ordering is safe and valuable here precisely because of the algebraic structure of `GROUP BY` with a summing aggregate. Each row contributes to exactly one bucket. As buckets are disjoint, there is no cross-bucket dependence that another thread might need to observe in order. Within a bucket, the only operation is `+=`, which is both associative and commutative, so any interleaving of `fetch_adds` from different rows produces the same result.

SYCLDB trades Crystal's locality optimization for code uniformity and backend portability. Instead of two different implementations that depend on the group size, *SYCLDB* in contrast, uses the `sycl::atomic_ref` SYCL feature to achieve the same effect in a portable fashion. An `atomic_ref<T, Order, Scope, Space>` is a *non-owning* reference that re-interprets reads, writes, and read-modify-writes through it as atomic operations on the underlying storage. A key template parameter taken by `atomic_ref` is the choice of memory model. The use of `memory_order::relaxed` results in the SYCL compiler producing the optimal code for each GPU backend, namely the same PTX instruction as CUDA `atomicAdd` on NVIDIA GPUs, a global atomic without an explicit `s_waitcnt vmcnt(0)` on AMD CDNA devices, and a Level-Zero atomic without cache-line invalidation on Intel Xe GPUs. *SYCLDB* uses `atomic_ref` to perform grouped aggregation in a single `parallel_for` over the input column with no intra-block reduction and no explicit synchronization. In order to do this, *SYCLDB* assumes a star-schema workload configuration identical to Crystal [15], where each dimension column exhibits a small, contiguous range of integer codes. Hence, the Cartesian product of the group-by columns fits in a flat array, allowing each active row to map directly to its slot via collision-free mixed-radix arithmetic. Listing 3 shows this GROUP BY implementation. After computing the slot, each row issues two relaxed device-scope atomics: an `exchange` that elects the first writer responsible for installing the representative group keys, and a `fetch_add` that accumulates the numeric aggregate.

2.4 Interpreted Query Execution

To execute SQL queries dynamically on modern GPU accelerators, *SYCLDB* employs a decoupled server-client query planning and execution architecture.

```
q.parallel_for(range, sycl::reduction(sum, sycl::plus<>()),
  [=](sycl::id<1> id, auto& sum) { sum += data[id]; });
```

Listing 2: Modular aggregation using the high-level SYCL 2020 reduction API

```
q.parallel_for(N, [=](sycl::id<1> idx) {
    const auto i = idx[0];
    if (!flags[i]) return;

    int hash = 0, mult = 1;
    for (int j = 0; j < G; ++j) {
        hash += (group_cols[j][i] - min[j]) * mult;
        mult *= max[j] - min[j] + 1;
    }

    sycl::atomic_ref<unsigned, sycl::memory_order::relaxed,
        sycl::memory_scope::device,
        sycl::access::address_space::global_space> first(flags[hash]);
    if (first.exchange(1) == 0)
        for (int j = 0; j < G; ++j) keys[j][hash] = group_cols[j][i];

    sycl::atomic_ref<uint64_t, sycl::memory_order::relaxed,
        sycl::memory_scope::device,
        sycl::access::address_space::global_space> sum(agg[hash]);
    sum.fetch_add(value[i]);
});
```

Listing 3: *SYCLDB* GROUP BY implementation.

A Java Virtual Machine based optimizer using Apache Calcite [2] parses and optimizes the incoming SQL query, applying cost-based relational rules to perform join and operator reordering. The resulting optimized physical execution plan is serialized and transmitted via Apache Thrift RPC to the C_{++} execution engine, which deserializes this plan and constructs a directed acyclic graph (DAG) representing the physical operator execution order. *SYCLDB* executes the DAG by dynamically traversing it in topological order and dispatching precompiled, template-based general-purpose operators directly to the device queue. Thus, *SYCLDB* performs kernel-at-a-time execution to evaluate any given SQL query. It is important to note that while we do kernel-at-a-time execution, we do not perform full materialization after each kernel due to use of selection flags. Instead, materialization happens at natural pipeline boundaries (such as join probes). Currently, the prototype targets a high-performance subset of core relational operators optimized for fixed-width numeric attributes; we detail our exact feature boundaries and schema limitations in Sect. 4.

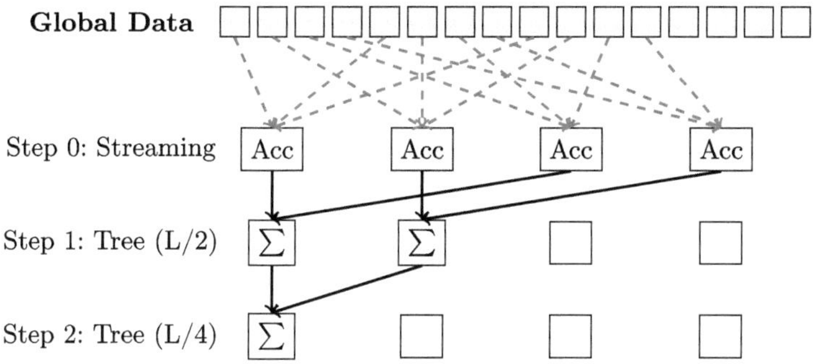

Fig. 1. SYCL2020 Reduction: Register Streaming + Shared-Memory Tree

3 Evaluation

Hardware Platforms. We evaluate *SYCLDB* across three heterogeneous GPU architectures, each connected via a PCIe Gen4 x16 interconnect (31.5 GB/s theoretical bi-directional bandwidth). The host system is equipped with a dual-socket **Intel Xeon Platinum 8454H** processors (Sapphire Rapids, 32 cores/socket, 128 threads total, 3.4GHz boost), **1 TB DDR5 ECC** system memory, and a Gen4 NVMe SSD capable of 7,400 MB/s sequential reads, used for initial data staging into system memory.

- **NVIDIA L40S:** Based on the Ada Lovelace architecture, featuring **48 GB of GDDR6** memory with a peak bandwidth of **864 GB/s**. It operates at a 350W TDP and provides high-throughput FP32/INT32 compute units.
- **AMD Instinct MI210:** Built on the CDNA 2 architecture, providing **64 GB of HBM2e** memory with a peak bandwidth of **1.6 TB/s**. The HBM2e stack is critical for saturating the high-throughput requirements of analytical workloads at scale.
- **Intel Data Center GPU Flex 170:** Based on the Xe-HPG architecture, featuring **16 GB of GDDR6** memory with a peak bandwidth of **576 GB/s**. This platform represents a high-density, power-efficient acceleration point for moderate-scale datasets.

Dataset and Workload. We utilize the industry-standard Star Schema Benchmark (SSB) as our primary evaluation workload, because its data warehousing query patterns isolate the core microarchitectural bottlenecks of GPU-accelerated analytical execution: high-selectivity predicate pushdowns, multi-way pointer-chasing hash joins, and dense global aggregations.

Software Stack. We use **AdaptiveCpp 25.10.0** (compiled with LLVM 18) as our primary SYCL toolchain for NVIDIA, AMD, and Intel GPUs, targeting the CUDA backend (CUDA 12.6 SDK), HIP backend (ROCm 6.3.3), and OpenCL backend (Intel Compute Runtime), respectively [1,9].

Measurement Protocol and Baseline Normalization. To eliminate transient hardware noise and cold-start compilation overhead, each query is first executed as an unrecorded cold pass. Reported timings correspond to the steady-state performance averaged over 10 subsequent consecutive runs. Because the steady-state variance across execution loops was under 10%, error bars are omitted from results. Unless otherwise stated, query execution time excludes initial table loading from persistent storage and assumes that input columns are already resident in the memory space used by each engine. Once the data is entirely device-resident, there is no structural layout or storage-layer difference between the evaluated engines, successfully isolating pure compute and memory hierarchy performance. For GPU engines, kernel-only time includes only device kernel execution, while total time includes SQL planning where applicable, host-side operator orchestration, kernel launch overheads, synchronization points, and device-side intermediate materialization. For systems that perform JIT compilation, compilation overhead is excluded from kernel-only time and included in total time only when it occurs as part of the measured query execution path.

3.1 End-to-End Query Execution Performance

To evaluate *SYCLDB* under a large-scale analytical workload, we benchmarked the execution time of *SYCLDB*, HeavyDB (industry-grade GPU database engine with compiled query execution) [7], SiriusDB (composable analytics engine based on composing dataframe kernels) [19], Crystal [15], and DuckDB (state-of-the-art CPU-based analytical engine) [12] under the SSB benchmark [11]. For this analysis, we use Scale Factor 100 (SF100), corresponding to approximately 600 million rows. The results are shown in Fig. 2.

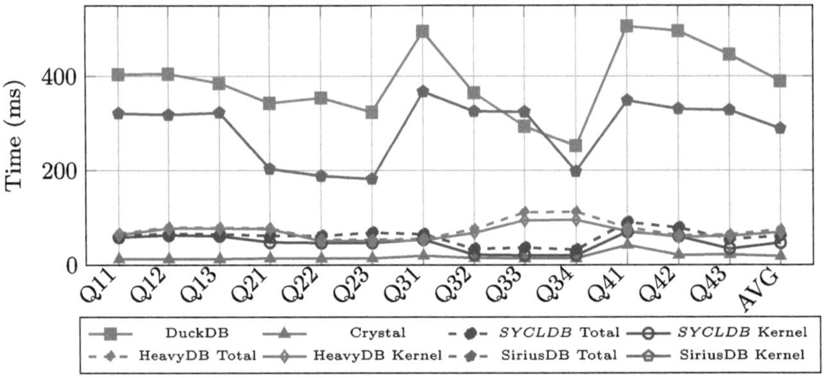

Fig. 2. Query execution performance at SF100 scale on NVIDIA L40S. The solid lines report kernel execution time, assuming that the input data is already resident in device memory. The dashed lines include the additional query frontend overhead (SQL parsing, optimization, kernel launches, etc.).

DuckDB provides a strong reference point for CPU query execution as it is a highly-optimized, state-of-the-art, open-source in-memory analytical engine. Compared with DuckDB, *SYCLDB* achieves substantially lower execution times across the benchmark with a speedup between 4.7× and 10.7×. These results show the potential of GPUs for analytical query execution and underscore potential for further improvements, especially given the fact that *SYCLDB* performs straight-forward kernel-at-a-time execution without optimizations like pipelining, kernel fusion, or indexing. On average, DuckDB requires 389.92 ms per query, whereas *SYCLDB* Total requires 61.23 ms (and 46.47 ms for Kernel time only), which represents a 6.37× speedup in overall end-to-end execution (8.39× speedup in kernel-only execution) over the CPU baseline.

Crystal, on the other hand, represents a specialized GPU implementation in which SQL queries are directly implemented as hard-coded CUDA kernels, thus, removing SQL parsing, query planning, frontend processing, dynamic specialization, and most general-purpose operator-boundary costs. While Crystal is not built to be a general-purpose query execution engine, it acts as an absolute lower-bound baseline for specialized GPU execution time. As expected, Crystal achieves the lowest execution times across the benchmark, with *SYCLDB*'s kernel time between 1.46× and 4.93× higher than Crystal across the entire benchmark. For several complex join queries such as Q3.2, Q3.3, Q3.4, the gap is small with *SYCLDB* only about 1.46×–1.47× slower than the manual Crystal baseline. These results show that the *SYCLDB* preserves generality while providing performance competitive with a highly specialized implementation for several queries. Comparing their averages, the hand-written Crystal baseline achieves a mean query time of 15.88 ms, while *SYCLDB*'s interpreted kernel-only execution averages 46.47 ms. This demonstrates that *SYCLDB* remains competitive within a 2.93× factor of a specialized CUDA reference. Crucially, as isolated in our performance portability analysis (Sect. 2), this execution gap is not a limitation of the SYCL abstraction layer, but rather represents the necessary query orchestration and relational modularity tax of a fully interpreted database engine running over independent operator boundaries.

Comparing *SYCLDB* to SiriusDB, we see that SiriusDB is 4× - 16.0× slower than *SYCLDB*. The gap is especially visible for Q3.2 and Q3.3, where SiriusDB requires 325.72 ms and 324.53 ms, while *SYCLDB* executes the same kernel workloads in 21.31 ms and 20.25 ms, corresponding to speedups of 15.3× and 16.0×, respectively. This is due to the cost of materializing intermediate states across operator boundaries. In *SYCLDB*, general-purpose execution propagates intermediate condition outcomes across operators through device-resident flag arrays, with additional write and read from global device memory between successive operators. This cost is even more pronounced in SiriusDB, which relies on chaining highly optimized `libcudf` library functions. Although each individual primitive is optimized, the pipeline is fragmented across external library calls. Consequently, intermediate outputs produced by filters and join probes must be materialized in global device memory before the next library operator can begin, leading to substantially higher execution times across the benchmark. Considering kernel execution time, the comparison shows that *SYCLDB*'s approach of building on SYCL compiler and runtime toolchain is more efficient than a dataframe-library composition model adopted by SiriusDB, as *SYCLDB*'s specialized relational kernels keep execution closer to the physical query plan and avoid the overhead incurred by chaining general-purpose library primitives. In terms of macro-level averages, SiriusDB exhibits a mean execution time of 289.08 ms, which is 4.72× slower than *SYCLDB*'s end-to-end average of 61.23 ms and 6.22× slower than *SYCLDB*'s kernel-only average of 46.47 ms, highlighting the significant VRAM materialization tax of dataframe library chaining.

HeavyDB follows a completely different design strategy by using a custom LLVM [9] backend to generate JIT-compiled fused kernels. Comparing *SYCLDB* and HeavyDB, we see that *SYCLDB* remains highly competitive. In raw kernel execution time, *SYCLDB* outperforms HeavyDB on 11 out of the 13 evaluated SSB queries with a significant speedup for the Q3 query family: for Q3.2, *SYCLDB* executes the kernel workload in 21.31 ms compared to 67.60 ms for HeavyDB (3.2× faster), while for Q3.3 and Q3.4 it requires 20.25 ms and 20.21 ms compared to 94.30 ms and 95.10 ms for HeavyDB, corresponding to speedups of 4.7× in both cases. HeavyDB is slightly faster in kernel time for Q3.1 and Q4.2, but the difference is less than 5%: 52.50 ms versus 53.79 ms for Q3.1, and 59.20 ms versus 60.45 ms for Q4.2. These results show the potential of SYCL for developing GPU-based analytical engines and open the door for further performance optimizations that can be achieved by using JIT compilation to fuse SYCL kernels in the future. Looking at the overall benchmark averages, HeavyDB requires an average of 74.75 ms for end-to-end execution (and 68.98 ms for kernel time), whereas *SYCLDB* requires 61.23 ms (and 46.47 ms for kernel time), showing that *SYCLDB* achieves a 1.22× speedup in end-to-end execution and a 1.48× speedup in kernel execution over HeavyDB's custom-generated LLVM query pipeline.

Finally, the gap between the dashed lines and the solid lines quantifies the overhead of the frontend and kernel orchestration. In *SYCLDB*, each relational operator is submitted as a separate SYCL kernel and followed by an explicit synchronization point used to enforce execution order and collect profiling information. This overhead includes kernel dispatch, synchronization, and intermediate state management. Across the benchmark, this overhead ranges from approximately 3.4 ms to 21.6 ms, with an average of about 13.2 ms per query. The smallest overheads appear in Q1.1–Q1.3, where the gap between kernel time and total time is only about 3–4 ms, while more complex queries such as Q2.3 and Q4.1–Q4.3 incur larger orchestration costs. Even with this overhead, *SYCLDB* remains substantially faster than DuckDB and SiriusDB across all queries, indicating that the general-purpose execution path and the composable front end both remain practical and efficient for large-scale analytical workloads.

3.2 Performance Portability and Cross-Vendor Analysis

In this section, we analyze the performance portability of *SYCLDB* across diverse hardware architectures, validating that (i) the same codebase executes seamlessly across multiple vendor stacks, and (ii) portable SYCL implementations can compete with or outperform native, highly specialized GPU baselines. We compare the full *SYCLDB* engine against an evaluation-only SYCL-Hardcoded reference implementation. SYCL-Hardcoded is not a separate execution path exposed by *SYCLDB*; rather, it uses the same *SYCLDB* relational primitives inside hand-written query kernels similar to Crystal to estimate the performance available without a SQL front end.

To demonstrate cross-vendor portability, we execute the full SSB benchmark on three distinct GPU architectures: the NVIDIA L40S, the AMD Instinct MI210, and the Intel Data Center GPU Flex 170. We select Scale Factor 40 (SF40) for the Intel Flex 170 to match the device's 16 GB physical memory capacity boundary, while evaluating the high-throughput NVIDIA and AMD platforms at SF100. We used the ROCm HIPIFY tool[2] to convert the CUDA Crystal baseline into its HIP version for AMD evaluation. Notably, the hand-written CUDA baseline (Crystal) and its HIP translation are entirely vendor-locked and cannot run on the Intel Flex 170. This highlights the role of open standards like SYCL in building general-purpose, cross-vendor database engines.

As shown in Fig. 3, the portable SYCL-Hardcoded reference consistently matches or outperforms the native CUDA and HIP baselines. On NVIDIA L40S, SYCL-Hardcoded achieves a mean execution time of 8.33 ms, representing a 1.91× speedup over native CUDA-based Crystal (15.88 ms average). Similarly, on AMD Instinct MI210, SYCL-Hardcoded averages 14.31 ms, securing a 1.13× speedup over native Hipified Crystal (16.17 ms average). This performance advantage is driven by the structural limitations of Crystal's manual tile-based implementation, which relies on explicit shared-memory synchronization and loop structures. In contrast, the SYCL compiler (AdaptiveCpp) dynamically inlines the *SYCLDB* relational primitives used by the hardcoded kernels, performing aggressive global register allocation and instruction scheduling. This eliminates active thread barriers and produces extremely tight, barrier-free machine instructions that saturate the hardware's execution units.

Comparing *SYCLDB* with SYCL-Hardcoded isolates the cost of general-purpose query execution. This overhead is microarchitecturally driven by two main factors: intermediate materialization and instruction inflation. In the full *SYCLDB* engine, relational operators are scheduled across independent kernels and the engine must write and read back row selection flag vectors across operator boundaries. In the SYCL-Hardcoded reference, operators that scan or probe the same table are combined into a per-table kernel, while joins and table-to-table transitions remain separate kernel boundaries. Per-table selection flags are implemented as local variables similar to Crystal, resulting in them being resident in registers. For Q1.1 at SF100, the full engine generates 28.60 GB of global DRAM traffic. In contrast, SYCL-Hardcoded keeps selection flags resident in registers, reducing global DRAM traffic to 9.60 GB leading to a uniform 66% reduction across all architectures. Furthermore, *SYCLDB* requires launching up to 18 distinct kernels per query, introducing substantial instruction inflation

[2] https://github.com/ROCm/HIPIFY.

(up to 11.6× on AMD and 9.3× on NVIDIA) and boundary synchronization fences that serialize execution. The SYCL-Hardcoded reference removes these per-operator materialization points where they occur within the same table leading to better performance. Similar to the monolithic compilation strategy by HeavyDB [7], these microarchitectural insights point to a natural direction for future work: runtime compilation to dynamically fuse adjacent multi-operator blocks into a single device kernel. This approach would allow *SYCLDB* to provide the performance of the hardcoded reference while preserving declarative relational generality.

4 Discussion and Future Work

In this work, we presented *SYCLDB*, an end-to-end analytical database engine built entirely on the open SYCL standard. By implementing core relational oper-

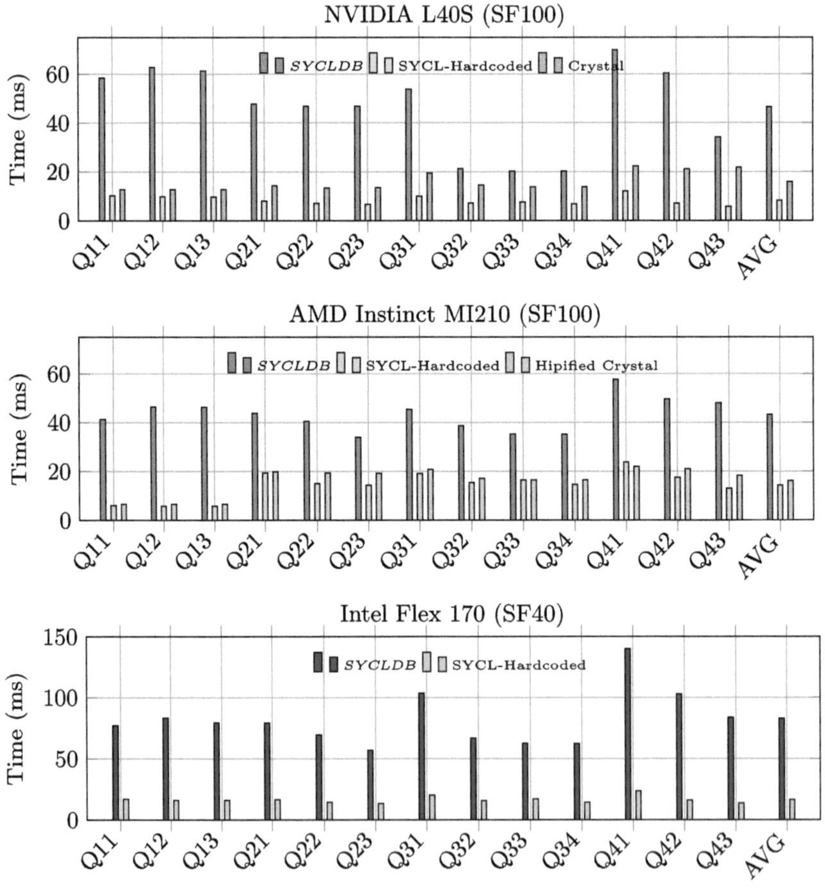

Fig. 3. Cross-architecture execution performance comparison across SSB queries.

ators using modular SYCL primitives, and by integrating them with a composable SQL frontend based on Apache Calcite and Apache Thrift, SYCLDB demonstrates that an open-standard programming model can support fully interpreted, end-to-end SQL query execution on the GPU. Our evaluation across NVIDIA, AMD, and Intel hardware demonstrates seamless portability and competitive execution speeds compared to proprietary, vendor-locked reference engines [7,15,19]. However, the current prototype exhibits operational boundaries that outline key avenues for future development:

Workload Diversity and SQL Coverage. Broader schema configurations and query patterns, such as those in TPC-DS [18], are currently outside the scope of our execution library. At present, *SYCLDB* excludes complex relational features like comprehensive `NULL` semantics, non-equi joins, variable-length strings, sparse-key grouping (requiring dynamic hash-collision resolution), and User-Defined Functions (UDFs). Integrating these capabilities and data types remains a primary path for future work. Furthermore, we plan to extend beyond standard relational boundaries to natively support convergent AI workloads.

Modularity and Optimization Paradigms. The observed 2.93× performance gap relative to Crystal's specialized CUDA references represents the relational modularity and orchestration tax of an interpreted query engine, rather than an inherent limitation of the SYCL language abstraction. Future work can eliminate this overhead by taking advantage of AdaptiveCpp's recently introduced just-in-time (JIT) compiler support for kernel fusion[3].

Lakehouse Integration and Storage Heterogeneity. Modern analytics are rapidly shifting toward decentralized data lakes and cloud lakehouse architectures [20]. Future iterations of *SYCLDB* will investigate native data streaming and zero-copy ingestion from open table formats (such as Apache Iceberg or Delta Lake) directly into device-accessible memory spaces. Leveraging SYCL's Unified Shared Memory (USM) properties alongside networked file systems will allow our portable execution layer to process massive, remote data lakes directly, making *SYCLDB* a highly generic acceleration plug-in for cross-platform data meshes.

Heterogeneous Multi-GPU Execution. While this work proves performance portability by evaluating separate hardware platforms independently, modern large-scale clusters increasingly deploy diverse accelerators in tandem pipelining a single query plan across concurrent GPUs from different vendors.

Taken together, our results demonstrate that open, standards-based GPU programming is now a mature foundation for the next generation of cross-vendor analytical database systems.

[3] https://github.com/AdaptiveCpp/AdaptiveCpp/releases/tag/v24.06.0.

References

1. Alpay, A., Heuveline, V.: Sycl beyond opencl: the architecture, current state and future direction of hipsycl. In: Proceedings of the International Workshop on OpenCL (2020). https://doi.org/10.1145/3388333.3388658
2. Begoli, E., Camacho-Rodríguez, J., Hyde, J., Mior, M.J., Lemire, D.: Apache calcite: a foundational framework for optimized query processing over heterogeneous data sources. In: Proceedings of the 2018 International Conference on Management of Data (SIGMOD) (2018). https://doi.org/10.1145/3183713.3190662
3. Crisci, L., Carpentieri, L., Thoman, P., Alpay, A., Heuveline, V., Cosenza, B.: Sycl-bench 2020: benchmarking sycl 2020 on amd, intel, and nvidia gpus. In: Proceedings of the 12th International Workshop on OpenCL and SYCL (2024). https://doi.org/10.1145/3648115.3648120
4. Deakin, T., McIntosh-Smith, S.: Evaluating the performance of hpc-style sycl applications. In: Proceedings of the International Workshop on OpenCL (2020). https://doi.org/10.1145/3388333.3388643
5. Deakin, T., McIntosh-Smith, S., Alpay, A., Heuveline, V.: Benchmarking and extending sycl hierarchical parallelism. In: 2021 IEEE/ACM International Workshop on Hierarchical Parallelism for Exascale Computing (HiPar), pp. 10–19 (2021). https://doi.org/10.1109/HiPar54615.2021.00007
6. Esmaeilzadeh, H., Cao, T., Yang, X., Blackburn, S.M., Burger, D.: Dark silicon and the end of multicore scaling. In: Proceedings of the 38th Annual International Symposium on Computer Architecture (ISCA), pp. 365–376 (2011). https://doi.org/10.1145/2000064.2000108
7. HEAVY.AI: Heavydb (2025). https://www.heavy.ai/
8. Lal, S., et al.: Sycl-bench: a versatile cross-platform benchmark suite for heterogeneous computing. In: European Conference on Parallel Processing (2020). https://api.semanticscholar.org/CorpusID:220444462
9. Lattner, C., Adve, V.: Llvm: a compilation framework for lifelong program analysis & transformation. In: Proceedings of the International Symposium on Code Generation and Optimization: Feedback-Directed and Runtime Optimization, CGO '04, p. 75. IEEE Computer Society (2004)
10. Marinelli, E., Appuswamy, R.: Xjoin: portable, parallel hash join across diverse xpu architectures with oneapi. In: Proceedings of the 17th International Workshop on Data Management on New Hardware (2021). https://doi.org/10.1145/3465998.3466012
11. O'Neil, P., O'Neil, E., Chen, X., Revilak, S.: The star schema benchmark and augmented fact table indexing. In: Technology Conference on Performance Evaluation and Benchmarking (TPCTC), pp. 237–252 (2009)
12. Raasveldt, M., Mühleisen, H.: Duckdb: an embeddable analytical database. In: Proceedings of the 2019 International Conference on Management of Data (SIGMOD), pp. 1981–1984 (2019). https://doi.org/10.1145/3299869.3320212
13. Reinsel, D., Gantz, J., Rydning, J.: The digitization of the world: From edge to core. In: IDC White Paper (2018). International Data Corporation. Document number: US44413318. Forecasts the Global Datasphere to grow to 175 ZB by 2025, Framingham, MA
14. Reyes, R., Brown, G., Burns, R., Wong, M.: Sycl 2020: more than meets the eye. In: Proceedings of the International Workshop on OpenCL (IWOCL '20) (2020). https://doi.org/10.1145/3388333.3388870

15. Shanbhag, A., Madden, S., Yu, X.: A study of the fundamental performance characteristics of gpus and cpus for database analytics. In: Proceedings of the 2020 ACM SIGMOD International Conference on Management of Data, pp. 1617–1632 (2020). https://doi.org/10.1145/3318464.3380595
16. Slee, M., Agarwal, A., Kwiatkowski, M.: Thrift: Scalable Cross-Language Services Implementation. White paper, Facebook (2007)
17. Stone, J.E., Gohara, D., Shi, G.: Opencl: a parallel programming standard for heterogeneous computing systems. Comput. Sci. Eng. **12**(3), 66–73 (2010)
18. Transaction Processing Performance Council (TPC): TPC Benchmark DS (TPC-DS) Specification (2021). http://www.tpc.org/tpc_documents_current_versions/pdf/tpc-ds_v3.2.0.pdf. Accessed 23 June 2026
19. Yogatama, B., et al.: Rethinking analytical processing in the gpu era. In: 14th Conference on Innovative Data Systems Research (CIDR '26) (2026)
20. Zaharia, M.A., Ghodsi, A., Xin, R., Armbrust, M.: Lakehouse: a new generation of open platforms that unify data warehousing and advanced analytics. In: Conference on Innovative Data Systems Research (2021). https://api.semanticscholar.org/CorpusID:229576171

Elastic Scheduling of Intermittent Query Processing in a Cluster Environment

Saranya Chandrasekaran[1,2](✉) and S. Sudarshan[2]

[1] U R Rao Satellite Centre, ISRO, Bengaluru, India
[2] IIT Bombay, Mumbai, India
{saranyac,sudarsha}@cse.iitb.ac.in

Abstract. Many applications process a stream of tuples over a window duration and require the results within a specified deadline after the end of the window. For such scenarios, processing tuples intermittently (in batches) instead of eagerly processing tuples as they arrive significantly reduces the overall cost. Earlier work on intermittent query processing has addressed only fixed environments.

In this paper, we propose scheduling schemes for batched processing of tuples in an elastic parallel environment, scaling nodes up or down. Our scheduling schemes ensure we meet the deadlines while incurring minimum cost. Our schemes also handle multiple concurrent queries, the arrival of new queries, and input rate variations.

We have implemented our schemes on top of Apache Spark, in the AWS EMR environment. Our experimental results show that our scheduling algorithms significantly outperform alternatives, such as using a fixed set of nodes without elasticity or using Spark streaming.

Keywords: Stream processing · Intermittent query processing

1 Introduction

Many applications have a set of analysis queries that are run on a regular basis, where results are needed only at deadlines and not required on a per tuple basis. Stream processing engines such as Apache Spark and Apache Flink update the aggregate/status as and when a new tuple arrives or when a micro batch of tuples arrives. This method of processing eagerly can lead to significant overhead.

Instead, the fact that results are needed only by a deadline can be utilized to reduce overhead. If there is sufficient time to process all tuples together, starting after the window end, then a single batch is sufficient to complete the processing. However, in general, there may not be sufficient time to process the entire data in the gap between the end of the window and the query deadline.

In such cases, tuples may be collected and processed in batches, and then the partial aggregates on each batch can be further aggregated to get the final result. Tang et al. [13] refer to this method of processing queries in parts and combining the intermediate results as *Intermittent Query Processing*.

G. Vargas-Solar et al. (Eds.): ADBIS 2026, LNCS 16937, pp. 48–64, 2027.
https://doi.org/10.1007/978-3-032-39820-8_5

Our earlier work [2] presented scheduling strategies for intermittent query processing that minimizes cost for an environment with a single node or a fixed set of nodes, while ensuring deadlines are met.

To handle large ingestion rates, we need to use parallel processing. Processing in batches means that in between batch executions, the system may be idle, waiting for enough tuples to arrive. Further, in case there is a spike in the load, with a fixed set of nodes, deadlines may get missed.

A parallel elastic platform where nodes can be added or removed based on demand can be used to address both the above-mentioned problems, reducing cost, while being able to scale up to handle load spikes. While fixed resource scheduling, as in [2], requires a large number of nodes to handle stringent deadlines or higher input rates, our present work proposes an elastic scheduling methodology that initially uses a default number of nodes and further adds or removes nodes based on demand. The Elastic Map Reduce (EMR) platform provided by Amazon Web Services (AWS) is an example of such a platform, where resources are billed based on usage. Our performance results in Sect. 7.5 show that using an elastic configuration can significantly reduce cost compared to a minimal fixed configuration that can meet the deadline.

While fewer nodes may result in a longer processing time, the overall cost incurred may be lower compared to processing with a larger number of nodes, but at the risk of missing deadlines. At the other end, processing all tuples together in a single batch after the window end may require a large number of nodes to meet the deadline, thereby incurring a very high cost, since speedup is often sub-linear in the number of nodes.

Our goal is to schedule the execution of tuple batches at appropriate times on an appropriate number of nodes to minimize the cost while meeting deadlines.

In this paper, we propose an elastic scheduling approach that is based on a simulation model. Given a set of queries, the input rate and initial configuration, the simulation model is used to estimate the appropriate batch size and number of nodes required over different time points to meet the deadline. Our approach is to run the simulation model for different configurations and choose the one that incurs the least cost while ensuring the deadline constraint is met.

Based on the simulation results, our scheduler does the node management by issuing appropriate node resize requests. In general, the addition or removal of nodes in an elastic platform takes a few minutes to set up or release. Our scheduler handles this delay to ensure that the required number of nodes are available when needed.

Our contributions are as follows:

1. We propose strategies to derive the cost model for different configurations.
2. We have devised a simulation model in Sect. 3 to determine the best configuration along with the appropriate batch size.
3. We describe the schedule execution with the addition and deletion of nodes in Sect. 4 and handling of variable input rates in Sect. 5.
4. We implemented the scheduling strategies on Apache Spark, executed on AWS EMR. We present experiments with the TPC-H dataset, including different

input rate profiles and deadline scenarios. The results show the significant benefits of our approach compared to alternatives (Sect. 7).

Related work is discussed in Sect. 6, while Sect. 8 summarizes the conclusions and future work.

2 Background

In this section, we explain the problem description and the factors that affect query scheduling.

2.1 Problem Description

We consider the problem of processing queries with deadlines, on streaming data, intermittently, on an elastic cloud platform. A batch of input tuples for a query is processed at a time, in parallel across multiple nodes. We assume only one query is processed at a time; extensions to consider schedules with concurrent processing of multiple queries are part of future work.

An elastic schedule is a sequence of entries, where each entry consists of the following 4 attributes: (query ID, batch start time, batch size, number of nodes), which represents the execution of the selected query on a batch of specified size, on the specified number of nodes. Our goal is to derive an elastic schedule that incurs the minimum cost, while meeting query deadlines.

The number of alternative configurations (number of nodes) is quite large. To minimize the optimization cost, we consider only some fixed set of configurations, for example, configurations with 2, 4, 10, 14, and 20 nodes. Let these configurations be represented as Cf_i where i varies from 1 to n, s.t. each configuration Cf_{i+1} has more nodes than Cf_i.

Typically, multiple queries need to be processed. We assume that the queries are independent of each other, each with its own deadline. We consider queries that are incremental in nature, allowing tuples to be processed in batches, i.e., incrementally, and combining intermediate results, subsequently, to get the final results; this property is referred to as incrementability in [12].

Queries often run on a single input stream, but may access multiple stored or static relations. We assume that the static data does not change over the period of query execution. Hence, each input stream batch is joined against the static data to get the join results.

Queries that run on multiple streams require stream-to-stream joins. In general, tuples in one batch of a stream could potentially match tuples from any other batch of the stream, which can be very expensive. Similar to [2], for simplicity, our implementation assumes that batches of all streams are aligned, and tuples in a batch of one stream can only match tuples in the same batch of any other stream. Details on handling late arriving tuples are covered in Sect. 5.

Since many analysis queries are recurrent in nature, the cost model of a query can be learnt from the past execution logs, as explained in Sect. 7.2. For simulation, the input rate can be modeled as uniform or non-uniform. While the uniform input rate model assumes that the number of tuples arriving per second does not vary, the non-uniform input rate model can accommodate changing arrival rates, for example, peak versus non-peak hour traffic. Initially, we consider the input rate is known ahead of time, and later in Sect. 5, we address handling dynamically varying input rate.

2.2 Factors Affecting Query Scheduling

The main decisions to be made as part of query scheduling are the batch sizes, their scheduling time points, and the number of nodes for each batch.

In general, we process tuples in batches, numbered $1 \ldots B$, each with its own number of tuples t_{bi}, and number of nodes p_{bi}. Then the cost of a batch can be defined as a function $Cost_b(p_{bi}, t_{bi})$. We note that a batch can be scheduled only after all the tuples in the batch have arrived. Once all batches are processed, the final aggregation is done. The total cost of processing the batches, including the final aggregation cost, $AggCost$, is then defined as in Eq. 1 below.

$$TotalCost = \sum_{b=1}^{B} Cost_b(p_{bi}, t_{bi}) + AggCost \tag{1}$$

We execute each query with different batch sizes on different number of nodes and learn the cost function by fitting these measurements to a linear or piecewise linear cost model (see Sect. 7.2 for more details). Then, using the cost models, we generate the schedule for query processing as explained in Sect. 3.

3 Execution Simulation

The scheduler simulates the processing of the given set of queries in batches, based on batch readiness times, for the given batch sizes. The simulation helps determine the node requirement at each time point to meet the deadline. In this section, we focus on the simulation aspect. The actual scheduling of query batches for execution is discussed later in Sect. 4.

We first explain the generation of a schedule for a given batch size and initial configuration, i.e. initial number of nodes, in Sect. 3.1, and the optimization of the generated schedule and the overall simulation process in Sect. 3.2

3.1 Schedule Generation

We consider a non-preemptive scheduler where once a batch execution begins, it is allowed to complete without interruption. We upper bound the batch size for each query such that each batch can be processed within a maximum duration called C_{max}. This ensures that any new query can be considered for processing within an interval of C_{max} (plus the simulation time) from its arrival.

Algorithm 1. *GenBatchSchedule(simuQList[], &qryBatchSch, batchSizeFactor, C_{max}, simuStartTime, schStartIndex, numNodes)*

```
Output: posSlack (true or false) : denotes whether all query batches completed
  with positive slack time.
simuTime = simuStartTime
For each query in simuQList determine its batchSize based on batchSizeFactor
  and C_max
while (simuQList.length ¿ 0) do
  for (i=0; i¡SimuQList.length; i++) do
    Determine simuQList[i].NextBRT based on batchSize and input rate
    Determine simuQList[i].BCT, simuQList[i].FAT with numNodes
    Determine simuQList[i].BST using Eq. 2
    Determine simuQList[i].SQSlackTime using Eq. 3
  end for
  Pick the query, selQry, with the least slack time, from among those which are
    ready at simuTime. If none of the queries is ready at simuTime, pick the one
    with the (lexicographically) least value of (NextBRT, slack time).
  if (selQry.SQSlacktime ¡ 0) then
    return false
  else
    Update simuTime and selQry.BET using Eq. 4
    Update pendingTuples in selQry based on batchSize
    Assign attributes of qryBatchSch[schStartIndex] from the corresponding
      attributes in selQry {BST, queryID, BST, BET, batchSize, numNodes,
      pendingTuples}     // Add selQry to qryBatchSch with attributes {time,
      qryID, BST, BET, batchSize, reqNodes, pendingTuples}
    if selQry.pendingTuples == 0 then
      Update simuTime for final aggregation & remove selQry from simuQList
    schStartIndex++
end while
return true
```

Let the duration for processing a batch of size x for a query Q, using configuration Cf_i, be denoted as $Dur(Cf_i, x)$. The minimum time for processing the entire input of N tuples with configuration Cf_1 would be by using a single batch of size N, in time $Dur(Cf_1, N)$. To minimize overheads due to small batches, we choose a batch size, X, which is the minimum value of x such that $\lceil N/x \rceil * Dur(Cf_1, x) \leq 2 * Dur(Cf_1, N)$. We upper bound the batch size to the maximum batch size x such that $Dur(Cf_1, x) < C_{max}$.

The batch size determined based on the above scheme is referred to as batch size factor 1X. We also consider larger batch sizes that are multiples of the above size, up to the maximum batch size. For example, with the batch size factor of 2X, the batch size is computed as 2 times the 1X batch size. Simulation is carried out for different configurations, i.e. number of nodes, say Cf_i to Cf_n and batch size factors, say from 1X to SX, as explained in Sect. 3.2.

We now present an algorithm for finding an elastic schedule that minimizes the cost. We first describe the GenBatchSchedule() function, and later explain how it is used in the GenSchedule() function to generate the final schedule.

Function GenBatchSchedule: Function GenBatchSchedule() shown in Algorithm 1, generates the schedule for the input query list, *simQList*, based on execution simulation for the given initial number of nodes and batch size factor, provided it is feasible. If the schedule is not feasible, it returns failure, and it is rerun with a larger number of nodes, as explained later in Function *GenSchedule()*.

The query batch execution schedule, *qryBatchSch*, contains the list of query batches that are scheduled, each defined with the primary attributes of a schedule and a few additional attributes, such as the time, query ID, batch size, batch computation start and end times, pending tuples, and most importantly, the number of nodes required for processing that query batch.

GenBatchSchedule() carries out simulation from *schStartIndex* in *qryBatchSch*. Initially, qryBatchSch contains a single entry with the simulation start time and the initial number of nodes and *schStartIndex* is set to zero.

The algorithm determines the actual batch size of each query based on the batch size factor and C_{max}. Then, the algorithm determines the next batch readiness time (i.e. the batch to be scheduled), $NextBRT$, for each query based on the batch size and the estimated input rate. Let BCT denote its Batch Computation Time and FAT denote the Final Aggregation Time. BCT and FAT are computed using the cost model of the corresponding configuration, Cf_i, where i is based on the number of nodes passed to the function GenBatchSchedule().

Let BST and BET denote the Batch Start Time and Batch End Time, respectively, corresponding to each query batch execution. BST for each query batch is determined as in Eq. 2, and then the slack time of the query is computed, as in Eq. 3 w.r.t. its BST, as follows; here n denotes the total number of batches pending for processing.

$$Q_i.BST = \begin{cases} SimuTime & \text{if } SimuTime > Q_i.NextBRT \\ Q_i.NextBRT & \text{else} \end{cases} \tag{2}$$

$$Q_i.SQSlacktime = Q_i.Deadline - Q_i.BST - (\sum_{j=1}^{n} BCT + FAT) \tag{3}$$

If query batches are ready at *simuTime*, then the query with the least slack time among such query batches is scheduled for processing (in the simulation). If none of the query batches are ready at *simuTime*, then sorting is based on the minimum lexicographic order of *(NextBRT, SQSlacktime)* (line 11 in Algorithm 1). The query batch thus selected is scheduled for processing, provided it has positive slack time.

Thus, we choose the query with the least slack time, thereby using Least Laxity First (LLF) scheduling. (We can alternatively use Earliest Deadline First for scheduling, where, among the queries whose batches are ready, the query with the earliest deadline is chosen for processing.)

The simulation time progresses as the processing of each query batch is simulated, as shown in Eq. 4

$$SimuTime = Q_i.BET = Q_i.BST + Q_i.BCT \tag{4}$$

Once all tuples of a query are processed, the final aggregation of intermediate results is done and the query is removed from *simuQList* (lines 18 and 19 in Algorithm 1). As each query batch gets scheduled, it is added to *qryBatchSch* (line 17 in Algorithm 1) and the *schStartIndex* gets incremented.

If all query batches could be scheduled with non-negative slack time, then *GenBatchSchedule* returns true, and the cost is computed based on the number of nodes and their usage. If a feasible schedule could not be generated with the given batch size factor and number of nodes, *GenBatchSchedule* returns false.

Function GenSchedule: If *GenBatchSchedule* returns false, i.e. the slack time of a query is negative, then we add additional nodes to earlier query batches. The intention to add additional nodes to earlier query batches is to complete these batches earlier, thereby getting sufficient slack for the current query batch (the one with negative slack time with the current schedule) with fewer nodes than requiring a higher number of nodes for speeding up only the current batch.

Then the simulation is repeated, where *GenSchedule* invokes the function *GenBatchSchedule* and the simulation is rerun from the last query batch by setting it to the next configuration, i.e. Cf_{i+1}. If the slack time still remains negative, then the simulation is run with a higher configuration for the successively earlier batches until a positive slack time is achieved, or we reach the first batch. On reaching the first batch, if the slack time is still negative, we rerun the process above with the next higher configuration, starting from the last batch backwards. This process continues until a feasible schedule is obtained, or if a feasible schedule is not possible even on reaching the maximum number of nodes, then the simulation returns an empty schedule. Details on Algorithm *GenSchedule*, which invokes *GenBatchSchedule*, can be referred to in the full version of our paper [1].

3.2 Schedule Optimization

The simulation generates the schedule for the given batch size factor and initial configuration. To determine the appropriate batch size factor and initial configuration, we run the simulation (accounting for optimizations described later in this section), for different batch size factors from 1X to some maximum value, say 6X, starting with the different initial configuration, e.g. Cf_1 to Cf_5, and choose the configuration and the batch size factor that minimizes overall cost, while meeting deadlines.

Running the simulation for all possible batch size factors and initial number of nodes may be expensive and hence we run the same for a chosen set of batch size factors and initial configurations. Also, the simulation can be run in parallel to the query execution to reduce the additional delay due to the simulation.

We now consider some optimizations. We first consider the release of nodes when not required. If the number of nodes required for each query batch in *qryBatchSch* is the same as the initial number of nodes, then the schedule is already optimized, as it does not require additional nodes.

If the number of nodes required for any query batch in *qryBatchSch* is greater than the initial number of nodes, then there can be scope for optimization. For such schedules, we verify their utilization by computing the idle time between the completion and start of consecutive query batches, for batches that were scheduled with a higher number of nodes.

If idle time exists, the simulation is rerun from the start of the idle period with the initial number of nodes. If the initial number of nodes is not sufficient, then the appropriate number of nodes required is determined by the simulation as explained earlier. This is repeated for each segment with idle time before it, and the final optimized schedule is obtained by merging the schedules generated for each segment.

In addition, for idle periods where no inputs arrive or if there are sufficient gaps between consecutive query batches scheduled for execution, then the additional nodes are released and acquired later when needed.

We note that while our algorithms implement several techniques to minimize the cost of execution, proving how close the result is to optimal is part of future work.

3.3 Partial Aggregation

Though aggregation is done only once after processing all tuples in Algorithm 1, we can do partial aggregation on intermediate results to bring down the final aggregation time. The number of batches after which the partial aggregation can be done is made configurable. Then the batch end time for batches where partial aggregations are carried out can be computed as in Eq. 5, where PAT denotes Partial Aggregation Time.

$$Q_i.BET = Q_i.BST + Q_i.BCT + Q_i.PAT \tag{5}$$

During simulation, in Function *GenBatchSchedule()* we generate a schedule by accommodating PAT in BET computation. More details are available in the full version of our paper [1].

4 Schedule Execution

In this section, we explain the execution of the schedule generated using simulation. The scheduler carries out node management and scheduling of query batches for processing, based on batch readiness.

The schedule contains the number of nodes required at any given point in time. Although the simulation considers that nodes can be acquired and released instantaneously, cluster platforms require a certain duration to allocate or release a node. Here, we explain how such delays are accommodated.

The scheduler keeps track of the latest number of nodes requested to the cluster. If the required number of nodes changes at any point in the chosen schedule, the scheduler issues appropriate node resize requests as follows.

Addition of Nodes: If the currently requested number of nodes is less than the required number of nodes, then more nodes have to be added. A new node allocation request may have an associated delay; upto 6 min delay has been observed on AWS EMR from request to allocation of a node. To accommodate such delays, the scheduler issues requests for new nodes correspondingly ahead of the time when the nodes are required in the schedule. The time ahead of which the request has to be placed can be tuned based on the cluster requirements.

Release of Nodes: Similarly, nodes have to be released if the current number of nodes is greater than the required number of nodes at some point in the schedule. Actual release of nodes happens when there is no active job running on the nodes. The release operation takes around 1 or 2 min for completion on AWS EMR. Thus, nodes are released provided that these nodes remain idle for a certain duration. As node allocation takes a considerable duration, this idle period is set to at least twice the node allocation time.

Execution of query batches is managed by the scheduler. The scheduler checks the currently available tuples for each of the queries and determines the queries whose batches are ready for processing. Then, the scheduler computes the slack time of the queries. The query with the least slack is chosen and scheduled for processing, following the LLF policy.

On processing the query batch, its result, referred to as an intermediate result, is stored. Once all the batches of the query have been processed, the final aggregation is done on the intermediate results, and the query is removed from the scheduler queue.

5 Handling Variable Input Rate

So far, we have assumed that the input data rate is known and the total number of tuples is fixed. But the actual input rate may vary dynamically. In an optimistic model, if the input rate is faster, we assume that tuples arrive early, but the total number of tuples in the window remains the same; if the input rate is slower, we assume that the total number of tuples in the window is smaller. On the other hand, in a pessimistic model, if we see a higher input rate, we assume the higher input rate will continue, resulting in an increase in the number of tuples in the window; if the input rate is slower, we assume that more tuples will arrive later for the same window and the total number of tuples in the window remains the same.

With a pessimistic model, if we see a higher input rate, we rerun the simulation with an increased total number of tuples. If we see a slower input rate, we continue with the existing schedule until the input rate increases, which will happen under the pessimistic model, at which point we rerun the simulation.

During runtime, the actual input rate is determined by averaging the total number of tuples received over a given time duration. When the observed rate is significantly higher than the assumed rate, the simulation is rerun, and a new schedule is generated. For multiple streams, the simulation is rerun when at least one of the input rates varies beyond the maximum supported rates.

The time duration for input rate estimation depends on the time taken for node allocation in the elastic cluster. For AWS, the node allocation time is observed up to 6 min; we use a duration of 3 min for the estimation of input rate to allow reasonably fast adaptation to changing rates, while being relatively close to the node allocation time.

If the input rate varies frequently, the simulation could get rerun repeatedly. To avoid this, as part of the simulation, we also determine the maximum input rate that can be supported by the chosen schedule. During runtime, we rerun the simulation only when the actual input rate exceeds the maximum supported rate.

In stream-to-stream joins, we assume that matching tuples from different streams arrive in the same batch. In case tuples arrive late in some streams, late arriving tuples can be handled as follows: in each batch, the late arriving tuples, i.e. tuples whose timestamp is earlier compared to the normal start timestamp of the batch, are identified and joined against the previous batches of other streams.

6 Related Work

Tang et al. [13] and [12] introduce incrementability and intermittent query processing, where a query can be processed in parts, and the partial results can be combined to get the consolidated result. Though we do intermittent processing, our work schedules jobs within deadlines, while [13] and [12] do not consider deadlines.

Similarly, Shang et al. [10], Tang et al. [8], propose Crocodile DB, which utilizes query slackness to reduce resource consumption. Sotolongo et al. [6] propose to generate incremental views periodically based on user input target lags. But, unlike ours, these works, [8,10] and [6] do not consider deadlines.

YARN [11] caters to generic resource management and job scheduling, but does not support deadline based scheduling.

The general job scheduling techniques are EDF and LLF. While our scheduling is based on LLF; unlike [9], we perform batching to minimize the overall cost in addition to meeting deadlines.

Grosbeak [7] schedules routine analysis jobs in non-peak hours based on the history of resource utilization. We also process jobs in batches, but details on scheduling are not discussed in [7].

Work has been done in the past to reduce resource consumption in a cluster environment under deadline bound scenarios, [5,9,14,15] and [16]. Unlike these works, our methodology processes jobs in appropriate batches, thereby minimizing the node requirement while ensuring deadlines are met.

Zhu et al. [4] propose scheduling jobs on an elastic platform with the aim of meeting deadlines while minimizing node requirements. Unlike [4], we consider streaming jobs where batches are scheduled based on the availability of tuples.

Huang et al. [3] propose scheduling queries at times when the price is lower on cloud platforms with variable pricing policies. Elastic scheduling based on deadlines is not considered by [3]. In addition, while ours is a streaming scenario where inputs arrive continuously, allowing us to choose batch sizes, [3] considers the arrival of data at discrete points when scheduling is done.

The closest related work is our earlier work [2], which considers batching and scheduling for intermittent query processing, but on a single node or a fixed set of nodes. The benefits of processing in batches, showing that scheduling queries with EDF and LLF without a minimum batch size may lead to deadline misses, are demonstrated in [2]. However, it does not address elastic scheduling, which is a focus of our work. In addition, we consider the monetary cost in a cloud platform and design scheduling techniques to minimise the actual cost incurred.

While there has been prior work in scheduling jobs to meet deadlines, our work of scheduling based on tuple arrival in a streaming system with a simulation model to add or remove nodes based on demand is a unique contribution. To the best of our knowledge, none of the earlier work considers the combination of batching and elastic scheduling to minimize cost while meeting deadlines.

7 Performance Evaluation

We present our performance results in this section, using the TPC-H benchmark queries along with some custom queries.

7.1 Experimental Setup

Our experiments are carried out in AWS EMR, which consists of a Primary node (P), and 1 or more Core (C) nodes and 0 or more Task (T) nodes; computation is carried out on core and task nodes, while core nodes can also access HDFS storage. We used EMR version emr-6.13.0, and each of the P/C/T nodes is of type m5.xlarge with 4 virtual cores and 16 GiB memory.

The scheduling algorithm is implemented as part of a Custom Scheduler module that runs on top of Apache Spark. It comprises three components, namely the Query Scheduler, the Schedule Optimizer and the Query Repository. Code may be found at https://github.com/saranyacsekar/ElasticScheduler.

The Query Scheduler carries out the schedule execution, and the Schedule Optimizer does the simulation comprising schedule generation and optimisation. The Query Repository contains the metadata of the queries to be processed and their Spark operations since the current implementation is based on Apache Spark. The Query Scheduler also monitors for the addition or deletion of queries or input rate variations in the existing queries and invokes the Schedule Optimizer for carrying out the simulation, if required.

Since batch sizes are chosen such that no batch takes more than C_{max} time, the Query Scheduler performs these tasks periodically within a maximum interval of C_{max} plus the time taken for simulation. We used $C_{max} = 120$ s.

In our performance study, we consider the following configurations: 1P-1C-1T, 1P-1C-3T, 1P-1C-9T, 1P-1C-13T and 1P-1C-19T denoted as Cf_1, Cf_2, Cf_3, Cf_4 and Cf_5, with 2, 4, 10, 14 and 20 worker nodes, respectively. Input data is read from and the results are written to an S3 bucket. We chose On-Demand pricing model to ensure the instances cannot be terminated based on demand.

We use a slightly modified version of the TPC-H Dataset, considering a timestamp in each record of Orders and Lineitem, to model a streaming input. We consider 4500 files (25 GB of data), where each file of orders and lineitem is about 1.2 MB and 5 MB, respectively, with an input rate of 1 file of Orders and 1 file of Lineitem per second. Other relations are considered to be static information that does not change during query execution.

A subset of TPC-H queries that support incremental processing, including queries with joins, as in [2], has been considered. Apart from these TPC-H queries, some custom queries, as in [2], shown in Table 1, were also used. For queries with joins, similar to [2], we assume that matching tuples between Orders and Lineitem are within the same input batch. However, late arriving tuples in stream-to-stream join can be handled as described in Sect. 5.

Table 1. Custom Queries

QryID	Query
CQ1	*SELECT count(∗) as totalOrders FROM orders*
CQ2	*SELECT count(∗) as totalItems, partKey FROM lineItems GROUP BY partKey*
CQ3	*SELECT count(∗) as totalItems, suppKey FROM lineItems GROUP BY suppKey*
CQ4	*SELECT count(∗) as totalOrders, orderPriority FROM orders GROUP BY orderPriority*

7.2 Cost Modeling for TPC-H Queries in EMR

For each query, we determine its cost model for different configurations by measuring time (processing duration without aggregation) and monetary cost. As queries are executed in a recurring fashion, the cost of executing them to fit the cost model gets amortized across a large number of actual executions.

We experimentally measure the time taken for processing the input by varying in steps of 250 files, where each file is as described earlier, in each run in different configurations. Using linear regression, the measurements were fit into a linear model, including queries with joins, as streaming joins are window based. Run-to-run variations were observed. For example, processing time measurements for TPC-Q1 had a variance of 4 with respect to the modelled value of

16.5 s. Aggregation duration was modelled as a piecewise linear model based on the number of batches and nodes. Methods to derive the cost model with fewer runs are explained in [1].

Once the processing duration is determined, the monetary cost incurred can be computed. AWS EMR monetary cost has two components: AWS EC2 node billed on a per-second basis, with a minimum of 1 min, which depends on the type of compute node and per-node cost for using EMR. For e.g., the hourly rates for Amazon EC2 On-Demand instances and EMR, for m5.xlarge instances in the Asia Pacific region, are $0.202 and $0.048, respectively. Based on the number of instances used and their duration, the total cost is computed.

7.3 Experiments with Different Deadline Scenarios and Input Rates

Experiments were carried out by considering 9 TPC-H queries and the 4 custom queries together. The minimum duration required for processing all tuples in a single batch starting at the window end using Cf_5 is set as Deadline, 1D. Further cases were generated where the deadlines are reduced to 0.8D, 0.6D, 0.4D and 0.3D. Further, we ran experiments by increasing the input rate to two (2FR) and four times (4FR) of the baseline input rate (FR).

For each of these cases, the simulation was carried out with different batch size factors (BSF) and initial number of nodes and the schedule that incurs the least cost was chosen for execution. Simulation results covering all combinations are available in the full version of our paper [1]. Table 2 shows the comparison between the simulation and the actual runs. The initial number of nodes (INN) is set to 2, while max number of nodes (MNN) is determined by our scheduler. The batch size factor is chosen based on the minimal cost as per the simulation. All cases were completed within deadlines and the results of the actual runs match well with the simulation results. For all these cases, a simulation was run once at the beginning of each run. The longest simulation time was for the 4FR case, at 233 s, while the total run duration was 4610 s.

Table 2. Experimental Results with Different Deadline and Input Rates

Deadline	InputRate	INN	MNN	BSF	SimuCost($)	ActualCost($)
1D	1FR	2	2	2X	0.94	1.12
0.8D	1FR	2	2	2X	0.94	1.23
0.6D	1FR	2	4	2X	1.14	1.27
0.4D	1FR	2	10	2X	1.55	1.53
0.3D	1FR	2	14	8X	1.74	1.62
1D	2FR	2	4	16X	1.34	1.10
1D	4FR	2	14	32X	2.99	2.72

7.4 Experiments with Variable Input Rates

We also carried out experiments with variable input rates, as shown in Fig. 1. VR1 starts with an input rate slower than 2FR and subsequently varies up to 8 times 2FR, while in the VR2 profile, the input rate varies up to 8 times 2FR and the total number of tuples exceeds the 2FR case. The input rate fed to the simulation was 2FR and the schedule generated was the same as that of the 2FR case. Further, during the runtime, the scheduler measures the input rate by averaging the number of tuples received over the last 3-minute duration. If the measured input rate is more than the estimate i.e. 2FR, by 2%, then the simulation is rerun and a new schedule is generated. Further, the new schedule continues until the input rate varies again. It was observed that the rerunning of simulation was triggered multiple times (5 times for VR1 and 9 times for VR2).

As shown in the Fig. 1, while 2FR completed with 4 nodes, VR1 and VR2 required 14 and 10 nodes, respectively. Both runs were successful. Table 3 shows the experimental results. Additional details are available in [1].

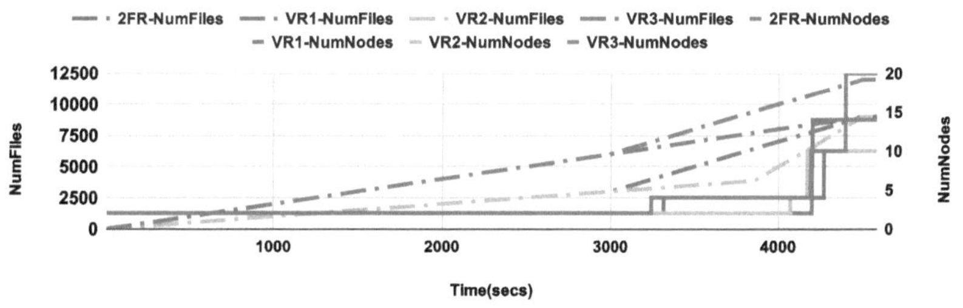

Fig. 1. Variable Input Rate Profiles and Node Requirements

Table 3. Experimental Results with Variable Input Rates

Case	INN	MNN	BSF	SimuCost($)	ActualCost($)
2FR	2	4	16X	1.34	1.10
VR1	2	14	16X	1.34	1.51
VR2	2	10	16X	1.34	1.33

7.5 Comparison With Other Approaches

We now compare our scheduling algorithm to alternative approaches.

Comparison with Fixed Configuration. Here, we compare our elastic scheduling to a fixed configuration, with both approaches using batch size determination as explained in Sect. 3.1. For each of the cases considered in Table 4, we carried out a simulation using a fixed configuration. In Table 4 FN represents a fixed number of nodes, while Elastic represents our approach with a variable number of nodes. Table 4 shows the cost incurred with each fixed configuration, provided the deadlines were met successfully. For each of the cases, our approach incurs cost less than the cost incurred by the minimum fixed configuration that meets the deadline. Thus, our approach generates the best elastic configuration to meet the deadline while minimising the cost incurred.

Table 4. Simulation Results for Cost ($) with Fixed vs Elastic Configuration **Notation: Case**: InputRate:Deadline; **FN:n** Fixed n Nodes **MNN**: Max Number of Nodes

Case	FN:2	FN:4	FN:10	FN:14	FN:20	Elastic	Elastic MNN
1FR:0.6D	-	2.05	5.11	6.11	8.13	1.14	4
1FR:0.4D	-	-	5.10	6.10	8.11	1.55	10
1FR:0.3D	-	-	-	6.10	8.11	1.74	14
2FR:1D	-	2.06	5.11	6.11	8.12	1.34	4
4FR:1D	-	-	5.13	6.13	8.15	2.99	14

LLF Without Batch Size Determination: To evaluate the importance of batching used in our approach, we compare our strategy with using LLF without batch size determination, where the currently available tuples are processed based on LLF (minimum batch size is 1 file having around 9400 tuples, as input is simulated as files/sec). We use a fixed configuration for this experiment. Execution completed within the deadline (1D case) for the 20 nodes configuration and failed for lower configurations, while our approach completed with 2 nodes.

Comparison with EMR Auto Scaling Mode. Here, we compare our elastic scheduling with the auto scaling feature of EMR. We experimented on the FR:1D case, enabling the EMR auto scaling feature. Since deadline based rules were not available in EMR, we defined rules for scaling in and out based on the percentage of YARN Memory available. While our scheduler completed the same case with 2 nodes, incurring 1.12 dollars, auto scaling acquired 10 nodes, incurring 2.28 dollars for the same run. While, our approach meets deadline with cheaper cost, auto scaling, in general, gives no guarantees of meeting deadlines.

Comparison with Spark Streaming. We experimented using Spark Streaming for the 1D case by enabling auto scaling based on the percentage of YARN Memory available. Spark Streaming uses micro batching, with a single file of about 9500 records as the minimum size. While with our approach, the 1D case completed all queries within their deadlines using 2 nodes, Spark Streaming could not compute the results for queries with joins within the deadline duration. Another run considering queries without joins in Spark Streaming mode completed with 20 nodes, incurring 12 times more cost compared to our approach. Thus, our approach is more efficient in minimizing cost while meeting deadlines.

7.6 Other Experiments

We also carried out experiments demonstrating the release of nodes and the significance of partial aggregation. In addition to TPC-H, we also carried out experiments with the Yahoo Streaming Dataset. For lack of space, we omit the results here, but details are available in the full version of our paper [1].

8 Conclusion and Future Work

Intermittent query processing is ideal for situations where data over a window period has to be analyzed within some deadlines. We have proposed scheduling techniques for intermittent query processing in an elastic environment where the processing is done with the appropriate number of nodes to ensure deadlines are met while reducing the overall cost incurred. Our experimental results establish the benefits of our approach. As part of future work, we plan to extend the scheduling to support the simultaneous execution of different queries on different subsets of nodes in the cluster. Evaluating our algorithm with dynamic query arrivals is part of future work. Optimising the simulation time, as well as proving the optimality of our scheduling algorithm, are areas of future work.

Disclosure of Interests. The authors have no competing interests to declare that are relevant to the content of this article.

References

1. Saranya, C., Sudarshan, S.: Elastic scheduling of intermittent query processing in a cluster environment (2026). https://doi.org/10.48550/arXiv.2605.08601
2. Chandrasekaran, S., Sudarshan, S.: Scheduling of intermittent query processing. In: International Database Engineered Applications Symposium 2024 (2024)
3. Huang, B., et al.: Agamotto: scheduling of deadline-oriented incremental query execution under uncertain resource price. In: VLDB 2025 (2025)
4. Zhu, J., et al.: Scheduling stochastic multi-stage jobs to elastic hybrid cloud resources. IEEE Trans. Parallel Distrib. Syst. (2018)
5. Hou, X., et al.: Dynamic deadline-constraint scheduler for Hadoop YARN. In: IEEE SmartWorld/SCALCOM/UIC/ATC/CBDCom/IOP/SCI 2017 (2017)
6. Sotolongo, D., et al.: Streaming democratized: ease across the latency spectrum with delayed view semantics and snowflake dynamic tables. In: ACM SIGMOD 2025 (2025)

7. Wang, Z., et al.: Grosbeak: a data warehouse supporting resource-aware incremental computing. In: ACM SIGMOD 2020 (2020)
8. Tang, D., et al.: CrocodileDB in action: resource-efficient query execution by exploiting time slackness. In: Proceedings Of The VLDB Endowment 2020 (2020)
9. Wang, G., et al.: A hard real-time scheduler for Spark on YARN. In: 18th IEEE/ACM International Symposium on Cluster, Cloud and Grid Computing 2018 (2018)
10. Shang, Z., et al.: CrocodileDB: efficient database execution through intelligent deferment. In: CIDR (2020)
11. Vavilapalli, V., et al.: Apache Hadoop Yarn: yet another resource negotiator. In: Proceedings of the 4th Annual Symposium On Cloud Computing 2013 (2013)
12. Tang, D., et al.: Thrifty query execution via incrementability. In: ACM SIGMOD International Conference on Management of Data 2020 (2020)
13. Tang, D., Shang, Z., Elmore, A., Krishnan, S., Franklin, M.: Intermittent query processing. In: Proceedings of the VLDB Endowment 2019 (2019)
14. Dimopoulos, S., et al.: Justice: a deadline-aware, fair-share resource allocator for implementing multi-analytics. In: IEEE International Conference on Cluster Computing 2017 (2017)
15. Sidhanta, S., et al.: A deadline-aware cost optimization model for spark. In: 16th IEEE/ACM International Symposium on Cluster, Cloud and Grid Computing 2016 (2016)
16. Islam, M., et al.: dSpark: deadline-based resource allocation for big data applications in Apache Spark. In: IEEE 13th International Conference on E-Science 2017 (2017)

BPG: Efficient and Scalable Property Graph Serialization

Dominik Tomaszuk(✉)

University of Bialystok, Bialystok, Poland
d.tomaszuk@uwb.edu.pl

Abstract. Property graphs are widely used for heterogeneous, schema-flexible data, but their common exchange formats remain predominantly text-oriented, repeat structural information, and require full parsing before analytical access. These costs matter when property graphs are published, archived, moved between systems, or queried in data-processing pipelines without first loading them into a graph DBMS. In this paper, we present Binary Property Graph (BPG), a Parquet-based serialization that preserves property-graph constructs while exposing nodes, edges, labels, and properties to compact columnar storage and direct analytical scans. BPG stores graph structure as typed Parquet files, annotates values with Graph Query Language (GQL)-oriented metadata, and optionally packages the files into a single integrity-protected container. Experiments on eight real-world property graphs and five synthetic scale graphs show that BPG substantially reduces storage compared with CSV and GraphML baselines, while preserving efficient analytical access through standard columnar tooling.

Keywords: Property graphs · Binary serialization · Apache Parquet · Graph data management · Data compression

1 Introduction

Property graphs model data as nodes, relationships, labels, and key-value properties, and are used in domains ranging from biomedical knowledge graphs to social networks and investigative data management [2,4]. Even when the primary workload runs inside a graph DBMS, graph snapshots still move through data lakes, ETL pipelines, notebooks, benchmark suites, archives, and publication repositories. A physical exchange format is therefore not a substitute for a DBMS, but an interoperability layer that determines how much work is needed before another tool can inspect, validate, or query the graph.

Existing formats leave a gap for large property graphs that should be both portable and directly analyzable. Mainstream property-graph serializations such as GraphML [8], GraphSON [40], and YARS-PG [35] are useful for interchange, but they repeat markup for nodes, edges, labels, and properties, require full parsing before scans, and cannot expose column pruning to analytical engines. General binary formats improve compactness [43], but they usually encode records,

G. Vargas-Solar et al. (Eds.): ADBIS 2026, LNCS 16937, pp. 65–82, 2027.
https://doi.org/10.1007/978-3-032-39820-8_6

messages, or tree-shaped documents rather than a reusable property-graph layout. A consumer must then know application-specific choices such as where node labels are stored, how edge-property values are typed, how multi-valued properties are encoded, and which fields are identifiers before it can execute efficient scans or joins.

In this paper, we propose Binary Property Graph (BPG), a serialization that maps property-graph structure to Apache Parquet. BPG gives nodes and edges a graph-specific Parquet profile, stores graph and value semantics in metadata, and can be read by columnar engines such as DuckDB, Spark, or Arrow-based tools without implementing a new low-level parser. The contribution is the reusable graph-specific columnar layout, not only a conversion pipeline. This conservative choice is deliberate: Parquet already provides compression codecs, typed columns, row-group statistics, and column pruning, which directly support count queries, label filters, property scans, and simple edge-node joins over exported graph snapshots.

The contributions are as follows: **C1** we derive design criteria for binary property-graph exchange from limitations of existing formats and analytical workloads; **C2** we define a Parquet-based BPG representation for nodes, edges, labels, properties, and GQL-oriented value metadata; **C3** we add an optional container for single-file exchange and integrity checking; and **C4** we evaluate BPG on real-world and synthetic datasets with respect to conformance, storage footprint, write throughput, analytical queries, and container overhead.

This paper is structured as follows. Section 2 defines the requirements, Sect. 3 discusses related work, Sect. 4 introduces BPG, Sect. 5 evaluates it, and Sect. 6 concludes.

2 Design Requirements

The design follows the property-graph model in which nodes and edges may carry labels and properties [4]. The requirements summarize three observations from the motivation. First, an exchange format must preserve property-graph semantics rather than only serialize generic records. Second, analytical consumers should be able to scan identifiers, labels, endpoints, and selected properties without reparsing complete text files. Third, published graph snapshots need predictable compression, validation, and integrity checks when they are moved outside a DBMS. We separate functional requirements from operational requirements so that expressiveness can be evaluated independently from storage and processing efficiency.

FR1 Nodes. Nodes must be represented with unique identifiers.
FR2 Edges. Edges must be represented as relationships between nodes and may have identifiers; BPG adopts mandatory edge identifiers for unambiguous management.
FR3 Node labels. Node labels must be supported.
FR4 Edge labels. Edge labels must be supported.
FR5 Node properties. Nodes must support named property values.

FR6 Edge properties. Edges must support named property values.
FR7 Property values. Single-value and multi-value properties must be representable.

The non-functional requirements capture the resulting operational goals.

NFR1 Conciseness. The representation should avoid repeated textual markup and reduce storage and processing overhead.
NFR2 Compression. The format should support multiple compression algorithms so that users can choose between compact and fast-access profiles.
NFR3 Performance. Reads and writes should support efficient scan-heavy and graph-oriented analytical workloads.
NFR4 Scalability. The format must handle large graphs efficiently.
NFR5 Interoperability. The format should work with existing data processing systems.
NFR6 Integrity and recoverability. The format should support integrity verification and limited recovery when corruption is localized.
NFR7 Efficiency. Encoding and decoding should minimize unnecessary CPU, memory, and I/O overhead.

3 Related Work

Binary serialization has a long history, from schema-driven encodings such as ASN.1 [29] to language-specific object serialization and modern data-exchange formats. The common motivation is to reduce parsing cost and storage overhead, but the design space differs substantially depending on whether a format targets messages, documents, tabular analytics, or graph data. BPG is positioned in this space as a graph-aware physical representation that reuses a mature columnar format rather than defining a new byte-level encoding.

General-purpose binary serializations improve on plain text in different ways. Avro [44], Protobuf [11], and Thrift [32] emphasize schema-driven data interchange and remote communication. FlatBuffers [23] emphasizes fast object access. MessagePack [9], CBOR [7], BSON [10], and EXI [24] compact JSON-like or XML-like trees. ORC [38] is closer to BPG because it is columnar, but BPG uses Parquet because of its broad analytical ecosystem and metadata model. These systems can encode graph records, but they require application-specific conventions for labels, edge properties, multi-valued property values, identifiers, and graph metadata; consequently, they do not provide a directly reusable property-graph exchange layout (Table 1).

Binary graph serializations have been studied most extensively for RDF [13]. HDT [13], ERI [12], k^2-TRIPLES [1], and RDS [14] exploit RDF-specific structure and compression opportunities. HDT separates headers, dictionaries, and triples; k^2-TRIPLES compresses sparse adjacency-like structures; ERI and RDS focus on stream-oriented RDF exchange. These approaches are less suitable for property graphs because RDF triples do not directly capture labels, edge properties, and multi-valued property values without reification or additional modelling conventions. TinkerPop's Gryo and GraphBinary address property-graph

Table 1. General-purpose and tree-oriented binary formats in relation to BPG. The cited formats are referenced in the surrounding text.

Format	Orientation	Schema	Compression	Selective access	Interoperability
Avro [44]	Row-oriented data interchange	Yes	External/supported	Limited	High
FlatBuffers [23]	In-memory objects	Yes	No native support	Object-level	Medium
Protobuf [11]	Message interchange	Yes	External	Limited	Very high
ORC [38]	Columnar analytics	Yes	Yes	Yes	Medium
ASN.1 [29]	General binary encoding	Yes	Depends on rules	Limited	Medium
MessagePack [9]	JSON-like binary trees	No	No native support	Limited	High
CBOR [7]	JSON-like binary trees	No	No native support	Limited	High
BSON [10]	Binary JSON documents	Partial	Limited	Limited	High
EXI [24]	Binary XML	Optional	Yes	Limited	Medium
BPG	Parquet property graphs	Yes	Yes	Yes	High

objects [39,41], but their primary use is tied to TinkerPop object exchange rather than columnar analytical access, independent Parquet readers, or compression profiles supported by data-lake tooling (Table 2).

Table 2. Binary graph serializations primarily targeting RDF, compared with BPG.

Format	Target model	Binary	Compression focus	Query orientation	Fit for PG
HDT [13]	RDF	Yes	High	Partial	Low
ERI [12]	RDF streams	Yes	High	Low	Low
k^2-TRIPLES [1]	RDF	Yes	High	Specific graph queries	Low
RDS [14]	RDF streams	Yes	High	No	Low
BPG	Property Graph	Yes	High	Analytical/columnar	High

Schema languages are complementary rather than competing work: SHACL [22], ShEx [33], SQL/PGQ [20], GQL [21], openCypher schema [6], PG-Schema [2], XML Schema [25], RELAX NG [19], JSON Schema [30], and GraphQL [16] can constrain valid data or query types, but they do not define a compact physical layout, compression strategy, or column-pruning behavior.

Recent text-based property-graph formats such as YARS-PG [35] and PGDF [3] address platform-independent publication and exchange. BPG is complementary: it focuses on a binary, columnar representation for compact storage and direct analytical access over graph snapshots (Table 3).

4 BPG Serialization

This section separates the inherited Parquet binary envelope from the BPG-specific graph profile: first the physical payload, then node and edge schemas, metadata, and the optional container.

Table 3. Property-graph serialization formats most directly comparable to BPG because they encode property-graph data rather than only generic records or RDF triples.

Format	Text/bin.	PG-native	Labels & props	Multi-value props	Compression	Ecosystem
GraphML [8]	Text	Yes	Yes	Limited/indirect	External	Broad
GraphSON [40]	Text	Yes	Yes	Yes	External	TinkerPop-oriented
Gryo [41]	Binary	Yes	Yes	Yes	Limited	Narrow
GraphBinary [39]	Binary	Yes	Yes	Yes	Limited	Narrow/medium
BPG	Binary	Yes	Yes	Yes	Parquet codecs	Broad analytical ecosystem

4.1 Parquet Background and Use in BPG

Apache Parquet is a column-oriented binary file format designed for large analytical datasets [5]. Each generated BPG node and edge payload is a standard Parquet file with the binary envelope in Listing 1.1. The four-byte header and footer are Parquet magic markers; `RowGroups` stores columnar data; and `FileMetadata` records schema, offsets, sizes, statistics, compression, and BPG key-value metadata such as `name`, `version`, and `gql`.

Listing 1.1. Binary envelope of generated BPG Parquet payloads.

```
Header[4]                                  mandatory
RowGroups[row_groups_size]                 mandatory
FileMetadata[file_metadata_size]           mandatory
MetadataLength[4]                          mandatory
Footer[4]                                  mandatory
```

Within `RowGroups`, each row group is an independently readable horizontal partition; each row group contains one column chunk per column; and each column chunk is split into compressed pages. Thus a query that needs only identifiers or labels can skip unrelated columns and many pages.

BPG uses Parquet as the physical substrate and adds a property-graph profile. Node identifiers become an integer `id` column, labels become repeated string columns, endpoints become edge columns, and properties become nested key/-value columns. This layout is natural for graph snapshots because identifiers, labels, relationship tokens, and property keys contain many repeated values that Parquet encoders and codecs can compress well. Columnar storage addresses **NFR1**, Parquet codecs address **NFR2**, typed scans and joins address **NFR3**, row groups address **NFR4**, and the Parquet ecosystem addresses **NFR5**. Metadata-guided typing and the optional container provide the integrity and efficient-access mechanisms needed for **NFR6** and **NFR7**.

4.2 Logical Graph Representation

BPG stores a property graph as two self-contained Parquet files: `nodes.parquet`, with one logical row per node, and `edges.parquet`, with one logical row per edge. Logically, a BPG instance consists of node and edge sets, label sets assigned to nodes and edges, and property maps from keys to finite value lists. Figure 1 gives the logical entity–relationship view, while Table 4 shows how one small graph is represented physically. The node row contains the node identifier and a nested property list; the nested entry is not a second node row, but a repeated value inside the same logical node row. Query engines can use the same layout directly: a node count reads `nodes.id`, a label filter reads `nodes.label`, and a one-hop join reads edge endpoints plus the target-node `id`.

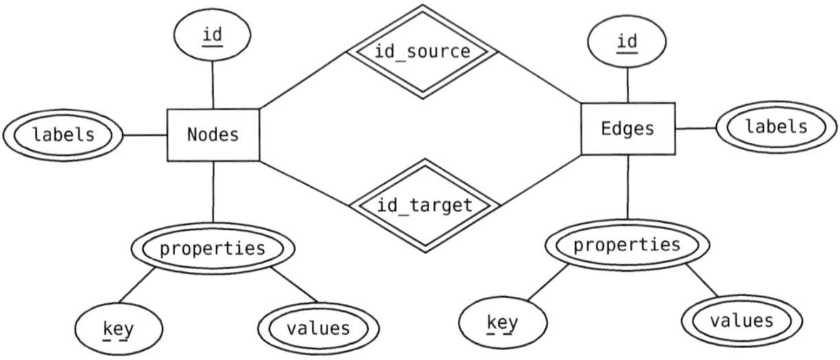

Fig. 1. Logical entity–relationship view of BPG.

Table 4. Central BPG example: a property graph fragment is represented by node and edge Parquet rows with nested labels/properties and file-level metadata.

Graph fragment	nodes.parquet	edges.parquet
(1:Person {name: Alice})	row: id=1, label=[Person], properties=[{key:name, values:[Alice]}]	
-[7:KNOWS {since:2020}]->	row: id=2, label=[Person], properties=[]	row: id=7, source=1, target=2, label=[KNOWS], properties=[{key:since, values:[2020]}]
file metadata	name=BPG, version=1.0, gql={...}	same keys, edge-column descriptors

Each file contains file-level metadata `name=BPG`, `version=1.0`, and a `gql` manifest. The manifest is UTF-8 JSON stored in the Parquet footer key-value metadata under key `gql`. It has required fields `version` and `columns`; optional fields describe the GQL dialect, temporal defaults, and column descriptors. A column descriptor records the original GQL type, physical Parquet representation, encoding, nullability, numeric precision/scale, temporal unit, time zone, compatibility column, and list or record parameters. Field-level metadata keys with prefix `gql:*` can locally refine the manifest; readers prefer field metadata when it conflicts with the manifest and should report the conflict.

Listing 1.2. Illustrative BPG metadata stored in Parquet file and field metadata.

```
file key_values:
  name = BPG
  version = 1.0
  gql = {"version":"1.0.1","dialect":"ISO/IEC 39075",
         "columns":{"properties.values.value":
           {"originalType":"string",
            "physical":"BYTE_ARRAY(STRING)",
            "nullable":true}}}
field properties.values.value:
  gql:type = string
  gql:codec = utf8
```

Standard Parquet logical types are preferred whenever they preserve GQL semantics. Metadata-guided binary carriers are used only when Parquet lacks a native representation, for example for wider integers or specialized temporal values. Graph reference concepts are encoded structurally by identifiers and endpoints; the `gql` metadata profile covers value typing.

Listings 1.3 and 1.4 use Parquet message type notation: `required`, `optional`, and `repeated` define cardinality, `group` defines nesting, and `binary (UTF8)` denotes byte arrays with a string logical annotation. In the node schema, `id` satisfies **FR1**, `label` satisfies **FR3**, `properties` satisfies **FR5**, and nested `values` satisfies **FR7**. The `value` field is a carrier interpreted with `gql` metadata rather than an untyped byte string.

Listing 1.3. BPG node schema in Apache Parquet notation.

```
message Node {
  required int64 id;
  repeated binary label (UTF8);
  repeated group properties {
    required binary key (UTF8);
    repeated group values {
      optional binary value;
    }
  }
}
```

Edges have mandatory identifiers, source and target node references, labels, and properties. Although some property-graph definitions allow edge identifiers to be omitted, BPG adopts mandatory edge identifiers to support unambiguous edge-level properties, comparisons, and references. In Listing 1.4, `id`, `source_node_id`, and `target_node_id` satisfy **FR2**; `label` satisfies **FR4**; `properties` satisfies **FR6**; and nested `values` again satisfies **FR7**.

Listing 1.4. BPG edge schema in Apache Parquet notation.

```
message Edge {
  required int64 id;
  required int64 source_node_id;
  required int64 target_node_id;
  repeated binary label (UTF8);
  repeated group properties {
    required binary key (UTF8);
    repeated group values {
      optional binary value;
    }
  }
}
```

4.3 BPG Container

For publication, transport, and archival, BPG can package the two Parquet files and optional metadata into one binary artifact. The container does not alter the graph model or Parquet schemas; it only records section offsets and adds artifact-level integrity checking.

Listing 1.5. Logical structure of a BPG container.

```
Header[256]
Metadata[metadata_size]      optional
Nodes[nodes_size]            mandatory
Edges[edges_size]            mandatory
CRC32[4]
```

The 256-byte header starts with magic signature `BPG`, stores the container version `1.0`, and records sizes and offsets for metadata, node, and edge sections. The metadata section is optional UTF-8 YAML; the node and edge sections are mandatory Parquet payloads conforming to the BPG profile. The trailing CRC32 verifies the header and all payload sections, allowing readers to detect truncation or accidental modification before extraction or query processing.

5 Experiments

The experiments evaluate whether BPG satisfies the non-functional requirements introduced in Sect. 2. They answer three questions: *RQ1* whether BPG preserves the expected graph structure, *RQ2* how much storage it saves and how quickly it can be written, and *RQ3* how it behaves for direct analytical reads, joins, and container packaging. We therefore consider conformance, storage footprint, write throughput, read and query performance, and container overhead. In contrast to a purely synthetic benchmark, the evaluation uses real datasets and supplements them with deterministic synthetic scale graphs.

5.1 Experimental Setup

Table 5 summarizes the benchmark inputs [42]. The real group contains eight property graphs: *StarWars* [26], *POLE* [27], *MB6* [36], *FIB25* [37], *HET.IO* [17], *ICIJ* [18], *Cord19* [15,45], and *Twitch* [28]. These datasets cover a small sanity graph, investigative and biomedical graphs, multi-label connectomes, large literature-derived data, and a large social graph. The synthetic group contains five scale graphs with 250 thousand to 8 million nodes and 1 to 40 million edges. They were generated by local scripts using a deterministic Knows-style layout [34]: colon-separated node label sets, typed directed edges, and scalar properties that are converted to the generic BPG key-value property representation.

The real datasets provide CSV and GraphML materializations used as the reported storage baselines. For BPG, each dataset is written as `nodes.parquet` and `edges.parquet`; both files include file-level `name=BPG`, `version=1.0`, and

Table 5. Datasets used in the evaluation. GraphML baselines are available for real datasets; synthetic datasets are compared against their generated CSV source.

Dataset	Kind	$\|V\|$	$\|E\|$	CSV (MB)	GraphML (MB)
StarWars	real	260	365	0.1	0.2
POLE	real	61521	105840	18.2	27.1
MB6	real	486267	961571	167.1	235.6
FIB25	real	802473	1625428	270.5	393.2
HET.IO	real	47031	2250197	265.1	510.9
ICIJ	real	2016523	3339267	1254.0	2146.4
Cord19	real	5485296	5720776	1791.8	2210.8
Twitch	real	4680870	10076938	622.8	1625.5
Syn-250K	synthetic	250000	1000000	63.7	–
Syn-1M	synthetic	1000000	5000000	297.6	–
Syn-2M	synthetic	2000000	10000000	608.3	–
Syn-4M	synthetic	4000000	20000000	1229.7	–
Syn-8M	synthetic	8000000	40000000	2472.9	–

`gql` metadata. Storage experiments compare uncompressed Parquet with Snappy, Gzip, Zstd, Brotli, LZ4, and LZ4_RAW BPG variants. Write throughput, read and query performance, and container overhead use Snappy because it is the fast default for columnar analytics. GraphML is used only as a storage-size exchange-format baseline because XML graph files require parsing and transformation before comparable columnar scans. Queries are executed with DuckDB [31] because it can read CSV and Parquet directly in-process, which keeps the benchmark focused on local file access rather than server setup or data loading into a separate DBMS.

All timed experiments were repeated ten times. Tables report the arithmetic mean and sample standard deviation where timing variability is relevant; write measurements additionally report the median and interquartile range. The measurements were run on an Intel Core Ultra 7 265 machine with 20 cores and 30 GiB RAM, Linux 6.17, Python 3.12.3, and DuckDB 1.5.0. Query timings include DuckDB process startup and file opening overhead for both BPG and CSV. We did not force cold-cache eviction, so the results should be interpreted as warm-cache local-file measurements.

5.2 Correctness and Conformance

Before measuring performance, each BPG pair, i.e., the corresponding `nodes.parquet` and `edges.parquet` files, was validated against structural invariants: expected node and edge counts, duplicate node identifiers, duplicate edge identifiers, orphan edge endpoints, and required BPG file metadata. All thirteen datasets passed these checks. The validation covered 28.8 million nodes and 100.1 million edges in total, with no duplicate identifiers and no orphan endpoints. For the query benchmark, BPG and CSV results were also compared for every workload after exact label and relationship-token matching; all corresponding result counts were identical.

5.3 Storage Footprint

Table 6 compares BPG compression variants on the real datasets, with CSV and GraphML sizes reported in Table 5. Brotli produced the smallest BPG files for every real graph in this benchmark. Relative to CSV, the best BPG variant is 5.94–37.03 times smaller; relative to GraphML, it is 10.36–53.83 times smaller. Snappy and LZ4 are larger than Gzip, Zstd, and Brotli, but they remain useful fast-access profiles for analytics-oriented workflows (Fig. 2).

Table 6. Storage footprint on real datasets by Parquet codec. Sizes are in MB; CSV/best is the CSV-to-smallest-BPG size ratio.

Dataset	uncompressed	snappy	gzip	zstd	brotli	lz4	lz4_raw	CSV/best
StarWars	0.1	0.0	0.0	0.0	0.0	0.0	0.0	5.94
POLE	8.6	4.1	2.2	2.1	1.7	4.1	4.1	10.44
MB6	52.8	16.3	7.8	7.7	4.8	16.5	16.5	34.56
FIB25	78.4	25.5	12.0	11.5	7.3	25.8	25.8	37.03
HET.IO	69.3	35.7	22.3	20.8	17.3	35.9	35.9	15.33
ICIJ	600.2	167.1	94.3	85.9	61.7	156.1	156.1	20.32
Cord19	645.0	322.9	185.9	171.8	116.9	317.5	317.5	15.32
Twitch	266.0	156.7	85.3	77.6	62.7	156.8	156.8	9.93

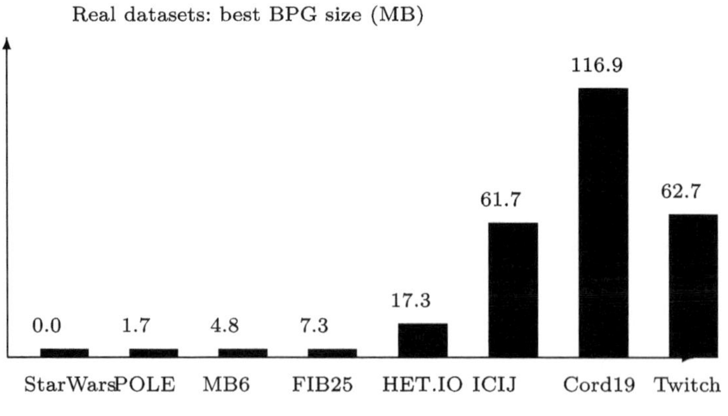

Fig. 2. Best compressed BPG size for the real datasets.

Table 7 reports the synthetic scale results. The synthetic graphs use CSV as the reported baseline because producing additional large text materializations would mostly measure text generation cost. Brotli is again the smallest codec, reducing CSV size by 10.31–11.79 times across the five synthetic graphs. The ratio remains stable from `Syn-250K` to `Syn-8M`, indicating that the storage effect is not an artifact of a single small instance.

Table 7. Storage footprint on synthetic scale datasets by Parquet codec. Sizes are in MB; CSV/best is the CSV-to-smallest-BPG size ratio.

Dataset	uncompressed	snappy	gzip	zstd	brotli	lz4	lz4_raw	CSV/best
Syn-250K	55.1	21.5	11.4	9.4	6.2	21.3	21.3	10.31
Syn-1M	250.0	102.2	53.9	43.8	26.1	101.2	101.2	11.39
Syn-2M	501.0	203.5	108.2	88.1	52.4	201.6	201.6	11.61
Syn-4M	1003.0	408.9	215.8	175.7	104.3	404.5	404.5	11.79
Syn-8M	2007.6	815.5	434.0	349.6	209.9	807.6	807.6	11.78

The storage results support **NFR1** and **NFR2**. The gap between GraphML and BPG is especially large because XML repeats structural markup for every node, edge, and property. BPG benefits from Parquet's columnar encoding because repeated labels, property keys, and numeric identifiers are stored in homogeneous columns instead of repeated textual records.

5.4 Write Throughput

Table 8 reports the time required to materialize Snappy BPG from the CSV representation. The smallest real graph, *StarWars*, is written in 0.05 s on average. Larger real datasets remain within seconds: *ICIJ* takes 8.66 s and *Cord19* takes 11.58 s despite having more than 5 million nodes. The synthetic benchmark shows near-linear scaling: `Syn-250K` takes 0.81 s, `Syn-1M` takes 3.44 s, `Syn-2M` takes 6.82 s, `Syn-4M` takes 13.40 s, and `Syn-8M` takes 26.83 s.

These results support **NFR4**. Write time is driven primarily by the number of records and properties rather than by the file size of the original text materialization. For example, *Twitch* has a smaller CSV file than *Cord19*, but more edges; its 5.26 s write time reflects that record structure rather than only the input byte size. The low standard deviations in Table 8 also show that the conversion path is stable under repeated local execution.

5.5 Read and Query Performance

The query benchmark uses four workload classes. `count-nodes` computes `COUNT(*)` on the node file. `label-filter` counts nodes whose label list contains a dataset-specific label token. `property-exists` counts nodes that contain

Table 8. Snappy BPG write time over ten repetitions.

Dataset	Mean (s)	Std. (s)	Median (s)	IQR (s)
StarWars	0.05	0.00	0.05	0.00
POLE	0.30	0.01	0.30	0.01
MB6	1.60	0.01	1.59	0.01
FIB25	2.58	0.04	2.56	0.04
HET.IO	3.18	0.05	3.20	0.08
ICIJ	8.66	0.06	8.66	0.07
Cord19	11.58	0.08	11.60	0.10
Twitch	5.26	0.03	5.27	0.03
Syn-250K	0.81	0.01	0.81	0.02
Syn-1M	3.44	0.04	3.43	0.06
Syn-2M	6.82	0.03	6.81	0.03
Syn-4M	13.40	0.08	13.38	0.10
Syn-8M	26.83	0.15	26.78	0.10

a dataset-specific property key. `one-hop-join` joins edges to their target nodes for a dataset-specific relationship token. Thus, each table row is one instantiated query template for one dataset, not a set of multiple hidden queries.

The BPG variant reads Snappy-compressed Parquet files directly. Listing 1.6 presents DuckDB SQL templates and equivalent Cypher patterns illustrating how graph predicates map to BPG columns: the label filter reads `label` without touching `properties`, while the one-hop query reads only edge labels, target endpoints, and target-node identifiers/labels.

Listing 1.6. DuckDB SQL templates and equivalent Cypher patterns for label filtering and one-hop traversal over BPG.

```
SELECT count(*) FROM read_parquet('nodes.parquet')
WHERE list_contains(label, 'Person');
-- or
MATCH (n:Person) RETURN count(n);

SELECT count(*) FROM read_parquet('edges.parquet') e
JOIN read_parquet('nodes.parquet') n ON e.target_node_id = n.id
WHERE list_contains(e.label, 'KNOWS') AND list_contains(n.label, 'Person');
-- or
MATCH ()-[:KNOWS]->(n:Person) RETURN count(n);
```

The CSV baseline reads the original CSV materializations through DuckDB using the same logical predicates and exact token matching, without first converting CSV to Parquet. Tables 9 and 10 report mean latency, standard deviation, result cardinality, and speed-up defined as CSV mean latency divided by BPG mean latency.

The results support **NFR3** for scan-heavy and join-oriented analytical workloads. Full node counts and exact label filters consistently favor BPG. On the largest real graphs, the count speed-up is 45.18 for *ICIJ*, 61.09 for *Cord19*, and

Table 9. Query latency on real datasets over ten repetitions. μ is the arithmetic mean and σ the sample standard deviation, both in seconds. Result is the output cardinality. Speed-up values above one favor BPG.

Dataset	Query	BPG $\mu(\sigma)$ s	CSV $\mu(\sigma)$ s	Speed-up	Result
StarWars	count-nodes	0.010 (0.001)	0.027 (0.001)	2.72	260
StarWars	label-filter	0.010 (0.003)	0.029 (0.003)	2.80	82
StarWars	property-exists	0.014 (0.002)	0.028 (0.001)	1.96	254
StarWars	one-hop-join	0.011 (0.001)	0.047 (0.004)	4.41	162
POLE	count-nodes	0.010 (0.001)	0.077 (0.002)	7.67	61521
POLE	label-filter	0.011 (0.001)	0.077 (0.003)	7.32	369
POLE	property-exists	0.057 (0.003)	0.077 (0.002)	1.35	1369
POLE	one-hop-join	0.014 (0.002)	0.139 (0.003)	9.79	586
MB6	count-nodes	0.010 (0.001)	0.106 (0.004)	10.63	486267
MB6	label-filter	0.013 (0.001)	0.107 (0.004)	8.21	160516
MB6	property-exists	0.220 (0.004)	0.108 (0.007)	0.49	0
MB6	one-hop-join	0.023 (0.002)	0.209 (0.007)	8.96	160516
FIB25	count-nodes	0.011 (0.001)	0.146 (0.006)	13.58	802473
FIB25	label-filter	0.014 (0.001)	0.146 (0.006)	10.73	349032
FIB25	property-exists	0.288 (0.007)	0.151 (0.006)	0.53	0
FIB25	one-hop-join	0.035 (0.001)	0.308 (0.007)	8.86	349032
HET.IO	count-nodes	0.010 (0.002)	0.153 (0.008)	14.99	47031
HET.IO	label-filter	0.011 (0.001)	0.147 (0.006)	13.27	47031
HET.IO	property-exists	0.068 (0.001)	0.151 (0.006)	2.21	47031
HET.IO	one-hop-join	0.017 (0.001)	0.281 (0.006)	16.04	124335
ICIJ	count-nodes	0.011 (0.001)	0.476 (0.023)	45.18	2016523
ICIJ	label-filter	0.012 (0.001)	0.471 (0.012)	39.78	814344
ICIJ	property-exists	2.858 (0.060)	0.478 (0.021)	0.17	1837546
ICIJ	one-hop-join	0.016 (0.002)	0.795 (0.046)	49.34	12145
Cord19	count-nodes	0.010 (0.001)	0.604 (0.021)	61.09	5485296
Cord19	label-filter	0.013 (0.002)	0.562 (0.014)	41.82	128492
Cord19	property-exists	3.663 (0.068)	0.601 (0.026)	0.16	2686361
Cord19	one-hop-join	0.027 (0.004)	1.087 (0.034)	40.55	128492
Twitch	count-nodes	0.010 (0.001)	0.283 (0.015)	28.00	4680870
Twitch	label-filter	0.012 (0.002)	0.273 (0.013)	22.05	4678779
Twitch	property-exists	1.524 (0.051)	0.269 (0.018)	0.18	4680867
Twitch	one-hop-join	0.025 (0.005)	0.516 (0.023)	20.53	5696

28.00 for *Twitch*. One-hop joins also favor BPG across all datasets, with speed-ups of 49.34 on *ICIJ*, 40.55 on *Cord19*, and 20.53 on *Twitch*. The synthetic scale datasets show the same direction: the one-hop speed-up rises from 5.57 on `Syn-250K` to 12.09 on `Syn-8M`.

Table 10. Query latency on synthetic datasets over ten repetitions. μ is the arithmetic mean and σ the sample standard deviation, both in seconds. Result is the output cardinality. Speed-up values above one favor BPG.

Dataset	Query	BPG $\mu(\sigma)$ s	CSV $\mu(\sigma)$ s	Speed-up	Result
Syn-250K	count-nodes	0.010 (0.001)	0.072 (0.002)	6.92	250000
Syn-250K	label-filter	0.011 (0.001)	0.074 (0.002)	7.03	50000
Syn-250K	property-exists	0.199 (0.004)	0.071 (0.004)	0.36	250000
Syn-250K	one-hop-join	0.025 (0.001)	0.140 (0.002)	5.57	200000
Syn-1M	count-nodes	0.011 (0.001)	0.165 (0.010)	15.34	1000000
Syn-1M	label-filter	0.012 (0.001)	0.159 (0.009)	13.44	200000
Syn-1M	property-exists	0.697 (0.012)	0.163 (0.007)	0.23	1000000
Syn-1M	one-hop-join	0.039 (0.002)	0.333 (0.015)	8.63	1000000
Syn-2M	count-nodes	0.010 (0.001)	0.302 (0.017)	28.90	2000000
Syn-2M	label-filter	0.012 (0.001)	0.291 (0.019)	24.18	400000
Syn-2M	property-exists	1.300 (0.037)	0.294 (0.015)	0.23	2000000
Syn-2M	one-hop-join	0.043 (0.001)	0.516 (0.027)	12.06	2000000
Syn-4M	count-nodes	0.011 (0.002)	0.485 (0.017)	45.52	4000000
Syn-4M	label-filter	0.013 (0.002)	0.471 (0.029)	36.79	800000
Syn-4M	property-exists	2.492 (0.040)	0.480 (0.026)	0.19	4000000
Syn-4M	one-hop-join	0.072 (0.003)	0.834 (0.028)	11.58	4000000
Syn-8M	count-nodes	0.011 (0.002)	0.761 (0.027)	71.90	8000000
Syn-8M	label-filter	0.016 (0.003)	0.708 (0.028)	45.01	1600000
Syn-8M	property-exists	5.128 (0.107)	0.761 (0.021)	0.15	8000000
Syn-8M	one-hop-join	0.128 (0.008)	1.543 (0.098)	12.09	8000000

The property-existence workload exposes an important limitation of the current generic property representation. CSV keeps each known property as a scalar column, so DuckDB evaluates the predicate as a column test. BPG stores properties as a list of key-value records, so the equivalent query must unnest the nested `properties` list and test `properties.key`. This is acceptable for small datasets and remains faster for *HET.IO*, but it is slower on multi-label and large irregular datasets such as *ICIJ*, *Cord19*, and *Twitch*. The result does not weaken the storage and join advantages, but it shows that frequently queried properties should either be projected into dedicated typed columns or supported by an additional indexing/profile mechanism.

5.6 Container Overhead

The optional `.bpg` container stores the metadata payload, the two Parquet payloads, a 256-byte header, and a 4-byte CRC32 checksum. In all cases, CRC verification succeeded after extraction. The measured structural overhead is exactly

260 bytes beyond the embedded payloads, so the relative overhead is negligible for all but toy-sized graphs.

For the largest real Parquet pair, *Cord19*, the Snappy BPG payload is 322.9 MB and the complete container is also 322.9 MB at the displayed precision. Mean creation time is 0.099 s and mean extraction time is 0.193 s. For `Syn-8M`, the corresponding times are 0.269 s and 0.484 s. The container therefore adds integrity checking and single-file transport without materially affecting storage footprint or dominating the conversion cost. These results support **NFR6**.

5.7 Summary of Findings

The experiments show that BPG provides substantial storage savings over the reported CSV and GraphML baselines on real property graphs, while synthetic scale graphs confirm the same trend under controlled growth up to 8 million nodes and 40 million edges. Brotli gives the most compact files in this benchmark, Zstd and Gzip offer intermediate footprints, and Snappy/LZ4 provide larger fast-access variants. Query results favor BPG for counts, label filters, and one-hop joins because Parquet avoids reparsing large CSV files and exposes typed columns to DuckDB. The main observed weakness is selective filtering over generic nested properties; this motivates future BPG profiles that expose frequently queried properties as typed columns or indexes. The container experiment confirms that packaging BPG as a single integrity-protected file adds only constant-size structural overhead and preserves CRC integrity in every run.

6 Conclusions

BPG is a Parquet-based binary serialization for property graphs. It preserves the core property-graph constructs required by **FR1**–**FR7**, reuses Parquet metadata for GQL-oriented typing, and provides an optional single-file container with CRC-based integrity checking. The evaluation shows that BPG addresses **NFR1**–**NFR7** in a practical way: it is concise, codec-flexible, efficient for analytical reads, scalable on large graphs, interoperable with existing columnar tools, and inexpensive to package as an integrity-protected artifact. Future work will focus on typed property projections, index profiles for selective property predicates, and broader integration with graph query engines.

Acknowledgments. This work was supported by the project "BPG: High-Performance Graph Data Format for Storage and Processing Optimization", carried out at the University of Bialystok. The project received funding from the Grant Fund under the project "Regional project for building the potential of the PPO region", no. FEPD.01.01-1Z.00-0011/24, implemented by the Marshal's Office of the Podlaskie Voivodeship within the European Funds for Podlaskie 2021–2027 Programme.

Disclosure of interest. The author has no competing interests to declare that are relevant to the content of this article.

References

1. Álvarez-García, S., Brisaboa, N., Fernández, J.D., Martínez-Prieto, M.A., Navarro, G.: Compressed vertical partitioning for efficient RDF management. Knowl. Inf. Syst. **44**(2), 439–474 (2015)
2. Angles, R., et al.: PG-schema: schemas for property graphs. Proc. ACM Manage. Data **1**(2), 1–25 (2023)
3. Angles, R., Ferrada, S., Burgos, I.: The property graph data format (PGDF). IEEE Access **12**, 159267–159279 (2024). https://doi.org/10.1109/ACCESS.2024.3485095
4. Angles, R., Thakkar, H., Tomaszuk, D.: Mapping RDF databases to property graph databases. IEEE Access **8**, 86091–86110 (2020)
5. Apache Software Foundation: Apache Parquet documentation (2026). https://parquet.apache.org/docs/. Accessed 17 May 2026
6. Bonifati, A., Furniss, P., Green, A., Harmer, R., Oshurko, E., Voigt, H.: Schema validation and evolution for graph databases. In: Laender, A.H.F., Pernici, B., Lim, E.-P., de Oliveira, J.P.M. (eds.) ER 2019. LNCS, vol. 11788, pp. 448–456. Springer, Cham (2019). https://doi.org/10.1007/978-3-030-33223-5_37
7. Bormann, C., Hoffman, P.E.: Concise binary object representation (CBOR). RFC 8949, December 2020. https://doi.org/10.17487/RFC8949, https://www.rfc-editor.org/info/rfc8949
8. Brandes, U., Eiglsperger, M., Herman, I., Himsolt, M., Marshall, M.S.: GraphML progress report structural layer proposal. In: Mutzel, P., Jünger, M., Leipert, S. (eds.) GD 2001. LNCS, vol. 2265, pp. 501–512. Springer, Heidelberg (2002). https://doi.org/10.1007/3-540-45848-4_59
9. Ching, T., Eddelbuettel, D.: RcppMsgPack: MessagePack headers and interface functions for R. R J. **10**(2) (2018)
10. Chodorow, K.: MongoDB: The Definitive Guide. O'Reilly (2013)
11. Currier, C.: Protocol buffers. In: Mobile Forensics–The File Format Handbook: Common File Formats and File Systems Used in Mobile Devices, pp. 223–260. Springer, Cham (2022). https://doi.org/10.1007/978-3-030-98467-0_9
12. Fernández, J.D., Llaves, A., Corcho, O.: Efficient RDF interchange (ERI) format for RDF data streams. In: Mika, P., et al. (eds.) ISWC 2014, Part II 13. LNCS, vol. 8797, pp. 244–259. Springer, Cham (2014). https://doi.org/10.1007/978-3-319-11915-1_16
13. Fernández, J.D., Martínez-Prieto, M.A., Gutiérrez, C., Polleres, A., Arias, M.: Binary RDF representation for publication and exchange (HDT). J. Web Semant. **19**, 22–41 (2013)
14. Fernández, N., Arias, J., Sánchez, L., Fuentes-Lorenzo, D., Corcho, Ó.: RDSZ: an approach for lossless RDF stream compression. In: Presutti, V., d'Amato, C., Gandon, F., d'Aquin, M., Staab, S., Tordai, A. (eds.) ESWC 2014. LNCS, vol. 8465, pp. 52–67. Springer, Cham (2014). https://doi.org/10.1007/978-3-319-07443-6_5
15. Gütebier, L., et al.: CovidGraph: a graph to fight COVID-19. Bioinformatics **38**(20), 4843–4844 (2022). https://doi.org/10.1093/bioinformatics/btac592
16. Hartig, O., Pérez, J.: Semantics and complexity of GraphQL. In: Proceedings of the 2018 World Wide Web Conference, pp. 1155–1164 (2018)
17. Himmelstein, D.S., et al.: Systematic integration of biomedical knowledge prioritizes drugs for repurposing. eLife **6**, e26726 (2017). https://doi.org/10.7554/eLife.26726
18. International Consortium of Investigative Journalists: Offshore leaks database (2016). https://offshoreleaks.icij.org/pages/database. Accessed 17 May 2026

19. ISO/IEC: ISO/IEC 19757-2:2008 – information technology – document schema definition language (DSDL) – part 2: Regular-grammar-based validation – RELAX NG. ISO/IEC 19757-2:2008, ISO/IEC, December 2008
20. ISO/IEC: ISO/IEC 9075-16:2023 – information technology – database languages SQL – part 16: Property graph queries (SQL/PGQ). ISO/IEC 9075-16:2023, ISO/IEC, June 2023
21. ISO/IEC: ISO/IEC 39075:2024 – information technology – database languages – GQL. ISO/IEC, December 2008
22. Kontokostas, D., Knublauch, H.: Shapes constraint language (SHACL). W3C recommendation, W3C, Jul 2017. https://www.w3.org/TR/2017/REC-shacl-20170720/
23. Koparkar, C.: Efficient data representation using FlatBuffers. XRDS Crossroads ACM Mag. Students **29**(2), 50–51 (2023)
24. Kyusakov, R., Kamiya, T., Schneider, J., Peintner, D.: Efficient XML interchange (EXI) format 1.0 (second edition). W3C recommendation, W3C, February 2014. https://www.w3.org/TR/2014/REC-exi-20140211/
25. Maloney, M., Gao, S., Thompson, H., Sperberg-McQueen, M., Beech, D., Mendelsohn, N.: W3C XML schema definition language (XSD) 1.1 part 1: Structures. W3C recommendation, W3C, April 2012. https://www.w3.org/TR/2012/REC-xmlschema11-1-20120405/
26. Neo4j Graph Examples: Star wars graph example dataset (2022). https://github.com/neo4j-graph-examples/star-wars. Accessed 17 May 2026
27. Neo4j Graph Examples: POLE: crime investigation graph example dataset (2024). https://github.com/neo4j-graph-examples/pole. Accessed 17 May 2026
28. Neo4j Graph Examples: Twitch graph example dataset (2024). https://github.com/neo4j-graph-examples/twitch. Accessed 17 May 2026
29. Neufeld, G., Vuong, S.: An overview of ASN.1. Comput. Netw. ISDN Syst. **23**(5), 393–415 (1992)
30. Pezoa, F., Reutter, J.L., Suarez, F., Ugarte, M., Vrgoč, D.: Foundations of JSON schema. In: Proceedings of the 25th International Conference on World Wide Web, pp. 263–273 (2016)
31. Raasveldt, M., Mühleisen, H.: DuckDB: An embeddable analytical database. In: Proceedings of the 2019 International Conference on Management of Data, pp. 1981–1984 (2019). https://doi.org/10.1145/3299869.3320212
32. Rakowski, K.: Learning Apache Thrift. Packt Publishing Ltd (2015)
33. Staworko, S., Boneva, I., Gayo, J.E.L., Hym, S., Prud'hommeaux, E.G., Solbrig, H.R.: Complexity and expressiveness of ShEx for RDF. In: 18th International Conference on Database Theory, ICDT 2015, 23–27 March 2015, Brussels, Belgium, pp. 195–211 (2015)
34. Szeremeta, Ł: Knows: a flexible and reproducible property graph generator. SoftwareX **33**, 102510 (2026). https://doi.org/10.1016/j.softx.2026.102510
35. Szeremeta, Ł, Tomaszuk, D., Angles, R.: YARS-PG: property graphs representation for publication and exchange. IEEE Access **12**, 73386–73399 (2024). https://doi.org/10.1109/ACCESS.2024.3403924
36. Takemura, S., et al.: A connectome of a learning and memory center in the adult Drosophila brain. eLife **6**, e26975 (2017). https://doi.org/10.7554/eLife.26975
37. Takemura, S., et al.: Synaptic circuits and their variations within different columns in the visual system of Drosophila. Proc. Nat. Acad. Sci. **112**(44), 13711–13716 (2015).https://doi.org/10.1073/pnas.1509820112

38. Thusoo, A., et al.: Hive-a petabyte scale data warehouse using Hadoop. In: 2010 IEEE 26th International Conference on Data Engineering, ICDE 2010, pp. 996–1005. IEEE (2010)
39. TinkerPop: IO reference — GraphBinary (2024). https://tinkerpop.apache.org/docs/3.7.2/dev/io/#graphbinary. Accessed 07 May 2024
40. TinkerPop: IO reference — GraphSON (2024). https://tinkerpop.apache.org/docs/3.7.2/dev/io/#graphson-3d0. Accessed 07 May 2024
41. TinkerPop: IO reference — Gryo (2024). https://tinkerpop.apache.org/docs/3.7.2/dev/io/#gryo. Accessed 07 May 2024
42. Tomaszuk, D.: Property Graph Datasets. Figshare dataset, June 2026. https://doi.org/10.6084/m9.gshare.32816693.v1, https://gshare.com/articles/dataset/Property_Graph_Datasets/32816693. Accessed 28 June 2026
43. Viotti, J.C., Kinderkhedia, M.: A benchmark of JSON-compatible binary serialization specifications. arXiv preprint arXiv:2201.03051 (2022)
44. Vohra, D., Vohra, D.: Apache Avro. Practical Hadoop Ecosystem: A Definitive Guide to Hadoop-Related Frameworks and Tools, pp. 303–323 (2016)
45. Wang, L.L., et al.: CORD-19: the COVID-19 open research dataset. In: Proceedings of the 1st Workshop on NLP for COVID-19 at ACL 2020 (2020)

Agentic Architecture for Data-Centric AutoML

Mattia Matteini[1], Matteo Magnini[2], Matteo Francia[1(✉)], Giovanni Ciatto[1], and Andrea Omicini[1]

[1] Department of Computer Science and Engineering, Alma Mater Studiorum—Università di Bologna, Cesena, Italy
{mattia.matteini,m.francia,giovanni.ciatto,andrea.omicini}@unibo.it
[2] Department of Computer Science Faculty of Science, Technology and Medicine, University of Luxembourg, Esch sur Alzette, Luxembourg
matteo.magnini@uni.lu

Abstract. Data-Centric Artificial Intelligence (AI) focuses on improving data quality and curation as the main driver of Machine Learning (ML) performance Although Automated Machine Learning (AutoML) has reduced the cost of model selection and hyper-parameter tuning, most systems remain model-centric and poorly aligned with Machine Learning Operations (MLOps) requirements such as controllability, traceability, and process-level explainability: automated choices about preprocessing, pipeline structure, and validation are often opaque and difficult to revise, despite their strong influence on model behaviour. We propose AGE-ML, a specification-driven, *agentic* architecture for Data-Centric AI. AGE-ML is data-centric in the sense that pipeline construction is conditioned on the data at hand: the selected workflow may include preprocessing, feature handling, rebalancing, and other data-preparation steps required by the dataset properties and by the selected estimators. A human-readable specification language enables data scientists to encode assumptions, constraints, evaluation criteria, and design preferences across the pipeline. From the specification, a search space for pipeline generation is algorithmically constructed and explored to support controlled automation and reproducible execution traces. Then, Large Language Models (LLMs) operate within a controlled agent loop to interpret specifications, generate and validate pipelines, and produce structured explanations for them. Results show improved traceability of pipeline generation, iterative pipeline refinement, and stronger integration with MLOps practices such as experiment tracking and reproducibility. Finally, we discuss limitations and future directions for AGE-ML.

Keywords: MLOps · Data-centric AI · Agentic AI · AutoML · LLMs

1 Introduction

Data-centric AI emphasises the improvement of data quality and curation as the primary driver of the performance of machine learning models [18]. In this

G. Vargas-Solar et al. (Eds.): ADBIS 2026, LNCS 16937, pp. 83–99, 2027.
https://doi.org/10.1007/978-3-032-39820-8_7

paradigm, the role of the data scientist extends beyond model selection and hyper-parameter tuning to the design of effective data preprocessing, feature engineering, and validation. Injecting domain knowledge and a-priori experience into ML pipelines is therefore essential. However, modern ML systems are characterised by a fundamental tension between integrating human expertise and automation. On one hand, data scientists possess domain knowledge, a-priori experience, and contextual understanding that are indispensable for designing robust and trustworthy pipelines [3]. On the other hand, the increasing scale and velocity of data demand *automation* to ensure efficiency, reproducibility, and scalability [6].

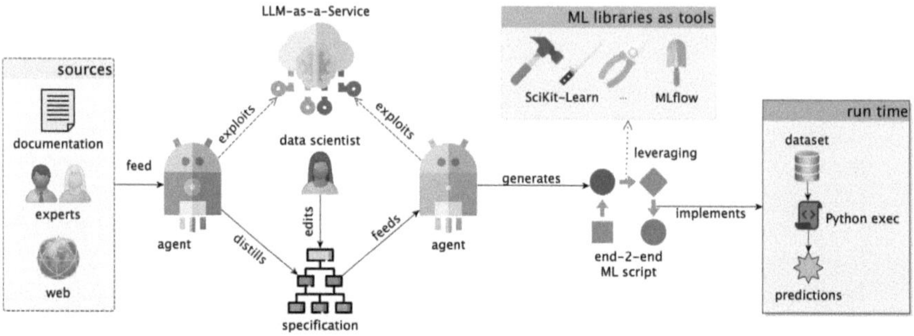

Fig. 1. AGE-ML: data scientists encode their ML knowledge in a structured specification. It lets agents (green) generate end-to-end ML code through well-known ML libraries. LLMs support code generation and reasoning about the data. Generated code is automatically run on actual datasets to produce predictions. Solid arrows denote data/control flow; open-headed dashed arrows denote LLM-mediated interactions. (Color figure online)

In this context, our perspective is to reposition human effort toward high-value tasks rather than low-level coding, repetitive experimentation, and manual orchestration of workflow components. Automation should amplify expertise while preserving meaningful human control over the structure and logic of the pipeline. Despite their empirical effectiveness, many AutoML systems [18] exhibit a mismatch with data-centric AI principles. Traditional AutoML approaches primarily focus on model selection and hyper-parameter optimisation, often treating the dataset as fixed and immutable. While this strategy can yield strong benchmark results, it overlooks the iterative and data-focused processes that characterise real-world machine learning practice and the well-established principles of CRISP-DM [13].

In this paper, we propose AGE-ML, an *agentic* architecture for automatic *end-to-end* pipeline generation and execution that aligns with data-centric AI principles. Here, "data-centric" means that pipeline construction is tailored to the data at hand, including preprocessing, feature handling, rebalancing, and other data-preparation steps required by dataset properties and by the selected estimators. Thanks to LLM-based intelligent agents, AGE-ML (i) enables structured integration of expert knowledge into automated processes (e.g., via YAML plus natural language), (ii) reduces operational load for data scientists (by automating generation and execution of low-level coding and tuning tasks), and (iii) supports modularity and reusability of knowledge (data scientists' knowledge can be encoded, extended, and shared over time).

In particular, AGE-ML (Fig. 1) delegates the design and implementation of ML pipelines to a Multi-Agent System (MAS) where agents interleave symbolic reasoning, intuitive reasoning, text generation (as provided by LLMs), and the execution of generated code to automate and document ML pipeline construction. Crucially, AGE-ML enables structured human knowledge injection during pipeline creation, via an *ad-hoc* specification language. Domain experts can constrain search spaces, define preferred preprocessing strategies, or embed domain rules directly into their specification file. This paradigm combines the automated optimisation capabilities of AutoML with guided expertise, producing pipelines that are not only performant but also inspectable, well-documented, adaptable, and aligned with domain requirements.

The remainder of the paper is organised as follows. Section 2 provides background on data-centric AI, AutoML, and agentic AI. Section 3 introduces the architecture of AGE-ML, whereas Sect. 4 evaluates it also against state-of-the-art approaches. Section 5 concludes the paper and discusses future work.

2 Related Work

Data-centric AI prioritises improving data quality and representativeness over focusing primarily on ML models [18]. It shifts the main optimisation target from model design to data quality, treating high-quality data as a powerful lever for improving system performance. In this perspective, practitioners may keep the model family fixed while revising preprocessing, feature handling, labelling assumptions, or sampling choices in response to dataset properties.

In this context, AutoML reduces the manual effort of building and tuning ML models by automating parts of the development process. However, most approaches focus primarily on Hyper-Parameter Optimization (HPO) and model selection, improving predictive performance through the exploration of model families, preprocessing strategies, and hyper-parameters. While effective, this remains largely model-centric and does not explicitly address reproducibility, auditability, or controllability across the broader ML lifecycle. Moreover, AutoML rarely incorporates knowledge about data semantics, provenance, or quality, often treating datasets as static and reliable inputs. As a result, it struggles to support data-centric refinement and reasoning about the suitability of the data itself. Existing AutoML systems rely on structured algorithmic search spaces, which provide reproducibility and computational efficiency. TPOT [12], Auto-WEKA [14], and Auto-Sklearn [2] are built on top of the Combined Algorithm Selection and Hyperparameter optimization (CASH) problem, which extends both the 'Algorithm selection' problem and the HPO, by searching for both the best algorithm and its hyper-parameters for a given dataset. Other frameworks (e.g., Auto-Keras [7]) focus more on searching for deep learning models and support multimodal and multitask learning. More recently, FLAML [16] has outperformed the above-mentioned approaches. Newer AutoML frameworks also focus on end-to-end automation, such as [4] and [3] where AutoML for end-to-end pipelines was introduced and formalised.

Other recent frameworks address end-to-end machine learning pipelines through LLM-driven and multi-agent approaches. DS-Agent [5] leverages case-based reasoning [8] to iteratively construct and refine pipelines by retrieving and adapting prior solutions, incorporating human insights (e.g., from Kaggle) and execution feedback. CBR operates by retrieving similar past problems, reusing their solutions for the current problem, evaluating the effectiveness, revising the solution, and retaining successful solutions. MLZero [1] extends this paradigm with a multi-agent architecture that combines perception, semantic memory, and episodic memory to iteratively generate, evaluate, and improve code, enabling both domain knowledge integration and error-driven learning. The semantic memory enhances the LLM's parametric knowledge with domain-specific information from external knowledge that is not constructed by humans but rather by the summarisation agent and the condensation agent. Similarly, AutoML-Agent [15] adopts a coordinated multi-agent strategy to automate the full pipeline, from data processing and model selection to deployment, by decomposing the task into specialised roles.

Despite these advances, current approaches still exhibit key limitations, particularly opaque optimisation processes and limited integration of constraints and domain semantics provided by data scientists, motivating the need for more traceable and data-centric AutoML solutions. A detailed comparison of older contributions can be found in [15].

Distinguishing Features of AGE-ML. Non-LLM approaches such as HAMLET and FLAML provide constrained generation and hot-start capabilities, although only HAMLET supports end-to-end automation with a largely black-box optimisation process. Existing LLM-based systems enable flexible end-to-end pipeline construction and often include validation mechanisms, but they typically lack explicit constraints, reducing reliability and reproducibility. Moreover, data scientists usually provide only the initial task specification, with limited involvement in later optimisation and refinement stages, while resulting pipeline-generation processes are often neither well documented nor searchable.

AGE-ML combines the strengths of both paradigms. Unlike prior LLM-based methods, it introduces *constrained generation* to improve robustness and enforce well-defined rules, while preserving full end-to-end automation and integrating *human-centred design*. It also supports *inspectable pipeline construction*, *pipeline validation*, and *searchability* through the data catalog. Finally, its *zero-data cold start capabilities* enable reuse of prior knowledge when available, while still supporting adoption through default specifications alone.

Another distinguishing feature of AGE-ML is explainability. In this work, explainability refers to the traceability and natural-language documentation of the pipeline-generation process, rather than to post-hoc explanation of individual model predictions. This is a key aspect of AGE-ML's design, allowing data scientists to understand and audit automated ML processes.

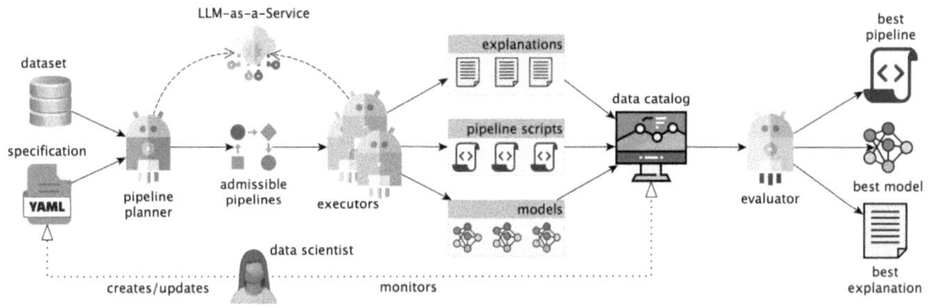

Fig. 2. Overview of the agentic architecture for specification-driven AutoML. Androids represent agents and open-headed dashed arrows denote interactions with LLMs.

3 Agentic Architecture for Specification-Driven AutoML

Figure 2 shows the proposed architecture for specification-driven AutoML. The system takes as input: (i) a dataset, (ii) a **specification**, and (iii) a computational budget and returns the best model found among the admissible pipelines. Admissibility is determined by the data-science knowledge encoded in the specification, whereas optimality is assessed empirically on the dataset at hand. Additionally, the architecture consists of three agent types and one reactive component. The **pipeline planner** agent parses the specification, resolves dataset-dependent conditions, and generates admissible pipeline plans. The **pipeline executor** agent turns each plan into executable code, runs it, and stores the resulting artefacts. The **data catalog** records execution traces, including generated scripts, hyper-parameters, intermediate artefacts, metrics, and natural-language explanations. Finally, the **evaluator** agent compares the produced models on a held-out test set and selects the best model, together with its corresponding pipeline and explanation. The planner and evaluator are singleton modules, whereas executors can be instantiated in parallel, thereby supporting budgeted exploration of multiple admissible pipelines.

3.1 Specification

We adopt a YAML-like concrete syntax to keep specifications readable by practitioners, parsable by software components, and amenable to LLM-based generation and revision. This specification style is inspired by SKI-Lang [9], which uses a YAML-like language to encode knowledge injected into a neural predictor. The file comprises four main sections: `pipeline`, `ordering`, `constraints`,

Listing 7.1. Excerpt from specification.

```
pipeline:
  steps:
    normalization:
      candidates:
        min-max:
          params: {feature_range: [[0, 1]]}
    classification:
      mandatory: true
      candidates:
        knn:
          params:
            n_neighbors: [5, 11]
            weights: [uniform, distance]
ordering:
  - sequence: [imputation, normalization, features]
  - {before: features, after: classification}
constraints:
  - if: {step: {classification: knn}}
    require: [normalization, features]
  - if:
      dataset:
        has_feature:
          named_like: [class, target]
          data_type: [categorical, integer]
    require: [classification]
budgets:
  pipelines: 5
  generation_attempts: 10
  time: {hours: 2, minutes: 5, seconds: 30}
```

and `budgets`. Listing 7.1 reports only the core constructs needed to understand the architecture; a complete account of the syntax and formal semantics of the specification language is omitted for space reasons and delegated to an extended version of this work. Listing 7.1 shows an excerpt from the specification. The `pipeline` block specifies the admissible steps, their candidate implementations, and their hyper-parameter domains. The `ordering` block specifies that the pipeline must first perform *imputation* to handle missing data, then apply *normalisation* to scale the features, and afterward execute the *features* step for feature engineering or feature selection. The `constraints` block states that when the classification algorithm is KNN, the pipeline must include both *normalisation* and *features* steps, since KNN is sensitive to feature scaling and often benefits from feature preparation. Additionally, if the dataset contains a target feature whose name resembles *class* or *target* and whose data type is categorical or integer, then the pipeline must use *classification*. The `budgets` block defines execution budgets and resource limits for an automated search process, allowing at most 5 candidate pipelines to be evaluated, and up to 10 attempts to generate valid pipeline code.

AGE-ML currently assumes that experts collaborate to produce a *single*, *coherent*, and *consistent* specification. Supporting independently authored, reusable, or partially conflicting specification modules would require additional language mechanisms for decomposition, abstraction, priority, and conflict handling, which we leave to future engineering work.

3.2 Pipeline Planner

Pipeline planning is the phase in which the system turns a specification into a set of admissible candidate pipelines. Intuitively, the planner agent reads the specification, checks which rules apply to the input dataset, and enumerates the pipelines that are compatible with the specification's constraints. Most notably, the planner agent samples the set of all admissible pipelines according to the budget constraints, so the output of this agent is a *subset* of the pipelines that satisfy the specification, whose cardinality is determined by the `pipelines` budget. Informally, we refer to this set as the "pipeline execution plan", because it contains the pipelines that will be executed in the next phases.

Pipeline Admissibility. A pipeline is admissible when it is compatible with the data-science knowledge encoded in the specification: it contains all mandatory steps, respects the required ordering among steps, and satisfies the declarative constraints relating dataset properties, steps, and candidate algorithms. The planner resolves these requirements before execution, so that downstream components receive only pipelines that are structurally valid with respect to the specification.

A pipeline can still be seen as a finite sequence of step–candidate pairs, where each step denotes a phase of the workflow, and each candidate denotes the concrete algorithm or operation selected for that phase. However, the purpose of the planner is not to optimise hyper-parameters directly. Rather, it defines the admissible region of the workflow space: which steps may appear, in which order, and with which candidate implementations. Hyper-parameter optimisation is then delegated to the pipeline executor agent.

Finding Admissible Pipelines via CSP. The planner models "admissibility" as a finite-domain Constraint Satisfaction Problem (CSP) tailored to the input YAML specification file. It then leverages a CSP solver – currently, the Z3 theorem prover [11] – to compute admissible pipelines efficiently.

Additional implementation details on the CSP encoding are available in the project repository; here we provide only an informal sketch of its main components and constraints. For each possible step, the CSP records whether the step is selected, where it appears in the pipeline, and which candidate implements it. The constraints ensure that: (i) every selected step has exactly one selected candidate; (ii) skipped steps have no candidate and no position in the pipeline; (iii) selected steps occupy distinct positions while being totally ordered; (iv) mandatory steps are always selected; (v) precedence relations from the specification among steps are respected; and (vi) declarative constraints from the specification are enforced, along with their require/forbid implications. Thus, constraints such as "if the classifier is knn, then normalisation is required" are compiled into logical constraints over the corresponding step and candidate variables.

Once a satisfying assignment is obtained, the planner reconstructs the corresponding pipeline by ordering the selected steps according to their assigned positions and attaching to each step its selected candidate. The resulting sequence is then passed to the pipeline executor, which generates and runs the corresponding code.

3.3 Pipeline Executor

The pipeline executor is responsible for synthesising and executing pipelines.

Code Generation. Code generation aims to bridge the gap between the symbolic representation of a pipeline and a concrete training procedure that can be executed on actual data. Given an admissible pipeline, the executor agent produces a Python script implementing exactly the candidate algorithms in the prescribed order. The generated script is parametric with respect to the hyper-parameters associated with the candidates in the target pipeline according to the user-provided specification. The generated code exposes one parameter for each hyper-parameter, so that the pipeline can be re-executed multiple times with different hyper-parameter values during the subsequent execution phase.

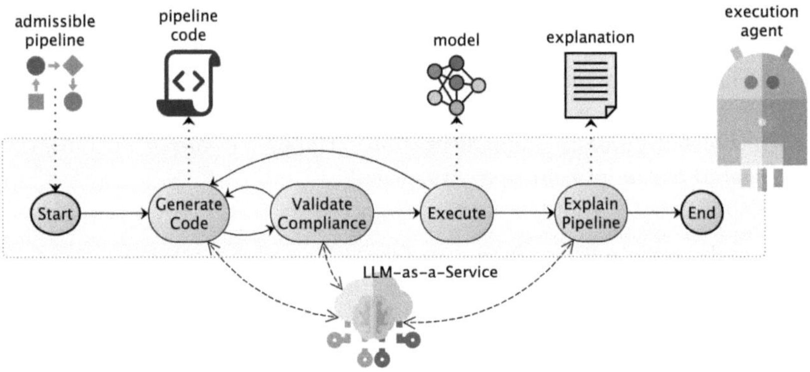

Fig. 3. State machine governing the behaviour of executor agents. Starting from an admissible pipeline for the dataset at hand, the agent iteratively generates Python code, validates its compliance with respect to the pipeline, executes it on the training set – multiple times, exploring different hyper-parameter assignments –, and finally produces a textual explanation of the outcome.

Figure 3 depicts the state machine governing the behaviour of executor agents, focusing on the control loop of an executor agent, not the whole multi-agent architecture. The figure highlights that code generation is not treated as a single-shot translation problem, but rather as an iterative synthesis procedure in which generation, semantic validation, runtime validation, and explanation are tightly coupled. The generation process starts by collecting the information needed to condition the synthesis task. This includes: (i) a compact description of the dataset's structure, (ii) the parsed specification (which includes budget constraints, e.g. on the amount of retries allowed in the generation process, as well as time limitations), (iii) the admissible pipeline selected by the planner, and (iv) the target feature. The compact dataset description is computed from deterministic metadata and summary statistics, such as column names, inferred types, cardinalities, missingness, and small samples; LLMs are used only to interpret semantic predicates when needed. This information is used by executor agents to build the prompt context for some underlying LLM, which is then asked to produce Python code, with a fixed interface and well-defined responsibility.

After code is generated, executor agents perform an automatic validation step aimed at checking semantic compliance. Rather than relying on syntactical correctness alone, the generated program is inspected against the intended pipeline specification to verify that it contains *exactly* the expected steps and *no unintended* ones. This validation can be formulated as a combination of (i) a judgment problem in which a LLM is asked to compare the admissible pipeline and the generated code, and to determine whether the latter faithfully implements the former;[1] and (ii) a matching problem in which the generated code is matched against a number of regular expressions, to ensure that it matches the desired syntax, and that all necessary hyper-parameters are mentioned. Whenever any of these checks fail, the feedback is injected back into the conversational context, and a new generation attempt is performed, until the retry limit is reached.

Reproducibility is addressed at the artefact and execution level rather than by assuming deterministic LLM behaviour: AGE-ML constrains code generation through explicit prompts, fixed interfaces, automated validation, runtime testing, and complete logging of generated code, hyper-parameters, metrics, and artefacts.

Pipeline Execution. Pipeline execution starts once an executor agent has successfully generated and validated a parametric script for some admissible pipeline. At this point, the script is assumed to expose a fixed training interface, as discussed above, and to contain one parameter for each hyper-parameter associated with the candidates occurring in the pipeline. The executor then attempts to run the script on the input dataset. As shown in Fig. 3, execution is still part of the agentic control loop: runtime failures are not treated as terminal errors by default, but as feedback for the executor agent. Whenever execution fails, the agent backtracks to the generation phase, unless the retry budget has already been exhausted.

[1] In particular, the LLM-as-a-judge approach is employed, to check that all necessary candidates appear in the code, and that no extraneous candidate is present.

Parallelism. The execution process is parallelised at the pipeline level. Given the set of admissible pipelines selected by the planner, the system spawns as many executor agents as the number of pipelines to be explored, within the limits imposed by the computational budget. Consequently, code generation, validation, runtime repair, and execution may proceed concurrently for different pipelines. This form of parallelism is deliberately coarse-grained: each executor agent is responsible for one admissible pipeline, including all its hyper-parameter assignments, while the global budget bounds the number of pipelines, generation retries, and executions that may be attempted.

Explanation Generation. The executor finally produces a natural-language explanation of the whole generation–validation–execution process. In doing so, the agent steers the LLM to summarise the whole conversational context, including the initial pipeline specification, the generated code, the validation feedback (in case of failed validation), the execution feedback (in case of failed execution), and the variations across generation attempts.

Examples of generated explanations are available in the project repository.

3.4 Data Catalog

All execution artefacts are tracked in the data catalog, currently implemented using `MLflow` [17], in a hierarchical way.[2] The logged structure mirrors the 3-level hierarchy of the exploration process, as shown in fig. 4. At the first level, one experiment corresponds to the AutoML problem instance, namely: user-provided specification plus input dataset; possibly including metadata such as the date-time of execution. At the second level, there is one entry for each admissible pipeline selected by the planner. Each pipeline is associated with metadata describing its steps and candidates, together with its generated code and explanation. At the third level, there is one entry for each run of each pipeline script, where metadata include hyper-parameter values, trained model artefacts, and their training statistics and performance.

This hierarchical logging scheme serves two purposes. First, it makes the resulting executions reproducible at the artefact level: for each trained model, one can recover the dataset split, the generating script, the pipeline structure, the hyper-parameter assignment, and the runtime trace that produced it. Second, it provides the evaluator agent with a structured metadata organisation, aimed at simplifying the identification of the best model, as described in the next subsection.

3.5 Evaluator

The evaluator agent is responsible for selecting the final model, and therefore the best pipeline, among those actually generated and executed by the execu-

[2] `MLflow` acts as a model/pipeline registry that treats AI models as tracked assets with governed access, auditing, and lineage.

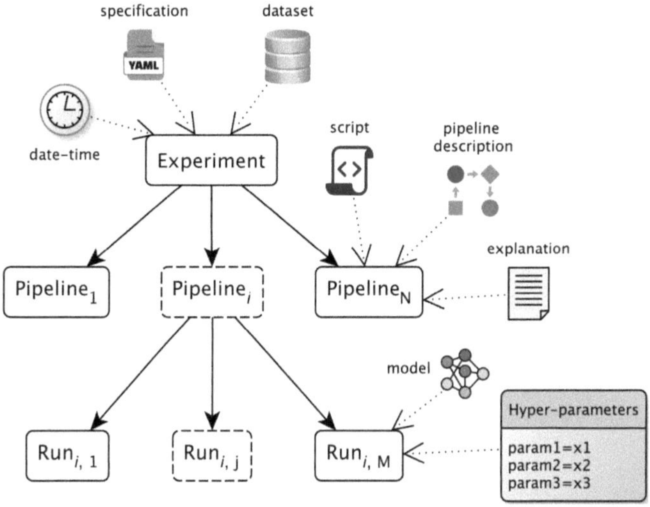

Fig. 4. Hierarchical logging scheme for the execution artefacts produced during specification-driven AutoML. Dotted arrows denote metadata associations for entries at different levels of the hierarchy.

tor agents. This selection is empirical: the chosen solution is the one that performs best with respect to the runs completed for the current AutoML problem instance —in compliance with budget limitations.

To this end, the evaluator traverses the aforementioned hierarchy of logged artefacts (see fig. 4) from the leaves to the root, assessing the performance metrics of the trained models on the test set and propagating the best values up to the experiment level. The particular performance metric to be optimised is specified as a launch parameter of the system.

4 Experimental Evaluation

We empirically evaluate the implementation of AGE-ML, both in *absolute* terms – by assessing the predictive performance achieved by AGE-ML on a collection of well-known benchmark datasets –, and in *relative* terms—by comparing the performance of AGE-ML against a state-of-the-art AutoML system (HAMLET [4]).

In particular, AGE-ML consists of a Python system, using `LangChain` [10][3] and `LangGraph`[4] for agent orchestration, `Z3` for CSP solving, `MLflow` as the data catalog, `scikit-learn` as the ML library for generated pipelines, and our implementations of the pipeline planner, pipeline executor, and evaluator agents, in compliance with the architecture from Sect. 3. The project repository[5] provides

[3] https://www.langchain.com.
[4] https://www.langchain.com/langgraph.
[5] https://github.com/Mala1180/age-ml.

the source code of AGE-ML, reproduction instructions, scripts, prompts, configuration files, and implementation details under an open-source licence.

Experimental setup. The system is evaluated under a fixed computational budget defined in the experimental configuration, including: a maximum of 30 pipelines to explore, up to 8 parallel workers, a maximum of 10 generation attempts per pipeline, and a total time budget of 2 h per run. All executions are fully tracked using a data catalog (based on MLflow in the implementation), enabling artefact-level reproducibility and post-hoc analysis of both predictive outcomes and explanation artefacts. Balanced accuracy is used for classification tasks and RMSE for regression tasks. Although several examples focus on classification for brevity, AGE-ML is not restricted to classifiers: in practice, any estimator following the `scikit-learn` fitting interface can be used as a candidate, and our experiments cover classification and regression as common and easily interpretable use cases.

Table 1. Overview of the benchmark datasets used in the experimental evaluation. The datasets cover both classification (C) and regression (R).

Dataset	Problem	Features	Instances	Numeric	Discrete
Wilt	C	5	4839	5	0
Texture	C	40	5500	40	0
Madelon	C	500	2600	500	0
HAR	C	561	10299	561	0
Adult	C	14	48842	6	8
MNIST_784	C	784	70000	784	0
Ames Housing	R	80	2930	37	43
California Housing	R	8	20640	8	0
Auto MPG	R	7	398	6	1

We evaluate AGE-ML on a diverse collection of benchmark datasets commonly used in the machine learning literature, covering both classification and regression tasks, with varying dimensionality and feature types. Table 1 summarises the main characteristics of each dataset, including the number of instances, features, and the type of task.

Language Models and Prompts. The experimental evaluation relies on LLMs to support (i) translation of semantic constraints, (ii) code generation, (iii) validation, and (iv) explanation within the executor agents. In particular, we employ two models from the Gemini family, namely *Gemini 2.5 Flash* and *Gemini 3.1 Flash Lite*, which are used across experiments without task-specific fine-tuning. We deliberately choose small models to demonstrate that AGE-ML does not require large-scale LLMs to be effective, and to keep the financial budget manageable.

Our agents interact with a small set of task-specific system prompts, designed to enforce clear responsibilities. In particular: (i) a code-generation prompt instructs the model to produce executable Python code implementing a given pipeline with a fixed interface, (ii) a validation prompt frames the task as a compliance check between the intended pipeline and the generated code (LLM-as-a-judge), and (iii) an explanation prompt requires the model to produce a structured, human-readable description of the final pipeline and its design rationale.

Prompts are intentionally kept simple and consistent across experiments, relying on the surrounding agentic loop to enforce correctness through iterative validation and feedback; full prompt definitions are available in the project repository[5].

Results. Tables 2 and 3 report the results obtained with *Gemini 3.1 Flash Lite* and *Gemini 2.5 Flash*, respectively, across six classification and three regression datasets. Balanced accuracy is used for classification tasks, where higher is better, whereas RMSE is used for regression tasks, where lower is better. Column 'AGE-ML' reports the best score obtained by AGE-ML on the dataset, column 'Baseline' reports the comparison system, column 'Actual P.' denotes the number of pipelines successfully generated, validated, and executed within the budget, whereas columns '* Token' report aggregate LLM usage, while 'Putative Cost' is estimated from token usage times the per-token cost of the underlying LLM Application Programming Interface (API). For the baseline, we use the performance of HAMLET [4] or Kaggle notebooks (where HAMLET is not available). In particular, for *Ames Housing* we consider Gus Martins' results,[6] for Auto MPG we use Ertuğrul Demir's work,[7] for California Housing we report Ahmed Mahmoud's notebook.[8]

Table 2. Results obtained with Gemini 3.1 Flash Lite.

Dataset	AGE-ML	Baseline	Actual P.	Input Tokens	Output Tokens	Total Tokens	Putative Cost ($)
Wilt	**0.983**	0.975	30	615,707	33,780	649,487	0.614
Texture	0.992	0.997	30	2,017,288	35,480	2,052,768	1.208
Madelon	0.863	0.875	30	14,266,818	32,835	14,299,653	2.207
HAR	**0.987**	0.959	30	22,220,902	33,979	22,254,881	4.180
Adult	**0.822**	0.805	30	2,674,441	81,671	2,756,112	1.876
MNIST_784	0.971	0.972	25	17,785,846	27,616	17,813,462	5.615
California Housing	**67,675.641**	69,838.844	30	955,318	41,872	997,190	0.868
Ames Housing	30,189.152	29,660.363	29	4,071,760	65,523	4,137,283	2.017
Auto MPG	**2.148**	2.508	30	1,490,934	44,644	1,535,578	1.253

[6] https://www.kaggle.com/code/gusthema/house-prices-prediction-using-tfdf.
[7] https://www.kaggle.com/code/datafan07/auto-mpg-eda-feature-engineering-and-regressions/notebook.
[8] https://www.kaggle.com/code/ahmedmahmoud16/california-housing-prices.

Table 3. Results obtained with Gemini 2.5 Flash.

Dataset	AGE-ML	Baseline	Actual P.	Input Tokens	Output Tokens	Total Tokens	Putative Cost ($)
Wilt	0.966	0.975	30	413,432	119,853	533,285	0.656
Texture	0.995	0.997	30	1,645,606	135,529	1,781,135	1.075
Madelon	0.863	0.875	18	7,368,780	80,067	7,448,847	1.855
HAR	**0.981**	0.959	12	8,305,395	66,378	8,371,773	2.864
Adult	**0.813**	0.805	30	3,533,767	864,794	4,398,561	3.933
MNIST_784	0.966	0.972	11	5,932,213	47,113	5,979,326	1.610
California Housing	**69,331.032**	69,838.844	30	1,620,167	492,151	2,112,318	2.258
Ames Housing	31,970.630	29,660.363	30	4,504,694	640,509	5,145,203	3.431
Auto MPG	**2.283**	2.508	30	1,662,359	244,199	1,906,558	1.694

Both models generate competitive pipelines under a constrained computational budget and without task-specific tuning. Across classification tasks, *Gemini 3.1 Flash Lite* improves over the baseline on *Wilt*, *HAR*, and *Adult*, while *Gemini 2.5 Flash* improves on *HAR* and *Adult* and remains competitive elsewhere. On regression tasks, both models improve over the baseline on *California Housing* and *Auto MPG*, whereas *Ames Housing* remains more challenging.

A key difference between the two models lies in their ability to explore the search space. *Gemini 3.1 Flash Lite* consistently executes the full pipeline budget (30 pipelines in almost all datasets), whereas *Gemini 2.5 Flash* often fails to reach the maximum number of valid pipelines (e.g., 12 on *HAR* and 11 on *MNIST_784*). The number of actually executed pipelines depends not only on the nominal exploration budget, but also on whether generated code passes semantic validation and runtime tests within the retry budget. This reduced exploration may directly affect performance on more complex datasets. *Gemini 3.1 Flash Lite* reaches the pipeline budget more consistently while producing fewer output tokens than *Gemini 2.5 Flash* in our runs.

Token usage shows the same trade-off: *Gemini 3.1 Flash Lite* generally uses more input tokens due to broader exploration, whereas *Gemini 2.5 Flash* produces substantially more output tokens, leading to comparable or higher overall costs despite exploring fewer pipelines.

Discussion. The results show that the proposed approach generalises across heterogeneous datasets, with particularly clear gains in scenarios requiring coordinated preprocessing steps such as *Adult* and *HAR*. An important factor affecting performance is the number of successfully executed pipelines. Datasets where fewer valid pipelines are generated (e.g., *HAR* and *MNIST_784* with *Gemini 2.5 Flash*) exhibit lower performance, indicating that pipeline validity and executability are critical bottlenecks in LLM-driven AutoML. This highlights the importance of the validation loop not only as a correctness mechanism, but also as a key enabler of effective search.

5 Conclusion and Future Work

This paper presents AGE-ML: an agentic AutoML approach focused on process-level explainability and data-centric process automation from an MLOps perspective. AGE-ML enables practitioners to guide pipeline exploration through a high-level specification language designed to express custom constraints and ML best practices. Given time and cost budgets, the system explores the space of admissible pipelines defined by the specification to identify high-performing solutions for the target task. Experiments show that AGE-ML can generate competitive pipelines across heterogeneous datasets, while providing traceable pipeline-generation rationale and a transparent optimisation process.

The main contributions of this work are: (i) a specification language for data-centric AutoML pipeline exploration, (ii) symbolic enumeration of feasible pipelines, (iii) automated code generation and execution, and (iv) logging of runs, artefacts, results, and explanations.

Future work will explore several directions to enhance the system's capabilities and applicability, including (in chronological order of execution): (i) agent-assisted authoring of modular, reusable, and priority-aware specifications from natural-language sources; (ii) support for human editing of generated pipeline scripts and selective re-execution of only the affected runs, while preserving provenance in the data catalog; (iii) analysing repeated-run variability and budget sensitivity, extending the evaluation across multiple LLMs, reducing latency and token usage through prompt compression and caching, and ranking admissible pipelines with heuristic or diversity-aware search; (iv) direct evaluation of data-quality improvement, cleaning effectiveness, and bias mitigation.

Acknowledgements. Matteo Magnini was supported by the Luxembourg National Research Fund (FNR) through the project "A DJ for Machine Ethics: the Dialogue Jiminy" (O24/18989918/DJ4ME).

Experiments have been enabled by our friend and colleague Dr. Gianluca Aguzzi (currently employed at the Universit di Bologna), who kindly provided us with access to his credits for LLMs usage on Google AI Studio, as provided by his Gemma Academic Program Award 2025.

References

1. Fang, H., et al.: MLZero: A multi-agent system for end-to-end machine learning automation. CoRR **abs/2505.13941** (2025). https://doi.org/10.48550/ARXIV.2505.13941
2. Feurer, M., Eggensperger, K., Falkner, S., Lindauer, M., Hutter, F.: Auto-Sklearn 2.0: Hands-free AutoML via meta-learning. J. Mach. Learn. Res. **23**, 261:1–261:61 (2022). https://jmlr.org/papers/v23/21-0992.html

3. Francia, M., Giovanelli, J., Golfarelli, M.: AutoClues: Exploring clustering pipelines via AutoML and diversification. In: Yang, D., Xie, X., Tseng, V.S., Pei, J., Huang, J., Lin, J.C. (eds.) Advances in Knowledge Discovery and Data Mining - 28th Pacific-Asia Conference on Knowledge Discovery and Data Mining, PAKDD 2024, Taipei, Taiwan, May 7-10, 2024, Proceedings, Part I. Lecture Notes in Computer Science, vol. 14645, pp. 246–258. Springer (2024). https://doi.org/10.1007/978-981-97-2242-6_20
4. Francia, M., Giovanelli, J., Pisano, G.: HAMLET: A framework for human-centered automl via structured argumentation. Future Gener. Comput. Syst **142**, 182–194 (2023). https://doi.org/10.1016/J.FUTURE.2022.12.035
5. Guo, S., Deng, C., Wen, Y., Chen, H., Chang, Y., Wang, J.: DS-Agent: Automated data science by empowering large language models with case-based reasoning. In: Salakhutdinov, R., Kolter, Z., Heller, K.A., Weller, A., Oliver, N., Scarlett, J., Berkenkamp, F. (eds.) Forty-first International Conference on Machine Learning, ICML 2024, Vienna, Austria, July 21-27, 2024, pp. 16813–16848. Proceedings of Machine Learning Research, PMLR / OpenReview.net (2024). https://proceedings.mlr.press/v235/guo24b.html
6. He, X., Zhao, K., Chu, X.: AutoML: A survey of the state-of-the-art. Knowl. Based Syst **212**, 106622 (2021). https://doi.org/10.1016/J.KNOSYS.2020.106622
7. Jin, H., Song, Q., Hu, X.: Auto-Keras: An efficient neural architecture search system. In: Teredesai, A., Kumar, V., Li, Y., Rosales, R., Terzi, E., Karypis, G. (eds.) Proceedings of the 25th ACM SIGKDD International Conference on Knowledge Discovery & Data Mining, KDD 2019, Anchorage, AK, USA, August 4-8, 2019, pp. 1946–1956. ACM (2019). https://doi.org/10.1145/3292500.3330648
8. Kolodner, J.L.: An introduction to case-based reasoning. Artif. Intell. Rev. **6**(1), 3–34 (1992). https://doi.org/10.1007/BF00155578
9. Matteini, M., Ciatto, G., Magnini, M., Kuru, E., Aydoğan, R., Omicini, A.: A domain-specific language for nesy focussing on symbolic knowledge injection. In: ANSyA 2025: Advanced Neuro-Symbolic Applications, pp. 84–92. CEUR Workshop Proceedings (2025).D https://ceur-ws.org/Vol-4125/paper_21.pdf
10. Mavroudis, V.: LangchainD (2024). https://doi.org/10.20944/preprints202411.0566.v1
11. de Moura, L.M., Bjørner, N.S.: Z3: an efficient SMT solver. In: Ramakrishnan, C.R., Rehof, J. (eds.) Tools and Algorithms for the Construction and Analysis of Systems, 14th International Conference, TACAS 2008, Held as Part of the Joint European Conferences on Theory and Practice of Software, ETAPS 2008, Budapest, Hungary, March 29-April 6, 2008. Proceedings, pp. 337–340. Lecture Notes in Computer Science, Springer (2008). https://doi.org/10.1007/978-3-540-78800-3_24
12. Olson, R.S., Moore, J.H.: TPOT: A tree-based pipeline optimization tool for automating machine learning. In: Hutter, F., Kotthoff, L., Vanschoren, J. (eds.) Automated Machine Learning - Methods, Systems, Challenges, pp. 151–160. The Springer Series on Challenges in Machine Learning, Springer (2019). https://doi.org/10.1007/978-3-030-05318-5_8

13. Schröer, C., Kruse, F., Gómez, J.M.: A systematic literature review on applying CRISP-DM process model. In: Cruz-Cunha, M.M., Martinho, R., Rijo, R., Peres, E., Domingos, D., Coelho, N.M. (eds.) CENTERIS 2020 - International Conference on ENTERprise Information Systems / ProjMAN 2020 - International Conference on Project MANagement / HCist 2020 - International Conference on Health and Social Care Information Systems and Technologies 2020, Vilamoura, Portugal. Procedia Computer Science, vol. 181, pp. 526–534. Elsevier (2021). https://doi.org/10.1016/J.PROCS.2021.01.199
14. Thornton, C., Hutter, F., Hoos, H.H., Leyton-Brown, K.: Auto-WEKA: combined selection and hyperparameter optimization of classification algorithms. In: Dhillon, I.S., et al., (eds.) The 19th ACM SIGKDD International Conference on Knowledge Discovery and Data Mining, KDD 2013, Chicago, IL, USA, August 11-14, 2013. pp. 847–855. ACM (2013). https://doi.org/10.1145/2487575.2487629
15. Trirat, P., Jeong, W., Hwang, S.J.: AutoML-agent: A multi-agent LLM framework for full-pipeline AutoML. In: Singh, A., et al., (eds.) Forty-second International Conference on Machine Learning, ICML 2025, Vancouver, BC, Canada, July 13-19, 2025. Proceedings of Machine Learning Research, PMLR / OpenReview.net (2025). https://proceedings.mlr.press/v267/trirat25a.html
16. Wang, C., Wu, Q., Liu, X., Quintanilla, L.: Automated machine learning & tuning with FLAML. In: Zhang, A., Rangwala, H. (eds.) KDD '22: The 28th ACM SIGKDD Conference on Knowledge Discovery and Data Mining, Washington, DC, USA, August 14 - 18, 2022, pp. 4828–4829. ACM (2022).https://doi.org/10.1145/3534678.3542636
17. Zaharia, M., et al.: Accelerating the machine learning lifecycle with mlflow. IEEE Data Eng. Bull. **41**(4), 39–45 (2018). http://sites.computer.org/debull/A18dec/p39.pdf
18. Zha, D., et al.: Data-centric artificial intelligence: a survey. ACM Comput. Surv. **57**(5), 129:1–129:42 (2025). https://doi.org/10.1145/3711118

Similarity, Topic Modeling and Knowledge Graphs

AQUA: Adaptive Query Rewriting Advisor with Schema-Driven Clustering and Contextual Bandits

Soumia Benkrid[1(✉)], Alfredo Cuzzocrea[2], and Nabil Tiaiba[1]

[1] LCSI, École Nationale Supérieure d'Informatique (ESI), Algiers, Algeria
{s_benkrid,n_tiaiba}@esi.dz
[2] DEA Lab, University of Calabria, Rende, Italy
alfredo.cuzzocrea@unical.it

Abstract. Query rewriting improves database performance by transforming SQL queries into semantically equivalent but more efficient forms. Recent ML- and LLM-based approaches achieve promising results, but they often process queries independently, rely on unreliable optimizer cost estimates, and incur high online inference overhead. We propose AQUA, an adaptive query rewrite strategy selection framework based on schema-driven clustering and contextual bandits. Queries are grouped by structural similarity using join predicate patterns, and each cluster maintains a shared LinUCB bandit that learns the most effective rewriting strategy from direct execution feedback. AQUA adaptively selects among join order selection, Common Table Expression (CTE) introduction, and hybrid rewrites without offline retraining or online LLM inference. Experiments on the TPC-H benchmark show that AQUA reduces average query execution time by up to 56.1% over original queries and 29.0% over the state-of-the-art LLM-based rewriting system QUITE, while achieving substantially lower rewrite overhead.

Keywords: Query Rewriting · Contextual Bandits · Adaptive Query Optimization · Workload Clustering · Database Systems

1 Introduction

AI-driven optimization techniques such as workload forecasting [21], cardinality estimation [33], learned cost modeling [22], plan enumeration [37],and query optimization in distributed/parallel environments [5,9] aim to improve DBMS performance by adapting optimization strategies to workload and data characteristics. However, these approaches typically depend on historical training data, making them sensitive to workload drift and often requiring expensive retraining.

Query rewriting [12,30,35] provides a complementary and more robust optimization layer by transforming SQL queries at the logical level (e.g., removing redundant operators or pulling up subqueries) into semantically equivalent but more efficiently executable forms. This can substantially reduce execution time

G. Vargas-Solar et al. (Eds.): ADBIS 2026, LNCS 16937, pp. 103–118, 2027.
https://doi.org/10.1007/978-3-032-39820-8_8

and expose learned optimizers to more diverse query patterns, improving their generalization. From a broader perspective, such generalization is increasingly relevant as ML-driven techniques are applied to large-scale OLAP analytics [17]. Classical query rewriting is NP-hard [24], and early methods applied predefined rules in fixed orders [4,14], often resulting in local optima and limited generalization. More recent approaches train machine learning models on rewriting histories to predict which rules to apply and in what order [35], while large language models (LLMs) have been explored for reasoning over rule selection and rewriting strategy generation [19,27].

Despite these advances, both ML and LLM-based rewriting approaches face critical limitations. They rely on DBMS optimizer cost estimates as substitutes for execution performance, which are known to be unreliable for multi-join queries where intermediate result sizes dominate [16]. Moreover, both families treat each query independently, rebuilding search structures or re-running inference pipelines from scratch at every query arrival. As shown in Fig. 1(a), ML-based methods incur a rewrite latency of 6.1–69.8 ms per query [35], a non-trivial overhead in high-throughput environments, particularly when compounded by frequent retraining, whereas LLM-based approaches average 291.59 seconds per query with performance directly tied to third-party API availability and pricing [27], incurring an average API cost of $6.76 per workload. As illustrated in Fig. 1(b), these per-query costs scale linearly with workload size regardless of structural similarity between queries.

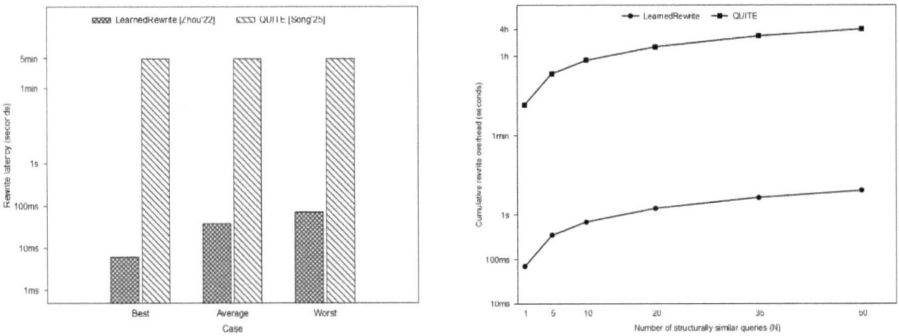

(a) Per-query rewrite latency (log scale)

(b) Cumulative rewrite overhead

Fig. 1. Performance comparison between LearnedRewrite [35] and QUITE [27].

A fundamental cause of these limitations is that existing methods treat each query in isolation, failing to identify and reuse rewriting strategies learned from structurally similar queries. In analytical settings, query execution performance is critically sensitive to common subexpressions. However, the optimal strategy for rewriting them is neither fixed nor universal. The literature has addressed this challenge from different angles: some works propose join order selection (JOS)

[34], others focus on Common Table Expression (CTE) introduction, and others on hybrid combinations. In practice, the best strategy depends on the specific query structure and the current data distribution, a strategy that effectively reduces execution time under one distribution may become suboptimal as table cardinalities shift and value skew changes. Yet existing approaches commit to a single rewriting strategy without any mechanism to learn which one works best for a given structural query pattern or to adapt as data evolves.

To address these challenges, we propose AQUA, an Adaptive QUery Advisor for query rewriting based on cluster-level contextual bandits. Rather than optimizing each query independently, AQUA groups structurally similar queries using join predicate patterns and enables them to share rewriting experience through a common LinUCB model. Queries are partitioned offline using Apriori-based feature extraction and K-Modes clustering, producing schema-driven groups that remain stable across data distribution changes. Within each cluster, a Multi-Armed Bandit (MAB) learns from direct execution feedback to adaptively select among join reordering, CTE introduction, and hybrid rewriting strategies. By relying on observed execution latency instead of optimizer cost estimates, AQUA continuously adapts rewrite strategy selection online while avoiding expensive retraining and repeated LLM inference.

Our main contributions are as follows:

- We formulate adaptive query rewrite selection as a cluster-level contextual bandit problem that enables knowledge sharing across structurally similar SQL queries.
- We introduce a schema-driven workload clustering approach based on join predicate patterns, allowing stable query grouping independent of data statistics.
- We implement and evaluate AQUA on TPC-H, showing substantial reductions in execution time and rewrite overhead compared with state-of-the-art LLM-based rewriting systems.

The remainder of this paper is organized as follows. Section 2 reviews related work. Section 3 presents the overall system architecture. Sections 3.2 and 3.3 detail the workload partitioning and MAB-based strategy selection components, respectively. Section 4 reports experimental results, and Sect. 5 concludes.

2 Related Work

2.1 Query Rewrite

Query rewriting transforms a SQL query into a semantically equivalent form with improved execution performance and has long been studied as a core component of query optimization [14,24]. Heuristic-based systems apply rewrite rules in fixed orders using pattern matching over logical query trees [4,25]. While computationally efficient, these methods cannot generalize to unseen query structures, are sensitive to rule ordering, and remain limited to predefined relational transformations [11].

ML-Driven Approaches. Learning-based systems attempt to better navigate the rewrite search space. WeTune [30] automatically discovers and verifies rewrite rules using algebraic reasoning, but supports only limited operator classes. Equality saturation methods [23] and user-guided tools such as QueryBooster [3] broaden the rewrite space but lack full autonomy across diverse workloads. LearnedRewrite [35] formulates rewriting as a Monte Carlo Tree Search (MCTS) problem guided by a learned cost-reduction model over query operators and metadata. Although effective on TPC-H and JOB workloads, its performance depends heavily on learned cost estimation quality and degrades on larger search spaces such as DSB. Moreover, these approaches remain confined to predefined rewrite rules and cannot generalize beyond their rewrite vocabulary [11,27].
LLM-Driven Approaches. Recent work incorporates LLMs to improve rewrite coverage and rule selection. GenRewrite [20] uses LLMs to generate rewrite rules in natural language but suffers from expensive candidate evaluation and limited equivalence verification. LLM-R2 [19] retrieves similar historical queries to guide rule selection through in-context learning, while R-Bot [28] combines retrieval-augmented generation with reflective reasoning. However, both remain restricted to predefined rewrite templates and are sensitive to workload distribution shifts. QUITE [27] departs from rule-based rewriting entirely by using LLM agents to directly generate semantically equivalent rewrites through a multi-stage reasoning and verification pipeline integrating SQLSolver [10]. Although QUITE substantially improves rewrite coverage and execution performance, it incurs significant online inference overhead due to repeated LLM invocation.

2.2 Bandit-Based Optimization

Multi-Armed Bandit (MAB) algorithms provide a principled framework for sequential decision-making under uncertainty by balancing exploration and exploitation [2,15]. Classical methods such as UCB [2] and Thompson Sampling [29] rely solely on reward statistics, whereas contextual variants such as LinUCB [18] incorporate feature representations of the current context. Several works combine clustering with contextual bandits to enable knowledge sharing across structurally similar instances. Bouneffouf et al. [8] partition the input space into clusters and apply contextual bandits within each cluster to accelerate convergence. More recently, bandits have been integrated with LLMs for prompt optimization [26], fine-tuning data selection [31], and adaptive exploration [7]. In database systems, bandit-based methods have been applied to learned query optimization and hint selection [22], but these approaches optimize queries independently without exploiting workload-level structural similarity.

In contrast, our approach formulates rewrite strategy selection as a cluster-level contextual bandit problem, where structurally similar queries are grouped by join predicate patterns and share a common LinUCB model. This shared learning framework enables execution-feedback-driven adaptation across related queries while avoiding repeated retraining and expensive online LLM inference.

3 AQUA: Adaptive Query Rewriting with Cluster-Level Contextual Bandits

In this section, we present AQUA, a lightweight adaptive framework for query rewrite strategy selection based on cluster-level contextual bandits. AQUA enables structurally similar queries to collaboratively learn rewrite preferences through shared execution feedback, allowing newly arriving queries to immediately benefit from previously observed workload behavior. The framework consists of two components: (i) schema-driven workload clustering for knowledge sharing, and (ii) contextual bandit learning for adaptive rewrite strategy selection.

3.1 Problem Setting

We consider the problem of adaptive query rewriting. At each time step t, a query q_t arrives with a feature vector $\mathbf{x}_t \in \{0,1\}^d$ encoding its structural characteristics (e.g., join predicates [6,36]). The system must select a rewriting strategy $a_t \in \mathcal{A} = \{a_1, \ldots, a_{|\mathcal{A}|}\}$ to optimize execution time while preserving semantic equivalence.

In this work, we instantiate $\mathcal{A} = \{\text{JOS}, \text{CTE}, \text{Hybrid}\}$, representing join reordering, Common Table Expression (CTE) introduction, and a hybrid combination of both, respectively. Join reordering and CTE introduction are well-studied rewriting problems [13,32,34]. Each arm corresponds to a deterministic rewrite module. JOS applies join reordering transformations, CTE introduces reusable subexpressions, and Hybrid first applies join reordering followed by CTE introduction, following the procedures described in [13,34].

We focus on the orthogonal problem of adaptive strategy selection: given a query, which rewriting approach yields the best execution performance under the current data distribution? All three strategies share a common design objective: reducing the volume of intermediate results produced during query execution, a dominant cost driver in analytical multi-join workloads [16]. JOS controls *when* large intermediates appear in the plan by reordering joins, whereas CTE controls *how many times* a given intermediate is materialized by eliminating redundant subexpression recomputation. The optimal strategy is query- and distribution-dependent, which is precisely the uncertainty the LinUCB bandit resolves through direct execution feedback.

After applying the selected strategy, the system observes a reward:

$$r_t = \max\left(0, \frac{t_{\text{orig}}(q_t) - t_{\text{rew}}(q_t, a_t)}{t_{\text{orig}}(q_t)}\right)$$

where $t_{\text{orig}}(q_t)$ and $t_{\text{rew}}(q_t, a_t)$ denote the execution times of the original and rewritten query, respectively. This ratio captures the relative reduction in execution time achieved by the selected strategy, a direct proxy for intermediate result volume reduction, since smaller intermediates translate proportionally to lower execution cost in multi-join workloads [16]. A positive reward indicates improvement; a zero reward indicates that the selected strategy failed to improve execution time. The objective is to maximize cumulative reward over T steps: $\max \sum_{t=1}^{T} r_t$.

We advocate a periodically updated clustering approach for adaptive query rewriting. In this approach, the workload is partitioned into K clusters based on structural query features, specifically, frequent join predicates discovered via Apriori. Queries assigned to the same cluster share a common LinUCB model, enabling execution-feedback knowledge to transfer across structurally similar workload patterns. This allows ad-hoc queries to benefit from the accumulated knowledge of structurally similar queries without requiring their own historical data. Moreover, as workload characteristics evolve, query assignments are dynamically updated based on join predicate features, enabling queries to switch to clusters that better reflect current workload patterns and allowing cluster assignments to remain aligned with evolving workload structure. As illustrated in Fig. 2, AQUA addresses this problem in two steps: **(i)** an offline phase that partitions the query workload into structural clusters to enable knowledge sharing, and **(ii)** an online phase in which a cluster-level bandit continuously learns and adapts the optimal rewriting strategy from direct execution feedback.

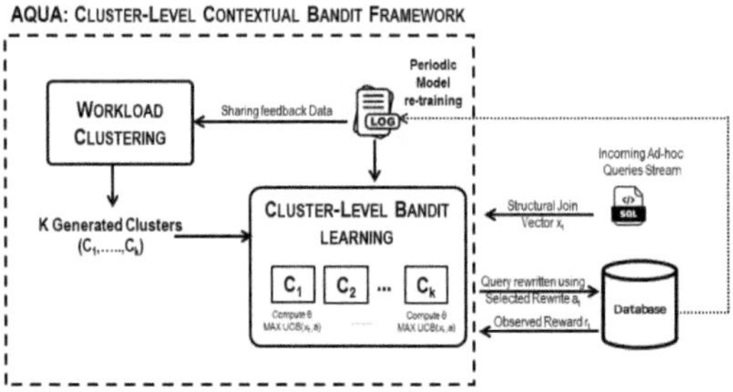

Fig. 2. Overview of AQUA.

3.2 Knowledge Sharing via Workload Clustering

We design a periodic workload reclustering method to enable long-term effectiveness of the query rewriting engine. Without knowledge sharing, each query would need extensive historical feedback to learn optimal rewriting strategies, an impractical requirement for ad-hoc and infrequent queries. By grouping structurally similar queries, our approach allows them to collectively benefit from shared rewriting experience as workload patterns evolve.

Feature Representation. Each query q is represented as a binary vector $\mathbf{x} \in \{0,1\}^d$, where d is the number of distinct join predicates discovered across the workload via the Apriori algorithm, and $x_i = 1$ if predicate i appears in q, and 0 otherwise. This representation captures the structural join pattern of each query in a compact, schema-grounded form.

Cluster Assignment. We assume K structural clusters. Each query q is assigned to the nearest cluster center $\mathbf{c}_k$ under Hamming distance, which is the natural dissimilarity measure for binary vectors and the metric underlying K-Modes clustering:

$$k(q) = \arg\min_k H(\mathbf{x}, \mathbf{c}_k), \quad \text{where } H(\mathbf{x}, \mathbf{c}_k) = \sum_{i=1}^{d} |x_i - c_{k,i}|$$

Queries assigned to the same cluster share a LinUCB bandit, enabling collective learning of rewriting strategies across structurally similar workload members.

Selecting the Number of Clusters K. We employ two complementary methods:

- **Elbow Method**: Plots the within-cluster sum of Hamming distances against K; the optimal K is identified at the elbow where the rate of decrease significantly slows.
- **Silhouette Coefficient**: For query i, defined as:

$$s(i) = \frac{b(i) - a(i)}{\max(a(i), b(i))}$$

  where $a(i)$ is the mean Hamming distance to queries in the same cluster, and $b(i)$ is the mean distance to queries in the nearest neighboring cluster. Values range from -1 (poor fit) to $+1$ (excellent fit); we select K that maximizes the mean silhouette score across all queries.

Periodic Reclustering. To sustain performance under distributional drift, we introduce periodic reclustering at interval Δ. As workload characteristics shift, cluster centers are recomputed and queries are reassigned to reflect current structural trends, ensuring that each query consistently benefits from the most relevant collective knowledge without requiring manual reconfiguration.

This framework achieves two complementary objectives: *knowledge sharing*, enabling new queries to benefit from accumulated experience of structurally similar patterns, and *dynamic adaptation*, maintaining cluster relevance as workloads evolve, both without manual reconfiguration. Rewrite selection is then modeled as a contextual bandit problem over shared cluster-level feedback, where separate per-cluster models prevent reward signals from dissimilar queries from interfering with one another. Knowledge sharing occurs through shared LinUCB sufficient statistics $(M_{k,a}, b_{k,a})$ maintained at the cluster level.

3.3 Bandit Learning for Strategy Selection

Contextual Bandit Formulation. Building on the cluster partition introduced in Sect. 3.2, we formulate strategy selection as a *contextual bandit* problem operating at the cluster level. Each cluster k maintains a shared bandit that accumulates the execution experience of all its member queries. When query q_t is assigned to cluster k_t, it immediately benefits from the collective reward history of all structurally similar queries that preceded it, without requiring its own execution history. The system learns from the sequence of observations $\langle \mathbf{x}_t, a_t, r_t \rangle$ accumulated across all queries in cluster k_t, with no reward observed for strategies not selected at step t. Crucially, r_t is derived from measured execution time rather than optimizer cost estimates, directly addressing the reliability gap identified in prior work.

The objective is equivalently expressed as minimizing total cumulative regret:

$$\text{Regret}(T) = \sum_{t=1}^{T} \left[r_t(a^*) - r_t(a_t) \right]$$

where a^* is the optimal rewriting strategy and $r_t(a^*)$ is the reward that would have been obtained by selecting the best arm at step t. Lower regret indicates faster convergence to the best strategy.

We adopt LinUCB [18] as our bandit framework, modeling the expected reward of arm a in cluster k as a linear function of the context. Let $x_t \in \mathbb{R}^d$ denote the query feature vector, $M_{k,a} \in \mathbb{R}^{d \times d}$ the regularized Gram matrix associated with arm a in cluster k, and $b_{k,a} \in \mathbb{R}^d$ the corresponding reward-weighted context accumulator. The expected reward is estimated as:

$$\hat{r}(k, a, \mathbf{x}_t) = \hat{\boldsymbol{\theta}}_{k,a}^{\top} \mathbf{x}_t \tag{1}$$

where $\hat{\boldsymbol{\theta}}_{k,a} \in \mathbb{R}^d$ is the regression coefficient vector learned from all queries previously assigned to cluster k that selected arm a. To balance exploitation of high-reward strategies with exploration of uncertain ones, LinUCB selects the arm maximizing an upper confidence bound over the cluster-level parameters:

$$a_t = \arg\max_{a \in \mathcal{A}} \left[\hat{\boldsymbol{\theta}}_{k_t,a}^{\top} \mathbf{x}_t + \alpha \sqrt{\mathbf{x}_t^{\top} \mathbf{M}_{k_t,a}^{-1} \mathbf{x}_t} \right] \tag{2}$$

where $\mathbf{M}_{k,a} \in \mathbb{R}^{d \times d}$ is the regularized gram matrix initialized as $\mathbf{M}_{k,a} = \lambda \mathbf{I}$ (with $\lambda > 0$ a regularization parameter), $\mathbf{b}_{k,a} \in \mathbb{R}^d$ is the reward-weighted context accumulator initialized as $\mathbf{b}_{k,a} = \mathbf{0}$, and α controls the exploration-exploitation trade-off, set as $\alpha = 1 + \sqrt{\ln(2/\delta)/2}$ with confidence level $1 - \delta = 0.95$.

After selecting a_t and observing reward r_t, only the parameters of the selected arm in cluster k_t are updated:

$$\mathbf{M}_{k_t,a_t} \leftarrow \mathbf{M}_{k_t,a_t} + \mathbf{x}_t \mathbf{x}_t^{\top}, \quad \mathbf{b}_{k_t,a_t} \leftarrow \mathbf{b}_{k_t,a_t} + r_t \mathbf{x}_t, \quad \hat{\boldsymbol{\theta}}_{k_t,a_t} = \mathbf{M}_{k_t,a_t}^{-1} \mathbf{b}_{k_t,a_t} \tag{3}$$

Reward Acquisition and the Role of Δ. Computing r_t requires executing both the original query and its rewrite, a cost too high to incur on every query online. AQUA therefore computes rewards and updates $(\mathbf{M}_{k,a}, \mathbf{b}_{k,a})$ offline, in batch, every Δ queries, reusing the same maintenance window already used for reclustering (Sect. 3.2). Online serving only performs cluster assignment and arm scoring against the most recently committed $\hat{\boldsymbol{\theta}}_{k,a}$, with no additional query execution.

This selective update ensures that reward signals from one structural query group do not contaminate the learned strategies of another.

The full procedure, integrating cluster-level bandit updates, Hamming-distance-based query assignment, and periodic reclustering, is formalized in Algorithm 1.

Algorithm 1. AQUA: Cluster-Level Contextual Bandit Framework for Adaptive Query Rewriting

Require: $K, \alpha, \lambda, \Delta$
Ensure: Optimal rewriting strategy per query
Initialize K clusters via K-Modes on historical query predicates
Initialize $\mathbf{M}_{k,a} = \lambda \mathbf{I}$, $\mathbf{b}_{k,a} = \mathbf{0}$ for all k, a
for $t = 1$ **to** T **do**
  Observe query q_t with feature vector $\mathbf{x}_t$
  Assign q_t to nearest cluster: $k_t = \arg\min_k H(\mathbf{x}_t, \mathbf{c}_k)$
  for all arm $a \in \mathcal{A}$ **do**
    Compute $\hat{\boldsymbol{\theta}}_{k_t,a} = \mathbf{M}_{k_t,a}^{-1} \mathbf{b}_{k_t,a}$
    Compute $\mathrm{UCB}_{k_t,a}(\mathbf{x}_t) = \hat{\boldsymbol{\theta}}_{k_t,a}^{\top} \mathbf{x}_t + \alpha \sqrt{\mathbf{x}_t^{\top} \mathbf{M}_{k_t,a}^{-1} \mathbf{x}_t}$
  end for
  Select $a_t = \arg\max_{a \in \mathcal{A}} \mathrm{UCB}_{k_t,a}(\mathbf{x}_t)$
  Execute rewritten query, observe reward r_t
  Update $\mathbf{M}_{k_t,a_t} \leftarrow \mathbf{M}_{k_t,a_t} + \mathbf{x}_t \mathbf{x}_t^{\top}$, $\mathbf{b}_{k_t,a_t} \leftarrow \mathbf{b}_{k_t,a_t} + r_t \mathbf{x}_t$
  if $t \bmod \Delta = 0$ **then**
    Recompute cluster centers and reassign all queries
  end if
end for

4 Experimental Evaluation

4.1 Experimental Setup

All experiments were conducted on a MacBook Pro equipped with an Apple M-series processor, 16 GB of RAM, and PostgreSQL v14.13. We used a TPC-H benchmark at scale factor SF10 ($\sim$10 GB), consisting of eight tables, as our experimental benchmark.

To ensure result stability and reproducibility, the database system was restarted prior to each query execution to clear all caches. Each query evaluation consisted of one warm-up run to mitigate cold-start effects, followed by ten measured executions, over which we report the average execution time. Queries exceeding 300 s were terminated and capped at that value, following the methodology of [19,27]. Each rewritten query was verified to produce results identical to the original.

AQUA Configuration. The offline clustering phase was initialized using K-Modes on the full TPC-H query workload, with K selected via silhouette analysis as described in Sect. 3.2, yielding $K = 8$ clusters. We set $\lambda = 1$ following standard LinUCB practice [15,18], $\alpha = 1 + \sqrt{\ln(2/\delta)/2}$ with $\delta = 0.05$, and $\Delta = 10$, recomputing cluster centers every 10 query arrivals to balance adaptation speed against computational overhead.
Baseline. We select QUITE [27] as our primary baseline, as it represents the current state of the art in LLM-based query rewriting and has been shown to outperform LearnedRewrite [35], LLM-R2 [19], and R-Bot [28]. QUITE was re-run on our hardware under identical experimental conditions and configured according to its original paper, using GPT-4o as the underlying language model.

4.2 Rewriting Selection System Efficiency

We evaluate the full query workload derived from all templates of the TPC-H benchmark, comparing AQUA against QUITE across multiple statistical measures (Table 1). AQUA consistently outperforms both the original queries and QUITE, reducing mean execution time by 56.1% over the original baseline and by 29.0% over QUITE. These gains confirm that directly targeting intermediate result volume through adaptive selection among JOS, CTE, and Hybrid strategies. is an effective optimization objective for analytical multi-join workloads, without requiring LLM inference or cost-estimate-based guidance. The advantage is most pronounced at the tail: the 95th-percentile latency drops from 276.98 s (QUITE) to 79.54 s (AQUA), a reduction of 71.3%, indicating that QUITE's LLM-generated rewrites occasionally produce plans that trigger query timeouts, whereas AQUA's execution-feedback-driven selection avoids such pathological cases.

To isolate the effect of timeout queries, we additionally report results on the filtered workload. Even under this more favorable setting for QUITE, AQUA maintains a lower mean execution time (27.43 s vs. 29.47 s) and better 75th-percentile latency (37.67 s vs. 41.40 s), confirming that its gains reflect a consistently superior rewriting selection strategy rather than mere timeout avoidance.

Table 1. Performance comparison of query rewrite methods.

Methods	Full Workload				Excluding Timeouts			
	Mean	Median	75th	95th	Mean	Median	75th	95th
Original	68.79	42.80	65.42	300.00	44.45	42.00	48.68	148.70
AQUA	**30.20**	**28.34**	**37.84**	**79.54**	**27.43**	**28.26**	**37.67**	**69.73**
QUITE	42.52	30.11	43.27	276.98	29.47	28.89	41.40	69.77

4.3 Robustness Study

Rewriting Time Analysis To evaluate inference-time efficiency, we measure end-to-end rewriting time across two query sets: *ad-hoc queries* sampled from TPC-H templates, and *drift queries* with modified join patterns. A key property of AQUA is that rewriting overhead is decoupled from query complexity: strategy selection reduces to a single Hamming-distance cluster lookup followed by a closed-form UCB computation.

Ad-hoc queries. Table 2 reports results on 30 ad-hoc queries. AQUA reduces mean rewriting time by 11.0% (11.20 s vs. 12.59 s) and median by 42.0% (4.70 s vs. 8.10 s), as shared cluster-level knowledge allows arriving queries to immediately inherit accumulated rewriting experience. At the 95th percentile, QUITE is marginally faster (35.14 s vs. 35.87 s), suggesting that for structurally complex queries, the three intermediate-result-oriented arms do not fully cover the rewriting space. Extending the action space with complementary rules such as predicate pushdown or subquery unnesting represents a natural next step, as the cluster-level bandit accommodates additional arms without architectural changes.

Table 2. Rewriting time (seconds) on 30 ad-hoc queries (online stage).

Method	Mean	Median	75th	95th
AQUA	**11.20**	**4.70**	**19.50**	35.87
QUITE	12.59	8.10	20.10	**35.14**

Drift queries. As illustrated in Fig. 3, AQUA imposes a constant 0.1 s overhead per query, accumulating to 3.0 s across 30 drift queries. QUITE incurs variable overhead of 19.9 s–71.5 s per query, accumulating to 1145.7 s, a **381**× increase. Because clusters are defined by join predicate patterns rather than data statistics, drift queries are immediately routed to the nearest structural cluster and served by accumulated bandit knowledge, eliminating any LLM re-invocation and making AQUA particularly suited to latency-sensitive environments with evolving workloads.

Generalization Across Database Scales A key property of AQUA's schema-driven clustering is that the cluster partition does not drift under distributional shift: because clusters are defined by join predicate patterns rather than data statistics, the partition computed at SF1 remains valid at SF10 without recomputation, contrasting with statistics-based approaches that require recomputation as table cardinalities shift. To validate this, we evaluate a policy learned on SF1 (∼1GB) directly on SF10 (∼10GB) without offline retraining. As shown in Table 3, performance degrades marginally at the median (+2.1%) and mean (+8.4%), confirming that query routing remains correct across scales and accumulated bandit knowledge stays applicable. The only notable gap appears at the

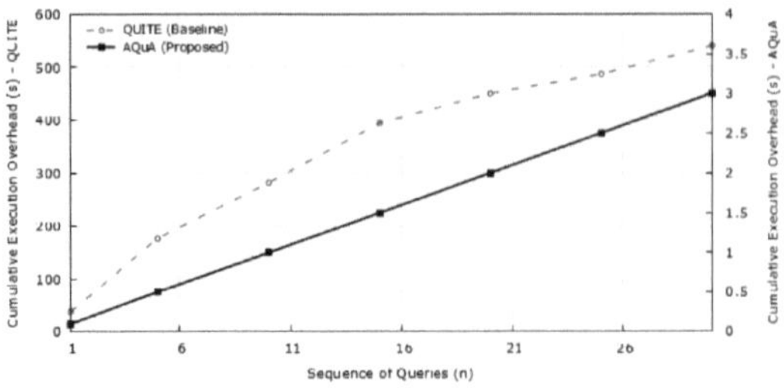

Fig. 3. Cumulative execution overhead.

95th percentile (+45.5%), attributable to tail queries underrepresented in SF1, a gap that closes automatically as the bandit accumulates online feedback at SF10, with no manual intervention required.

Table 3. Policy learned on SF1 evaluated on SF10 without offline retraining .

Configuration	Mean	Median	75th	95th
SF10 (matched)	**30.20**	**28.35**	**37.84**	**79.54**
SF1 (transferred)	32.73	28.94	39.39	115.70
Δ (%)	+8.4%	+2.1%	+4.1%	+45.5%

4.4 Ablation Study

Bandit Algorithm Selection and Convergence Analysis. To validate the choice of LinUCB as AQUA's cluster-level strategy selector, we compare it against three alternatives:

- *Linear Thompson Sampling* (LinTS) [1], a Bayesian contextual variant that samples from a Gaussian posterior rather than optimizing a confidence bound;
- *Upper Confidence Bound* (UCB) [2], a non-contextual baseline selecting strategies solely on per-arm reward statistics;
- *Thompson Sampling* (TS) [29], a non-contextual Bayesian baseline maintaining a Beta posterior per arm, ignoring query structural features entirely.

As shown in Fig. 4 (a), LinUCB achieves the lowest cumulative regret over the full TPC-H workload. The gap between contextual and non-contextual methods is pronounced: UCB and TS treat every query identically and require far more observations to distinguish among strategies, whereas LinUCB and LinTS leverage binary join predicate features to transfer accumulated experience immediately to structurally similar queries. Among contextual methods, LinUCB outperforms LinTS as its deterministic confidence-bound selection provides more stable convergence than stochastic posterior sampling, which can over-explore in early rounds.

To verify that LinUCB's advantage is not an artifact of timeout queries, we repeat the analysis by excluding TS. As shown in Fig. 4 (b), LinUCB retains the lowest cumulative regret, confirming that its superiority reflects genuine policy quality. These results validate the combination of cluster-level knowledge sharing and confidence-bound-driven exploration as well-suited to the adaptive query rewriting setting.

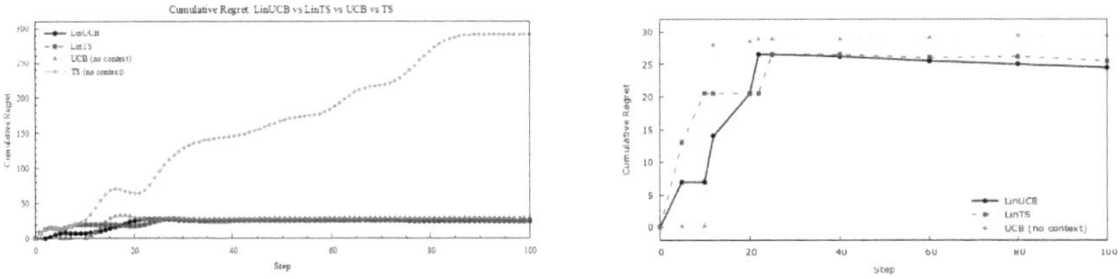

(a) Algorithm Comparison. (b) Algorithm Comparison (Without TS).

Fig. 4. Bandit algorithm ablation within AQUA.

Table 4. Sensitivity to the number of clusters K.

Configuration	Total	Mean	Median	75th	95th
Original	844.49	44.45	42.00	48.68	148.70
$K = 1$	554.74	29.20	28.35	38.03	74.94
$K = 4$	528.52	27.82	28.26	37.54	74.94
AQUA ($K = 8$)	**521.15**	**27.43**	**28.26**	37.76	**69.73**
$K = 12$	523.68	27.56	28.26	**36.81**	69.73

Sensitivity to the Number of Clusters *K*. To isolate the contribution of clustering granularity, we evaluate AQUA across $K \in \{1, 4, 8, 12\}$ on the filtered workload. Results are reported in Table 4 and reveal three consistent findings. First, even $K = 1$ substantially outperforms the original queries (mean: 29.20 s vs. 44.45 s, −34.3%), confirming that execution-feedback-driven strategy selection is the primary performance driver. Second, clustering provides consistent additional gains: performance improves monotonically from $K = 1$ to $K = 8$, which achieves the best mean (27.43 s) and 95th-percentile latency (69.73 s), confirming that grouping structurally similar queries prevents reward signals from dissimilar patterns from interfering with bandit learning. Third, $K = 12$

yields diminishing returns rather than collapse (mean: 27.56 s, identical 95th-percentile), indicating robustness to mild over-clustering, a desirable property when the optimal K is not known precisely.

These results empirically validate the silhouette-based selection described in Sect. 3.2: the analytically derived $K = 8$ coincides with the empirically optimal configuration without requiring exhaustive search.

5 Conclusion

We presented AQUA, a lightweight adaptive framework for query rewrite strategy selection based on schema-driven clustering and cluster-level contextual bandits. By grouping structurally similar queries via join predicate patterns and sharing rewriting experience through a common LinUCB bandit, AQUA learns from direct execution feedback without offline retraining or LLM inference. Experiments on TPC-H demonstrate that AQUA substantially reduces query execution time over both unoptimized queries and the state-of-the-art LLM-based rewriting system QUITE, while imposing dramatically lower rewriting overhead per query. The schema-driven partition generalizes across database scales without recomputation, making it robust to distributional shift. Ablation studies confirm that LinUCB is the most effective bandit variant for this setting, and that silhouette-based cluster selection yields an empirically optimal workload partition. These results establish that targeting intermediate result volume through adaptive bandit-driven strategy selection is an effective and practical alternative to LLM-based rewriting in latency-sensitive environments, achieving superior execution performance without the cost, latency, or external dependencies of online LLM inference.

Several directions remain open for future work. First, extending the action space beyond the three intermediate-result-oriented strategies considered here, for instance, incorporating predicate pushdown or materialized view matching, would broaden AQUA's rewriting coverage, as the cluster-level bandit naturally accommodates additional arms without architectural changes. Second, a timeout-aware fallback mechanism that temporarily merges sparse clusters during cold-start phases could further stabilize tail-query performance. Third, evaluating AQUA on more diverse benchmarks such as JOB or TPC-DS would establish broader generalization beyond the TPC-H setting studied here. We release our implementation to facilitate reproducibility and further research in adaptive query rewriting.

References

1. Agrawal, S., Goyal, N.: Thompson sampling for contextual bandits with linear payoffs. In: International Conference on Machine Learning, pp. 127–135. PMLR (2013)
2. Auer, P., Cesa-Bianchi, N., Fischer, P.: Finite-time analysis of the multiarmed bandit problem. Mach. Learn. **47**(2), 235–256 (2002)

3. Bai, Q., Alsudais, S., Li, C.: Querybooster: Improving SQL performance using middleware services for human-centered query rewriting. arXiv preprint arXiv:2305.08272 (2023)
4. Begoli, E., Camacho-Rodríguez, J., Hyde, J., Mior, M.J., Lemire, D.: Apache calcite: A foundational framework for optimized query processing over heterogeneous data sources. In: Proceedings of the 2018 International Conference on Management of Data, pp. 221–230 (2018)
5. Bellatreche, L., Benkrid, S., Crolotte, A., Cuzzocrea, A., Ghazal, A.: The f&a methodology and its experimental validation on a real-life parallel processing database system. In: 2012 Sixth International Conference on Complex, Intelligent, and Software Intensive Systems, pp. 114–121. IEEE (2012)
6. Benkrid, S., Mestoui, Y., Bellatreche, L., Ordonez, C.: A genetic optimization physical planner for big data warehouses. In: 2020 IEEE International Conference on Big Data (Big Data), pp. 406–412. IEEE (2020)
7. Bouneffouf, D., Féraud, R.: A tutorial on multi-armed bandit applications for large language models. In: Proceedings of the 30th ACM SIGKDD Conference on Knowledge Discovery and Data Mining, pp. 6412–6413 (2024)
8. Bouneffouf, D., Laroche, R., Urvoy, T.,. Féraud, R., Allesiardo, R.: Contextual bandit for active learning: Active thompson sampling. In: International Conference on Neural Information Processing, pp. 405–412. Springer (2014)
9. Chatzimilioudis, G., Cuzzocrea, A., Gunopulos, D., Mamoulis, N.: A novel distributed framework for optimizing query routing trees in wireless sensor networks via optimal operator placement. J. Comput. Syst. Sci. **79**(3), 349–368 (2013)
10. Ding, H.: Proving query equivalence using linear integer arithmetic. Proc. ACM Manage. Data **1**(4), 1–26 (2023)
11. Dong, R., Liu, J., Zhu, Y., Yan, C., Mozafari, B., Wang, X.: Slabcity: Whole-query optimization using program synthesis. Proc. VLDB Endowment **16**(11) (2023)
12. eatrice Finance, B., Gardarin, G.: A rule based query rewriter in an extensible DBMS. In: Proceedings of the 7th International Conference on Data Engineering. IEEE (1991)
13. El-Helw, A., Raghavan, V., Soliman, M.A., Caragea, G., Gu, Z., Petropoulos, M.: Optimization of common table expressions in MPP database systems. Proc. VLDB Endowment **8**(12), 1704–1715 (2015)
14. Graefe, G., McKenna, W.J.: The volcano optimizer generator: Extensibility and efficient search. In: Proceedings of IEEE 9th International Conference on Data Engineering, pp. 209–218. IEEE (1993)
15. Lattimore, T., Szepesvári, C.: Bandit algorithms, Cambridge University Press (2020)
16. Leis, V., Gubichev, A., Mirchev, A., Boncz, P., Kemper, A., Neumann, T.: How good are query optimizers, really? Proc. VLDB Endowment **9**(3), 204–215 (2015)
17. Leung, C.K., Chen, Y., Hoi, C.S., Shang, S., Cuzzocrea, A.: Machine learning and OLAP on big covid-19 data. In: 2020 IEEE International Conference on Big Data (Big Data), pp. 5118–5127. IEEE (2020)
18. Li, L., Chu, W., Langford, J., Schapire, R.E.: A contextual-bandit approach to personalized news article recommendation. In: Proceedings of the 19th International Conference on World Wide Web, pp. 661–670 (2010)
19. Li, Z., Yuan, H., Wang, H., Cong, G., Bing, L.: LLM-r2: a large language model enhanced rule-based rewrite system for boosting query efficiency. Proc. VLDB Endowment **18**(1), 53–65 (2024)
20. Liu, J., Mozafari, B.: Genrewrite: Query rewriting via large language models. Proc. ACM Manage. Data **4**(1 (SIGMOD):1–26 (2026)

21. Ma, L., Van Aken, D., Hefny, A., Mezerhane, G., Pavlo, A., Gordon, G.J.: Query-based workload forecasting for self-driving database management systems. In: Proceedings of the 2018 International Conference on Management of Data, pp. 631–645 (2018)
22. Marcus, R., Negi, P., Mao, H., Tatbul, N., Alizadeh, M., Kraska, T.: Bao: Making learned query optimization practical. In: Proceedings of the 2021 International Conference on Management of Data, pp. 1275–1288 (2021)
23. Nandi, C., et al.: Rewrite rule inference using equality saturation. Proc. ACM Programm. Lang. **5**(OOPSLA), 1–28 (2021)
24. Pirahesh, H., Hellerstein, J.M., Hasan, W.: Extensible/rule based query rewrite optimization in starburst. ACM SIGMOD Rec. **21**(2), 39–48 (1992)
25. PostgreSQL Global Development Group (2024). PostgreSQL 14 Documentation
26. Shi, C., Yang, K., Chen, Z., Li, J., Yang, J., Shen, C.: Efficient prompt optimization through the lens of best arm identification. Adv. Neural. Inf. Process. Syst. **37**, 99646–99685 (2024)
27. Song, Y., et al.: Quite: A query rewrite system beyond rules with LLM agents. arXiv preprint arXiv:2506.07675 (2025)
28. Sun, Z., Zhou, X., Li, G., Yu, X., Feng, J., Zhang, Y.: R-bot: An LLM-based query rewrite system. Proc. VLDB Endow. **18**(12), 5031–5044 (2025)
29. Thompson, W.R.: On the likelihood that one unknown probability exceeds another in view of the evidence of two samples. Biometrika **25**(3/4), 285–294 (1933)
30. Wang, Z., et al.: Wetune: Automatic discovery and verification of query rewrite rules. In: Proceedings of the 2022 International Conference on Management of Data, pp. 94–107 (2022)
31. Xia, Y., et al.: Which LLM to play? convergence-aware online model selection with time-increasing bandits. In: Proceedings of the ACM Web Conference, pp. 4059–4070 (2024)
32. Yan, Z., Uotila, V.J.E., Lu, J.: Join order selection with deep reinforcement learning: Fundamentals, techniques, and challenges. Proc. VLDB Endowment **16**(12), 3882–3885 (2023)
33. Yang, Z., et al.: Deep unsupervised cardinality estimation. arXiv preprint arXiv:1905.04278 (2019)
34. Yu, X., Li, G., Chai, C., Tang, N.: Reinforcement learning with tree-LSTM for join order selection. In: 2020 IEEE 36th International Conference on Data Engineering (ICDE), pp. 1297–1308. IEEE (2020)
35. Zhou, X., Li, G., Chai, C., Feng, J.: A learned query rewrite system using Monte Carlo tree search. Proc. VLDB Endow. **15**(1), 46–58 (2021)
36. Zhu, J., Cai, S., Shen, Y., Chen, G., Deng, F., Ooi, B.: In-context adaptation to concept drift for learned database operations. Proc. Mach. Learn. Res. **267**, 79699–79726 (2025)
37. Zhu, R.: LERO: A learning-to-rank query optimizer. Proc. VLDB Endow. **16**(6), 1466–1479 (2023). Feb

Data Cleaning, Semantic Discovery and AutoML

Similarity Denial Constraints for Detecting Violations in Noisy Data

Leonardo Ferreira Luciano[1(✉)], Eduardo Henrique Monteiro Pena[2], and Eduardo Cunha de Almeida[1]

[1] Federal University of Paraná, Curitiba, Paraná, Brazil
{lfluciano,eduardo}@inf.ufpr.br
[2] Federal University of Technology, Campo Mourõ, Paraná, Brazil
eduardopena@utfpr.edu.br

Abstract. Integrity constraints (ICs) play an important role in data cleaning and data exploration. Various works focus on the automatic discovery of ICs or on detecting violations of provided ICs. However, most existing approaches cannot handle a problem commonly found in real datasets: noisy textual data, i.e., data containing multiple strings that represent the same real-world entity. To address this problem, we present *Similarity FAst Constraint-based Error DeTector* (`SimFACET`), which detects violations of denial constraints (DCs) that contain similarity predicates. By focusing on DCs, a first-order logic formalism for ICs with high expressive power, our work introduces the notion of string similarity to address constraints not covered by existing research. `SimFACET` efficiently evaluates DCs containing similarity predicates using exact and approximate algorithms for performing similarity joins. To determine string similarity, the detector supports the edit distance between strings or the cosine distance between text embeddings. We also explore different strategies for the placement of similarity operator processing in the pipeline. To evaluate the proposed algorithms and strategies, we have conducted experiments across multiple datasets and using DCs with different characteristics. The results show that `SimFACET` maintains high accuracy while consistently reducing detection time, executing up to 4× faster than baselines.

Keywords: Denial Constraints · Similarity · Violations Detection

1 Introduction

Integrity constraints (ICs) have been used in many data-related tasks, such as query optimization [20], inconsistency measurement [24], and data cleaning [1]. Enforcing a set of meaningful ICs increases data consistency and quality, enabling more reliable insights and better data-driven decisions in organizations.

To illustrate the applicability of ICs, consider the `Employees` relation shown in Table 1, which stores employee records for a fictional company. Consider that this company has some employee-related policies, translated into the following

G. Vargas-Solar et al. (Eds.): ADBIS 2026, LNCS 16937, pp. 121–136, 2027.
https://doi.org/10.1007/978-3-032-39820-8_9

data rules: (1) each employee must have a unique identifier; (2) employees from the same department must work at the same location; and (3) no employee must receive a salary lower than the salary of another employee who started after him in the same department. All these data rules can be expressed using different IC formalisms. In this work, we focus on *denial constraints* (DCs) [5], as they can express many constraints, subsuming multiple other formalisms [9].

Table 1. The `Employees` relation.

	id	name	department	location	start_year	salary
t_1	101	Smith	Information Technology	San Francisco	2021	9000
t_2	102	Williams	Sales	New York	2022	9500
t_3	103	Jones	Sales	New York	2023	8000
t_4	104	Johnson	IT	San Francisco	2024	10000

If we consider only the exact-value comparison for the records, there are no violations of any of the three data rules. However, we should be more careful and consider the semantic value of data. In this case, we notice that the values of the `department` column in tuples t_1 (*Information Technology*) and t_4 (*IT*) refer to the same real-world entity, the Information Technology department. So, in the real world, the tuple pair (t_1, t_4) is a violation of rule (3), which has not been detected because of noisy data, in this case, different representations of a department name.

This example illustrates a limitation of traditional DCs. Most works use DCs based on the following set of operators $(=, \neq, <, \leq, >, \geq)$ and do not consider similarity-based operators [9,23,25,30,32]. The works that define DCs with more flexible operators, theoretically allowing the notion of similarity, do not further explore this subject [4,13,34]. The absence of similarity operators has a significant impact on DC violations detection when dealing with columns whose values are strings, as it is common for real data in these columns to be noisy, i.e., to contain typos, abbreviations, acronyms, or variations representing the same real-world entity. Therefore, considering string similarity in DC predicates can improve their usefulness in real datasets, enabling the detection of integrity violations even in the presence of noisy data.

To address these questions, we present *Similarity FAst Constraint-based Error DeTector* (`SimFACET`), a system capable of detecting violations of DCs containing predicates with similarity operators. Similarity can be measured in multiple ways. `SimFACET` measures it using two of the most commonly used similarity distance metrics for strings and categorical data: edit distance and cosine distance. Edit distance is faster but limited to syntactic distance, while cosine distance increases detection time but considers semantic distance. To detect DC similarity violations across large datasets, we propose exact and approximate algorithms that efficiently evaluate similarity operators by leveraging indexing techniques to perform similarity joins. We integrate these algorithms into a robust detector of traditional DC violations and explore different strategies for planning the processing order of the similarity operators. In summary, our main contributions are:

- A system for detecting DC violations using similarity operators in large noisy datasets (Sect. 3);
- Exact and approximate algorithms that leverage indexing techniques to efficiently evaluate similarity operators, supporting both edit distance and cosine distance for text embeddings (Sect. 3);
- An experimental evaluation on multiple real and synthetic datasets, comparing detection time, accuracy of approximate approaches, and the impact of operator execution order (Sect. 4).

We provide background in Sect. 2, discuss related work in Sect. 5, and conclude in Sect. 6.

2 Background

2.1 Denial Constraints

Denial constraints (DCs) can be defined as a set of predicates that cannot be true at the same time for any pair of distinct tuples from a table. In this work, we follow [30] and [23], restricting our DCs to contain only predicates that compare different tuples, without allowing predicates that compare tuples with a constant. Let r be a table with schema R and n tuples; A and B be columns of r; and t and t' be tuples in r, with $t \neq t'$. We denote $dom(A)$ the set of values of column A in table r; and $t.A$ the value of tuple t in column A. Given predicates $p_1, \cdots, p_m$ of the form $p : t.A\ f\ t'.B$, where $f : dom(A) \times dom(B) \rightarrow \{true, false\}$ is an operator, a DC φ is defined as follows:

$$\varphi : \forall t, t' \in r, \neg(p_1 \wedge \cdots \wedge p_m)$$

A tuple pair (t, t') satisfies a DC φ if it evaluates to true for φ. A violation of a DC φ is a tuple pair (t, t') that does not satisfy φ. We say that a DC φ holds on a table r if no pair of distinct tuples violates it in r. A table r is inconsistent with respect to a DC φ if φ does not hold on r.

Similarity Operator. Given columns A and B, let function $d : dom(A) \times dom(B) \rightarrow \mathbb{R}$ be a similarity distance metric and $\tau_d \in \mathbb{R}$ be a similarity distance threshold. Given tuples t and t', we define the similarity operator $\approx_{d,\tau_d}$: $dom(A) \times dom(B) \rightarrow \{true, false\}$ such that a predicate $p : t.A \approx_{d,\tau_d} t'.B$ evaluates to true if, and only if, $d(t.A, t'.B) \leq \tau_d$. Therefore, the similarity operator $\approx_{d,\tau_d}$ determines similarity by verifying whether the distance given by the similarity distance metric d is less or equal than the similarity distance threshold τ_d.

Similarity DCs. Traditionally, DCs are defined with $f \in \{=, \neq, <, \leq, >, \geq\}$ [6,9,23]. In this work, we extend this set of operators, supporting $f \in \{=, \neq, <, \leq, >, \geq, \approx_{d,\tau_d}\}$. We call similarity DCs those DCs containing at least one predicate using a similarity operator. Back to the data rules defined in Sect. 1 for table `Employees`, we can now write them as DCs, using similarity DCs to handle noisy data:

$$\varphi_1 : \neg(t.\texttt{id} = t'.\texttt{id})$$
$$\varphi_2 : \neg(t.\texttt{department} \approx_{d,\tau_d} t'.\texttt{department} \wedge t.\texttt{location} \neq t'.\texttt{location})$$
$$\varphi_3 : \neg(t.\texttt{department} \approx_{d,\tau_d} t'.\texttt{department} \wedge t.\texttt{start\_year} < t'.\texttt{start\_year} \wedge t.\texttt{salary} < t'.\texttt{salary})$$

Consider that the operator $\approx_{d,\tau_d}$ is perfect, i.e., evaluates to true if, and only if, the compared values represent the same entity in the real world. In this case, these DCs capture the data rules of the `Employees` table despite the noisy data. As the data rules (1) and (2), the DCs φ_1 and φ_2 have no violations. Furthermore, as rule (3), DC φ_3 is violated by the tuple pair (t_1, t_4), because $t_1.\texttt{department} \approx_{d,\tau_d} t_4.\texttt{department}$ (*Information Technology* $\approx_{d,\tau_d}$ *IT*); $t_1.\texttt{start\_year} < t_4.\texttt{start\_year}$ (2021 < 2024); and $t_1.\texttt{salary} < t_4.\texttt{salary}$ (9000 < 10000).

2.2 Similarity Distance Metrics

Edit Distance. Proposed in [22], we define it as the minimum number of operations required to transform one string into another [7]. An operation is a character insertion, deletion, or substitution. We write the edit distance between two strings s and s' as $ed(s, s')$. The edit distance can be used to measure syntactic distance between strings, but it does not directly account for semantic distance. Note that, if DC φ_3 uses this metric in the similarity operator ($\approx_{ed,\tau_{ed}}$), it will require $\tau_{ed} \geq 20$ to detect the violation (t_1, t_4), given that $ed(\textit{Information Technology}, \textit{IT}) = 20$. Such a high threshold will lead to incorrect violations being detected, as $ed(\textit{Information Technology}, \textit{Sales}) = 20$.

Cosine Distance. Embeddings are high-dimensional dense vectors of numbers that can represent multiple types of data, including text, which is the focus of this work. Embedding models [10,27,33] are capable of, by using contextual information, converting text into vectors in a way that the distance between these vectors expresses the semantic distance between the text they represent. Multiple similarity distance metrics can be used to compare two embeddings [11]. We use cosine distance, which measures the distance between two nonzero vectors using the cosine of the angle between them. Given two nonzero vectors $\mathbf{v}, \mathbf{v}' \in \mathbb{R}^l$ and θ being the angle between them, the cosine similarity between $\mathbf{v}$ and $\mathbf{v}'$ is $cos(\theta)$. The cosine distance between two embeddings $\mathbf{v}$ and $\mathbf{v}'$ is noted as $cd(\mathbf{v}, \mathbf{v}') = 1 - cos(\theta)$. We consider $cd(s, s') = cd(\mathbf{v}, \mathbf{v}')$ when, using the same embedding model, embeddings $\mathbf{v}$ and $\mathbf{v}'$ have been generated from strings s and s', respectively. Depending on the quality of the embedding model in use, it is possible to define a threshold τ_{cd} such that using this metric in the similarity operator ($\approx_{cd,\tau_{cd}}$) of DC φ_3 allows for the correct detection of its violations in table `Employees`.

3 Detecting DC Violations with Similarity Predicates

Several systems exist for detecting violations of traditional DCs [23,30,31]. For `SimFACET`, we follow the design and implementations of `FACET` [30] due to its pipelined architecture, which enables natural integration of similarity operators. We reuse its implementations of traditional operators and extend the framework with new algorithms for similarity-based predicates. We first introduce the key structural concepts used in our system for representing DC violations, then present the technical details of our algorithms.

3.1 Refinements

Following `FACET`, we use refinements to evaluate predicates. Refinements are special operators that operate over compact representations of tuple pairs using different algorithms depending on the predicate being evaluated.

Representing Tuple Pairs. Instead of storing each tuple pair individually, we use clusters for a compact representation. A cluster is a set of tuples in a table r. Given the clusters C_1 and C_2, a cluster pair (C_1, C_2) represents the set of all tuple pairs (t_1, t_2) such that $t_1 \in C_1$, $t_2 \in C_2$, and $t_1 \neq t_2$. A partition is a set of cluster pairs that denotes the union of all sets of tuple pairs represented by the cluster pairs in the partition. Formally, the partition $P = \{(C_1, C_2), \cdots, (C_{2m-1}, C_{2m})\}$ represents the set of tuple pairs $\bigcup_{(C_i,C_j)\in P}(C_i, C_j)$. For example, given the clusters $C_1 = \{t_1, t_2\}$, $C_2 = \{t_1, t_3, t_4\}$, $C_3 = \{t_4\}$ and $C_4 = \{t_1\}$, the partition $\{(C_1, C_2), (C_3, C_4)\}$ represents $(C_1, C_2) \cup (C_3, C_4)$, i.e., the union of $(C_1, C_2) = \{(t_1, t_3), (t_1, t_4), (t_2, t_1), (t_2, t_3), (t_2, t_4)\}$ and $(C_3, C_4) = \{(t_4, t_1)\}$.

Refinements Pipeline. A refinement receives a partition P and a predicate p, and returns a partition P' that denotes the set of all tuple pairs represented by P that evaluate to true for the predicate p. To detect the violations of a DC $\varphi = \neg(p_1 \wedge \cdots \wedge p_m)$ in a table r, we use a refinements pipeline, where each refinement receives as input the output of the previous refinement. We refer to the mapping from the predicates of φ to the refinements of the pipeline as refinements evaluation plan.

Pipelined Execution. Consider the relation `Employees` and the DC φ_3. Let $p_1 : t.\texttt{department} \approx_{d,\tau_d} t'.\texttt{department}$, $p_2 : t.\texttt{start\_date} < t'.\texttt{start\_date}$ and $p_3 : t.\texttt{salary} < t'.\texttt{salary}$. The refinements pipeline will be (ref_1, ref_2, ref_3). Consider that the refinements evaluation plan is such that the refinements ref_1,

ref_2 and ref_3 receive, respectively, the predicates p_1, p_2 and p_3. The first refinement on the pipeline must receive a partition representing all the pairs of distinct tuples in the evaluated relation, so the detection starts with the refinement ref_1 receiving the partition $P_{Employees} = \{(\{t_1, t_2, t_3, t_4\}, \{t_1, t_2, t_3, t_4\})\}$. After evaluating the predicate p_1, refinement ref_1 returns the partition $P_1 = \{(\{t_1, t_4\}, \{t_1, t_4\}), (\{t_2, t_3\}, \{t_2, t_3\})\}$, that represents all tuple pairs from partition $P_{Employees}$ that evaluate true for predicate p_1. After, the refinement ref_2 receives the partition P_1 returned by ref_1 and returns the partition $P_2 = \{(\{t_1\}, \{t_4\}), (\{t_2\}, \{t_3\})\}$, that represents all tuple pairs from partition P_1 that evaluate true for predicate p_2. Finally, the refinement ref_3 receives the partition P_2 and returns the partition $P_3 = \{(\{t_1\}, \{t_4\})\}$. The detection is then finished, with the partition P_3 containing all violations of DC φ_3 in relation `Employees`.

3.2 Implementing Similarity Operators

We implement the similarity operator ($\approx_{d,\tau_d}$) using edit distance ($\approx_{ed,\tau_{ed}}$) and cosine distance ($\approx_{cd,\tau_{cd}}$), considering empirically defined thresholds τ_{ed} and τ_{cd}. Next, we present our implementations of the similarity refinements. For simplicity of exposition, we present these algorithms with a single cluster pair (C_A, C_B) as input. In practice, they are executed for each cluster pair in a refinement input partition P. Furthermore, the similarity indexes are always built using the combination of a column and a cluster with the smaller cardinality. However, for easy presentation, we convey that the indices are built using column A and cluster C_A.

The algorithms use the same input and output types. They receive a cluster pair (C_A, C_B) representing the tuple pairs to be evaluated on predicate $p : t.A \approx_{d,\tau_d} t'.B$ using the similarity distance metric d and similarity distance threshold τ_d, and return a partition P' representing all the tuple pairs that evaluate true to p given d and τ_d. Consider value sets $V = \bigcup_{t \in C_A} t.A$ and $V' = \bigcup_{t' \in C_B} t'.B$. Internally, the algorithms we present perform the similarity join $V \bowtie V'$, which dominates the predicate evaluation time for similarity predicates. Given that, we present index-based strategies to reduce the time needed to perform this join and, consequently, improve detection performance.

3.3 Edit Distance Algorithm

Our implementation of refinements for similarity operators using edit distance ($\approx_{ed,\tau_{ed}}$) is based on the index used in the `FastSSwC` algorithm [7]. Given a string s, a string set S', and a threshold τ_{ed}, `FastSSwC` efficiently finds all strings $s' \in S'$ such that $ed(s, s') \leq \tau_{ed}$. The time complexity of building a `FastSSwC` index with a threshold τ_{ed} is $O(|S'| \times l^{\tau_d})$, where l is the average length of strings S'.

`EDFastSS` is our algorithm for similarity refinements using edit distance. First, we initialize an empty partition P', which will store the final result. After, we build a hash table H_A that maps the string value $t.A$ of each tuple t in C_A to all the tuples t' in C_A such that $t'.A = t.A$. Similarly, we build a hash table H_B for column B and cluster C_B. Then, using the keys from H_A and the threshold

τ_{ed}, we build a FastSSwC index I. Next, we iterate over the keys from H_B. For each string s_B from H_B, we create a cluster C'_B with the tuples indexed in H_B by s_B, and initialize an empty cluster C'_A. Using index I, we find all strings s_A such that $ed(s_B, s_A) \leq \tau_{ed}$. For each string s_A, we add the tuples indexed in H_A by s_A to the cluster C'_A. After iterating over all strings s_A, we add the cluster pair (C'_A, C'_B) to the partition P'. After iterating over all strings s_B, we return the partition P' and EDFastSS terminates.

3.4 Cosine Distance Algorithms

For similarity operators using cosine distance ($\approx_{cd,\tau_{cd}}$), we preprocess target column values by converting strings to embeddings. For efficiency, our implementations use approximate indexes. We discuss the limitations of exact indexes for our problem in Sect. 5.

To evaluate the efficiency and accuracy of our approximate algorithms, we present CDFlat, an exact baseline algorithm using nested loops. We initialize a partition P', and create hash tables H_A and H_B similarly as done in EDFastSS. Next, we iterate over the keys from H_B. For each embedding $\mathbf{v_B}$ from H_B, we create a cluster C'_B with the tuples indexed in H_B by $\mathbf{v_B}$, and initialize an empty cluster C'_A. Then, from the keys from H_A, we filter the embeddings $\mathbf{v_A}$ such that $cd(\mathbf{v_B}, \mathbf{v_A}) \leq \tau_{cd}$. For each embedding $\mathbf{v_A}$, we add the tuples indexed in H_A by $\mathbf{v_A}$ to the cluster C'_A. After iterating over all embeddings $\mathbf{v_A}$, we add the cluster pair (C'_A, C'_B) to the partition P'. After iterating over all embeddings $\mathbf{v_B}$, we return the partition P' and CDFlat terminates.

Our approximate algorithms rely on inverted file (IVF) indexes, more specifically, IVFFlat [11,37]. The idea behind using an IVF index is to create lists of embeddings indexed by a key embedding in a way that, if a query embedding is close to a key embedding, then it is close to the embeddings in the list indexed by it. So, we only need to calculate the distance between the query embedding and the key embeddings, and search for embeddings close to the query embedding only within the lists indexed by the closest key embeddings. To create those lists, we cluster the embeddings using k-means [38]. The k-means clusters will be our lists, and their centroids will be our key embeddings. For the number of lists used in our implementation, we chose a value commonly used as a starting point for IVF indexes: the square root of the number of embeddings being indexed [11].

CDAllIVF is our first algorithm for similarity refinements using cosine distance between embeddings. Similarly to EDFastSS and CDFlat, we start by initializing an empty partition P', and creating hash tables H_A and H_B. After, we use all keys from H_A to create an IVF index I. Then, we iterate over the keys from table H_B. For each embedding $\mathbf{v_B}$ from H_B, we create a cluster C'_B with the tuples indexed in H_B by $\mathbf{v_B}$, and initialize an empty cluster C'_A. Then, we calculate the cosine distance between $\mathbf{v_B}$ and each key in I, order the keys based on smaller distance, and get the lists L indexed by 1% of the keys from I closer to $\mathbf{v_B}$. We iterate over each list L and filter the embeddings $\mathbf{v_A}$ from L such that $cd(\mathbf{v_B}, \mathbf{v_A}) \leq \tau_{cd}$. For each embedding $\mathbf{v_A}$, we add the tuples indexed in H_A by $\mathbf{v_A}$ to the cluster C'_A. After iterating over all lists L, we add the cluster pair (C'_A, C'_B) to the partition P'. After iterating over all embeddings $\mathbf{v_B}$, we return the partition P' and `CDAllIVF` terminates.

`CDSampledIVF` is a variation of `CDAllIVF`. In `CDAllIVF`, we execute `k-means` with all the key embeddings from H_A. It creates a better IVF index, i.e., an IVF index that, given an embedding $\mathbf{v}$, has lists L where the average distance between $\mathbf{v}$ and the embeddings in L is highly proportional to the distance between $\mathbf{v}$ and the indexing key of L. However, the use of all embeddings also increases the execution time of `k-means` and, therefore, elevates the IVF index building time. As the index building time dominates the detection time, reducing it can lead to relevant performance improvements. `CDSampledIVF` addresses this question by using only 10% of the embeddings in the `k-means` execution. The used embeddings are randomly selected from all keys from H_A. After the clusterization, each of the embeddings $\mathbf{v}$ that was not used in `k-means` is added to the list with the key closer to $\mathbf{v}$. It reduces the quality of the IVF index, but also significantly reduces the building time of the index. To compensate for the reduction in the index quality, we verify more lists in `CDSampledIVF`. While in `CDAllIVF`, as described, we verify only 1% of the lists, in `CDSampledIVF` we increase this fraction to 10%.

3.5 Integrating Similarity Operators Into the Refinements Pipeline

While refinements can be evaluated in any order, we strategically order them in the pipeline based on predicate selectivitythe proportion of tuple pairs a predicate filters out. Predicates that evaluate to true for fewer tuple pairs have higher selectivity. We order refinements with traditional operators from most to least selective, following [30]: equalities $(=)$, inequalities $(<, \leq, >, \geq)$, and non-equalities $(\neq)$. This ordering allows for fewer intermediates to be processed in the pipeline, which is expected to reduce detection time.

Predicates using similarity operators $(\approx_{d,\tau_d})$ are expected to have selectivity only slightly lower than equalities. Therefore, because equalities are highly selective, similarities are also expected to be highly selective. However, since the indexes employed in similarity algorithms are more complex than those used for other operators, processing similarity refinements is expected to be slower than other refinements. To understand the impact of these two factors, we explore three distinct strategies for planning the pipeline with similarity refinements. The first strategy, labeled "I", prioritizes reducing the number of intermediates by applying similarity refinements immediately after equalities. The second, named "C", focuses on delaying the cost of similarity refinements as much as possible, placing them at the end of the pipeline, after non-equalities. Finally, the third strategy, referenced "B", represents a balance between the other two, with similarity refinements placed right after inequalities but before non-equalities.

4 Experimental Evaluation

4.1 Experimental Settings

Table 2 shows the datasets used in our experiments. It includes column cardinalities, which affect algorithmic complexity by determining the number of distinct values being processed. It also contains the column values' average lengths, i.e., the average number of characters in the column values, which impact the complexity of `EDFastSS`. Table 3 presents the DCs, along with the datasets on which they are evaluated.

Table 2. Datasets used in our experiments.

Dataset	Number of rows	Column	Col. cardinality	Col. values avg. length
Flights [30]	1M	custom_origin custom_destination distance	42k 19k 2k	28 25 -
Tax [30]	1M	custom_city salary rate	30k 10k 851	20 - -
Inspections [8]	286k	aka_name dba_name	32k 33k	19 -
Contacts [29]	782k	business_city business_street_name business_house_number type first_name last_name	5k 49k 22k 9 50k 71k	10 12 - - 7 8
Jobs [28]	27k	job_description other_description initial_cost total_est_fee	22k 870 4k 5k	135 11 - -

Table 3. Similarity DCs used in our experiments.

DC number	Dataset	Denial constraint
φ_1	Flights	$\neg(t.\text{custom\_origin} \approx_{d,\tau_d} t'.\text{custom\_destination} \wedge t.\text{custom\_destination} \approx_{d,\tau_d} t'.\text{custom\_origin} \wedge t.\text{distance} \neq t'.\text{distance})$
φ_2	Tax	$\neg(t.\text{custom\_city} \approx_{d,\tau_d} t'.\text{custom\_city} \wedge t.\text{salary} > t'.\text{salary} \wedge t.\text{rate} < t'.\text{rate})$
φ_3	Inspections	$\neg(t.\text{aka\_name} \approx_{d,\tau_d} t'.\text{aka\_name} \wedge t.\text{dba\_name} \neq t'.\text{dba\_name})$
φ_4	Contacts	$\neg(t.\text{business\_city} \approx_{d,\tau_d} t'.\text{business\_city} \wedge t.\text{business\_street\_name} \approx_{d,\tau_d} t'.\text{business\_street\_name} \wedge t.\text{business\_house\_number} = t'.\text{business\_house\_number} \wedge t.\text{type} = t'.\text{type} \wedge t.\text{first\_name} \approx_{d,\tau_d} t'.\text{first\_name} \wedge t.\text{last\_name} \approx_{d,\tau_d} t'.\text{last\_name})$
φ_5	Jobs	$\neg(t.\text{job\_description} \approx_{d,\tau_d} t'.\text{job\_description} \wedge t.\text{other\_description} \approx_{d,\tau_d} t'.\text{other\_description} \wedge t.\text{initial\_cost} < t'.\text{initial\_cost} \wedge t.\text{total\_est\_fee} > t'.\text{total\_est\_fee})$

We ran all experiments on a server with an AMD EPYC 7401 virtualized with KVM (2.0 GHz, eight cores, eight threads, 512 KiB of private L1d cache, 512 KiB of private L1i cache, 4 MiB of private L2 cache, 128 MiB of private L3 cache); 32 GB of RAM; 1 TB of SDD; Debian GNU/Linux 12; OpenJDK 64-Bit Server VM 17.0.14+7-Debian-1deb12u1 with the JVM head size set to 16 GB. We terminated any execution exceeding one hour. Each reported time is the average of six executions. For the embeddings-based algorithms, all the string values have been previously converted to embedding values using the embedding model `paraphrase-mpnet-base-v2` [15]. As any embeddings-based algorithm requires creating embeddings from strings, and as we focus on the impact of our algorithms on similarity join execution, we do not report the time required to create embeddings in our experiments. Unlike the time spent creating embeddings, the time required to build the indexes is a central aspect of our analysis; therefore, we present it for all algorithms.

4.2 Detection Time

Figure 1 shows the detection time for each combination of algorithm and refinement pipeline planning strategy.

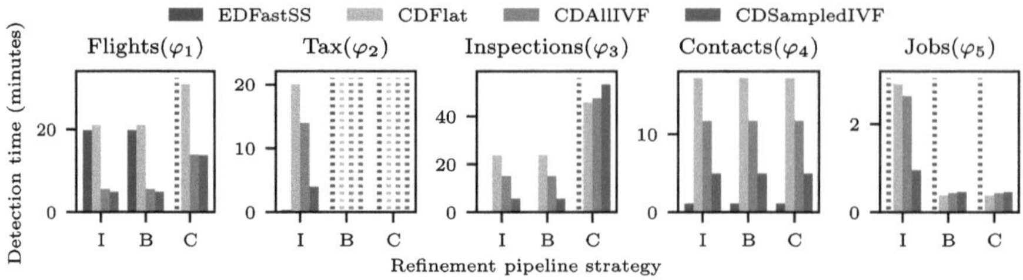

Fig. 1. Detection time of similarity algorithms for each refinement pipeline planning strategy. The dashed lines represent cases that exceed the execution time limit of one hour. For `EDFastSS`, the τ_{ed} threshold used was 2. For `CDFlat`, `CDAllIVF` and `CDSampledIVF`, the τ_{cd} threshold used was 0.15.

For similarity based on edit distance, the results show the impact of string length on `EDFastSS` detection time. No matter the pipeline planning strategy, `EDFastSS` did not finish the detection for `Jobs`(φ_5) because of the high average length of values in column `job_description`. The string's length is also contributing to the timeout of `EDFastSS` in `Flights`(φ_1) and `Inspections`(φ_3) when similarities are processed after the non-equalities, as they generate a large amount of cluster pairs for the similarity refinements, forcing the building of many small indexes with relatively long strings. The timeout in `Tax`(φ_2) had a different origin, occurring because of the long processing time of the pair of inequalities.

For similarity based on cosine distance, the results show that, in general, indexing with `CDAllIVF` reduces the detection time compared to `CDFlat`, with speedups of 1.9× for "I", 1.7× for "B", and 1.3× for "C". Using sampling with `CDSampledIVF` improves performance even more than `CDAllIVF`, with speedups of 4.0× for "I", 2.8× for "B", and 1.7× for "C". Two exceptional cases occur in `Inspections`(φ_3) and `Jobs`(φ_5) when the similarities are processed later in the pipeline, where the detection time increases with the use of indexing and sampling. In both cases, the increase in detection time is caused by a large number of cluster pairs containing small cardinality clusters being generated by the previous operators. The time cost of indexing and sampling does not pay off for these small cardinality clusters, making `CDFlat` the better option in this situation. As occurs for edit distance, for strategies "B" and "C", none of the algorithms for cosine distance finish their detection within the time limit for `Tax`(φ_2) because of the cost of processing the inequalities.

For both edit distance and cosine distance, the results show that the strategy "I" generally achieves the lower detection times. It occurs becauses, by processing the highly selective similarity predicates earlier, strategy "I" reduces the total number of tuple pairs being evaluated and consequently shortens the detection time. The exceptional result in `Jobs`(φ_5), where the detection time is short when processing the cosine distance similarities later, can be explained by the low selectivity of the similarity predicates in DC φ_5 for the dataset `Jobs`, which contains many similar values in the columns `job_description` and `other_description`.

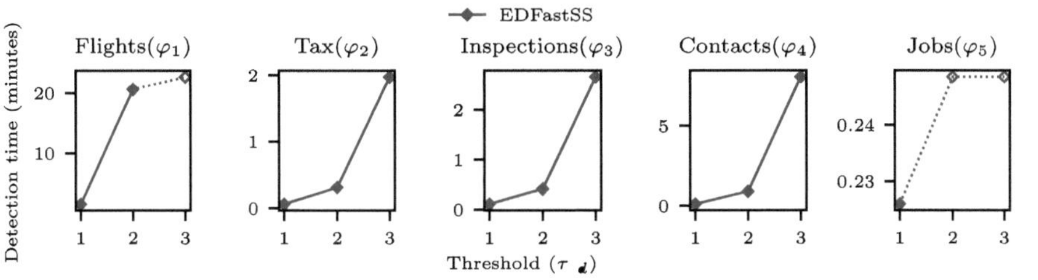

Fig. 2. Detection time of similarity algorithm based on edit distance when varying the τ_{ed} threshold. The dashed lines and unfilled markers represent cases that exceed the execution time limit of one hour. The refinement pipeline strategy adopted was "I".

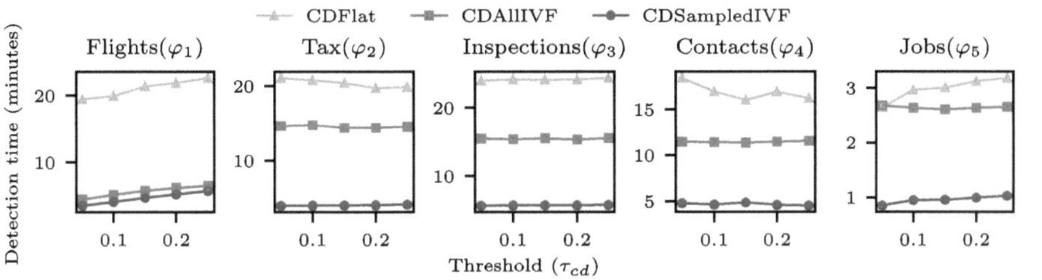

Fig. 3. Detection time of similarity algorithms based on cosine distance when varying the τ_{cd} threshold. The dashed lines and unfilled markers represent cases that exceed the execution time limit of one hour. The refinement pipeline strategy adopted was "I".

Given the low selectivity of those predicates, reducing the number of intermediates in evaluating similarities earlier in the pipeline does not compensate for the time cost of processing the similarity operators with a larger number of pairs.

Figure 2 shows the detection times for the edit distance algorithm when varying the τ_{ed} threshold from 1 to 3. The results indicate that the time required for detection increases rapidly as the threshold increases. This is an expected result, as the threshold is directly related to the size and build time of the `FastSSwC` index. For datasets with larger strings, the detection time rapidly exceeds the one hour limit, as occurs for `Flights`(φ_1) with $\tau_{ed} = 3$, and for `Jobs`(φ_5) with $\tau_{ed} = 2$ and $\tau_{ed} = 3$.

Figure 3 shows the detection times of the cosine distance algorithms when varying the τ_{cd} threshold from 0.05 to 0.25. As expected, the results indicate that increasing the threshold has a low impact on the algorithms' detection time, as it has no influence on the size or build time of the IVF index, and only slightly affects the number of intermediates passed to the next operators in the refinement pipeline. Besides, those results demonstrate that the improvements from using indexing and sampling shown in Fig. 1 are consistent across multiple thresholds, reinforcing the contribution of the `CDSampledIVF` algorithm.

4.3 Approximate Indexes Accuracy

Figure 4 presents the F1 score with respect to the exact algorithm `CDFlat` of the approximate algorithms `CDAllIVF` and `CDSampledIVF`. The results show that `CDAllIVF` and `CDSampledIVF` algorithms allow for a reliable detection in almost any case. Furthermore, the sampling approach used in `CDSampledIVF` slightly improves detection compared to `CDAllIVF`.

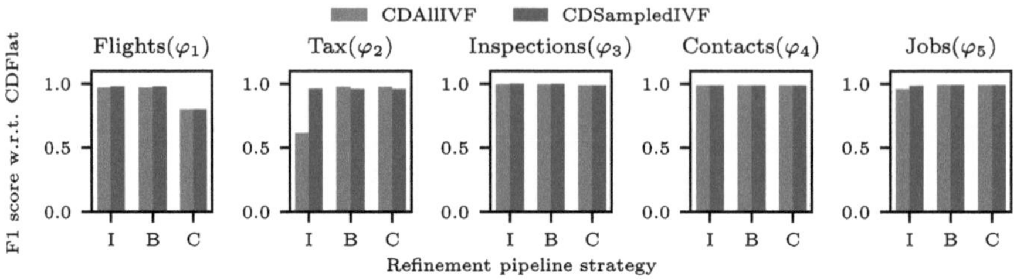

Fig. 4. F1 score with respect to `CDFlat` of approximate similarity algorithms based on cosine distance for each refinement pipeline planning strategy. The F1 score was calculated over detected violations. The τ_{cd} threshold used was 0.15.

Figure 5 shows the F1 score with respect to the exact algorithm `CDFlat` of the approximate algorithms `CDAllIVF` and `CDSampledIVF` when varying the τ_{cd} threshold from 0.05 to 0.25. The results indicate that the detection reliability is negatively affected by increasing the similarity distance threshold. The reason is that there are more embeddings in lists that are not being verified because their key embeddings are not so similar to the query embedding. Here we see again that the sampling approach from `CDSampledIVF` improves the F1 score, making the detection more reliable as the threshold increases.

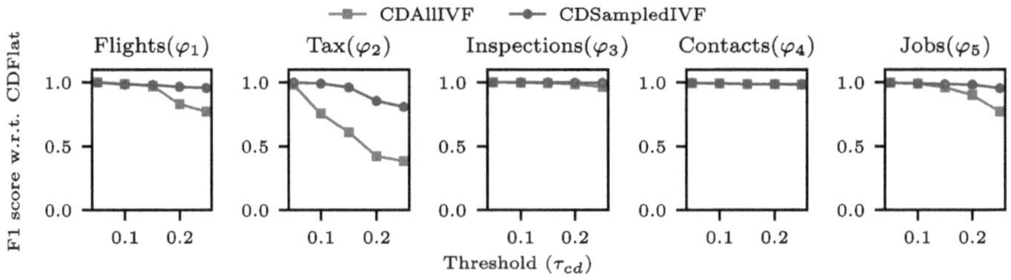

Fig. 5. F1 score with respect to `CDFlat` of approximate similarity algorithms based on cosine distance when varying the τ_{cd} threshold. The F1 score was calculated over detected violations. The refinement pipeline strategy adopted was "I".

5 Related Work

Other works proposed the relaxation of existing formalisms to accommodate similarity, as matching dependencies (MDs) [12,36], similarity inclusion dependencies (sINDs) [19], and differential dependencies (DDs) [21,39]. None of them, however, can express all the constraints expressed by DCs. In DCs, some works use relaxed definitions, theoretically allowing for similarity DCs, but none of them further explore this subject [4,13,34]. `HoloDetect` [14] uses embeddings to detect violations of DCs with similarity operators, but it requires training, which is not necessary for `SimFACET`.

As the processing of the similarity refinements requires a similarity join, we investigate both the literature on similarity indexes and on similarity joins. For edit distance, according to the results presented by [17], `FastSS` [7] is the fastest alternative for performing string similarity joins using edit distance for strings with the length range we are interested in. Approximate alternatives exist [43], but we decided not to explore them, as the exact algorithms for edit distance are already fast when compared with cosine distance. For cosine distance, there are exact join algorithms [2,3] and tree-based indexes, but they are not efficient for embeddings, as embeddings are both dense [35] and have high dimension [18,41]. Hash-based indexes as `LSH` [11,16] suffer from accuracy issues [18]. Graph-based indexes as `HNSW` [11,26,35] have elevated accuracy and are one of the current faster alternatives in terms of similarity search, but their high building time [42] is prohibitive for us, given that the index building time is part of the violations detection time in `SimFACET`. Finally, we have inverted file (`IVF`) indexes [11,37], which achieve good accuracy and balance fast search time with acceptable build time [42]. Both `IVF` and `HNSW` are used by modern SGBDs as `PostgreSQL` [42] and `Milvus` [40].

6 Conclusion

In this work, we presented `SimFACET`, a system that detects violations of DCs in noisy data using similarity. We have shown that our system can detect DC similarity violations across large datasets. For cosine-based similarity, we also demonstrate that our approximate algorithms reduce detection time compared with exact alternatives while maintaining high accuracy. We also extracted insights indicating that processing similarity operators before less-selective operators can reduce detection time in most cases.

Acknowledgments. This work was supported by PROEX CAPES and CNPq under grants 302909/2022-2 and 444192/2024-7, and by the Araucria Foundation for Support to Scientific and Technological Development of the State of Paran and the Serrapilheira Institute, through the Young Scientists Support Program (Protocol No. SER2023371000001/PI 28/2023).

References

1. Abedjan, Z., et al.: Detecting data errors: where are we and what needs to be done? Proc. VLDB Endow. **9**(12), 993–1004 (Aug 2016). https://doi.org/10.14778/2994509.2994518
2. Anastasiu, D.C., Karypis, G.: L2ap: Fast cosine similarity search with prefix l-2 norm bounds. In: 2014 IEEE 30th International Conference on Data Engineering, pp. 784–795 (2014). https://doi.org/10.1109/ICDE.2014.6816700
3. Bayardo, R.J., Ma, Y., Srikant, R.: Scaling up all pairs similarity search. In: Proceedings of the 16th International Conference on World Wide Web, pp. 131–140. WWW '07, Association for Computing Machinery, New York, NY, USA (2007). https://doi.org/10.1145/1242572.1242591
4. Bertossi, L.: Database Repairing and Consistent Query Answering. Morgan & Claypool Publishers (2011)
5. Bertossi, L., Chomicki, J.: Query answering in inconsistent databases, pp. 43–83. Springer Berlin Heidelberg, Berlin, Heidelberg (2004). https://doi.org/10.1007/978-3-642-18690-5_2
6. Bleifuß, T., Kruse, S., Naumann, F.: Efficient denial constraint discovery with hydra. Proc. VLDB Endow. **11**(3), 311–323 (Nov 2017). https://doi.org/10.14778/3157794.3157800
7. Bocek, T., Hunt, E., Stiller, B.: Fast similarity search in large dictionaries. University of Zurich (2007)
8. ChicagoDataPortal: Food inspections (2025). https://data.cityofchicago.org/Health-Human-Services/Food-Inspections/4ijn-s7e5/about_data
9. Chu, X., Ilyas, I.F., Papotti, P.: Discovering denial constraints. Proc. VLDB Endow. **6**(13), 1498–1509 (Aug 2013). https://doi.org/10.14778/2536258.2536262
10. Devlin, J., Chang, M., Lee, K., Toutanova, K.: BERT: pre-training of deep bidirectional transformers for language understanding. In: Burstein, J., Doran, C., Solorio, T. (eds.) Proceedings of the 2019 Conference of the North American Chapter of the Association for Computational Linguistics: Human Language Technologies, NAACL-HLT 2019, Minneapolis, MN, USA, June 2-7, 2019, Volume 1 (Long and Short Papers), pp. 4171–4186. Association for Computational Linguistics (2019). https://doi.org/10.18653/V1/N19-1423
11. Facebook: Faiss (2025). https://github.com/facebookresearch/faiss/wiki
12. Fan, W.: Dependencies revisited for improving data quality. In: Proceedings of the Twenty-Seventh ACM SIGMOD-SIGACT-SIGART Symposium on Principles of Database Systems, pp. 159–170. PODS '08, Association for Computing Machinery, New York, NY, USA (2008). https://doi.org/10.1145/1376916.1376940
13. Giannakopoulou, S., Karpathiotakis, M., Ailamaki, A.: Cleaning denial constraint violations through relaxation. In: Proceedings of the 2020 ACM SIGMOD International Conference on Management of Data, pp. 805–815. SIGMOD '20, Association for Computing Machinery, New York, NY, USA (2020).https://doi.org/10.1145/3318464.3389775
14. Heidari, A., McGrath, J., Ilyas, I.F., Rekatsinas, T.: Holodetect: Few-shot learning for error detection. In: Proceedings of the 2019 International Conference on Management of Data, pp. 829–846. SIGMOD '19, Association for Computing Machinery, New York, NY, USA (2019). https://doi.org/10.1145/3299869.3319888
15. HuggingFace: paraphrase-mpnet-base-v2 (2025). https://huggingface.co/sentence-transformers/paraphrase-mpnet-base-v2

16. Indyk, P., Motwani, R.: Approximate nearest neighbors: towards removing the curse of dimensionality. In: Proceedings of the Thirtieth Annual ACM Symposium on Theory of Computing. p. 604–613. STOC '98, Association for Computing Machinery, New York, NY, USA (1998). https://doi.org/10.1145/276698.276876
17. Jiang, Y., Li, G., Feng, J., Li, W.S.: String similarity joins: an experimental evaluation. Proc. VLDB Endow. **7**(8), 625–636 (Apr 2014). https://doi.org/10.14778/2732296.2732299
18. Jégou, H., Douze, M., Schmid, C.: Product quantization for nearest neighbor search. IEEE Trans. Pattern Anal. Mach. Intell. **33**(1), 117–128 (2011). https://doi.org/10.1109/TPAMI.2010.57
19. Kaminsky, Y., Pena, E.H.M., Naumann, F.: Discovering similarity inclusion dependencies. Proc. ACM Manag. Data **1**(1) (May 2023). https://doi.org/10.1145/3588929
20. Kossmann, J., Papenbrock, T., Naumann, F.: Data dependencies for query optimization: a survey. VLDB J. **31**(1), 1–22 (2021). https://doi.org/10.1007/s00778-021-00676-3. Jun
21. Kuang, S., Yang, H., Tan, Z., Ma, S.: Efficient differential dependency discovery. Proc. VLDB Endow. **17**(7), 1552–1564 (Mar 2024). https://doi.org/10.14778/3654621.3654624
22. Levenshtein, V.I.: Binary codes capable of correcting deletions, insertions and reversals. Soviet Phys. Doklady **10**, 707–710 (1966)
23. Liu, Z., Deep, S., Fariha, A., Psallidas, F., Tiwari, A., Floratou, A.: Rapidash: Efficient detection of constraint violations. Proc. VLDB Endow. **17**(8), 2009–2021 (May 2024). https://doi.org/10.14778/3659437.3659454
24. Livshits, E., Kochirgan, R., Tsur, S., Ilyas, I.F., Kimelfeld, B., Roy, S.: Properties of inconsistency measures for databases. In: Proceedings of the 2021 International Conference on Management of Data, pp. 1182–1194. SIGMOD '21, Association for Computing Machinery, New York, NY, USA (2021). https://doi.org/10.1145/3448016.3457310
25. Luciano, L., Moro, W., de Almeida, E.C., Pena, E.: Projeção eficiente de violações de restrições de negação. In: Anais do XXXVIII Simpósio Brasileiro de Bancos de Dados, pp. 390–395. SBC, Porto Alegre, RS, Brasil (2023). https://doi.org/10.5753/sbbd.2023.233388
26. Malkov, Y.A., Yashunin, D.A.: Efficient and robust approximate nearest neighbor search using hierarchical navigable small world graphs. IEEE Trans. Pattern Anal. Mach. Intell. **42**(4), 824–836 (2020). https://doi.org/10.1109/TPAMI.2018.2889473. Apr
27. Mikolov, T., Chen, K., Corrado, G., Dean, J.: Efficient estimation of word representations in vector space. In: Bengio, Y., LeCun, Y. (eds.) 1st International Conference on Learning Representations, ICLR 2013, Scottsdale, Arizona, USA, May 2-4, 2013, Workshop Track Proceedings (2013). http://arxiv.org/abs/1301.3781
28. NYCOpenData: Dob job application filings (2025). https://data.cityofnewyork.us/Housing-Development/DOB-Job-Application-Filings/ic3t-wcy2/about_data
29. NYCOpenData: Registration contacts (2025). https://data.cityofnewyork.us/Housing-Development/Registration-Contacts/feu5-w2e2/about_data
30. Pena, E.H.M., de Almeida, E.C., Naumann, F.: Fast detection of denial constraint violations. Proc. VLDB Endow. **15**(4), 859–871 (Dec 2021). https://doi.org/10.14778/3503585.3503595

31. Pena, E.H.M., Lucas Filho, E.R., de Almeida, E.C., Naumann, F.: Efficient detection of data dependency violations. In: Proceedings of the 29th ACM International Conference on Information & Knowledge Management, pp. 1235–1244. CIKM '20, Association for Computing Machinery, New York, NY, USA (2020). https://doi.org/10.1145/3340531.3412062
32. Pena, E.H.M., Porto, F., Naumann, F.: Fast algorithms for denial constraint discovery. Proc. VLDB Endow. **16**(4), 684–696 (Dec 2022). https://doi.org/10.14778/3574245.3574254
33. Reimers, N., Gurevych, I.: Sentence-BERT: Sentence embeddings using Siamese BERT-networks. In: Inui, K., Jiang, J., Ng, V., Wan, X. (eds.) Proceedings of the 2019 Conference on Empirical Methods in Natural Language Processing and the 9th International Joint Conference on Natural Language Processing (EMNLP-IJCNLP), pp. 3982–3992. Association for Computational Linguistics, Hong Kong, China (Nov 2019). https://doi.org/10.18653/v1/D19-1410
34. Rekatsinas, T., Chu, X., Ilyas, I.F., Ré, C.: Holoclean: holistic data repairs with probabilistic inference. Proc. VLDB Endow. **10**(11), 1190–1201 (Aug 2017). https://doi.org/10.14778/3137628.3137631
35. Santana, D., Ribeiro, L.: Approximate similarity joins over dense vector embeddings. In: Anais do XXXVIII Simpósio Brasileiro de Bancos de Dados, pp. 51–62. SBC, Porto Alegre, RS, Brasil (2023). https://doi.org/10.5753/sbbd.2023.232512
36. Schirmer, P., Papenbrock, T., Koumarelas, I., Naumann, F.: Efficient discovery of matching dependencies. ACM Trans. Database Syst. **45**(3) (Aug 2020). https://doi.org/10.1145/3392778
37. Sivic, Zisserman: Video google: a text retrieval approach to object matching in videos. In: Proceedings Ninth IEEE International Conference on Computer Vision, pp. 1470–1477 vol.2 (2003). https://doi.org/10.1109/ICCV.2003.1238663
38. Smile: Clustering (2025). https://haifengl.github.io/clustering.html
39. Song, S., Chen, L.: Differential dependencies: Reasoning and discovery. ACM Trans. Database Syst. **36**(3) (Aug 2011). https://doi.org/10.1145/2000824.2000826
40. Wang, J., et al.: Milvus: A purpose-built vector data management system. In: Proceedings of the 2021 International Conference on Management of Data. p. 2614–2627. SIGMOD '21, Association for Computing Machinery, New York, NY, USA (2021). https://doi.org/10.1145/3448016.3457550
41. Weber, R., Schek, H.J., Blott, S.: A quantitative analysis and performance study for similarity-search methods in high-dimensional spaces. In: Proceedings of the 24rd International Conference on Very Large Data Bases, pp. 194–205. VLDB '98, Morgan Kaufmann Publishers Inc., San Francisco, CA, USA (1998)
42. Yang, W., Li, T., Fang, G., Wei, H.: Pase: Postgresql ultra-high-dimensional approximate nearest neighbor search extension. In: Proceedings of the 2020 ACM SIGMOD International Conference on Management of Data, pp. 2241–2253. SIGMOD '20, Association for Computing Machinery, New York, NY, USA (2020).https://doi.org/10.1145/3318464.3386131
43. Zhang, H., Zhang, Q.: Minjoin: Efficient edit similarity joins via local hash minima. In: Proceedings of the 25th ACM SIGKDD International Conference on Knowledge Discovery & Data Mining, pp. 1093–1103. KDD '19, Association for Computing Machinery, New York, NY, USA (2019). https://doi.org/10.1145/3292500.3330853

AstraClean-RAG: Integrating Domain Knowledge and Correction Log for Tabular Data Cleaning

Bingxiang Chen(✉) and Toni Taipalus

Tampere University,Tampere, Finland
{bingxiang.chen,toni.taipalus}@tuni.fi

Abstract. AstraClean-RAG is a human-in-the-loop framework for tabular data cleaning that combines two distinct external memory sources: a *Domain Knowledge Base* (DKB) encoding stable domain constraints and a *Correction Log* (CL) capturing validated historical repairs. This study extends our earlier proof-of-concept by formalizing the complementary roles of these sources through a design inspired by rule-based and case-based reasoning and by evaluating the approach at a broader scale. The evaluation considers multiple datasets, selected dirty columns, and conflict scenarios in which the two evidence sources provide different repair signals. The DKB provides rule-like support for consistency and canonicalization, while the CL provides case-like support for reuse of recurring correction patterns. Results suggest that treating the two sources separately improves reliability over LLM-only and single-source baselines. When the sources disagree, the framework surfaces the disagreement explicitly for human review rather than resolving it automatically. Overall, the findings suggest that the two sources provide complementary support for tabular data cleaning.

Keywords: Data cleaning · Retrieval-augmented generation · Human-in-the-loop · Large language models

1 Introduction

Data cleaning remains one of the most labor-intensive and error-prone stages in modern data preparation workflows [27]. Industry studies consistently show that practitioners invest substantial effort in cleaning before downstream analysis or modeling can begin [7], and recent work further shows that automated cleaning can improve downstream predictive performance [16]. Effective cleaning requires not only identifying potential errors but also the application of domain-specific corrections that depend on both formal constraints and contextual knowledge [8]. For decades, the dominant paradigm has been rule-based, relying on explicit constraints, integrity rules, and dependency specifications [27]. Prior work on data profiling has studied how metadata, dependencies, and constraints can be discovered from relational data [3]. These methods support consistency and transparency, but they still impose authoring, validation, and maintenance burdens.

G. Vargas-Solar et al. (Eds.): ADBIS 2026, LNCS 16937, pp. 137–152, 2027.
https://doi.org/10.1007/978-3-032-39820-8_10

As real-world data evolves, new exceptions emerge, conventions shift, and maintaining rule bases becomes increasingly expensive.

Recent advances in large language models (LLMs) have created new opportunities for data cleaning. LLMs can generate context-aware repair suggestions without task-specific training [29]. However, direct application of LLMs in this setting raises several challenges. First, the same logical error may receive different repairs across runs, undermining consistency. Second, LLM outputs may be weakly grounded in domain-specific constraints and can produce hallucinated values [14]. Third, LLMs have no native mechanism to accumulate and reuse institutional memory across cleaning sessions, meaning that human corrections are not systematically preserved.

Retrieval-augmented generation (RAG) addresses some of these limitations by grounding LLM outputs in retrieved evidence [19]. In data cleaning, existing retrieval-based approaches rely on a user-provided data lake to retrieve similar tuples for repair generation [10], and do not explicitly model stable domain constraints or historical correction practice as separate knowledge sources. This may be limiting in settings where a large-scale reference corpus is unavailable. By contrast, `AstraClean-RAG` separates domain knowledge from correction history into two distinct sources. The DKB can be initialized from a small stratified sample of relatively clean rows, or constructed manually by domain experts. The Correction Log requires no pre-existing data: it starts empty and grows incrementally as human-validated corrections accumulate during cleaning sessions.

This study reports the second-stage development of `AstraClean-RAG`. An earlier proof-of-concept prototype, preserved as version 1.0 in the project repository, introduced the basic idea of combining domain knowledge and correction history for LLM-assisted tabular data cleaning and provided a small-scale feasibility study [5]. The present version advances that prototype in two substantive ways. First, it makes explicit the complementary roles of rule-like domain knowledge and case-like correction history through a dual-source retrieval design inspired by rule-based and case-based reasoning (RBR/CBR). Second, it broadens the empirical evidence through a larger evaluation across multiple datasets and cleaning scenarios. In this study, we address the following research question:

> **RQ:** How does dual-source retrieval, combining stable domain knowledge and reusable historical corrections, affect the reliability of LLM-assisted data cleaning?

The main contributions of this study are: *(1)* an RBR/CBR-inspired conceptualization of dual-source retrieval for tabular data cleaning, where the DKB acts as a rule-like source of stable constraints and the Correction Log (CL) acts as a case-like source of validated historical corrections, *(2)* an extended `AstraClean-RAG` design that preserves and reuses correction history as an evolving external memory, and *(3)* a broader empirical evaluation than in the initial proof-of-concept, covering multiple datasets, columns, and conflict scenarios. The proof-of-concept implementation and evaluation code are available in our public repository.[1]

The rest of the study is organized as follows. Section 2 reviews related work, and Sect. 3 describes the system design, followed by the empirical evaluation in Sect. 4. Section 5 discusses the practical implications and limitations of the study. Section 6 concludes the study.

2 Related Work

2.1 Earlier Approaches to Data Cleaning

Data cleaning research has evolved along several complementary directions, each addressing different aspects of the problem. We position our work by surveying these traditions and identifying gaps that motivate our hybrid approach. In the following subsections, we consider different data cleaning approaches starting from traditional methods and moving towards recent LLM-assisted approaches.

Classical tabular data cleaning has relied heavily on explicit constraints, external knowledge, and probabilistic inference [27]. Early work surveyed the problem space and established cleaning as a core data-management task. Later systems operationalized different forms of external or structured knowledge: `KATARA` uses knowledge bases and crowdsourcing to interpret and repair table values [8], `HoloClean` frames cleaning as probabilistic inference by combining integrity constraints with statistical signals to estimate the most likely clean database [28], and `Llunatic` provides a general chase-based framework for data cleaning under integrity constraints and related repair settings [11]. `Auto-Detect` takes a different direction by leveraging statistics from large corpora of clean tables to detect anomalies without requiring manually specified constraints [15]. Recent work further questions some common assumptions in constraint-based repair, showing that minimum-change repairs are not always the most appropriate cleaning outcomes [6]. Broader deployment-oriented evaluations also show that automatic data repair methods vary substantially across error rates, error types, and downstream tasks [25]. These systems demonstrate the value of grounding cleaning decisions in structured evidence. However, they generally do not treat validated historical corrections as a separate, append-only memory source that grows through iterative human feedback and can be retrieved alongside stable domain knowledge.

2.2 Example-Driven and Semi-supervised Cleaning

A complementary line of work reduces the burden of manually specifying rules by learning from limited user supervision. `Raha` formulates error detection as a configuration-free classification problem that combines signals from multiple pre-existing error detection strategies without requiring task-specific rule authoring [23], while more recent work has explored few-shot and meta-learning

[1] https://github.com/bingxiangch/AstraClean-RAG.

formulations for tabular error detection [2]. ED2 studies active learning strategies for error detection, prioritizing labeling effort to maximize detection performance [24], and Baran performs semi-supervised error correction by learning from a small number of example repairs using a unified contextual representation [22]. Recent work has also examined how to accelerate Raha and Baran through task and data parallelism, highlighting both their practical relevance and the computational challenges of scaling such cleaning pipelines [4]. This literature is important for AstraClean-RAG because it shows that small amounts of validated human feedback can be generalized effectively. Our work differs in that it preserves validated corrections as an explicit case-like memory and combines them with a separate rule-like knowledge source, rather than using supervision solely to train a detection or correction model.

2.3 LLM-Assisted and Retrieval-Grounded Cleaning

Recent work has begun to explore LLM-assisted cleaning and retrieval-grounded repair. RetClean retrieves similar tuples from data lakes to support LLM-based cleaning [10], IterClean uses an iterative detectorverifierrepairer workflow [26], and Cocoon decomposes data cleaning into semantically structured sub-tasks for LLM orchestration [29]. Domain-specific studies also suggest that LLMs can be effective for cleaning structured personal contact data [12]. Other recent work has examined costquality trade-offs in LLM-based cleaning [13], and broader surveys now place such approaches within the emerging landscape of LLMs for table processing [21]. Compared with these systems, AstraClean-RAG does not rely on a large pre-existing clean reference lake as its only external source. Instead, it separates stable domain knowledge from evolving correction history and treats disagreements between them as first-class signals for review.

2.4 RBR/CBR as a Conceptual Lens for Dual-Source Cleaning

To clarify the architecture, we use rule-based reasoning (RBR) and case-based reasoning (CBR) as a conceptual lens rather than claim a full classical expert system. In classical CBR, new problems are handled through the cycle of retrieving, reusing, revising, and retaining prior cases [1]. RBR, by contrast, applies explicitly represented general knowledge, such as rules or constraints, to new instances [9,18,20]. The two paradigms are widely treated as complementary in hybrid reasoning systems, as rules support consistency and explicit normative knowledge, whereas cases support contextual reuse and adaptation [18]. In AstraClean-RAG, the DKB is therefore *rule-like* rather than 'retrieved text', and the Correction Log is *case-like* rather than 'history'. The novelty of our design lies in keeping these sources separate, mediating between them, and allowing validated corrections to accumulate as future cases.

Human-in-the-loop design is central here not only as a safeguard against incorrect autonomous repair, but also as the mechanism by which the case base evolves over time through validated corrections. Our work differs by positioning the LLM as a mediator that integrates evidence from multiple sources and presents it to the user, rather than making autonomous repair decisions. In this sense, human participation is not only a safeguard, but also a mechanism for maintaining and extending the case base over time through validated corrections.

3 System Design

3.1 Design Goals and Architecture Overview

`AstraClean-RAG` is designed around four goals: grounded suggestions, cumulative learning, transparent conflict handling, and human authority. Grounded suggestions ensure that outputs are supported by retrieved evidence rather than parametric knowledge alone. Cumulative learning allows validated corrections to be reused when similar error patterns recur. Transparent conflict handling makes disagreements between evidence sources visible instead of resolving them silently. Human authority ensures that final cleaning decisions remain with the reviewer.

To support these goals, the system combines two complementary knowledge sources within a unified retrieval and mediation pipeline. The first is a *Domain Knowledge Base* (DKB), which stores stable domain rules such as format conventions, valid ranges, and canonical representations. The second is a *Correction Log* (CL), which stores human-verified corrections made during previous cleaning sessions together with their context and provenance.

Figure 1 shows the overall workflow. Given a user-selected target column and lightweight cleaning instructions, the system generates a repair suggestion for each cell value by retrieving evidence from both the DKB and the CL and passing it to an LLM-based mediation layer. The human reviewer then determines whether each suggested repair represents a true error and whether to accept, modify, or reject it.

3.2 Core Data Structures

`AstraClean-RAG` relies on two complementary knowledge sources: a Domain Knowledge Base and a Correction Log. The DKB is a static, rule-based repository that captures stable domain constraints and conventions, while the CL is an append-only repository that stores human-verified corrections together with contextual metadata and provenance. The DKB stores stable domain rules for each dataset. Each entry contains a rule description, the target column, the rule type, and a short textual summary used for retrieval. The rule types include format constraints, valid ranges, canonical representations, and domain-specific constraints. The DKB is initialized once per dataset and remains fixed during cleaning.

The CL stores human-verified corrections collected during cleaning. Each entry records the dirty value, the verified clean value, the target column, the surrounding row context, and metadata such as reviewer identity and timestamp. The CL grows monotonically, and entries are never deleted or modified. This

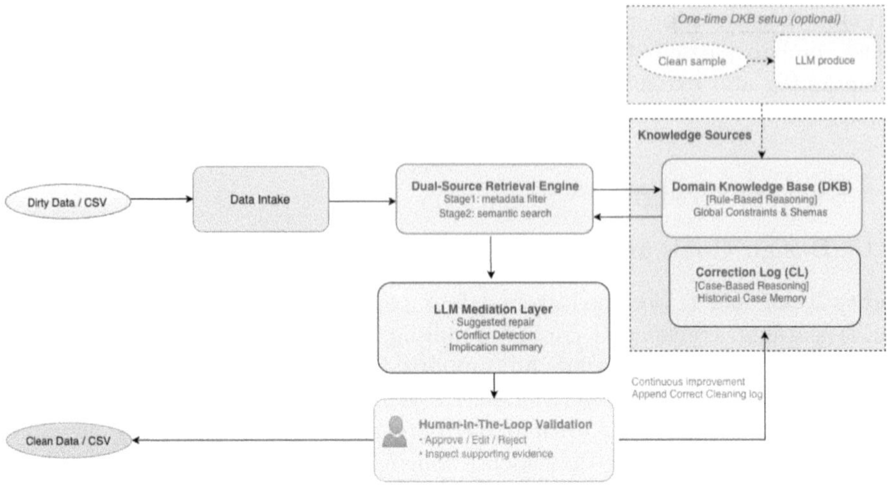

Fig. 1. High-level architecture and workflow of `AstraClean-RAG`; the system combines stable domain knowledge (DKB) and evolving correction history (CL) through dual-source retrieval and LLM-based mediation

design preserves a complete audit trail and supports both case-based reasoning, through retrieval of similar past corrections, and interpretability, through traceable evidence. To support semantic search, both DKB and CL entries are embedded and stored in separate vector indices within a persistent vector database such as `Qdrant`.

3.3 Domain Knowledge Base Construction

In many practical settings, formal domain documentation is incomplete or unavailable. `AstraClean-RAG` therefore constructs the DKB through a lightweight semi-automated process based on clean data samples.

Given a dataset $\mathcal{D}$, the system first draws a stratified sample $\mathcal{S} \subseteq \mathcal{D}$:

$$|\mathcal{S}| = \max(0.1 \cdot |\mathcal{D}|, 100 \text{ rows}) \quad (1)$$

This sample is intended to preserve the distribution of major categorical attributes so that the generated rules are not dominated by overrepresented cases. The sampled rows are then provided to an LLM, which proposes candidate rules for each column. These rules may describe expected value formats, unit conventions, valid ranges, canonical forms, and simple domain-specific restrictions. The generated rules are treated strictly as candidates rather than final knowledge. Before indexing, a human reviewer inspects each candidate rule together with its target column and supporting sample values. The reviewer may accept, revise, merge, delete, or manually add rules. Poor rules, including rules that are overly general, unsupported by the sample, or inconsistent with known domain conventions, are revised or removed. If candidate rules are contradictory, they are not committed automatically; the reviewer either resolves the contradiction by rewriting the rule set or excludes the conflicting rules when the available evidence is insufficient. Thus, the DKB construction process is semi-automated rather than fully automatic: the LLM reduces the authoring burden, while the reviewer remains responsible for validating the rules that enter the knowledge base.

3.4 Dual-Source Retrieval and LLM-Based Mediation

For each candidate cell under review, `AstraClean-RAG` retrieves evidence from both the DKB and the CL. A key design challenge is avoiding cross-column noise during retrieval. For example, a value such as '12.0' in a volume column should not retrieve semantically similar but contextually irrelevant entries from a temperature column, where the same number would represent a different type of measurement. To reduce such mismatches, retrieval is carried out in two stages. The first stage is metadata filtering. Before vector similarity is computed, the search space is restricted to entries associated with the same target column. This removes most irrelevant matches before semantic retrieval begins. The second stage is vector search within the filtered candidates. The query embedding is constructed from the target column, the dirty value, and row context:

$$\text{query} = \text{embed}(\text{“column: } c \text{ — dirty: } v_{\texttt{dirty}} \text{ — context: } x\text{”}) \quad (2)$$

where $v_{\texttt{dirty}}$ is the anomalous cell value and x denotes relevant row-level context from the same record. The system retrieves the top-k results from each source independently. By default, $k = 3$ for the DKB and $k = 3$ for the CL. This value was selected to balance retrieval coverage and prompt length.

The retrieved evidence is then passed to an LLM-based mediation layer. Rather than making a fully autonomous cleaning decision, the LLM compares the retrieved DKB and CL evidence and classifies the case as either `aligned` or `conflicting`. A case is treated as `aligned` when both sources support the same target value or compatible normalization rationale. A case is treated as `conflicting` when the DKB and CL suggest different target values, incompatible formats, or different normalization policies. In aligned cases, the system generates a grounded repair suggestion with a short justification and supporting evidence identifiers. In conflicting cases, the system does not choose one source automatically; instead, it produces a structured conflict summary describing the DKB interpretation, the CL pattern, and the nature of the disagreement, leaving the final decision to the human reviewer. The mediation procedure is summarized in Algorithm 1.

3.5 Human Review and Feedback Loop

`AstraClean-RAG` is designed as a decision-support system in which final authority remains with the human reviewer. The review interface presents the cell value

Algorithm 1. LLM-Based Mediation

```
procedure MEDIATE(results_dkb, results_cl)
    context_dkb ← format_evidence(results_dkb)
    context_cl ← format_evidence(results_cl)
    output ← LLM(mediation instruction, {context_dkb, context_cl})
    if output.mode = aligned then
        return format_suggestion(output)
    else
        return format_conflict_summary(output)
    end if
end procedure
```

under review, its target column, the surrounding row context, the system output, and the retrieved evidence from both the DKB and the CL.

The human reviewer may then approve the suggestion, modify it before approval, or reject it and enter a different clean value manually. Each validated decision is then appended to the CL together with its context, metadata, and provenance. The recorded provenance includes which DKB rules were retrieved, which historical corrections were shown, what action the reviewer took, and when the decision was made. This feedback loop allows the CL to grow over time and makes repeated correction patterns easier to reuse in later sessions. At the same time, it preserves an auditable record of how decisions were supported and finalized.

3.6 Proof-of-Concept Implementation

We implemented a proof-of-concept web interface for `AstraClean-RAG`, shown in Fig. 2. In the data cleaning view, users can upload a CSV file, select a target column, provide lightweight cleaning instructions, and review flagged anomalies one by one. For each candidate cell under review, the interface displays the suggested repair, the retrieved evidence, and, when applicable, a structured conflict summary. More importantly, it presents the retrieved evidence alongside each suggestion so that reviewers can inspect the basis of the system output rather than treating it as a black box.

Figure 3 illustrates the data index management view. This module is used to maintain the two main evidence sources in the system: domain knowledge and correction history. Through this interface, users can create, update, and delete `domain_kb` and `history_log` entries. In addition, the module supports domain knowledge construction from clean data samples. Candidate rules are generated by an LLM, presented to the user for optional review and editing, and then saved in JSONL format and added to the retrieval index for subsequent cleaning.

The backend uses `FastAPI` (Python), and the frontend uses `React` (JavaScript). For retrieval, we use the `sentence-transformers/all-MiniLM-L6-v2` embedding model to generate dense vector representations, and `Qdrant` as the vector database for indexing and similarity search. We use GPT-

3.5 as the underlying language model. These implementation choices reflect the objective of this study, which is to evaluate the effect of dual-source retrieval and evidence integration rather than model-specific improvements. Therefore, we rely on lightweight and widely used components instead of optimizing for the strongest possible model performance.

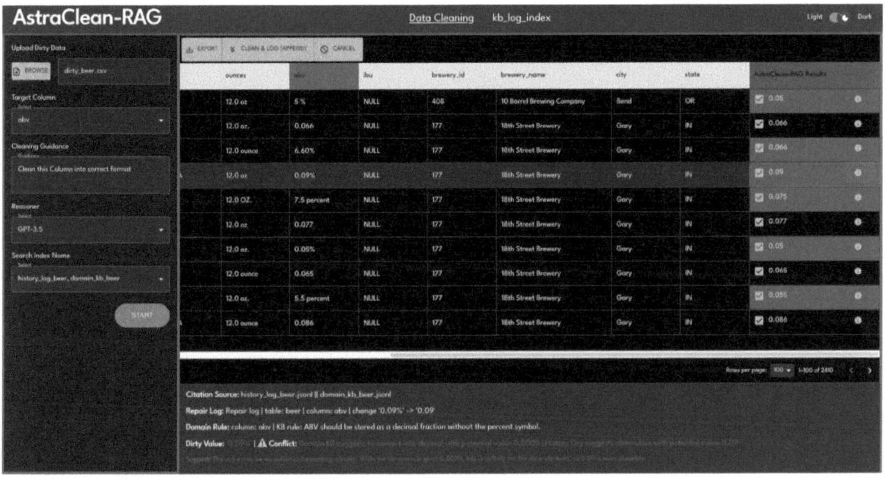

Fig. 2. Proof-of-concept interface of `AstraClean-RAG`, showing a suggested repair, retrieved evidence from DKB rules and CL corrections, and a conflict indicator for cases where the two sources suggest different resolutions

4 Empirical Evaluation

4.1 Datasets

We evaluate `AstraClean-RAG` on three datasets, summarized in Table 1, selected to cover complementary data cleaning scenarios. The dataset *Beers* focuses primarily on numeric normalization and unit conversion, including inconsistent representations of ounces, precision variations in alcohol content, and missing values. *Hospital* emphasizes textual and semi-structured cleaning problems, including typographical errors, abbreviation inconsistency, entity normalization, malformed phone numbers, and identifier format violations. *Tax* provides a larger and more rule-intensive setting, where cleaning decisions depend on stricter structural constraints such as zip code formatting and numeric standardization. For each dataset, the domain knowledge base is initialized from a clean sample with lightweight human verification. The correction log is initialized as empty and populated progressively during evaluation. Although these datasets are commonly used in data cleaning research, recent work has argued that benchmark error models may not fully reflect realistic tabular data errors [17]. We therefore

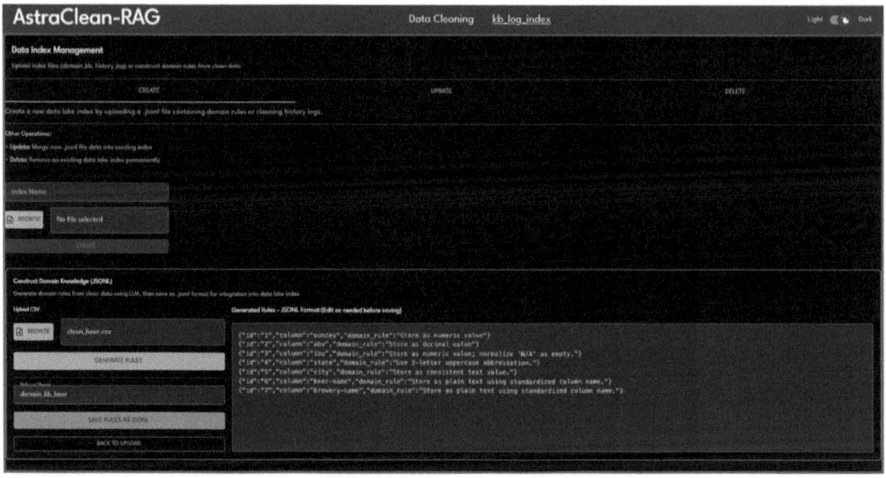

Fig. 3. Data index management interface of `AstraClean-RAG`, allowing users to manage domain knowledge and correction logs and to construct domain rules from clean data using an LLM with optional human review before indexing

interpret the evaluation as a controlled benchmark study of dual-source retrieval behavior rather than as a definitive assessment of performance in all real-world cleaning settings.

Table 1. Datasets used in the evaluation, adapted from benchmark settings in `Baran` [22]

Dataset	Rows	Cols	Dirty Cells	Error Types
Beers	2,410	9	~270	Units, precision, missing values
Hospital	1,000	20	~330	Typos, abbreviations, malformed fields
Tax	2,000	15	~800	ZIP format, rate precision, normalization

4.2 Baselines and Main Results

We evaluate `AstraClean-RAG` against three baselines: LLM-only (zero-shot), which uses GPT-3.5 without any retrieval; DKB-only, which retrieves from the domain knowledge base alone; and CL-only, which retrieves from the correction log alone. The main results are reported on two representative dirty columns from each dataset, chosen to reflect different cleaning challenges within the same domain. For *Beers*, we evaluate on *ounces* and *abv*; for *Hospital*, on *city* and *measure_name*; and for *Tax*, on *zip* and *rate*. These columns were selected because they capture recurring but distinct forms of noise, including unit inconsistency, numeric formatting, typographical errors, and rule-intensive normalization.

For both CL-only and `AstraClean-RAG`, the correction log is initialized as empty and populated progressively from previously validated corrections in the training split. For the main results, each method uses 20 historical corrections per selected column. At each evaluation stage, both methods access the same amount of historical correction data, ensuring a fair comparison without exposure to future corrections. Precision (P) measures the fraction of suggested repairs that are correct; Recall (R) measures the fraction of true errors for which a correct repair was suggested; F1 is their harmonic mean.

Table 2. Main results on two representative dirty columns from each dataset, evaluated using precision (P), recall (R), and F1-score

	Beers			Hospital			Tax		
Method	P	R	F1	P	R	F1	P	R	F1
LLM-only	0.75	0.82	0.78	0.83	0.87	0.85	0.71	0.79	0.75
DKB-only	0.82	0.80	0.81	0.88	0.85	0.86	0.89	0.84	0.86
CL-only	0.86	0.89	0.87	0.86	0.88	0.87	0.81	0.85	0.83
`AstraClean-RAG`	0.89	0.91	0.90	0.88	0.89	0.88	0.91	0.86	0.88

Table 2 summarizes the results. Across all datasets, `AstraClean-RAG` achieves the highest overall F1-score, while exhibiting a more balanced precision–recall trade-off than the single-source baselines. On the *Beers* dataset, improvements are most evident in columns such as *ounces* and *abv*. The *ounces* column contains recurring unit inconsistencies (e.g., "12.0 oz", "12.0 oz.", "355 ml", "0.355L"), where similar correction patterns appear repeatedly. This favors case-based reuse and helps explain the relatively strong performance of CL-only. In contrast, the *abv* column involves format normalization (e.g., "0.05" vs "0.05%"), where domain constraints provide stronger guidance.

On the *Hospital* dataset, the gains are more moderate due to the diversity and irregularity of errors. For example, the *city* column contains spelling variations (e.g., "birminghxm", "sheffxeld"), while *measure_name* includes longer and less structured textual noise (e.g., "caxxed", "bxockers", "hospitax"). Such errors are less repetitive and therefore harder to capture through either rules or historical reuse alone, resulting in smaller but still consistent improvements.

On the *Tax* dataset, DKB-only achieves relatively high precision, reflecting the importance of explicit structural constraints in rule-intensive settings. For instance, the *zip* column requires consistent formatting with leading zeros (e.g., "01907" vs "1907"), and the *rate* column exhibits precision inconsistencies (e.g., "5", "5.3", "6.84", "1.9519792"). In this setting, domain rules provide strong guidance, while the correction log contributes additional coverage for recurring edge cases.

Overall, these results indicate that the two knowledge sources provide complementary benefits: domain knowledge supports precision through stable constraints, while historical corrections improve coverage by capturing recurring patterns.

4.3 Longitudinal Analysis

Unlike the main results in Table 2, which are aggregated over two representative columns, this analysis focuses only on the *ounces* column of the *Beers* dataset. We simulate system performance as the correction log grows over time under the full system configuration, where both the domain knowledge base and the correction log are used (Table 3).

Table 3. Longitudinal performance on the *ounces* column of the *Beers* dataset

Number of corrections in CL	F1
0	0.78
10	0.85
20	0.88
50	0.89

The results show that performance improves rapidly in the early stage, with F1 increasing from 0.78 to 0.88 within the first 20 corrections. This indicates that frequent error patterns are quickly captured and reused. Further gains beyond 20 corrections are smaller, suggesting that most common patterns have already been covered and that additional corrections mainly address less frequent cases. The results suggest that the correction log is most beneficial in the early stage, while the DKB provides stable support before sufficient historical corrections accumulate.

4.4 Conflict Analysis

We analyze cases where the domain knowledge base and the correction log suggest different repairs. Such conflicts arise when global constraints and historical corrections provide inconsistent signals. For example, in the *rate* column of the *Tax* dataset, domain rules may favor a fixed numeric precision, while historical corrections reflect varying but previously accepted levels of precision. Similarly, in the *ounces* column of the Beers dataset, domain rules may favor a canonical unit representation, while a particular historical correction may preserve a previously accepted converted form. In both cases, the disagreement does not necessarily indicate an error in either source. Rather, it reflects different but reasonable normalization choices. Instead of resolving these disagreements automatically, `AstraClean-RAG` presents both interpretations to the reviewer and leaves the final decision to human judgment.

5 Discussion

5.1 Practical Implications

In real-world data cleaning workflows, organizations often lack large-scale clean reference resources, while knowledge about how to resolve recurring errors remains scattered across people, documents, and past decisions. `AstraClean-RAG` explores one possible way to address this by externalizing two complementary forms of knowledge: stable domain conventions in a Domain Knowledge Base and validated historical corrections in a Correction Log. By representing these as explicit external knowledge sources rather than leaving them implicit in model behavior, the framework suggests a possible direction for retrieval-grounded LLM-assisted cleaning in settings where a large pre-cleaned reference repository is unavailable, but limited clean examples, domain documentation, or expert-reviewed samples can still be used to initialize lightweight domain knowledge. This also makes the basis of repair suggestions more explicit and easier to review. This may be particularly useful in settings where important cleaning knowledge is internal to the organization, such as private conventions, validated historical decisions, or domain-specific business logic.

The dual-source design also points to a different way of using human effort in the cleaning process. Instead of requiring experts to specify all rules upfront or repeatedly resolve similar issues manually, the framework allows knowledge support to develop incrementally through reviewed rules and validated corrections. Over time, this may help shift part of the human role from repeated manual cleaning toward knowledge curation, while preserving reviewer authority over final decisions. By surfacing the specific domain rule or historical correction behind each suggestion, the framework may also contribute to a more transparent and auditable cleaning workflow over time.

5.2 Limitations

This work has several limitations. First, the effectiveness of `AstraClean-RAG` depends on the quality and coverage of its two knowledge sources. The system is less effective when both the DKB and the CL provide weak or noisy signals, especially for errors that are neither covered by domain rules nor sufficiently similar to prior corrections. Moreover, the current DKB construction process relies on limited clean examples, domain documentation, or expert-reviewed samples. Therefore, `AstraClean-RAG` should not be interpreted as requiring no clean information at all; rather, it reduces reliance on a large pre-existing clean reference repository by combining lightweight, inspectable domain knowledge with an evolving correction log.

Second, the empirical evaluation is limited in scope. Although we evaluate the framework on multiple datasets, the main results are reported on selected representative columns rather than all dirty attributes, and the benchmark datasets are relatively small. These datasets also may not fully capture realistic tabular errors. Future work should therefore evaluate the framework on larger datasets, a fuller range of dirty columns, and more realistic error models [17].

Third, the current study does not directly evaluate reviewer interaction or robustness across model backbones. We do not include a user study of reviewer decision time, cognitive effort, or the effect of structured conflict summaries compared with raw LLM suggestions. In addition, all experiments use GPT-3.5 as the underlying language model. While newer models may provide stronger reasoning capabilities, our objective is to evaluate the effect of dual-source retrieval rather than model-specific improvements. We reduce output variability by using a fixed model configuration and deterministic decoding where supported, with temperature set to 0; however, this does not guarantee fully identical outputs across runs. Future work should examine whether stronger LLMs reduce the marginal benefit of retrieval, or whether explicit DKB and CL evidence continues to improve grounding, traceability, and conflict visibility.

6 Conclusion

We presented `AstraClean-RAG`, a human-in-the-loop framework for tabular data cleaning that combines a fixed DKB and an append-only CL through dual-source retrieval and LLM mediation. By integrating rule-based and case-based reasoning, the framework is designed to balance consistency with adaptability in practical data cleaning scenarios. The empirical results indicate that combining domain knowledge with accumulated correction history can improve cleaning performance over single-source approaches on the evaluated tasks. In addition, the framework supports incremental learning from human feedback and treats conflicts between knowledge sources as signals to be exposed rather than automatically resolved. While the current evaluation focuses on selected columns and a single LLM backbone, the results suggest that structuring human–LLM collaboration around explicit evidence and complementary knowledge sources is a promising direction for knowledge-intensive data management tasks.

Acknowledgments. This work has been supported by FAST, the Finnish Software Engineering Doctoral Research Network, funded by the Ministry of Education and Culture, Finland.

Disclosure of Interests. The authors have no competing interests to declare that are relevant to the content of this article.

References

1. Aamodt, A., Plaza, E.: Case-based reasoning: Foundational issues, methodological variations, and system approaches. AI Commun., (1994)
2. Abdelaal, M., Ktitarev, T., Städtler, D., Schöning, H.: SAGED: Few-shot meta learning for tabular data error detection. In: Proceedings of the 27th International Conference on Extending Database Technology (EDBT 2024), pp. 386–398. OpenProceedings.org (2024). https://doi.org/10.48786/EDBT.2024.34
3. Abedjan, Z., Golab, L., Naumann, F.: Profiling relational data: a survey. VLDB J. **24**(4), 557–581 (Aug 2015). https://doi.org/10.1007/s00778-015-0389-y

4. Ahmadi, F., Mandirali, Y., Abedjan, Z.: Accelerating the data cleaning systems Raha and Baran through task and data parallelism. Proc. VLDB Endowment. ISSN **2150**, 8097 (2024)
5. Chen, B., Taipalus, T.: AstraClean-RAG: Supporting human-LLM collaboration in tabular data cleaning through dual-source retrieval. In: Proceedings of the 2026 ACM CHI Conference on Human Factors in Computing Systems (CHI'26), Co-Data: Cultivating Effective Human-LLM Collaboration for Collaborative Data Processing, ACM (2026) in press
6. Chen, J., Sun, Y., Song, S., Zhang, H., Yuan, X.: Minimum Change $\neq$ Best Cleaning: Parallel and incremental error detection under integrity constraints. Proc. ACM Manag. Data **3**(4) (Sep 2025). https://doi.org/10.1145/3749174
7. Chu, X., Ilyas, I.F., Krishnan, S., Wang, J.: Data cleaning: Overview and emerging challenges. In: Proceedings of the 2016 International Conference on Management of Data, pp. 2201–2206 (2016)
8. Chu, X., et al.: KATARA: Reliable data cleaning with knowledge bases and crowdsourcing. Proc. VLDB Endowment **8**(12), 1952–1955 (2015). https://doi.org/10.14778/2824032.2824109
9. Dutta, S., Bonissone, P.P.: Integrating case-and rule-based reasoning. Int. J. Approx. Reason. **8**(3), 163–203 (1993)
10. Eltabakh, M.Y., Naeem, Z.A., Ahmad, M.S., Ouzzani, M., Tang, N.: RetClean: Retrieval-based data cleaning using LLMs and data lakes. Proc. VLDB Endowment **17**(12), 4421–4424 (2024). https://doi.org/10.14778/3685800.3685890
11. Geerts, F., Mecca, G., Papotti, P., Santoro, D.: Cleaning data with Llunatic. VLDB J. **29**(4), 867–892 (2020)
12. Glock, A.C., Dominka-Kiss, C., Korom, P., Ehrlinger, L.: Detecting and cleaning errors in personal contact information with large language models. In: Proceedings of the 2nd International Workshop on Data-driven AI (DATAI 2025) at VLDB 2025. VLDB Endowment (2025). https://www.vldb.org/2025/Workshops/VLDB-Workshops-2025/DATAI/DATAI25_12.pdf
13. Hu, T., et al.: A multi-objective optimization framework for data cleaning using large language models. Big Data Mining Anal. (2025). https://doi.org/10.26599/BDMA.2025.9020074
14. Huang, L., Yu, W., Ma, W., et al.: A survey on hallucination in large language models: Principles, taxonomy, challenges, and open questions. arXiv preprint arXiv:2311.05232 (2023)
15. Huang, Z., He, Y.: Auto-Detect: Data-driven error detection in tables. In: Proceedings of the 2018 International Conference on Management of Data, pp. 1377–1392. ACM (2018). https://doi.org/10.1145/3183713.3196889
16. Jäger, S., Biessmann, F.: From data imputation to data cleaning — automated cleaning of tabular data improves downstream predictive performance. In: Proceedings of The 27th International Conference on Artificial Intelligence and Statistics. Proceedings of Machine Learning Research, vol. 238, pp. 3394–3402. PMLR (2024). https://proceedings.mlr.press/v238/jager24a.html
17. Jung, P., Jäger, S., Chandler, N., Biessmann, F.: Towards realistic error models for tabular data. J. Data Inform. Qual. **17**(4) (Dec 2025) https://doi.org/10.1145/3774914
18. Kaoura, G., Kovas, K., Boutsinas, B., Hatzilygeroudis, I.: A new hybrid reasoning model based on rules, cases and processes: application to care of individuals facing autism spectrum disorders. Knowl. Inf. Syst. **67**, 371–401 (2025). https://doi.org/10.1007/s10115-024-02228-x

19. Lewis, P., et al.: Retrieval-augmented generation for knowledge-intensive NLP tasks. Adv. Neural. Inf. Process. Syst. **33**, 9459–9474 (2020)
20. Liao, S.H.: Expert system methodologies and applications—a decade review from 1995 to 2004. Expert Syst. Appl. **28**(1), 93–103 (2005)
21. Lu, W., Zhang, J., Fan, J., Fu, Z., Chen, Y., Du, X.: Large language model for table processing: a survey. Front. Comput. Sci. **19**, 192350 (2025). https://doi.org/10.1007/s11704-024-40763-6
22. Mahdavi, M., Abedjan, Z.: Baran: Effective error correction via a unified context representation and transfer learning. Proc. VLDB Endowment **13**(12), 1948–1961 (2020). https://doi.org/10.14778/3407790.3407801
23. Mahdavi, M., et al.: Raha: A configuration-free error detection system. In: Proceedings of the 2019 International Conference on Management of Data, pp. 865–882. ACM (2019). https://doi.org/10.1145/3299869.3324956
24. Neutatz, F., Mahdavi, M., Abedjan, Z.: ED2: A case for active learning in error detection. In: Proceedings of the 28th ACM International Conference on Information and Knowledge Management, pp. 2249–2252. ACM (2019). https://doi.org/10.1145/3357384.3358129
25. Ni, W., Miao, X., Zhao, X., Wu, Y., Liang, S., Yin, J.: Automatic data repair: Are we ready to deploy? Proc. VLDB Endow. **17**(10), 2617–2630 (Jun 2024). https://doi.org/10.14778/3675034.3675051
26. Ni, W., Zhang, K., Miao, X., Zhao, X., Wu, Y., Yin, J.: IterClean: an iterative data cleaning framework with large language models. In: Proceedings of the ACM Turing Award Celebration Conference - China 2024. ACM (2024). https://doi.org/10.1145/3674399.3674436
27. Rahm, E., Do, H.H.: Data cleaning: problems and current approaches. IEEE Data Eng. Bull. **23**(4), 3–13 (2000)
28. Rekatsinas, T., Chu, X., Ilyas, I.F., Ré, C.: HoloClean: Holistic data repairs with probabilistic inference. Proc. VLDB Endowment **10**(11), 1190–1201 (2017). https://doi.org/10.14778/3137628.3137631
29. Zhang, S., Huang, Z., Wu, E.: Data cleaning using large language models. In: 2025 IEEE 41st International Conference on Data Engineering Workshops (ICDEW), pp. 28–32. IEEE (2025). https://doi.org/10.1109/ICDEW67478.2025.00008

Inclusion Dependency Discovery with Semantic Column Representations

Gregully Willian(✉), Igor L. de Oliveira, and Eduardo Henrique Monteiro Pena

Federal University of Technology – Paraná (UTFPR), Curitiba, Brazil
{gregulywillian,igooli,eduardopena}@utfpr.edu.br

Abstract. Inclusion dependencies (INDs) reveal foreign keys, meaningful joins, and integration opportunities across datasets. However, they are often unknown and must be discovered, for example, from data. Most IND discovery methods still rely on exact value containment. Even relaxed variants, such as approximate and similarity INDs, mainly modify the satisfaction criterion rather than the candidate generation process. As a result, discovery remains dominated by syntactic signals, with limited use of semantic information. In this work, we propose a hybrid method for IND discovery that combines representation learning with deterministic validation. We first map columns into vector spaces designed to capture both value distributions and semantic characteristics, and then use proximity in those spaces to pre-select candidate pairs. Then, we validate these candidates on the data to determine which ones form valid INDs. In our experiments, the proposed method consistently reduces false positives while maintaining competitive recall, resulting in better overall F1 than syntactic IND discovery baselines across diverse datasets. It also achieves competitive, and often superior, performance relative to recent embedding-based join-discovery methods, despite relying solely on pre-trained embeddings and no dataset-specific fine-tuning.

Keywords: Data Profiling · Inclusion Dependencies · Column representations

1 Introduction

Inclusion dependencies (INDs) are a classical class of relational data dependencies [5]. They express containment between attribute sets, that is, whether every value combination on one side of the dependency also appears on the other side. INDs support several data management tasks, including referential integrity enforcement [6], foreign key discovery [7], data integration [14], query optimization [13]. They are also closely related to join discovery, since exact, approximate, or similarity-based containment between columns can provide evidence that two tables are joinable [15,23]. However, INDs are rarely declared explicitly in practice, and this has led to a large body of work on automatically discovering them from data [10].

G. Vargas-Solar et al. (Eds.): ADBIS 2026, LNCS 16937, pp. 153–168, 2027.
https://doi.org/10.1007/978-3-032-39820-8_11

Many *IND discovery algorithms* focus primarily on scalability, improving the generation, pruning, and verification of candidate INDs [10]. Most of these methods still adopt the classical notion of IND satisfaction based on exact domain containment, which implicitly assumes that related attributes use identical value representations. Although faithful to the formal definition of INDs, this assumption is often too restrictive for real-world data, where noise, formatting differences, and heterogeneous coding conventions are common. As a result, exact-containment methods are highly sensitive to representational differences and may fail to recover relationships that are semantically meaningful but not extensionally identical. Recent work has relaxed exact containment, for example, by allowing limited violations [27], or by using token-based similarity measures such as Jaccard similarity [15]. However, these approaches still remain largely *syntactic*, since they assess candidate relationships mainly through domain overlap rather than a broader notion of semantic relatedness between attributes.

A purely syntactic view of IND discovery can be too limited for real-world data. Several semantically related attributes often exhibit limited syntactic overlap due to formatting differences, abbreviations, naming conventions, or data errors. As a result, meaningful inclusion dependencies may be missed. Conversely, substantial syntactic overlap alone does not necessarily imply attribute relatedness, which can lead to spurious INDs.

Figure 1 illustrates these limitations using two relations from a university admission process, one containing course catalog information and the other containing student application records. Although semantically related, an exact containment-based IND discovery method would only retrieve trivial matches such as `Degree` since the values of `Applications[Degree]` are contained in `CourseCatalog[Degree]` or spurious ones such as `Exam Room` contained in `Seats Offered`, where the containment is maintained by accidental numerical overlap, and not because the attributes represent the same concept. Furthermore, it would not detect a match between `ProgramApplied` and `ProgramName` whose values differ due to lexical variations, abbreviations, and data errors, such as *English* versus *English Language* and *Food Processing* versus *Food Production*. These examples show that syntactic signals alone are not sufficient to identify meaningful INDs, motivating methods that combine the data domain with related semantics.

CourseCatalog

Degree	ProgramName	Seats Offered
Licensure	Mathematics	30
Technology	Food Processing	40
Licensure	English	20
Bachelor	Electrical Eng.	50

Applications

Degree	Program Applied	Exam Room
Licensure	mathematics	10
Licensure	English Language	20
Technology	Food Production	30
Bachelor	Electrical Eng.	50

Fig. 1. Sample relations from a university admission process illustrating the limitations of syntactic IND discovery.

In response to these challenges, we present SEIND[1], a system for discovering inclusion dependencies that leverages semantic representations to improve IND generation and syntactic validation to ensure reliability. In particular, we make the following contributions:

1. We propose SEIND, an embedding-based approach for inclusion dependency discovery that leverages semantic similarity for candidate generation;
2. We define a notion of valid inclusion dependencies that accounts for challenges observed in real-world datasets;
3. We present a comprehensive evaluation of SEIND, comparing our approach to state-of-the-art algorithms for IND and join discovery.

2 Background and Related Work

This section revisits inclusion dependencies, algorithmic approaches for their discovery, and motivates the notion of semantic inclusion discovery.

2.1 Inclusion Dependencies and Semantic Inclusion Discovery

Classical Inclusion Dependencies. Given two relation instances r over schema R and s over schema S, and attribute lists X and Y with $|X| = |Y|$, an inclusion dependency (IND) of the form $R[X] \subseteq S[Y]$ states that every value occurring in the projection $r[X]$ also occurs in the projection $s[Y]$, i.e., $\forall u \in r, \exists v \in s : u[X] = v[Y]$. Unary INDs involve one attribute on each side, while n-ary INDs involve aligned attribute lists. When the referenced attributes (Y) form a key, an IND captures referential inclusion and is therefore closely related to foreign-key constraints. At the same time, INDs are strictly weaker than foreign keys in two respects. First, they do not require the referenced attributes to form a key: the same value set may appear in a non-key column. Second, exact value containment alone does not imply a structurally enforced referential relationship [5,18].

Why Exact Validity is not Enough. The set of valid INDs in an instance is usually much larger than the set of *useful* ones. Most profiling algorithms enumerate all valid dependencies, which are often INDs that are irrelevant for tasks such as schema understanding, foreign-key identification, or a join. Many formally valid INDs are accidental or spurious, arising from small domains, status codes, booleans, coarse categories, or unrelated identifier spaces whose values happen to be nested. Thus, extensional validity alone does not distinguish genuine relational structure from incidental domain containment.

IND Variants. The literature extends the basic notion of INDs in several directions. Conditional inclusion dependencies restrict validity to tuples that satisfy additional value conditions [2,4]. Approximate INDs relax exact containment

[1] Code and artifacts are available at https://github.com/GregullyW/SEIND.git.

by allowing a controlled proportion of values on the dependent side to be missing from the referenced side, instead of requiring full inclusion [27]. Similarity inclusion dependencies (sINDs) replace exact equality with a similarity condition when comparing values [15]. These variants reflect the fact that strict extensional containment is often too rigid for real data.

Toward Meaningful Inclusion. The discovery of meaningful INDs should distinguish between two questions: whether a dependency is sufficiently satisfied extensionally in the data, and whether it represents a meaningful relational connection. In practice, an exact IND may be formally valid yet uninformative because it may arise from accidental overlap in small or low-information domains. Conversely, a candidate that reflects the intended relationship may fail to achieve exact containment due to missing tuples, dirty values, or heterogeneous representations. Existing variants, such as approximate and similarity INDs, relax the satisfaction condition, but they still do not directly address the task of selecting those inclusions that correspond to plausible referential or join relationships. This gap motivates the *semantic IND discovery* problem defined next.

Semantic IND Discovery. Let $\mathcal{D}$ be a collection of relation instances, and let M denote metadata and contextual evidence associated with them, such as attribute names, table names, sample values, and table statistics. Since IND satisfaction was defined earlier, we treat it here as a component of our discovery definition. In this work, we instantiate that component using tuple-level approximate containment. For two relation instances $r, s \in \mathcal{D}$ over schemas R and S, respectively, for attribute lists X and Y with $|X| = |Y|$, and for a threshold $\rho \in (0,1]$, we say that

$$R[X] \subseteq_\rho S[Y]$$

holds if at least a fraction ρ of the tuples in $r[X]$ also appear in $s[Y]$. When $\rho = 1$, this reduces to exact IND satisfaction. Other satisfaction notions could be used within the same framework.

To capture semantic and structural evidence, let

$$\Gamma(R[X], S[Y], M) \in [0,1]$$

be a compatibility score measuring how strongly $R[X]$ and $S[Y]$ are semantically related and structurally compatible given the evidence in M. Let $\tau \in [0,1]$ denote the minimum compatibility score required for a candidate to be considered meaningful. We then define the *semantic IND discovery* problem as computing

$$\mathcal{S}(\mathcal{D}, M, \rho, \tau) = \{R[X] \subseteq_\rho S[Y] \mid R[X] \subseteq_\rho S[Y] \text{ holds and } \Gamma(R[X], S[Y], M) \geq \tau\}.$$

Semantic IND discovery targets containments that are meaningful for a given task, such as foreign-key discovery. The exact case is recovered when $\rho = 1$, while lower values allow the formulation to retain meaningful candidates in noisy or heterogeneous settings. In this way, semantic IND discovery preserves the classical extensional basis of inclusion dependencies while refining the discovery objective with semantic and structural evidence.

2.2 Discovery Algorithms

Discovering all inclusion dependencies in a relational dataset is a fundamental data profiling task [1]. The search space is already $O(m^2)$ for unary INDs over a schema with m attributes, and extending discovery to n-ary INDs makes the problem exponentially harder [10]. Several algorithms address this with a two-phase structure that enumerates satisfied unary INDs and then lifts the remaining candidates to higher arities, using different validation strategies to improve efficiency. Sort-merge approaches, such as Spider [3], validate INDs by sorting attribute domains and performing linear merge scans to test set containment, enabling efficient sequential access patterns. In contrast, hash-based strategies, such as BINDER [22], partition attribute values into buckets and leverage hash indexes to accelerate containment checks and prune candidate pairs early. The comprehensive study of Drsch et al. [10] confirms that hash-based approaches dominate in terms of runtime and scalability. One way to accelerate exact IND discovery is to replace precise set-containment tests with probabilistic approximations. FAIDA takes this approach, using sketches to estimate column containment, achieving a significant speedup over exact methods [10].

Discovery algorithms for relaxed IND variants must also quantify the degree to which it does or does not hold. Su et al. [27] defines approximate INDs by measuring violations under insertion semantics (missing distinct values) and deletion semantics (tuples with unmatched values), providing two complementary notions of error. It leverages partition-based validation with frequency-aware buckets to incrementally compute violations and prune candidates early, enabling scalable approximate IND discovery. Kaminsky et al. [15] discovers similarity-based INDs by replacing exact value containment with similarity string such as edit distance or Jaccard similarity. It leverages a segmented inverted index and length-based filtering to efficiently retrieve candidate value pairs, validating only those that share common segments and pruning dissimilar pairs early.

IND discovery is also closely connected to the task of join discovery in data lakes [11,29]. Both problems begin by searching for column pairs whose value sets exhibit strong containment or overlap. Scalable overlap-search methods such as LSH Ensemble [30] and JOSIE [29] can likewise be viewed as candidate-generation mechanisms for approximate or exact IND-like relationships. However, these approaches also expose the weakness of purely syntactic evidence: substantial value overlap does not necessarily imply a meaningful relational connection. As a result, they often return spurious matches. Representation-learning methods such as DeepJoin [9] and OmniMatch [16] address this limitation by encoding column contents and metadata into learned embeddings and retrieving candidates based on semantic proximity. In particular, DeepJoin encodes column values into dense representations using transformer-based models and performs similarity search in the embedding space relying on fine-tunning to improve accuracy. OmniMatch extends this paradigm by integrating multiple signals, including column values, metadata, and structural context, into unified representations, enabling more robust matching in heterogeneous and noisy scenarios. Their output, however, is a ranked set of potentially joinable column pairs rather than a directed, data-validated inclusion constraint. Our view is that semantic IND discovery lies between these two perspectives, retaining the structural properties of classical INDs while incorporating semantic evidence to distinguish meaningful referential relationships from accidental domain overlap.

3 Discovering Semantic INDs

We propose `SEIND`, a two-stage method for discovering semantically meaningful INDs. The method first generates candidates using embeddings and then validates them through approximate value inclusion over normalized domains. We focus on unary INDs because they capture most inclusion relationships of practical interest and serve as the basis for n-ary discovery. Extension to n-ary INDs is left for future work.

3.1 Why and How We Use Column Representation for INDs?

Classical IND discovery methods operate on raw column values and are therefore sensitive to noise. Approximate methods address some of this through a violation threshold, but the appropriate threshold is hard to set because the level of noise differs across columns, and a single global threshold may be too strict for dirty columns and too loose for clean ones [8]. Moreover, for an IND to be useful in practice (e.g., for a join or a foreign key constraint), a large fraction of values must actually match. The values that do not are candidates for repair, not evidence that the dependency should be discarded. Our position is that a threshold alone cannot distinguish genuine noise from a fundamentally incompatible pair.

We therefore represent each column as normalized text combining its name with a sample of its values, following standard practice in table discovery and schema matching [9,12,17]. This representation feeds the semantic stage, which identifies compatible pairs, while the data-level stage then verifies that enough values actually match. Together, the two stages separate the question of whether two columns are about the same thing from the question of whether their values are consistent enough to support a join or key relationship.

For each column, we drop null values and empty strings, convert the remaining entries to strings, and normalize them by lowercasing, stripping whitespace, and cleaning non-ASCII and non-alphanumeric characters. Then, we sample up to $k = 50$ distinct values without replacement from the resulting unique non-null values to prevent frequent duplicates from dominating the representation. The choice of k is discussed in 4.

The serialized text follows one of two templates depending on column type. Numeric values often carry little meaning on their own, so when all sampled values parse as numeric, we concatenate each value with the column name before listing. Otherwise, we list the sampled values directly. In both cases, the string begins with the column name, which gives the representation its main semantic cue. This choice makes the column description more informative for the embedding model. Preliminary experiments showed that including the table name in the representation did not improve accuracy performance, so we disabled it.

3.2 Candidate Generation

Classical IND discovery algorithms prune the search space through syntactic criteria. They sort and scan value lists, count violations, and discard a candidate as soon as the violation threshold is exceeded [10,27]. Column metadata is not used at all, even though it is present in most real datasets. This works well when columns share a common format, but it does not when the same domain is expressed differently across tables, and wastes the semantic information available in column names. `SEIND` takes a complementary approach, pruning based on semantic similarity. Thus, only column pairs whose representations are sufficiently close in embedding space are passed to data-level validation. Pairs that are semantically dissimilar are unlikely to satisfy inclusion regardless of their syntactic properties, and checking them against the data results in wasted computation.

`SEIND` encodes each column's serialized text with a pre-trained sentence embedding model [26]. Such models have been used to estimate semantic relatedness between columns and have shown strong empirical performance in similar tasks [17]. We map each column to a dense vector summarizing its serialized description and normalize all vectors so that similarity reduces to cosine similarity. For each column, we retrieve its k most similar columns ($k = 20$) and generate directed candidate pairs $A \rightarrow B$. We then apply a similarity threshold, α, to the candidate pairs, retaining only those whose cosine similarity exceeds α. A higher α produces a smaller, more precise candidate set, at the risk of missing true INDs between columns that are semantically related but not close in embedding space. The role of this stage is not to decide whether an IND holds, but to identify which pairs are worth checking against the data.

3.3 Approximate Inclusion Validation

Semantic similarity is a necessary but not sufficient condition for an IND. Two columns may be topically related yet fail inclusion if their actual value sets diverge. We therefore impose a direct data-level criterion on every candidate that passes the similarity threshold.

For each candidate $A \rightarrow B$, we construct the domain of each column as the set of distinct non-null values after normalization: we lowercase, strip whitespace, and decompose each string using Unicode compatibility decomposition, which breaks composite characters into their base forms and separate combining marks. This normalization targets case and accent variation while preserving punctuation and numeric structure.

We accept a candidate if the fraction of values in $D(A)$ absent from $D(B)$ does not exceed a threshold ϵ:

$$\frac{|D(A) \setminus D(B)|}{|D(A)|} \leq \epsilon.$$

When $\epsilon = 0$, this reduces to exact inclusion. Positive values of ϵ tolerate noise, missing entries, and residual formatting differences that remain after normalization. These conditions arise routinely in real-world datasets where the same domain is represented across tables with slight inconsistencies.

The thresholds α and ϵ govern complementary aspects of the discovery. α controls which candidates reach validation, whereas ϵ controls which candidates pass it. A pair rejected by α is never checked against the data, and a pair accepted by α but rejected by ϵ was semantically plausible but not data-supported. We analyze the sensitivity of results to both parameters in Sect. 4.

4 Experimental Evaluation

We evaluate `SEIND` against three IND discovery algorithms with different IND satisfiability criteria and two embedding-based join discovery systems–solutions that represent the current state-of-the-art in each respective approach. Our evaluation addresses two questions: (i) whether our semantic approach improves IND discovery effectiveness relative to syntactic baselines, and (ii) whther it generalizes without dataset-specific fine-tuning.

4.1 Experimental Setup

Datasets. Our experiments use eight real-world datasets from [19]: *Carcinogenesis*, *Financial*, *Hepatitis* and *IMDB*, *Comercy* [20], *Airlines*[2], *CATH* [24], *SISU* [25] and the synthetic dataset *TPC-H* [28], spanning diverse domains and scales. Among these, SISU is a Brazilian dataset that aggregates information on universities and student applications within a national admissions system. Table 1 summarizes the characteristics of the datasets used in our experiments. For each dataset, the reported statistics correspond to the aggregation across all its tables, including the total number of tuples, attributes, and distinct values. Datasets were selected to cover a range of schema sizes, tuple counts, and levels of data heterogeneity, including datasets with irregular or noisy attribute values and inconsistent naming conventions.

Ground Truth. For evaluation, we manually annotated a set of valid INDs as ground truth for each dataset. When available, we leveraged Entity-Relationship (ER) diagrams to identify referential relationships and directly derive the corresponding INDs. This was possible for the TPC-H, Carcinogenesis, IMDB, Hepatitis, and Financial datasets. For datasets without available ER diagrams (SISU, CATH, Comercy, and Airline), we manually examined pairs of attributes by considering domain compatibility, dependency direction, attribute cardinality, and value inclusion. An IND $R[A] \subseteq S[B]$ was included in the ground truth only when both domain compatibility and value inclusion were clearly satisfied. The final ground truth is represented as ordered attribute pairs, following the format adopted by Metanome framework [21].

Baselines. We compare `SEIND` against three IND discovery tools: BINDER [22], SAWFISH [15], and AINDD [27]. We also include two embedding-based join

[2] https://openflights.org/data.php#other.

Table 1. Datasets used in the experimental evaluation.

Dataset	#Tables	Size (MB)	#Tuples	#Attributes	#Distinct Values
Airlines	3	1.50	14,597	31	7,646
Carcinogenesis	6	0.79	13,562	23	13,562
CATH	1	0.71	18,473	12	18,473
Comercy	9	106.00	1,000,163	52	717,613
Financial	8	13.00	177,648	55	177,648
Hepatitis	7	0.20	5,691	26	5,691
IMDB	7	102.90	2,510,976	21	1,174,610
SISU	2	63.31	323,944	43	141,737
TPC-H	1	1836.78	6,001,215	55	4,580,667

discovery methods, DeepJoin [9] and OmniMatch [16], to assess whether systems designed for joinable column search transfer to the semantic IND setting. For these methods, we take the ranked join pairs and convert them into candidate attribute pairs. These candidates are then subjected to the same syntactic inclusion validation used by IND discovery tools. For DeepJoin, we limit the number of evaluated candidates by selecting the top-k ranked joins, with $k \in \{3, 5, 10\}$.

All IND baselines are implemented in Java and executed within the Metanome framework to ensure a consistent environment. Each method is configured according to its original publication and, where applicable, further tuned. Specifically, for SAWFISH, we perform a grid search over the similarity threshold in $[0.4, 1.0]$ across all similarity modes; for BINDER, we vary the bucket count between 10 and 20 (which only impacts runtime); and for AINDD, we tune both the bucket count and the violation threshold.

All experiments are restricted to unary INDs. For each method, *we perform a grid search over its parameter space and report the best-performing configuration.* AINDD, BINDER, and SAWFISH are deterministic and produce a single result per configuration. SEIND, DeepJoin, and Omnimatch are non-deterministic, so we average results across three runs with different random seeds. We note, however, that the variance across runs was negligible in all our experiments.

Evaluation Metrics. We report precision, recall, and F1-score against the ground-truth INDs. A discovered IND $R[A] \subseteq S[B]$ is counted as a true positive only if it appears in the ground truth for the corresponding dataset. We also report the number of false positives, since they reflect unnecessary candidate validations and directly affect the computational cost of IND discovery.

Hardware. All experiments were performed on an Intel Core i5-13450HX machine with 16 GB RAM and 10 cores at 2.4 GHz.

4.2 End-To-End Effectiveness

Figure 2 reports the best F1 score achieved by each method across all datasets. `SEIND` achieves the best F1 in most cases and remains competitive elsewhere, with only small differences from the strongest baseline. The largest gains are observed on datasets with heterogeneous schemas and noisy attribute representations, such as Airlines, Hepatitis, and SISU.

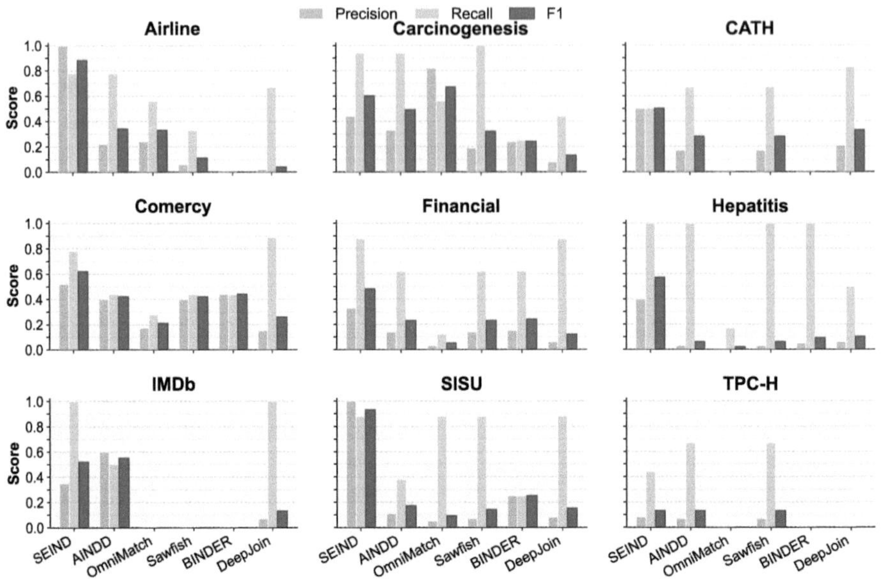

Fig. 2. Comparison of SEIND with inclusion dependency and join discovery methods across multiple datasets. For each method, Precision, Recall, and F1 scores are reported at the configuration achieving the highest F1. Missing bars denote cases where the method did not produce results or did not execute.

Syntactic IND discovery methods (in our experiments, AINDD, Sawfish, and Binder) typically achieve high recall but low precision. They generate a large candidate space and rely on syntactic validation to prune it, which allows them to recover most true INDs but also produces many false positives. This happens because these methods generate candidates based on value overlap or token similarity, without considering semantic attribute relatedness. BINDER enumerates all type-compatible pairs, SAWFISH filters pairs using Jaccard similarity over tokens, and AINDD relaxes containment through a violation budget. All three rely only on data-level signals and therefore cannot distinguish semantically unrelated attributes that happen to share values by coincidence. In contrast, `SEIND` selects candidate pairs by proximity in the embedding space and applies syntactic validation only to this reduced set. As a result, it reduces false positives by approximately 40% to 90% relative to competing methods while maintaining competitive recall.

A key aspect of our evaluation is that `SEIND` is compared against two distinct families of baselines: classical IND discovery methods and recent join discovery methods. This is important because SEIND sits between these two lines of work. It uses semantic representations to generate plausible candidate pairs, as in join discovery, but validates them by checking their inclusion in the data, as in IND discovery. Across datasets, this hybrid design yields more stable behavior than either family alone: it avoids the large false-positive counts typical of syntactic IND discovery methods, while also showing less variability than join discovery baselines. This is particularly clear in the comparison with DeepJoin and OmniMatch, two of the strongest recent join-discovery methods. When adapted for IND discovery, both achieve competitive F1 scores across several datasets, indicating that learned representations provide useful signals for candidate generation. However, their performance is less stable than SEIND's. One reason is that they were designed for joinability rather than IND satisfaction, so their representations are not well aligned with the containment-based nature of INDs.

4.3 Semantic Pre-filtering of IND Candidates

The end-to-end results above evaluate our method as a complete pipeline. We now isolate the role of the semantic component by using it only as a pre-filter for existing IND discovery methods. For each dataset, we first retain the unary attribute pairs that pass the embedding-based semantic filter, and then run AINDD, SAWFISH and BINDER only on this reduced candidate space. The downstream discovery and validation logic remain unchanged, so any performance difference reflects only the effect of semantic candidate reduction.

Figure 3 demonstrates that incorporating semantics is a crucial factor in discovering INDs, improving the balance between precision and recall. We observe a significant improvement in the accuracy of the SISU dataset and an increase in the F1 score across all datasets. By eliminating semantically implausible candidates before syntactic validation, methods become more selective and produce fewer spurious matches. We observe a reduction of up to 80% in the number of false positives.

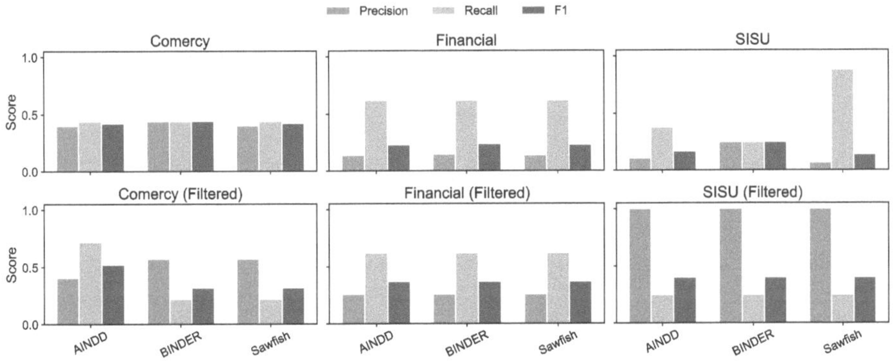

Fig. 3. Performance of IND discovery methods for the three most representative datasets in terms of number of attributes after applying the semantic pre-filter.

The gains come with a modest recall trade-off in some cases. A small number of valid INDs is removed because the corresponding attribute pairs satisfy value inclusion but are assigned low semantic compatibility by the embedding model. Still, the overall effect is positive: semantic pre-filtering serves as an effective front-end for traditional IND discovery methods, improving the precision–recall trade-off by reducing the candidate space prior to syntactic validation.

4.4 Robustness Under Schema Perturbation

SEIND methods exploit both attribute names and data values. To assess how much each signal contributes, we replace all attribute names with generic identifiers (col1, col2, ...), removing schema-level semantics while preserving data values. We compared the results with the best configuration of each tool. Table 2 reports results for the original, perturbed, and best-baseline configurations.

Table 2. Effect of schema perturbation on the proposed method for some of the most representative datasets in terms of number of attributes. Each group of datasets shows: original, perturbed (column names replaced by generic identifiers), and best baseline.

Dataset	Configuration	F1	Recall	Precision	TP	FP	FN
Carcinogenesis	Original	0.57	0.94	0.41	15	22	1
	Perturbed	0.57	0.94	0.41	15	19	1
	Best baseline	0.49	0.94	0.33	15	30	1
Comercy	Original	0.62	0.78	0.52	14	13	4
	Perturbed	0.35	0.50	0.27	9	24	9
	Best baseline	0.44	0.44	0.44	8	10	10
SISU	Original	0.93	0.88	1.00	7	0	1
	Perturbed	0.59	1.00	0.42	8	11	0
	Best baseline	0.25	0.25	0.25	2	6	6
Airlines	Original	0.88	0.78	1.00	7	0	2
	Perturbed	0.63	0.67	0.60	6	4	3
	Best baseline	0.34	0.78	0.22	7	25	2

The results show that our method uses schema-level and data-level semantics in a complementary way. When attribute names are removed, performance degradation varies significantly between datasets, indicating different degrees of dependence on each signal. For the Carcinogenesis dataset, performance remains unchanged, suggesting that value-based semantics alone are sufficient to identify valid INDs. In this case, attribute names consist mainly of abbreviations and short codes, contributing little to semantic representation. We observe the same pattern in other datasets with similar characteristics, suggesting that attribute names dominated by abbreviations and short codes provide a limited semantic signal. In contrast, the Comercy dataset exhibits a substantial drop in F1-score, accompanied by increases in both false positives and false negatives, indicating a stronger reliance on schema-level information. A particularly notable behavior is observed in SISU, where recall increases from 0.88 to 1.00 under perturbation, while precision drops sharply due to a significant rise in false positives. This suggests that attribute names act as an important precision filter, helping to eliminate semantically implausible candidates. Similarly, in the Comercy and Airlines datasets, attribute names help constrain the search space to semantically consistent pairs, improving the quality of the evaluated candidates.

Overall, these results reinforce that the combination of name-based and value-based semantics is complementary, as while data values sustain coverage, attribute names are essential for controlling precision.

4.5 Parameter Configuration and Model Selection

SEIND uses pre-trained models to generate column embeddings. Preliminary experiments with different models showed variations in both performance and execution time, with SentenceTransformer `all-mpnet-base-v2` producing the most consistent results. We also evaluated the impact of the sampling parameter k using a grid ranging from 5 to 100. Unlike schema matching approaches such as Magneto [17], the discovery of semantic INDs relies on an adequate representation of the observed domain. Larger samples reduce the likelihood of omitting relevant column values. Although smaller values of k (e.g., 20) reduce execution time, we observed a decline in discovery quality metrics. Consequently, we adopted $k = 50$ as a trade-off between computational cost and domain coverage.

SEIND uses two parameters to balance semantic similarity and syntactic inclusion during candidate generation and validation. The cosine similarity threshold α controls how semantically similar two columns must be to be considered candidates, with lower values yielding larger candidate sets and higher values restricting the search to strongly related columns. The parameter ϵ defines the tolerated level of inconsistency during inclusion validation; $\epsilon = 0$ corresponds to exact INDs, and larger values allow approximate containment. Figure 4 shows the impact of both parameters across different datasets and settings.

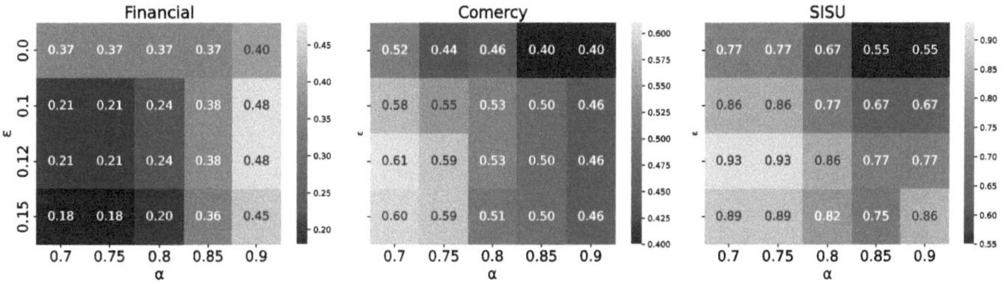

Fig. 4. F1 score (α versus ϵ) for some of the most representative sets in terms of number of attributes.

In general, moderately permissive values of α, such as 0.7 and 0.75, achieve the best performance, as they allow the method to capture inclusion relationships beyond strictly identical value sets, unlike more restrictive thresholds such as 0.95. For the Financial dataset, however, stricter settings lead to a noticeable improvement. This behavior can be explained by the high alignment of attributes across tables, a pattern also observed in datasets that contain columns with abbreviations or short codes. When $\epsilon = 0$, the method behaves similarly to an exact approach such as BINDER. As ϵ increases, performance improves by allowing a controlled level of data inconsistency.

4.6 Runtime Analysis

Table 3 presents the execution times for the four most representative datasets by number of attributes, highlighting scalability across different scenarios. The IND baselines are faster than SEIND because they rely exclusively on strategies optimized for contention and pruning during verification, whereas SEIND introduces an additional candidate-generation stage before extensional verification. This overhead is most pronounced on larger datasets such as TPC-H, where generation becomes the dominant cost, but remains moderate on smaller ones and is offset by the accuracy gains shown earlier. Join discovery methods sit at the other extreme: they rely entirely on semantic signals and are substantially slower. SEIND occupies the middle ground, paying a moderate overhead over IND baselines in exchange for more accurate and robust discovery, while avoiding the full cost of purely semantic approaches.

Table 3. Execution time comparison (s).

Tool	Dataset	Time (s)	Tool	Dataset	Time (s)
SEIND	TPC-H	126.60	SEIND	Financial	1.80
AINDD	TPC-H	102.30	AINDD	Financial	0.53
SAWFISH	TPC-H	89.50	SAWFISH	Financial	0.50
BINDER	TPC-H	–	BINDER	Financial	1.60
Omnimatch	TPC-H	–	Omnimatch	Financial	693.20
DeepJoin	TPC-H	–	DeepJoin	Financial	42.60
SEIND	Comercy	16.90	SEIND	SISU	8.03
AINDD	Comercy	2.70	AINDD	SISU	1.34
SAWFISH	Comercy	2.80	SAWFISH	SISU	1.42
BINDER	Comercy	4.90	BINDER	SISU	2.34
Omnimatch	Comercy	552.20	Omnimatch	SISU	930.93
DeepJoin	Comercy	149.30	DeepJoin	SISU	72.50

5 Conclusion

We studied the discovery of semantically meaningful inclusion dependencies and argued that exact and approximate containment, taken alone, are insufficient to distinguish genuine referential structure from accidental domain overlap. Building on this observation, we introduced SEIND, a two-stage method that pairs embedding-based candidate generation with approximate value inclusion over normalized domains, where the first stage decides which column pairs to check and the second decides which pairs are supported by the data. The evaluation indicates that SEIND matches or exceeds the accuracy of the IND and join discovery baselines, with the largest gains on heterogeneous, noisy schemas. Also, when used as a front-end to existing IND tools, the embedding stage reduces false positives with little impact on recall.

Acknowledgments.. This study was supported by the Araucria Foundation for Support to Scientific and Technological Development of the State of Paraná and by the Serrapilheira Institute, through the Young Scientists Support Program (Protocol No. SER2023371000001/PI 28/2023).

References

1. Abedjan, Z., Golab, L., Naumann, F.: Profiling relational data: a survey. VLDB J. **24**(4), 557–581 (2015). https://doi.org/10.1007/s00778-015-0389-y
2. Bauckmann, J., Abedjan, Z., Leser, U., Müller, H., Naumann, F.: Discovering conditional inclusion dependencies. In: CIKM '12, pp. 2094–2098. ACM (2012).https://doi.org/10.1145/2396761.2398580
3. Bauckmann, J., Leser, U., Naumann, F., Tietz, V.: Efficiently detecting inclusion dependencies. In: IEEE 23rd International Conference on Data Engineering, pp. 1448–1450 (2007). https://doi.org/10.1109/ICDE.2007.369032
4. Bravo, L., Fan, W., Ma, S.: Extending dependencies with conditions. In: PVLDB, pp. 243–254 (2007). https://doi.org/10.5555/1325851.1325882
5. Casanova, M.A., Fagin, R., Papadimitriou, C.H.: Inclusion dependencies and their interaction with functional dependencies. In: Proceedings of the 1st ACM SIGACT-SIGMOD Symposium on Principles of Database Systems (PODS '82), pp. 171–176 ACM (1982). https://doi.org/10.1145/588111.588141
6. Casanova, M.A., Tucherman, L., Furtado, A.L.: Enforcing inclusion dependencies and referencial integrity, pp. 38–49. VLDB (1988)
7. Chen, Z., Narasayya, V., Chaudhuri, S.: Fast foreign-key detection in microsoft SQL server powerpivot for excel. PVLDB **7**(13), 1417–1428 (2014). https://doi.org/10.14778/2733004.2733014
8. Ding, X., Lu, Y., Wang, H., Wang, C., Liu, Y., Wang, J.: Dafdiscover: Robust mining algorithm for dynamic approximate functional dependencies on dirty data. PVLDB **17**(11), 3484–3496 (JulY 2024). https://doi.org/10.14778/3681954.3682015
9. Dong, Y., Xiao, C., Nozawa, T., Enomoto, M., Oyamada, M.: Deepjoin: Joinable table discovery with pre-trained language models. PVLDB **16**(10), 2458–2470 (2023). https://doi.org/10.14778/3603581.3603587

10. Dürsch, F., et al.: Inclusion dependency discovery: An experimental evaluation of thirteen algorithms. In: CIKM '19. pp. 219–228. ACM (2019). https://doi.org/10.1145/3357384.3357916
11. Fan, G., Wang, J., Li, Y., Miller, R.J.: Table discovery in data lakes: State-of-the-art and future directions. In: Companion of the 2023 International Conference on Management of Data, pp. 69–75 (2023)
12. Fan, G., Wang, J., Li, Y., Zhang, D., Miller, R.J.: Semantics-aware dataset discovery from data lakes with contextualized column-based representation learning. PVLDB **16**(7), 1726–1739 (2023). https://doi.org/10.14778/3587136.3587146
13. Gryz, J.: Query folding with inclusion dependencies. In: Proceedings 14th International Conference on Data Engineering, pp. 126–133. IEEE (1998)
14. Hassanzadeh, O., Pu, K.Q., Yeganeh, S.H., Miller, R.J., Popa, L., Hernández, M.A., Ho, H.: Discovering linkage points over web data. PVLDB **6**(6), 445–456 (2013)
15. Kaminsky, Y., Pena, E.H.M., Naumann, F.: Discovering similarity inclusion dependencies. Proc. ACM Manage. Data **1**(1), 1–24 (2023). https://doi.org/10.1145/3588929
16. Koutras, C., et al.: Omnimatch: Joinability discovery in data products. PVLDB **18**(11), 4588–4601 (2025). https://doi.org/10.14778/3749646.3749715
17. Liu, Y., Pena, E.H.M., Santos, A., Wu, E., Freire, J.: Magneto: Combining small and large language models for schema matching. PVLDB **18**(8), 2681–2694 (2025). https://doi.org/10.14778/3742728.3742757
18. Lopes, S., Petit, J., Toumani, F.: Discovering interesting inclusion dependencies: Application to logical database tuning. Inf. Syst. (2002). https://doi.org/10.1016/S0306-4379(01)00027-8
19. Motl, J., Schulte, O.: The CTU Prague relational learning repository (2024). https://arxiv.org/abs/1511.03086
20. Olist, S., A.: Brazilian e-commerce public dataset by olist (2018). https://doi.org/10.34740/KAGGLE/DSV/195341
21. Papenbrock, T., Bergmann, T., Finke, M., Zwiener, J., Naumann, F.: Data profiling with metanome. PVLDB **8**(12), 1860–1863 (2015)
22. Papenbrock, T., Kruse, S., Quiané-Ruiz, J., Naumann, F.: Divide & conquer-based inclusion dependency discovery. PVLDB **8**(7), 774–785 (2015). https://doi.org/10.14778/2752939.2752946
23. Paton, N., Chen, J., Wu, Z.: Dataset discovery and exploration: a survey. ACM Comput. Surv. (2023). https://doi.org/10.1145/3626521. Oct
24. Pearl, F.M.: The CATH database: an extended protein family resource for structural and functional genomics. Nucleic Acids Res. **31**(1), 452–455 (2003)
25. SISU: SISU - data. https://dadosabertos.mec.gov.br/sisu?start=50
26. Song, K., Tan, X., Qin, T., Lu, J., Liu, T.Y.: MPNet: masked and permuted pre-training for language understanding. In: Proceedings of the 34th International Conference on Neural Information Processing Systems. NIPS '20, Curran Associates Inc, Red Hook, NY, USA (2020)
27. Su, Q., Wang, Z., Tan, Z., Ma, S.: Discovering approximate inclusion dependencies. PVLDB **18**(4), 1210–1222 (2024). https://doi.org/10.14778/3717755.3717777
28. TPC: TPC-H Benchmark. http://www.tpc.org/tpch/
29. Zhu, E., Deng, D., Nargesian, F., Miller, R.J.: Josie: Overlap set similarity search for finding joinable tables in data lakes. In: Proceedings of the SIGMOD '19, pp. 847–864. ACM (2019). https://doi.org/10.1145/3299869.3300065
30. Zhu, E., Nargesian, F., Pu, K.Q., Miller, R.J.: LSH ensemble: Internet-scale domain search. PVLDB **9**(12), 1185–1196 (2016). https://doi.org/10.14778/2994509.2994534

Conversational Data Management: A Multi-agent Natural Language Interface for Semantic Data Lakes

Sayed Hoseini[1(✉)], Niels Mittelstädt[2], Vincent Herrmann[1], Stefan Decker[3], and Christoph Quix[1,3]

[1] Niederrhein University of Applied Sciences, Krefeld, Germany
christoph.quix@hsnr.de
[2] RWTH Aachen University, Aachen, Germany
[3] Fraunhofer FIT, St. Augustin, Germany

Abstract. While modern data lakes offer powerful capabilities for handling heterogeneous datasets, interacting with them can be challenging, especially for users without technical expertise. Large Language Models (LLMs) offer a promising solution: conversational access to complex data systems using plain language. This paper presents a novel natural language interface for semantic data lakes, designed to complement their existing user interface and lower the technical barrier for users. The system integrates LLMs into a modular, multi-agent architecture using retrieval-augmented generation and tool calling to decompose queries, plan workflows, and translate natural language into structured operations in the data lake. This enables seamless execution of tasks such as integration, discovery, and analytics without requiring users to understand system internals. We implemented the approach within our semantic data lake SEDAR, demonstrating its feasibility in a real data-centric environment. At the same time, the underlying multi-agent architecture is designed to be transferable and can be applied to other data-centric platforms. Evaluation on representative queries and multiple metrics shows that current LLMs can automate multi-step workflows, enhance accessibility, and robustly handle linguistic ambiguity. Our contribution is a reusable and system-independent agentic design pattern for helping to democratize data science for non-expert users.

1 Introduction

Rapid advancements in data science and AI have led to the proliferation of data lakes, which are centralized repositories that store vast amounts of raw data in original format [7]. Despite offering powerful capabilities, data lakes often remain inaccessible to non-technical users due to steep learning curves, limited interfaces, and complex workflows. This usability gap prevents organizations from broad adoption and from fully leveraging their data assets and motivates the need for more intuitive, self-service interaction paradigms [9].

G. Vargas-Solar et al. (Eds.): ADBIS 2026, LNCS 16937, pp. 169–185, 2027.
https://doi.org/10.1007/978-3-032-39820-8_12

Recent developments in natural language (NL) processing and the emergence of Large Language Models (LLMs) have opened new avenues for simplifying data interactions. LLMs have demonstrated remarkable capabilities in understanding and generating human-like text as well as programming code, making them suitable for various applications, including data management [17]. LLM-based agents [27] combine reasoning and NL understanding with goal-oriented behaviors and tool integration. Agents are designed not only to interpret user intents, but also to autonomously plan and execute multi-step tasks by invoking external tools. Recent frameworks [11,23] have demonstrated the viability of equipping LLMs with agentic behaviors to perform data-intensive tasks, from question answering to data transformation and ML pipeline orchestration.

In this paper, we explore how such agents can be leveraged to create a more intelligent interface for semantic data lakes. The interface facilitates general data management tasks (such as data ingestion, discovery, integration, and ML) by using LLMs to convert user queries into actions executed on the system.

This work introduces a novel multi-agent, LLM-driven interface that explicitly targets NL interaction, data integration, and exploration in semantic data lakes. Unlike prior systems that hard-code query templates or narrow use cases [18], our natural language interface (NLI) introduces a transferable design pattern: decomposing queries into modular agent tasks, grounding them in API calls of the underlying system, and evaluating them with reasoning-focused metrics. The same pattern could be applied to other domains, such as the Azure SDK, where complex systems and APIs present a similar challenge for non-expert users.

The approach is applied in our *Semantic Data Reservoir* (SEDAR [12]), which has been designed as a modular data lake system using open-source technologies, making it suitable as a workbench for research on scalable data architectures. Originally a classical data lake, SEDAR has evolved to support semantic data management and ontology-based data access, aligning with key features of semantic data lakes [5]. SEDAR streamlines the ML life cycle using MLOps principles, applies AutoML [13], and is applied in production as part of a cyber-physical system for an Industry 4.0 case [14].
Our contributions are twofold:

1. **Methodological contribution:** We introduce a multi-agent design applicable to any API-centric platform, together with an evaluation protocol including (i) semantically varied query datasets, (ii) parameter-efficient finetuning for adaptation, and (iii) metrics for reasoning consistency and robustness.
2. **System contribution:** To verify the approach, we have implemented an NLI that integrates LLMs with retrieval and tool execution for semantic data lakes that enables end-to-end tasks such as discovery, ML and semantic querying. Code, datasets, and evaluation results are available on GitHub.

The rest of this article is structured as follows: Sect. 2 reviews related work, introduces the SEDAR system and defines functional components of the NLI. Section 3 describes the design and implementation of the NLI. Finally, Sect. 4 presents an analysis of the systems capabilities and limitations.

2 Related Work and Background

LLMs have been shown to be effective for various tasks in data management [17]. We focus on approaches using either NL or multi-agent systems.

Natural Language Interfaces for Databases [18] allow querying databases in NL, which is addressed in the broad research field of text-to-SQL [19]. Some approaches go beyond generating SQL queries and offer more advanced data management functions. LOTUS [22] adds semantic operators to the relational model, enabling complex queries over structured and unstructured data with language models. SYMPHONY [3], on the other hand, enables NL querying of multi-modal data lakes without prior integration. QueryArtisan [25] enable explainable, multi-modal data exploration in NL for data lakes. DataScout [1] introduces an interactive system where an LLM-based agent acts as an NLI for data platforms. However, most existing approaches focus on specific tasks rather than providing a unified NLI across the entire functionality of a data lake system. The most closely related work is the Apache Iceberg-based approach [16], which also relies on semantic annotations. Unlike that approach, our annotations are directly defined in the source code, avoiding the need for a separate semantic layer.

Multi-Agent Systems (MAS) [26] equip multiple interacting agents with tools and external knowledge to interact with their environment, receive feedback from their actions, and communicate with each other to coordinate tasks and achieve shared goals. Each agent has distinct roles and expertise that are provided to the LLM. MetaGPT [10] introduces such a role-based collaboration system where agents simulate roles of a software development team, such as the Data Interpreter [11].

LLM Tool-Calling refers to LLMs that invoke external tools, APIs or functions such as a calculator or database query engine, or to request external information [28]. Gorilla [23] and Toolformer [24] are approaches where finetuning was used to create a model specialized in API tool calling, while He et al. [8] show that LLMs can be taught to call external tools without any finetuning.

Our *semantic data lake* SEDAR has been deployed in various settings, but especially in the chemical domain [13,14]. The system provides an API to simplify integration with industrial processes, allowing developers to focus on building automation solutions which include data management and ML. This programmatic interface for the backend is called the SEDAR-API. Both the SEDAR-API as well as the frontend remain a critical bottleneck for many users. Interacting with these interfaces often requires familiarity with internal data structures, functions, APIs, and workflows, posing a significant barrier not only for non-technical users but also for analysts and researchers. To simplify access to the system, there is a need for a more intuitive interaction. An NLI bridges this gap by allowing users to express their information needs in everyday language. By converting NL into actionable commands, the NLI lowers the cognitive and technical threshold required to engage with the system. This NLI is implemented as a chat-based interface embedded within the existing UI. For example, a domain expert may want to retrieve all datasets containing information on solvents used in experiments. In current systems, this would require knowing the exact table names and schema details. With our multi-agent NLI, which also leverages semantic annotations of datasets, the same task can be expressed as a single query in plain language, e.g., *"List all datasets that include solvent information."*

Ingestion and Data Discovery:
- Ingest my file into the appropriate storage system.
- Upload the datasets X & Y and run their ingestion concurrently.
- Retrieve the versions of dataset X. What are their differences?
- What is the lineage of dataset X?
- Look at dataset X and add a description to it.
- Given dataset X, find all datasets related to it.
- Name all datasets that contain data about chemicals.

Machine Learning:
- Use the dataset X and create an AutoML run to predict the target T.
- Perform binary classification based on dataset X to predict T.
- Which ML experiments exist for the dataset X? Explain them.

Semantic Data Management:
- Create a new ontology O by uploading the file F.
- Find a fitting semantic label from Ontology O for dataset X.
- Create a semantic model to join the datasets X, Y and Z.
- Using the OBDA functionality join the datasets X, Y and Z.

Fig. 1. Representative queries for ingestion, ML, and semantic data management.

For evaluation, we have defined a set of representative queries that covers a broad range of data management functions (see Fig. 1). For example, the first query in *Data Discovery* requires first retrieving all available datasets, and their metadata to then reason for relatedness on the gathered information. Each query maps to backend API functions. For ML tasks, this includes dataset uploads (with labels for classification/regression on tabular and image data) and the creation of ML pipelines [13]. The last items in *Semantic Data Management* are the running example for Sect. 3.

3 Multi-agent System: Concepts and Realization

We first describe the general architecture, followed by a brief description of each agent, an explaination of the retrieval pipeline, chat interface, and finally finetuning and prompt compression.

Architecture. A central challenge in designing MAS is balancing autonomy and alignment: agents must produce outputs consistent with system goals while retaining flexibility to handle diverse tasks in dynamic environments.

In our setting, an agent is an LLM-based component that reasons over the system state and interacts with the SEDAR API to perform task-specific actions. The overall system is organized as a directed graph (Fig. 2), where each node corresponds to an agent invocation. Agents operate with dedicated prompts, access shared state and tools, and communicate indirectly through the workflow.

A key design decision concerns the trade-off between retrieval-based approaches and explicit task decomposition across multiple agents. Pure retrieval simplifies orchestration but limits flexibility, while highly specialized agents increase coordination overhead.

To address this, we adopt a hybrid architecture that combines retrieval techniques with lightweight coordination. API classes are registered via decorators, and their methods, implementations, and docstrings are embedded into a vector store. This enables class-based retrieval of relevant functionality at runtime [20], avoiding excessive agent fragmentation while maintaining scalability: new capabilities require only updating embeddings rather than architectural changes.

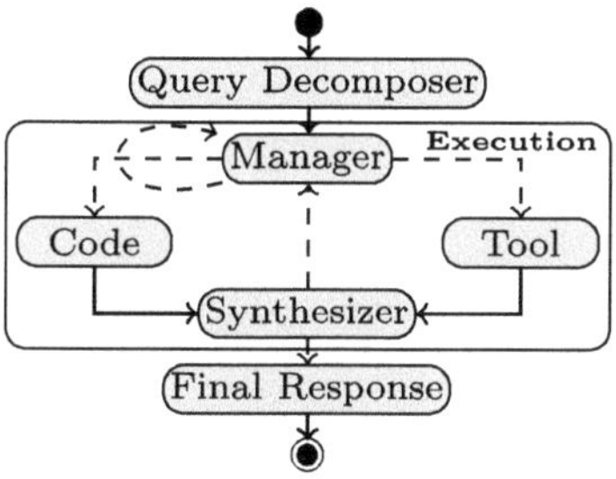

Agent	Role	Input	Output
Query Decomp.	Break query into subtasks	Query, API context	Subtasks
Manager	Assign subtasks	Subtasks, cache	Tool/code decision
Tool	Execute API call	API context, cache	API call result
Code	Run custom code	API context, cache	Code result
Synthesizer	Merge results	Agent outputs	Summary
Final Resp.	Deliver response	Summary	Reply

Fig. 2. Multi-Agent Architecture (solid edges indicate primary control flow & dashed represent conditional edges) and Agent Overview

Tools, i.e., external functions, can be registered as callable nodes. Conditional edges (dashed) are supported and traversed based on evaluations over the current state to enable feedback loops, iterative processing, retries, and adaptive logic. The particular agent decomposition was guided by the observation that retrieved tool and knowledge subsets tend to cluster around distinct functional and semantically coherent domains such as ingestion, dataset handling, or AutoML. All agents use Retrieval-Augmented-Generation (RAG) to access the context about the API relevant to the task. Tool Agents operate over a narrow, class-specific scope, reducing the number of functions the LLM must reason about at once. Execution feedback, including intermediate outputs, results and errors, is passed among agents to refine outputs iteratively, following the ReAct pattern [29]. By limiting the number of tools or functions the LLM must consider at each step, this design reduces redundancy and lowers reasoning complexity.

The architecture comprises six agents. Every user query is first processed by the *Query Decompose Agent*, which decomposes the query into atomic subtasks based on information about the API retrieved from a vector store. In the best case, each subtask can be answered by a single API call. For this agent, we use a mix of top-7 retrieval and passing only the names of the methods to the LLM, so that the agent then knows about relevant classes of the API and their methods. For example, for the query "Show me all datasets", the `get_all_datasets` function from the `Dataset` class should be in the top-7 retrieved functions. These methods and their classes are passed to the LLM together with descriptions and information about the parameters.

The next unanswered subquery is retrieved from the state and passed to the *Manager Agent*. Executed functions often return instances of API classes, which play a central role by storing intermediate objects from function calls or code executions in an `object_cache`. These cached instances can later be reused by the Tool or Code Agents as parameters or inputs in subsequent steps. In addition to the object cache, various message arrays serve as memory structures that retain the interaction history of each agent to inform and guide decisions.

However, not all messages are relevant to every agent at every step. For example, the Code Agent may only receive messages from the Manager, while the Synthesizer aggregates messages from all agents to form a final response. This selective context passing is made possible through the LangGraph framework, which allows fine-grained control over the shared state.

The Manager determines the next action by analyzing the current query, the retrieved function context, and the available objects in the cache. As depicted in Fig. 2, the Manager has three possible outgoing conditional edges: The Tool Agent is preferred when a matching function is available, as it is more reliable and operates on a specific object from the cache, while the Code Agent is more flexible and capable of arbitrary code generation, but is also more error-prone. If the Manager produces an invalid output, such as failing to select either Tool or Code, generating invalid JSON, or referencing an object that is not present in the cache, the self-loop edge is taken. This conditional routing enables the Manager to robustly handle errors and adaptively select the most appropriate step based on the current context and state.

The *Tool Agent* receives the query, the object cache, and the API context selected by the Manager. The Tool Agent then determines which function to invoke on the selected objects. The system avoids listing functions in the prompt by using native tool-calling features of model providers (e.g., Ollama, OpenAI, Anthropic), where functions are registered in advance. Function calls may reference cached objects. After execution, the agent updates the global statelogging messages and the cache. If the function fails or the query remains unresolved, prior attempts and outputs are utilized for iterative refinement. Due to numerous parameters or intricate behavior, some API functions are unsuitable for direct use by the Tool Agent. To address this, *custom tool agents* invoke an equivalent of the intended function.

The Code Agent is selected by the Manager when a query cannot be resolved by a single API call or requires complex logic, such as conditionals or composition of multiple functions. When invoked, it receives the same context as the Manager, i.e., the top-7 relevant functions, information about the associated API class, and the names of all available functions to generate custom code. The Code Agent also has access to the full object cache. The agent is equipped with helper functions to load, store and update objects, typically via a custom `print` function that preserves intermediate results. If the code fails or does not resolve the query, the previous code and its output are included in the next iteration.

The Synthesize Agent determines whether the query has been successfully addressed. It receives the full context: the initial and current queries, decisions by the Manager, steps taken, and resulting outputs. If the query is fulfilled, the Synthesizer summarizes the execution and routes control to the *Final Response Agent*, which answers the original user query based on the summary. Otherwise, if errors occur or the result is assessed as insufficient by the Synthesizer, it passes control back to the Manager to retry using the updated context and feedback.

Retrieval Pipeline. In our system, agents are entirely dependent on the candidates of the retrieved functions to construct meaningful responses. If a relevant function is not retrieved, the agent will either fail to answer or hallucinate functionality. Hence, a strong retrieval pipeline is essential to ensure high-quality responses. The pipeline consists of four main parts: the indexing of API functions, the vector store for retrieval, the cross-encoder for re-ranking, and the cache. Before any retrieval for a given query is performed, we check whether the retrieval results are already in *cache*. If a cache hit occurs, the stored results are returned immediately to improve response time.

The API functions need to be *indexed*. For this, we use a custom Python decorator (`@cacheable`) that registers the classes to be indexed. All public methods of each registered class that are not excluded explicitly are indexed. For each function, a document is created that contains the full source code of the function. It also includes metadata such as the class name, the function name, and an ID. For computing the *embedding*, we rely on Nomic Embed. With a context length of 8192 tokens, it outperforms OpenAI's Ada-002 and text-embedding-3-small on both short and long context tasks and ranks well on the MTEB [21] leaderboard for retrieval tasks. In our initial tests, it has shown better performance than other models such as BGE M3 [2] or OpenAI's text-embedding-3-large. The extended context length allows us to embed any API function; the embeddings with 768 dimensions are then stored in a Qdrant vector store.

The main *retrieval* process uses cosine similarity for similarity search. The retriever is employed in two main ways within our system. First, general retrieval of functions from the API is used by both the Query Decompose Agent and the Manager. This method allows specifying the search query, the parameter k (denoting the number of top-matching documents to retrieve), and whether to include short descriptions of other relevant methods and classes not directly retrieved. Second, tool retrieval for a specific class is provided to the Tool Agent. In this case, a class and its associated tools are provided, and only the tools matching the retrieved functions for the query are returned. In the initial retrieval, to avoid missing any relevant functions, a larger k value such as 20 worked well for us but can be tuned based on system size or domain specificity. To enhance retrieval precision, we apply re-ranking using FlashRank on retrieved functions before passing them to the LLM to narrow down the top-7 results.

Chat Interface and Example Walkthrough. The user interface (UI) for conversational interaction is implemented via Chainlit, which seamlessly integrates with LangGraph. Figure 3 shows the chat interface integrated in the existing SEDAR frontend. The chat window shows an intermediate step from the example below, where the system suggests some labels for datasets that can be accepted or declined through the UI. The action bar allows files to be uploaded, for example, to create a new ontology or dataset.

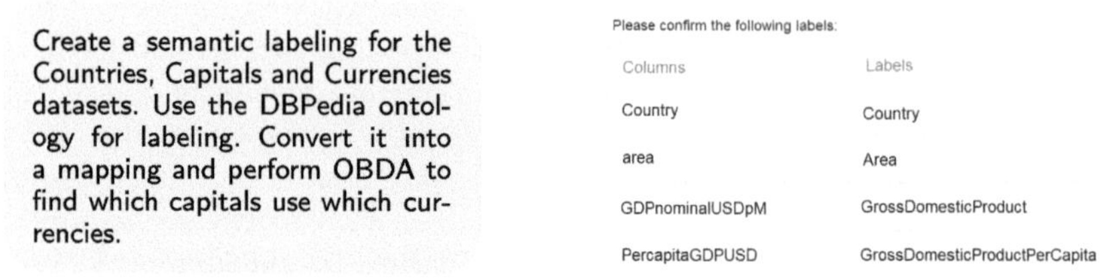

Fig. 3. Integrated chat interface with semantic-label confirmation

The Chainlit backend wraps the LangGraph MAS and communicates with the frontend only. Communication with the SEDAR's backend only happens from within the MAS through the SEDAR-API. To illustrate the multi-agent workflow in practice, we present a walkthrough (video) of a sample user query and the corresponding system steps. The example query from Fig. 3 requires the system to search for specific datasets, locate an ontology, create a semantic model, perform attribute labeling, convert the semantic model into an RML mapping, and create a query for ontology-based data access (OBDA) that joins the data involving several interdependent subtasks:
Step 1 - Query Submission: The user submits the query in the chat.
Step 2 - API Function Retrieval: The system retrieves relevant API functions from the vector store and re-ranks to prioritize the most relevant candidates, e.g., `label_modeling_attributes`, `datasets_search`.
Step 3 - Query Decomposition: Based on the retrieved context, the query is decomposed into subtasks and passed to the subsequent agents:

- Search for the dataset *Countries*/*Capitals*/*Currencies*
- Get all ontologies and find the DBpedia ontology.
- Create a semantic model for the datasets.
- Label the attributes of the datasets using the DBpedia ontology.
- Convert the semantic model into an RML mapping.
- Create and execute an OBDA query that joins the data and returns the capitals and their currencies.

Step 4 - Subtask Execution: Each subtask is processed through the Execution loop. API functions contextually relevant to the current subtask are retrieved and re-ranked. The Manager determines whether the subtask can be solved by

calling an API function or requires generating custom code. In this example, the Tool Agent is always chosen, as each subtask can be handled by single API functions. Some functions, such as `execute_obda_query`, are implemented as tools to handle complex tasks that require multiple LLM invocations or function calls. For the final subtask, the Tool Agent invokes this tool, which orchestrates the OBDA query generation and execution process. The Synthesizer evaluates whether the subtask was completed. If not, the agents can iteratively refine their approach or fix errors.
Step 5 - Response: Once all subtasks are completed and validated, the Final Response Agent aggregates the results and generates a user-friendly summary. The example's response begins as follows:
Ive completed the semantic annotation (using the DBpedia ontology), generated an RML mapping and ran an OBDA SPARQL query to link capitals to their currencies. Here are the first ten as examples:
1. Albania: Capital - Tirana, Currency - Lek ...

Finetuning and Prompt Compression. In our experience, even models with >70B parameters often struggle with complex and long-context tasks like tool calling, structured data handling, code generation, and multi-agent coordination which require specialized reasoning. By finetuning current LLMs on a custom dataset that closely matches these workflows, we aim to improve the handling of extended contexts and specialized tasks.

With SEDAR populated by sample data, we run the MAS against representative queries (Fig. 1). For these runs, we use high-performing "teacher" models (GPT-4o & Gemini 2.0) and fetch successful LLM calls. Each run contains a complete LLM interaction including the system message, any tool definitions, the prompt as well as any context about the object cache or API functions, and past messages from other agents. First, the data is stored in the more generic sharegpt format and then converted into a model-specific format. All entries are then manually reviewed to ensure high quality, resulting in a dataset of 535 samples reflecting the types of reasoning tasks performed by agents in our system, i.e., tool calling, code generation, and response synthesis.

We finetuned Llama3.3:70B and Qwen2.5:72B with an Intel Xeon 8468 Sapphire CPU, 450 GB RAM, and a single NVIDIA H100 GPU with 96 GB VRAM using Unsloth by following the official training notebooks with only minor adjustments for our use case. We employed QLoRA [4] for parameter-efficient finetuning. Configuration details can be seen in Table 1. Maximum sequence length was set to 65,536 tokens and the batch size per device was set to 2, with gradient accumulation yielding effectively 16.

The training strategy used selective masking, i.e., each training sample included the entire conversational history, but only the final assistant response was unmasked for loss computation to ensure models learned to interpret long, multi-turn contexts. Early experiments without adequate masking or with shorter sequence lengths (e.g., 2,000 tokens) led to hallucinations and perfor-

Table 1. Finetuning configurations and results.

Configuration	Llama 3.3 70B	Qwen 2.5 72B
LoRA Rank (r)	32	64
Epochs	2	3
Trainable Parameters	414M (1.13%)	842M (2.19%)
Adapter Weight Size	1.5 GB	3.1 GB
Training Time	104 min	156 min
Quantized Size	~40 GB	~44 GB

mance degradation, highlighting the importance of these design choices. Upon completion of training, we exported the LoRA adapter weights and merged them into the base models using 4-bit quantization. This allowed local inference on a single NVIDIA Quadro RTX 8000 GPU (48 GB VRAM).

To address the challenges of long prompts in our MAS, such as the *lost in the middle* effect, we incorporated *prompt compression* [15]. Especially with smaller models, important context can be overlooked when buried in the middle of long inputs. Prompt compression reduces the number of tokens while aiming to retain critical information. LLMLingua [15] computes token importance using a smaller LLM and removes low-importance tokens, producing compressed inputs that remain interpretable for the model but are often unintelligible to humans. To preserve reliability, we apply compression selectively, with a moderate compression rate (retain 60%) to balance efficiency and accuracy. User queries, retrieved API responses, function signatures, and cache object keys are excluded from compression to avoid errors. Only compressible content such as docstrings can be reduced in size.

4 Evaluation and Discussion

To rigorously assess the performance and robustness of our system, we conduct a quantitative evaluation based on a set of NL queries. These queries cover the systems key functionalities and are semantically varied to test generalization beyond fixed templates.

A key goal of this evaluation is not only to check whether the final answer is correct, but also how robust the system is to linguistic variation, i.e., whether it can correctly interpret semantically equivalent queries phrased in different ways. This reflects real-world usage, where users express the same intent using varied phrasing. The guiding question here is: **How consistent is the performance when users phrase the same request differently?** While comparisons with existing approaches are desirable, most related work focuses on isolated tasks such as text-to-SQL or dataset discovery, making direct comparisons difficult. Furthermore, runtime measurements were not considered meaningful in our setting, as the experiments were executed using locally hosted LLMs

Table 2. Model performance.

Model	TOK↓	ACC↑	LACC↑	P@1↑	P@2↑
llama3.3:latest	25,455	0.12	0.16	0.12	0.26
finetunedllama:latest	**24,093**	0.16	0.16	0.21	0.31
qwen2.5:72b	32,959	0.30	0.35	0.27	0.40
finetuned-qwen:latest	34,959	0.33	0.31	0.28	0.43
command-a	42,015	0.87	0.84	**0.93**	**0.96**
gpt-4o-mini	35,428	0.70	0.70	0.77	0.82
gpt-4.1-mini	29,896	0.85	**0.87**	**0.93**	0.95
gemini-2.0-flash	31,656	0.67	0.68	0.73	0.74
o4-mini-high	50,466	**0.90**	0.84	0.91	0.95
gpt-4o	33,922	0.81	0.76	0.83	0.85
gpt-4.1	32,709	0.87	**0.87**	0.91	0.92
claude-3-7-sonnet	42,321	0.89	**0.87**	0.92	0.93
gemini-2.5-pro-preview	39,691	0.79	0.76	0.86	0.90
gpt-4.1-PC	27,175	0.74	0.76	0.79	0.83

on resource-constrained hardware, causing execution times to be dominated by hardware-specific limitations rather than the proposed approach itself. Therefore, our evaluation focuses on the correctness and robustness of the generated results across different natural language formulations.

We began by manually deriving 27 base queries that span major functional areas from the representative queries (see Fig. 1). For each base query, four semantically distinct rephrasings were created, either manually or with the help of an LLM. Each variations must remain sufficiently close to the base query for the corresponding ground-truth to remain valid and applicable. To quantify semantic distance, we encode each query using a Sentence Transformer model, then compute the cosine similarity between each variation and its corresponding base query. Only those variations with similarity below 0.85 remain to ensure sufficient linguistic diversity. This methodology is grounded in prior work on embedding-based semantic similarity [6]. The final dataset consists of 135 queries (27 base + 108 filtered variations) with an average similarity of 0.78.

To understand the reliability and efficiency of the system, we analyze the entire trajectory taken, including intermediate decisions, tool usage, and communication between agents. To ensure consistency and reproducibility, we apply a reset mechanism for the whole data lake before each evaluation run. We use the following metrics (Table 2): Token usage (**TOK**) denotes the average number of tokens used. It reflects the verbosity and efficiency of the system and correlates with inference cost. We use two metrics to assess whether a task was completed successfully. **ACC** is a manually annotated accuracy score. Each run is labeled either correct or incorrect, while also taking the underlying reasoning into account. **LACC** serves the same purpose but is computed automatically by

Table 3. Node and tool metrics for all models. ↑ higher is better; ↓ lower is better.

	Node metrics						Tool metrics					
Model	EM↑	JS↑	LCS↑	ED↓	US↑	ES↑	EM↑	JS↑	LCS↑	ED↓	US↑	ES↑
llama3.3:latest	0.02	0.19	0.14	0.86	0.30	0.31	0.02	0.13	0.11	0.90	0.31	0.32
finetunedllama:latest	0.04	0.21	0.19	0.81	0.34	0.36	0.08	0.16	0.15	0.85	0.36	0.36
qwen2.5:72b	0.00	0.34	0.22	0.78	0.44	0.45	0.07	0.21	0.18	0.83	0.47	0.47
finetuned-qwen:latest	0.00	0.37	0.25	0.75	0.50	0.52	0.09	0.29	0.24	0.77	0.53	0.53
command-a	**0.71**	**0.93**	**0.88**	**0.12**	**0.95**	**0.96**	**0.63**	**0.84**	**0.80**	**0.21**	**0.96**	**0.96**
gpt-4o-mini	0.38	0.76	0.67	0.33	0.83	0.83	0.41	0.63	0.59	0.41	0.84	0.84
gpt-4.1-mini	0.56	0.88	0.84	0.17	**0.95**	**0.96**	0.53	0.80	0.75	0.25	**0.96**	**0.96**
gemini-2.0-flash	0.53	0.73	0.69	0.31	0.75	0.75	0.48	0.63	0.60	0.40	0.75	0.75
o4-mini-high	0.23	0.84	0.66	0.34	0.92	0.93	0.19	0.72	0.54	0.46	0.95	0.95
gpt-4o	0.53	0.81	0.75	0.25	0.85	0.85	0.50	0.68	0.67	0.33	0.86	0.86
gpt-4.1	0.63	0.89	0.82	0.18	0.92	0.92	0.53	0.73	0.71	0.29	0.93	0.93
claude-3-7-sonnet	0.64	0.91	0.83	0.17	0.92	0.93	0.53	0.74	0.72	0.29	0.93	0.93
gemini-2.5-pro-preview	0.56	0.88	0.80	0.20	0.90	0.91	0.44	0.72	0.67	0.33	0.91	0.91
gpt-4.1-PC	0.47	0.81	0.71	0.29	0.84	0.85	0.37	0.61	0.58	0.42	0.85	0.85

prompting a capable LLM (GPT-4o in our case) to judge the correctness of the answer. While this approach enables large-scale evaluation, it may not match the precision of human annotations. The **Pass@k** metrics assess whether the system produced the correct tool calls or code snippets and whether they succeeded within k attempts. We do not apply metrics for evaluating code generation (e.g., CodeBLEU), because we prioritize tool invocation over code synthesis since generated code is short and tightly scoped to individual subtasks. Thus, correctness is more effectively captured through the Pass@k and sequence metrics.

Node and tool metrics are shown in Table 3. *Node sequence evaluation* focuses on the agent nodes visited during the reasoning process. We compare the predicted node sequence to a ground truth reference; both sequences are extracted from the messages of the run and ground truth example, where the order of messages determines the order of nodes in the sequence. For *Tool sequence evaluation* we apply the same set of metrics and again compare to the ground truth sequence. The sequence for the run to be evaluated is constructed by iterating over the messages: if the message's `source_node` is `"tool_agent"`, the tool name is added; if it is `"code_agent"`, tool names from the example are added if they appear in the message content, otherwise a placeholder is used. Sequences are evaluated with the following metrics:

Exact Match (EM): Binary match score (1 if identical, 0 otherwise).

Jaccard Similarity (JS): Overlap of predicted and reference nodes.

Longest Common Subsequence (LCS): Relative length of the longest common subsequence.

Edit Distance (ED): Normalized Levenshtein distance, giving 0 for identical sequences and 1 for completely different ones.

Unmatched Steps (US): Measures how many steps in the predicted sequence do not align with the reference via $1 - \frac{u}{L_{\max}}$, where u is the number of unmatched steps and $L_{\max}$ is the maximum sequence length set to 200 across all runs.

ES (Extra Steps): Measures how many extra steps e were predicted compared to the reference, via $1 - \frac{e}{L_{\max}}$.

All step-based metrics are normalized to 1, making them comparable across runs and tasks of varying lengths. For evaluation, we report average scores computed over all queries and runs. This enables robust comparisons across models and configurations. Together, these metrics provide a comprehensive view of system performance capturing not only whether the system reaches right answer, but also how it arrives at that answer.

The selection of models is based on those capable of tool calling, a necessary feature for our system. Tables 3 and 2 summarize the evaluation results across all models. The first five entries correspond to open-source models including fine-tuned versions. While LLaMA and Qwen are fully open-source, we treat Command-A as an intermediate case: not fully open-source, but available for local inference. The remaining models are closed-source and include models from OpenAI, Anthropic (which requires a custom parsing mechanism), and Google DeepMind. Models are roughly ordered by parameter size. The final row shows results for our prompt compression approach using GPT-4.1.

Discussion of Results. The results show that 70B open-source models, such as Llama 3.3 and Qwen 2.5, are approaching their limits for complex, multi-step, and long-context tasks. While Qwen consistently outperforms Llama across most metrics, its accuracy remains insufficient. The marginal improvements from finetuning indicate that the current model scale and/or the available finetuning dataset are not enough to bridge the gap to production readiness. Qualitative inspection reveals frequent hallucinations and schema violations, particularly in scenarios involving long contexts, such as selecting objects from cache or synthesizing outputs from large JSON structures, even with larger models.

There is a notable performance jump between the 70B-class models and Coheres Command-A model (111B), which ranks among the top-3 overall in terms of accuracy and achieves the best scores across both node and tool sequence metrics. Additionally, Command-A attains the highest pass@1 and pass@2 rates, indicating that its tool calls and generated code are the least likely to fail. These results underscore the benefits of scaling up model size and improving pretraining quality, particularly for structured, tool-driven multi-agent workflows.

Closed-source models consistently outperform the smaller open-source models across all evaluation metrics. The highest accuracy was achieved by `o4-mini` (0.90) with the reasoning effort parameter set to `high`. However, this setting results in significantly higher token usage (50,466 tokens on average) and slower inference times, making it unsuitable for interactive applications where quick responses are expected. In contrast, models such as GPT-4.1 and Claude 3.7 Sonnet offer a strong balance between accuracy and efficiency. Notably, GPT-4.1-mini provides a cost-effective option, maintaining high performance while reducing resource consumption compared to its larger variants. A general trend is observed where models with higher accuracy also consume more tokens and vice versa. This is likely due to their ability to complete more steps, generate more detailed reasoning, and avoid premature failures.

Despite reducing the average token count, applying prompt compression led to a significant drop in accuracy and other metrics (GPT-4.1-PC). This is mainly because many critical prompt elements (e.g., function signatures, object cache, user queries, API responses) cannot be compressed without introducing errors.

A positive finding is that LLM-based accuracy (LACC) closely matches human-annotated accuracy, suggesting that LLMs can reliably self-assess the correctness of their outputs in this setting.

In our setting, finetuning open-source models led to only marginal improvements. This could be due to factors such as limited dataset size, model capacity, or the specific finetuning strategy used. Given both annotation effort and compute cost, the current cost-benefit trade-off limits the practical value of finetuning. Again, model scale and pretraining quality remain the most important factors for accuracy and reliability.

Overall, accuracy remains the decisive metric for judging model readiness in our multi-agent setting. As shown in Table 2, open-source models achieve limited accuracy (0.12–0.33), even when fine-tuned, confirming that they are not yet competitive for complex, multi-step workflows. In contrast, proprietary models consistently surpass 0.70, with GPT-4.1, Claude 3.7 Sonnet, `o4-mini-high`, and Coheres Command-A all achieving accuracies of 0.87 or higher. Among them, Command-A, a relatively small model (111B) matches GPT-4.1 at 0.87 and is only slightly outperformed by Claude 3.7 Sonnet (0.89) and o4-mini-high (0.90). This demonstrates that top proprietary models are currently necessary for reliable execution in our setting, while open-source alternatives remain behind. Notably, the models with the highest accuracy also achieve the best `pass@1` and `pass@2` scores, meaning they converge faster and with fewer failed attempts.

Beyond accuracy, the node and tool sequence metrics reveal important qualitative differences between models. Command-A achieves high accuracy and also shows good alignment with ground-truth sequences (EM 0.71, JS 0.84), indicating that its reasoning process closely mirrors the intended workflow. This reflects Cohere's training choices, which emphasized extensive instruction-tuning and tool use with the explicit goal of reproducible, API-like outputs for enterprise use cases rather than open-ended free-form text generation.

By contrast, open-source models often deviate substantially from the correct node and tool order, even when they occasionally produce the right final answer. This suggests brittle reasoning and low robustness to linguistic variation. GPT-4.1 and Claude 3.7 balance high accuracy with strong sequence metrics, showing that they can reach both the correct result and follow a plausible reasoning trajectory. Interestingly, token-heavy models like o4-mini-high achieve strong final answers but weaker sequence alignment, implying that sheer verbosity can compensate for reasoning mistakes. It often deviates from the expected path, with extra steps, repeated tool calls, or slightly different orderings. Instead of following a direct route, the model works through several alternatives until it arrives at the correct result. These results underscore the importance of evaluating not just correctness but also reasoning consistency, efficiency, and robustness, which are critical for MAS where interpretability and reproducibility matter.

5 Conclusion and Future Work

We proposed a novel NLI that enables users to interact with a semantic data lake through chat. The MAS orchestrates LLM-driven agents using LangGraph to decompose, plan, and execute complex user queries. It employs a RAG pipeline, combining semantic search, re-ranking, and context-aware function invocation. We curate a finetuning dataset by leveraging teacher LLMs and adapt open-source models to the specific requirement using parameter-efficient finetuning. We propose an evaluation protocol tailored to multi-agent, tool-using LLM systems. It covers correctness, reasoning trajectories, tool invocation sequences, and robustness to semantic variation, systematically assessing the system's ability to handle diverse user queries. We find the LLM Command-A to be competitive even against the most capable closed-source models.

However, limitations remain: tool invocation is sensitive to retrieval quality, object cache coordination is error-prone in long workflows, smaller models often struggle with robustness and large models can be costly. While error handling was graceful, the system lacked mechanisms for clarifying user intent or suggesting alternatives. Some components introduce latency such as re-ranking and large reasoning models, especially when not run on dedicated hardware. The current prompt compression method reduces token usage at the cost of accuracy and finetuning helped only marginally. Currently, the system decomposes user queries into subtasks only once, without adapting to intermediate results or failures. Adding adaptive planning could improve robustness. While the NLI lowers the technical barrier, users still require some domain knowledge to formulate effective queries. Further extensions could include domain-aware agents that clarify user intent, explain available functionalities, translate vocabulary, or suggest next steps.

As LLMs and retrieval methods mature, we can expect even more powerful NLIs for complex data systems. The NLI methodology layered on top of it, which lowers technical barriers for domain experts and thereby raises the potential to democratize data science for non-experts.

Acknowledgements AND GenAI Disclosure. This work has been sponsored by the German Federal Ministry of Research, Technology and Space in the funding program "Forschung an Fachhochschulen", project i2DACH (grant no. 13FH557KX0). The authors used ChatGPT 5 to improve the writing, make suggestions, and re-phrase. The authors reviewed and edited the content as needed and take full responsibility for the content of the publication.

References

1. Chen, C., Liu, Y., Shi, D., Cao, S., Cao, N.: Datascout: Automatic data fact retrieval for statement augmentation with an LLM-based agent. arXiv preprint arXiv:2504.17334 (2025)
2. Chen, J., Xiao, S., Zhang, P., Luo, K., Lian, D., Liu, Z.: M3-embedding: Multi-linguality, multi-functionality, multi-granularity text embeddings through self-knowledge distillation. In: ACL 2024, pp. 2318–2335., Bangkok, Thailand (2024). https://doi.org/10.18653/v1/2024.findings-acl.137
3. Chen, Z., Gu, Z., Cao, L., Fan, J., Madden, S., Tang, N.: Symphony: Towards natural language query answering over multi-modal data lakes. In: CIDR (2023)
4. Dettmers, T., Pagnoni, A., Holtzman, A., Zettlemoyer, L.: Qlora: efficient finetuning of quantized LLMs. In: Proceedings of the NeurIPS (2023)
5. Diamantini, C., et al.: A knowledge-based approach to support analytic query answering in semantic data lakes. In: Proceedings of the ADBIS (2022). https://doi.org/10.1007/978-3-031-15740-0_14
6. Elekes, A., Schaeler, M., Boehm, K.: On the various semantics of similarity in word embedding models. In: Proceedings of the AMC JCDL (2017). https://doi.org/10.1109/JCDL.2017.7991568
7. Hai, R., Koutras, C., Quix, C., Jarke, M.: Data lakes: a survey of functions and systems. IEEE Trans. Knowl. Data Eng. (2023). https://doi.org/10.1109/TKDE.2023.3270101
8. He, S.: Achieving tool calling functionality in LLMs using only prompt engineering without fine-tuning. arXiv preprint arXiv:2407.04997 (2024)
9. Hechler, E., Weihrauch, M., Wu, Y.: Data Fabric and Data Mesh Approaches with AI. Apress Berkeley, Berkeley, CA, USA (2023)
10. Hong, S., et al.: Metagpt: Meta programming for A multi-agent collaborative framework. In: Proceedings of the ICLR (2024). https://openreview.net/forum?id=VtmBAGCN7o
11. Hong, S., et al.: Data interpreter: An LLM agent for data science. In: Proceedings of the ACL (2025). https://aclanthology.org/2025.findings-acl.1016/
12. Hoseini, S., Ali, A., Shaker, H., Quix, C.: SEDAR: A semantic data reservoir for heterogeneous datasets. In: Proceeding of the CIKM (2023). https://doi.org/10.1145/3583780.3614753
13. Hoseini, S., Ibbels, M., Quix, C.: Enhancing machine learning capabilities in data lakes with automl and LLMs. In: Proceedings of the ADBIS, Springer (2024)
14. Hoseini, S., et al.: Coatings intelligence: Data-driven automation for chemistry 4.0. In: Proceedings of the ICPS. IEEE (2024). https://doi.org/10.1109/ICPS59941.2024.10640053
15. Jiang, H., Wu, Q., Lin, C.Y., Yang, Y., Qiu, L.: LLMLingua: Compressing prompts for accelerated inference of large language models. In: Proceedings of the EMNLP (2023). https://doi.org/10.18653/v1/2023.emnlp-main.825

16. Kataria, V., Kumar, N.: Democratizing cloud data lake analytics: natural language access to Apache iceberg via LLM agents. Front. Big Data **9** (2026). https://doi.org/10.3389/fdata.2026.1785710
17. Li, G., Zhou, X., Zhao, X.: LLM for data management. In: Proceedings of the VLDB Endow (2024). https://doi.org/10.14778/3685800.3685838
18. Liu, M., Wang, X., Xu, J., Yi, W., Wolfson, O.: A systematic review of natural language interfaces for databases. Frontiers Comput. Sci. (2026). https://doi.org/10.1007/S11704-025-50592-W
19. Liu, X., et al.: A survey of Text-to-SQL in the era of LLMs: Where are we, and where are we going? IEEE Trans. Knowl. Data Eng. (2025). https://doi.org/10.1109/TKDE.2025.3592032
20. Lumer, E., Subbiah, V.K., Burke, J.A., Basavaraju, P.H., Huber, A.: Toolshed: Scale tool-equipped agents with advanced rag-tool fusion and tool knowledge bases. Pro. ICAART (2025). https://doi.org/10.5220/0013303000003890
21. Muennighoff, N., Tazi, N., Magne, L., Reimers, N.: MTEB: massive text embedding benchmark. In: Proceedings of the EACL (2023). https://doi.org/10.18653/V1/2023.EACL-MAIN.148
22. Patel, L., Jha, S., Guestrin, C., Zaharia, M.: Lotus: Enabling semantic queries with LLMs over tables of unstructured and structured data. arXiv preprint arXiv:2407.11418 (2024)
23. Patil, S.G., Zhang, T., Wang, X., Gonzalez, J.E.: Gorilla: Large Language Model Connected with Massive Apis. Proc, NeurIPS (2024)
24. Schick, T., et al.: Toolformer: Language Models Can Teach Themselves to Use Tools. Proc, NeurIPS (2023)
25. Tang, X., et al.: Queryartisan: Generating data manipulation codes for ad-hoc analysis in data lakes. In: Proceedings of the VLDB Endow (2024). https://doi.org/10.14778/3705829.3705832
26. Tran, K., Dao, D., Nguyen, M., Pham, Q., O'Sullivan, B., Nguyen, H.D.: Multi-agent collaboration mechanisms: a survey of LLMs. CoRR (2025). https://doi.org/10.48550/ARXIV.2501.06322
27. Xi, Z., et al.: The rise and potential of large language model based agents: a survey. Sci. China Inf. Sci. (2025). https://doi.org/10.1007/S11432-024-4222-0
28. Yang, R., Song, L., Li, Y., Zhao, S., Ge, Y., Li, X., Shan, Y.: Gpt4tools: Teaching large language model to use tools via self-instruction. Proc, NeurIPS (2023)
29. Yao, S., et al.: React: Synergizing reasoning and acting in language models. In: Proceedings of the ICLR (2023)

Energy Plateaus and Privacy Cliffs in Deep-Learning Privacy-Preserving Record Linkage

Alexandros Karakasidis[1](✉) and Chairi Kiourt[2]

[1] Department of Applied Informatics, University of Macedonia, Thessaloniki, Greece
a.karakasidis@uom.edu.gr
[2] Athena Research Center, Xanthi, Greece
chairiq@athenarc.gr

Abstract. Deep-learning approaches to Privacy-Preserving Record Linkage (PPRL) deliver strong matching performance but incur computational costs that raise sustainability concerns. In this paper, we provide a model-driven characterisation of the energy – accuracy surface induced by a representative deep-learning PPRL pipeline. We show that the high-quality region of the configuration space forms a broad *plateau* in which energy costs vary substantially while matching quality does not, and we identify a sharp accuracy cliff concentrated at high differential-privacy noise. Both findings are formalised through phase-separated scaling-law cost models and a threshold-based accuracy model.

Keywords: Green AI · Privacy-Preserving Record Linkage · Energy Modeling · Differential Privacy

1 Introduction

Record linkage–the identification of records that refer to the same real-world entity across distinct datasets–is a foundational operation in healthcare, governance, and many domains where data integration is required. When the entities being linked are individuals, the operation must additionally preserve the privacy of personal information, giving rise to the problem of Privacy-Preserving Record Linkage (PPRL). PPRL has been the subject of sustained research over the past two decades, with approaches based on Bloom filters, locality-sensitive hashing, secure multi-party computation, and more recently, machine learning.

The deep-learning approach to PPRL introduced in [14] combines Bloom-filter encodings with differential-privacy noise injection and a neural-network classifier operating on similarity features. While this approach achieves strong matching performance, its reliance on neural-network training raises concerns about computational cost–concerns that fit into the broader Green AI agenda, which calls for explicit accounting of the energy and environmental costs of machine-learning research [16].

G. Vargas-Solar et al. (Eds.): ADBIS 2026, LNCS 16937, pp. 186–201, 2027.
https://doi.org/10.1007/978-3-032-39820-8_13

Practitioners deploying such a pipeline must navigate a configuration space spanning Bloom-filter geometry, differential-privacy strength, and neural-network architecture, with the joint impact on energy, matching quality, and privacy guarantees largely uncharacterised. In this paper, we provide that characterisation. We run the pipeline across four dataset sizes (2,000–20,000 records) over a 1,296-point factorial grid with three independent replicates per configuration, and we use the resulting measurements to fit interpretable scaling-law models that predict the cost and quality of unseen configurations.

The central finding is that the energy–accuracy surface has structure. The high-quality region of the configuration space forms a broad plateau in which energy costs vary by factors of three to four while matching quality does not, and the only sharp transition in the surface appears along the privacy axis, at high differential-privacy noise. Both observations are formalised through regression models with engineered, theory-derived predictors, and validated empirically through held-out-scale cross-validation.

Contributions. The contributions of this paper are:

1. A **systematic empirical evaluation** of deep-learning PPRL energy consumption across four dataset sizes (2,000 to 20,000 records), with three replicates per configuration over a 1,296-point factorial grid covering Bloom-filter geometry, differential-privacy noise, and neural-network architecture.
2. An **empirical characterisation** of the energy–accuracy surface, demonstrating that comparably-performing configurations form a broad plateau and identifying a sharp accuracy cliff at high differential-privacy noise.
3. **Phase-separated scaling-law cost models with held-out validation.** Cost is modelled separately for the feature-generation and neural-network phases of the pipeline using engineered, theory-derived predictors. Out-of-sample generalisation is established through leave-one-N-out cross-validation, with both models extrapolating to held-out dataset scales within bounds appropriate for practitioner use. A complementary threshold-based accuracy model allows practitioners to verify quality targets for unseen configurations.
4. A **reusable experimental dataset** of 1,296 PPRL configurations with three replicates, with energy measured via RAPL across both feature-generation and neural-network phases.[1]

The remainder of the paper is structured as follows. Section 2 reviews relevant work. Section 3 contains the background for this work. Section 4 presents the experimental setup. Section 5 develops the cost models and reports their validation. Section 6 characterises the energy–accuracy surface and the role of privacy. Section 7 discusses implications and limitations. Section 8 concludes.

[1] Available at: https://github.com/akarakasidis/pprl-energy-surface.

2 Related Work

2.1 Privacy-Preserving Record Linkage

A comprehensive survey of modern PPRL techniques may be found in [6]. Among existing approaches, Bloom filter-based methods utilizing n-grams have been particularly influential due to their balance of matching accuracy and computational efficiency [14,15]. Although effective, Bloom-filter-based PPRL has known vulnerabilities, motivating a range of hardening techniques [5]. Alternative approaches include MinHash-based pseudonymisation [17], two-step hash encodings [13], and cryptographic methods such as homomorphic encryption and garbled circuits [2,4,12]. While these provide stronger formal guarantees, they typically incur increased computational cost or reduced matching flexibility.

2.2 Deep Learning and LLMs for Entity Resolution

Entity resolution has increasingly adopted deep-learning approaches, including Siamese architectures and neural matching models [10,11]. More recently, large language models have been explored for entity resolution [9], although privacy-preserving variants remain largely unexplored. Within PPRL specifically, the deep-learning architecture of Ranbaduge et al. [14] represents one of the principal neural approaches and forms the basis of the present study.

2.3 Green AI and Empirical Cost Evaluation

Green AI frames computational and environmental cost as a first-class evaluation metric alongside predictive performance [16]. More broadly, Green Deep Learning has emerged as an active research area that seeks to reduce the computational, energy, and carbon costs of deep learning through efficient model architectures, training strategies, inference techniques, and data utilization [19]. Subsequent work has introduced reporting standards and large-scale empirical analyses of ML energy consumption [8]. Energy measurement in ML systems commonly relies on Intel's RAPL interface [3], `perun` [7], used in this work. Despite growing interest in sustainable ML, the intersection of Green AI and PPRL remains underexplored. Prior work in [18] provided an initial energy evaluation of a deep-learning PPRL pipeline at a single dataset scale. The present work goes beyond this direction by developing predictive models for energy and quality estimation across configurations.

3 Background

This section describes the PPRL pipeline under evaluation and the measurement methodology used to assess its energy consumption.

3.1 The Deep-Learning PPRL Pipeline

We evaluate the pipeline introduced in [14]. The pipeline assumes two data-holders who wish to identify matching records without revealing the underlying entities, mediated by a Linkage Unit.

Each record is tokenized into bigrams and encoded into a Bloom filter parameterized by a *capacity* (the maximum expected number of elements) and an *error rate* (the target false-positive rate). These parameters jointly determine the bit-array size m and the number of hash functions k via the standard Bloom-filter formulas. Privacy is introduced through randomized response: each bit is flipped independently with probability p_{flip}, a mechanism proven to provide ε-differential privacy at the Bloom-filter level [14], with $p_{\text{flip}} = 1/(1 + e^{\varepsilon/2nk})$ for k hash functions and at most n q-grams per record. A larger flip probability thus corresponds to a smaller ε and stronger privacy.

Candidate matches are generated by taking the Cartesian product of the two encoded datasets–no blocking is employed, unlike the reference design [14], to limit experimental factors. For each candidate pair, three similarity features are computed from the encoded Bloom filters: Jaccard similarity, Dice similarity, and Hamming distance. These three scalars are the input to a binary classifier—a feed-forward neural network with a configurable number of hidden layers and neurons per layer—trained with binary cross-entropy with logits on a class-weighted objective to address the imbalance between matching and non-matching pairs.

3.2 Energy Measurement

Energy consumption is measured using the Perun software [7], which exposes RAPL counters. Our analysis focuses on energy as the headline cost metric. We measure these quantities separately for the two computationally distinct phases of the pipeline: the *feature-generation* phase (Bloom-filter encoding plus candidate-pair similarity computation), and the *training-and-evaluation* phase (neural-network training plus prediction over the candidate set), whose scaling depends jointly on N and the network configuration.

4 Experimental Setup

4.1 Datasets

We use samples from the North Carolina voters dataset[2]. We construct four matched pairs of samples, with dataset sizes N = 2,000, 5,000, 10,000, and 20,000 records. In each pair, 25% of records are shared between the two samples (the true matches), and the second sample is corrupted using the German Record Linkage Center's data corrupter [1] with one edit-distance operation applied to a random field per record, ensuring that exact joins on the matching attributes

[2] Available at: https://dl.ncsbe.gov/?prefix=data.

return empty results. The 25% overlap ratio is held constant across dataset sizes so that scale is the only varying factor relevant to the matching task. The matching attributes are *last name*, *first name*, *middle name*, *address*, and *suburb*.

4.2 Configuration Grid

The full configuration grid varies seven factors, summarised in Table 1. We refer to the number of hidden layers as the network's *depth* (L) and the number of neurons per hidden layer as its *width*. The training batch size is fixed at 8192, the optimizer is Adam with learning rate 0.001, and candidate record pairs are split 60:20:20 for training, validation, and testing. Class weights are applied during training to account for the substantial imbalance between matching and non-matching pairs.

4.3 Matching Quality Metrics

For each configuration we record true positives, false positives, true negatives, and false negatives on the test set, and derive precision, recall, and F1. In the small number of cases where a model predicts no positives on the test set ($\mathrm{TP} + \mathrm{FP} = 0$), we set precision to zero and F1 to zero accordingly; this convention is applied consistently throughout.

4.4 Hardware and Software Environment

All experiments were run on a single physical machine to eliminate hardware-induced variability across measurements. Our host features an Intel i9 CPU with 64 GB of RAM on Ubuntu 24.04, running python 3.10 and PyTorch 2.8. Perun 0.8.10 was used for RAPL-based energy measurement.

5 Energy Cost Models

The two phases of the pipeline have different cost structures and are measured separately. We model them with two regressions, one per phase, fit to data with the appropriate unit of analysis: feature-generation cost is modelled on the 48 unique feature-generation measurements (one per (N, capacity, error rate, flip probability) combination), and NN-phase cost is modelled on the 1,296 NN measurements (one per full configuration). A practitioner-facing total cost is obtained by composing the two predictions arithmetically. Throughout, the modelling philosophy is that of empirical scaling-law analysis: predictors are engineered from the algorithm's data-generating process, functional forms are chosen to match theoretical expectations, and out-of-sample generalisation is established through held-out cross-validation.

Table 1. Configuration grid. The Cartesian product yields 1,296 distinct configurations, each run with three independent replicates.

Factor	Levels
Dataset size N	2000, 5000, 10000, 20000
Bloom filter capacity	100, 200
Bloom filter error rate	0.01, 0.1
Flip probability (DP noise)	0, 0.01, 0.1
Hidden layers	1, 2, 3
Neurons per hidden layer	4, 8, 16
Training epochs	5, 10, 20

5.1 Functional Forms

We model the energy of each phase as a function of its driving configuration factors. Let E_{fg} and E_{nn} denote the feature-generation and NN-phase energy in joules, L the number of hidden layers, and m and k the Bloom filter size and hash-function count from Sect. 3. The β terms are empirical scaling coefficients to be estimated from the data, α is a multiplicative constant with log-space form $\alpha' = \log \alpha$, and η is a zero-mean regression error term.

The feature-generation phase is dominated by the Cartesian product of two N-record datasets and per-pair Bloom-filter similarity computations whose cost scales with the bit-array size m and number of hash functions k. We posit a multiplicative cost model

$$E_{\text{fg}}(N, m, k) = \alpha \cdot N^{\beta_N} \cdot m^{\beta_m} \cdot k^{\beta_k} \cdot \exp(\eta), \tag{1}$$

which in log space is linear in the log-transformed predictors:

$$\log E_{\text{fg}} = \alpha' + \beta_N \log N + \beta_m \log m + \beta_k \log k + \eta. \tag{2}$$

The NN phase has two cost components with different scaling behaviour. Training repeats over the candidate pairs once per epoch, so its cost scales jointly with the number of pairs ($\Theta(N^2)$), the network architecture (depth L and width), and the number of epochs. Test-set evaluation runs once at the end of training regardless of the number of epochs, contributing a fixed $\Theta(N^2)$ overhead. The neural network operates on three scalar similarity features per candidate pair regardless of Bloom-filter size, so the Bloom-filter parameters have no mechanical route into either component. A log-linear specification

$$\log E_{\text{nn}} = \alpha' + \beta_N \log N + \beta_{\text{ep}} \log \text{epochs} + \beta_L \log L + \beta_{\text{neu}} \log \text{neurons} + \eta \tag{3}$$

captures both components in a single equation. As Sect. 5.4 shows, the dependence on network width is non-monotonic, motivating a specification in which width is treated categorically.

Choice of Estimator. We adopt ordinary least squares regression in log space rather than more flexible alternatives (polynomial regression, generalised additive models, decision-tree ensembles, neural surrogates) for three reasons. First, the dominant scaling behaviour is theory-predicted ($\Theta(N^2)$ from the Cartesian product), so a flexible estimator would primarily recover what is already known from the algorithm structure. Second, the resulting coefficients are directly interpretable as scaling exponents—how cost grows with each factor—which a practitioner can reason about without consulting a model artefact. Third, the log-linear specification is the standard form for scaling-law analyses in empirical machine-learning research, and adopting it makes the present results directly comparable to the broader Green AI literature. We report fit quality on the log scale (variation explained) and prediction error on the original joule scale (percentage error), the latter obtained by converting model predictions back from log space to joules before comparing them with measurements.

5.2 Variance Decomposition

Before fitting parametric models, we use analysis of variance (ANOVA) to decompose variation in each response. We fit an additive model with all relevant factors entered categorically and no interaction terms, attributing each factor's share of the total sum of squares (η^2). The categorical encoding makes no assumption about functional formfor example, the share attributed to N does not presuppose N^2 scalingso the decomposition identifies *which* factors matter, leaving *how* each enters the cost to the regressions that follow. Because the grid is a balanced full factorial, the factors are orthogonal and the shares are independent of entry order. Table 2 reports the results.

Table 2. Share of variation in each response explained by each factor (%).

Factor	$\log E_{\text{fg}}$ (%)	$\log E_{\text{nn}}$ (%)	F_1 (%)
N	97.0	94.7	0.4
capacity	1.9	0.0	0.0
error rate	0.9	0.0	5.9
p_{flip}	0.0	0.0	52.4
epochs	—	3.7	2.5
L	—	0.9	0.5
neurons	—	0.5	0.3
Residual	0.2	0.2	37.9

Four observations follow. First, energy is dominated by dataset scale: N alone accounts for 97% of the variance in feature-generation energy and 95% of the variance in NN-phase energy, while the evaluated factors leave residual variance below 0.2% in both phases. Second, the phase separation is substantiated by the decomposition: the dominant non-N factor differs between phases–Bloom-filter geometry for feature generation and epochs for the NN phase–whereas the architectural factors (epochs, layers, and neurons) together account for only about 5% of NN-phase energy variance. Third, F_1 behaves fundamentally differently from energy: p_{flip} alone accounts for 52% of the variance, with no other evaluated factor contributing more than 6%. Finally, residual F_1 variance remains substantial (38%), indicating variability not explained by the evaluated configuration factors. As discussed in Sect. 6, this pattern is consistent with stochastic neural-network training rather than systematic effects of the evaluated design.

5.3 Feature-Generation Cost Model

Feature-generation energy fits a log-linear model in N and the Bloom-filter parameters:

$$\log E_{\text{fg}} = -13.02 + 2.001 \log N + 0.682 \log m - 0.264 \log k, \tag{4}$$

matching the measured energy of the 48 unique feature-generation configurations to within about 1% of the variability in the data. The estimated exponent on N is 2.001 and is pinned tightly by the data: the four measured scales constrain it to within roughly ± 0.04 of this value. The result recovers the N^2 cost predicted by the Cartesian product over N-record datasets, and is consistent with the dashed slope-2 reference line in Fig. 1(a).

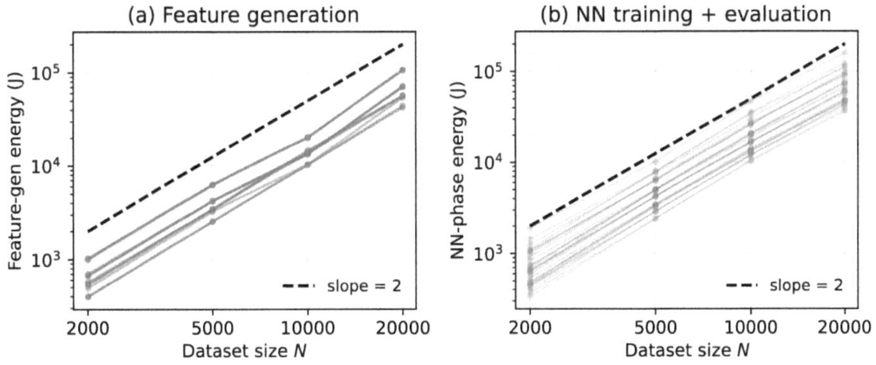

Fig. 1. Energy versus dataset size N on log-log axes, for (a) the feature-generation phase and (b) the NN training-and-evaluation phase. Each line shows one configuration of the non-N factors. The dashed reference lines have slope 2 and are placed alongside the data for visual comparison. Both phases scale as N^2 within tight tolerances.

5.4 NN-Phase Cost Model

Neuron width affects NN energy non-monotonically: 8 neurons are about 23% cheaper than 4, with no further reduction at 16. No single continuous slope can fit this shape, so a continuous-width specification misfits at every width level; we therefore treat neurons categorically, which gives the working model:

$$\log E_{\text{nn}} = -9.99 + 1.993 \log N + 0.596 \log \text{epochs} + 0.356 \log L + \gamma_{\text{neu}}, \quad (5)$$

where γ_{neu} is a constant set by the neuron count (Table 3); for example, an 8-neuron model subtracts 0.259 from the predicted log-energy, making it about 23% cheaper than the 4-neuron baseline. The model accounts for 99.7% of the variation across the 1,296 NN measurements. Energy again rises with the square of the dataset size—doubling N roughly quadruples NN-phase energy—as expected when every record must be compared against every other. The fit is tight. Adding training epochs costs less than proportionally: doubling the number of epochs adds only about 50% to NN-phase energy, not 100%, because the one-time cost of evaluating the test set is paid once no matter how many epochs are run, softening the effect of each extra epoch. Adding hidden layers also costs less than proportionally: going from 1 to 2 layers adds about 28%, and from 1 to 3 layers about 48%.

Table 3. Categorical offsets in the NN-phase energy model. The 4-neuron level is the baseline (offset 0); the values below are relative to it.

Level	Offset on $\log E_{\text{nn}}$
neurons = 8	−0.259
neurons = 16	−0.283

The 4-Neuron Penalty. The per-width constants capture a substantive finding: 4-neuron configurations cost 25–38% more than 8-neuron configurations depending on dataset size, with no further reduction at 16 (Fig. 2). The penalty is largest at the smallest dataset size ($N = 2{,}000$). We attribute it to the narrowest width underusing the hardware's matrix-multiply throughput—at width 4 the matrices may be too small to be processed efficiently—though we do not measure this directly. The absolute magnitude is therefore implementation-specific, depending on the underlying linear-algebra (BLAS) library, while the direction of the effect should generalise.

5.5 Leave-One-N-Out Cross-Validation

A model can describe the data it was trained on well yet still predict poorly. To test prediction at unseen scales, we refit each cost model with one dataset size held out, then use the refit model to predict energy at the held-out scale. Table 4 reports, for each held-out scale, the median percentage gap between predicted and measured energy across the held-out configurations. Errors are computed on the original joule scale after converting predictions back from log space.

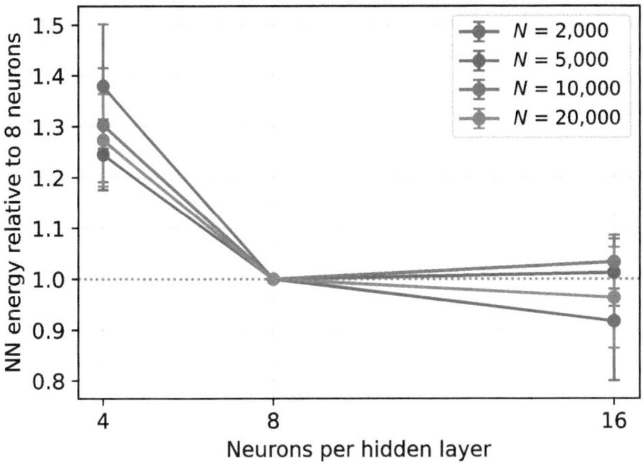

Fig. 2. NN-phase energy as a function of width, expressed as a ratio relative to the 8-neuron baseline at the same $(N, L, \text{epochs}, m, k, p_{\text{flip}})$. Configurations with 4 neurons cost 25–38% more than those with 8 neurons depending on dataset size; configurations with 16 neurons are essentially equivalent to those with 8. The pattern is consistent across dataset sizes.

The two phases behave differently. Feature-generation prediction is accurate at the smaller scales (median error under 7%). NN-phase prediction is accurate when the held-out scale falls between measured ones (5–8% median error) but degrades at the upper and lower boundaries (16–20%), reflecting the genuine difficulty of forecasting training cost beyond the measured range with only three other scales as anchors.

5.6 Composite Total Energy

For the practitioner-facing analyses in Sect. 6, total energy is the unit of interest. We predict it by estimating each phase from its own model, converting each prediction back from log space to joules, and adding the two:

$$\hat{E}_{\text{total}} = \exp(\widehat{\log E_{\text{fg}}}) + \exp(\widehat{\log E_{\text{nn}}}). \tag{6}$$

Total energy is therefore not a separate regression but the sum of two predictions, and it inherits the prediction error of each.

6 The Energy–Accuracy Surface

The cost models of Sect. 5 describe what configurations cost. This section examines what they buy in matching quality and how energy, accuracy, and privacy interact.

6.1 Matching Quality Across Configurations

Figure 3 shows the joint distribution of F_1 and total energy at each dataset size. We highlight the Pareto-optimal configurations: those for which no other configuration is both cheaper and higher-quality. Taken together they form the Pareto frontier—the set of configurations a cost-conscious practitioner need consider, since every other configuration is beaten on both axes by some point on the frontier. Two features are visible at every scale: the high-quality region forms a horizontal band near $F_1 = 1$ that spans a wide range of energies, and the frontier contains only 8–10 of the 324 configurations at each N. The horizontal band is the more consequential of the two: many configurations reach near-maximal quality while differing several-fold in energy, so quality alone does not single out an efficient configuration. Next, we develop this plateau and its implications.

Table 4. Prediction accuracy for the phase-separated cost models when each dataset size is held out from the training data in turn. Errors are median percentage gaps between predicted and measured energy across the held-out configurations.

Phase	Held-out N	Test type	Median error
Feature-generation	2,000	extrapolate down	6.2%
	5,000	interpolate	5.1%
	10,000	interpolate	14.7%
	20,000	extrapolate up	16.3%
NN training + evaluation	2,000	extrapolate down	16.2%
	5,000	interpolate	5.0%
	10,000	interpolate	8.4%
	20,000	extrapolate up	20.5%

6.2 The Plateau

Across all four dataset sizes, the configurations achieving $F_1 \geq 0.9$ form a substantial subset of the grid—between 144 and 183 of the 324 configurations at each N, roughly half. Within this high-quality region, total energy varies by a factor of 3.3 to 4.1 between the cheapest and most expensive configuration, yet F_1 barely moves: more energy buys at best a negligible quality gain, far too small to justify the several-fold cost.

The breadth of this plateau means practitioners have real choice among efficient operating points rather than a single best configuration. The cheapest configurations meeting the threshold share the same profile at every dataset size: capacity-100, error-rate-0.1 Bloom filters with single-layer networks of 8 or 16 neurons, trained for 5 epochs at zero or low privacy noise. That this profile recurs across all four scales indicates efficiency favours simple configurations and

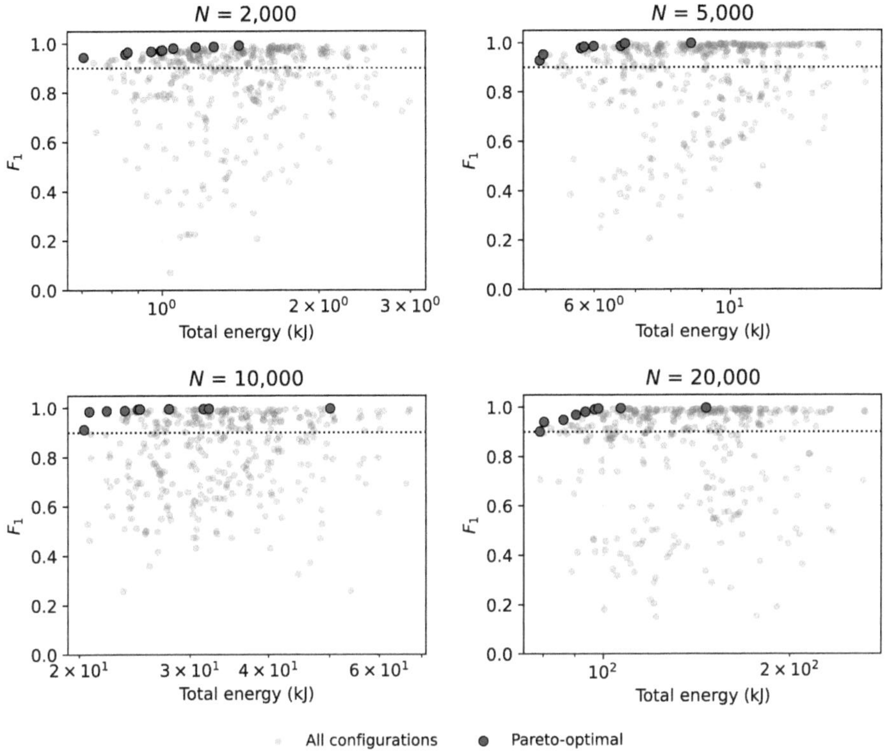

Fig. 3. F_1 versus total energy for all configurations at each dataset size. Pareto-optimal configurations (those for which no other configuration at the same N has both lower energy and higher F_1) are highlighted in red. The dotted reference line marks $F_1 = 0.9$. (Color figure online)

is not an artefact of any single dataset size—and that the larger, more expensive Bloom-filter geometries are not needed to reach high quality.

A likely explanation is that matching quality saturates. The classifier sees only a few similarity scores computed from each Bloom-filter pair, not the filters themselves; once those scores carry enough signal to separate matches from non-matches, enlarging the filter adds detail the classifier cannot use. Larger filters then cost more energy to compute without improving quality. We do not test this mechanism directly, but it is consistent with the flat energy–quality relationship across the plateau.

6.3 The Privacy Cliff

While the energy–accuracy face of the surface is largely flat, the privacy axis behaves very differently. Figure 4 shows mean F_1 as a function of flip probability at each dataset size. At flip probabilities of 0 and 0.01, mean F_1 stays between about 0.90 and 0.95 at every dataset size. At $p_{\text{flip}} = 0.1$ it falls to 0.59–0.68. Yet, energy is unaffected by flip probability: adding privacy noise changes matching quality but not the amount of computation, so it costs essentially no extra energy.

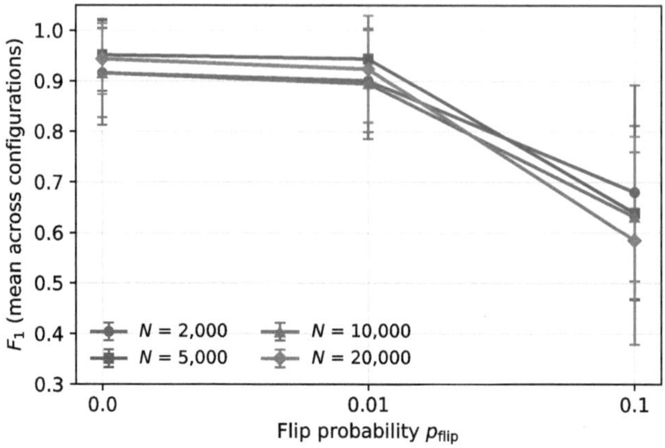

Fig. 4. Mean F_1 across configurations as a function of flip probability, at each dataset size. Error bars show one standard deviation across the configurations at the given (N, p_{flip}) combination. The behaviour is consistent across scales: F_1 is essentially flat between $p_{\text{flip}} = 0$ and $p_{\text{flip}} = 0.01$, then drops sharply at $p_{\text{flip}} = 0.1$.

The practical consequence is asymmetric. Low privacy noise is close to free: a flip probability up to about 0.01 leaves both matching quality and energy essentially unchanged. Strong privacy is not: pushing the flip probability to 0.1 collapses matching quality at a single step. Practitioners can therefore adopt flip probabilities up to roughly 0.01 without meaningful trade-off, but reaching 0.1 means either accepting badly degraded matching or switching to a different privacy mechanism.

6.4 A Threshold Model of Matching Quality

For practitioners, the question is usually not a configuration's exact F_1 but whether it clears a quality threshold. We model the probability that a configuration achieves $F_1 \geq 0.9$ as a logistic function of the configuration parameters.

The fitted model correctly predicts whether a configuration clears the threshold 83% of the time, against 52% for a baseline that always guesses the majority outcome—a 31-point improvement. The dominant predictor is flip probability: moving to $p_{\text{flip}} = 0.1$ makes a configuration about 130 times less likely to clear the threshold relative to no privacy noise (roughly 70 to 230 times), while moving to $p_{\text{flip}} = 0.01$ has only a small effect. The cliff seen in Sect. 6.3 reappears here through a different method, confirming the same feature.

Going from 4 to 8 neurons makes a configuration about 1.7 times more likely to clear the threshold, so the 4-neuron penalty seen in energy carries over into matching quality. Dataset size, once the other factors are fixed, has no appreciable effect. Combined with the cost models of Sect. 5, the threshold model gives a practitioner two things about an unseen configuration: an expected energy cost and a probability of meeting a chosen quality target.

6.5 Synthesis

The surface induced by this pipeline has three structural features, each quantified in the analyses above. First, energy cost depends almost entirely on dataset size and a few training parameters; the Bloom-filter parameters and the privacy mechanism barely affect it. Second, matching quality is driven most strongly by the privacy mechanism, with a sharp drop at $p_{\text{flip}} = 0.1$, while the remaining configuration parameters have a smaller and smoother effect. Third, within the high-quality region, energy varies several-fold while quality does not, so energy can be cut without sacrificing matching performance—mainly by not enlarging the Bloom filter beyond what the classifier can use.

Several observations reinforce these features. The high-quality plateaus are broad (144–183 of 324 configurations reach $F_1 \geq 0.9$), so many efficient operating points exist rather than a single best configuration. The energy scaling with N recovered here matches the N^2 scaling established analytically in Sect. 5. Efficient configurations favour simple architectures at every dataset size, and the threshold and Pareto analyses agree on the dominant factor (p_{flip}) and on the same secondary pattern (cheap configurations use small filters and modest networks). The structure is not a too-clean fit: a large share of F_1 variation (38%) is left unexplained by any configuration factor, consistent with the training-stability noise discussed earlier. Finally, the configuration reported as a single-scale sweet spot in earlier work on this method [18] sits within the plateau characterised here.

7 Discussion

7.1 Practical Recommendations

The results above support a few concrete configuration recommendations for practitioners deploying deep-learning PPRL. For matching quality at $p_{\text{flip}} \leq 0.01$, the cheapest configurations use capacity-100 Bloom filters with error rate 0.1 and single-layer networks of 8 or 16 neurons trained for 5 epochs. Going narrower (4 neurons) costs more energy and matches worse; going wider still (beyond 16) is unnecessary. Adding layers adds energy without improving threshold-clearing odds, and training beyond 5 epochs adds energy with diminishing returns. Stronger privacy ($p_{\text{flip}} = 0.1$) is feasible but carries an accuracy cost that no configuration choice can offset.

7.2 Limitations

Several limitations warrant explicit mention. Experiments are conducted on a single physical machine; this controls for hardware variability but makes the absolute energy figures machine-specific, including the size of the 4-neuron penalty, which depends on the BLAS implementation. The scaling exponents on N and epochs are theory-driven and should transfer; the intercepts will not. All experiments use one underlying dataset; the plateau and cliff may differ in shape for data with different attribute structures or match difficulty, and external validity rests on the theoretical scaling arguments rather than direct demonstration. Finally, we evaluate on the full Cartesian product, whereas the reference design [14] uses locality-sensitive-hashing blocking. Blocking reduces the candidate set below the full product and so lowers the $\Theta(N^2)$ feature-generation cost; the plateau itself, which arises from how much the classifier can use rather than from the number of pairs, should persist, though confirming this is left to future work.

8 Conclusion and Future Work

We have provided a systematic empirical characterisation of the energy–accuracy surface, and its privacy implications, induced by a representative deep-learning PPRL pipeline, supported by phase-separated cost models and a threshold-based accuracy model with held-out validation. The principal findings are that the high-quality region of the configuration space forms a broad plateau of comparably-performing configurations whose energy costs vary by several-fold; that the privacy mechanism produces a sharp accuracy drop at $p_{\text{flip}} = 0.1$ while leaving energy unchanged; and that the energy cost of the pipeline can be predicted to within roughly 5 to 20% median error at held-out dataset scales, using interpretable regression models with theory-derived predictors. The cost models account for almost all of the variation in energy (a residual under 0.2%), consistent with replicate-level measurement noise.

Several directions for future work follow naturally. External validation on additional datasets would strengthen the generalisability of the findings. Adding blocking would alter the cost structure substantially and is worth investigating in the same framework. Finally, comparing energy against other PPRL methods would give practitioners a broader basis for choosing among approaches.

Acknowledgment. This publication is based on work supported by the COST Action CA24161: Improving Neuroimaging Data for Sharing (INDoS).

Disclosure of Interests. The authors have no competing interests to declare that are relevant to the content of this article.

References

1. Bachteler, T., Reiher, J.: A test data generator for evaluating record linkage methods. Tech. rep., German RLC Working Paper No. wp-grlc-2012-01 (2012)
2. Chen, F., et al.: Perfectly secure and efficient two-party electronic-health-record linkage. IEEE Internet Comput. **22**(2), 32–41 (2018)

3. David, H., Gorbatov, E., Hanebutte, U., Khanna, R., Le, C.: RAPL: Memory power estimation and capping. In: Proceedings of the 16th ACM/IEEE International Symposium on Low Power Electronics and Design (ISLPED), pp. 189–194 ACM (2010)
4. Essex, A.: Secure approximate string matching for privacy-preserving record linkage. IEEE Trans. Inf. Forensics Secur. **14**(10), 2623–2632 (2019)
5. Franke, M., Sehili, Z., Rohde, F., Rahm, E.: Evaluation of hardening techniques for privacy-preserving record linkage. In: 24th International Conference on Extending Database Technology, pp. 289–300 OpenProceedings.org (2021)
6. Gkoulalas-Divanis, A., Vatsalan, D., Karapiperis, D., Kantarcioglu, M.: Modern privacy-preserving record linkage techniques: an overview. IEEE Trans. Inf. Forensics Secur. **16**, 4966–4987 (2021)
7. Gutiérrez Hermosillo Muriedas, J.P., Flügel, K., Debus, C., Obermaier, H., Streit, A., Götz, M.: Perun: Benchmarking energy consumption of high-performance computing applications. In: Cano, J., Dikaiakos, M.D., Papadopoulos, G.A., Pericàs, M., Sakellariou, R. (eds.) Euro-Par 2023: Parallel Processing, pp. 17–31. Springer Nature Switzerland, Cham (2023)
8. Henderson, P., Hu, J., Romoff, J., Brunskill, E., Jurafsky, D., Pineau, J.: Towards the systematic reporting of the energy and carbon footprints of machine learning. J. Mach. Learn. Res. **21**(248), 1–43 (2020)
9. Li, H., et al.: On leveraging large language models for enhancing entity resolution. arXiv preprint arXiv:2401.03426 (2024)
10. Li, X., Talburt, J.R., Li, T., Liu, X.: When entity resolution meets deep learning, is similarity measure necessary? In: Advances in Artificial Intelligence and Applied Cognitive Computing: Proceedings from ICAI'20 and ACC'20, pp. 127–140. Springer (2021)
11. Lv, Y., Qi, L., Huo, J., Wang, H., Gao, Y.: Joint multi-field Siamese recurrent neural network for entity resolution. In: PRICAI 2018: Trends in Artificial Intelligence, Part II, pp. 482–490. Springer (2018)
12. Mullaymeri, X., Karakasidis, A.: Using fuzzy vaults for privacy preserving record linkage. In: The 23rd International Workshop on Design, Optimization, Languages and Analytical Processing of Big Data. CEUR Workshop Proceedings, vol. 2840, pp. 101–110. CEUR-WS.org (2021)
13. Ranbaduge, T., Christen, P., Schnell, R.: Secure and accurate two-step hash encoding for privacy-preserving record linkage. In: Advances in Knowledge Discovery and Data Mining — 24th Pacific-Asia Conference. Lecture Notes in Computer Science, vol. 12085, pp. 139–151. Springer (2020)
14. Ranbaduge, T., Vatsalan, D., Ding, M.: Privacy-preserving deep learning based record linkage. IEEE Trans. Knowl. Data Eng. **36**(11), 6839–6850 (2024)
15. Schnell, R., Bachteler, T., Reiher, J.: Privacy-preserving record linkage using bloom filters. BMC Med. Inform. Decis. Mak. **9**, 41 (2009)
16. Schwartz, R., Dodge, J., Smith, N.A., Etzioni, O.: Green AI. Communications of the ACM **63**(12), 54–63 (2020)
17. Smith, D.: Secure pseudonymisation for privacy-preserving probabilistic record linkage. J. Inform. Security Appl. **34**, 271–279 (2017)
18. Sokorelis, E., Karakasidis, A., Protopapadakis, E., Kiourt, C.: An evaluation of energy consumption for deep learning-based privacy preserving record linkage. In: European Conference on Advances in Databases and Information Systems, pp. 171–180. Springer (2025)
19. Xu, J., Zhou, W., Fu, Z., Zhou, H., Li, L.: A survey on green deep learning (2021). https://arxiv.org/abs/2111.05193

Multi-algorithm GNN Aggregation Pipeline for Information Quality Enhancement

Rihab Ayed[1(✉)], Guilherme Medeiros Machado[1], Hassan Soubra[1], and Mohand-Said Hacid[2]

[1] LyRIDS, ECE Engineering School, OMNES Education, Paris, France
{rayed,gmedeirosmachado,hsoubra}@ece.fr

[2] Universit Claude Bernard Lyon 1, CNRS, LIRIS, UMR5205, 69100 Villeurbanne, France
mohand-said.hacid@univ-lyon1.fr

Abstract. Graph Neural Networks (GNNs) employ diverse aggregation strategies to transform node-level embeddings into graph-level representations. While heterogeneous GNNs like MAGNN or SMCD leverage metapath-based semantic aggregation, algorithms like EGAI focus on edge pruning to improve aggregate structural quality. Prior work shows that naive algorithm combinations can degrade performance. For example, directly combining meta-path-based (HAN) and meta-path-free (SimpleHGN) methods often degrades performance due to information redundancy, excessive parameterization, inadequate weighting mechanisms, and error propagation across stages. Strategies for combining GNN aggregation algorithms remain insufficiently studied. While individual algorithms achieve strong performance through combined aggregation strategies, principled approaches to integrate the complementary strengths of different as-is GNN algorithms have not been systematically studied. We propose a two-stage aggregation pipeline that integrates two GNN aggregation strategies: metapath-based aggregation (MAGNN, SMCD) and denoising of target node embeddings (using EGAI). This pipeline would reduce information noise while preserving heterogeneous graph semantics. We evaluate our approach on standard benchmarks (DBLP, IMDB) for the node classification task, comparing our results against standalone algorithms. We show that our principled sequential fusion strategy slightly outperforms the individual methods.

Keywords: Graph Neural Networks · Heterogeneous Aggregation · Embedding Quality · Metapath Learning · Structural pruning · Node classification

1 Introduction

Data aggregation [6] on graphs is fundamental to knowledge discovery, recommendation systems, and predictive analytics [8,9]. Graph Neural Networks

G. Vargas-Solar et al. (Eds.): ADBIS 2026, LNCS 16937, pp. 202–212, 2027.
https://doi.org/10.1007/978-3-032-39820-8_14

(GNN) [5,7] achieve this through neighborhood aggregation, updating node embeddings by combining information from neighboring nodes. To ameliorate the quality of aggregates, GNN aggregation algorithms employ diverse aggregation strategies oriented towards different objectives, such as Semantic preservation (e.g., MAGNN [2], HAGNN [9], SMCD [1]) and regularization techniques such as edge pruning (EGAI [4], BDE [3]),

A naive idea might be to combine these algorithms to leverage the benefits of different strategies. Recent work [9] demonstrates that the naive combination of GNN aggregation algorithms degrades performance due to information redundancy and conflicting inductive biases. Principled fusion aggregation strategies remain insufficiently studied. This raises a critical question: Can we design principled combination strategies that preserve the complementary strengths of different aggregation algorithms? This hypothesis leads us to propose a two-stage aggregation pipeline that integrates metapath-based aggregation (*e.g.* MAGNN, SMCD) with denoising mechanisms on target node types (*e.g.* EGAI) to reduce information noise while preserving heterogeneous graph semantics. We evaluate our approach on standard benchmarks (DBLP, IMDB) for node classification task, demonstrating when and why algorithm combinations can outperform or match individual methods. The main contributions of this paper are:

1. Dimensionality reduction insight: Show that collapsing to the target node type preserves performance while enabling focused refinement
2. Empirical analysis: Systematic evaluation on two benchmarks with different configurations
3. Design principles: Guidelines for when algorithm combinations could improve embedding quality

In the remainder of this paper, we present the related works (Sect. 2), the problem formulation (Sect. 3), the proposed pipeline (Sects. 4 and 5), and the achieved results and observations (Sects. 6 and 7), followed by the conclusions (Sect. 8).

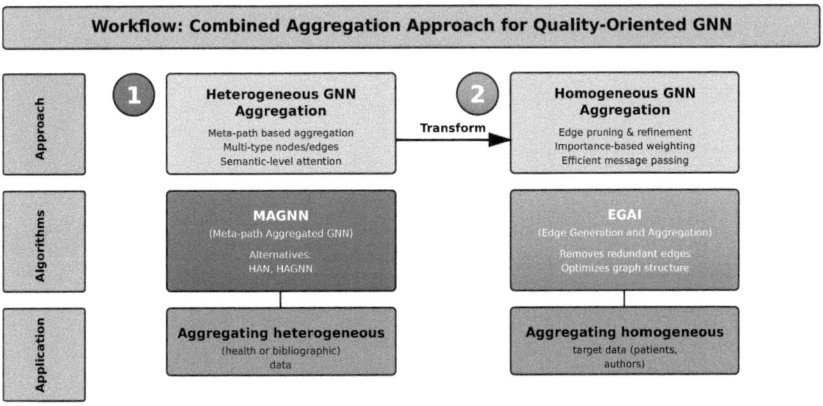

Fig. 1. Workflow for Combined Aggregation Approach for Quality-Oriented GNN

2 Related Works

We are interested in the two-stage pipeline which combines two strategies in GNN aggregation: *semantic preservation* and *noise reduction*. Algorithms such as MAGNN [2] use metapath-based aggregation with intra-metapath and inter-metapath attention mechanisms to capture complex semantic relationships (Fig. 1).

HAGNN [9] addresses information redundancy by combining inter-type and intra-type aggregation with fusion layers. SMCD [1] introduces semantic-aware meta-path augmentation by generating auxiliary meta-paths and perturbing core meta-path structures through diffusion based on semantic similarity. It also performs contrastive learning over multi-view meta-path embeddings to denoise representations and produce robust node embeddings. These GNN algorithms [1,2,9] output embeddings that already encode heterogeneous semantics, so we can safely collapse to the target type and apply homogeneous refinement without losing semantic information.

In the second stage, we studied noise reduction algorithms that are integrated into homogeneous GNN algorithms. The purpose is to clean the graph topology after its construction from node embeddings of the first stage. Regularization techniques such as EGAI [4] eliminate harmful edges by using inter- and intra-class nodes and pseudo-labeling prior to each GNN aggregation layer. Other techniques, such as AEE+BDE [3], have also been proposed for mitigating the over-smoothing of embeddings.

Prior attempts at combining complementary GNN architectures for better quality performance, such as in [9], conclude that naive combinations of GNN embeddings (e.g., metapath-based and metapath-free) can fail due to redundant information and misaligned embedding spaces. Success requires explicit fusion mechanisms that resolve conflicts between aggregation strategies. [9] proves that concatenating the embeddings of two aggregation algorithms can yield good performance.

3 Problem Formulation

The problem of quality-oriented heterogeneous graph aggregation can be formalized as follows. Given a heterogeneous graph $G = (V, E, T_V, T_E)$ where:

- V: node set with type function $\phi : V \to T_V$
- E: edge set with type function $\psi : E \to T_E$

Let $t^* \in T_V$ denote the target node type (e.g., authors in DBLP, patients in medical networks, movies in IMDB), and $V_{t^*} = \{v \in V : \phi(v) = t^*\}$ be the set of target nodes.

Goal: Learn embeddings $h_v \in \mathbb{R}^d$ for target nodes that maximize the quality for downstream tasks (*e.g.* node classification, link prediction).

4 Architecture

We present our architecture addressing the challenges from Sect. 2. We investigate two pipeline designs for combining GNN algorithms: aggregate fusion and sequential composition. Our approach sequences metapath-based semantic aggregation before edge-pruning-based noise reduction, motivated by two insights:

Insight 1: Semantic-First Ordering. Metapath aggregation must precede edge pruning: (i) metapaths capture high-order semantics lost if edges are pruned early, (ii) heterogeneous structure provides richer signals for identifying important connections, and (iii) collapsing to the target node type yields a refined homogeneous graph suited for denoising assessment.

Insight 2: Dimensionality Reduction without Performance Loss. Metapath aggregation first allows safe projection onto a homogeneous graph over target nodes, as learned embeddings already encode cross-type semantic information, eliminating the need to retain the full heterogeneous structure downstream.

4.1 Stage 1: Metapath-Based Embedding Extraction

Given a heterogeneous graph and predefined metapaths, we apply a metapath-based encoder to obtain target-node embeddings. The encoder aggregates information along each metapath and then fuses the resulting representations (see Algorithm 1).

Algorithm 1: Metapath-Based Embedding Extraction

Input: Heterogeneous graph G, metapaths $\mathcal{P}$, target type t^*
Output: Initial target-node embeddings $H^{(t^*)}$
for *each metapath* $P \in \mathcal{P}$ **do**
  Collect neighbors of target nodes following P;
  Compute metapath-specific embedding for target nodes;
Fuse all metapath-specific embeddings;
return $H^{(t^*)}$;

4.2 Stage 2: Edge Pruning and Homogeneous GNN

The embeddings from Stage 1 (metapath-based aggregation) are used to build a homogeneous graph for a target node type, using *k-NN* embedding similarity or *Wmeta* with metapath-neighbors that are above a minimum embedding similarity weight. EGAI prunes inter-class and uninformative intra-class edges using labels and pseudo-labels. A GCN trains on the pruned graph (Algorithm 2).

Algorithm 2: Edge Pruning and Homogeneous GNN

Input: Embeddings $H^{(t^*)}$, node $\in$ {k-NN, Wmeta}, pruning ratio r
Output: Refined embeddings $H^{(2)}$
Construct homogeneous graph using selected mode;
for *each epoch* **do**
  Score edges by similarity and class consistency;
  Remove bottom-r% edges;
  Train GCN with labels + pseudo-labels;
return $H^{(2)}$;

5 Experimental Setup

5.1 Training Hyperparameters

We report the configurations used for MAGNN [2], SMCD [1], and EGAI [4] to ensure reproducibility. In the following, bolded values indicate parameters that were modified from the released code defaults [1].

Stage 1 *MAGNN* [2]: Adam ($\eta = 0.005$, $\lambda = 0.001$), hidden dim 64, 2 layers, 8 attention heads, dropout 0.5, 100 epochs, 10 runs, seed 1566911444.
SMCD [1]: Adam ($\eta = 0.001$ IMDb, 0.0008 DBLP), $\lambda = 0$, 950 epochs, 5 runs, hidden dim 64, $d_{\text{emb}} = 8$, feat_drop = 0.4, attn_drop = 0.3/0.35. Modified parameters: $\boldsymbol{\theta}_{\text{mp}} = \mathbf{0.3}$ (IMDb), 0.7 (DBLP); $\boldsymbol{\lambda}_{\text{mp}} = \mathbf{0.8}$; $\boldsymbol{\lambda}_{\text{ic}} = \mathbf{0.5}$ (IMDb), 1.0 (DBLP); $\lambda_{\text{cg}} = 5\times10^{-6}$ (IMDb), 10^{-5} (DBLP); $\tau = 0.5$ (IMDb), 0.9 (DBLP). Diffusion: $T = 50$, sampling steps = 50 (IMDb), 0 (DBLP). Evaluation: 200 epochs, $\eta = 0.25$, seed 0.

Stage 2 *EGAI / MAGNN+EGAI* [4]: Adam ($\eta = 0.01$, $\lambda = 0.0005$), input dim 64, hidden dim 16, 2-layer GCN, patience 10. Pruning ratios and pseudo-label percentages $\in \{10\%, 50\%, 80\%\}$; 18 configurations (2 seeds $\times$ 3 ratios $\times$ 3%); mean results reported.
SMCD+EGAI: Adam ($\eta = 0.01$), hidden dim $\in \{\mathbf{16}, \mathbf{64}\}$, dropout 0.5, 200 epochs, **no early stopping**, seed 0, $k \in \{5, 10, 15, 20\}$. Pruning ratios and pseudo-label percentages $\in \{10\%, 50\%, 80\%\}$, 2 seeds. Best validation results reported.

5.2 Baselines

MAGNN or SMCD embeddings feed into EGAI under two edge construction schemes: **(kNN)** k-nearest neighbors by embedding similarity, **(Wmeta)** weighted metapath fusion with similarity threshold, to verify gains are not solely from kNN.

5.3 Datasets

We rely on two versions of preprocessed DBLP and IMDB datasets[1,2] provided by MAGNN and SMCD authors, respectively (see Table 1).

Table 1. Datasets used in experiments.

	Dataset	Nodes	Meta-paths
MAGNN	DBLP	A/P/T/V: 4K/14K/8K/20	APA, APTPA, APVPA
	IMDB	M/A/D: 4K/5K/2K	MDM, MAM
SMCD	DBLP	A/P/V: 4K/14K/20	APA; APVPA, PAP
	IMDB	M/A/D: 5K/6K/2K	MAM, MDM; AMA, DMD

5.4 Evaluation Protocol

Each algorithm (MAGNN, SMCD, EGAI) was evaluated using its native protocol for the node classification task. For MAGNN+EGAI, we adopt EGAI's evaluation protocol with its as-is parameters, which evaluates embeddings inline during generation. For SMCD+EGAI, we evaluate the results with both SMCD and EGAI native protocols. SMCD evaluation protocol trains a logistic regression classifier over 200 epochs on the frozen embeddings. The paper results rely on downstream performance for node classification, the same metrics (Macro-F1, Micro-F1) used for assessing MAGNN, SMCD and EGAI are used here.

6 Results

The reported F1 scores are evaluated on the test set corresponding to each training split.

6.1 MAGNN-Driven Pipeline

For training splits, we report results for the smallest and largest splits provided by MAGNN and EGAI: 20% and 80%. Tables 2 and 3 reveal consistent patterns across both metrics. On DBLP, *MAGNN+EGAI (k-NN)* achieves the strongest results, reaching 94.19% Macro-F1 and 94.66% Micro-F1 at 80% training, a gain of more than 12 pp over standalone EGAI (k-NN) and roughly 1 pp over MAGNN alone. In contrast, *MAGNN+EGAI (Wmeta)* performs poorly on DBLP (77.63% Macro-F1 at 20%, 86.46% at 80%), despite improving over standalone EGAI (Wmeta).

This underperformance can be attributed to DBLP's sparse and heterogeneous structure, where metapath-based edge construction introduces noisy or irrelevant connections that degrade the quality of the augmented graph,

Table 2. Node classification results (Macro-F1 %) - MAGNN variants

Method	Train %	DBLP	IMDB
MAGNN	20%	92.74 ± 0.35	58.01 ± 0.84
	80%	93.34 ± 0.80	**60.04 ± 1.62**
EGAI (k-NN)	20%	81.55 ± 0.57	53.30 ± 1.50
	80%	81.96 ± 0.45	54.86 ± 0.47
EGAI (Wmeta)	20%	42.34 ± 17.01	58.95 ± 0.55
	80%	70.48 ± 3.39	59.30 ± 0.63
MAGNN+EGAI (k-NN)	20%	**93.93 ± 0.21**	59.30 ± 0.29
	80%	**94.19 ± 0.25**	59.13 ± 0.27
MAGNN+EGAI (Wmeta)	20%	77.63 ± 8.14	**60.05 ± 0.33**
	80%	86.46 ± 2.11	**60.51 ± 0.32**

Table 3. Node classification results (Micro-F1 %) - MAGNN variants

Method	Train %	DBLP	IMDB
MAGNN	20%	93.28 ± 0.33	58.07 ± 0.82
	80%	93.81 ± 0.78	**60.16 ± 1.68**
EGAI (k-NN)	20%	82.22 ± 0.52	53.78 ± 1.05
	80%	82.70 ± 0.42	54.60 ± 0.46
EGAI (Wmeta)	20%	51.60 ± 13.88	59.05 ± 0.55
	80%	73.75 ± 2.17	59.29 ± 0.66
MAGNN+EGAI (k-NN)	20%	**94.45 ± 0.16**	59.97 ± 0.25
	80%	**94.66 ± 0.21**	59.87 ± 0.22
MAGNN+EGAI (Wmeta)	20%	84.51 ± 4.23	**60.83 ± 0.29**
	80%	88.68 ± 1.65	**61.18 ± 0.34**

whereas k-NN relies on embedding similarity and is more robust to such sparsity. On IMDB, *MAGNN+EGAI (Wmeta)* delivers the highest scores (60.51% Macro-F1, 61.18% Micro-F1 at 80%), marginally surpassing MAGNN while substantially reducing its variance. IMDB's two metapaths (MAM, MDM) capture complementary semantic relationships actor and director co-occurrence providing diverse relational signals for Wmeta edge construction. In contrast, DBLP's metapaths (APA, APTPA, APVPA) all revolve around author-paper co-authorship, making them more redundant and prone to introducing noisy edges.

6.2 SMCD-Driven Pipeline

For *SMCD+EGAI*, results are reported under the edge pruning ratio and pseudo-label node percentage that yielded the best validation performance.

Unlike *MAGNN+EGAI*, which outperforms MAGNN on average across parameter configurations, *SMCD+EGAI* only surpasses SMCD under specific settings, reflecting the limited margin left by SMCD's already strong baseline.

Table 4. Effect of evaluation learning rate on SMCD performance (IMDB) (percent 80%, ratio 80%, k=10, d=64) - SMCD evaluation protocol.

Method	Eval LR	Macro-F1	Micro-F1
SMCD	0.25	**73.82 ± 0.22**	**77.95 ± 0.09**
	0.01	53.72 ± 1.35	70.49 ± 0.41
SMCD+EGAI	0.25	**74.89 ± 0.48**	**77.93 ± 0.20**
	0.01	73.42 ± 0.12	77.91 ± 0.11

Learning rate variation : Standalone SMCD collapses by 20 pp Macro-F1 when evaluated at $\eta = 0.01$ instead of its native $\eta = 0.25$ (Table 4).

SMCD+EGAI remains more stable across both rates (74.89% vs. 73.42%, Table 4). EGAI refinement therefore absorbs the evaluation-protocol sensitivity of the Stage 1 backbone, making the pipeline less sensitive to learning rate choice at inference time.

Table 5. Embedding size, k, and evaluation protocol effects on SMCD variants performance (percent 80%, ratio 80%) - IMDB

Method	k	Dim	Macro-F1	Micro-F1
EGAI evaluation protocol				
SMCD + EGAI	5	16	71.97 ± 0.30	77.36 ± 0.08
	5	64	74.07 ± 0.20	**78.09 ± 0.13**
	10	64	73.85 ± 0.05	77.54 ± 0.06
	15	64	**74.16 ± 0.25**	77.83 ± 0.04
SMCD evaluation protocol				
SMCD	-	16	70.47 ± 0.10	74.06 ± 0.17
SMCD	-	64	73.78 ± 0.13	77.92 ± 0.08
SMCD + EGAI	5	64	**74.13 ± 0.39**	77.88 ± 0.22

Embedding dimension and k-NN variations: Across both datasets, `dim=` 64 consistently outperforms `dim=` 16, with a ~2 pp gain on IMDB (71.97 → 74.07, Table 5) and ~1.8 pp on DBLP (95.47 → 97.24, Table 7), confirming that embedding size is a key factor regardless of the dataset.

Table 6. Overall performance of SMCD+EGAI ($k = 5$, mean ratios) - IMDB - EGAI evaluation protocol

Method	Dim	Train %	Macro-F1	Micro-F1
SMCD+EGAI	64	80%	73.98 ± 0.16	77.85 ± 0.20
		20%	73.46 ± 0.57	77.73 ± 0.30
SMCD +EGAI	16	80%	72.18 ± 0.37	77.51 ± 0.16
		20%	*60.72 ± 4.75*	*73.47 ± 1.52*

The effect of k is however dataset-dependent: on IMDB, varying k from 5 to 15 yields a decrease in Macro-F1 (78.09 to 77.83), whereas on DBLP performance improves incrementally with larger k, peaking at $k = 20$ (97.62 under EGAI protocol, Table 7). Table 6 confirms that `dim`= 64 yields stronger and more stable results than `dim`= 16 on the mean ratios of edge pruning. At `dim`= 16, performance degrades sharply at 20% training (60.72% Macro-F1), suggesting that a small embedding size combined with limited pseudo-labeled data from EGAI leads to unstable representations in the SMCD+EGAI pipeline.

Table 7. Embedding size, k, and evaluation protocol effects on SMCD variants performance (ratio, percent set at best performance) - DBLP

Method	Train %	Prune Ratio	***k***	Dim	Macro-F1	Micro-F1
			SMCD evaluation protocol			
SMCD	-	-	-	16	95.47 ± 0.11	95.75 ± 0.11
SMCD	-	-	-	64	97.24 ± 0.03	97.46 ± 0.03
SMCD+EGAI	80%	80%	5	64	97.44 ± 0.08	97.65 ± 0.07
	50%	80%	20	64	**97.55 ± 0.05**	**97.74 ± 0.04**
			EGAI evaluation protocol			
SMCD+EGAI	80%	80%	5, 10	64	97.36 ± 0.02	97.59 ± 0.01
	80%	80%	15	64	97.49 ± 0.05	97.69 ± 0.05
	50%	80%	20	64	**97.62 ± 0.05**	**97.82 ± 0.04**

Evaluation protocol variation: Tables 5 and 7 show that the choice of evaluation protocol has a marginal effect on SMCD+EGAI performance. For example, on IMDB, the EGAI protocol yields 74.16% Macro-F1 compared to 74.13% under the SMCD protocol. In both cases, the EGAI evaluation protocol produces slightly higher scores, though the differences remain negligible.

7 Discussion

Why the Pipeline should be further pushed: (1) EGAI prunes homogeneous graphs; applying MAGNN or SMCD first constructs refined homogeneous graphs over target nodes, enabling effective pruning while preserving semantic paths. (2) Metapaths capture long-range dependencies; edge pruning handles local noise. (3) Sequential design avoids embedding space misalignment inherent in naive combinations [9]. (4) The pipeline improves robustness over the standalone backbone: SMCD+EGAI remains stable across evaluation learning rates where standalone SMCD collapses by 20 pp Macro-F1 (Table 4), suggesting that edge pruning and pseudo-label refinement absorb sensitivity to evaluation hyperparameters introduced by Stage 1. (5) Combining the outputs of complementary aggregation strategies has been widely shown to improve performance in the literature [9]. Our sequential design currently uses Stage 1 embeddings as input to Stage 2; a promising future direction is to explicitly combine SMCD and EGAI embeddings for instance through concatenation or attention-based fusion to further leverage the complementary strengths of both aggregation strategies.

8 Conclusion

The framework validates principled GNN algorithm combination as an alternative to monolithic architectures, opening paths for multi-stage pipelines where specialized algorithms compose as modular components. Several directions remain open: (1) the choice of Stage 2 edge construction strategy (k-NN vs. Wmeta) is a basic approach, graph structure learning strategies could further improve results; (2) explicitly concatenating Stage 1 and Stage 2 embeddings could yield additional gains; (3) EGAI yields modest gains in its original formulation, and substituting it with stronger denoising algorithms in Stage 2 could unlock more substantial improvements. Future work should evaluate the updated pipeline on additional tasks (e.g., link prediction) and diverse heterogeneous graph datasets to extract guidelines for effective sequential GNN aggregation. To facilitate reproducibility, all code and datasets will be publicly available at HybAgg Github.

Disclosure of Interests. The authors have no competing interests to declare.

References

1. Ding, G., Tang, R., Mo, X.: Enhancing heterogeneous graph learning with semantic-aware meta-path diffusion and dual optimization. Knowl. Based Syst. pp. 115385 (2026). gitHub: https://github.com/Ding-guang-hua/SMCD
2. Fu, X., Zhang, J., Meng, Z., King, I.: MAGNN: metapath aggregated graph neural network for heterogeneous graph embedding. In: Proceedings of The Web Conference (WWW) (2020). gitHub: https://github.com/cynricfu/MAGNN

3. Hoseinnia, F., Ghatee, M., Chehreghani, M.H.: Mitigating over-smoothing in graph neural networks for node classification through adaptive early embedding and biased dropedge procedures. Knowl.-Based Syst. **320**, 113615 (2025)
4. Liu, C., Wu, J., Liu, W., Hu, W.: Enhancing graph neural networks by a high-quality aggregation of beneficial information. Neural Netw. **142**, 20–33 (2021). gitHub: https://github.com/liucoo/egai
5. Wang, X., et al.: Heterogeneous graph attention network. In: The World Wide Web Conference, pp. 2022–2032 (2019)
6. Wen, T.: Data aggregation. Encylopedia of Big Data. Springer, Cham (2020)
7. Wu, Z., Pan, S., Chen, F., Long, G., Zhang, C., Philip, S.Y.: A comprehensive survey on graph neural networks. IEEE trans. neural netw. learn. syst. **32**(1), 4–24 (2020)
8. Zequn Sun, Chengming Wang, W.H.M.C.J.D.W.Z.Y.Q.: Knowledge graph alignment network with gated multi-hop neighborhood aggregation. In: AAAI, pp. 222–229 (2020)
9. Zhu, G., Zhu, Z., Chen, H., Yuan, C., Huang, Y.: HAGNN: hybrid aggregation for heterogeneous graph neural networks. IEEE Trans. Neural Netw. Learn. Syst. (2024)

Text, GNNs, Privacy and Ethereum Analytics

Can Data Postdiction Extend to Text? An Experimental Evaluation of Vectorization Strategies

Brian T. Nixon(✉) and Panos K. Chrysanthis

University of Pittsburgh, Pittsburgh, PA 15213, USA
{nixon.b,panos}@cs.pitt.edu

Abstract. Data postdiction is a lossy compression technique that replaces stored values with ML models under per-value error guarantees, but its applicability to textual data is unexplored. This paper investigates extending it to text via LLMs and vectorization approaches. LLMs are ruled out due to hallucination, unpredictable training costs, and poor scalability. Evaluating Word2Vec, UTF-8 binary encoding, and Qwen3 embeddings on real-world datasets, none reliably recover semantically meaningful text. We conclude that data postdiction, similar to traditional lossy compression methods, does not generalize well to textual data, and for the time being, lossless compression remains the recommended approach .

Keywords: data postdiction · lossy text compression · vectorization

1 Introduction

The challenge of reducing large volumes of textual data efficiently is a long-standing problem in data management. As relational databases increasingly store free-text attributes alongside numerical data, the need for effective compression of textual columns has grown substantially. While lossless compression methods remain the predominant strategy for reducing textual data, they face fundamental storage reduction limits, motivating the exploration of lossy alternatives.

Data postdiction has emerged as a promising lossy compression technique for numerical data, replacing stored values with trained regression models while enforcing per-value relative error guarantees (Fig. 1). Baskin et al. [2] extended this approach with clustering, outlier detection, and accuracy tuning, demonstrating strong storage reductions on numerical datasets. However, the applicability of data postdiction to textual attributes remains an open question.

A natural candidate for extending postdiction to textual data is the use of large language models (LLMs), which have demonstrated remarkable generative capabilities across diverse domains. However, directly applying LLMs to textual data postdiction introduces *hallucination*, *storage overhead* from model parameters, and *poor scaling* with dataset size, raising concerns about their practical viability for textual compression.

G. Vargas-Solar et al. (Eds.): ADBIS 2026, LNCS 16937, pp. 215–231, 2027.
https://doi.org/10.1007/978-3-032-39820-8_15

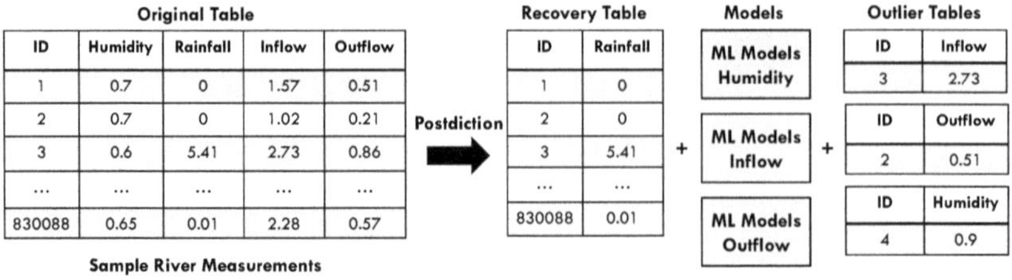

Fig. 1. Example of basic data postdiction on river measurements.

This paper investigates whether data postdiction can be extended to textual data through vectorization-based approaches, which encode text as numerical representations compatible with the existing data postdiction pipeline. Specifically, we evaluate *Word2Vec* [15], binary *UTF-8* encodings, and Qwen3 embeddings [1] as vectorization techniques and assess their effectiveness across two textual datasets. We also explore the use of fine-tuned LLMs.

Our key finding is that current data postdiction approaches, similar to traditional lossy compression methods, fail to generalize effectively to textual data. Consequently, lossless compression remains the only reliable option at present.

The paper is organized as follows. Section 2 reviews compression techniques and the postdiction pipeline. Sections 3–4 discuss LLMs and our vectorization approaches. Sections 5–7 detail the experimental evaluation and concludes.

2 Background and Related Work

2.1 Common Compression Techniques

Compression methods broadly split into *lossless* and *lossy* techniques. *Lossless compression* recovers data exactly, using techniques that fall into a few main families: statistical methods (Huffman, Arithmetic Coding) assign shorter codes to frequent symbols; run-length and Rice coding handle repeated sequences; dictionary approaches (LZ77/78, LZW) store recurring patterns in codebooks; and transform methods like Burrows-Wheeler rearrange data to expose redundancy. Hybrids like DEFLATE and Zstandard combine these. A newer method, LeCo [13], fits regression models over data partitions and stores only predictions and residuals. The fundamental limit of all lossless methods is that they cannot distort data, which limits how much they can compress.

Lossy compression trades accuracy for greater size reduction. Transform methods (DCT, wavelets) apply irreversible math to signals. Predictive methods estimate values from context, e.g., MPEG stores frame differences in video, LPC captures only resonance moments in speech. For numerical data, SZ [11] fits polynomial regression to neighbors and quantizes errors within a user-defined bound, while ZFP [12] uses a block transform with fixed-rate encoding. For time series specifically, Sim-Piece [10] merges similar line segments and PAA [24] replaces segments with mean values. A further specialized approach, data postdiction, targets time-series telecom data [5] by first spatially clustering records by proximity to cell towers, then temporally ordering them within each cluster so that stale, low-utility values can be replaced by predictions of the LSTM model. None of these lossy methods, however, extend to text.

Recent work has explored LLM-based semantic compression for text, including prompt-level compression [8], context window extension via summarization models [7], and lossy LLM-decompressible codes [20]. Unlike these approaches, which target prompt efficiency or context window extension for LLM inference, our work evaluates vectorization strategies for database-oriented data postdiction, where the goal is storage reduction under per-value error guarantees.

2.2 Data Postdiction Pipeline

We generalized data postdiction (Fig. 2) to numerical datasets beyond telco data by utilizing *feature selection*, *outlier detection*, *clustering*, and *accuracy tuning* with per-value error guarantees [2,16]. *Feature selection* determines which attributes to replace and which to preserve as inputs. *Outlier detection* removes anomalous values before or after model training to improve prediction quality. *Clustering* groups similar values within a column to allow models to replace them with lower distortion. Each cluster has an independently trained model. *Accuracy Tuning* enforces a user-specified per-value relative error threshold by maintaining values whose predictions fall outside the threshold in a separate outlier table. Any values stored within an outlier table are not replaced by models.

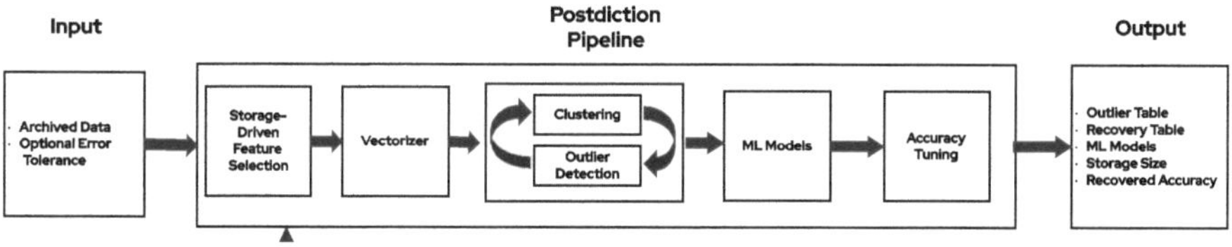

Fig. 2. Data Postdiction Pipeline

3 LLMs Fall Short

The first technique that was used in our attempt to handle textual data was fine-tuned GPT models through OpenAI [17]. We initially trained the first 100 rows of a wine description dataset. Each training example consisted of a prompt encoding all predictor column values in a structured natural-language format, with the target column value as the expected response. This prompt structure was designed to generalize across any target column.

Several limitations made this approach infeasible at scale. Training on just 100 examples required 13 min via the OpenAI API. Extrapolating to the full

130,000-row dataset, with multiple training rounds required by the clustering pipeline, renders the approach computationally impractical. Beyond timing, the reliance on external compute introduced inconsistency entirely outside the pipeline's control. Early evaluations also revealed quality issues: while some predictions matched exactly, others hallucinated plausible-sounding but incorrect content, and responses occasionally contained spurious special characters.

These results expose a fundamental tension between LLMs and the postdiction pipeline's requirements. LLMs are designed for open-ended generation rather than precise value retrieval, making hallucination an intrinsic risk rather than an incidental one. Their reliance on external compute also introduces latency and variability incompatible with a tightly controlled pipeline. Rather than a limitation of this particular implementation, these shortcomings suggest that LLMs are structurally ill-suited as a postdiction step, motivating the search for more deterministic, self-contained alternatives.

4 Textual Data Postdiction

This section describes our exploration of a textual postdiction pipeline implemented using textual encodings and embeddings as shown in Fig. 2.

4.1 Relative User Dissimilarity

The original error metric [2] replaces a value when an ML model predicts it within specified bounds, but does not capture textual semantics such as word similarity, context, and sentence structure. We adopted cosine similarity due to its ability to capture semantic similarity in vectorized text and its widespread use in NLP. Cosine similarity ranges from -1 (completely dissimilar) to 1 (identical), with 0 representing neutral similarity. Given a user's *relative dissimilarity tolerance*, ϵ, the relative error is mapped onto cosine similarity's range as:

$$\text{similarity\_error\_threshold} = 1 - (2 \times (\epsilon \times \frac{1}{100})) \quad (1)$$

A predicted vector is considered acceptable if its cosine similarity to the original vector exceeds the computed threshold.

4.2 Word2Vec Encodings

The first approach utilizes Word2Vec models [15] to transform each word within a textual value to a dimension of a numerical vector. It involves using a multi-layered neural network to find relationships between terms used in a corpus, and using those relationships, assigns a vector to each term such that words close to each other in the vector space are semantically similar.

Given the reliability of Word2Vec in the NLP space, if the original vector representation of a piece of text is sufficiently similar to that of a recovered vector from the ML model, these vectors should be semantically similar. Although these

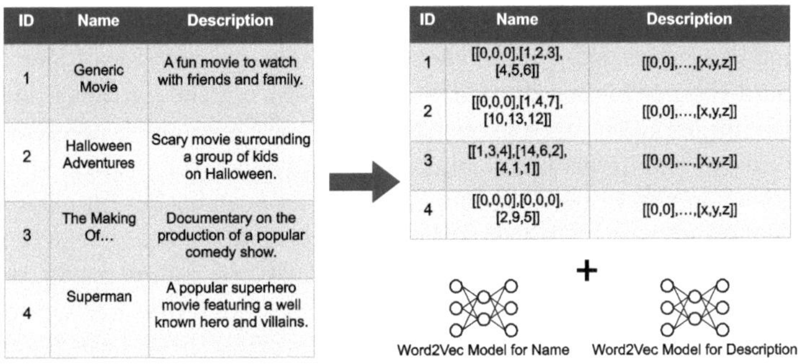

Fig. 3. Using Word2Vec to Convert Textual Columns to Numerical Vectors

models allow postdiction to be performed on textual data, the use of Word2Vec models also introduces additional storage overheads for the encoding models to convert the generated vectors back to text, as seen in Fig. 3. Within the *Vectorizer* module, textual attributes are used as a corpus to train a Word2Vec model with each attribute training an independent Word2Vec model. To ensure vectors of the same length, a requirement for LR and LSTM models, each attribute is scanned for the maximum number of words within a single value before training Word2Vec models. If the textual data contains a smaller sentence with fewer words than the maximum length, the vector is padded using zeros to ensure equal length vectors. As each batch updates the training of the Word2Vec model, values within the batch are converted to numerical vectors based on the mappings generated by the Word2Vec model. From there, the batched vector data are mapped to clusters within the replaced attribute.

With the updated relative dissimilarity error metric, the Accuracy Tuning module was updated to utilize the cosine similarity error metric when determining whether a value should be marked as an outlier. That is, if the cosine similarity between a vector generated from the original word and the ML model predicted vector satisfies the similarity threshold defined in Eq. 1, the data point would be replaced by the cluster and ML model.

Calculating the final size of the pipeline's output was also updated to reflect the textual data type. Since each predicted vector will always be padded to the maximum number of words within a value and assuming that each numerical representation is eight bytes, the total size of a replaced column is computed by:

$$\text{Replacement Column Size} = (8 \times \text{max vector length}) \times \text{cardinality}$$

The original dataset size, without reductions, assumes that each character requires one byte and sums the length of each textual value during the *fitting* phase. However, the Word2Vec models produced for encoding each attribute would also need to be preserved, so that values can be recovered by predicting vectors from the ML models and transforming predictions to textual data with the Word2Vec models. The Word2Vec model size introduces an additional storage overhead on top of the storage costs of ML models and outlier values. If a textual dataset is too small, adding a Word2Vec model would result in expansion, rather than reduction, in the sense that the storage size of the pipeline's output would require higher storage costs than storing the dataset in its original format. It is important to note that although Word2Vec models are generated for each attribute of the determinant and dependent, only the Word2Vec model for the dependent attribute needs to be saved in the postdiction pipeline's output. Since we will still have the full input corpus after postdiction, the determinant's Word2Vec model(s) can be regenerated if recovery of values in the dependent attribute is necessary. However, this introduces a tradeoff between storage costs and the performance of textual retrievals, since storing the determinant's encoding models avoids repeated computations at the cost of added storage overheads.

4.3 Binary Encodings

In contrast to the Word2Vec encoding approach, our second approach builds off the observation that *textual data are stored internally as a binary representation.* We extended the *Vectorizer* module to transform each textual value into a binary sequence vector using UTF-8's dynamic encoding rather than ASCII, which has a limited set of encodings using a fixed byte for each character. Specifically, each textual value is converted to a Big-Endian UTF-8 byte sequence. While converting the byte sequence into a single unsigned integer value would reduce the storage overheads of LR models (since each dimension introduces an additional eight byte slope), values were often extremely large and led to Overflow Errors when maintaining the values in memory. For this reason, we treat each byte within the byte sequence as a separate unsigned integer dimension in the vector, however, given the need for equal length vectors for ML models, we pad the initial bytes with zeros for a Null value.

Similar to the approach using Word2Vec, a scan of the dataset to determine the maximum byte sequence length is needed prior to training and fitting onto clusters. Unlike the Word2Vec approach, textual values do not need to update a separate embedding model and each batch is immediately processed after the values are encoded as a UTF-8 byte sequence based on UTF-8's mappings.

When using the binary encoding approach, the final output size is calculated based on the maximum byte sequence length and the number of bytes required at each sequence. In the worst-case, a single UTF-8 sequence will require four bytes, so we assume that every sequence requires four bytes. The total size of the replaced column can be computed by:

$$\text{Replacement Column Size} = (4 \times \text{max sequence length}) \times \text{cardinality}$$

Since UTF-8 is a standard encoding format, it does not require an external encoding model to map values between textual and byte representations. This avoids the storage overheads of preserving encoding models for future data recovery. However, the binary encoding approach achieves this storage reduction by sacrificing the multi-layered neural networks of Word2Vec models, intended to capture the semantics of textual data, with a purely numerical approach. Furthermore, the removal of an external encoding model avoids the tradeoff between storage costs and the performance of textual retrievals, since UTF-8 supports the reversal of byte sequences to textual data.

4.4 Qwen3 Embeddings

Our third approach uses embedding models. Unlike the previous approaches, embedding models compress text into fixed-size vectors regardless of input length. As a result, embedded columns lack a clear inverse mapping and rely on Nearest-Neighbor queries to identify similar textual values. Unlike Word2Vec [15] which maps individual words to static vectors using a shallow neural model to capture co-occurrence statistics, Qwen3 [1] utilizes large transformer-based embedding models trained using unsupervised and supervised data to generate contextual embeddings beyond words for sentences, paragraphs, or documents.

With the motivation to reduce the costs of storing data, as discussed in Sect. 1, we did not consider embedding models that require paid licenses (e.g., OpenAI [18], Gemini [9]) as they would incur additional fees on top of the added storage costs of preserving complex embedding models. Instead, we explored the use of Qwen3 [1] from Ollama as a state-of-the-art and free textual embedding model that has seen wide adoption due to its support of 201 languages and dialects. At its core, Qwen3 uses a decoder-only transformer with a dual-encoder design to extract semantic representations from the state of the final token, while the reranking model uses a cross-encoder structure that takes query-document pairs as input and outputs a relevance score. Since the embedding model can be stored locally from Ollama (rather than accessed through an API), we utilized the smallest pretrained Qwen3 model, Qwen3-0.6B which contains 0.6 billion weights, instead of the larger Qwen3-4B and Qwen3-8B variants.

Unlike the Word2Vec models, Qwen3 models are already pretrained on large datasets and are not retrained as each batch of textual data is processed. Furthermore, Qwen3 models support the specification of vector dimensions through the use of Matryoshka Representation Learning for flexible dimension reduction, allowing it to avoid the maximum length scans required for Word2Vec and UTF-8 encodings. Within the postdiction pipeline, the vector dimensionality was set to 32 as the smallest size supported by Qwen3 since each additional dimension contributes an additional 8 bytes per row in storage costs.

When using the Qwen3 embedding approach, the final size of the data postdiction pipeline's output is determined by the pre-specified vector dimensionality and number of bytes required for each dimension. Assuming that each numerical representation is eight bytes and vector dimensionality is set to 32, the total size of a replaced column can be calculated by:

$$\text{Replacement Column Size} = (8 \times 32) \times \text{cardinality}$$

Since Qwen3 models can be accessed using Ollama's API, we do not include the model size in the calculation of the pipeline's output size.

Table 1. Datasets for evaluating Textual Postdiction

Dataset	Cardinality	Arity	Size	Nulls	Predictor	Outlier_Attributes
Wine	129,971	13	51.56 MB	107,447	winery	N/A
Wiki	4,133,298	5	2.42 GB	81	page_title	N/A

5 Experimental Setup

In this section, we detail the experimental setup for evaluating our exploration of a textual postdiction pipeline.

Hardware and Software. Experiments were run on a laptop with an Intel Ultra 7 155H CPU (22 logical processors), 64 GB of RAM, and an NVIDIA RTX 500 Ada GPU under Windows Subsystem for Linux (WSL2) with 22 processes. The pipeline is implemented in Python 3.12 using default configurations of *Keras* and *Scikit-learn* for LSTM and LR models. Datasets are batched and loaded as parquet files using *Dask*. We utilize the NLTK library for Word2Vec models, Python's standard library for UTF-8 encoding, and Ollama for Qwen3. Embeddings were locally cached per batch to speed up subsequent experiments. The source code has been made available at the ADMT Lab's GitHub Organization.

Datasets. The textual extension was evaluated on several datasets with varying characteristics, two of which are reported here in Table 1. The *Wine* [23] dataset contains wine reviews and the *Wiki* [3] dataset comprises Wikipedia pages focused on STEM topics. The *Wine* dataset includes attributes such as a wine's *description*, *designation*, *variety*, and *winery* while the *Wiki* dataset contains a *content ID*, *page title*, *section title*, *breadcrumb*, and the *text* within a section. *Wine* is the smaller textual dataset with 107,447 missing values while Wiki is the larger dataset with only 81 missing values. As in prior work, index and categorical columns were excluded, as they require complete accuracy or a prespecified mapping of similar classes. Null values in either dataset are stored as outliers.

Configuration Variables. The following configurations were used to evaluate the textual extensions unless otherwise noted.

- *Relative Dissimilarity Tolerance*: Set to 5.0%, a cosine similarity of 0.90.
- *Clustering Algorithm*: K-Means for unsupervised clustering with a predefined number of clusters and the Simple Split approach [16] for unsupervised clustering without a predefined number of clusters.
- *ML Model*: LSTMs and LR models, given their usage in earlier versions of the data postdiction pipeline.

- *Data Fitting Method*: *KD-Tree Indexing* [16], as determinant and dependent attributes are vectors rather than scalar values.
- *Batch Size*: 32 MB based on prior observations [16] that smaller batches require less time per-column. The smaller batch size also ensures Qwen3's GPU usage fits within the 4 GB memory limit.
- *Vector Dimensionality*: The size of vectors per word in Word2Vec and the output vector length in Qwen3. Binary encoding is unaffected by this parameter. Word2Vec defaults to one value per word; Qwen3 defaults to 32.

Predictor features were selected via AFDs and the Feature Selection algorithm discussed by Nixon [16], with the best features shown in Table 1. There were no outlier attributes detected in any of the textual datasets.

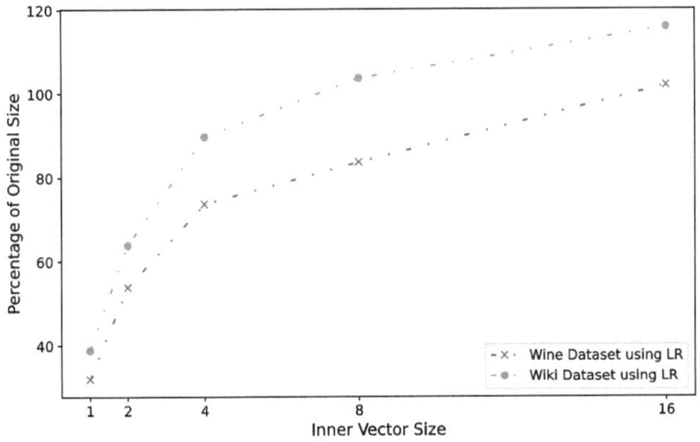

Fig. 4. Impact of Inner Vector Size with Word2Vec Encoding

6 Experimental Evaluation

With the experimental setup established, this section evaluates the textual extensions of the postdiction pipeline. In particular, we evaluate the data reductions of both datasets using each *Vectorization* method along with LRs and LSTMs. In addition, we examine data reductions across a range of error thresholds, analyze a snapshot of recovered data using Word2Vec and binary encoding, and discuss the significance of textual data distortion.

6.1 Word2Vec Parameters

The use of Word2Vec involves the adoption and refinement of two parameters, *min_count* and *vector_size* associated with the encoding models. The *min_count* parameter determines how many times a word must appear in the text corpus that the Word2Vec model is trained on, for the value to be mapped to a vector.

A higher *min_count* value means that a word must appear more times for it to have a mapping, but would require less storage space for the Word2Vec model itself, since it would have less mappings. However, if the *min_count* is set to any value greater than one, words that only appear a single time within the dataset would not be mapped and impossible to recover from LR models. Since any value above one goes against our goal of allowing replaced data to be recovered for future data accesses, we utilize a *min_count* of one for all experiments.

To tune the inner *vector_size* of Word2Vec models, we trained LR models on both datasets, clustered using the unsupervised *train-and-split* approach, and measured the pipeline's output size with several potential vector sizes: 1, 2, 4, 8, 16. As shown in Fig. 4, an inner vector size of one yielded the lowest storage costs, as each additional dimension incurs eight bytes per row. Vectors of eight dimensions expanded the Wiki dataset, and sixteen dimensions expanded both datasets. Higher dimensions also increase vector variability, reducing the likelihood of matching within the dissimilarity threshold and yielding more outliers.

With these results, we utilize a *vector_size* of one (i.e., one dimension per word) for each remaining experiment. Tuning the inner vector size is only necessary for Word2Vec since UTF-8 is a dynamic byte sequence where each byte is represented as a single dimension and Qwen3 produces one dimensional vectors.

6.2 Data Postdiction Reductions with Vectorization

To assess the reduction capabilities of postdiction, we measure the pipeline's output storage size using Word2Vec, UTF-8, and Qwen3. Table 2 summarizes the full set of experimental parameters used in this evaluation. We experimented with both K-Means and *train-and-split* clustering methods during the *training* phase along with LSTMs and LR models. Since K-Means partitions into a predefined number of clusters, we tested each vectorization method using 1, 2, 4, and 8 clusters per attribute. Once data was transformed to a vector representation, batches are fit onto clusters with *KD-Tree Indexing* [16] across a range of relative dissimilarity thresholds. Lastly, we compare the storage reductions of the best performing ML model(s) for each dataset and vectorization approach against standard lossless compression (LZMA [21], Gzip [6], Bzip2 [4], Zstd [14]) and state-of-the-art learned lossless compression (LeCo [13]). Lossy compression was not included since previous methods (ZFP [12], SZ [11,19]) do not support textual data. Figures pertaining to the Wine dataset were omitted due to space limitations[1]; however, the results for both datasets are discussed in this section.

Word2Vec: The results for using Word2Vec encoding models can be seen in Figs. 5 through 7. All three vectorization methods shared a common pattern across datasets: LSTM models tended to expand storage on smaller datasets due to model overhead, while LR models achieved more consistent reductions. The methods diverge in their best-case performance as detailed below.

LR models were less erratic across varying error thresholds and illustrated a storage decline with higher error thresholds. Notably, all cluster sizes reduced

[1] All figures are available in Nixon [16].

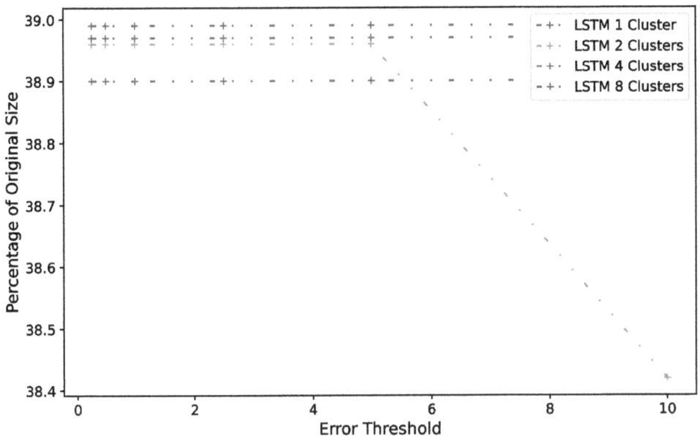

Fig. 5. Wiki Dataset: Word2Vec Encodings and LSTMs

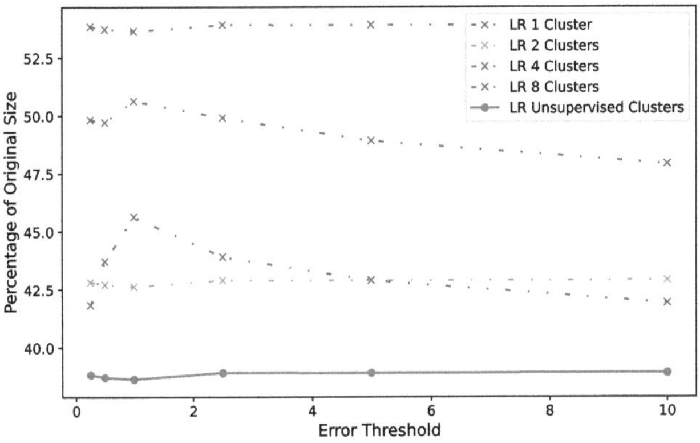

Fig. 6. Wiki Dataset: Word2Vec Encodings and LR

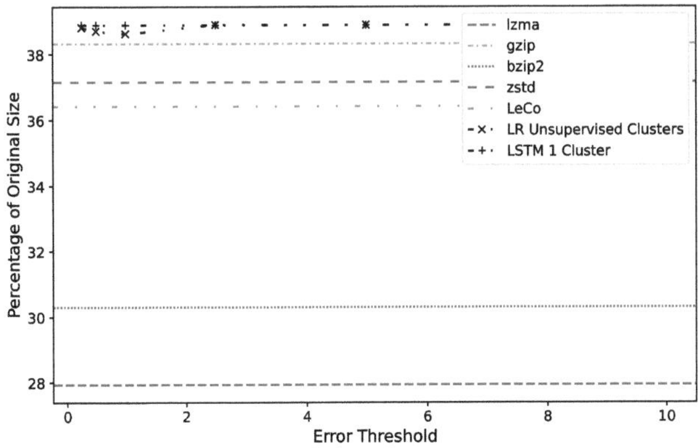

Fig. 7. Wiki Dataset: Word2Vec vs. Lossless Compression

Table 2. Experimental parameters for the Vectorization module.

Parameter	Values
Vectorization method	Word2Vec, UTF-8, Qwen3
Clustering method	K-Means, Train-and-split
ML model	LSTM, LR
Clusters per attribute	1, 2, 4, 8
Indexing structure	KD-Tree
Dissimilarity thresholds	0.25%, 0.5%, 1%, 2.5%, 5%, 10%
Lossless baselines	LZMA, Gzip, Bzip2, Zstd, LeCo

storage as low as 30.44% of the original size below 1% relative dissimilarity. At 1% error, every cluster size expanded the storage costs of the Wine dataset with the *train-and-split* approach yielding higher storage costs than K-Means clustering. With higher dissimilarity tolerances, the use of two LR models produced the best storage reductions with data postdiction outputting 59.7% of the original dataset size at 5% error and 30.44% at 10% error.

On the larger Wiki dataset, LSTMs performed better. Each cluster size reduced the dataset by at least 61%, with a single LSTM performing slightly better below 5% error. At 10% error, two LSTMs yielded a lower storage size of 38.43% due to the split clusters replacing more values and reducing the number of outlier values. Across both datasets, lossless compression outperformed all Word2Vec configurations in both storage reduction and construction time.

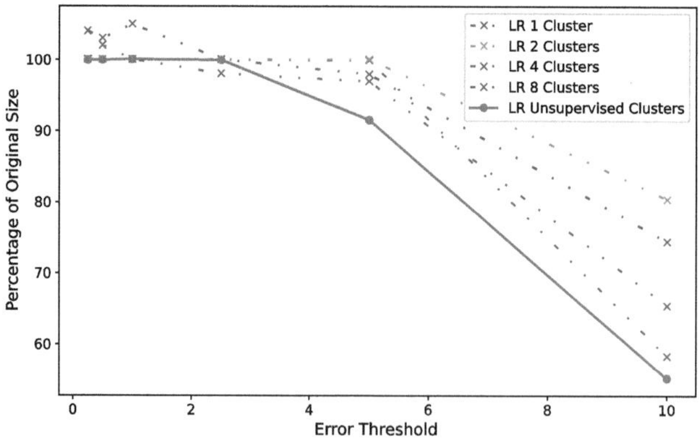

Fig. 8. Wiki Dataset: UTF-8 Encodings and LR

UTF-8: The results of using UTF-8 in the data postdiction pipeline are illustrated in Figs. 8 and 9. Unlike the use of LSTMs with UTF-8 encoding, LR models reduced the storage costs of the Wine dataset across every relative

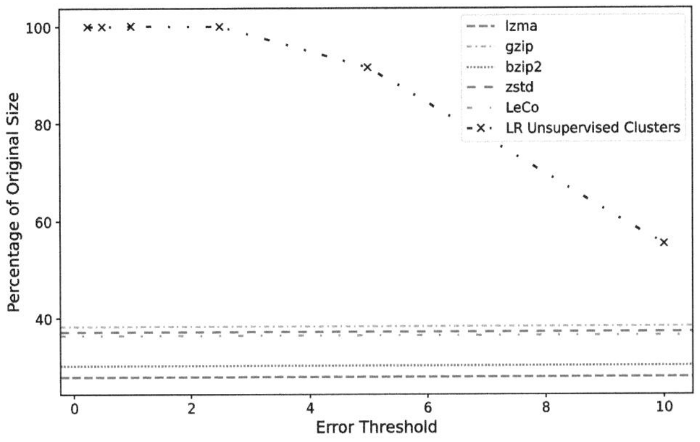

Fig. 9. Wiki Dataset: UTF-8 vs. Lossless Compression

error threshold. As the relative error threshold increased, the storage reductions using LR models also increased. While all cluster sizes illustrated similar trends, the use of eight LR models reduced the dataset by 90.15% at 10% error and by 4.78% at 1% error. Unlike LSTMs, where more models incurred higher overhead, deploying more LR models reduced outliers without significantly increasing storage costs. This distinction highlights a trade-off between the two encoding approaches: LSTMs paired with Word2Vec encodings achieved stronger compression performance on the Wine dataset, whereas LR models proved more effective when combined with UTF-8 encodings.

The Wiki dataset followed the same trends. A notable exception, however, emerged with LR models employing the unsupervised clustering approach with three clusters. This configuration achieved the lowest storage costs among all tested methods, retaining only 55% of the original dataset size (Figs. 6 and 11).

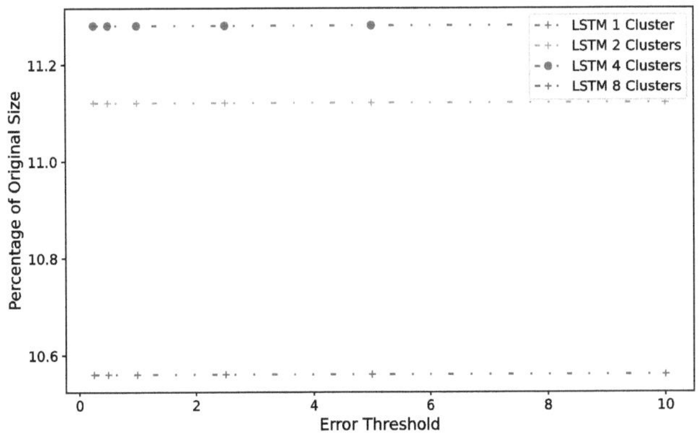

Fig. 10. Wiki Dataset: Qwen3 Embeddings and LSTMs

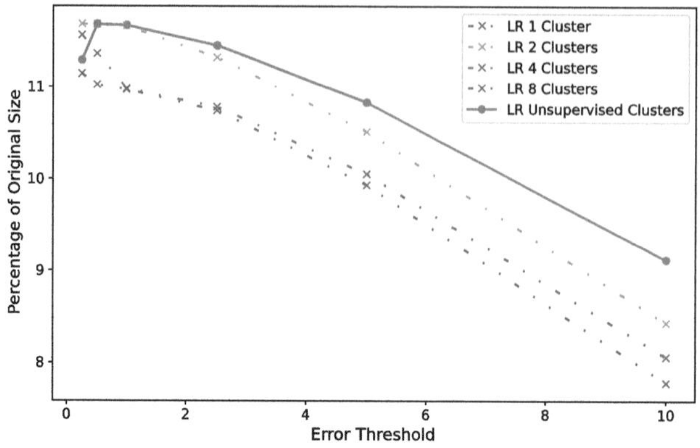

Fig. 11. Wiki Dataset: Qwen3 Embeddings and LR

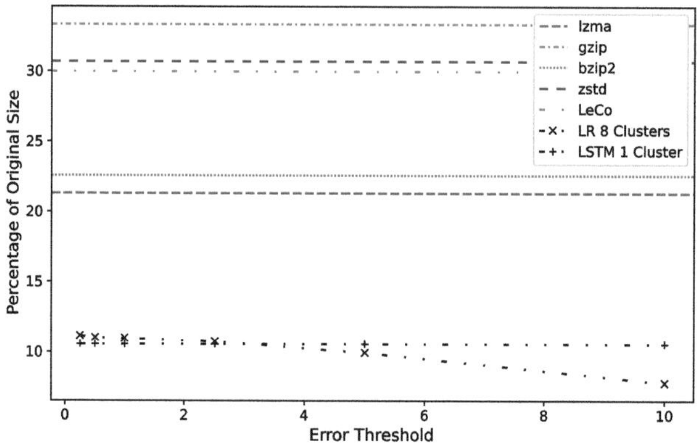

Fig. 12. Wiki Dataset: Qwen3 vs. Lossless Compression

Qwen3: Lastly, the results of textual data postdiction using Qwen3-0.6B embedding models are displayed in Figs. 10 through 12. Qwen3 diverged from the prior two approaches with a single LSTM reducing the Wine dataset by 60.99% and the Wiki dataset by 89.44%. LR models employing the unsupervised *train-and-split* clustering approach achieved the lowest storage costs on the Wine dataset beyond the 1% error threshold, yielding a 79.04% storage reduction, while eight LR models achieved the best storage reductions across all relative dissimilarity tolerances on the Wiki dataset, reaching a 92.22% reduction.

For the Wine dataset, LZMA performed best overall, though data postdiction with Qwen3 and LR models achieved a marginally higher storage reduction at 10% relative dissimilarity. For the Wiki dataset, Qwen3 embedding models outperformed every lossless compression method on this dataset, with LSTMs yielding lower storage costs below 2.5% dissimilarity and LRs achieving lower storage costs beyond that threshold.

This performance advantage comes with important practical caveats. Although the pipeline's use of Qwen3 embeddings achieved lower storage costs, its construction time (35,764 ms on the Wine dataset and 1,953,112 ms on the Wiki dataset) was slower than LZMA's. More critically, Qwen3 introduces a hidden retrieval cost absent in Word2Vec and UTF-8 encodings. Because Qwen3 performs dynamic feature reduction, values cannot be directly decoded. Instead, recovery relies on the assumption that embeddings are stored alongside unmodified data to support Nearest-Neighbor queries, which identify the most similar text to a predicted embedding vector. This requirement would introduce additional storage overheads across the entire data management pipeline, as an extra column would need to be added for every replaced attribute within the dataset's schema, with each value represented as a vector of at least 32 dimensions for Qwen3-0.6B. For these reasons, our overall recommendation remains to utilize lossless compression, specifically LZMA, for reducing textual data.

6.3 Recovered Textual Data

We examine the recovery of the *country* attribute in the Wine dataset using Word2Vec and UTF-8 encodings; Qwen3 was excluded for the reasons discussed in Sect. 6.2. Unlike numerical data distortion, which results in a slight shift in value, textual data distortion undermines the semantic meaning associated with each value entirely. With Word2Vec, several values were replaced with semantically adjacent terms. For instance, "France" was recovered as "Spain" and "Spain" as "Portugal", while others such as "US" returned <`Unknown`>.

There is no guarantee that the predicted vector appears in the model's corpus. Training on every potential value would necessitate a substantially larger corpus and higher storage overheads. The inability to recover textual values, combined with the storage costs required to even attempt it, directly contradicts the goals of minimizing storage overhead and preserving user accuracy constraints.

While UTF-8 encodings avoid this issue, recovered strings bore no resemblance to the original countries. For example, "France" was recovered as "GnX", "HnV", and "HmT", illustrating that text carries semantic meaning that cannot be approximated through bounded recovery alone. The high storage costs, slower construction times, and inability to recover textual values collectively reaffirm that data postdiction is not suited for textual data in its current state. Consequently, lossless compression remains the de facto approach for textual data reduction for the time being.

7 Conclusion

We investigated Word2Vec, UTF-8, and Qwen3 as vectorization strategies for extending postdiction to text. None generalized effectively to text: each introduced storage overhead, failed to reconstruct values, or produced semantically meaningless outputs. Lossless compression (LZMA) remained the strongest option and suggests that future pipelines should apply data postdiction and lossless compression according to data type. Given the limitations of the Qwen3 approach, future work could also explore LoRA-based [22] fine-tuning of pretrained LLMs to recover semantic content without retaining the original text.

Acknowledgments.. This work was partially funded by NIH award R01HL159805. The authors would like to thank Vasilis Sarris, Trevor Petersen, and Robbie Fishel from the ADMT Lab at the University of Pittsburgh for their helpful discussions.

References

1. Alibaba: Qwen3 embedding model (2026). https://ollama.com/library/qwen3
2. Baskin, A.: Remembering the forgotten: Clustering, outlier detection, and accuracy tuning in a postdiction pipeline. In: ADBIS **1850**, 46–55 (2023)
3. Biswas, R., Bamba, U., Broad, N.: Wiki stem corpus (2024). https://www.kaggle.com/datasets/conjuring92/wiki-stem-corpus
4. Burrows, M., Wheeler, D.: A block-sorting lossless data compression algorithm. SRS Research Report 124 (1994)
5. Costa, C.: Decaying telco big data with data postdiction. In: MDM, pp. 106–115 (2018)
6. Deutsch, L.P.: DEFLATE Compressed Data Format Specification version 1.3 (1996). https://doi.org/10.17487/RFC1951
7. Fei, W., et al.: Extending context window of large language models via semantic compression (2023). https://arxiv.org/abs/2312.09571
8. Gilbert, H., et al.: Semantic compression with large language models (2023). https://arxiv.org/abs/2304.12512
9. Google: Gemini text embeddings. https://ai.google.dev/gemini-api/
10. Kitsios, X., et al.: Sim-Piece: highly accurate piecewise linear approximation through similar segment merging. PVLDB **16**(8), 1910–1922 (2023)
11. Liang, X., et al.: Sz3: a modular framework for composing prediction-based error-bounded lossy compressors. IEEE Big Data **9**(2), 485–498 (2023)
12. Lindstrom, P.: Fixed-rate compressed floating-point arrays. IEEE TVCG **20**(12), 2674–2683 (2014)
13. Liu, Y., Zeng, X., Zhang, H.: Leco: Lightweight compression via learning serial correlations. Proc. ACM Manag. Data **2**(1), (2024)
14. Meta: Zstd - real-time data compression (2017), http://facebook.github.io/zstd/
15. Mikolov, T.: Efficient estimation of word representations in vector space. ICLR (2013)
16. Nixon, B.T.: Reducing data archival costs using machine learning. In: PhD Dissertation, pp. 1–168. University of Pittsburgh (2026)
17. OpenAI: GPT-4 technical report (2023). https://doi.org/10.48550/arXiv.2303.08774
18. OpenAI: OpenAI text embeddings (2026). https://developers.openai.com/api/
19. Tao, D.: Significantly improving lossy compression for scientific data sets based on multidimensional prediction and error-controlled quantization. IPDPS, pp. 1129–1139 (2017)
20. Trukhina, N., Vashkelis, V.: Semanticzip: A pilot framework for lossy text compression with LLMS as semantic decompressors (2026). https://arxiv.org/abs/2605.24541

21. Welch, T.: A technique for high-performance data compression. Computer **17**(6), 8–19 (1984)
22. Xu, Y., et al.: QA-LoRA: quantization-aware low-rank adaptation of large language models (2023). https://doi.org/10.48550/arXiv.2309.14717
23. Zackthoutt: Wine reviews. https://www.kaggle.com/datasets/zynicide/wine-reviews
24. Zhang, C., et al.: An improvement of PAA on trend-based approximation for time series. In: ICA3PP, pp. 248–262 (2018)

Personalized SQL Exercise Generation with Large Language Models and Constraint-Based Validation

Davide Ponzini(✉), Elisa Calza, Barbara Catania, and Giovanna Guerrini

DIBRIS - Universit di Genova, Genova, Italy
davide.ponzini@edu.unige.it, {barbara.catania,giovanna.guerrini}@unige.it

Abstract. SQL learners often require targeted practice to avoid recurring syntactic and semantic errors. However, generating personalized SQL exercises remains a challenging and time-consuming task. While Large Language Models (LLMs) enable scalable automatic content generation, they provide limited guarantees on the correctness and consistency of the produced exercises. This paper presents a personalized exercise generation component for LensQL, a framework for SQL learning centered on student error analysis. The proposed component automatically generates SQL assignments and reference solutions by combining LLM-based generation with a validation layer enforcing structural and pedagogical constraints at both schema and query levels.

1 Introduction

SQL is a fundamental component of database education, but many students experience persistent difficulties in formulating correct queries. Typical mistakes range from syntactic issues to deeper semantic and logical misunderstandings involving joins, aggregation, nested queries, or ambiguous attribute references. Overcoming these challenges usually requires extensive targeted practice, timely feedback, and progressively more complex exercises.

Recent advances in Large Language Models (LLMs) created opportunities to automatically generate educational SQL material, including schemas, datasets, exercises, and candidate solutions. Existing approaches [6,20] demonstrate the potential of LLMs for the automatic generation of educational SQL material, but, by largely relying on prompting strategies, suffer from limitations in terms of reliability, controllability, and structural guarantees, providing limited mechanisms for enforcing precise relational and pedagogical properties. Generated artifacts may thus contain inconsistent schemas, logically incorrect queries, or exercises whose complexity does not match the intended learning objectives.

These challenges are closely related to a long-standing problem in database research: the controlled generation of SQL workloads. Traditional benchmarks like TPC [3,12] rely on carefully designed schemas and workloads to expose specific relational characteristics, while more recent approaches [8,11] explore

G. Vargas-Solar et al. (Eds.): ADBIS 2026, LNCS 16937, pp. 232–248, 2027.
https://doi.org/10.1007/978-3-032-39820-8_16

controllable workload synthesis through constraints and validation mechanisms. However, the target is system evaluation rather than educational objectives.

This paper proposes a constraint-guided approach to personalized SQL exercise generation. The proposed method is implemented as a component of LensQL [13], a generative AI-based framework for SQL learning that places student errors at the center of the learning process. Starting from learner interaction traces and recurring error patterns, the component automatically generates SQL assignments and reference solutions tailored to specific errors and difficulty levels. The approach combines the flexibility of LLM-based generation with deterministic validation mechanisms. The LLM generates schemas, datasets, and SQL exercises from high-level specifications, while a validation layer enforces structural and pedagogical constraints at both schema and query levels. Constraints describe properties such as the presence of specific joins, aggregations, subqueries, ambiguous attributes, or query complexity patterns, enabling controlled generation of educational SQL workloads with desired characteristics.

The main contributions of the paper are the following: (i) a constraint-guided framework for personalized SQL exercise generation integrating learner analytics and LLM-based generation; (ii) a validation mechanism enforcing structural and pedagogical constraints on both generated schemas and SQL queries; (iii) an experimental evaluation assessing the reliability of the generation process and the quality of the generated exercises.

The remainder of the paper is organized as follows. Section 2 discusses related work. Section 3 presents the overall design and architecture of the component. Section 4 describes how personalized exercise plans can be configured and Sect. 5 discusses how exercises can be generated and validated. Section 6 presents the experimental evaluation, while Sect. 7 concludes.

2 Related Work

Educational SQL Systems and Error Taxonomies. Several approaches support SQL teaching through automatic query grading [4,10], error repair [15], hint generation [7], and, more recently, LLM-based correction [2,5]. Other studies investigate frequent SQL errors and the reasoning behind them [17]. The taxonomy by Taipalus et al. [18], later revised for automatic error categorization [14], classifies errors as syntactic, semantic, logical, or overly complex. While these systems support tutoring and feedback, they generally do not aim at generating SQL exercises and datasets. LensQL [13] integrates error categorization, learner analytics, and personalized assignment generation; this paper focuses on its generation component.

LLM-Based SQL Generation and Constraint Validation. The use of LLMs for SQL generation has attracted considerable attention [9], with benchmarks evaluating text-to-SQL capabilities [21]. Recent approaches combine LLMs with symbolic constraints through constrained decoding [16] or execution-guided generation and repair [19], enforcing syntactic or execution correctness during or immediately after decoding. In contrast, our approach applies constraints after generation, enabling the enforcement of higher-level structural and semantic properties and supporting the controlled generation of pedagogically targeted SQL exercises.

Benchmark and Workload Generation. Database research has extensively investigated synthetic workload and benchmark generation for system evaluation. Traditional benchmarks such as TPC-H [3] and TPC-DS [12] rely on carefully designed schemas and parameterized query templates, while recent approaches [8,11] explore synthetic SQL workload generation and constrained query synthesis. Unlike these systems, our objective is pedagogically driven workload generation, where relational structures and query properties are controlled to target specific student recurring errors and misconceptions.

Personalized SQL Exercise Generation with LLMs. Early work [1] demonstrated the feasibility of using GPT-3.5 to generate schemas, synthetic data, and SQL queries, while highlighting structural inconsistencies and logical errors. More recent approaches, such as PLAS [20], exploit stronger LLMs and structured generation pipelines, improving robustness but still showing degraded reliability for complex queries involving joins, nested subqueries, and aggregations. Complementary approaches generate SQL comprehension questions rather than complete exercises [6]. Although these systems improve educational support, they remain inherently probabilistic and do not enforce structural constraints. In contrast, our approach combines structural validation with learner analytics to generate personalized exercise plans driven by student error patterns.

3 LensQL Assignment Generation Module

LensQL is a generative AI-based web application designed to support SQL learning by placing student errors at the center of the educational process [13]. It is developed in Python and is integrated with the `gpt-5.4-nano` LLM. The platform stores student-related information, e.g., their domains of interests, and continuously collects and analyzes student interactions, including submitted queries and execution outcomes. Submitted queries are automatically classified according to the SQL error taxonomy proposed in [14]. Student interactions and associated errors are processed by the LensQL `Learning Analytics` module, which performs Extract-Transform-Load operations to integrate analytics into a dedicated data warehouse and build learner profiles capturing recurring errors and student performance patterns. Learner profiles constitute the basis for the automatic and personalized exercise generation process, which is the focus of this paper. They are exploited by the `Assignment Generation` module to support teachers in automatically generating student-specific exercises.

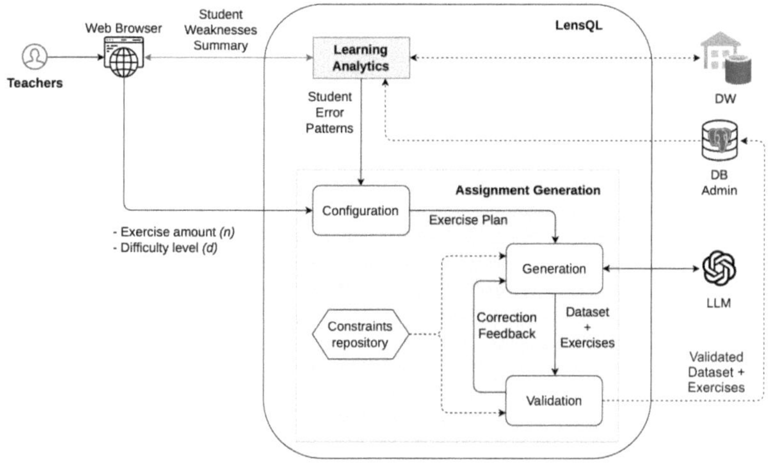

Fig. 1. Architecture of the LensQL `Assignment Generation` module.

As shown in Fig. 1, teachers interact with the system through a web browser and specify some high-level pedagogical parameters to guide the generation process. We consider two complementary dimensions: (i) the amount of reinforcement provided for each error category, expressed as the target number of exercises to generate for each student's most frequent error (n); and (ii) the cognitive complexity required to solve the generated exercises, including both the involved SQL concepts and the complexity of the underlying schema, expressed by a target difficulty level (d) with three possible values: `easy`, `medium`, and `hard`. Optionally, the teacher can also provide an SQL script containing dataset definition and population statements, to be used for exercise generation.

Teacher-defined parameters are then translated into student-specific SQL exercises through three main components. The `Configuration` component transforms the teacher-defined constraints into a *personalized exercise plan*, considering student-specific *error patterns* collected by the `Learning Analytics` component. Each pattern specifies how many exercises should target a given *learning objective*, defined in terms of an error category and a difficulty level.

The resulting exercise plan is then passed to the `Assignment Generation` module, which orchestrates the generation of both the dataset (if an SQL script is not provided by the teacher) and the corresponding exercises. The `Generation` module interact with an LLM to produce the required artifacts, while relying on a `Constraints Repository` that associates each learning objective with structural and pedagogical constraints guiding the generation process. Generated datasets and exercises are subsequently processed by the `Validation` component, which exploit the same repository to verify their consistency, validity, and educational quality with respect to the exercise plan. Validation results are fed back to the generation modules through iterative correction loops, enabling progressive refinement whenever inconsistencies or constraint violations are detected. Once validated, the dataset and exercises are stored and integrated into the LensQL ecosystem for subsequent student interaction and learning analytics.

4 Personalized Exercise Plan Configuration

The purpose of the `Configuration` module is to transform teacher-provided high-level pedagogical objectives, defined in terms of the provided parameter values, and student-specific learning needs, defined in terms of student-specific *error patterns*, into a *personalized exercise plan*, that guides the LLM-based generation and validation process, using a given *configuration function*. This configuration step is necessary because teacher-defined pedagogical objectives are intentionally specified at a high (e.g., class) level and cannot directly capture the heterogeneous learning needs of individual students. For instance, two students may exhibit different error categories or the same error category with substantially different frequencies, persistence levels, or correction behaviors. Consequently, generating the same exercises for both students could lead either to insufficient reinforcement or to unnecessary repetition. The `Configuration` module therefore acts as an adaptation layer between global instructional objectives and student-specific generation requirements, allowing the system to dynamically personalize the exercise category, the quantity, and the complexity of the generated exercises.

Student *error patterns* correspond to statistical information related to their top-k (where k is a system-defined parameter) most frequent SQL error categories [14], determined by the `Learning Analytics` component. For each top-k error category e_i ($i = 1, \ldots, k$) of a student s, the error pattern corresponds to a pair (e_i, A_i), where $A_i = [a_{i_1}, \ldots, a_{i_m}]$ is a list of analytics associated with error e_i for student s. Typical analytics include frequency, recency, and persistence in time. Given the teacher-defined parameters (n, d) and a top-k error pattern, the *configuration function* returns a *personalized exercise plan element* for that error pattern. The plan thus consists of k triples (e_i, d_i, n_i), one for each top-k student frequent error, where e_i denotes the error category, d_i the associated difficulty level, and n_i the number of exercises to be generated for reinforcing the corresponding concept. The pair (e_i, d_i) is called *learning objective*.

The choice of the configuration function depends on the intended pedagogical objectives. For instance, it may exploit learner analytics to provide additional reinforcement for recurring misconceptions while reducing unnecessary practice on already mastered concepts. Assuming that each error pattern includes the relative frequency $freq(e_i) \in [0, 1]$ of the error category e_i, a simple configuration function may assign more, easier exercises to frequent errors and fewer, more challenging exercises to infrequent ones. Formally:

$$f(e_i, A_i, n, d) = \begin{cases} (e_i, \texttt{easy}, n+1) & \text{if } freq(e_i) > \tau_h \\ (e_i, d, n) & \text{if } \tau_l \leq freq(e_i) \leq \tau_h \\ (e_i, \texttt{hard}, \max(1, n-1)) & \text{if } freq(e_i) < \tau_l \end{cases}$$

Algorithm 1 Personalized exercise plan configuration

Input:
Teacher parameters (n, d)
Student error patterns $P_s = \{(e_i, A_i) \mid i = 1, \ldots, k\}$
Configuration function f
Output: Exercise plan Π_s

$\Pi_s \leftarrow \emptyset$
for $i = 1, ..., k$ **do**
  $\Pi_s \leftarrow \Pi_s \cup \{f(e_i, d_i, n_i)\}$
end for
return Π_s

where τ_l and τ_h are scenario-dependent thresholds. On the other hand, a function which ignores learner analytics and simply propagates the teacher-defined values of the exercise amount and difficulty to every learning objective (called *identity-based function*) is appropriate when the pedagogical objective is to provide all students with the same amount of practice and target difficulty while adapting only the concepts being reinforced. This configuration is currently used in our prototype and serves as a simple baseline for future extensions.

Example 1. Suppose that the teacher specifies the parameters ($n = 3, d =$ `medium`), meaning that up to three medium-difficulty exercises should be generated for the most frequent student error categories. Suppose that the `Learning Analytics` component identifies the following top-2 error patterns for a student s, correspond to missing join conditions and usage of ambiguous columns:[1]

$$(\texttt{Missing join condition}, [\texttt{freq} = 30])$$
$$(\texttt{Ambiguous column}, [\texttt{freq} = 6]).$$

Based on these analytics, different configuration functions might generate different personalized exercise plans. For example, using the frequency-based function and setting $\tau_h = 25$ and $\tau_l = 10$, we obtain:

$$(\texttt{Missing join condition}, \texttt{easy}, 4)$$
$$(\texttt{Ambiguous column}, \texttt{hard}, 2).$$

The first category receives more exercises but easier ones, since the student repeatedly fails on the same fundamental concept. The second error instead receives fewer but moderately more complex exercises, reflecting a less persistent misconception. With the identity-based function, both error categories will be associated with the input parameters `medium, 3)`.

5 Constraint-Based Generation and Validation

Personalized exercise generation starts from the execution plan, generated by the `Configuration` component, and exploits the interaction with an LLM to produce a reference dataset and a set of SQL exercises, each composed of a

[1] This error arises when the student omits table qualification when referencing attributes appearing in multiple tables.

natural language request and a reference SQL query solution, tailored to the generated personalized plan. To guide the generation and the validation process, any possible learning objective (e_i, d_i) is associated with a set of structural and pedagogical constraints, stored in a `Constraints Repository`, ensuring the consistency, validity, and educational quality of the produced assignments.

5.1 Constraints Repository

For each learning objective $l_i = (e_i, d_i)$, the `Constraints Repository` stores a predefined and student independent set of constraints $C_i = \{c_i^1, ...c_i^m\}$, each defining a property that an SQL exercise for the learning objective l_i must satisfy. Each constraint c_i^j is associated with a predicate, composed of a name and some parameters, and a natural language description, to be used with LLM interactions.

Constraints provide a reusable mechanism for specifying the structural and educational properties of exercises generated for l_i. They serve two complementary purposes: making error e_i plausible through suitable dataset and query structures, and controlling exercise complexity based on d_i. Accordingly, constraints may refer either to the dataset (*dataset constraints*) or to the SQL query solution (*exercise constraints*) of the generated exercises.

Dataset Constraints. Table 1 summarizes the currently used set of dataset constraints. A first group of constraints specifies table properties. The `MinTables`, `MinColumns`, `MaxColumns`, and `MinChecks` constraints provide the schema shape and offer a coarse but important form of control. For example, an exercise requiring joins cannot be generated over a single-table dataset, while an easy exercise should not be based on tables with an excessive number of

Table 1. Dataset constraints.

Constraint	(Simplified) constraint description for the LLM
Tables	
`MinTables(n)`	At least n tables are defined.
`MinColumns(n,t)`	At least t tables contain at least n columns.
`MaxColumns(n)`	No table contains more than n columns.
`MinChecks(n,m)`	Between n and m `CHECK` constraints are defined ($m = *$ corresponds to no upper bound).
`ComplexColumnName(n)`	At least n tables names contain at least 15 characters and an underscore.
`SameColumnNames(n)`	At least n pairs of non-key columns share the same name across tables, but no semantic correlation.
Values	
`MinRows(n)`	Each table contains at least n rows.

attributes. The `ComplexColumnName` and `SameColumnNames` constraints impose restrictions on column names. On the other hand, the `MinRows` constraint refers to table instances and prevents the generation of datasets that are structurally valid but practically unusable or meaningless because they contain too little data.

Exercise Constraints. Table 2 summarizes the currently used exercise constraint groups. Most of them refer to structural information of the SQL query solution and cover the main SQL constructs involved in the exercises, namely: table references and joins, projections, selection conditions, grouping, ordering, aggregation, set operations, subqueries. Constraints of the group *Rows* refer to the result of the SQL query. They allow one to specify whether the result must contain duplicate rows, since if it does not contain duplicates we cannot trigger errors related to the usage (or lack) of the `DISTINCT` clause.

Mapping Learning Objectives to Sets of Constraints. When mapping a learning objective to constraints, the target error category determines the set of schema and exercise constraints required to make the error plausible, while the difficulty level controls the overall cognitive complexity of the exercise. Easy difficulty configurations include only the schema and query elements strictly necessary to trigger the target error, thus minimizing the reasoning effort required to derive the solution. Medium and hard difficulty configurations progressively introduce additional relational constructs and reasoning steps that are not directly related to the target misconception, such as larger schemas, additional filtering conditions, aggregation, joins, nested subqueries, and potential distractors. As a result, higher difficulty levels require students to reason over more complex relational structures while still focusing on the same underlying misconception.

Example 2. Consider the learning objective `(Ambiguous column, easy)`. Since the difficulty level is `easy`, minimal constraints necessary to trigger the target error category are considered. Such constraints, listed in Table 3, at the dataset level specify that the dataset must contain at least two tables, with at least one table having at least two columns, while keeping low the total number of allowed columns, setting it to four. Additionally, the dataset must contain at least one repeated non-key column name across different tables. At the query level, the reference SQL solution of the proposed exercise must involve two table references and one selection condition while complex structures like subqueries and `HAVING` clauses are forbidden. When moving to the `medium` or `hard` difficulty levels, the cognitive load is increased by specifying constraints that introduce additional reasoning elements. This is possible by increasing the number of pairs of repeated column names (2 or 3) and specifying that the reference solution must contain multiple filtering conditions (2 or 3) together with at least one aggregation operator and no subqueries (at the `medium` level) or both subqueries and at least one aggregation operator (at the `hard` level).

Table 2. Exercise constraints ($m = *$ corresponds to no upper bound).

Constraint	(Simplified) constraint description for the LLM
Table references	
`TableReferences(n,m)`	Between n and m tables are referenced.
`LeftJoin(n,m)`	Between n and m `LEFT JOIN`s.
`RightJoin(n,m)`	Between n and m `RIGHT JOIN`s.
`SelfJoin(n,m)`	Between n and m self-joins.
Projection	
`SelectedColumns(n,m,s)`	Between n and m columns are projected. s specifies if self-joins are counted as two distinct tables or not.
`Alias(n,m)`	Between n and m projected columns are aliased.
`OriginalName(n,m)`	Between n and m projected columns are not aliased.
Conditions	
`Conditions(n,m)`	Between n and m `WHERE` conditions of any kind.
`StringComparison(n,m)`	Between n and m comparisons against string literals.
`EmptyStringComparison(n,m)`	Between n and m comparisons against empty strings.
`NullComparison(n,m)`	Between n and m `IS NULL` predicates.
`NotNullComparison(n,m)`	Between n and m `IS NOT NULL` predicates.
`NoLike()`	Absence of `LIKE` operators.
`Not(n,m)`	Between n and m negations.
`Exists(n,m)`	Between n and m `EXISTS` predicates.
`NotExists(n,m)`	Between n and m `NOT EXISTS` predicates.
`MathOperators(n,m)`	Between n and m predicates use arithmetic operators.
`ExistsNotExists_InNotIn(n1,n2,m1,m2)`	Between $n1$ and $m1$ `EXISTS` or `IN` predicates, and between $n2$ and $m2$ `NOT EXISTS` or `NOT IN` predicates.
`WilcardCharacters(n,c)`	At least n `LIKE` patterns contain the characters c.
`WilcardLength(n,m)`	`LIKE` patterns contain between n and m non-wildcard characters.
`MultipleConditionsOnSameColumn(n)`	At least n conditions refer to the same column.
`InAnyAll(n)`	At least n `IN`, `ANY`, or `ALL` predicates.
Grouping	
`GroupBy(n,m)`	Between n and m columns used for grouping.
`Having(n,m)`	Between n and m `HAVING` conditions are used.
Ordering	
`OrderBy(n,m)`	Between n and m columns are used for ordering.
`OrderByASC(n,m)`	Between n and m columns are ordered ascending.
`OrderByDESC(n,m)`	Between n and m columns are ordered descending.
Aggregation	
`Aggregation(n,m,f)`	Between n and m aggregate functions, among those listed in f.
Rows	
`Duplicates()`	The result contains duplicate rows.
`NoDuplicates()`	The result is unique, even without using `DISTINCT`.
`Distinct()`	Result uniqueness is achieved using `DISTINCT`.
Set operations	
`Union(n,m,a)`	Between n and m union operators are used. a allows optional filtering of only `UNION` or `UNION ALL` operators.
Subqueries	
`Subqueries(n,m)`	Between n and m subqueries are used.
`NestedSubqueries(n,m)`	Between n and m nested subqueries are used.

5.2 Generation and Validation Pipeline

Given a student-specific exercise plan, the `Generation` and `Validation` components use the `Constraints Repository` as an operational interface between pedagogical objectives and LLM-based generation to produce personalized exercises. For each exercise plan, if the teacher does not provide an SQL script, the system generates and populates a dataset in one of the students domains of interest through LLM interaction. All exercises generated from the same plan share this dataset, avoiding isolated artificial schemas and supporting a more coherent and realistic sequence of assignments within a common relational context (Table 3).

Table 3. Constraints for the (`Ambiguous column, easy`) learning objective.

Dataset Constraints	Exercise Constraints
`MinTables(2)`	`TableReferences(2,2)`
`MinColumns(2,1)`	`Conditions(1,1)`
`MaxColumns(4)`	`Subqueries(0,0)`
`MinRows(3)`	`Having(0,0)`
`SameColumnNames(1)`	

Each SQL exercise consists of: (i) a natural language request; and (ii) a reference SQL query solution over the generated dataset. The request describes the information need presented to the learner, while the reference solution is used both for exercise validation and subsequent student assessment.

The system produces artifacts satisfying the constraints associated with the learning objectives derived from the exercise plan, thus ensuring that exercises target the intended misconceptions at the appropriate difficulty level. Figure 2 summarizes the overall workflow. The process is divided into two main phases: *dataset preparation*, responsible for generating and populating the dataset, and *exercise preparation*, devoted to exercise generation. In both phases, generation (purple for datasets and light blue for exercises) and validation (red) iteratively interact to ensure that all generated artifacts satisfy the required constraints. To keep the process automatic, no additional correctness checks besides constraint validation are performed on generated query solutions. The SQL dialect, the natural language used for generation, and the database instance used for SQL code validation can all be easily customized within LensQL.

Dataset Preparation. The `Generation` module first retrieves from the `Constraints Repository` the dataset constraints associated with each learning objective (e_i, d_i) derived from the exercise plan. Constraints of the same type are then merged into a single unified specification by retaining the strongest compatible requirement and conflicts, if any, are resolved. For example, if one learning

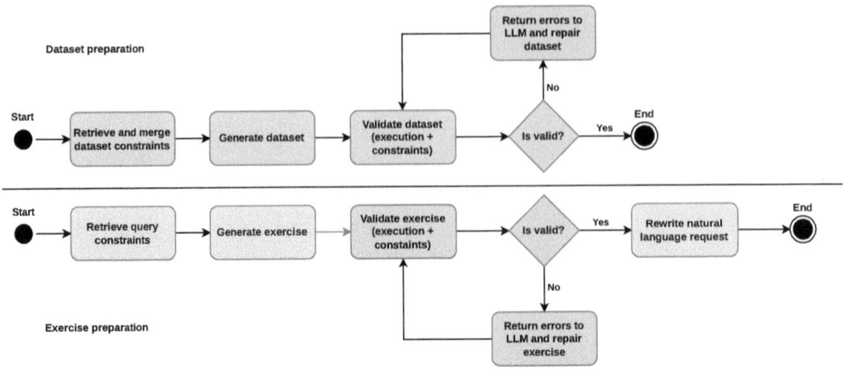

Fig. 2. Overview of the generation and validation workflow.

objective requires at least two tables and another requires between three and five tables, the resulting dataset specification requires between three and five tables. The LLM is then prompted to generate a SQL script for one of the student's domains of interest, guided by the textual description of each constraint.

The generated SQL script is then passed to the `Validation` component for a double check. First, the script is executed on the target database. If the execution fails, the database error message is returned to the LLM, which is asked to repair the script. Once the script executes successfully, the `Validation` component checks whether all dataset constraints are satisfied, by parsing the SQL script, counting structural components and comparing their number with what requested by the merged constraints. If some constraints are violated, it generates a diagnostic message describing the missing requirements and, when possible, suggesting concrete changes. The LLM is then asked to revise the dataset accordingly. This generate–validate–repair loop continues until the dataset satisfies all constraints or a maximum number of retries is reached. In the second case, the process terminates with an error and no exercise is returned.

Exercise Preparation. Once a valid dataset is available, the control passes again to the `Generation` component. Now, for each triple (e_i, d_i, n_i) in the exercise plan, n_i exercises for the reference dataset, targeting the e_i misconception, are generated at difficulty level d_i, by interacting with the LLM. Figure 2 shows the process for the generation of a single exercise for a pair (e_i, d_i).

The exercise generation and validation process is similar to that described for dataset preparation, considering now exercise constraints, that are primarily validated by inspecting the query abstract syntax tree of the generated SQL query solution for the exercise. Once an exercise has been validated through execution and constraint checking, a final rewriting step is applied to its natural language request. Indeed, preliminary experiments showed that LLM-generated requests often suffer from two opposite problems: some are too close to SQL syntax and implicitly reveal the solution strategy, while others are too vague about the expected output. To address this issue, the `Validation` component prompts the LLM to rewrite the generated request. The rewritten version of the request must describe the information need at a conceptual level, without suggesting how to solve it, while explicitly specifying the expected output columns and aliases. This produces exercises that are less leading for students while remaining precise enough for automated evaluation.

Example 3. Consider an exercise plan containing the following triple: `(Ambiguous columns, medium, 1)`. According to the constraints associated with the underlying learning objective (see Example 2), the generated dataset for a job-related domain might have the following schema:

```
departments(dept_id, name, city, budget)
employees(emp_id, name, city, salary, dept_id)
```

where both `name` and `city` are repeated non-key attributes, `emp_id` and `dept_id` are the primary keys, and `employees.dept_id` references `departments.dept_id`. A validated exercise might correspond to the following natural language request:

> *"For each department in New York, return the department name and the average salary of its employees. Only include departments where the budget exceeds 100000."*

with the following reference solution:

```
SELECT departments.name, AVG(salary)
FROM departments d JOIN employees e ON e.dept_id = d.dept_id
WHERE departments.city = 'New York' AND budget > 100000
GROUP BY departments.name;
```

We observe that this exercise may easily trigger an ambiguous column error for students who often omit table qualification in predicates or projections. The aggregation operator and the additional filtering condition increase the reasoning complexity compared to an easy configuration, while still avoiding the higher cognitive load associated with the usage of subqueries.

Table 4. Dataset and exercise generation success rate for different exercise plan lengths.

Dataset generation					Exercise generation				
k	Successes	Failures	Total	Rate	k	Successes	Failures	Total	Rate
1	777	3	780	99.62%	1	715	62	777	92.02%
2	73	27	100	73.00%	2	136	10	146	93.15%
3	55	45	100	55.00%	3	154	11	165	93.33%
4	42	58	100	42.00%	4	158	10	168	94.05%
5	32	68	100	32.00%	5	147	13	160	91.88%
10	1	99	100	1.00%	10	9	1	10	90.00%

6 Experimental Evaluation

We evaluated the proposed `Generation` component along three dimensions: (i) the ability of the system to generate valid datasets and exercises satisfying the required constraints; (ii) the pedagogical quality of the generated exercises, assessed through expert judgments; (iii) preliminary student interaction data, used to analyze whether intended difficulty levels are reflected in solving behavior.

6.1 Generation and Validation Pipeline Evaluation

The first evaluation assesses the reliability of the generation and validation pipeline. Dataset generation is considered successful when the generated SQL script executes correctly and satisfies all required dataset constraints. Exercise generation is considered successful when the generated request and reference solution execute correctly and satisfy all associated exercise constraints.

We consider six settings with an increasingly longer exercise plan length $k = 1, 2, 3, 4, 5, 10$. Error categories are sampled from a subset of 65 taxonomy nodes, corresponding to SQL mistakes that are both pedagogically relevant and supported by the current `Constraints Repository`. When $k = 1$, we create an exercise plan for each combination of the error categories and difficulty levels. For each learning objective, the pipeline is executed 4 times, in order to account for the stochastic nature of LLM-based generation while keeping the experimental cost manageable. Thus, the process is executed $65 \times 3 \times 4 = 780$ times in total. When $k > 1$, each run consists of a single exercise plan containing k randomly selected learning objectives. For each setting, 100 randomly created exercise plans are created. Under all settings, for each exercise plan the system first generates the shared dataset and, if successful, it proceeds with exercise generation.

Table 4 shows that dataset generation is effective when targeting a single learning objective. For $k = 1$, the system generates valid datasets in 99.62% of the cases. As the exercise plan length increases, dataset generation becomes harder because a single dataset must satisfy several heterogeneous constraint sets simultaneously. In particular, the success rate decreases to 73.00% for $k = 2$ and 55.00% for $k = 3$, then drops more sharply for larger plans, getting only one successful case for $k = 10$. These results suggest that the current pipeline can reliably support small personalized exercise plans. We observe that this is also a realistic setting since a limited number of recurring errors is usually sufficient to characterize a student's main weaknesses.

Table 4 also reports the results for exercise generation. As expected, the total number of exercise generation attempts depends on the number of successfully generated datasets. For example, for $k = 5$, 32 successful datasets produce $32 \times 5 = 160$ exercise generation attempts. Once a valid dataset is available, exercise generation remains highly reliable: across all settings, the success rate stays above 90%. This indicates that the main limitation for longer exercise plans concerns shared dataset generation rather than individual exercise generation.

6.2 Expert Evaluation

To assess the pedagogical quality of the generated exercises, we conducted an expert evaluation with six participants. Experts are PhD students (not involved in this research) and recent graduates who are proficient in SQL and familiar with the learning outcomes of a Bachelor-level introductory database course. Experts solved 35 generated exercises (a total of 189 queries) without access to the reference solutions and then rated *task clarity* and *perceived difficulty* on a four-point Likert scale (for task clarity, higher values indicate better quality while, for perceived difficulty, 1 corresponds to "not at all difficult" and 4 to "very difficult"). Additionally, we asked the experts to: (1) compare the results of their SQL queries with those of the generated reference solutions when executed on the generated dataset; a reference solution is considered *result-based correct* if its output matches that of the expert solution on the same dataset; (2) manually verify the *semantic correctness* of the generated reference solutions. Indeed, matching the reference output on a given dataset does not guarantee semantic correctness, since the query may produce different results on other datasets and may still contain unnecessary constructs, such as redundant joins.

Table 5. Expert evaluation of generated exercises by difficulty level.

Difficulty	Task clarity	Perceived difficulty	Result-based correctness
`easy`	3.80	1.12	100%
`medium`	3.37	2.26	100%
`hard`	3.50	3.04	91.66%
Overall	3.55	2.13	97.22%

Table 5 summarizes the results, reporting task clarity and perceived difficulty scores, together with the percentage of result-based correct solutions. Generated exercises are generally clear and solvable, with high task clarity across all difficulty levels (overall average 3.55). Perceived difficulty is consistent with the difficulty levels. These results provide preliminary evidence that the constraint-based definition of difficulty captures meaningful differences in cognitive load. All easy and medium exercises, and most hard exercises, were validated successfully in terms of result-based correctness. However, manual inspection revealed that a few medium and hard exercises did not satisfy semantic correctness since they contained unnecessary complications or minor logical flaws that could lead to incorrect behavior on other datasets. This suggests that result-based validation, while useful, is insufficient on its own and motivates stronger semantic validation in future versions of the system.

6.3 Student Interaction Analysis

As a preliminary validation in an authentic learning setting, we analyzed interaction traces collected while students worked on generated exercises. The validation is performed in the context of a second-year introductory database course within the Bachelors degree program in Computer Science at the University of Genova, Italy (around one hundred enrolled students).

In LensQL, we consider an exercise *solved* by a student if the student manages to write a query that is executed by the DBMS and is result-based correct with respect to the reference solution.[2] For each exercise solved by a student, we consider three indicators computed over the time interval between the students first submitted query and the time at which the exercise is solved: (i) the number of attempts that are not result-based correct, when compared with the reference solution through a dedicated LensQL functionality; (ii) the total number of executed queries that were not explicitly compared with the reference solution; (iii) the total completion time, measured in minutes. Attempts corresponding to solving times longer than two hours were treated as outliers and excluded from the analysis.

Table 6. Average student interaction indicators by generated difficulty.

Difficulty	Incorrect attempts	Intermediate queries	Time (minutes)
`easy`	0.55	3.45	7.42
`medium`	1.75	6.83	24.64
`hard`	0.88	7.13	28.83

The results, shown in Table 6 provide partial support for the intended difficulty calibration. The number of intermediate queries increases while increasing the exercise difficulty, from 3.45 for easy exercises to 7.13 for hard exercises. Solving time follows the same trend, increasing from 7.42 to 28.83 min. These indicators suggest that harder exercises require more exploration and refinement before students reach a solution. Incorrect attempts show a less regular pattern: they increase from easy to medium exercises, but decrease for hard exercises. This does not necessarily mean that hard exercises were easier. Rather, considered together with the higher number of intermediate queries and longer solving times, it suggests that students may approach harder exercises more cautiously, testing intermediate queries before submitting a final answer.

6.4 Threats to Validity

This evaluation is preliminary, and its validity is limited from a number of perspectives. For what concerns internal validity, we point out that usage by the students was in unsupervised setting. In terms of external validity, expert assessment was conducted on a limited set of exercises, and student interaction data only provide an initial indication of difficulty rather than evidence of learning

[2] Students are informed that matching the reference output on a given dataset does not guarantee semantic correctness, as defined above.

gains. Moreover, a single course is considered, thus, results cannot be generalized. Finally, the set of considered metrics could have been extended, including a systematic evaluation of semantic correctness.

7 Concluding Remarks

We presented a framework for personalized SQL exercise generation within LensQL. Recurring student SQL errors are transformed into exercise plans that are translated into schema- and query-level constraints, guiding LLM-based dataset and exercise generation. Through iterative validation and repair, the system produces executable artifacts aligned with the learning objectives. The evaluation demonstrates the approach feasibility: the system reliably generates valid datasets and exercises for short plans, expert judgments indicate that exercises are clear and aligned with intended difficulty, and student traces suggest that higher generated difficulty corresponds to higher cognitive demand. Limitations include the lack of direct learning-effect measurements, the preliminary student evaluation, and the scalability of shared dataset generation. Moreover, constraint-based validation reduces, but does not eliminate, the risk of semantically incorrect or pedagogically weak generated exercises, especially for complex queries. Future work will address these issues by improving constraint management and assessing the long-term impact of personalized exercises on recurring SQL errors.

References

1. Aerts, W., Fletcher, G., Miedema, D.: A feasibility study on automated SQL exercise generation with ChatGPT-3.5. In: Proceedings of the 3rd International Workshop on Data Systems Education, pp. 13–19 (2024)
2. AlRabah, A., Yang, S., Alawini, A.: Optimizing database query learning: a generative AI approach for semantic error feedback. In: ASEE Annual Conference and Exposition, Conference Proceedings. American Society for Engineering Education (2024)
3. Boncz, P., Neumann, T., Erling, O.: TPC-H analyzed: hidden messages and lessons learned from an influential benchmark. In: Nambiar, R., Poess, M. (eds.) TPCTC 2013. LNCS, vol. 8391, pp. 61–76. Springer, Cham (2014). https://doi.org/10.1007/978-3-319-04936-6_5
4. Chandra, B., Chawda, B., Kar, B., Reddy, K.M., Shah, S., Sudarshan, S.: Data generation for testing and grading SQL queries. VLDB J. **24**(6), 731–755 (2015)
5. Chen, Z., et al.: Text-to-SQL error correction with language models of code. In: Proceedings of the 61st Meeting of the Association for Computational Linguistics, pp. 1359–1372 (2023)
6. Goodfellow, M., Lambert, A., Fagan, A., Booth, R.: AI-assisted generation of SQL comprehension questions. In: Proceedings of the 5th International Workshop on Data Systems Education (2026)
7. Hu, Y., Gilad, A., Stephens-Martinez, K., Roy, S., Yang, J.: Qr-Hint: actionable hints towards correcting wrong SQL queries. In: Proceedings of the ACM Conference on Management of Data **2**(3), 1–27 (2024)

8. Lao, J., Trummer, I.: SQLBarber: a system leveraging large language models to generate customized and realistic SQL workloads. In: Proceedings of the ACM Symposium on Management of Data, vol. 4, pp. 1–27 (2026)
9. Liu, X., et al.: A survey of text-to-SQL in the era of LLMs: where are we, and where are we going? IEEE Trans. Knowl. Data Eng. (2025)
10. Manikani, K., Chapaneri, R., Shetty, D., Shah, D.: SQL Autograder: web-based LLM-powered autograder for assessment of SQL queries. Int. J. Artif. Intell. Educ., 1–31 (2025)
11. Mehta, K., Mankodi, A.: SynQL: a controllable and scalable rule-based framework for SQL workload synthesis for performance benchmarking. arXiv preprint arXiv:2604.08021v1 (2026)
12. Nambiar, R.O., Poess, M.: The making of TPC-DS. In: VLDB, vol. 6, pp. 1049–1058 (2006)
13. Ponzini, D., Catania, B., Guerrini, G.: Enhancing SQL learning through generative AI and student error analysis. In: Chrysanthis, P.K., Nørvåg, K., Stefanidis, K., Zhang, Z., Quintarelli, E., Zumpano, E. (eds.) New Trends in Database and Information Systems, ADBIS 2025. CCIS, vol. 2676. Springer, Cham (2026). https://doi.org/10.1007/978-3-032-05727-3_12
14. Ponzini, D., Guerrini, G., Catania, B.: A proposal for revising SQL error taxonomies based on automated detection. In: Proceedings of the 5th International Workshop on Data Systems Education (2026)
15. Presler-Marshall, K., Heckman, S., Stolee, K.: SQLRepair: identifying and repairing mistakes in student-authored SQL queries. In: Proceedings of 43rd International Conference on Software Engineering: Software Engineering Education and Training, pp. 199–210 (2021)
16. Scholak, T., Schucher, N., Bahdanau, D.: PICARD: parsing incrementally for constrained auto-regressive decoding from language models. In: Proceedings of the Conference on Empirical Methods in Natural Language Processing, pp. 9895–9901 (2021)
17. Taipalus, T.: Explaining causes behind SQL query formulation errors. In: 2020 IEEE Frontiers in Education Conference (FIE), pp. 1–9. IEEE (2020)
18. Taipalus, T., Siponen, M., Vartiainen, T.: Errors and complications in SQL query formulation. ACM Trans. Comput. Educ. **18**(3), 1–29 (2018)
19. Wang, B., Shin, R., Liu, X., Polozov, O., Richardson, M.: Execution-guided neural program decoding. In: Proceedings of the Workshop on Neural Machine Translation and Generation, pp. 83–92 (2018)
20. Wardani, N.W., et al.: An SQL query description problem with AI assistance for an SQL programming learning assistant system. Information **17**(1) (2026)
21. Yu, T., et al.: Spider: a large-scale human-labeled dataset for complex and cross-domain semantic parsing and text-to-SQL task. In: Proceedings of the Conference on Empirical Methods in Natural Language Processing, pp. 3911–3921 (2018)

Balancing Privacy and Utility in Synthetic Genotype Data Generation by Adaptive Optimization

Mohamed Sabri Hafidi(✉), Anton Dignös, Johann Gamper, and Ozan Kahramanoğulları

Free University of Bozen-Bolzano, Bolzano, Italy
{hmohamedsabri,anton.dignoes,johann.gamper,okahramanogullari}@unibz.it

Abstract. Since genetic data is highly sensitive, collaborative processing pipelines require robust privacy-preserving strategies. To this end, we introduce an adaptive framework for synthesizing genotype data that balances utility and privacy guarantees. The framework incorporates an adaptive model tuning mechanism with a state-persistent rollback strategy. Our methodology manages the data generation process by iteratively refining synthetic outputs using utility metrics and privacy constraints, preventing model divergence while preserving multivariate correlations. We evaluate the framework by benchmarking three generative paradigms: a statistical frequency-based approach, a shuffling-based reconfiguration, and a Wasserstein generative adversarial network. Privacy risk is quantified through membership inference attacks, while data utility is assessed via the preservation of linkage disequilibrium patterns and minor allele frequency distributions. An experimental evaluation shows that our methodology preserves complex genomic structures while maintaining a quantified privacy trade-off.

Keywords: Genomic Privacy · Synthetic Data · GWAS · WGAN-GP · Membership Inference Attack

1 Introduction

The rapid advancement of genomic technologies has transformed our understanding of human biology and disease. Genomic data holds immense potential for personalized medicine, drug discovery, and population-scale research. Yet its uniquely identifying nature, which can reveal sensitive information about individuals and their relatives, raises profound ethical and privacy concerns [7,14]. The central challenge is to enable scientific progress by facilitating the sharing of data among interested parties while protecting individuals' privacy.

This tension is particularly acute in large-scale genomic data management. Population-level repositories are essential for benchmarking algorithms and conducting statistical analyses. Still, the regulatory frameworks, such as the

G. Vargas-Solar et al. (Eds.): ADBIS 2026, LNCS 16937, pp. 249–265, 2027.
https://doi.org/10.1007/978-3-032-39820-8_17

GDPR [11] and HIPAA [25], heavily restrict the sharing of data. These regulations classify genotypes as sensitive personal data, creating a fundamental trade-off: researchers must preserve the utility of complex multivariate genomic structures while minimizing re-identification risks.

Synthetic data offers a promising path forward. By generating artificial genotypes that mimic the statistical properties of real cohorts, researchers can facilitate data sharing without exposing individual genomes [27]. Existing approaches range from simple frequency-based sampling to advanced deep generative models, such as Generative Adversarial Networks [13]. However, achieving both biological fidelity and adversarial robustness remains challenging, particularly given the high dimensionality and skewness of genomic data [23], i.e., the vast majority of variants match the reference genome, represented as 0.

To address these limitations, we propose an adaptive framework that governs the data generation process through an iterative optimization loop. More specifically, our main contributions can be summarized as follows:

- We introduce an adaptive model-tuning mechanism with a state-persistent rollback strategy. The proposed meta-algorithm calls a data generation model, which is iteratively refined by jointly evaluating the utility and privacy of the generated data at each step.
- We design a Wasserstein generative adversarial network with gradient penalty (WGAN-GP) adapted to genomic data. The model handles discrete genotypes and high dimensionality through stability-oriented architectural choices that preserve complex genomic structure.
- We use a Membership Inference Attack protocol using a universal shadow pool that leverages likelihood-ratio signals to estimate membership risk. This feature enables efficient weakest-link privacy analysis by identifying the most vulnerable individuals.
- We benchmark our approach against state-of-the-art generative baselines and show that the returned model is stable, consistently producing high-utility and privacy-preserving synthetic datasets.

Our results show that the proposed framework captures complex genomic correlation structures while maintaining a quantified trade-off between privacy and utility. Our framework provides a scalable, model- and dataset-agnostic solution for genomic data management and secure data dissemination.

The rest of the paper is structured as follows: Sect. 2 introduces useful background information. In Sect. 3 we discuss related work, followed by the presentation of the generative framework in Sect. 4. Section 5 discusses the results of our experimental evaluation, and Sect. 6 concludes the paper.

2 Background

Genomic Variation and Representation. Genomic datasets primarily track positions where the DNA sequence differs among individuals. In most eukaryotes, nuclear genetic information is typically inherited through homologous chromosome pairs, with one set contributed by each parent. Consequently, each genetic coordinate (locus) is represented by two values, or alleles, which together form a *genotype* [19]. For computational purposes, this information is typically encoded into a discrete two-dimensional matrix [24] and stored in so-called VCF files. In this structure, rows represent specific genetic variants and columns represent individual samples [21].

The Variant Call Format (VCF). VCF is the de facto standard for managing large-scale genomic data [10]. VCF files achieve data efficiency through a reference-based encoding scheme: rather than storing the complete sequence, the format only records positions that differ from a standard reference assembly [21]. As illustrated in Fig. 1, a VCF file is structured into three segments:

- *Meta-information:* System-level headers defining file versions and technical specifications for data fields.
- *Fixed Fields:* Feature metadata, including chromosome (`CHROM`), physical position (`POS`), and the reference (`REF`) vs. alternative (`ALT`) states.
- *Samples Block:* The data matrix where genotypes are encoded numerically relative to the reference (`0` for reference, `1` or higher for mutations).

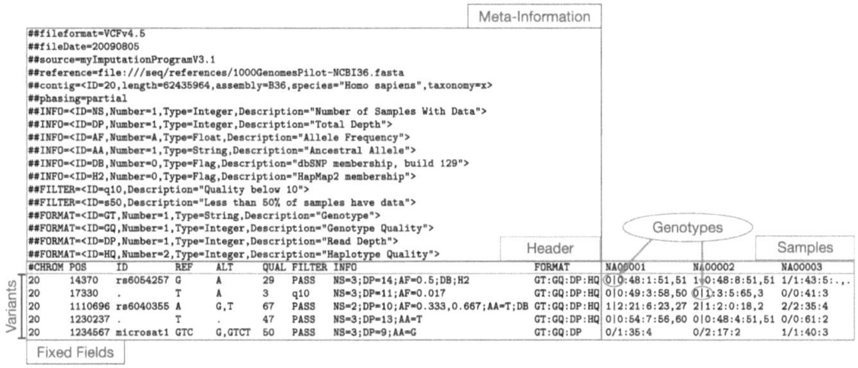

Fig. 1. Structure of a Variant Call Format (VCF) file.

Structural Dependencies. The genomic data contained within the *Samples Block* is not a collection of independent variables. Due to the biological process of inheritance over many generations, certain variants on a chromosome tend to be transmitted together as blocks, a phenomenon known as *Linkage Disequilibrium* (LD) [22]. These correlations manifest as complex multivariate dependencies, meaning that the presence of a specific allele at one position is a strong statistical predictor of alleles at correlated positions. In other words, the observed allele at one locus serves as a significant statistical predictor of alleles at other loci in high LD. For any data synthesis effort, preserving these LD patterns is the primary benchmark of quality; failing to capture these non-random associations results in "hallucinated" genetic profiles that violate the structural integrity of real human populations [27].

Biological Utility: MAF and Structural Dependencies. The scientific validity of synthetic genomic data depends upon the faithful preservation of the statistical properties of the source population, in particular LD and *Minor Allele Frequency* (MAF). MAF characterizes the marginal distribution of the less common allele at a specific genomic coordinate [15]. Maintaining this distribution is essential for the synthetic dataset to reflect the allelic diversity of the original cohort [2]. Furthermore, as discussed above, genomic sequences are not independent variables but exhibit intricate LD correlations. Consequently, the accurate replication of these patterns serves as the primary benchmark for structural integrity. A failure to capture these utility markers leads to the generation of biologically inconsistent profiles that deviate from the structural constraints of real populations [27].

Privacy Threat Model. Genomic sequences are inherently vulnerable to *Membership Inference Attacks* (MIA) [3,23] due to their high-dimensional and identifying properties. In this threat model, we assume an adversary attempts to determine if a specific record (x) was part of the original training cohort (D_{org}) by analyzing the synthetic output (D_{syn}). In our analysis, we adopt a conservative approach to identifying information leaks, prioritizing worst-case analysis. This design choice contrasts with potential alternatives such as average-case privacy. By quantifying the maximum re-identification risk among the most vulnerable individuals in a cohort, we establish a robust privacy lower bound for our generative framework.

3 Related Work

The generation of synthetic genomic data has transitioned from simple probabilistic sampling to complex deep learning architectures. Existing literature generally follows three methodological trajectories, each presenting distinct trade-offs between biological utility and privacy resilience.

Frequency-Based and Algorithmic Baselines. The most direct approach to genotype synthesis relies on observed population statistics. Independent variant sampling, governed by MAF, serves as the foundational baseline for generating artificial cohorts. While computationally simple and effective at masking the specific sequences of correlated variants, also known as *haplotypes*, these methods inherently destroy the *LD* required for downstream genome-wide association studies (GWAS) [27]. To address this, shuffling and permutation-based algorithms were introduced to preserve local sequence structure by reconfiguring existing haplotypes [23]. However, these algorithmic approaches are limited by their inability to generate novel genetic manifolds; they essentially re-sample the existing population, which can lead to residual re-identification risks if the permutation blocks are insufficiently randomized [14]. Consequently, the primary limitation of these baselines is their failure to capture global multivariate correlations and their vulnerability to identity disclosure through record matching.

Deep Generative Paradigms. The advent of Generative Adversarial Networks (GANs) shifted the focus toward learning the high-dimensional latent distribution of genotypes. Early successes in discrete data, such as *medGAN* [6], demonstrated that adversarial training could capture complex correlations in tabular health records. Yelmen et al. [27] further extended this to genomics, demonstrating that GANs and Restricted Boltzmann Machines (RBMs) could outperform traditional statistical models in capturing population structure. Despite these gains, standard GANs are prone to mode collapse and training instability in the sparse, high-dimensional space of single-nucleotide polymorphisms. To mitigate these issues, Wasserstein-based architectures [13] have been explored, offering a more stable loss metric that correlates with the biological realism of the output. Nevertheless, these architectures lack inherent interpretability and formal constraints, making it difficult to guarantee that the learned distributions do not passively memorize rare, identifiable genomic sequences.

The Privacy-Utility Trade-Off. A critical challenge in current research is the tension between data fidelity and privacy. While differential privacy provides formal guarantees, its application to genomic GANs often requires injecting significant noise, which can degrade the multivariate correlations and population-level structures vital for genomic utility [23]. Recent studies have highlighted that high-fidelity synthetic data is particularly vulnerable to MIA [3]. The main weakness in current literature is that privacy and utility are treated as independent post-processing steps rather than integrated objectives, often resulting in models that either preserve biological structure at the cost of high privacy risk or ensure privacy by rendering the data unusable for downstream analysis.

Unlike existing static models that evaluate privacy post-hoc, our work uses an adaptive tuning approach. By integrating an MIA-based worst-case privacy evaluator directly into the synthesis pipeline, we address a significant gap in the literature: the lack of a standardized, computationally efficient framework that balances analytical utility with measurable individual-level privacy.

4 Generative Framework for Synthetic Genomic Data

4.1 A Meta-algorithm for Adaptive Model Tuning

Training generative models for genomic data is inherently challenging due to the high dimensionality and skewness of variant matrices, as well as the competing objectives of privacy and utility. To address these challenges, we introduce an adaptive model-tuning mechanism equipped with a rollback strategy that preserves the best-performing model state (Algorithm 1). The algorithms takes as input a real-world dataset D, a generative model M, a privacy function $\mathcal{P}$, a utility function $\mathcal{U}$, a privacy threshold δ_p, and a utility threshold δ_u, and it returns a synthetic dataset that mimics the real-world input data together with a model to generate more synthetic datasets with the same properties.

The core intuition is to initialize the process with a real dataset D and iteratively improve the best-so-far synthetic dataset D_{bsf}, ensuring that privacy and utility remain above user-defined thresholds as the synthetic data progressively improves. Unlike conventional generative architectures that map noise to a fixed latent distribution [12], our generative model M is *state-aware*: at each iteration, it produces a new candidate dataset by applying its current parameters to the best-so-far dataset D_{bsf}. This conditioning mechanism enables incremental refinement of genomic structures while maintaining a stable optimum model state M_{bsf}, which stores the best configuration discovered across the N iterations.

At each iteration, the candidate dataset D is evaluated using the privacy and utility functions $\mathcal{P}$ and $\mathcal{U}$ against the thresholds δ_p and δ_u. A candidate is accepted only if it satisfies both thresholds and strictly improves upon the current best-so-far dataset D_{bsf}, prioritizing utility and using privacy as a tie-breaker. When this occurs, both D_{bsf} and the model checkpoint M_{bsf} are updated. Conversely, if the candidate violates a threshold or degrades performance, the algorithm rolls back to the last accepted dataset D_{bsf} and its corresponding model state M_{bsf}. This mechanism prevents divergence, enforces monotonic utility improvement, and ensures that the optimization trajectory remains grounded in a biologically valid and privacy-preserving state.

Algorithm 1: Adaptive Model Tuning

Input: dataset D, generative model M, privacy $\mathcal{P}(\cdot)$, utility $\mathcal{U}(\cdot)$, privacy threshold δ_p, utility threshold δ_u, number of iterations N

Output: Synthetic dataset D_{bsf}, optimized generative model M_{bsf}

1 $D_{bsf} \leftarrow D$;
2 $M_{bsf} \leftarrow M$;
3 **for** $i = 1$ **to** N **do**
4     $D \leftarrow M(D_{bsf})$;
5   **if** $\mathcal{P}(D) < \delta_p \vee \mathcal{U}(D) < \delta_u$ **then**
6         $M \leftarrow M_{bsf}$;
7   **else if** $\mathcal{U}(D) > \mathcal{U}(D_{bsf}) \vee \mathcal{U}(D) = \mathcal{U}(D_{bsf}) \wedge \mathcal{P}(D) > \mathcal{P}(D_{bsf})$ **then**
8         $D_{bsf} \leftarrow D$;
9         $M_{bsf} \leftarrow M$;
10     $M \leftarrow \text{Update}(M, D_{bsf})$;
11 **return** (D_{bsf}, M_{bsf});

Update Mechanism. Following each iteration, the framework applies an update step (line 10) that adjusts the generative model based on the current best-so-far dataset D_{bsf}. This operation ensures that the model remains synchronized with the most recently validated synthetic state and incorporates the feedback obtained from the privacy–utility evaluation. Only generators whose parameters evolve with the synthetic dataset participate in this update; fixed-parameter models are excluded. The update mechanism provides the link between feedback and model refinement, enabling the framework to steer the generation process toward higher-quality synthetic data progressively. The concrete update rules for each generator type are described in the subsequent subsections.

4.2 Generation Methods

We consider three types of generation models M: frequency-based, shuffling-based, and neural networks. Each method produces synthetic genotypes through a distinct mechanism and interacts differently with the adaptive tuning framework.

Frequency-Based Generation. This generator provides a simple statistical baseline by reproducing the empirical genotype distribution observed in the real dataset. For each variant, we compute the relative frequency of each genotype category (e.g., 0/0, 0/1, 1/1) across all individuals, and synthetic samples are generated independently by sampling from these empirical distributions. During adaptive tuning, the update step resets the generator to the original frequencies, maintaining a stable anchor for marginal distribution matching. This method preserves per-variant statistics and serves as a lightweight baseline for assessing how more expressive generators improve upon simple distributional matching.

Shuffling and Recombination. This family of methods generates synthetic individuals by rearranging existing genetic material. Our *Shuffling* generator operates at the variant level (column-wise): a shuffling ratio determines the proportion of individuals whose alleles are fully permuted across the cohort, while the remaining individuals are copied directly from the original dataset. This ratio provides a smooth continuum between fully randomized genotypes and exact replicas of real individuals. During adaptive tuning, the update step aligns the shuffling ratio with the value stored in the current best-so-far model M_{bsf}. In contrast, the shuffling itself always operates on the original dataset to avoid drift. We contrast this with the recombination-based Reshape method of Cavinato et al. [4], which uses a Poisson process to simulate chromosomal crossover. By stitching together segments from multiple source individuals, this method creates synthetic mosaics that maintain the biological integrity of contiguous genomic blocks.

Neural Networks. Neural models aim to learn patterns in the joint distribution of genomic variants to generate new samples that reflect the structure of the real data [12]. We evaluate two architectures as independent generators: Restricted Boltzmann Machines (RBMs) and a Wasserstein GAN with Gradient Penalty (WGAN-GP), which we adapt to the characteristics of genotype matrices.

RBMs offer a simple probabilistic framework for modeling co-occurrence patterns between variants. Their two-layer structure forces all variants to interact through a shared set of latent units, allowing the model to learn common genotype configurations without assuming any spatial ordering or local neighborhood structure. This aspect makes RBMs a useful baseline for assessing how much genomic structure can be recovered using a lightweight model focused on lower-order relationships, and they have been shown to capture population-level patterns in genomic data [27].

To capture complex dependencies, we adapt a WGAN-GP architecture to genotype matrices. We first map discrete genotypes into a numerical space to enable continuous gradient-based learning. We use fully connected layers rather than convolutional layers because CNNs are designed for data (e.g., images) in which local patterns repeat across positions [17,18]. In contrast, genomic correlations (e.g., LD) are region-specific and do not recur uniformly across the genome [8,22]. This design avoids imposing an artificial image-like locality on the data. Finally, we use the Wasserstein objective with Gradient Penalty to ensure stable training on the sparse, high-dimensional distributions characteristic of genotype matrices [1,13], preventing the training collapse often observed in simpler GAN formulations.

4.3 Utility Metrics

To evaluate the utility of a synthetic dataset, we use three complementary measures that capture population diversity, marginal variant statistics, and multivariate genomic structure, respectively.

Genomic Diversity Distance. We measure how well the synthetic data preserves population diversity using the Kolmogorov-Smirnov (KS) statistic. For each pair of individuals, we compute the fraction of genomic positions on which their genotypes differ, corresponding to the normalized Hamming distance between their genotype vectors. Let $F_{\text{real}}(x)$ and $F_{\text{syn}}(x)$ denote the cumulative distribution functions of these pairwise distances, where x is any possible distance value. The KS distance is the maximum difference between these two distributions:

$$\textit{KS distance}: \; D_{\text{KS}} = \sup_x \left| F_{\text{real}}(x) - F_{\text{syn}}(x) \right| .$$

Values close to 0 indicate that the synthetic data reproduces the diversity and relatedness structure of the real population.

Allele Frequency Preservation. We evaluate how well the synthetic data preserves variant-level statistics by comparing the minor allele frequencies (MAF) of the real and synthetic datasets. The MAF of a variant is the proportion of chromosomes that carry its less common allele. For each variant i, we compute the MAF in the real and synthetic data, and take the absolute difference between them. The mean absolute difference is obtained by averaging these differences over all m variants:

$$\textit{Mean Absolute Difference}: \quad \mathrm{MAD}_{\mathrm{MAF}} = \frac{1}{m}\sum_{i=1}^{m}\left|\mathrm{MAF}_i^{\mathrm{real}} - \mathrm{MAF}_i^{\mathrm{syn}}\right|.$$

Lower values indicate that the synthetic data closely matches the allele frequency spectrum of the real dataset.

Linkage Disequilibrium Preservation. We assess how well the synthetic data preserves linkage disequilibrium (LD) by comparing the LD values computed by PLINK [5] for the real and synthetic datasets. PLINK reports an LD score for each pair of variants within a sliding genomic window (e.g., 1 Mb), and we merge the real and synthetic LD outputs on matching variant pairs. LD preservation is quantified using two complementary metrics: the Pearson Correlation Coefficient (PCC), which measures how well the overall LD pattern aligns between the two datasets, and the Mean Squared Error (MSE), which captures the average squared deviation between corresponding LD values. Using both metrics is important since PCC evaluates pattern similarity and MSE absolute accuracy.

Let each matched pair of variants be indexed by $k = 1, \ldots, K$, and let L_k^{real} and L_k^{syn} denote their LD values in the real and synthetic datasets, respectively. Then we get the following measures:

$$\textit{Pattern similarity (PCC):} \qquad \mathrm{PCC}_{\mathrm{LD}} = \left|\mathrm{corr}\left(\{L_k^{\mathrm{real}}\}, \{L_k^{\mathrm{syn}}\}\right)\right|.$$

$$\textit{Absolute accuracy (MSE):} \qquad \mathrm{MSE}_{\mathrm{LD}} = \frac{1}{K}\sum_{k=1}^{K}\left(L_k^{\mathrm{real}} - L_k^{\mathrm{syn}}\right)^2.$$

A higher PCC indicates stronger alignment between the relative LD patterns, while a lower MSE reflects a more accurate reproduction of absolute LD values.

4.4 Privacy Metric

Generative models trained on genomic data may inadvertently memorize specific individuals, allowing an adversary to infer whether a given genome was used during training. To quantify this risk, we use a membership inference attack (MIA) framework, which evaluates how easily an attacker can distinguish *training* individuals from *non-training* individuals based solely on the model's outputs. MIAs are widely used to assess privacy leakage in machine learning systems and provide a principled way to measure the extent of unintended memorization [3].

Classical MIA Setting. In a standard shadow-model MIA [20,26], the attacker trains multiple "shadow models" that mimic the behavior of the target generative model. Each shadow model is trained on a dataset where the attacker *knows* which individuals are included (IN) and which are excluded (OUT). By observing how the shadow models behave on IN versus OUT individuals, the attacker learns a decision rule that predicts membership for new samples. However, high-precision MIAs often require training a separate set of shadow models for each target individual, making them computationally infeasible for large cohorts.

Universal Shadow Pool. To overcome this limitation, we use a *universal shadow pool*: a fixed pool of K shadow models trained once on random subsets of the population. Because each shadow model sees a different subset, the pool collectively induces the empirical IN and OUT distributions for *every* individual in the cohort. This design eliminates the need to retrain models per target record and makes full-cohort privacy evaluation computationally tractable.

Likelihood Ratio Attack (LiRA). For each individual t, we apply the Likelihood Ratio Attack (LiRA) [3], which compares how likely the generative model's outputs appear under the IN versus OUT distributions. The resulting log-likelihood ratio indicates how strongly the model behaves as if it had seen t during training. Because raw LiRA values are theoretically unbounded, we convert each score into a probability using a logistic transformation, which maps the log-likelihood ratio into the interval $[0, 1]$. This step yields a membership probability $p(t)$ that reflects the likelihood that the model will treat t as part of the training set.

Weakest-link Privacy Gain. To maintain the convention that higher values correspond to stronger privacy, we invert the membership probability into an individual-level privacy score. For a dataset D with individuals $t \in D$, we define the weakest-link Privacy Gain as:

$$PG(D) = \min_{t \in D} (1 - p(t)) .$$

This metric captures the privacy of the "weakest link", i.e., the least-protected individual t in the dataset D. Values close to 1 indicate strong privacy, while values near 0 reveal that at least one individual remains vulnerable to membership inference. By focusing on the minimum gain, we ensure our adaptive framework protects the most exposed outliers in the cohort.

5 Experimental Evaluation

5.1 Environment

Experiments were performed on a high-performance computing cluster node running Ubuntu 24.04.4 LTS. To support training adversarial models and processing high-dimensional genomic matrices, we used a dedicated NVIDIA A100-SXM4-80GB GPU. The compute infrastructure featured an AMD EPYC 7543P 32-Core Processor and 200 GiB of allocated system memory, backed by a 1 PB Ceph storage system for scalable data management. The software stack was built on CUDA 12.4 and cuDNN 8.9.7. The generative framework and evaluation pipelines were implemented in Python 3.10, leveraging PyTorch for neural network operations and Scikit-learn for privacy risk assessment.

5.2 Datasets

We evaluate our framework on three publicly available genomic datasets that differ in organism, scale, missingness, and genotype complexity, providing a broad benchmarking environment for assessing generative performance under different conditions. Genotype complexity refers to the number and diversity of genotype encodings observed at each variant. Higher complexity increases the difficulty of modeling discrete genomic data. The *Mouse Genomes Project (MGP)* dataset [16] contains near-complete genotype calls for inbred laboratory strains, resulting in no missing values and very low genotype complexity, with only a small set of distinct genotype classes appearing across variants. This controlled setting enables a baseline evaluation of structural fidelity. The *HapMap Phase 3* dataset [9] offers high-quality, fully imputed human genotypes and moderate genotype complexity, consisting mostly of a limited number of common genotype classes per variant. This aspect makes it well-suited for benchmarking under stable, QC-filtered conditions. Finally, the *1000 Genomes Project (Phase 3)* dataset [8] provides real-world whole-genome variation with substantial population diversity and high genotype complexity due to multi-allelic variants [19], rare genotypes, and missing values. In our experiments, we use chromosome 22 (1 kG Chr22), which retains the dataset's characteristics while reducing computational cost. This dataset captures the full complexity of human genomic structure and therefore represents the most challenging setting for evaluating privacy–utility trade-offs. Together, these datasets span controlled reference-quality genotypes, imputed population data, and heterogeneous real-world variation, enabling a thorough assessment of our generative framework (Table 1).

Table 1. Summary of genomic datasets used in the experimental evaluation.

Dataset	Samples	Variants	Missing Values	Genotype Complexity
MGP	80	42,812	No	Low, 3 classes
HapMap3	1,184	1,387,466	Fully imputed	Moderate, 5 classes
1 kG Chr22	2,504	1,103,547	Yes	High, 23 classes

5.3 Results and Discussion

Optimization Path and Backtracking Dynamics. In the first experiment in Fig. 2 we analyze the performance of our meta-algorithm on real genomic data by evaluating it on the MGP dataset using the utility metrics MAD_{MAF} and PCC_{LD} and visualizing the rollback trajectories of our best-performing model WGAN-GP. The x-axis represents the training iteration, while the y-axis simultaneously reports the utility value for the selected metric and the corresponding privacy score computed at the same iteration. We also computed the KS distance, but its trajectory closely matches that of MAD_{MAF}, so we omit it here and focus on the two metrics that provide distinct diagnostic signal: MAD_{MAF} (lower is better) and PCC_{LD} (higher is better).

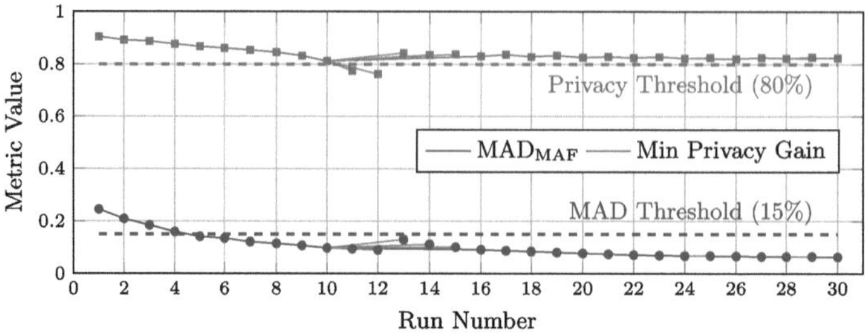

(a) MAD_{MAF} Rollback

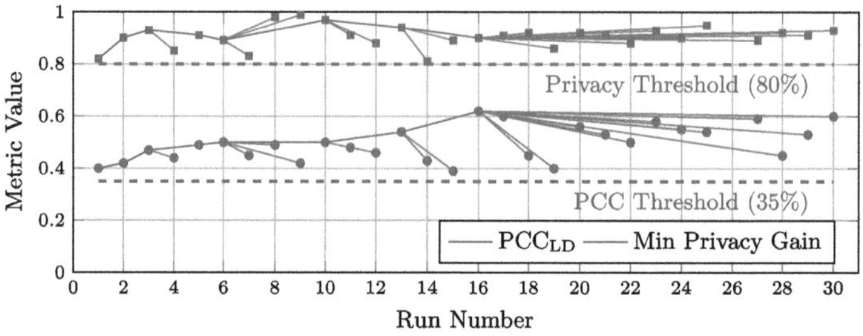

(b) PCC_{LD} Rollback

Fig. 2. Rollback trajectories of WGAN-GP under MAD_{MAF} and PCC_{LD}

The MAD_{MAF} trajectory in Fig. 2a shows a mostly smooth progression, with a mid-stage rollback at iterations 11–12 triggered by a drop in privacy below the threshold, followed by another rollback at iterations 13–14 where the MAD_{MAF} value exceeded the last acceptable state; these events illustrate how the system corrects brief deviations while maintaining overall stability in MAF fidelity.

In contrast, the PCC_{LD} trajectory in Fig. 2b exposes degradations in long-range genomic structure that are not visible in MAD_{MAF}, marked by late-stage rollback events beginning at iteration 16, where structural correlation collapsed and the system reverted to earlier, more stable states. This pattern reflects the greater difficulty of maintaining LD patterns during training. Notably, we find that the complementary MSE_{LD} metric remains consistently low across all runs, confirming it does not provide additional diagnostic information beyond PCC_{LD}. Taken together, the two subplots show that stabilizing MAD_{MAF} is relatively straightforward, whereas PCC_{LD} requires more careful intervention; the meta-algorithm adapts accordingly by selectively reverting to earlier states when LD fidelity deteriorates, ultimately converging to a stable, high-quality solution.

Privacy–Utility Comparison. In the next experiment in Fig. 3 we evaluate how the meta-algorithm optimizes the data generation models and how the resulting best-performing checkpoints compare against state-of-the-art baselines. For each dataset, the meta-algorithm explores the generator's parameter space and returns the strongest performing variants, while RBM and Reshape serve as external baselines. Frequency and Shuffling consistently yield very low utility (PCC_{LD} = 0.02–0.10), but their privacy levels vary widely across datasets, ranging from 0.40 to 0.98, indicating that simple perturbation-based generators do not reliably achieve strong privacy despite sacrificing structure. RBM and Reshape show the opposite pattern, achieving moderate to high LD preservation (0.20–0.88) but with limited privacy (0.10–0.82). In contrast, the WGAN-GP version of our generator, when optimized by the meta-algorithm, consistently identifies operating points that balance both objectives: it achieves high utility (0.57 on MGP, 0.86 on HapMap3, 0.71 on 1 KG Chr22) together with strong privacy protection (0.72–0.94). These results demonstrate that the adaptive feedback loop effectively steers our generator toward states that preserve population-level structure without substantially compromising individual-level privacy.

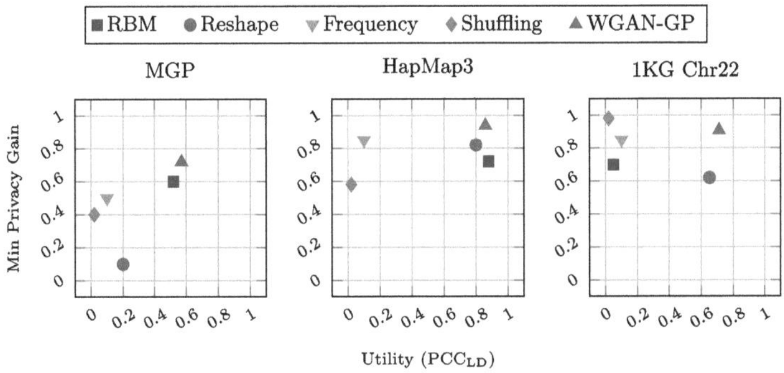

Fig. 3. Privacy-utility trade-off across different datasets.

MAF Distributional Fidelity. We evaluate distributional fidelity by comparing the MAF of generated variants against the ground truth. The results are shown in Fig. 4. Simple baselines such as *Shuffling* and *Frequency* generation achieve near-perfect linearity but lack the structural complexity required for meaningful genomic utility. Among the more expressive models, the WGAN-GP exhibits the highest precision (MAD: 0.0078), closely following the identity line across the full allele-frequency spectrum. In contrast, the RBM shows substantial dispersion (MAD: 0.0361), and the *Reshape* method displays a characteristic stair-step pattern indicative of discretization artifacts. These results confirm that our adaptive WGAN-GP approach preserves both first-order (MAF) and second-order (LD) statistical properties of the source population.

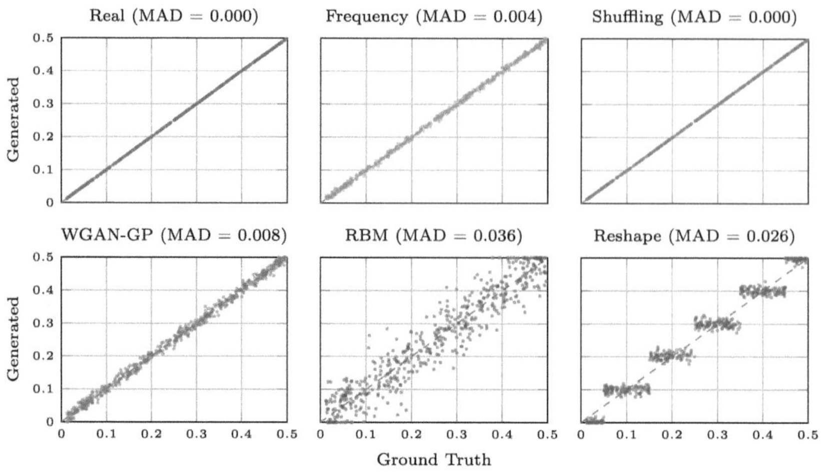

Fig. 4. Comparative analysis of MAF preservation. The diagonal line ($y = x$) represents perfect frequency fidelity.

Generative Consistency. To assess whether the best-performing model returned by the meta-algorithm produces stable outputs rather than a single favorable sample, we conducted an additional robustness experiment on the MGP dataset. The results are shown in Fig. 5. After determining the optimal checkpoint, which was found on iteration 16, we used this Model 16 to generate five independent synthetic datasets and evaluated each using PCC_{LD} and privacy gain. The results show tightly clustered PCC_{LD} values between 0.60 and 0.63, indicating consistent reconstruction of pairwise genomic structure across generations. Privacy scores likewise remain stable, ranging from 0.89 to 0.91, indicating that the model remains robust to membership inference attacks. Together, these findings confirm that the selected model exhibits reliable generative behavior, producing reproducible synthetic datasets that preserve structural fidelity while sustaining robust privacy guarantees.

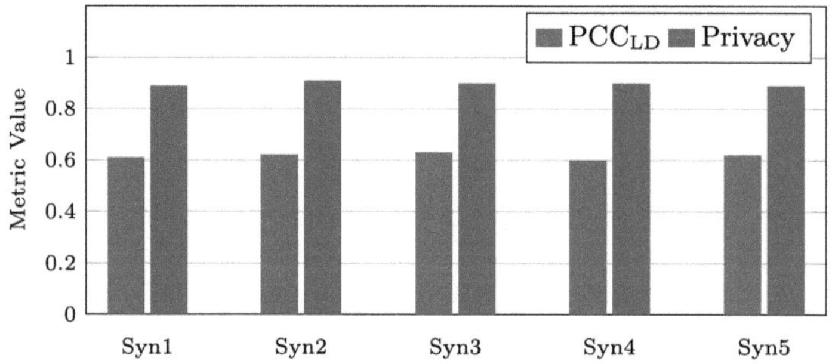

Fig. 5. WGAN-GP Model 16: Consistency Across Synthetic Datasets.

6 Conclusion

We presented a framework for iterative refinement of synthetic genomic data under explicit privacy constraints. A key strength of this framework is its plug-and-play design: it is agnostic to both the underlying generative architecture and the choice of privacy or utility metrics. Any metric can be incorporated as a monitoring signal, and the rollback mechanism adapts accordingly. Likewise, the method can wrap any generative architecture. The adaptive tuning algorithm guides the parameter updates through an iterative loop. We demonstrated this flexibility using a WGAN-GP architecture tailored to high-dimensional genotype matrices. Experimental evaluation demonstrates that our framework improves stability, particularly when preserving LD structure is challenging, and recovers higher-fidelity states through targeted rollbacks. To assess privacy, we compute membership-inference risk for all individuals simultaneously using a universal shadow pool, which provides the MIA scores needed to detect information leakage during the refinement process.

Future work will extend this framework in several directions. One avenue is to explore richer dimensions of utility, including downstream GWAS reproducibility metrics. Another direction of research involves evaluating the meta-algorithm across a broader class of architectures, such as diffusion models and autoregressive transformers. On the control level, future extensions can strengthen the refinement process itself. Adaptive rollback windows would allow the algorithm to scale the rollback distance based on the severity of a metric violation, rather than reverting to a fixed previous checkpoint. Finally, Pareto-frontier rollback controllers could replace single-threshold acceptance rules with multi-objective optimization.

Acknowledgments. This work was partially funded by the Autonomous Province of Bozen-Bolzano, call Joint Projects South Tyrol – Germany, project DyHealthNet, CUP I53C22002980003.

References

1. Arjovsky, M., Chintala, S., Bottou, L.: Wasserstein generative adversarial networks. In: Proceedings of the 34th International Conference on Machine Learning, ICML'17, vol. 70, pp. 214–223. JMLR.org (2017)
2. Auton, A., Brooks, L.D., Durbin, R.M., et al.: A global reference for human genetic variation. Nature **526**(7571), 68–74 (2015)
3. Carlini, N., Chien, S., Nasr, M., Song, S., Terzis, A., Tramer, F.: Membership inference attacks from first principles. In: 2022 IEEE Symposium on Security and Privacy (SP), pp. 1897–1914. IEEE (2022)
4. Cavinato, T., Rubinacci, S., Malaspinas, A.S., Delaneau, O.: A resampling-based approach to share reference panels. Nat. Comput. Sci. **4**(5), 360–366 (2024)

5. Chang, C.C., Chow, C.C., Tellier, L.C., Vattikuti, S., Purcell, S.M., Lee, J.J.: Second-generation plink: rising to the challenge of larger and richer datasets. Gigascience **4**(1), s13742-015 (2015)
6. Choi, E., Biswal, S., Glassman, B., Duke, J., Stewart, W.F., Sun, J.: Generating multi-label discrete patient records using generative adversarial networks. In: Proceedings of the 2nd MLHC, pp. 286–305. PMLR (2017)
7. Conboy, C.: Consent and privacy in the era of precision medicine and biobanking genomic data. Am. J. Law Med. **46**(2–3), 167–187 (2020)
8. The 1000 Genomes Project Consortium: A global reference for human genetic variation. Nature **526**(7571), 68–74 (2015)
9. The International HapMap 3 Consortium: Integrating common and rare genetic variation in diverse human populations. Nature **467**(7311), 52–58 (2010)
10. Danecek, P., et al.: The variant call format and VCFtools. Bioinformatics **27**(15), 2156–2158 (2011)
11. European Parliament and Council of the European Union: General data protection regulation (GDPR) (2016), regulation (EU) 2016/679. https://eur-lex.europa.eu/eli/reg/2016/679/oj. Accessed 10 Apr 2026
12. Goodfellow, I., Bengio, Y., Courville, A.: Deep Learning. MIT Press (2016). http://www.deeplearningbook.org
13. Gulrajani, I., Ahmed, F., Arjovsky, M., Dumoulin, V., Courville, A.C.: Improved training of Wasserstein GANs. In: Advances in Neural Information Processing Systems (NeurIPS), vol. 30 (2017)
14. Gymrek, M., McGuire, A.L., Golan, D., Halperin, E., Erlich, Y.: Identifying personal genomes by surname inference. Science **339**(6117), 321–324 (2013)
15. Hartl, D.L., Clark, A.G.: Principles of Population Genetics. Sinauer Associates, Sunderland, MA (2007)
16. Keane, T.M., Goodstadt, L., Danecek, P., et al.: Mouse genomic variation and its effect on phenotypes. Nature **477**(7364), 289–294 (2011)
17. LeCun, Y., Bengio, Y., Hinton, G.: Deep learning. Nature **521**(7553), 436–444 (2015)
18. Libbrecht, M.W., Noble, W.S.: Machine learning applications in genetics and genomics. Nat. Rev. Genet. **16**(6), 321–332 (2015)
19. Pierce, B.A.: Genetics: A Conceptual Approach. Macmillan Higher Education, New York, NY (2017)
20. Salem, A., Zhang, Y., Humbert, M., Berrang, P., Fritz, M., Backes, M.: ML-leaks: model and data independent membership inference attacks and defenses on machine learning models. In: Network and Distributed System Security Symposium (NDSS) (2019)
21. samtools: The variant call format specification VCFv4.4 and BCFv2.2 (2024). https://github.com/samtools/hts-specs. Accessed 10 Apr 2026
22. Slatkin, M.: Linkage disequilibrium—understanding the evolutionary past and informing the genetic future. Nat. Rev. Genet. **9**(6), 477–485 (2008)
23. Stadler, T., Oneto, L., Troncoso, C.: Synthetic data-anonymisation groundhog day. In: 31st USENIX Security Symposium (USENIX Security 22), pp. 1451–1468 (2022)
24. Tanjo, T., Kawai, Y., Tokunaga, K., Ogasawara, O., Nagasaki, M.: Practical guide for managing large-scale human genome data in research. J. Hum. Genet. **66**(1), 39–52 (2021)
25. US Department of Health and Human Services: Health insurance portability and accountability act of 1996 (HIPAA) (1996). Public Law 104-191. https://www.hhs.gov/hipaa/index.html. Accessed 10 Apr 2026

26. Ye, J., Maddi, A., Murakonda, S.K., Bindschaedler, V., Shokri, R.: Enhanced membership inference attacks against machine learning models. In: Proceedings of the 2022 ACM SIGSAC Conference on Computer and Communications Security, pp. 3093–3106 (2022)
27. Yelmen, B., et al.: Creating artificial human genomes using generative neural networks. PLoS Genet. **17**(2), e1009303 (2021)

Compression-Based Behavioral Similarity for Open-World Sybil Discovery on Ethereum

Michał Bartnicki(✉) and Jarosław A. Chudziak

Faculty of Electronics and Information Technology, Warsaw University of Technology, Warsaw, Poland
{michal.bartnicki.stud,jaroslaw.chudziak}@pw.edu.pl

Abstract. Sybil attackers are Blockchain actors that adopt the characteristics of regular users to exploit airdrops or influence governance. Current methods of Sybil actor detection include constructing graphs, which requires token transfers between examined wallets. Machine learning algorithms have been employed as well, but they treat the task as a closed-set classification problem, making them vulnerable to frequent changes in attack strategies or evasion tactics. We address the following questions: can compression-based similarity differentiate Sybil bots, organic users, and arbitrage bot wallets without direct financial links? What is the effect of high-signal contracts on the discovery of Sybils, and how robust are behavioral graphs under temporal drift and adversarial perturbations? Our approach synthesizes a symbolic Transaction Grammar from EVM (Ethereum Virtual Machine) traces, capturing separately transaction rhythm, execution structure, and functional intent. The high-signal contracts are filtered with our own protocol, called the Blind-Spot Protocol. Gzip-based NCD is used to construct a behavioral graph for Sybil discovery. We validate this framework against supervised machine learning baselines, a temporal split, and synthetic camouflage stress tests. Ultimately, we contribute a leakage-aware behavioral framework for Sybil candidate discovery. Its core NCD primitive requires no supervised training and can expand suspicious seed wallets without explicit funding links. We position the method as a training-free local discovery primitive for open-world blockchain audits, rather than as a formal open-set recognition system.

Keywords: Blockchain Analytics · Ethereum · Sybil Discovery · Normalized Compression Distance · Behavioral Similarity

1 Introduction

With DeFi and governance growth in Ethereum, Sybil attacks remain a persistent threat [8]. In these attacks, one entity controls many pseudonymous wallets to farm airdrops or manipulate DAO governance [18,20,28]. Aggregate statistics

G. Vargas-Solar et al. (Eds.): ADBIS 2026, LNCS 16937, pp. 266–282, 2027.
https://doi.org/10.1007/978-3-032-39820-8_18

or financial links expose simple cases, but evasive campaigns require coordination and execution-pattern analysis.

Current detection strategies primarily rely on explicit financial interaction graphs and closed-set supervised classifiers [1]. However, this framing is poorly aligned with blockchain audit settings where labels are incomplete, strategies evolve after deployment, and the goal is often candidate discovery rather than closed-set classification. [23]. Graph-based methods attempt to detect communities with common funding or value flow [27], although such indicators become weaker when value flows pass through centralized exchanges, disperser contracts, or other intermediates. Tabular feature-based supervised methods, including balance, transaction rate, gas expenditure, and number of interactions, have shown promise if representative labels exist [14,17]. Recent benchmarks suggest tree-based models remain the gold standard for such tabular blockchain data [10,24]. But such methods suffer from two weaknesses in audit-driven candidate discovery. First, models may exploit shortcut features, such as label-indicative contracts, instead of transferable behavior. The problem has parallels to more general issues around robustness of ML systems against adversarial distributional shortcuts [22]. Second, they remain reactive until representative labels are curated.

In this paper, we posit that Sybil discovery in this audit setting can be rephrased as pairwise behavioral similarity analysis rather than categorization of individual wallets. We define a wallet's behavior using a symbolic *Transaction Grammar* that encodes transaction rhythm, EVM execution trace structure, and function-level intent. Modeling wallet behavior as a sequence lets us measure similarity using Algorithmic Information Theory without training a classifier.

2 Related Work

The process of Sybil detection generally involves the use of explicit graphs, where each edge denotes an ETH or ERC-20 token transfer [5]. Community detection and clustering methods are used to detect Sybils with similar funding channels, whereas GNN pipelines classify Sybil accounts based on graph-based features [17, 27]. Although such techniques are effective, their performance depends heavily on visible funding flows and is significantly reduced when actors hide token transfers through intermediaries such as exchanges or dispersers.

The second method uses tabular machine learning to detect blockchain actors. Such algorithms operate with aggregate wallet statistics like number of transactions, transaction timings, gas usage, balance changes, and interaction frequencies [7,14,21]. The works on financial bot detection on Ethereum also confirm the efficiency of supervised and unsupervised machine learning approaches provided suitable features and labels are available. In particular, recent publications construct labeled Ethereum human/bot datasets using timing, frequency, gas price, and gas-limit features.

The current work on blockchain analytics seeks to leverage more advanced behavioral representations, taking into account that bots are characterized by their rhythm of activity and patterns of interaction, not the sheer rate of communication. Existing learning-based approaches have mostly been supervised and task-specific, labeling predefined classes of wallets, but failing to uncover new bot communities. This makes them inadequate for open-world blockchain audits, where new bot scripts may emerge before representative labels are available. Evaluations suffer from similar problems related to adversarial learning. One example is provided by TESSERACT, which highlights how incorrect experimental setups can cause an overestimation of performance because of space-time bias [22]. In the blockchain setting, a comparable pitfall is when learning algorithms take advantage of high-signal counterparts or blockchain peculiarities rather than extracting universal behavioral patterns.

Our approach is rooted in the methodological foundation of Normalized Compression Distance (NCD). The NCD evaluates similarity based on the compressibility of an artifact when compared to its counterpart; hence, the similarity of an object is measured depending on how well it can be compressed together with another artifact. Compression has been used before for various other purposes such as malware classification and cybersecurity; in all of those cases, similar structures of two different objects could have been identified despite their dissimilarity [6]. So far, there is no research related to compression and similarity of Ethereum Sybils.

In other words, our technique can be positioned between two well-established frameworks. First, contrary to explicit graph approaches, our method does not rely on explicit financial connections between wallets. Second, unlike supervised classifiers, no labeled training is needed in order to compute similarity scores between wallets. Instead, we define implicit graph where edges denote similarity of structural properties of transaction grammars. Such a construction allows local candidate generation from a suspicious seed wallet. Our approach targets audit scenarios where labels are rare, actor behaviors evolve, and transaction connections may be unavailable. Accordingly, graph neural baselines over explicit transfer or funding graphs are complementary rather than directly comparable to the disconnected behavioral-similarity task evaluated here.

3 Problem and Approach

This section presents our behavioral formulation of open-world Sybil discovery. We define the task as candidate discovery over wallet behavior, encode wallet histories as Transaction Grammars, compare them with Normalized Compression Distance, and construct an implicit behavioral graph. We then introduce the Blind-Spot protocol used to control leakage from high-signal contracts before evaluation.

3.1 Problem Formulation

Sybil attackers threaten blockchain ecosystems by operating many pseudonymous wallets that imitate ordinary users to farm airdrops or influence decentralized governance. The task is not simply bot detection: arbitrage-oriented MEV bots are also automated, but may represent benign or economically motivated activity. We therefore distinguish coordinated Sybil behavior from both Organic users and MEV automation.

Explicit financial graphs are effective when wallets share funding or transfer links, but coordinated campaigns may appear disconnected after using exchanges, dispersers, or intermediaries. Supervised classifiers require curated labels, retraining, and may exploit shortcut features such as class-indicative contracts. We instead formulate Sybil detection as training-free candidate discovery in an open-world audit setting: given wallet histories, identify groups that share behavioral grammar without requiring direct financial links or a closed-set classifier.

Each wallet W is represented as an ordered sequence $S_W = \{x_1, x_2, \ldots, x_L\}$, where each transaction x_t encodes rhythmic, structural, and intent-based properties from EVM traces. NCD then measures shared regularity between sequences and induces an implicit behavioral graph whose edges reflect script-level similarity rather than token flow.

This formulation leads to four empirical questions: whether Sybil wallets are internally more similar than Organic and MEV wallets; whether compression-based similarity supports candidate discovery without financial links; how much signal comes from high-signal contract leakage; and how stable the behavioral graph remains under temporal drift and adversarial camouflage.

3.2 Approach

Our framework operates by converting raw execution traces into compact behavioral patterns and analyzing them through information-theoretic distances. We first define a unified sequence modeling method to express multi-dimensional transaction properties as a structural script language. This representation is then used to construct an implicit behavioral graph and filter out global tracking bias, allowing for parameter-free malicious coordination discovery.

Transaction Grammar and Sequence Encodings. To capture on-chain behavior compactly, each transaction is encoded as $x_t = (\tau_t, \gamma_t, \nu_t)$: Rhythm, Structure, and Intent.

- **Rhythm** (τ_t): This component captures the temporal patterns of activity, ranging from high-frequency machine-speed bursts to human scales of dormancy. We compute the inter-arrival time Δt in seconds since the previous transaction and discretize it into 16 log-bins, ranging from `same-block` ($\Delta t = 0$) to `dormancy` ($\Delta t > 30$ days), with a unique `START` token for the beginning of a sequence.
- **Structure** (γ_t): To represent the inner workings of each transaction, we define nine properties from the EVM trace, including call depth, branching, and error rates. These metrics are discretized and concatenated into a unique composite string (e.g., `Cnt:2_Dp:4_Err:0`), effectively treating the "shape" of the execution trace as a word in our vocabulary.

- **Intent** (ν_t): This element encodes semantic intent through the 4-byte function selector of the call. In order to keep control of vocabulary size, the primary experiment uses a vocabulary of $|V| = 100$ most common selectors on a class-stratified basis, and less common selectors are treated as the generic `[UNK]`. We additionally verify that an unsupervised global-frequency vocabulary of the same size yields equivalent NCD retrieval quality, showing that the construction does not materially depend on class labels.

The grammar supports multiple sequence types: `rhythm_only`, `coarse_intent`, and `full_tokens`. The 16 logarithmic rhythm bins preserve activity scales from same-block bursts to long dormancy, while the $|V| = 100$ selector vocabulary keeps the symbolic alphabet compact enough for compression (Table 1).

Table 1. Transaction Grammar: Token Vocabulary Formulation

Token Type	Definition and Discretization Strategy
Rhythm (τ)	Log-binned Δt (16 bins): {`START`, `Same-Block`, ..., `30d+`}.
Structure (γ)	Composite string of 8 binned trace metrics: Complexity (Count, Depth, Branching), Outcome (Reverts, Root status), Op Types (Delegate, Static, Create ops).
Intent (ν)	Compact vocabulary of $\lvert V\rvert = 100$ frequent function selectors; global-frequency variant tested as ablation. Special: `[UNK]`, `NO_CALLDATA`.

Normalized Compression Distance. We quantify sequence similarity using Normalized Compression Distance (NCD) [6]. We use gzip as a deterministic, widely available LZ-family compressor that provides a reproducible baseline for detecting repeated symbolic motifs; alternative compressors are left for future work. For any two encoded wallet sequences x and y, the distance is defined as:

$$\mathrm{NCD}(x, y) = \frac{C(xy) - \min(C(x), C(y))}{\max(C(x), C(y))} \tag{1}$$

where $C(x)$ represents the byte length of the sequence x after compression with `gzip`, and xy denotes the concatenation of the two sequences. The NCD value ranges from 0 to 1, where lower values indicate higher structural similarity.

The efficacy of NCD in this context relies on the distinction between algorithmic regularity and human entropy. In our domain, organic users exhibit high natural entropy and diverse transaction grammars. Conversely, Sybil farmers rely on automated scripts that produce highly redundant sequences. When two such scripted sequences are concatenated (xy), the compressor identifies the shared structural motifs and achieves a higher compression ratio than it would for disparate organic traces, thereby yielding a low NCD score. This allows NCD to act as a coordination signal that is inherently robust to the exact timing or value of transactions, focusing instead on the shared "logic" of execution.

Implicit Behavioral Graph Construction. While traditional blockchain analytics focuses on explicit interaction graphs (i.e., value flow), we construct an *implicit behavioral graph* derived from the pairwise similarity of transaction grammars. For a given sample of $N = 900$ wallets, we compute a symmetric $N \times N$ distance matrix where each element D_{ij} is the NCD between wallet i and wallet j. We transform this distance into a similarity score $s = 1 - \text{NCD}$ to serve as the adjacency weight for our graph.

This implicit graph representation serves three primary downstream purposes:

- **Local Neighborhood Retrieval:** By examining the k-nearest neighbors (k-NN) of a suspect wallet in the NCD space, we can identify other actors within the same coordinated campaign. Our empirical results (H3) suggest that these local neighborhoods are significantly enriched with Sybil candidates, even when the actors have no direct on-chain funding links.
- **Global Community Discovery:** The similarity matrix serves as a primitive for unsupervised partitioning. We apply Spectral and Agglomerative clustering to detect larger pockets of coordination. Unlike isolated classification, this approach can identify emerging Sybil strategies by grouping wallets that exhibit similar "fingerprints" of structural regularity.
- **Robustness Analysis:** Treating similarity as a graph allows us to evaluate the structural resilience of the signal. By re-evaluating the graph connectivity before and after the application of the Blind-Spot protocol, we can quantify how much of the "coordination" is driven by shared utility (label leakage) versus the underlying algorithmic logic of the scripts.

By reinterpreting pairwise compression as a graph structure, we move from the classification of individual entities to the discovery of functional communities, making the framework particularly suitable for the open-world discovery of "orphaned" Sybil clusters.

Blind-Spot Protocol for Leakage-Free Evaluation. For leakage-controlled evaluation, our label-informed Blind-Spot protocol removes high-signal counterparties (e.g., popular DeFi protocols) that introduce label leakage by acting as shortcut features [9,15]. For instance, interactions with the Uniswap Router are a strong circular indicator of MEV arbitrage, while the ENS Controller is a primary signal for human-driven Organic identity.

The protocol systematically identifies and removes these high-signal interactions to force models to rely on authentic behavioral signatures, such as transaction timing and execution traces. In our implementation, this process resulted in the removal of 25.5% of the total transaction volume, targeting ubiquitous or class-specific contracts like OpenSea Wyvern and WETH9. By mitigating the influence of these specific counterparties, the protocol ensures that the predictive signal is derived from the structural regularity of the actor's behavior rather than superficial interaction targets.

4 Experiments and Results

This section evaluates the proposed compression-based behavioral similarity framework under both Raw and Blind-Spot-filtered settings. We first describe dataset construction and leakage filtering, then test behavioral separation, local candidate discovery, temporal stability, and robustness under synthetic camouflage.

4.1 Experimental Setup and Dataset

Our dataset was built by fetching the labels and addresses from two major sources. Organic and Sybil actors have been sourced from the Hop Protocol airdrop list [13]. The labels for the MEV Bots have been collected using the labeled datasets from Dune Analytics with a hard cutoff at May 13th, 2022, when Hop Protocol released its snapshot. We acquired addresses with labels indicating Arbitrage Bots. For downloading transaction's internal execution traces, we leveraged Google BigQuery. We initially excluded any wallet with less than $L_{\min} = 10$ transactions.

To refine this raw dataset and prevent label leakage, we applied our Blind-Spot Protocol. In the scope of this protocol, we calculated three key measures for each candidate address:

- **Support** (n): the total number of transactions related to an address. A minimum threshold of $n \geq 50$ is applied to ensure statistical relevance.
- **Max Class Share (Purity** P**)**: proportion of transactions that belong to the predominant actor class. Address with Purity value higher than $P \geq 0.95$ may be considered as leaking one's class.
- **Shannon Entropy** (H): uncertainty of class distribution measured as $H = -\sum p_i \log_2(p_i)$. Leaking addresses have entropy close to zero.

All transactions, including interactions with these "blind-spots" addresses, are removed from the histories of all wallets in the dataset. Applying this protocol removed 25.5% of all transaction volume and excluded 443 wallets that dropped below the minimum-history threshold ($L_{\min} = 10$). The final dataset statistics, comparing the raw and leakage-free wallet counts, are summarized in Table 2. For runtime context, computing a full $N = 900$ NCD matrix over 404,550 wallet pairs required 83–96 s across repeated runs, with a mean of 90.4 s, on a 2020 MacBook Pro with Apple M1 and 16 GB RAM.

Table 2. Dataset Statistics

Class	Raw Wallets Count	Leakage-Free Wallets Count
Organic	9,282	9,204
MEV Bot	3,558	3,202
Sybil	1,764	1,755
Total	**14,604**	**14,161**

4.2 Statistical Analysis of Behavioral Similarity

To test whether Sybil wallets are more behaviorally similar than Organic and MEV wallets, and whether this signal survives leakage control, we compare within-class NCD similarity before and after Blind-Spot filtering. Behavioral coordination is measured via within-class pairwise similarity $s = 1 - \text{NCD}$ using $N = 10$ random seeds (300 wallets per class, 44,850 pairs per class and seed). The separation of clusters is assessed through the mean similarity difference Δ between classes and Cliff's δ statistic, defined as:

$$\delta = \Pr(X > Y) - \Pr(X < Y). \tag{2}$$

Here, X and Y are two distributions of pairwise similarities. This effect-size statistic is suitable for non-normal data. Standard pairwise inference assumes independent observations, but each wallet appears in multiple comparisons. Therefore, we treat δ as a purely descriptive statistic and assess significance by testing whether the ten seed-level Δ values are significantly greater than zero using a one-sided Wilcoxon signed-rank test.

Table 3. Within-class similarity differences (Δ) and Cliff's δ effect sizes. Values are means $\pm$ standard deviations across $N = 10$ random seeds.

Encoding	Setting	Syb–Org Δ	Cliff's δ_{Org}	Syb–MEV Δ	Cliff's δ_{MEV}
`rhythm_only`	Raw	0.089 ± 0.008	0.392	0.092 ± 0.009	0.404
`rhythm_only`	LF	0.115 ± 0.010	0.483	0.117 ± 0.011	0.490
`rhythm+intent`	Raw	0.122 ± 0.011	0.384	0.118 ± 0.010	0.368
`rhythm+intent`	LF	0.233 ± 0.012	0.674	0.214 ± 0.013	0.640
`full_tokens`	LF[a]	0.091 ± 0.010	0.445	0.087 ± 0.009	0.428

LF denotes Leakage-Free. [a] We report `full_tokens` only in the leakage-free setting, where the complete transaction grammar is evaluated after removing utility-based shortcut interactions. Raw-vs-leakage comparisons are therefore limited to the first two encodings.

Table 3 indicates that Sybil wallets show higher within-class similarity than Organic and MEV wallets across all tested seeds. For the full_tokens leakage-free representation, this distributional shift is visualized in Fig. 1. For rhythm+intent profiles in the Leakage-Free setting, the observed $\delta = 0.674$ against Organic wallets corresponds to a common-language effect size of approximately 0.837, excluding ties. Thus, Sybil–Sybil pairs are more likely to be more similar than Organic–Organic pairs. This supports the hypothesis that behavioral scripts are reused more often in Sybil attacks.

When both Raw and Leakage-Free variants are available, the Blind-Spot protocol yields a larger effect size. For the `rhythm+intent` encoding, the Sybil–Organic similarity gap nearly doubles, increasing from +0.122 to +0.233 after the exclusion of high-signal global contracts. We interpret this as a denoising effect: removing universal contract counterparties, such as Uniswap, reduces shared "utility" similarity and reveals a clearer signal of repetitive script structure.

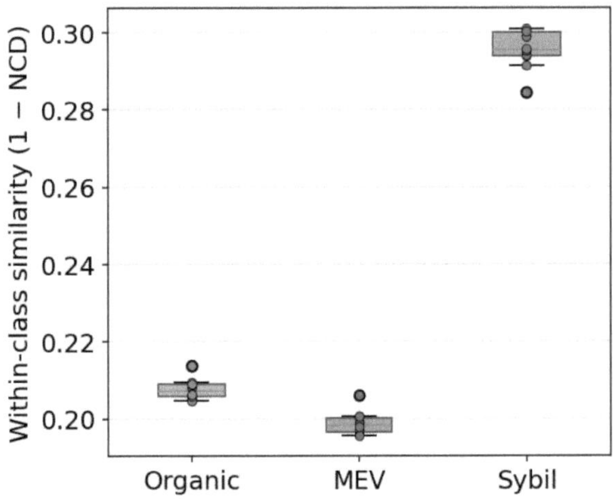

Fig. 1. Distribution of within-class behavioral similarity (1-NCD) for the Full Tokens grammar. The Sybil class exhibits a markedly higher similarity baseline compared to Organic and MEV actors.

4.3 Candidate Discovery and Comparative Analysis

To test whether compression-based similarity can support Sybil candidate discovery without financial links, we evaluate nearest-neighbor retrieval in the NCD behavioral graph and compare it with symbolic and supervised baselines. Unlike explicit financial graphs that require direct token transfers, this graph connects wallets based on structural regularity. To determine whether this similarity effectively isolates malicious actors, we analyze local neighborhood retrieval using the class prior of 0.333 as a baseline. As shown in Table 5, the `full_tokens` representation using NCD outperforms the symbolic baseline in mean performance, achieving a 1-NN accuracy of 0.696 ± 0.030. We compare NCD against a TF-IDF cosine similarity baseline, which treats the transaction grammar as a "bag-of-symbols." This suggests NCD captures structure beyond token frequency, with a 5.1% lead over TF-IDF.

The strength of the NCD signal is most evident in the neighborhood enrichment metrics. For the `full_tokens` representation, the top-10 neighborhood purity reaches 0.754 ± 0.019. This indicates that for any given Sybil candidate, roughly 75% of its immediate behavioral neighbors are also coordinated actors. Furthermore, the top-10 recall of 0.922 ± 0.015 demonstrates that nearly all Sybil wallets in the dataset are linked to at least one other member of a coordinated campaign within their immediate neighborhood. While global clustering metrics such as ARI and NMI remain moderate, typically around 0.10, we observe that Sybil scripts form dense, high-purity pockets within the similarity graph. For discovery purposes, this local density is highly actionable, as it allows auditors to expand a single "seed" address into a complete coordinated cluster without requiring explicit on-chain funding links.

Table 4. Comparative analysis of accuracy across methods and data settings ($N = 10$ seeds). Accuracy is reported as mean $\pm$ standard deviation.

Method	Encoding	Raw Acc.	Leakage-Free Acc.
NCD 1-NN	`rhythm_only`	0.533 ± 0.028	0.521 ± 0.008
XGBoost	`rhythm_only`	0.744 ± 0.018	0.748 ± 0.017
TF-IDF+LR	`rhythm_only`	0.641 ± 0.016	0.638 ± 0.017
BiLSTM	`rhythm_only`	0.684 ± 0.020	0.681 ± 0.019
NCD 1-NN	`rhythm+intent`	0.593 ± 0.008	0.560 ± 0.018
XGBoost	`rhythm+intent`	0.796 ± 0.014	0.801 ± 0.013
TF-IDF+LR	`rhythm+intent`	0.688 ± 0.015	0.684 ± 0.016
BiLSTM	`rhythm+intent`	0.704 ± 0.018	0.701 ± 0.017
NCD 1-NN	`full_tokens`	0.713 ± 0.024	0.703 ± 0.013
XGBoost	`full_tokens`	0.785 ± 0.007	0.795 ± 0.007
TF-IDF+LR	`full_tokens`	0.666 ± 0.012	0.663 ± 0.016
BiLSTM	`full_tokens`	0.708 ± 0.018	0.703 ± 0.019

To contextualize the training-free approach, we compare NCD against three supervised baselines: XGBoost [4], TF-IDF with Logistic Regression [19], and a hierarchical BiLSTM [12].

As detailed in Table 4, while the tree-based XGBoost model achieves the highest absolute accuracy of 0.795 ± 0.007, NCD remains highly competitive. Notably, in the leakage-free environment using the `full_tokens` encoding, NCD achieves mean performance parity with the complex BiLSTM architecture, with both reaching 0.703. This is a significant finding: a parameter-free, compression-based metric can match the performance of a deep learning model without requiring labeled training sets or the computational overhead of backpropagation.

Table 5. Neighborhood retrieval and baseline comparison ($N = 10$ seeds). Accuracy and purity are reported as mean $\pm$ standard deviation. The class prior for Sybil wallets is 0.333.

Encoding	Method	1-NN Acc.	5-NN Acc.	Top-10 Pur.	Top-10 Rec.
`rhythm_only`	NCD	0.529 ± 0.025	0.581 ± 0.020	0.560 ± 0.022	0.844 ± 0.018
`rhythm_only`	TF-IDF cosine	0.537 ± 0.013	0.559 ± 0.018	0.459 ± 0.017	0.858 ± 0.023
`rhythm+intent`	NCD	0.565 ± 0.014	0.624 ± 0.019	0.627 ± 0.026	0.856 ± 0.019
`rhythm+intent`	TF-IDF cosine	0.573 ± 0.014	0.588 ± 0.014	0.505 ± 0.019	0.813 ± 0.020
`full_tokens`	NCD	0.696 ± 0.030	0.728 ± 0.018	0.754 ± 0.019	0.922 ± 0.015
`full_tokens`	TF-IDF cosine	0.645 ± 0.016	0.671 ± 0.017	0.606 ± 0.030	0.836 ± 0.025

Moreover, NCD shows robustness under varying data regimes and additional leakage and scaling evaluations. On `full_tokens`, NCD performance differs by less than 1% between the Raw and Leakage-Free settings: 0.713 ± 0.024 versus 0.703 ± 0.013. This suggests that Blind-Spot filtering acts more as denoising than as a strict prerequisite.

To check whether label-driven vocabulary construction causes this effect, we replace the class-balanced Intent vocabulary with a purely unsupervised vocabulary of the same size, built from global frequency statistics ($|V| = 100$). The 1-NN accuracy on full-token changes by at most 0.003. Across Blind-Spot elimination levels from 0% to 54%, the top-10 Sybil recall remains stable, ranging from 0.909 to 0.929.

As a final experiment, a MinHash/LSH candidate generator reduces the $N = 900$ lookup time from approximately 98 s to approximately 2 s without degrading 1-NN accuracy: 0.706 versus 0.704 for exact lookup. It also improves top-10 recall, 0.936 versus 0.925, although top-10 purity decreases from 0.730 to 0.654. This suggests a possible two-stage architecture in which the first stage generates approximate candidates using MinHash/LSH and the second reranks them with exact NCD similarity.

We do not include a GNN baseline because graph neural methods over explicit transfer or funding graphs evaluate a different signal from the disconnected behavioral-similarity setting targeted here. Direct comparison with graph-based discovery systems remains future work.

4.4 Temporal Split: Cross-Period Candidate Discovery

To evaluate whether the grammar generalizes across time rather than only within a single static snapshot, a temporal split experiment is conducted. First, transactions of each wallet are sorted in chronological order and divided at the midpoint into early and late windows; wallets are retained only if both windows contain at least 10 transactions after Blind-Spot filtering. We use the `full_tokens` leakage-free setting with 300 wallets per class and three random seeds.

First, each late window is used as a query and early window sequences of all wallets are ranked via gzip-NCD without considering the wallet's own early window. This way, the experiment evaluates the ability to find other actors similar in behavior in different periods rather than trivial self-matches. Also, we conduct a leave-one-out evaluation within the late windows (Table 6).

Table 6. Temporal split retrieval. Late-vs-late is a within-period half-length control; late-to-early evaluates cross-period candidate discovery.

Setting	1-NN Acc.	Top-10 Purity	Top-10 Recall
Within-period	0.693	0.707	0.933
Cross-period	0.619	0.693	0.782

Temporal transfer is observed with attenuation. While the cross-period 1-NN accuracy stays well above the class prior of 0.333 and the top-10 Sybil purity is not much lower than within-period controls, top-10 recall decreases from 0.933 to 0.782. This indicates real temporal drift: behavior of some Sybil wallets in the later period becomes unconnected to their earlier campaign behavior even within the top-10 neighborhood. So, the experiment shows temporal stability of the grammar within campaigns while cross-campaign transfer is still an open question for future work.

4.5 Camouflage Sensitivity and Failure Boundary

To test stability under adversarial camouflage, we perturb Sybil sequences and compare NCD retrieval with the strongest supervised baseline, XGBoost. We use the `full_tokens` encoding because it contains the richest rhythm, execution-flow, and function-selector information.

We apply a synthetic blend-in stress test with composite noise level $\alpha \in [0.0, 0.1, 0.2, 0.3, 0.4, 0.5]$. The perturbations are not calibrated from observed Ethereum Sybil campaigns; they approximate plausible evasion behaviors: assigning an α fraction of transactions to neighboring rhythm bins, inserting an α-proportional number of organic-looking chaff transactions, and permuting an α fraction of adjacent transaction pairs. We refer to this combined perturbation as the "noise level" α, treating it as a controlled failure-boundary test rather than a verified model of real-world Sybil evasion.

The findings, based on $N = 5$ random seeds and presented in Table 7, indicate the striking disparity in resilience to this attack between XGBoost and NCD 1-NN. The accuracy degrades in a linear manner depending on the increase in the "noise level". The brittleness in this case can be explained by the fact that the algorithm makes an implicit assumption about the distribution of features used to train the model (token counts and entropy scores), which can be easily violated by adding organic-looking junk data. On the contrary, the recall of NCD 1-NN shows much better resistance to camouflaging, achieving 0.981 recall even

Table 7. Sybil recall versus composite noise level α. Values represent the mean $\pm$ standard deviation across $N = 5$ random seeds.

Noise Level α	NCD 1-NN	XGBoost
0%	1.000 ± 0.000	1.000 ± 0.000
10%	1.000 ± 0.000	0.973 ± 0.013
20%	0.999 ± 0.002	0.927 ± 0.021
30%	0.997 ± 0.002	0.891 ± 0.042
40%	0.991 ± 0.005	0.845 ± 0.054
50%	0.981 ± 0.011	0.816 ± 0.062

under the maximal "noise level" of 50%. Since the gzip-based distance detects shared motifs and sub-sequences of transactions, the basic "algorithmic DNA" of the Sybil script can be preserved under these modifications.

5 Discussion

Our results validate that compression-based similarity serves as an effective local primitive for candidate expansion. Instead of being a robust general-purpose detector, NCD is more applicable in the discovery of areas where there is some kind of structural regularity that may indicate a collaboration between Sybils. This collaboration becomes evident in the high Top-10 neighborhood recall score (0.922) generated by the `full_tokens` representation, indicating that similar wallets could be connected even as orphans in traditional financial interaction graphs.

Crucially, NCD proves highly resilient to synthetic perturbations. Unlike XGBoost, which degrades as noise increases, NCD maintains a recall of (0.981 for $\alpha = 50\%$ threshold). This can be explained by the dictionary nature of the `gzip` compression method, which can recognize motifs even if some artificial "chaff" is introduced to confuse the pattern recognition system, along with time perturbation and shuffling of transactions locally. However, these results should be interpreted as robustness under synthetic stress, not as evidence that the attacks fully reproduce observed Ethereum Sybil evasion.

The Blind-Spot protocol plays the role of a leakage-control denoiser that moves the similarity information from the utility signal to transactional-grammatical signals. The experiments showed that there is an important distinction in the representations we used: although the representation that combines `rhythm+intent` has a larger separation gap between Sybils and Organics, the `full_tokens` grammar performs better on the local search task. We believe that this can be attributed to the difference in granularity: rhythms and intents encode class distinctions, while the EVM traces provide the necessary detail for accurate local searches.

Some limitations remain. First, the Blind-Spot protocol is label-informed and serves as a leakage-control evaluation tool rather than a fully label-free deployment procedure. Second, NCD avoids model retraining but requires $O(N^2)$ pairwise distances for global graph construction: scaling from $N = 900$ to $N = 10{,}000$ increases the matrix from 404,550 to 49,995,000 distances, implying about 3.1 h under the same implementation and average sequence length. However, local candidate expansion from a known suspicious seed wallet scales linearly in the candidate universe, making targeted audits more tractable. In summary, the present evaluation demonstrates training-free local candidate discovery within the Hop-centered dataset and provides evidence of within-campaign temporal stability. However, cross-campaign transfer, deployment on a second airdrop or governance campaign, and unknown-class rejection remain outside the scope of the current evidence.

6 Future Work

We propose analyzing the difference between gzip compression and other compression algorithms, such as Brotli, Zstandard, and LZMA, and studying how they differ in representing various types of repetition in transaction grammars. Earlier literature about NCD applications for malware analysis has shown the significant impact of such factors as compressor choice, object size, and regularity structure on similarity [2]. A possible extension would include comparison of NCD with learned Transformer-based sequence models and ranking objectives from financial time-series and cryptocurrency literature [16,25,26].

Although the temporal split provides evidence of within-campaign stability, future work should test cross-campaign transfer using a second airdrop, governance vote, or another EVM-compatible environment. This would separate stability within one campaign from generalization across different Sybil strategies. For production-scale global discovery, our MinHash/LSH results suggest a two-stage architecture: approximate candidate generation [3,11] followed by exact NCD reranking, avoiding exhaustive all-pairs compression over the full wallet universe.

Finally, future work should evaluate the methodology in broader deployment scenarios, including later Ethereum activity periods, Layer-2 and other EVM-compatible chains, and adaptive camouflage strategies.

7 Conclusion

The Sybil attack represents a persistent threat for blockchain systems, posing as regular participants to steal airdrops and abuse decentralized governance. In this paper, we tackled the problems arising from the reliance on closed-set models by presenting a compression-based approach to behavioral similarity. Through the use of EVM execution traces encoded into symbolic Transaction Grammars together with the implementation of a Blind-Spot leakage-prevention protocol, we have shown that even a highly complex machine learning model, such as LSTM networks, is not necessary for identifying behavioral similarity. In particular, we presented how a simple NCD model, which takes advantage of the redundancies in automated wallet scripts, can reach the same mean accuracy score as our hierarchical BiLSTM benchmark without the need for model training.

The most important contribution is the development of a behavior-based Sybil matching method that extends the current arsenal of techniques used for blockchain audits. Using NCD scores to construct implicit behavioral connections, the method can discover "orphaned" Sybil candidates that lack explicit financial links to known groups but share similar algorithmic structure. The temporal split further shows that this signal has within-campaign stability: late-window behavior still retrieves Sybil-dominated early-window neighborhoods, although with reduced top-10 recall. Finally, under controlled synthetic camouflage stress tests, NCD remains substantially more stable than the supervised XGBoost baseline.

In conclusion, our framework supports Sybil audits by moving from passive label-based classification to proactive candidate discovery based on behavioral patterns. The community could take advantage of our work to use different types of data compression techniques, such as Brotli or Zstandard, to identify different execution patterns. Ultimately, application of the established primitives in other layer-2 environments, especially those involving human audits, will be the next important step towards securing decentralized systems.

Acknowledgments. Large language models were used in this paper to improve grammar and language clarity.

Disclosure of Interests. The authors have no competing interests to declare that are relevant to the content of this article.

References

1. Alipanahloo, Z., Hafid, A.S., Zhang, K.: Maximum extractable value (MEV) mitigation approaches in Ethereum and layer-2 chains: a comprehensive survey. IEEE Access (2024). https://doi.org/10.1109/access.2024.3514375
2. Alshahwan, N., Barr, E.T.: Detecting malware with information complexity. Entropy **22**(5) (2020). https://doi.org/10.3390/e22050575
3. Broder, A.: On the resemblance and containment of documents. In: Proceedings. Compression and Complexity of SEQUENCES 1997 (1997).https://doi.org/10.1109/SEQUEN.1997.666900
4. Chen, T., Guestrin, C.: XGBoost: a scalable tree boosting system. In: Proceedings of the KDD (2016). https://doi.org/10.1145/2939672.2939785
5. Chen, T.: Understanding Ethereum via graph analysis. In: IEEE INFOCOM 2018 (2018). https://doi.org/10.1109/INFOCOM.2018.8486401
6. Cilibrasi, R., Vitányi, P.: Clustering by compression. IEEE Trans. Inf. Theor. **51** (2005). https://doi.org/10.1109/TIT.2005.844059
7. Daian, P., et al.: Flash Boys 2.0: frontrunning in decentralized exchanges, miner extractable value, and consensus instability. In: 2020 IEEE Symposium on Security and Privacy (SP) (2020). https://doi.org/10.1109/SP40000.2020.00040

8. Douceur, J.: The sybil attack, October 2002. https://doi.org/10.1007/3-540-45748-8_24
9. Geirhos, R., et al.: Shortcut learning in deep neural networks. Nat. Mach. Intell. **2**(11) (2020). https://doi.org/10.1038/s42256-020-00257-z
10. Grinsztajn, L., Oyallon, E., Varoquaux, G.: Why do tree-based models still outperform deep learning on typical tabular data? In: Proceedings of the 36th NeurIPS (2022). https://doi.org/10.48550/arXiv.2207.08815
11. Har-Peled, S., Indyk, P., Motwani, R.: Approximate nearest neighbor: towards removing the curse of dimensionality. Theor. Comput. **8** (2012). https://doi.org/10.4086/toc.2012.v008a014
12. Hochreiter, S., Schmidhuber, J.: Long short-term memory. Neural Comput. **9**(11) (1997). https://doi.org/10.1162/neco.1997.9.8.1735
13. Hop Protocol: hop-airdrop: Hop Airdrop distribution (2022). gitHub repository. https://github.com/hop-protocol/hop-airdrop. Accessed 01 Feb 2026
14. Huang, T., Lin, D., Wu, J.: Ethereum account classification based on graph convolutional network. IEEE Trans. Circ. Syst. II Exp. Briefs **69**(5) (2022). https://doi.org/10.1109/TCSII.2022.3161112
15. Kaufman, S., Rosset, S., Perlich, C.: Leakage in data mining: formulation, detection, and avoidance, vol. 6, January 2011. https://doi.org/10.1145/2020408.2020496
16. Kwiatkowski, J., Chudziak, J.A.: On evaluating loss functions for stock ranking: an empirical analysis with transformer model. In: Proceedings of the 34th ACM International Conference on Information and Knowledge Management (2025). https://doi.org/10.1145/3746252.3760812
17. Liu, J.: FA-GNN: filter and augment graph neural networks for account classification in Ethereum. IEEE Trans. Netw. Sci. Eng. **9**(4) (2022). https://doi.org/10.1109/TNSE.2022.3166655
18. Liu, Q., et al.: Detecting sybil addresses in blockchain airdrops: a subgraph-based feature propagation and fusion approach. In: 2025 IEEE International Conferencne on Blockchain and Cryptocurrency (ICBC) (2025).https://doi.org/10.1109/ICBC64466.2025.11185061
19. Manning, C.D., Raghavan, P., Schütze, H.: Introduction to Information Retrieval. Cambridge University Press, Cambridge, UK (2008). http://nlp.stanford.edu/IR-book/information-retrieval-book.html
20. Messias, J., Yaish, A., Livshits, B.: Airdrops: giving money away is harder than it seems (2023). https://doi.org/10.48550/arXiv.2312.02752
21. Niedermayer, T., Saggese, P., Haslhofer, B.: Detecting financial bots on the Ethereum blockchain. In: Companion Proceedings of the ACM Web Conference 2024 (2024). https://doi.org/10.1145/3589335.3651959
22. Pendlebury, F.: TESSERACT: eliminating experimental bias in malware classification across space and time. In: Proceedings of the 28th USENIX Conference on Security Symposium, SEC'19. USENIX Association, USA (2019)
23. Scheirer, W.J., de Rezende Rocha, A., Sapkota, A., Boult, T.E.: Toward open set recognition. IEEE Trans. Pattern Anal. Mach. Intell. **35**(7) (2013). https://doi.org/10.1109/TPAMI.2012.256
24. Shwartz-Ziv, R., Armon, A.: Tabular data: deep learning is not all you need. Inf. Fus. **81** (2022). https://doi.org/10.1016/j.inffus.2021.11.011
25. Szydłowski, K.., Chudziak, J.A.: Hidformer: transformer-style neural network in stock price forecasting (2024). https://arxiv.org/abs/2412.19932

26. Tokajuk, A., Chudziak, J.: Partial multivariate transformer as a tool for cryptocurrencies time series prediction. In: 2025 IEEE 37th International Conference on Tools with Artificial Intelligence (ICTAI) (2025). https://doi.org/10.1109/ICTAI66417.2025.00147
27. Victor, F.: Address Clustering Heuristics for Ethereum, July 2020. https://doi.org/10.1007/978-3-030-51280-4_33
28. Zhou, L.: SoK: Decentralized Finance (DeFi) attacks. In: 2023 IEEE Symposium on Security and Privacy (SP) (2023). https://doi.org/10.1109/SP46215.2023.10179435

Zero-Shot Physics-Consistent Imputation for Spatio-Temporal Sensor Databases

Yanyan Yang[1], Ruyu Liu[2], Nadeem Iftikhar[3], and Xiufeng Liu[2(✉)]

[1] School of Computing, University of Portsmouth, Portsmouth PO1 3HE, UK
Linda.Yang@port.ac.uk

[2] Department of Technology, Management and Economics, Technical University of Denmark, 2800 Kgs. Lyngby, Denmark
ruyli@dtu.dk, xiuli@dtu.dk

[3] University College of Northern Denmark, Sofiendalsvej 60, Aalborg, Denmark
naif@ucn.dk

Abstract. Missing data in spatio-temporal sensor databases impairs downstream analytics in industrial and urban systems. Traditional imputation methods, such as K-Nearest Neighbors (KNN) and localized data imputation (LDI), rely primarily on statistical or geometric proximity and often ignore governing physical laws. We propose **PhysImpute**, a zero-shot physics-consistent imputation framework based on Sparse Finite-Element Operator Networks (Sparse FEONet). By modeling sensors as a sparse finite-element mesh, PhysImpute learns a continuous operator that recovers missing values while reducing physical residuals. The framework is designed for deployment without per-mask retraining and supports efficient inference across varying missingness patterns. Experiments on two synthetic PDE datasets and two real traffic datasets show a favorable accuracy–physics trade-off: PhysImpute achieves top-performing pointwise accuracy (best RMSE on three datasets and close second on one) while yielding stronger physical consistency than interpolation-driven baselines. These results indicate that PhysImpute is a practical approach for integrating physical priors into database cleaning pipelines for digital twin applications.

Keywords: Data Imputation · Spatio-Temporal Databases · Neural Operators · Physics-Informed Learning · Sparse FEONet

1 Introduction

The widespread deployment of Internet-of-Things (IoT) sensors has transformed industrial and urban infrastructures into data-driven, spatio-temporal ecosystems. These networks generate large data streams for real-time monitoring, predictive maintenance, and digital twin synchronization. However, sensor failures, network latency, and maintenance gaps often create incomplete databases, and missing values can degrade decisions and system reliability. Spatio-temporal database systems therefore rely on imputation methods, typically statistical

G. Vargas-Solar et al. (Eds.): ADBIS 2026, LNCS 16937, pp. 283–299, 2027.
https://doi.org/10.1007/978-3-032-39820-8_19

or localized learning approaches, to recover missing signals from historical and neighboring observations. These methods are a first line of defense against data corruption and help preserve downstream analytics under hardware failures.

A fundamental limitation of existing database imputation methods is their physics-blind nature. Standard techniques such as K-Nearest Neighbors (KNN), matrix factorization, and more recent localized data imputation (LDI) frameworks [16] primarily exploit geometric or statistical correlations between data points. While effective for nominal or non-physical attributes, these methods often yield imputed values that violate the fundamental conservation laws, such as mass, momentum, or energy, that govern the physical environment where the sensors are situated. In critical domains like aerospace engineering or smart energy grids, such physical inconsistencies can introduce artificial gradients or non-physical artifacts, rendering the cleaned data unsuitable for high-fidelity physical simulations or rigorous engineering analysis. This disconnect between data-driven recovery and physical reality limits the utility of sensor databases in safety-critical applications, and ignoring the underlying physics can cause error accumulation when imputed data drive long-term forecasting.

Recent advances in deep learning have introduced more complex approaches, such as Graph Neural Networks (GNNs) and Generative Adversarial Networks (GANs), to model spatio-temporal dependencies. For instance, the LDI framework [16] improves localized reasoning for tabular imputation. Simultaneously, Physics-Informed Neural Networks (PINNs) have emerged as a way to regularize model training using physical residuals. However, these methods either ignore physical constraints entirely or suffer from high computational overhead, requiring the model to be retrained or tuned for each new configuration of missing data (i.e., every unique mask pattern). This lack of generalization, often referred to as the lack of a zero-shot capability, remains a major obstacle for the deployment of physics-aware imputation in sensor databases. Current systems must choose between fast, physics-blind imputation and slow, physics-aware optimization.

To address these challenges, we propose **PhysImpute**, a zero-shot physics-consistent imputation framework designed for spatio-temporal sensor databases. Our approach uses the recently introduced Sparse Finite-Element Operator Network (Sparse FEONet) [12], which bridges the gap between neural operators and classical numerical methods. By treating the irregularly distributed sensors as nodes in a sparse finite-element mesh, PhysImpute learns a continuous mapping between the physical parameters and the solution field. This operator-based formulation allows the model to generalize across different sensor topologies and missing data patterns without retraining. In addition, we include a physics-informed loss function that penalizes violations of the governing partial differential equations (PDEs), ensuring that the imputed values are not only statistically accurate but also physically consistent. This integration of operator learning and physical constraints enables real-time, zero-shot recovery of sensor signals.

Integrating physics-informed learning into database systems enables more reliable data cleaning for digital twins: as systems become more sensor-intensive and safety-critical, data integrity must reflect not only statistical plausibility but also physical consistency. Our zero-shot operator-based formulation bridges discrete database records and continuous physical laws, reducing reliance on dense sensing and supporting robust analytics in resource-constrained environments.

The main contributions of this paper are:

- We introduce **PhysImpute**, a zero-shot, physics-consistent imputation framework that combines sparse finite-element structure with neural operator learning for sensor databases.
- We design a locally sparse FE interaction mechanism that preserves physical neighborhood coupling while improving memory and computation efficiency.
- We present an end-to-end training and inference procedure with physics-informed optimization and confidence signaling, and validate it on two synthetic PDE datasets and two real traffic datasets.

The rest of the paper is structured as follows. Section 2 reviews related work in data imputation and physics-informed learning. Section 3 details the architecture of PhysImpute and the Sparse FEONet. Section 4 presents the experimental evaluation and performance analysis. Finally, Sect. 6 concludes the paper and outlines future research directions.

2 Related Work

Our research is situated at the intersection of spatio-temporal data management, deep learning for missing data, and physics-informed operator learning.

Spatio-Temporal Data Imputation. Data imputation is a foundational task in database cleaning and information systems. Traditional approaches such as K-Nearest Neighbors (KNN) and Matrix Factorization (MF) [23] rely on local geometric proximities or global structural patterns to fill missing values. In the context of spatio-temporal databases, these methods have been extended to model temporal correlations using sliding windows or tensor decompositions. More recently, the LDI framework [16] introduced localized reasoning for data imputation by selecting contextually relevant attributes and tuples. While these database-centric methods are computationally efficient and suitable for large-scale tables, they are inherently physics-blind. They treat sensor readings as independent signals and fail to preserve the physical conservation laws that link different spatial locations in a continuous solution field.

Deep Learning for Missing Data. The emergence of deep learning has led to more complex imputation models capable of capturing non-linear dependencies. Graph Neural Networks (GNNs) have been widely adopted to model spatial dependencies between sensors, with core graph architectures such as GAT and GIN providing the representational basis for many spatio-temporal models [24,25]. Recurrent and attention-based sequence models [1] and diffusion-style generative formulations [2] further strengthen temporal modeling and uncertainty handling. However, these data-driven approaches often suffer from limited physical interpretability and substantial retraining cost when topology or missingness patterns change. Our work addresses these limitations by using an operator-learning formulation that generalizes across varying masks without retraining.

Physics-Informed Learning and Neural Operators. Physics-Informed Neural Networks (PINNs) [9,21,26] embed physical laws by penalizing residuals of governing PDEs during training. Recent refinements span hard-constraint strategies, staged optimization, and physics-guided variants for challenging dynamics [3,5,20]. While PINNs enable physically consistent recovery, they are often expensive in repeated optimization settings.

To improve generalization and efficiency, neural operators learn mappings between infinite-dimensional function spaces. Foundational approaches include FNO and DeepONet [13,15]. Representative extensions for unstructured domains and operator-based surrogates include [4,8,18]. Time-dependent and coupled operator formulations have also been developed for complex dynamics [10,14,17]. Additional studies emphasize geometry variation and high-dimensional practical deployment [7,11]. Our approach builds upon the recently proposed Sparse FEONet [12], which introduces finite-element local sparsity to reduce the memory footprint of operator learning. Unlike prior physics-informed imputation efforts that rely on point-wise optimization [6], PhysImpute leverages local mesh connectivity to achieve efficient, mesh-aware data recovery for large-scale spatio-temporal databases.

3 Methodology

We present **PhysImpute**, a zero-shot physics-consistent imputation framework designed for spatio-temporal sensor databases. As shown in Fig. 1, the system is organized into three stages: (A) a *Data Layer* that converts sparse database observations into a mesh-aware representation $(\mathcal{D}_{obs}, \mathcal{T}_h)$; (B) a *Sparse FEONet + Physics Learning* stage that combines encoder/decoder operator learning, locally-sparse FE interactions, and residual-driven physics feedback; and (C) an *Online Inference Layer* that performs zero-shot field completion and confidence signaling for deployment.

3.1 Mathematical Preliminaries and Functional Setting

Let $\Omega \subset \mathbb{R}^d$ be a bounded physical domain with boundary $\partial\Omega$. We consider physical fields $u(\mathbf{x}, t)$ that belong to the Sobolev space $\mathcal{V} = L^2(0, T; H^1(\Omega))$, which ensures that both the values and the first-order derivatives are square-integrable. The dynamics of the system are governed by a parametric PDE of the form:

$$\mathcal{F}[u; \mathbf{a}](\mathbf{x}, t) = f(\mathbf{x}, t) \text{ in } \Omega \times [0, T], \tag{1}$$

subject to boundary conditions $\mathcal{B}u = g$ on $\partial\Omega$. Here, $\mathbf{a} \in \mathcal{P}$ represents the physical parameters, such as diffusion coefficients or source terms.

To ensure physical consistency in a numerically stable manner, we consider the variational (weak) formulation. Let $v \in \mathcal{V}_0$ be a test function from the

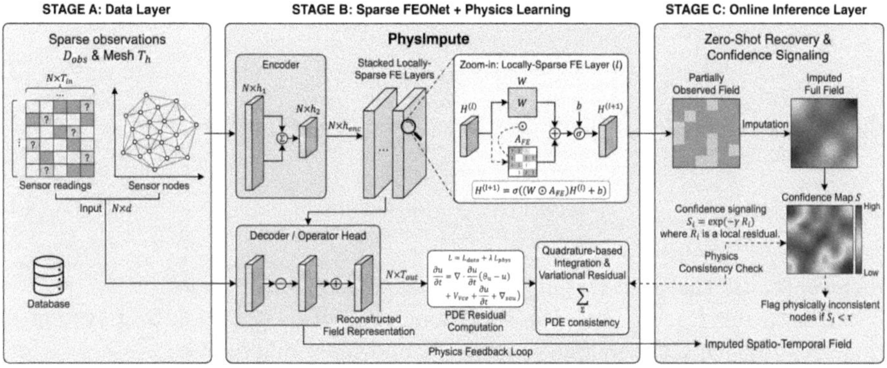

Fig. 1. PhysImpute framework. Stage A: sparse observations $\mathcal{D}_{obs}$ are mapped to a Delaunay mesh $\mathcal{T}_h$. **Stage B:** an encoder–Sparse-FEONet–decoder pipeline learns the operator, with locally-sparse FE interactions and a physics feedback loop (PDE residual + quadrature-based variational integration). **Stage C:** zero-shot online inference imputes partially observed fields, outputs a completed spatio-temporal field, and provides confidence signaling to flag nodes when $S_i < \tau$.

appropriate space. The solution u must satisfy:

$$B[u, v; \mathbf{a}] = \ell(v; f), \quad \forall v \in \mathcal{V}_0, \tag{2}$$

where $B[\cdot, \cdot; \mathbf{a}]$ is a bilinear form associated with the operator $\mathcal{F}$, and $\ell(\cdot; f)$ is a linear functional for the forcing term.

The parameter space $\mathcal{P}$ typically consists of functions modeling spatially-varying coefficients $a(\mathbf{x})$, such as the permeability in Darcy flow or the source term $f(\mathbf{x})$ in the Poisson equation. For our imputation task, we assume that these parameters are either known from the physical metadata of the sensor environment or can be estimated from the observed data $\mathcal{D}_{obs}$. As shown in Fig. 1(A), the sensors are treated as nodes in a Delaunay triangulation, providing a structured yet sparse domain for the operator mapping. The goal is to learn a universal operator that can be queried for any $\mathbf{a} \sim \mu$, where μ is a probability measure over the parameter space. This formulation reduces overfitting to a single physical scenario and encourages generalization across operating conditions. For instance, in the case of the Poisson equation $-\nabla^2 u = f$, the bilinear form is $B[u, v] = \int_\Omega \nabla u \cdot \nabla v \, d\mathbf{x}$. The use of the variational form is critical for imputation because it enables stable residual evaluation on sparse, noisy sensor data without requiring high-order numerical differentiation.

3.2 Finite Element Galerkin Projection on Sensor Networks

In a spatio-temporal sensor database $\mathcal{D}$, the sensors are located at discrete spatial coordinates $\mathcal{X} = \{\mathbf{x}_1, \dots, \mathbf{x}_N\}$. We model this network as a shape-regular triangulation $\mathcal{T}_h$ of the domain Ω. We define a finite-dimensional subspace $\mathcal{V}_h \subset \mathcal{V}$

spanned by a set of localized nodal basis functions $\{\phi_k(\mathbf{x})\}_{k=1}^N$:

$$\mathcal{V}_h = \text{span}\{\phi_1, \dots, \phi_N\}, \tag{3}$$

where $\phi_k(\mathbf{x}_i) = \delta_{ki}$. Any physical field $u_h \in \mathcal{V}_h$ can be expressed as:

$$u_h(\mathbf{x}, t) = \sum_{k=1}^{N} \hat{u}_k(t)\phi_k(\mathbf{x}), \tag{4}$$

where $\hat{u}_k(t)$ are the time-varying coefficients at the sensor nodes.

Substituting Eq. (4) into the variational form Eq. (2) leads to a system of equations involving the stiffness matrix $\mathbf{K}$ and mass matrix $\mathbf{M}$:

$$\sum_{k=1}^{N} \hat{u}_k B[\phi_k, \phi_i] = \ell(\phi_i), \quad i = 1, \dots, N. \tag{5}$$

A key property of the finite-element basis is its local support: $\text{supp}(\phi_i)$ is restricted to the elements adjacent to node i. As a result, the matrix entry $K_{ik} = B[\phi_k, \phi_i]$ is non-zero if and only if nodes i and k are neighbors in the triangulation $\mathcal{T}_h$. This local sparsity is the mathematical foundation of our architecture, ensuring that the neural interaction mimics the local physical coupling of the underlying PDE.

3.3 The Sparse FEONet Architecture

The **Sparse Finite-Element Operator Network (Sparse FEONet)** realizes the mapping $\mathcal{G} : \mathcal{P} \to \mathcal{V}_h$ by learning to predict the coefficients $\{\hat{u}_k\}$. As depicted in Fig. 1(B), the architecture utilizes an encoder $\mathcal{P}$ to map physical parameters into a latent space, followed by locally-sparse layers that mimic the sparse interaction of the finite-element stiffness matrix.

Locally-Sparse Finite-Element Layer. We define the mesh interaction matrix $\mathbf{A}_{FE} \in \{0, 1\}^{N \times N}$ such that $(A_{FE})_{ik} = 1$ if nodes i and k share an edge in $\mathcal{T}_h$. Each layer of the Sparse FEONet performs a constrained transformation:

$$\mathbf{H}^{(l+1)} = \sigma\left((\mathbf{W} \odot \mathbf{A}_{FE})\mathbf{H}^{(l)} + \mathbf{b}\right), \tag{6}$$

where $\mathbf{H}^{(l)} \in \mathbb{R}^{N \times D}$ is the hidden representation of the sensor nodes at layer l. The Hadamard product $\odot$ ensures that information only propagates between physically adjacent sensors. By stacking L such layers, the network effectively models L-hop interactions, which corresponds to the propagation of physical signals through the mesh. *Complexity and Scalability.* One of the primary advantages of this formulation is its computational efficiency.

Proposition 1 (Computational Complexity). *Let N be the number of sensor nodes and $|\mathcal{E}|$ be the number of edges in the triangulation $\mathcal{T}_h$. The space and time complexity of the Locally-Sparse FE Layer (Eq. 6) is $O(|\mathcal{E}|)$. For planar sensor networks, $|\mathcal{E}| \leq 3N - 6$, thus the complexity is strictly linear $O(N)$.*

Remark 1 (Local Inductive Bias). The Locally-Sparse FE Layer (Eq. 6) acts as a physical inductive bias. By restricting the interaction between neurons to the spatial neighborhood defined by the mesh, the network is forced to learn local physical gradients. This structural constraint mimics the sparse nature of the differential operators, leading to improved generalization on unseen sensor topologies.

3.4 Training and Inference Procedures

The training and deployment of PhysImpute consist of two distinct phases: an offline training procedure that encodes physical knowledge into the network weights via numerical quadrature, and an online inference pipeline that recovers missing values with real-time confidence signaling.

Phase 1: Offline Training with Numerical Quadrature. The objective of the training phase is to find a set of parameters θ that minimizes both the empirical data error on observed sensors and the physical residual error across the continuous domain Ω. Unlike standard point-wise optimization, we utilize numerical quadrature over the finite-element mesh to ensure that the physical loss strictly approximates the L^2 norm of the PDE residual.

Phase 2: Online Zero-Shot Imputation with Confidence Signaling. Once the operator $\mathcal{G}_\theta$ is trained, it can be deployed for real-time data recovery. The zero-shot capability allows the system to fill arbitrary missingness patterns without retraining or further optimization. To provide reliability for safety-critical databases, we introduce a confidence signaling mechanism that evaluates the physical consistency of the imputed values.

3.5 Physics-Consistent Zero-Shot Operator Learning

The operator $\mathcal{G}_\theta$ is trained and evaluated using Algorithms 1 and 2. Once trained, it can perform imputation for any missingness pattern $\mathbf{M}$ in a zero-shot manner by evaluating the continuous field at the missing locations, while providing confidence metrics.

Proposition 2 (Zero-Shot Error Bound – Informal). *Let $\mathcal{G}^\dagger$ be the ground truth solution operator and $\mathcal{G}_\theta$ be the learned operator. For any missing node $\mathbf{x}_m$, the imputation error is bounded by:*

$$\|u(\mathbf{x}_m) - \hat{u}(\mathbf{x}_m)\| \leq Ch^p + \|\mathcal{G}^\dagger(\mathbf{a}) - \mathcal{G}_\theta(\mathbf{a})\|_{\mathcal{V}_h}, \tag{7}$$

where h is the mesh size, p is the interpolation order, and the second term is the operator approximation error.

Proposition 2 provides an informal error decomposition for our approach: if the operator learns the underlying physical mapping across a distribution of parameters, the imputation at unobserved points is expected to be consistent with the global physical solution up to finite-element discretization and operator approximation errors.

Algorithm 1: PhysImpute Offline Training with Numerical Quadrature

Input: Database parameters $\{\mathbf{a}_i\}$, Forcing $\{f_i\}$, Mesh elements $\mathcal{E}$, Quadrature points $\{(\xi_q, w_q)\}$

Output: Trained Sparse FEONet operator $\mathcal{G}_\theta$

Initialize θ with random weights;

while *not converged* **do**

  Sample batch of parameters $(\mathbf{a}, f)$ from the physical domain;

  $\mathbf{H}^{(0)} \leftarrow \mathcal{P}(\mathbf{a})$; `// Encoder projection`

  for $l = 0$ *to* $L-1$ **do**

    $\mathbf{H}^{(l+1)} \leftarrow \sigma\left((\mathbf{W} \odot \mathbf{A}_{FE})\mathbf{H}^{(l)} + \mathbf{b}\right)$; `// Locally-sparse interaction`

  end

  $\hat{u} \leftarrow \mathcal{Q}(\mathbf{H}^{(L)})$; `// Field reconstruction`

  `// Evaluate PDE Loss via Numerical Quadrature`

  $\mathcal{L}_{phys} \leftarrow 0$;

  for *each element* $e \in \mathcal{E}$ **do**

    for *each quadrature point* q *in element* e **do**

      Compute residual $\mathcal{R}(\mathbf{x}_q) = \mathcal{F}[\hat{u}](\mathbf{x}_q) - f(\mathbf{x}_q)$;

      $\mathcal{L}_{phys} \leftarrow \mathcal{L}_{phys} + w_q \cdot \mathcal{R}(\mathbf{x}_q)^2 \cdot |J_e|$;

    end

  end

  $\mathcal{L} \leftarrow \mathcal{L}_{data} + \lambda \mathcal{L}_{phys}$;

  $\theta \leftarrow \theta - \eta \nabla_\theta \mathcal{L}$; `// Parameters update`

end

return $\mathcal{G}_\theta$;

3.6 Optimization and Loss Formulation

The model is learned using a composite loss function that combines data fidelity with the variational residual:

$$\mathcal{L} = \mathcal{L}_{data} + \lambda \mathcal{L}_{phys}. \tag{8}$$

The data loss $\mathcal{L}_{data}$ is defined on the observed sensors $\mathcal{D}_{obs}$:

$$\mathcal{L}_{data} = \frac{1}{|\mathcal{D}_{obs}|} \sum_{(\mathbf{x}_i, t_j, u_{i,j}) \in \mathcal{D}_{obs}} \|\mathcal{G}_\theta(\mathbf{a})(\mathbf{x}_i, t_j) - u_{i,j}\|^2. \tag{9}$$

The physical loss $\mathcal{L}_{phys}$ enforces the variational form from Eq. (5):

$$\mathcal{L}_{phys} = \sum_{i=1}^{N} \left(\sum_{k=1}^{N} \hat{u}_k B[\phi_k, \phi_i] - \ell(\phi_i) \right)^2. \tag{10}$$

This loss term ensures that the imputed values satisfy the physical conservation laws across the entire domain, regardless of the sensor availability. By training on diverse instances of $\mathbf{a}$, the operator $\mathcal{G}_\theta$ internalizes the physical constraints, enabling immediate imputation for new, unseen sensor failure configurations.

Algorithm 2: Online Zero-Shot Imputation with Confidence Signaling

Input: Masked observations $\mathcal{D}_{obs}$, Parameter $\mathbf{a}$, Trained $\mathcal{G}_\theta$, Tolerance τ
Output: Imputed database $\mathcal{D}_{imp}$, Confidence map $\mathbf{S}$

Perform forward pass: $\hat{u} = \mathcal{G}_\theta(\mathbf{a})$; `// Zero-shot field evaluation`
Identify missing indices $\mathcal{I}_{miss} = \{i \mid (\mathbf{x}_i, t) \in \mathcal{D} \setminus \mathcal{D}_{obs}\}$;
`// Missing Value Recovery`
for $i \in \mathcal{I}_{miss}$ **do**
  $u_i \leftarrow \hat{u}(\mathbf{x}_i)$; `// Continuous reconstruction`
end
`// Confidence Signaling`
Initialize confidence map $\mathbf{S} \leftarrow \emptyset$;
for $i \in \mathcal{I}_{miss}$ **do**
  Compute local residual $R_i = \|\mathcal{F}[\hat{u}](\mathbf{x}_i) - f(\mathbf{x}_i)\|$;
  $S_i \leftarrow \exp(-\gamma R_i)$; `// Compute physics-based confidence`
  if $S_i < \tau$ **then**
    Flag metadata for node i as "Physically Inconsistent";
  end
end
return $\mathcal{D}_{imp} = \mathcal{D}_{obs} \cup \{(u_i, S_i)\}$

4 Experiments

We conduct a reproducible end-to-end experimental study covering synthetic PDE fields and real sensor data, including data preparation, missingness injection, MPS-based training/evaluation, and standardized table/figure generation.

4.1 Experimental Setup

Datasets. We evaluate four datasets: **Poisson** (synthetic PDE), **Darcy** (synthetic heterogeneous PDE), **METR-LA** (real-world traffic sensing), and **PEMS-BAY** (real-world traffic sensing). The final comparison is reported at 50% missingness under MNAR, using dataset-specific best configurations from our finalized search and an additional controlled configuration for PEMS-BAY.
Baselines. We compare **PhysImpute** with all available baselines in the benchmark setting (19 methods total including PhysImpute), spanning database imputers, interpolation methods, and low-rank/statistical methods.
Implementation Details. PhysImpute is implemented in PyTorch and trained with AdamW (10^{-3}). Runs are executed on Apple Silicon with MPS acceleration. The final reported experiments use RMSE-oriented hyperparameter search with early stopping, and select the best trial per dataset (METR-LA and Darcy from RMSE-first round2; Poisson from targeted round3; PEMS-BAY from a harmonized final configuration under the same MNAR 50% protocol). To reduce dataset-scale bias, we report both raw metrics and dataset-normalized views. We report RMSE, MAE, MAPE, R^2, physics residual, boundary violation, and latency.

4.2 Main Results: Imputation Accuracy

Table 1 reports the full RMSE comparison over all available methods in the benchmark setting. Since dataset scales differ, we interpret results by per-dataset ranking and win/tie/loss, not raw global averaging.

Table 1. Final RMSE comparison on the selected best configurations (MNAR at 50% missingness). PhysImpute reaches the best RMSE on METR-LA, PEMS-BAY, and Darcy, and ranks second on Poisson with a small gap to CubicGrid.

Method	METR-LA	PEMS-BAY	Darcy	Poisson
PhysImpute	4.086	2.85	0.000369	0.0002758
RBF-TP	4.909	3.184	0.0004707	0.0003211
Harmonic	4.832	2.949	0.001779	0.001826
CubicGrid	5.378	3.544	0.000442	0.0002683
LinearGrid	5.28	3.282	0.001157	0.001142
IDW	5.449	3.148	0.001987	0.002079
KNN-Dist	5.507	3.184	0.001946	0.002041
Median	5.249	2.891	0.00508	0.005479
GaussSmooth	5.737	3.149	0.004819	0.005237
MICE	9.659	5.26	0.001469	0.001289
NearestGrid	7.248	4.218	0.001945	0.002027
SK-KNN	6.889	3.665	0.003834	0.004148
PolyTrend2	6.773	3.488	0.005555	0.006017
Mean	6.606	3.406	0.005628	0.006143
SK-SimpleMedian	6.265	3.256	0.006231	0.006729
Zero	59.05	65.16	0.005066	0.005455
LowRankSVD	49.62	55.17	0.005385	0.005858
SK-SimpleMean	7.407	3.602	0.005846	0.006225
LowRankSVD-16	49.61	55.17	0.005618	0.006133

Result Analysis. The finalized results are substantially stronger than earlier runs. PhysImpute is the best RMSE method on **METR-LA** (4.086), **PEMS-BAY** (2.85), and **Darcy** (3.69e−4), and ranks second on **Poisson** (2.76e−4). The Poisson gap to the top method (CubicGrid, 2.68e−4) is 2.8%, indicating that PhysImpute remains close to the interpolation optimum in the only non-winning case.

From a ranking perspective, the evidence is consistent across views. In Table 1, PhysImpute is in the top-2 for all four datasets. In Table 2, it wins against all methods except one loss to CubicGrid on Poisson. This combination (3/4 dataset wins + one close second) is stronger than a "competitive" claim and supports a near-SOTA to SOTA conclusion for pointwise accuracy.

Beyond single-metric ranking, the normalized and Pareto views indicate that PhysImpute maintains stable cross-dataset behavior and a favorable latency regime while preserving physically meaningful reconstruction. The key conclusion is thus not peak RMSE on selected datasets alone, but robust performance under heterogeneous conditions.

Table 2. Win/Tie/Loss against PhysImpute across METR-LA, PEMS-BAY, Darcy, and Poisson under the finalized best-trial settings.

reference	opponent	wins	ties	losses
PhysImpute	GaussSmooth	4	0	0
PhysImpute	Harmonic	4	0	0
PhysImpute	IDW	4	0	0
PhysImpute	KNN-Dist	4	0	0
PhysImpute	LinearGrid	4	0	0
PhysImpute	LowRankSVD	4	0	0
PhysImpute	LowRankSVD-16	4	0	0
PhysImpute	MICE	4	0	0
PhysImpute	Mean	4	0	0
PhysImpute	Median	4	0	0
PhysImpute	NearestGrid	4	0	0
PhysImpute	PolyTrend2	4	0	0
PhysImpute	RBF-TP	4	0	0
PhysImpute	SK-KNN	4	0	0
PhysImpute	SK-SimpleMean	4	0	0
PhysImpute	SK-SimpleMedian	4	0	0
PhysImpute	Zero	4	0	0
PhysImpute	CubicGrid	3	0	1

4.3 Cross-Dataset Ranking Overview

To complement per-dataset RMSE tables, we provide a normalized cross-dataset ranking view. Figure 2 reduces scale bias across METR-LA, PEMS-BAY, Darcy, and Poisson by normalizing RMSE within each dataset before aggregation.

The normalized view strengthens the main claim from Table 1: PhysImpute is consistently strong across heterogeneous settings, rather than being optimal on only one task profile. This is important for database deployment, where operating conditions are not fixed to one benchmark regime.

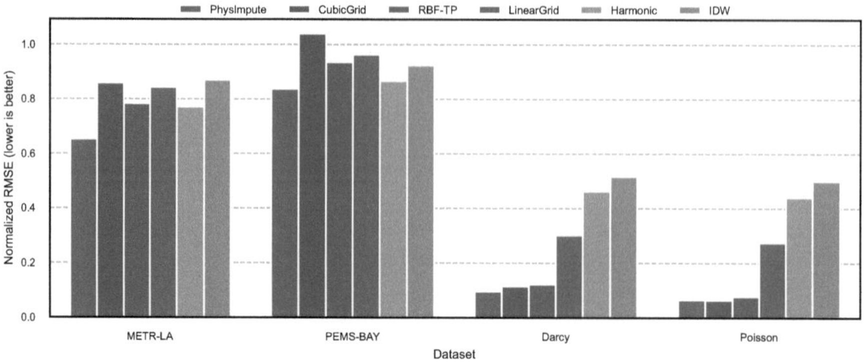

Fig. 2. Normalized RMSE comparison across METR-LA, PEMS-BAY, Darcy, and Poisson. After dataset-wise normalization, PhysImpute remains in the top tier across heterogeneous datasets, indicating that its gains are not driven by a single benchmark.

4.4 Computational Scalability and Efficiency

A key requirement for database information systems is low-latency inference under incomplete data. We report per-sample latency jointly with accuracy in a Pareto-style visualization.

Figure 3 shows a clear latency–accuracy stratification. Extremely lightweight imputers (e.g., constant or simple-statistics baselines) achieve very low latency but are separated from the leading methods by substantially worse normalized RMSE. PhysImpute is not the fastest method, yet it stays in a practical latency regime near the low-error frontier—a more relevant operating region for database imputation than latency minimization alone.

This behavior is consistent with the architectural design in Sect. 3.3. The sparse FE interaction pattern limits expensive dense global coupling and preserves scalable inference behavior as sensor networks grow, while still enabling multi-hop physical context aggregation. In database terms, this yields a useful trade-off: a moderate per-sample compute cost that buys a large gain in reconstruction quality compared with ultra-fast but high-error alternatives. Crucially, each new missingness pattern is imputed by a single operator forward pass rather than the per-instance optimization loop that PINN-based imputation requires, avoiding the repeated-solve overhead noted in Sect. 1, consistent with Fig. 3.

The latency view should be read jointly with the physics–accuracy analysis in Fig. 5: the former indicates whether a method meets latency constraints, the latter whether the recovered values remain physically credible. Together they support the claim that PhysImpute suits latency-constrained, reliability-sensitive spatio-temporal database settings.

4.5 Robustness Under Missingness and Physics–Accuracy Trade-Off

We further analyze robustness and trade-offs across missingness rates. Figure 4 summarizes normalized RMSE trajectories under increasing missingness in the

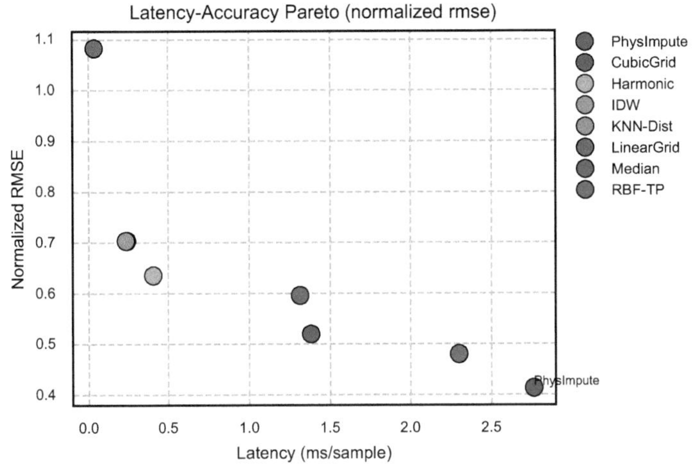

Fig. 3. Latency–accuracy trade-off under the finalized settings. PhysImpute is positioned near the low-latency, low-normalized-RMSE region, while some alternatives exhibit either higher error at similar latency or substantially higher latency.

ablation configuration, and Fig. 5 shows the RMSE–physics relationship in the finalized four-dataset setting.

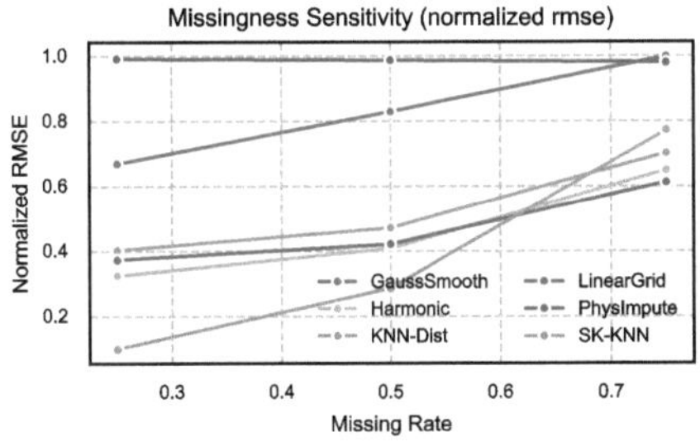

Fig. 4. Normalized RMSE sensitivity under increasing missingness in the ablation configuration. The curve highlights robustness differences across methods.

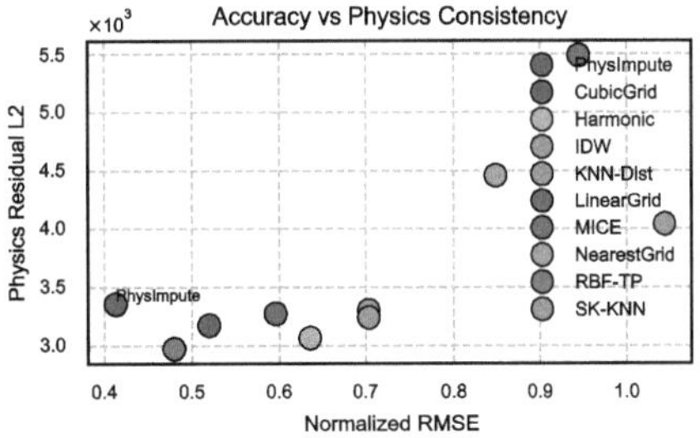

Fig. 5. Accuracy–physics frontier across methods in the finalized setting. PhysImpute stays in a favorable low-error region with meaningful residual control.

Taken together, these two views clarify the practical trade-off envelope. Under missingness stress tests, interpolation-heavy methods can remain very strong on pure pointwise RMSE. In contrast, the physics–accuracy frontier shows that PhysImpute maintains a favorable balance between competitive error and physically consistent reconstruction. This complements the main-table result (top performance on METR-LA, PEMS-BAY, and Darcy, and a close second on Poisson) by showing behavior beyond a single fixed evaluation slice.

4.6 Validity Checks

To reduce evaluation bias, we separate two experimental views: (i) the *finalized best-trial comparison* at 50% MNAR (Tables 1–2, Figs. 2–3), and (ii) the *missingness stress-test view* across 0.25/0.5/0.75 rates (Fig. 4), avoiding any mix of model-selection and robustness-trend conclusions.

We also clarify three validity boundaries. **Internal validity:** best-trial selection is performed per dataset, which improves practical tuning quality but can favor methods with larger search spaces. **Construct validity:** RMSE ranking captures pointwise error but does not fully represent physically plausible reconstruction; therefore we jointly analyze physics residuals (Fig. 5). **External validity:** current evidence covers two synthetic PDE families and two real traffic datasets; broader generalization to other sensing regimes (e.g., mobile sensors or multiphysics coupling) remains future work.

5 Discussion

PhysImpute is a practical framework for zero-shot physics-consistent imputation in spatio-temporal sensor databases. By leveraging the local sparsity of the finite-element mesh, it is designed for linear scalability while preserving physical structure in recovered fields.

Compared with global operators, a locally-sparse finite-element design highlights a key trade-off in spatio-temporal data management: broader receptive fields can improve fit, while localized interactions improve memory efficiency and deployment scalability. PhysImpute's advantage stems from the Locally-Sparse FE Layer, which models local physical gradients rather than dense global correlations, addressing scalability bottlenecks discussed in prior work [16] and aligning the imputer with the spatial locality of physical conservation laws.

More broadly, physics-informed operator learning can serve as a foundation for next-generation digital twin databases: integrating physical priors reframes database cleaning from pure statistical estimation to physics-constrained reconstruction. This is especially relevant for safety-critical applications, where data integrity is defined not only by numerical accuracy but also by physical realizability.

On statistical stability, randomness mainly comes from initialization, mini-batch ordering, and mask sampling, while explicit seed control and fixed preprocessing/evaluation ensure repeatable execution. We distinguish *ranking stability* (whether top methods remain top across runs) from *absolute metric stability* (numerical variation in RMSE/physics residuals); our conclusions rest on ranking evidence (top-2 across all datasets, three dataset-level wins), and future work can add multi-seed confidence intervals and significance tests.

Despite its advantages, PhysImpute has several technical limitations. First, the current architecture assumes that the sensor coordinates remain static over time; extending the framework to mobile sensors would require a real-time update of the sparse adjacency matrix $\mathbf{A}_{FE}$. Second, while the model is highly effective for physical variables (e.g., temperature, pressure), it does not directly handle nominal or categorical attributes that do not follow PDE laws. Third, the interpolation accuracy is bounded by the finite-element discretization error, which may become significant in regions with extremely sharp gradients or discontinuities. Relatedly, generalizing operator learning to highly irregular or complex geometries remains an open challenge; geometry-aware formulations such as Point-DeepONet [19] and finite-element eigenfunction networks [22] offer promising directions for extending mesh-based operators to such domains.

Future research will integrate PhysImpute into query optimization layers of spatio-temporal DBMS, use physical residuals to flag unrealistic imputations, and extend Sparse FEONet to multi-physics settings.

6 Conclusion

We introduced **PhysImpute**, a zero-shot physics-consistent imputation framework for spatio-temporal sensor databases. Built on Sparse FEONet, it models the sensor network as a sparse finite-element mesh and learns a continuous operator for missing-value recovery under physical constraints, with confidence-aware online inference validated across multiple datasets. PhysImpute achieves top-performing pointwise accuracy while delivering stronger physical consistency, a credible foundation for physics-aware data cleaning in large-scale databases.

Acknowledgments. The work was supported by MEDIC project funded by the Marie Sklodowska-Curie Postdoctoral Individual Fellowship under Grant No. 101284617.

References

1. Aizpurua, J.I.: Physics-informed machine learning for transformer condition monitoring – Part II: Physics-informed neural networks and uncertainty quantification (2025)
2. Biswas, S., Yadav, K.K.: A physics-informed U-Net-LSTM network for nonlinear structural response under seismic excitation (2026)
3. Chen, N., Cui, C., Ma, R., Chen, A., Wang, S.: Sharp-PINNs: staggered hard-constrained physics-informed neural networks for phase field modelling of corrosion. Comput. Methods Appl. Mech. Eng. **447**, 118346 (2025)
4. Chen, R., Kim, C.W., Wang, J.: Real-time surrogate model of vehicle-bridge interaction using a multiple-input neural operator. Autom. Constr. **180**, 106576 (2025)
5. Chen, Z., Lai, S.K., Yang, Z., Ni, Y.Q., Yang, Z., Cheung, K.C.: AT-PINN-HC: a refined time-sequential method incorporating hard-constraint strategies for predicting structural behavior under dynamic loads. Comput. Methods Appl. Mech. Eng. **436**, 117691 (2025)
6. Chrisnanto, J.E., Alia, S.R., Chrisnanto, Y.H., Faizal, F.: Unified spatiotemporal physics-informed learning (USPIL): a framework for modeling complex predator-prey dynamics (2025)
7. Duprez, M., Lleras, V., Lozinski, A., Vigon, V., Vuillemot, K.: *phi*-FEM-FNO: a new approach to train a neural operator as a fast PDE solver for variable geometries. Commun. Nonlinear Sci. Numer. Simul. **152**, 109131 (2026)

8. Haghighat, E., Adeli, M.H., Mousavi, S.M., Juanes, R.: STONet: a neural operator for modeling solute transport in micro-cracked reservoirs. Adv. Water Resour. **205**, 105046 (2025)
9. He, X., You, L., Tian, H., Han, B., Tsang, I., Ong, Y.S.: Lang-PINN: from language to physics-informed neural networks via a multi-agent framework (2025)
10. Hu, Z., Cao, Q., Kawaguchi, K., Karniadakis, G.E.: DeepOMamba: state-space model for spatio-temporal PDE neural operator learning. J. Comput. Phys. **540**, 114272 (2025)
11. Jiang, X., Wang, Z., Bao, W., Xu, Y.: Generalization of PINNs for elliptic interface problems. Appl. Math. Lett. **157**, 109175 (2024)
12. Ko, S., Kim, J., Shin, D.: Sparse FEONet: a low-cost, memory-efficient operator network via finite-element local sparsity for parametric PDEs (2026)
13. Li, Z., Kovachki, N., Azizzadenesheli, K., Liu, B., Bhattacharya, K., Stuart, A., Anandkumar, A.: Fourier neural operator for parametric partial differential equations (2020)
14. Liu, Q., Zhong, W., Koric, S., Meidani, H.: Sequential neural operator transformer for high-fidelity surrogates of time-dependent non-linear partial differential equations. Eng. Appl. Artif. Intell. **172**, 114428 (2026)
15. Lu, L., Jin, P., Pang, G., Zhang, Z., Karniadakis, G.E.: Learning nonlinear operators via DeepONet based on the universal approximation theorem of operators. Nat. Mach. Intell. **3**(3), 218–229 (2021)
16. Omidvartehrani, S., Nobari, A.D., Rafiei, D.: LDI: localized data imputation. In: Advances in Databases and Information Systems - 28th European Conference, ADBIS 2024 (2024)
17. Ouyang, W., Liu, S.W., Chan, S.L.: Second-order analysis method for pile-supported structures using neural-operator element method. Eng. Struct. **354**, 122385 (2026)
18. Ouyang, W., Shin, Y., Liu, S.W., Lu, L.: Neural-operator element method: efficient and scalable finite element method enabled by reusable neural operators (2025)
19. Park, J., Kang, N.: Point-DeepONet: predicting nonlinear fields on non-parametric geometries under variable load conditions. Neural Netw. **198**, 108560 (2026). https://doi.org/10.1016/j.neunet.2026.108560
20. Patel, J.M., Ramezankhani, M., Deodhar, A., Birru, D.: An extended physics-informed neural operator for accelerated design optimization in composites autoclave processing. Compos. B Eng. **308**, 112935 (2026)
21. Raissi, M., Perdikaris, P., Karniadakis, G.E.: Physics-informed neural networks. JCP (2019)
22. Salahshoor, H., Li, S.: Finite element eigenfunction network (FEENet): a hybrid framework for solving PDEs on complex geometries (2026). https://doi.org/10.2139/ssrn.6138934. sSRN preprint 6138934
23. Sundaram, R.C., Naghizade, E., Thuraisingham, B., Miller, T.J.: Harnessing spatio-temporal patterns in data for nominal attribute imputation. Int. J. Geogr. Inf. Sci. **34**(11), 2145–2170 (2020)

24. Veličković, P., Cucurull, G., Casanova, A., Romero, A., Lio, P., Bengio, Y.: Graph attention networks. In: ICLR (2018)
25. Xu, K., Hu, W., Leskovec, J., Jegelka, S.: How powerful are graph neural networks? In: ICLR (2019)
26. Zheng, J., Huang, Y., Yi, N.: IG-PINNs: interface-gated physics-informed neural networks for solving elliptic interface problems (2025)

Integration, Auditing, Diversification and Embeddings

VCFINTEGRATOR: Merging VCF Files with Conflict Resolution

Alina Skrylnik[1,2(✉)], Anton Dignös[1], Christian Fuchsberger[2], Giuseppe Tallini[1], and Johann Gamper[1]

[1] Free University of Bozen-Bolzano, Bolzano, Italy
{askrylnik,anton.dignoes,gtallini,johann.gamper}@unibz.it
[2] Eurac Research, Bolzano, Italy
{alskrylnik,christian.fuchsberger}@eurac.edu

Abstract. Genotype data are typically stored in so-called Variant Call Format (VCF) files and need to be integrated from different data sources for downstream analyses. Existing tools for merging multiple VCF files are not able to handle conflicts in the input data. In this paper, we propose the VCFINTEGRATOR algorithm, which solves conflicts in the input data by exploiting three different strategies: majority voting, probability scores provided in the input files, and user-defined preferences. An experimental evaluation shows that VCFINTEGRATOR is comparable to existing state-of-the-art competitors in terms of runtime, consumes less memory, and resolves conflicts, which none of the competitors is doing.

Keywords: Variant Call Format · Files merging · Genotype quality

1 Introduction

The sources of genetic data are numerous and are retrieved from diverse sources based on technologies such as whole exome sequencing [18], whole genome sequencing [16], or statistical methods like genotype imputation [11]. Such data are typically stored in so-called *Variant Call Format (VCF)* files [8,17], which have become the standard format for storing genomic variant data for large-scale genetic studies. To perform downstream analysis, data from different sources typically need to be merged into a single VCF file, which might reveal inconsistencies in the data that have to be solved.

A VCF file consists of two main parts (Fig. 1): a header with meta-data (lines starting with ##) and a table with genotype data, where rows represent genetic positions and columns represent samples. Each genotype is composed of a pair of nucleotides, which are represented by the letters A, T, C, and G. Instead of directly storing the nucleotides, VCF files store for each sample the variation wrt a reference sequence. Thus, the genotype table has the following fields: the number of the chromosome (*#CHROM*); the position of the genotype in the chromosome (*POS*); the nucleotide in the reference genome (*REF*); alternative nucleotides that can be present at this position (*ALT*); additional information

G. Vargas-Solar et al. (Eds.): ADBIS 2026, LNCS 16937, pp. 303–319, 2027.
https://doi.org/10.1007/978-3-032-39820-8_20

```
##fileformat=VCFv4.4
##fileDate=20090805
##source=myImputationProgramV3.1
##reference=file:///seq/references/1000GenomesPilot-NCBI36.fasta
##contig=<ID=20,length=62435964,assembly=B36,md5=f126cdf8a6e0c7f379d618ff66beb2da,species="Homo sapiens",taxonomy=x>
##phasing=partial
##INFO=<ID=NS,Number=1,Type=Integer,Description="Number of Samples With Data">
##INFO=<ID=DP,Number=1,Type=Integer,Description="Total Depth">
##INFO=<ID=AF,Number=A,Type=Float,Description="Allele Frequency">
##INFO=<ID=AA,Number=1,Type=String,Description="Ancestral Allele">
##INFO=<ID=DB,Number=0,Type=Flag,Description="dbSNP membership, build 129">
##INFO=<ID=H2,Number=0,Type=Flag,Description="HapMap2 membership">
##FILTER=<ID=q10,Description="Quality below 10">
##FILTER=<ID=s50,Description="Less than 50% of samples have data">
##FORMAT=<ID=GT,Number=1,Type=String,Description="Genotype">
##FORMAT=<ID=GQ,Number=1,Type=Integer,Description="Genotype Quality">
##FORMAT=<ID=DP,Number=1,Type=Integer,Description="Read Depth">
##FORMAT=<ID=HQ,Number=2,Type=Integer,Description="Haplotype Quality">
#CHROM POS     ID        REF    ALT     QUAL FILTER INFO                              FORMAT      NA00001        NA00002        NA00003
20     14370   rs6054257 G      A       29   PASS   NS=3;DP=14;AF=0.5;DB;H2           GT:GQ:DP:HQ 0|0:48:1:51,51 1|0:48:8:51,51 1/1:43:5:.,.
20     17330   .         T      A       3    q10    NS=3;DP=11;AF=0.017               GT:GQ:DP:HQ 0|0:49:3:58,50 0|1:3:5:65,3   0/0:41:3
20     1110696 rs6040355 A      G,T     67   PASS   NS=2;DP=10;AF=0.333,0.667;AA=T;DB GT:GQ:DP:HQ 1|2:21:6:23,27 2|1:2:0:18,2   2/2:35:4
20     1230237 .         T      .       47   PASS   NS=3;DP=13;AA=T                   GT:GQ:DP:HQ 0|0:54:7:56,60 0|0:48:4:51,51 0/0:61:2
20     1234567 microsat1 GTC    G,GTCT  50   PASS   NS=3;DP=9;AA=G                    GT:GQ:DP    0/1:35:4       0/2:17:2       1/1:40:3
```

Fig. 1. Sample VCF File [17]

about the specific genomic variants (*INFO*); the format of the genotype fields (*FORMAT*); and the genotype values of the samples (*NA00001, NA00002, ...*). The genotype values are represented by two numbers separated by a pipe (e.g., 0|0, 0|1) for phased genotypes or a slash (e.g., 0/0, 0/1) for unphased genotypes, indicating whether the allele's parental origin is known, respectively. The value 0 refers to the nucleotide in the *REF* field, a 1 refers to the first nucleotide in the *ALT* field, a 2 to the second nucleotide in the *ALT* field, etc.

Merging VCF files is straightforward if the datasets are disjoint, i.e., data from different samples or different genetic positions. However, if there is an overlap in the samples (columns) or genomic positions (rows), conflicts might occur. That is, the files might contain different information, such as duplicated genomic positions or different *REF*, *ALT*, and genotype values. This requires a careful conflict resolution during the merging.

There exist a number of tools for merging VCF files, most notably VCFtools [9], BCFtools [10], and Picard MergeVcfs [6], which have a similar functionality to the method proposed in this paper. However, these methods lack an appropriate conflict resolution mechanism. If different genotype values are present for a specific individual at the same position, existing tools fail to resolve the conflict and instead either discard the affected row or column, or simply copy it as it is. The former solution loses data, whereas the latter introduces redundancy, duplicates, or inconsistent data.

In this paper, we propose VCFIntegrator for merging multiple input VCF files that may contain overlapping data with potential conflicts. Conflicts arise if a sample in different files has different genotype data for the same position or if for a specific position there are different *REF* or *ALT* values in the input files. While previous approaches either discard data or introduce redundancy (without really solving conflicts), we propose a conflict resolution strategy that allows us to merge conflicting records from different input files into a single output record without losing information. Conflicts in genotype values are resolved by three different mechanisms: majority voting if a certain genotype value is present in most of the files; the use of additional information for the individual genotype values if they are provided in the input data; or user-specified preferences for the datasets. The other type of conflict (mismatch of *REF* or *ALT* values) is also handled by our algorithm. In case of *REF* mismatch, the rows are concatenated one after the other. If the *ALT* values in the merged input records vary, the corresponding output record stores the union of these values, which requires a remapping of the genotype values since they reference the *ALT* values.

A running example of merging three input VCF files is shown in Fig. 2. Since the input data is sorted by genomic position, our merging algorithm adopts a sort-merge strategy. This is very efficient and scales for large genomic datasets without compromising computational performance as the number of samples or variants increases. To the best of our knowledge, VCFINTEGRATOR is the first algorithm that offers lossless conflict resolution when merging multiple VCF files.

The technical contributions of this paper can be summarized as follows:

- We present a strategy for losslessly resolving conflicts when merging VCF files that contain overlapping genotype data. This allows us to keep all the data and information without introducing redundancy.
- We implement the conflict resolution strategy in an efficient and scalable merge algorithm, VCFINTEGRATOR, adopting a sort-merge approach.
- An experimental evaluation shows that our solution is on par with state-of-the-art competitors in terms of runtime and outperforms them in terms of memory, making it suitable for high-throughput genomic workflows.

The remainder of this paper is organized as follows. Section 2 discusses related work. Section 3 describes the conflict resolution and the conflict-aware merging algorithm. In Sect. 4 we discuss the results of our experimental evaluation, and Sect. 5 summarizes the results and outlines future work.

2 Related Work

Merging multiple VCF files has been studied in previous research. *Picard MergeVcfs* [6] is a command-line tool implemented in Java, which produces a result only for the intersection of samples from the input. Samples (columns) that are not present in all input files are discarded. The remaining data is copied to the output as is, regardless whether it is consistent, thereby introducing duplicated rows and redundancy.

VCFtools [9] provides two merging utilities: `vcf-merge`, which merges files by columns (samples), and `vcf-concat`, which appends rows (genomic positions). If a sample occurs in multiple files, the output file keeps all instances from the input files without merging duplicates into one column. Duplicates are renamed by prepending the name of the source file to the sample name, e.g., `filename_sample`. The tool supports both `.vcf` and `.vcf.gz` file formats and is implemented as a collection of Perl scripts.

BCFtools [10] applies the same conflict resolution strategy as VCFtools by offering `merge` and `concat` tools for integrating columns and rows, respectively. By default, the `merge` tool does not support duplicate samples, i.e., an error is

Table 1. Comparison of tools for merging VCF datasets.

Tool	Merges VCF files?	Requires only VCF files?	Handles conflicting genotype (GT) values?
BCFtools	✓	✓	✗
Picard MergeVcfs	✓	✓	✗
DRAGEN	✗	✗	✓
Minos	✓	✗	✓
VCFINTEGRATOR	✓	✓	✓

generated and the merge process stops if the same sample appears in more than one input file. The option `--force-samples` allows to overcome this problem by keeping, similar to the VCFtools, a copy of all samples and prepending an index that indicates the file number to the sample identifier, e.g., `2:sample`. Besides `.vcf` and `.vcf.gz` files, BCFtools also supports `.bcf` files, which is a binary version of the VCF format. The tool is implemented in C.

Minos [13] is a tool for adjudication between multiple VCF files. It uses sequencing reads from a single sample, a reference genome, and one or more VCF files containing candidate variants. It then determines which alleles are best supported by the available data. First, it merges and clusters overlapping SNPs [14] and indels [15] from the input VCFs into local variant regions. Next, it constructs a genome graph that includes the reference sequence and all candidate alleles, and maps the reads to this graph using gramtools. Based on allele-level read coverage and an error model, it selects the most strongly supported genotype, annotates the calls with confidence metrics, and outputs a filtered, single-sample VCF representing the adjudicated variant set. The tool heavily relies on additional files, such as the reference genome in FASTA format and read files (FASTQ) for each sample [1, Chapter 7, Sect. 7.1]. Moreover, it requires an external tool to combine these files into a single VCF. Therefore, it cannot rely solely on the VCF files themselves without the external supporting information.

DRAGEN [2] is primarily designed to handle structural variants (SVs) – large-scale changes involving more than 50 nucleotides [12] – rather than SNPs, which typically involve changes in one or two nucleotides. In contrast, SNP merging typically requires exact matching of (CHROM, POS, REF, ALT) or an ALT-union approach with genotype index remapping, which this tool does not implement. As a result, its parsing logic, matching strategy, and genotype consolidation model are not directly compatible with standard SNP-style VCF.

In the general context of *data fusion*, this paper focuses on conflict detection and resolution, i.e., merging records describing the same real-world entity into one consistent representation [5]. According to the classification of conflict-handling strategies into conflict *ignorance*, *avoidance*, and *resolution* [3,4], our VCFINTEGRATOR performs *resolution*, and more specifically, *deciding* resolution. In contrast, BCFtools, VCFtools, and Picard MergeVcfs only ignore conflicts, and either discard data, thereby losing information, or introduce duplicates, redundancies, or inconsistent data. Minos and DRAGEN resolve them but rely on evidence external to the VCF files. Table 1 summarizes the main features of VCF merging tools.

3 Merging VCF Files with Conflict Resolution

3.1 Conflict Resolution

When merging multiple VCF files, records that share the same genomic position (*CHR*, *POS*), i.e., a chromosome and a position within that chromosome, might contain various types of conflicts that need to be resolved and merged into one or more records in the output file. We use Fig. 2 as a running example, where groups of records with identical positions are indicated by colors. Files 1 and 2 contain data for four positions, whereas file 3 and the merged output file contain data for five positions.

`file1.vcf`

CHR	POS	REF	ALT	FMT	S1	S2
22	262	G	T	GT:GQ	0/1:85	1/0:70
22	262	AT	C	GT:GQ	1/1:60	0/0:50
22	262	TG	A	GT:GQ	0/0:90	1/0:65
22	417	G	A	GT:GQ	1/0:80	1/0:88
22	478	C	T	GT:GQ	0/0:95	1/1:40
22	480	G	A,T	GT:GQ	0/1:60	1/2:55

`file2.vcf`

CHR	POS	REF	ALT	FMT	S1	S2
22	262	TG	C	GT:PL	0/0:0,35,85	1/0:0,20,75
22	262	G	A,T	GT:PL	1/2:0,20,70	0/1:0,40,90
22	262	AT	C	GT:PL	1/0:0,25,80	1/1:60,15,0
22	417	G	T	GT:PL	1/1:60,10,0	0/1:0,30,85
22	478	C	A	GT:PL	0/1:0,20,70	1/1:80,25,0
22	480	G	A,T	GT:PL	0/1:0,40,95	0/2:0,30,85

`file3.vcf`

CHR	POS	REF	ALT	FMT	S1	S3
22	262	G	A,T	GT	1/2	1/2
22	262	AT	C	GT	1/1	0/0
22	417	G	T	GT	1/1	1/1
22	478	C	A	GT	0/0	1/1
22	480	G	A,T	GT	0/1	0/2
22	491	T	C	GT	0/1	0/0

`merged.vcf`

CHR	POS	REF	ALT	FMT	S1	S2	S3
22	262	G	A,T	GT:GQ:PL	1/2:20:0,20,70	2/0:70:.	1/2:.:.
22	262	AT	C	GT:GQ:PL	1/1:60:.	0/0:50:.	0/0:.:.
22	262	TG	A,C	GT:GQ:PL	0/0:90:.	1/0:65:.	./.:.:.
22	417	G	A,T	GT:GQ:PL	2/2:10:60,10,0	1/0:88:.	2/2:.:.
22	478	C	A,T	GT:GQ:PL	0/0:95:.	2/2:40:.	2/2:.:.
22	480	G	A,T	GT:GQ:PL	0/1:60:.	1/2:55:.	0/2:.:.
22	491	T	C	GT	0/1	./.	0/0

Fig. 2. Running example: merging three VCF files.

Conflicts in REF and ALT Values. The first group of conflicts concerns the *REF* and *ALT* values, which for a given position (*CHR*, *POS*) might differ in the input files. Since different *REF* values cannot be merged into a single record because each VCF file is based on a single reference genome, we produce an output record for each *REF* value occurring at that position. In contrast, *ALT* values are combined using union. Modifying the *ALT* value, however, requires updating the genotype values of samples since these are positional references to *REF* and *ALT* values for a record. For instance, 0/1 in the first input record of file 1 represents the genotype *G*/*T*.

Example 1. Consider position (22, 262), which in Fig. 2 is marked in blue. The input files 1 and 2 contain three records each with *REF* values G, AT, and TG, respectively, whereas file 3 has only two records with the *REF* values G and AT. This yields three output records, one for each of the different *REF* values.

As another example, consider position (22, 417), which is marked in red. It has exactly one record in each input file with *REF* value G, whereas the *ALT* value is A in file 1 and T in file 2 and file 3. This yields in the output record the *REF* value G and the *ALT* value A,T, i.e., the union of the *ALT* values from the three input records. Since the *ALT* value changed, the genotype values have to be adapted in the merged file. For instance, the genotype of the sample S1 is 1/1 in file 1 and 2, which corresponds to the alternative allele T. Since in the merged output record the alleles are ordered as *ALT* = A,T, the genotype value 1/1 from the input records is replaced by 2/2 in the output record (2 is now referring to allele T).

Conflicts in the Genotype Values. Once input records with the same *REF* value are aligned and the corresponding *ALT* values are combined, the genotype values of each individual sample in these records need to be analyzed and compared. If the genotype of a specific position (CHR, POS) and sample S_i differs across input records, we propose the following conflict resolution:

- *Majority Voting.* If one genotype value occurs more frequently than any other among matching input records, it is used in the output record. This is most reliable when the most frequent genotype calls are high quality.
- *Statistical Information.* If no most frequent genotype exists, the decision is based on the GQ (Genotype Quality) which measures the confidence in the genotype value and/or PL (Phred-scaled genotype likelihoods) values in the VCF files (if available). These values are used to select the GT corresponding to the higher quality score. PL values can be used to calculate the GQ values by subtracting the first most likely probability value from the second one [7]. These values represent the confidence of the variant caller in a particular GT value. The genotype value with the highest GQ among all input records is used in the output record.
- *User-specified Preferences.* If the above rules cannot be applied, the genotype value of the output is taken from a single input file according to a user-defined priority list. For simplicity, we assume in this paper that the order in which the input files are provided to the merging algorithm defines this priority list; that is, the first file is considered the most authoritative. If the first file does not resolve the conflict, the second file is considered, and so on. This option should be selected carefully by the user, as he/she should ensure that the variant calls used to generate the input VCF files are of sufficient quality for this approach to be reliable.

Example 2. Consider the genotype value at position (22, 480) of sample S_1 in Fig. 2. Since the genotypes in all three input files are 0/1, there is no conflict and 0/1 is taken as genotype value in the merged output record.

At position (22, 478) of sample S_1, we have the genotype value 0/0 in file 1 and file 3, and the value 0/1 in file 2. This conflict is solved by majority voting: two occurrences of 0/0 and one occurrence of 0/1 yield 0/0 as the merged genotype value in the output record.

Now consider position (22, 417) of sample S_2, for which we have the values 1/0 and 0/1 in the first two input files, respectively, and no value in file 3. Since majority voting cannot be applied, GQ is used. In file 1, the genotype value is 1/0 with $GQ = 88$, whereas file 2 has the genotype 0/1 with $PL = 0, 30, 85$. We compute the GQ value for file 2 as the difference between the PL values of the two most likely genotypes, which are 0/0 with $PL = 0$ and 0/1 with $PL = 30$. This yields $GQ = 30$. Since the value 1/0 in file 1 has a higher GQ than the value 0/1 in file 2, i.e. $88 > 30$, the genotype value including the GQ in the output record is set to 1/0 : 88.

3.2 Merging Algorithm

Algorithm 1 implements the merging process. The VCFINTEGRATOR algorithm takes as input a set $\mathcal{F} = \{F_1, F_2, \ldots, F_n\}$, $n \geq 2$, of VCF files, where the order of the files corresponds to the user-specified priority list. Each file is sorted by genomic position (CHR, POS). The output is a VCF file, where all input files are merged and conflicts are solved by applying the strategy described above.

Algorithm 1: VCFINTEGRATOR

Input: Set $\mathcal{F} = \{F_1, \ldots, F_n\}$ of VCF files
Output: Merged VCF file F

// Initialization
$p_i \leftarrow$ pointer to first record in F_i for $i = 1, \ldots, n$;
$\mathcal{S} \leftarrow$ set of sample IDs in all files F_i for $i = 1, \ldots, n$;
$F \leftarrow$ empty VCF file with a column for each sample in $\mathcal{S}$;

// Process all records with interleaved file scans
while *not all data processed* **do**
  $(chr, pos) \leftarrow$ position of least advanced pointer in $p_1, \ldots, p_n$;
  $G \leftarrow \emptyset$;
  foreach $F_i \in \mathcal{F}$ **do**
    $G \leftarrow G \cup \{r \in F_i \mid r.CHR = chr \wedge r.POS = pos\}$;
    Advance p_i to the record following (chr, pos);
  foreach $ref \in \{r.REF \mid r \in G\}$ **do**
    $R \leftarrow \{r \in G \mid r.REF = ref\}$;
    $F \leftarrow F \cup \{\text{MERGE}(R, \mathcal{S})\}$;
return F;

The initialization phase sets a pointer to the first record in each input file, determines the set $\mathcal{S}$ of samples across these files, and creates an empty VCF output file (line 1). Then, the input files are scanned simultaneously in an interleaved way, line by line, according to a sort-merge join strategy, thereby matching corresponding records and solving potential conflicts (lines 4–12).

First, we retrieve the genomic position (chr, pos) stored in the record of the least advanced pointer in $p_1, \ldots, p_n$ (line 5). Then, we collect in G all input records from all files that have the same genomic position (chr, pos), and the pointers p_i are advanced to the next position (line 7). Next, for each different *REF* value found in G, the set R of matching records is extracted from G. Note that all records in R have the same (*CHR*, *POS*) and *REF* values (line 10). A call of function Merge integrates all records in R into a single output record, which is added to the final VCF file (line 12).

Function Merge in Algorithm 2 takes as input a set R of records, which all have the same genomic position and the same *REF* value, and it returns a single record which is the result of merging the records in R by applying the conflict resolution strategy. Notice that R might have less records than n if some input files have no data for a given position.

Algorithm 2: Algorithm Merge

Input: Set $R = \{r_1, \ldots, r_m\}$ of records, set of samples $\mathcal{S}$
Output: Merged record r

1 $r \leftarrow$ empty record;
2 $r.CHR \leftarrow r_1.CHR$;
3 $r.POS \leftarrow r_1.POS$;
4 $r.REF \leftarrow r_1.REF$;
5 $r.ALT \leftarrow \{r'.ALT \mid r' \in R\}$;
6 $r.FORMAT \leftarrow r_1.FORMAT \circ \cdots \circ r_m.FORMAT$;
7 **foreach** *sample* $S \in \mathcal{S}$ **do**
8   **if** $r_1.S = \ldots = r_m.S$ **then**
9         $r.S \leftarrow r_1.S$;
10   **else if** $\nexists r' \in R$ *with a value* $r'.S$ **then**
11         $r.S \leftarrow$ ./.; `// empty value`
12   **else if** *majority of* $r_i \in R$ *has genotype* $r_i.S = v$ **then**
13         $r.S \leftarrow v$;
14   **else if** $\exists R' \subseteq R$ *with PL or GQ values for* $r \in R'$ **then**
15         $r.S \leftarrow$ genotype with highest PL or GQ value in R';
16   **else**
17         $r.S \leftarrow$ genotype of the first record in the user-specified preference list;
18   Remap $r.S$ to $r.ALT$ if (r.ALT changed wrt to the input records);
19 **return** r;

The first step is to set the *CHR*, *POS*, *REF*, *ALT*, and *FORMAT* values (lines 1–6). Since the first three values are identical across all records in R, they can be copied from any of the records. The *ALT* value of the output record is computed as the union of the *ALT* values of all input records (line 5). Similarly, the *FORMAT* of the output record is determined by concatenating all formats of the input records (line 6).

Next, the algorithm iterates over all samples in $\mathcal{S}$ (line 7). For each sample S_i, the corresponding genotype values in all input records are analyzed and, by applying our conflict resolution strategy, a single output value is determined. If all records r_i have the same genotype, this value is assigned to the output record (line 8). For the case that there is no input record in R that contains a value for sample S, the genotype of the output records is set to the empty value (line 10). Otherwise, majority voting, statistical information or user-specified priorities are applied to solve conflicts (lines 12, 14, 16). For majority voting, the most frequent genotype value is taken. For the statistical information, the genotype with the highest *PL* or *GQ* value is taken. Otherwise, the user-specified preference list is considered. To keep the pseudocode simple, we omit the user-specified preference list and assume that this information is carried over by the individual records. The final step is to map the genotype value to the new *ALT* value, if this has been modified (line 18).

Example 3. We illustrate algorithm VCFIntegrator by using the running example in Fig. 2. The first two input files contain samples S_1 and S_2, whereas file 3 has data for sample S_1 and sample S_3. All three files store data for the positions 262, 417, 478, and 480 of chromosome 22, and file 3 stores additionally data for position 491. Hence, there will be no conflicts for sample S_3 and for position 491.

First, the pointers p_i are set to the first record in each input file, and the set of samples is computed as $\mathcal{S} = \{S_1, S_2, S_3\}$. Next, we enter in the loop and determine the position of the first record as $(chr, pos) = (22, 262)$. We collect all records with this position, i.e., three records in files 1 and 2 and two records in file 3 (marked in blue). The corresponding set of different *REF* values is $\{G, AT, TG\}$. For each of these values, all corresponding records are collected and passed to the function Merge. The resulting tuple is added to the output.

Merge on its first invocation gets the first record of each input file, which have position $(22, 262)$, $REF = G$, and $ALT = T$ in file 1 and $ALT = A, T$ in file 2 and 3. The *ALT* value of the output record is computed as A, T, and the *FORMAT* values are concatenated. Then, the genotype values of the samples are considered. For sample S_1 majority voting yields the value 1/2. For sample S_2, which occurs only in file 1 and file 2, the *PL* and *GQ* values are considered. From the *PL* value in the second file (0,40,90), we can derive the *GQ* value by subtracting 0 from 40. We then select the GT corresponding to the higher *GQ* value, 1/0, and remap it, since *ALT* T is now in position 2, yielding 2/0:70:.

3.3 Efficient Implementation with Bitmaps

To efficiently implement the VCFIntegrator algorithm, we use a mapping table and a number of bitmap indices. First, we create a mapping table from sample positions in $\mathcal{S} = \{S_1, \ldots, S_n\}$ to sample positions in each file, which allows us to quickly determine the position of a certain sample in the individual files $\mathcal{F} = \{F_1, \ldots, F_n\}$. To further speed up the retrieval of all genotypes for a given sample we create a bitmap for each sample in $\mathcal{S} = \{S_1, \ldots, S_n\}$, where the positions in the bitmap indicate the input files and each bit indicates whether a sample is contained in an input file or not. For instance, in Fig. 2 we have the following mapping table and bitmaps:

	F_1	F_2	F_3
S_1	1	1	1
S_2	2	2	-
S_3	-	-	2

S_1	1	1	1
S_2	1	1	0
S_3	0	0	1

This mapping table and the bitmaps are created only once and allow MERGE to quickly identify for each sample S_i which files potentially contain input records using the bitmaps and find the corresponding position in the file using the mapping table. Not all files may contain a specific position (*CHR*, *POS*) and/or *REF* and thus may not need to be merged in line 12 of algorithm MERGE. Thus, we additionally maintain one bitmap when processing a position and one bitmap when processing a *REF* (line 8), where the positions in the bitmaps indicate the input files and each bit indicates whether a position or a *REF*, respectively, is contained in an input file. To find all genotypes in files at a specific (*CHR*, *POS*) and *REF* for a specific sample, we perform a bitwise-AND between these two bitmaps and the bitmap for the sample. For instance, in Fig. 2 when processing $(chr, pos) = (22, 262)$ and $REF = TG$, the position bitmap is $[1, 1, 1]$ and the *REF*-bitmap $[1, 1, 0]$. A bitwise-AND with the bitmap for S_1 results in $[1, 1, 0]$, i.e., only genotypes from files F_1 and F_2 need to be merged.

4 Experimental Evaluation

In this section, we report and discuss the results of extensive experiments, which compare VCFINTEGRATOR to existing competitors.

4.1 Setup

Datasets. We use compressed VCF files (`.vcf.gz`) derived from the HAPNEST dataset [19] containing synthetic genotype data. From this source, we generated datasets with varying numbers of positions and samples and different conflicts in terms of overlap, GT and REF-ALT conflicts. Table 2 gives an overview of the datasets. In the experiments, we vary one dimension at a time and, unless stated otherwise, use for the other dimensions the default value (bold face).

When we merge VCF files, we use input files with the same properties in the experiments. We have two parameters that determine the size of the input, i.e., the number of samples and the number of positions, where the number of samples translates to the number of columns and the number of position translates to the number of rows in the files. The overlap determines the size of the output, where for 100% overlap the output is as large as any of the input files and larger than any of the input files for less overlap since all samples and positions are retained in the output.

Table 2. Datasets

	Size		Conflicts		
	Samples [k]	Positions [k]	Overlap [%]	GT [%]	REF-ALT [%]
Small	0.5, 1, **1.5**, 2, 2.5	20, 35, **50**, 65, 80	90 – **100**	**0** – 50	**0** – 50
Large	5, 10, **15**, 20, 25	200,400,**600**,800,1000	90 – **100**	**0** – 50	**0** – 50

We generally consider three scenarios. The first scenario considers full overlap (all files contain the same samples and positions) with no genotype conflicts. The second scenario considers datasets with partial overlap of 90% in either samples or positions without genotype conflicts, introducing 10% of new samples or positions in each subset. The third scenario considers full overlap, as in the first scenario, but introduces a conflict rate of 20% for GT, meaning that 20% of GT values differ for certain samples and positions across the datasets. For VCFINTEGRATOR, we additionally run experiments with varying types and rates of conflicts. The first type involves conflicts in GT values, while the second involves simultaneous conflicts in REF and ALT values. We vary the conflict rates from 10% to 50% for each type.

Table 3. Runtime for BCFtools and VCFINTEGRATOR across scenarios.

Overlap	BCFtools	VCFINTEGRATOR	Diff. (%)
Full overlap (S)	4177.12	4197.57	+0.5
Full overlap (P)	4349.20	4238.31	-2.5
Partial overlap (S)	4063.74	4493.51	+10.6
Partial overlap (P)	4469.65	4556.65	+1.9
GT conflicts (S)	4541.09	4372.85	-3.7
GT conflicts (P)	4763.05	4459.68	-6.4

Each dataset used for merging consists of 3 subsets, which is the minimum number of files required to implement a majority vote. Each subset has identical sizes in terms of rows and columns, i.e., if we say 15k samples and 600k positions, then all three subsets have this size. Across all scenarios, we consider two settings: (1) a fixed number of samples (typically set to the default value) with varying number of positions, and (2) a fixed number of positions (typically set to the default value) with varying number of samples.

All approaches were run 5 times and we report the average runtime. We use `.vcf.gz` files as input files, as merging compressed files is inherently faster than the plain `.vcf` format.

Compared Methods. We compare our VCFINTEGRATOR algorithm[1], implemented in C, to three competitors. *Picard MergeVcfs* [6], which requires all input VCF files to contain exactly the same samples and simply discards conflicts. *VCFtools* [9] implemented in Perl, which includes all input data into the output file, regardless of producing duplicates. *BCFtools* [10] implemented in C, which applies the same merging strategy as *VCFtools.*

4.2 Results

Runtime. Figure 3 reports the runtime for varying numbers of genomic positions and samples for the small dataset. All methods scale linearly. VCFtools is by far the slowest solution, while the other methods are significantly more efficient. For this reason and since VCF files are typically much larger in reality, we exclude VCFtools in the following experiments.

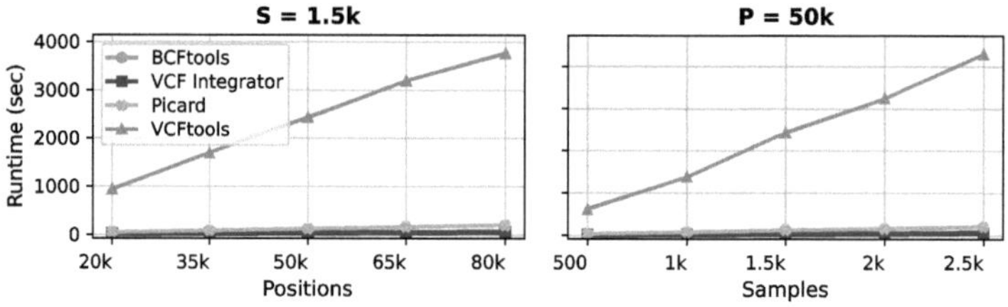

Fig. 3. Runtime experiments on small datasets

Next, we use the large dataset and report in Fig. 4 the runtime for varying the number of genomic positions and samples for different degrees of overlap. Picard MergeVcfs only supports settings where the samples in all files are exactly the same. It is therefore excluded from the experiment with partial overlap over fixed samples, where the overlap is on the samples and thus some samples differ. It is included in the partial overlap with fixed positions, where the overlap is on the positions and thus all samples are the same. In all cases Picard MergeVcfs is the slowest approach, while VCFINTEGRATOR and BCFtools are comparable in runtime over all settings.

[1] Code available at https://gitlab.inf.unibz.it/dbs/vcf-integrator.

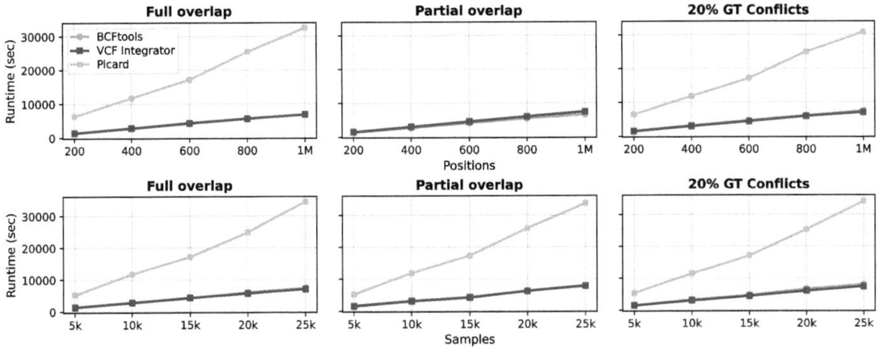

Fig. 4. Runtime for 3 scenarios: full overlap, partial overlap, and 20% GT conflicts

Since the runtimes of BCFtools and VCFIntegrator are very close, Tab. 3 provides a more detailed analysis of these two methods by comparing the average runtime in seconds over all data points for each scenario used in Fig. 4. BCFtools performed faster in scenarios involving partial overlap, i.e., when new positions or samples are introduced. In contrast, VCFIntegrator performs better in scenarios with full overlap and GT conflicts. These results demonstrate that BCFtools is generally more efficient at handling new information, particularly additional samples, whereas VCFIntegrator performs notably better when resolving conflicts within overlapping datasets.

Memory. Figure 5 reports the memory consumption for BCFtools, Picard MergeVcfs, and VCFIntegrator for the same settings as in the previous experiment. Picard MergeVcfs requires much more memory as compared to the other approaches with memory consumption up to 2.5 GB, however, the overall memory consumption remained manageable. In general, the memory consumption for varying number of positions remains constant, while it scales linearly with the number of samples. This is due to the sorted merge approach that needs to keep a few lines of the file in memory and the size of the line is influenced by the number of samples.

Overall, in terms of memory usage, VCFIntegrator demonstrates the best performance across all scenarios, consuming less memory compared to the other approaches.

VCFIntegrator Conflict Sensitivity. We now evaluate the scalability of VCFIntegrator in handling different types of conflicts. Other tools are not included since they do not properly resolve conflicts and the performance for discarding and replication has already been assessed in Figs. 4 and 5. We use the small dataset and vary the size in terms of number of positions and samples for different conflicts and also show the results for the large dataset with default values for varying conflicts.

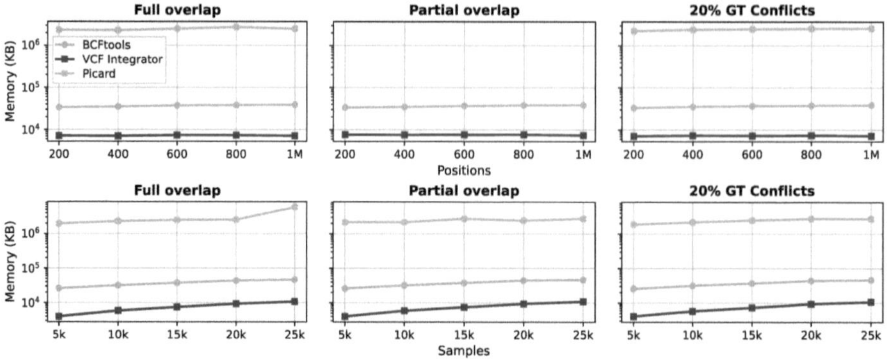

Fig. 5. Memory for 3 scenarios: full overlap, partial overlap, and 20% GT conflicts

Figure 6 shows the performance for different percentages of GT and REF/ALT conflicts. While as expected, the runtime increases linearly for larger number of positions and samples, it is only minimally affected by the number of conflicts. Figure 7 shows the same experiment for the large dataset, where we vary the number of conflicts. We can see that the runtime does increase, especially for resolving REF/ALT conflicts, since resolving larger numbers of conflicts requires additional logic and computation, but overall it can be resolved in a reasonable amount of time.

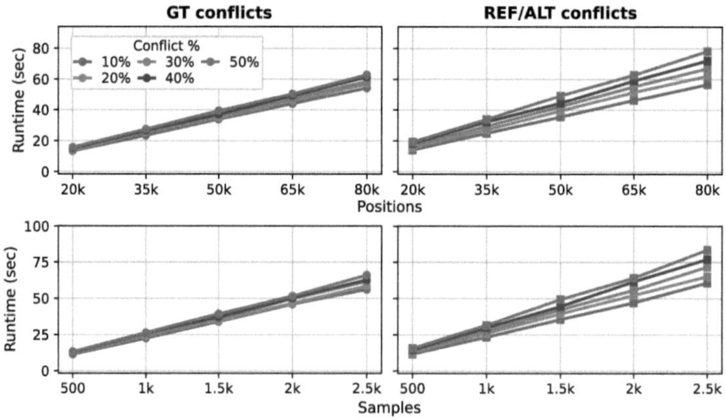

Fig. 6. Runtime VCFIntegrator for GT and REF/ALT conflicts (small data)

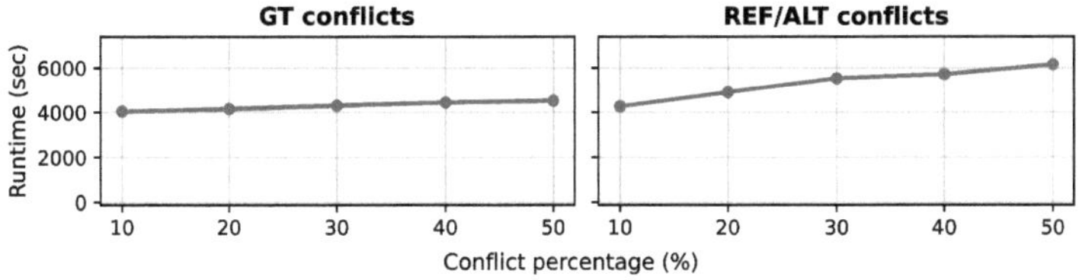

Fig. 7. Runtime VCFINTEGRATOR for GT and REF/ALT conflicts (large data)

Figure 8 shows the results for the memory consumption on the small dataset by varying the number of positions and samples. While memory is influenced by the number of samples, it is not influenced by the number of conflicts. Figure 9 confirms these results for the large dataset for a varying number of conflicts.

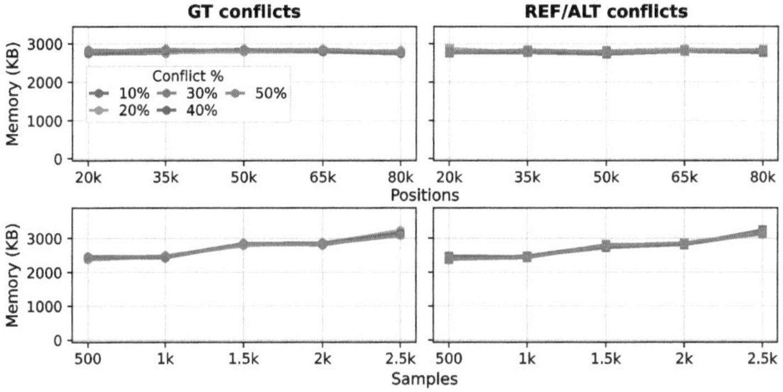

Fig. 8. Memory VCFINTEGRATOR for GT and REF/ALT conflicts (small data)

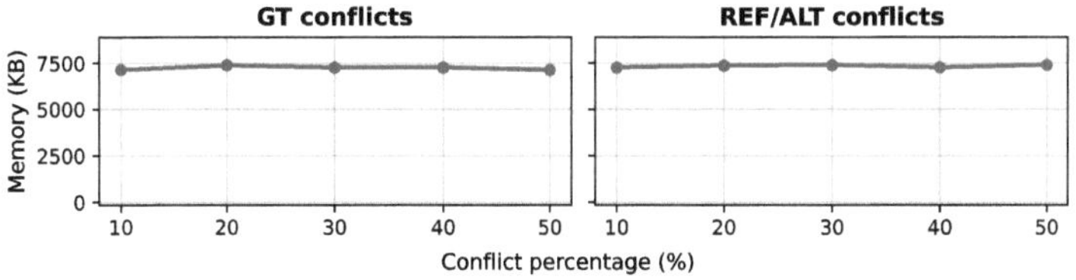

Fig. 9. Memory VCFINTEGRATOR for GT and REF/ALT conflicts (large data)

5 Conclusions

In this paper, we introduced the VCFINTEGRATOR tool for merging VCF files with built-in conflict resolution functionality. The tool demonstrated high efficiency in both runtime and memory consumption, outperforming the main competitor, BCFtools, by up to 79% in memory usage, while maintaining comparable runtime performance within a range of approximately ±6–10%. The tool performed very well in terms of runtime and memory consumption in conflicting scenarios, demonstrating efficient handling of conflicts in large-dimensional datasets and under high conflict rates.

Future research will primarily focus on integrating the .bcf format (the binary representation of VCF), which is expected to further improve the algorithm's runtime. Another direction involves extending the comparison of probability-related metrics beyond GQ: more sophisticated usage of PL and the inclusion of additional values such as DP, as well as accounting for insertions and deletions and their potential effects on GT values after normalization. Additionally, real-world datasets will be used to evaluate the VCFIntegrator algorithm to assess the reliability of each conflict-resolution strategy.

Acknowledgments. This work was funded in part by the Autonomous Province of Bozen-Bolzano, call Joint Projects South Tyrol – Germany, project DyHealthNet, CUP: I53C22002980003.

References

1. Akalin, A.: Computational Genomics with R. Chapman and Hall/CRC (2020). https://doi.org/10.1201/9780429084317
2. Behera, S., et al.: Comprehensive genome analysis and variant detection at scale using DRAGEN. Nat. Biotechnol. **43**(7), 1177–1191 (2025). https://doi.org/10.1038/s41587-024-02382-1
3. Bleiholder, J., Naumann, F.: Declarative data fusion – syntax, semantics, and implementation. In: Eder, J., Haav, H.-M., Kalja, A., Penjam, J. (eds.) ADBIS 2005. LNCS, vol. 3631, pp. 58–73. Springer, Heidelberg (2005). https://doi.org/10.1007/11547686_5
4. Bleiholder, J., Naumann, F.: Conflict handling strategies in an integrated information system. In: IIWeb (2006). https://doi.org/10.18452/2460
5. Bleiholder, J., Naumann, F.: Data Fusion. ACM Comput. Surv. **41**(1), 1–41 (2009). https://doi.org/10.1145/1456650.1456651
6. Broad Institute: Picard toolkit (2019). https://broadinstitute.github.io/picard/
7. Broad Institute: Phred-scaled quality scores (2023). https://gatk.broadinstitute.org/hc/en-us/articles/360035531872-Phred-scaled-quality-scores. Accessed 30 Jul 2025
8. Broad Institute: VCF – Variant Call Format (2024). https://gatk.broadinstitute.org/hc/en-us/articles/360035531692-VCF-Variant-Call-Format
9. Danecek, P., et al.: The variant call format and VCFtools. Bioinformatics **27**(15), 2156–2158 (2011). https://doi.org/10.1093/bioinformatics/btr330
10. Danecek, P., et al.: Twelve years of SAMtools and BCFtools. GigaScience **10**(2) (2021). https://doi.org/10.1093/gigascience/giab008
11. Das, S., et al.: Next-generation genotype imputation service and methods. Nat. Genet. **48**(10), 1284–1287 (2016). https://doi.org/10.1038/ng.3656
12. Escaramís, G., Docampo, E., Rabionet, R.: A decade of structural variants: description, history and methods to detect structural variation. Brief. Funct. Genomics **14**(5), 305–314 (2015). https://doi.org/10.1093/bfgp/elv014

13. Hunt, M., et al.: Minos: variant adjudication and joint genotyping of cohorts of bacterial genomes. Genome Biol. **23**(1), 147 (2022). https://doi.org/10.1186/s13059-022-02714-x
14. Komar, A.A.: Single Nucleotide Polymorphisms. Methods Mol. Biol. **578**(10), 978 (2009). https://doi.org/10.1007/978-1-60327-411-1
15. Mullaney, J.M., Mills, R.E., Pittard, W.S., Devine, S.E.: Small insertions and deletions (INDELs) in human genomes. Hum. Mol. Genet. **19**(R2), R131–R136 (2010). https://doi.org/10.1093/hmg/ddq400
16. Ng, P.C., Kirkness, E.F.: Whole Genome Sequencing. Genetic Variation: Methods and Protocols, pp. 215–226 (2010). https://doi.org/10.1007/978-1-60327-367-1_12
17. SAMtools: The Variant Call Format Specification (2024). https://samtools.github.io/hts-specs/VCFv4.4.pdf, version 4.4, October 9, 2024
18. Warr, A., Robert, C., Hume, D., Archibald, A., Deeb, N., Watson, M.: Exome sequencing: current and future perspectives. G3: Genes, Genomes, Genetics **5**(8), 1543–1550 (2015). https://doi.org/10.1534/g3.115.018564
19. Wharrie, S., et al.: HAPNEST: efficient, large-scale generation and evaluation of synthetic datasets for genotypes and phenotypes. Bioinformatics **39**(9), btad535 (2023). https://doi.org/10.1093/bioinformatics/btad535

Auditing Eye-Tracking Preprocessing Pipelines Using Intrinsic Data Quality Metrics

Jennifer Landes(✉) and Meike Klettke

Chair of Data Engineering, University of Regensburg, Regensburg, Germany
{jennifer.landes,meike.klettke}@informatik.uni-regensburg.de

Abstract. We propose a label-free audit for eye-tracking preprocessing based on interpretable before/after changes in intrinsic signal metrics. We evaluate 25 representative preprocessing pipelines combining missing-value handling, outlier handling, normalization, and optional smoothing or capping. For each recording, we quantify changes in trajectory dynamics, data retention, and spatial distribution structure. We further introduce a conservative composite screening score that penalizes excessive deletion and temporal distortion. The score is intended as a relative screening index within the evaluated pipeline set, not as an absolute measure of signal quality. Across five heterogeneous datasets, pipelines centered on Isolation Forest outlier handling combined with robust or z-score normalisation and mild Butterworth smoothing show recurring favourable trade-offs between dynamic stabilization and sample retention.

Keywords: Eye tracking · Signal preprocessing · Benchmarking · Robust metrics

1 Introduction

Quantifying the quality of eye-tracking (ET) time series is essential for valid inference about attention, perception, and oculomotor control. ET data quality is multi-dimensional—covering accuracy, precision, and data loss—and depends on device optics, calibration stability, and participant behaviour [8,9]. Unlike domains with explicit labels, raw gaze coordinates lack a ground-truth trajectory; preprocessing choices such as missing-value handling, outlier removal, normalisation, and smoothing therefore act as *modeling decisions* that can affect downstream analyses [1,10,14].

In practice, such choices are often inherited from tool defaults, tutorials, or lab-specific conventions and are rarely reported in sufficient detail. This is problematic because preprocessing can suppress jitter and artefacts, but also distort temporal structure, alter spatial distributions, or remove substantial portions of the data. We therefore treat preprocessing as an explicit, auditable object rather than a hidden implementation detail.

G. Vargas-Solar et al. (Eds.): ADBIS 2026, LNCS 16937, pp. 320–336, 2027.
https://doi.org/10.1007/978-3-032-39820-8_21

Existing evaluations of preprocessing are typically tied to downstream objectives such as event detection (fixations/saccades), gaze-event classification, or task-specific predictive performance [1,5,11,16]. While useful, such evaluations confound preprocessing quality with the choice of detector, labels, and task assumptions, and they do not answer a simpler upstream question: how strongly does a given pipeline reshape the intrinsic structure of the gaze signal? A label-free audit that makes these transformations explicit therefore provides a complementary tool for methodological validation and cross-dataset comparability.
Research Questions. We address four questions: (i) how strongly preprocessing pipelines reshape temporal, spatial, and distributional properties of gaze signals; (ii) whether these effects show recurring patterns across datasets with different sampling rates, tasks, and noise regimes; (iii) which intrinsic, label-free metrics are most informative for distinguishing pipelines; and (iv) which preprocessing families show favourable trade-offs within the evaluated label-free screening setting.

We introduce NIMBUS (*Noise-Informed Metric-Based Upstream Screening*), a label-free quality audit that evaluates preprocessing effects via intrinsic before/after changes and applies this audit to a representative set of 25 pipelines across five heterogeneous eye-tracking datasets. The audit is intended to support transparent pipeline screening and comparison, rather than to replace task-specific validation or ground-truth-based quality assessment.
Contributions. This work makes the following contributions:

- We frame eye-tracking preprocessing as an auditable object of analysis and propose a label-free evaluation protocol based on within-recording before/after changes in intrinsic signal metrics.
- We define a factorial preprocessing design space covering missing-value handling, outlier handling, normalisation, filtering, and capping, and select a diverse, reproducible subset of 25 representative pipelines via a deterministic maximin strategy.
- We introduce and analyse a suite of eight intrinsic quality metrics capturing complementary aspects of trajectory dynamics, spatial distribution structure, and data retention.
- We derive a conservative composite screening score for relative comparison within the evaluated pipeline set and explicitly distinguish this screening score from an absolute measure of signal quality.
- We provide a cross-dataset benchmark across five heterogeneous eye-tracking corpora (30–629 Hz) and identify recurring preprocessing families that show favourable trade-offs under the proposed intrinsic audit.

Structure of the Paper. The remainder of this paper is organised as follows: related work is discussed in Sect. 2. Section 3 describes the datasets, and Sect. 4 presents the methodology and implementation. Section 5 reports the results, Sect. 6 discusses the findings, and Sect. 7 concludes with limitations and future work.

2 Related Work and Previous Research

Eye-tracking (ET) data quality is commonly characterised along accuracy, precision, and data loss, and is known to depend strongly on calibration, protocol, and participant behaviour [8,9]. Accordingly, preprocessing pipelines typically address gap handling, spike and artifact removal, normalisation, and optional smoothing for gaze and pupil signals [10,14], with community guidance on task- and device-specific choices rather than universal filters. Recent work on streamlining eye-tracking data cleaning and analysis highlights the practical need for transparent, reproducible preprocessing workflows, particularly when downstream analyses depend on temporally structured gaze sequences [17].

Event detection algorithms based on velocity or dispersion thresholds are particularly sensitive to preprocessing, as small changes in filtering or outlier handling can substantially alter dynamic features [1,16]. Robust detectors for dynamic stimulation (e.g., REMoDNaV) therefore implicitly assume stable and well-behaved preprocessed input [5]. Large-scale repositories such as GazeBase enable cross-dataset and longitudinal benchmarking of preprocessing choices [6].

In our prior work, we examined eye-tracking preprocessing in two complementary directions. SeeME introduced a reusable graph schema for representing eye-tracking preprocessing workflows and supporting transparent, modular preprocessing documentation [7]. A separate downstream classification study showed that imputation, outlier handling, and normalisation can materially affect predictive performance, with KNN-based imputation and Isolation Forest often outperforming simpler baselines under high missingness [11,13]. The present paper introduces NIMBUS as a label-free audit framework that extends these lines of work: instead of focusing on schema representation or evaluating preprocessing through task-specific labels and downstream classifiers, it quantifies intrinsic before/after changes in gaze signal properties across heterogeneous datasets.

3 Datasets

We analysed five heterogeneous eye-tracking corpora (d1–d5, with gaps) spanning free viewing, reading, clinical assessment, film viewing, and everyday desktop interaction. Recordings were exported as raw CSV/TSV files with gaze coordinates (x, y), optional pupil diameter, and timestamps, with sampling rates between 30–629 Hz. The unit of analysis is a time-ordered gaze series per *(file × session × subject)* group. The evaluated corpora comprise d1 (EyeT4Empathy; 120 Hz, high missingness), d2 (Eye-Tracking Autism; 60 Hz, gaze+pupil), d3 (ETDD70; 250 Hz, controlled reading), d4 (Hollywood Gaze; high-frequency dynamic stimuli), and d5 (Desktop Activities; 30 Hz, naturalistic interaction).

Raw Data Characteristics. Across all datasets, we analysed 2,317 recording files. Sampling rates range from 30 Hz (d5) to 629 Hz (d4), and missing or invalid samples vary substantially between datasets (median 4.2%, maximum 37.9%). Higher sampling rates are associated with stronger short-interval jitter and velocity spikes, whereas low-frequency recordings exhibit spatial quantisation effects.

Table 1: Raw data characteristics before preprocessing: Number of files, median sampling frequency f (Hz), median duration T (s), fraction of missing samples (Miss, %), mean absolute successive difference (MASD), and spatial entropy (E).

Data	Files	f	T	Miss	MASD	E
d1	742	120	67.2	6.7	0.74	3.55
d2	311	60	41.9	5.1	0.59	3.22
d3	480	250	59.3	3.9	0.44	2.87
d4	516	629	31.4	10.8	1.92	4.12
d5	268	30	83.7	4.5	0.63	3.01

These differences motivate robust preprocessing and contextualise dataset-specific pipeline behaviour reported in Sect. 5 (Table 1).

4 Methodology

We treat eye-tracking preprocessing as an explicit object of analysis. Instead of relying on external labels—which are often unavailable or task-dependent—we quantify how preprocessing pipelines reshape intrinsic signal properties. Accordingly, our evaluation follows a *label-free, within-recording* design. For each recording and pipeline, we compute intrinsic quality metrics before and after preprocessing. All comparisons are relative to the unprocessed signal, supporting more controlled comparisons across datasets, devices, and sampling rates. We define a factorial preprocessing design space spanning missing-value handling, outlier handling, normalization, optional filtering, and capping. From this space, we select 25 representative pipelines to ensure broad coverage while avoiding near-duplicates.

4.1 Preprocessing Search Space

The preprocessing search space is defined as a factorial combination of common eye-tracking preprocessing operations, illustrated in Fig. 1. Each stage targets a distinct aspect of the signal, including missing data, outliers, coordinate scaling, temporal smoothness, and extreme values.

Pipelines are composed from five stages:

- **Missing-value handling (MV):** mean imputation, last-observation-carried-forward (LOCF), KNN-based imputation, or deletion of invalid samples.
- **Outlier handling (OUT):** univariate z-score thresholding, multivariate Isolation Forest on (x, y), percentile-based winsorization, or conservative deletion.
- **Normalisation (NORM):** robust scaling, z-score normalisation, or min–max scaling.

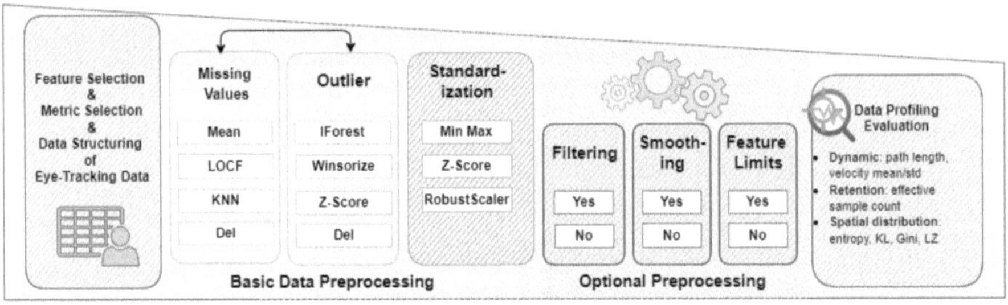

Fig. 1: Preprocessing workflow and factorial search space for eye-tracking data.

- **Temporal filtering (Filter):** no filtering, low-pass Butterworth filtering, or Fourier-domain smoothing. Butterworth and Fourier filtering are mutually exclusive.
- **Coordinate capping (Cap):** optional clipping to device-plausible screen ranges as a safeguard against extreme coordinate glitches.

The search space includes an explicit no-filtering option because temporal smoothing is optional and may distort gaze dynamics. Missing-value handling, outlier handling, and normalisation are treated as mandatory stages so that each pipeline yields finite, comparable coordinate series for metric computation. The stage order is fixed for all pipelines: missing-value handling, outlier handling, normalisation, and optional capping/ temporal filtering. This keeps method choices comparable and avoids confounding pipeline comparison with ordering effects; alternative stage orderings are left to future work. This combination yields

$$4(\text{MV}) \times 4(\text{OUT}) \times 3(\text{NORM}) \times 3(\text{Filter}) \times 2(\text{Cap}) = 288$$

valid preprocessing pipelines. From this space, a representative subset of 25 pipelines is selected as described in the following section.

4.2 Selection of Representative Pipelines

The full preprocessing design space comprises all valid combinations of the defined stages (MV, OUT, NORM, filtering, capping), yielding 288 feasible pipelines. To obtain a compact yet diverse subset without outcome-driven bias, we select 25 representative pipelines using a deterministic maximin strategy on the categorical design space [15]. Each pipeline is encoded as a one-hot vector over all stage levels, inducing a discrete design space in which diversity between pipelines is quantified via Hamming distance. Starting from a small set of fixed seed pipelines, candidates are added iteratively by maximising their minimum distance to the current selection. A light balance penalty discourages over-representation of individual stage levels, ensuring approximately uniform coverage across preprocessing families. After selection, pipelines are sorted deterministically and assigned stable identifiers (P01–P25), yielding a reproducible, space-filling subset that spans all major preprocessing choices while avoiding near-duplicate configurations (selected pipelines configurations are available at GitHub). The pipeline subset is not intended as an exhaustive search for the best configuration among all 288 candidates. It is a space-filling screening set for comparing major preprocessing families under identical conditions. This screening strategy was also motivated by prior experiments with larger pipeline grids, which indicated that family-level patterns can guide pipeline selection while avoiding the cost of exhaustive evaluation in every benchmark setting. Claims are consequently made at the family level; full-factorial evaluation of all 288 pipelines is left to future work and supported by the released implementation.

4.3 Quality Metrics

To quantify how strongly preprocessing pipelines reshape eye-tracking signals, we compute eight intrinsic, label-free quality metrics before and after preprocessing. The metrics capture complementary aspects of trajectory geometry, temporal dynamics, data retention, and spatial distribution structure, and are computed per recording without requiring ground-truth annotations [1,9].

The metrics do not estimate classical eye-tracking accuracy directly, because accuracy requires known target positions or calibration references. Instead, they capture signal properties that constrain data quality in practice: precision-related jitter, implausible velocity spikes, sample loss, spatial redistribution, and over-smoothing. We therefore interpret them as proximal, label-free indicators of preprocessing-induced signal distortion. NIMBUS is an upstream screening audit and should be complemented by calibration-based, event-level, or downstream validation whenever such references are available.

Let t_i denote strictly increasing timestamps and (x_i, y_i) the corresponding gaze coordinates. All metrics are computed on the longest contiguous subsequence of finite samples. We use N for the number of finite gaze samples and $K = N - 1$ for the number of successive gaze transitions. Spatial distribution metrics are computed on a two-dimensional screen grid, where p_{jk} denotes the empirical probability of samples falling into grid cell (j, k) and U_{jk} denotes the corresponding probability under a uniform reference distribution. For the Gini coefficient, $r_{(i)}$ denotes sorted radial distances from the screen centre. For Lempel–Ziv complexity, $c(N)$ denotes the number of distinct production steps in the symbolic scanpath sequence. An overview of all metrics, their definitions, and their interpretation in the eye-tracking context is given in Table 2.

Pupil diameter is not included as a core audit metric because it is not available consistently across all evaluated datasets and is more strongly affected by task context, illumination, and device-specific measurement properties. We therefore restrict the core metric set to gaze coordinates and timestamps, which are available across all corpora and allow a uniform cross-dataset audit.

Before/After Deltas. For each metric M, preprocessing effects are quantified via $\Delta M = M_{\text{after}} - M_{\text{before}}$, so that positive or negative deltas directly indicate how strongly a pipeline reshapes the corresponding signal property. All subsequent analyses are based on these within-recording deltas.

Table 2: Intrinsic quality metrics to audit preprocessing effects on eye-tracking signals. All metrics are computed per recording before &after preprocessing.

Metric	Definition	Interpretation in eye tracking
Path length	$L = \sum_{i=1}^{N-1} \sqrt{(x_{i+1} - x_i)^2 + (y_{i+1} - y_i)^2}$	Proxy for dynamic stability and noise; large values indicate jitter or spurious excursions [9, 16].
Velocity mean	$\bar{v} = K^{-1} \sum_{i=1}^{K} \Delta d_i / \Delta t_i$	Average gaze speed; sensitive to smoothing and large-amplitude artefacts [1].
Velocity variability	$\sigma_v = \sqrt{(K-1)^{-1} \sum_{i=1}^{K} (v_i - \bar{v})^2}$	Captures micro-jitter and spike noise; strongly affected by outlier handling [16].
Effective sample count	N_{after}	Measures data retention; penalises deletion-heavy preprocessing [8].
Spatial Shannon entropy	$H = -\sum_{j,k} p_{jk} \log_2 p_{jk}$	Quantifies spatial dispersion of gaze; low values indicate clustering or central bias [2].
KL divergence to uniform	$D_{\text{KL}}(P \Vert U) = \sum_{j,k} p_{jk} \log_2(p_{jk}/U_{jk})$	Measures deviation from uniform screen coverage; complements entropy [3].
Gini coefficient	$G = \frac{2\sum_{i=1}^{N} i r_{(i)}}{N \sum_{i=1}^{N} r_{(i)}} - \frac{N+1}{N}$	Captures inequality in radial gaze dispersion; highlights peripheral excursions [4].
Lempel–Ziv complexity	$C_{\text{LZ}} = c(N) \log_2(N)/N$	Measures temporal regularity of scanpaths; low values indicate over-smoothing or strong temporal constraints [12].

4.4 Composite Quality Score

To obtain a compact summary of preprocessing effects, we define a composite quality score that aggregates selected intrinsic delta metrics. The score is used as a relative screening index within the evaluated pipeline set and should not be interpreted as an absolute measure of eye-tracking signal quality. In particular, a higher score indicates a more favourable trade-off among the selected intrinsic metrics under the present audit design; it does not imply higher gaze accuracy, higher spatial precision, or better downstream task performance. Based on a preliminary variability analysis (reported in Sect. 5), we select five core metrics with the largest and most stable between-pipeline differences: path length, velocity mean, velocity standard deviation, effective sample count, and spatial Shannon entropy. For each (recording, pipeline) pair, before/after deltas ΔM are computed and z-standardised within the evaluated analysis setting before aggregation. Some metrics indicate favourable preprocessing effects when they decrease (path length, velocity mean, velocity variability, and sample count loss), while others improve when they increase (entropy), all deltas are oriented such that higher values correspond to more favourable changes within the audit. Deltas for path length, velocity mean, velocity standard deviation, and sample count loss are multiplied by -1 prior to aggregation. The composite quality score is defined as the mean of the five oriented, standardised delta metrics:

$$\text{QualityScore} = \frac{1}{5}\left(\tilde{\Delta}\text{path}^{\uparrow} + \tilde{\Delta}\text{vel\_std}^{\uparrow} + \tilde{\Delta}\text{vel\_mean}^{\uparrow} + \tilde{\Delta}\text{s\_count}^{\uparrow} + \tilde{\Delta}\text{entr}^{\uparrow}\right),$$

where the superscript $\uparrow$ denotes orientation such that higher values are preferable under the selected intrinsic metrics. Composite scores are first computed per recording and pipeline and then summarised within each dataset. Cross-dataset averages are reported only as descriptive aggregate screening summaries. They are used to identify recurring pipeline families, not to assign absolute quality levels to datasets or to claim that a single pipeline is universally optimal.

4.5 Implementation

All pipelines and quality metrics were implemented in Python 3.11 using `NumPy`, `pandas`, `scikit-learn`, and `SciPy`. As shown in Fig. 2, each recording is parsed into a uniform time series, processed independently by all 25 pipelines, evaluated via before/after intrinsic metrics, and exported in long-format tables. Dataset-specific extractors map vendor-specific columns to a common (t, x, y) representation, remove invalid samples, and enforce strictly increasing timestamps. Pipeline specifications are declarative and reproducible. The implementation is available at: https://github.com/eyetracking-data/Nimbus.

5 Results

This section reports the empirical evaluation of 25 preprocessing pipelines applied to five heterogeneous eye-tracking datasets (d1, d2, d3, d4, d5). For each (recording, pipeline) combination, we computed eight intrinsic quality metrics before and after preprocessing and analysed within-recording changes ΔM. The analyses address four questions: (i) how strongly pipelines differ in their overall impact on gaze signal structure, (ii) whether recurring patterns are visible across datasets with different sampling rates and tasks, (iii) which metrics carry the most discriminative information, and (iv) which preprocessing families show favourable trade-offs within the evaluated label-free screening setting. Interpretive remarks are kept brief and are further elaborated in the Discussion.

5.1 Global Preprocessing Effects and Composite Quality Score

For a compact overview of pipeline behaviour, we summarise results using the composite quality score defined in Sect. 4. The score aggregates five oriented, z-standardised delta metrics (path length, velocity mean, velocity SD, sample count loss, and Shannon entropy), where higher values indicate more favourable trade-offs within the evaluated audit setting. As discussed above, the score is

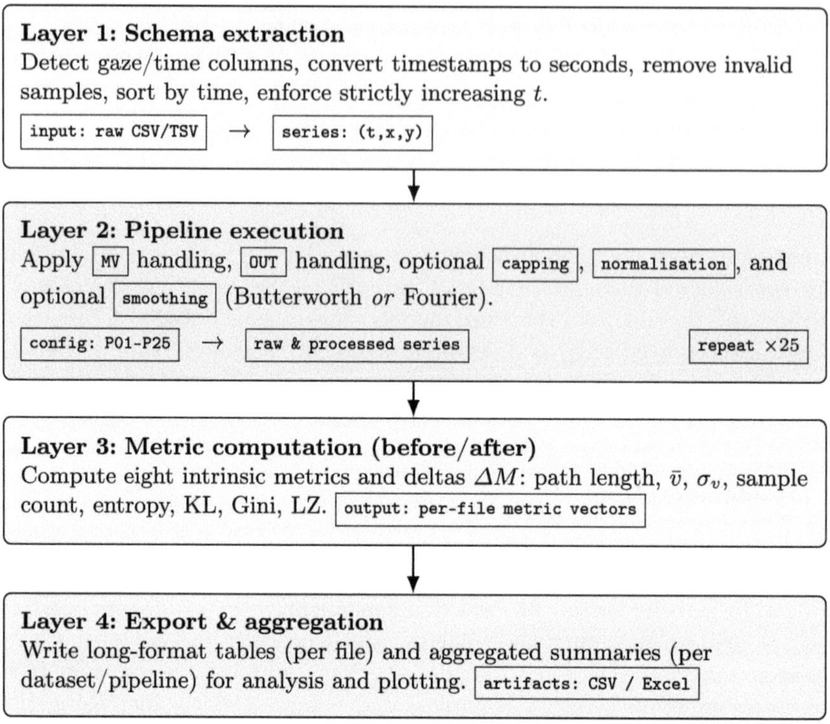

Fig. 2: Stage-based implementation architecture and data flow. Each recording is parsed into a uniform time series, processed by each pipeline configuration (P01–P25), evaluated via before/after intrinsic metrics, and exported in long-format tables for downstream analysis.

interpreted as a relative screening index rather than as an absolute measure of signal quality. Table 3 lists the Top-10 pipelines under the descriptive aggregate screening score. The table should be read as a compact summary of recurring patterns, not as an absolute cross-dataset quality ranking. Within this screening setting, pipelines using **Isolation Forest** for outlier handling repeatedly appear among the higher-ranked configurations, indicating favourable reductions in dynamic metrics (path length and velocity variability) without excessive loss of effective sample count. For each pipeline p, we compute a descriptive aggregate score as the mean of $\text{QualityScore}_{r,p}$ across recordings, after dataset-level summaries have been inspected. Pipelines are sorted in descending order of this aggregate in Fig. 3. Negative values indicate below-average performance relative to the evaluated pipeline set and selected metrics; they do not imply absolute degradation of signal quality. Because the composite score is standardised within the evaluated analysis setting, dataset-wise values are primarily meaningful for comparing pipelines within the same dataset. The mean column is used as a descriptive summary to inspect recurring family-level tendencies. It should not be read as evidence that a pipeline is universally optimal across datasets.

Table 3: Pipelines with high aggregate screening scores. Dataset-wise values show variation; mean is descriptive.

Pipe	d1	d2	d3	d4	d5	Mean
P23	0.254	0.929	−0.357	0.215	−0.043	0.200
P07	0.278	1.030	−0.234	0.987	−0.066	0.199
P22	0.277	1.030	−0.234	0.987	−0.066	0.199
P21	0.277	1.003	−0.274	0.950	−0.070	0.177
P10	0.253	0.931	−0.357	0.098	−0.068	0.171
P05	0.254	0.808	−0.323	0.130	−0.012	0.171
P09	0.254	0.873	−0.407	0.163	−0.051	0.166
P16	0.277	0.891	−0.270	0.975	−0.059	0.163
P06	0.156	0.899	−0.404	0.227	−0.089	0.158
P08	0.254	0.875	−0.407	0.049	−0.075	0.139

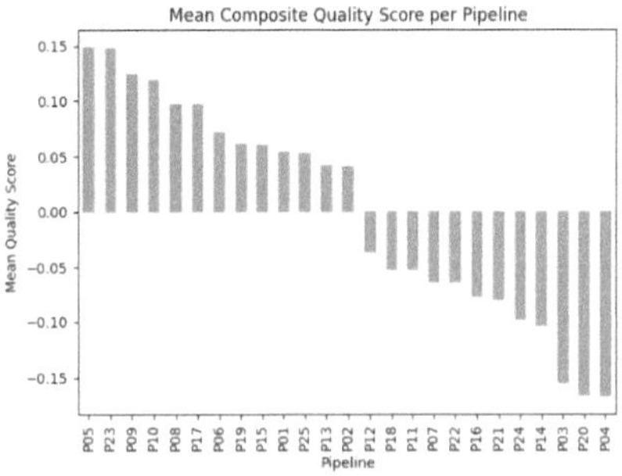

Fig. 3: Descriptive aggregate composite screening score per preprocessing pipeline.

Key Observation. Across both the Top-10 table and the aggregate overview, Isolation-Forest-based pipelines repeatedly appear among the higher-ranked configurations. In contrast, pipelines based on deletion-heavy strategies or LOCF are associated with less favourable trade-offs in the evaluated intrinsic metrics.

5.2 Variability and Redundancy of Delta Metrics

To assess which intrinsic metrics are most sensitive to preprocessing, we summarised the variability of all delta values across datasets and pipelines (Table 4). This reveals a recurring ordering of metric sensitivity.

Table 4: Standard deviation of delta metrics across all datasets and 25 pipelines.

Metric	$\sigma(\Delta)$	Metric	$\sigma(\Delta)$
Δ Path length	2.35×10^7	Δ Sample count	1.35×10^3
Δ Velocity std	8.30×10^5	Δ Shannon entropy	6.78×10^{-1}
Δ Velocity mean	$4.28e \times 10^4$	Δ KL divergence	6.78×10^{-1}
Δ Gini coefficient	1.18×10^{-1}	Δ LZ complexity	5.15×10^{-2}

The largest spread occurs for changes in path length and velocity-based metrics, indicating that dynamic properties of the gaze trajectory are strongly affected by preprocessing choices. Effective sample count also varies substantially, reflecting how aggressively different pipelines delete or retain data. In contrast, distributional metrics (entropy, KL, Gini, LZ) show smaller variability. Shannon entropy and KL divergence behave almost identically, indicating redundancy in this setting. Gini and LZ exhibit the weakest variability and primarily change under aggressive smoothing or deletion. Table 5 shows that a similar ordering is visible across datasets with sampling rates from 30–629 Hz: dynamic deltas dominate, followed by sample retention, while distributional metrics remain comparatively stable. Subsequent interpretations therefore emphasise path length (PL), velocity variability (VS), mean velocity (VM), sample count (SC), and spatial entropy (S), treating KL as redundant and Gini(G)/LZ as auxiliary descriptors.

Table 5: Standard deviation of delta metrics separated by dataset.

Data	$\sigma(\Delta$ PL)	$\sigma(\Delta$ VS)	$\sigma(\Delta$ SC)	$\sigma(\Delta$ VM)	$\sigma(\Delta$ S)	$\sigma(\Delta$ KL)	$\sigma(\Delta$ G)	$\sigma(\Delta$ LZ)
d1	4.58e7	1.89e4	5.56e2	6.78e3	0.631	0.631	0.121	0.028
d2	3.50e7	2.61e6	5.92e2	1.44e5	0.337	0.337	0.138	0.149
d3	3.71e5	3.53e3	3.81e2	6.36e2	0.188	0.188	0.030	0.021
d4	1.48e6	1.07e4	3.07e3	1.06e3	0.605	0.605	0.086	0.020
d5	1.51e5	6.53e2	3.82e1	4.90e2	0.596	0.596	0.128	0.038

5.3 Cross-Dataset Patterns

Across the five datasets (d1, d2, d3, d4, d5), recurring but not identical patterns are observed. Pipelines using **Isolation Forest** outlier handling, combined with robust or z-score normalisation and optional Butterworth filtering, often yield favourable changes in path length and velocity metrics without excessive sample loss. However, the magnitude and rank position of individual pipelines remain dataset-dependent. Qualitatively similar tendencies are observed across datasets, although their strength differs by sampling rate and task context. In low- and medium-frequency datasets (d1, d2, d5), differences between outlier-handling strategies account for much of the observed separation between pipelines, while smoothing yields smaller additional changes. In high-frequency datasets (d3, d4), the combination of outlier handling and Butterworth filtering is associated with reductions in path length and velocity variability without large reductions in sample count. Pipelines relying on Fourier smoothing without prior outlier removal show stronger alterations of dynamic metrics and should therefore be interpreted more cautiously.

5.4 Metric-Wise Effects

Dynamic Metrics: Path Length and Velocity. Across datasets, the largest between-pipeline variability is observed for Δpath length and Δvelocity standard deviation. Isolation-Forest-based pipelines are associated with substantial reductions in both metrics, consistent with suppressing spikes and micro-jitter while maintaining plausible mean velocity. Deletion-based pipelines may also reduce dynamic metrics but are associated with pronounced losses in effective sample count. LOCF-based pipelines exhibit patterns characterised by temporally introduced plateaus and distortions.

Distributional Metrics: Entropy, KL, Gini, LZ. Distributional metrics change less dramatically than dynamic ones but still capture systematic redistribution effects. Figure 4a summarises effect sizes for ΔGini and indicates moderate but consistent shifts across pipelines, broadly compatible with the removal of rare peripheral excursions or smoothing of extreme values. Figure 4b shows the distribution of ΔLZ complexity across pipelines; most medians remain near zero, with stronger negative shifts mainly for aggressive smoothing or deletion. Importantly, favourable shifts in entropy or Gini can coincide with substantial sample loss; distributional metrics therefore require joint interpretation with effective sample count.

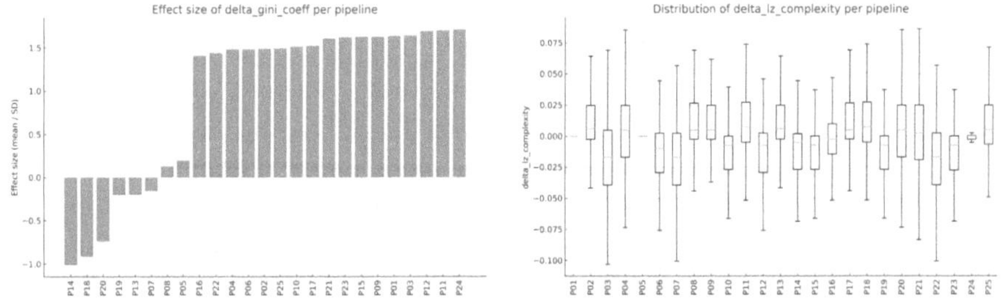

(a) Gini effect size.

(b) LZ complexity deltas.

Fig. 4: Distributional metric changes across pipelines. Left: effect size of ΔGini. Right: distribution of ΔLZ complexity.

5.5 Pipeline Families and Screening-Based Ranking

Table 6 lists five pipelines with high aggregate screening scores and shows their constituent stages. These pipelines share a recurring structure: multivariate outlier removal via Isolation Forest and robust or z-score normalisation, and—except for P16—moderate Butterworth smoothing. Missing-value handling varies among these configurations, while aggressive deletion is rare among the higher-ranked pipelines. Within the evaluated audit setting, three recurring pipeline families can be distinguished: (i) a favourable family combining Isolation Forest, robust/z-score normalisation, and moderate Butterworth filtering; (ii) an intermediate family using simpler univariate outlier strategies or weaker filtering; and (iii) less favourable configurations dominated by LOCF, deletion-only outlier handling, or Fourier-only smoothing without prior anomaly removal. These families should be interpreted as empirical patterns in the present benchmark rather than as universally valid preprocessing categories.

Table 6: Example pipelines with high aggregate screening scores and their preprocessing stages.

Pipeline	Rank	MV	OUT	NORM	Filter	Cap
P22	1	mean	iforest	zscore	Butterworth	yes
P07	2	knn	iforest	minmax	Butterworth	yes
P16	3	locf	iforest	zscore	none	yes
P21	4	mean	iforest	robust	Fourier	yes
P03	5	delete	iforest	robust	Butterworth	no

5.6 Stage-Wise Summary

Stage-wise inspection indicates that outlier handling accounts for much of the observed separation between pipelines. Isolation Forest repeatedly yields favourable changes, supporting the hypothesis that ET artefacts often appear as multivariate excursions in (x, y). Robust and z-score normalisation show favourable behaviour in the evaluated benchmark, while min–max scaling can interact more strongly with filtering. For missing values, mean and KNN imputation behave more stably than deletion or LOCF in most settings. Moderate Butterworth smoothing is associated with favourable behaviour in several datasets, whereas Fourier filtering shows higher variability without prior outlier handling. Capping remains useful as a safeguard against extreme coordinate glitches, but should not replace outlier handling.

The results support Isolation Forest combined with robust or z-score normalisation and optional moderate Butterworth filtering as a practical candidate baseline for label-free pipeline screening. This configuration should still be audited on the target dataset rather than treated as a universally optimal recipe.

6 Discussion

The present study shows that eye-tracking preprocessing pipelines differ systematically in how they reshape temporal, spatial, and distributional properties of gaze signals. Across 25 pipelines and five heterogeneous datasets, we observe recurring tendencies in preprocessing effects and identify pipeline families that show favourable trade-offs under the proposed intrinsic audit.

Answers to the Guiding Questions. Regarding Q1, pipelines differ markedly in their multivariate effect profiles, with the strongest separations driven by dynamic metrics (path length and velocity structure) and effective sample count.

For Q2, recurring tendencies are visible across datasets spanning 30–629 Hz and diverse task contexts, but the rank position and score magnitude of individual pipelines remain dataset-dependent. Concerning Q3, dynamic deltas carry most discriminative power, while spatial entropy provides a complementary distributional perspective; KL divergence closely mirrors entropy and adds little information in this benchmark. Finally, Q4 points to a favourable family combining multivariate outlier detection (Isolation Forest), robust or z-score normalisation, and moderate Butterworth smoothing, contrasted with less favourable deletion-heavy or LOCF-based strategies.

Pipeline-Family Effects. A recurring finding is the favourable behaviour of Isolation-Forest-based pipelines within the evaluated metric set. A plausible explanation is that eye-tracking artefacts often appear as multivariate excursions in (x, y) rather than as independent univariate anomalies. In combination with robust or z-score normalisation and moderate Butterworth smoothing, this reduces spikes and high-frequency noise while preserving sample count. By contrast, LOCF- and deletion-based strategies can introduce temporal plateaus, distort velocity profiles, or incur substantial retention loss.

Cross-Dataset Behaviour and the Role of Sampling Rate. Despite variation in sampling rate, stimulus type, and noise characteristics, the results suggest recurring family-level tendencies. Pipelines using multivariate outlier handling and robust or z-score normalisation often show favourable trade-offs under the intrinsic audit. However, individual rankings remain dataset-dependent: filtering plays a more prominent role in high-frequency recordings, whereas in lower-frequency datasets outlier handling often accounts for much of the observed improvement.

Interpretation of the Composite Score. The composite score should be understood as a relative screening instrument, not as an absolute quality measure. Its values summarise oriented changes in selected intrinsic metrics within the evaluated pipeline set. It is most useful for comparing preprocessing configurations within a dataset and for identifying recurring pipeline families across datasets; it does not replace validation against calibration accuracy, spatial precision, event-detection quality, or downstream task performance.

Practical Implications and Recommendations. The results suggest that researchers should use modular pipelines and intrinsic audits to make preprocessing-induced trade-offs explicit. Within the evaluated benchmark, a useful candidate baseline is: *Isolation Forest outlier handling + robust or z-score normalisation + optional moderate Butterworth filtering*, paired with conservative missing-value handling and optional capping for extreme glitches. This configuration should be audited on the target dataset and adapted when sampling rate, task context, or device characteristics require different trade-offs. Conversely, LOCF, deletion-heavy approaches, and Fourier-only smoothing without prior outlier handling should be treated cautiously as defaults.

7 Conclusion and Outlook

This paper frames eye-tracking preprocessing as an auditable object of study rather than a hidden implementation detail. We conducted a multimetric, label-free audit of 25 representative preprocessing pipelines across five heterogeneous datasets. Using intrinsic before/after metrics, we show that preprocessing choices are not neutral: they induce measurable changes in trajectory dynamics, sample retention, and spatial distribution structure.

Methodologically, we contribute an explicit preprocessing design space, a reproducible selection of representative pipelines, a within-recording delta protocol, a metric suite covering dynamic, retention-based, and distributional signal properties, and a conservative composite screening score. The score should be interpreted as an upstream screening instrument rather than as an absolute measure of eye-tracking signal quality.

Empirically, the benchmark reveals recurring family-level tendencies rather than a universally optimal preprocessing recipe. Pipelines combining Isolation Forest with robust or z-score normalisation and, where appropriate, moderate Butterworth smoothing often show favourable trade-offs between dynamic stabilisation and sample preservation. This pipeline family is therefore a practical candidate baseline to be audited and adapted on the target dataset.

By making preprocessing effects measurable without task-specific labels, NIMBUS supports transparent and reproducible pipeline selection. At the same time, the audit complements, but does not replace, validation against calibration accuracy, spatial precision, event-detection quality, or downstream task performance.

7.1 Limitations

Several limitations temper the generality of the results. First, the audit uses intrinsic before/after metrics and does not rely on external ground truth, calibration targets, or event-level annotations. This reflects the setting of many real eye-tracking corpora, where a true gaze trajectory is not available after acquisition. The audit therefore cannot determine whether a pipeline preserves the "true" gaze trajectory, improves spatial accuracy, or improves precision in the classical eye-tracking sense.

Second, the composite score is a relative screening index, not an absolute quality measure. Its values depend on the selected metrics, their orientation, the evaluated pipeline set, and the datasets included in the audit. Cross-dataset averages should therefore be interpreted as descriptive summaries for identifying recurring pipeline families, not as proof that one pipeline is universally optimal.

Third, all evaluated datasets are desktop or screen-based recordings. Mobile, wearable, or in-the-wild tracking may involve stronger head-motion artefacts, illumination changes, and nonlinear distortions. Finally, the analysis covers a curated subset of 25 pipelines from a larger space of 288 valid configurations and does not evaluate all possible preprocessing strategies or stage orderings.

The audit should therefore be understood as an upstream screening and documentation tool that complements, but does not replace, task-specific validation.

7.2 Future Work

Future work should link intrinsic preprocessing effects to external benchmarks and downstream performance, including calibration accuracy, spatial precision, fixation and saccade detection, gaze mapping, and predictive modelling. Such experiments would clarify which intrinsic metric changes translate into application-level improvements. A second direction is controlled perturbation analysis. Synthetic injections of noise, jitter, drift, outliers, and missingness would make it possible to assess how well pipelines recover known trajectories and to validate the composite screening score more directly. Finally, the design space should be extended beyond the 25 representative pipelines evaluated here by testing the full factorial set, alternative stage orderings, adaptive filters, nonlinear denoisers, and mobile or in-the-wild recordings. Integrating the audit into open-source tooling would further support reproducible preprocessing and transparent quality evaluation.

Declaration on Generative AI. Generative AI was used for language editing; all scientific content, analyses, and claims were verified by the authors.

References

1. Andersson, R., Larsson, L., Holmqvist, K., Stridh, M., Nyström, M.: One algorithm to rule them all? an evaluation and discussion of 10 eye movement event-detection algorithms. Behav. Res. Methods **49**(2), 616–637 (2017). https://doi.org/10.3758/s13428-016-0738-9
2. Coutrot, A., Hsiao, J.H.: Entropy-based measures of visual exploration. J. Vis. **18**(3), 1–17 (2018)
3. Cover, T.M., Thomas, J.A.: Elements of Information Theory. Wiley (2006)
4. Cowell, F.A.: Measuring Inequality. Oxford University Press (2011)
5. Dar, A.H., Wagner, A., et al.: REMoDNaV: robust eye-movement classification for dynamic stimulation. J. Vis. **20**(6), 10 (2020). https://doi.org/10.1167/jov.20.6.10
6. Griffith, H., et al.: GazeBase: a large-scale, multi-stimulus, longitudinal eye-movement dataset. Figshare Repository (2021). https://doi.org/10.6084/m9.figshare.12912257
7. Hausler, D., Landes, J., Klettke, M.: SeeME: a general, reusable graph schema for data preprocessing of eye-tracking data. In: BTW Workshops 2025, pp. 219–233 (2025). https://doi.org/10.18420/BTW2025-126
8. Hessels, R.S., Hooge, I.T.C.: Eye tracking data quality in infant research: a review of accuracy, precision and data loss. Infancy **20**(6), 601–633 (2015). https://doi.org/10.1111/infa.12093
9. Holmqvist, K., Nyström, M., Andersson, R., Dewhurst, R., Jarodzka, H., van de Weijer, J.: Eye Tracking: A Comprehensive Guide to Methods and Measures. Oxford University Press (2011)

10. Kret, M.E., Sjak-Shie, E.E.: Preprocessing pupil size data: guidelines and code. Behav. Res. Methods **51**(3), 1336–1342 (2019). https://doi.org/10.3758/s13428-018-1075-y
11. Landes, J., Klettke, M., Köppl, S.: Impact of preprocessing on classification results of eye-tracking-data. In: BTW 2025 Workshops. Lecture Notes in Informatics (LNI), vol. P-363, pp. 235–256 (2025). https://doi.org/10.18420/BTW2025-127
12. Lempel, A., Ziv, J.: On the complexity of finite sequences. IEEE Trans. Inf. Theory **22**(1), 75–81 (1976)
13. Liu, F.T., Ting, K.M., Zhou, Z.H.: Isolation forest. In: 2008 Eighth IEEE International Conference on Data Mining, pp. 413–422 (2008). https://doi.org/10.1109/ICDM.2008.17
14. Mathôt, S.: Pupillometry: psychology, physiology, and function. J. Cogn. **1**(1), 16 (2018). https://doi.org/10.5334/joc.18
15. Morris, M.D., Mitchell, T.J.: Exploratory designs for computational experiments. J. Stat. Plan. Inference **43**(3), 381–402 (1995)
16. Nyström, M., Holmqvist, K.: An adaptive algorithm for fixation, saccade, and glissade detection in eye-tracking data. Behav. Res. Methods **42**(1), 188–204 (2010). https://doi.org/10.3758/BRM.42.1.188
17. Rosalia, M.V.: Streamlining the cleaning and analysis of eye tracking data for cross-recurrence analysis. McNair Summer Research Program, University of San Diego (2025). https://digital.sandiego.edu/mcnair-summer/21/

PRIDE: Diversifying Similarity Queries in RDBMSs Using Pivots

Anna J. C. Lauton(✉), Willian D. Oliveira, Agma J. M. Traina, and Caetano Traina Jr.

University of São Paulo (USP), São Carlos, SP, Brazil
annalauton@usp.br, {willian,agma,caetano}@icmc.usp.br

Abstract. Including diversity in similarity query results reduces redundancy and increases user relevance. For instance, medical imaging diagnostics benefit from retrieving similar cases across varying diseases or exams, and recommender systems are more effective when suggestions are varied. However, Relational Database Management Systems (RDBMSs) offer limited support for such queries because diversification steps introduce significant computational overhead and are difficult to integrate efficiently into relational execution engines. To address this, we propose Pivot-Ring Indexable Diversified Exploration (PRIDE), a technique for executing diversified similarity queries within RDBMSs. PRIDE models a metric space using a set of pivots and intersecting distance rings, associating each data element with a "radical" that encodes its relative position. Leveraging this mapping, the method prunes candidates to select the element closest to the query center for each distinct radical. In this way, our method preserves result relevance while reducing local redundancy and promoting diversity. Furthermore, by relying solely on metric properties and structures native to relational environments, PRIDE enables highly efficient processing. Experimental results demonstrate that our method outperforms existing approaches in most scenarios, achieving execution-time speed-ups of over 400×.

Keywords: Similarity Queries · Diversification · RDBMS · Metric Spaces

1 Introduction

Similarity queries play a fundamental role in several applications requiring handling large data volumes. Consider, for example, a rental platform where a user wants to find accommodations similar to a selected one. For this purpose, the search may consider attributes such as location, price, and number of rooms, retrieving candidates based on similarity criteria. When only similarity is used, candidates tend to be very similar, making it difficult for the user to identify distinct yet relevant characteristics.

Diversity can help reduce the problem, leading to *Diversified Similarity Queries (DSQs)*. The target of these queries is not only relevance with respect to

G. Vargas-Solar et al. (Eds.): ADBIS 2026, LNCS 16937, pp. 337–353, 2027.
https://doi.org/10.1007/978-3-032-39820-8_22

the reference element, but also diversity among the returned elements, avoiding local redundancies and promoting better coverage of the search space.

Similarity-based retrieval is widely used in several domains, including Natural Language Processing [1], Information Retrieval [2], Machine Learning [3], and Data Analysis [4]. Despite its relevance, support for diversified similarity queries remains limited in Relational Database Management Systems (RDBMSs). Moreover, diversification based on pairwise candidate comparisons increases computational cost by turning an inherently linear process (each candidate is compared to the query center) into a quadratic one. Existing approaches were originally designed outside the relational model, which further complicates their integration into RDBMS environments. Key challenges include: (i) how to define diversification mechanisms that avoid iterative comparisons between candidates; (ii) how to effectively exploit access structures, such as indexes, during execution; and (iii) how to ensure scalability in large datasets.

In this context, this work proposes *Pivot-Ring Indexable Diversified Exploration (PRIDE)*, a technique for processing DSQs directly in an RDBMS core engine. The method maps a metric space using pivots and radial discretization, allowing the organization of candidates into structured regions and the efficient selection of representatives, promoting diversity without compromising result relevance and requiring no iterative comparisons among previous candidates. Furthermore, PRIDE was designed to exploit native RDBMS index structures, enabling efficient execution and integration with a relational environment.

2 Background and Related Work

This section presents the main concepts and related work underpinning this research, including similarity queries and result diversification, along with the use of indexing structures and pruning techniques to accelerate them.

2.1 Similarity Comparison in RDBMSs

RDBMSs are designed to work with scalar attributes A (such as numbers, text or dates), which are often compared using identity or order-based operators, represented by $\theta \in \{=, \neq, <, \geq \ldots\}$. To work with attributes that store complex data S (such as images, audio or video), similarity-based operators are typically used, which require the definition of a distance coefficient or function d that quantifies how close (similar) two elements are to each other [5].

To enable efficient data comparisons, the domain is commonly modeled as a metric space. This allows the integration of specialized index structures designed to optimize element access and comparisons [6]. A metric space is defined as a pair $M = \langle \mathbb{S}, d \rangle$, where $\mathbb{S}$ is the domain of the complex attribute S ($Dom(\mathsf{S}) = \mathbb{S}$) and d is a metric. For any element $s_i \in \mathbb{S}$, d is a metric when it satisfies the following properties [7]: (i) *non-negativity*, $d(s_1, s_2) \geq 0$, with $d(s_1, s_2) > 0$ for $s_1 \neq s_2$; (ii) *identity*, $d(s_1, s_2) = 0 \Leftrightarrow s_1 = s_2$; (iii) *symmetry*, $d(s_1, s_2) = d(s_2, s_1)$; and (iv) *triangle inequality*, $d(s_1, s_2) \leq d(s_1, s_3) + d(s_3, s_2)$. Given an attribute S belonging to relation T, the active domain of S is denoted as $\mathbf{S} = \overset{*}{Dom}(\mathsf{S})$, where $\mathbf{S} \subseteq \mathbb{S}$ represents the subset of values $t[\mathsf{S}] \in \mathbb{S}$ present in at least one tuple t of T.

Within this framework, similarity queries over S in T are expressed using similarity comparison operators, denoted as θ_s, defined over pairs of complex elements. Generally, two primary similarity comparison operators are widely used in the literature and in data retrieval systems. Given a predicate $(s_1\ \theta_s\ s_2)$ over a pair of complex elements s_1, s_2, where s_2 serves as the reference element (the query center), these operators are defined as follows:

- **Similarity range comparison operator** ($\theta_s = Rng\,[d, \xi]$): where $\xi > 0$ is a similarity threshold. It returns TRUE whenever the comparison $(s_1 Rng\,[d, \xi]\ s_2)$ indicates that $d(s_1, s_2) \leq \xi$;
- k**-nearest neighbors comparison operator** ($\theta_s = k\text{-}NN\,[d, k]$): where $k > 0$ is a quantity of elements. It returns TRUE for the comparison $(s_1\ k\text{-}NN\,[d, k]\ s_2)$ whenever s_1 belongs to the set of the k nearest elements to s_2 in $\mathbf{S}$.

2.2 Result Diversification

In similarity queries, the returned items are often highly similar to one another, particularly in large datasets with dense regions. This happens because nearby objects tend to share many characteristics, resulting in a low-variability result set. Such homogeneity can hinder analysis, forcing users to refine their queries multiple times to uncover more relevant or diverse information.

The goal of *DSQs* is to find a subset $R \subseteq \mathbf{S}$ that simultaneously maximizes similarity to the query element s_q while also promoting diversity among the returned items. Computing the exact solution is NP-hard, as it requires evaluating a combinatorial number of possible result subsets [8].

Approaches to result diversification are commonly classified into two main strategies. In separation-distance-based approaches, the user defines a minimum distance threshold between result elements, ensuring that the selected objects are sufficiently dissimilar. In influence-region-based approaches, element dependencies define dynamic exclusion regions, so that selecting an object prevents the inclusion of redundant items according to the properties of the metric space.

First-Match (FM) [9] and *Better Results with Influence Diversification (BRID)* [10] are representative examples of each strategy. *FM* follows a separation-distance approach, aiming to retrieve a set of k elements that are both similar to the query and mutually dissimilar. It requires a minimum pairwise distance Φ among selected elements. Candidates are ranked by similarity to the query object, and each candidate is included only if its distance to all previously selected elements exceeds Φ. *BRID* is based on influence regions, dynamically modeling the trade-off between similarity and diversity. It defines exclusion regions by quantifying the influence of already selected elements over the remaining candidates, discarding objects that are excessively similar to those already chosen. *BRID* has two main variants: (i) $BRID_K$, which returns a diversified set of k nearest neighbors; and (ii) $BRID_R$, which retrieves diversified elements within a predefined similarity radius.

2.3 Quality Evaluation Metrics

There are many aspects involved in quantifying diversity in a result set, and several metrics have been proposed to quantify them in the literature. Among them, the *Intra-List Diversity (ILD)* [11] quantifies the internal diversity of a result set as the average pairwise distance among its elements. Higher ILD values indicate greater dispersion, whereas lower values suggest higher redundancy. Given a result set R and a distance function $d(r_i, r_j)$ between elements $r_i, r_j \in R$, ILD is defined as: $\text{ILD}(R) = \frac{2}{|R|(|R|-1)} \sum_{i<j} d(r_i, r_j)$.

The *harmonic quality* measures the balance between similarity and diversity [12]. Let $Sim(R)$ denote the similarity of the elements in R to the query center, and $Div(R)$ the diversity among the elements in R. The harmonic quality is defined as $\frac{2 \cdot Sim(R) \cdot Div(R)}{Sim(R)+Div(R)}$. This metric penalizes unbalanced result sets, favoring those that simultaneously achieve high similarity and high diversity. Consequently, it evaluates an algorithm's ability to preserve proximity to the query center while maintaining diversity among the returned elements.

2.4 Indexing Structures in RDBMSs

To accelerate query execution and reduce data access, RDBMSs employ indexing structures such as B^+-tree and R-trees. The B^+-tree is widely used for indexing scalar attributes and efficiently supports exact-match and order-based queries [13]. For multidimensional attributes, structures such as the R-tree are more appropriate, as they organize data into hierarchical spatial regions, enabling efficient proximity and intersection queries [14].

The *Generalized Search Tree (GiST)* framework [15] provides a unifying abstraction for implementing diverse index structures within a RDBMS. It decouples the definition of structure-specific behaviors from the underlying indexing infrastructure, allowing developers to extend the system with new access methods without reimplementing core index management. *PostgreSQL* incorporates GiST as a native extensibility mechanism and employs it in extensions such as `CUBE`[1]. It supports representing points and hyper-rectangular regions in multidimensional spaces, enabling efficient R-tree-based indexing. It provides multiple distance metrics—including Euclidean, Manhattan and Chebyshev, enabling the execution of similarity queries directly within the relational engine.

2.5 Pruning Techniques in Metric Spaces

Pruning techniques complement indexing structures by reducing the cost of similarity queries in metric spaces. They exploit distance properties, particularly the

[1] https://www.postgresql.org/docs/current/cube.html.

triangle inequality, to avoid unnecessary calculations. The *Omni-Technique* [16] is a pivot-based approach that accelerates queries by precomputing distances. It selects a pivot set P and computes the distances from each data object to each pivot, forming vector representations known as *Omni-coordinates.* Pivots are drawn from the dataset S, forming a pivot set $P = \{p_1, \ldots, p_\ell\} \subseteq S$, with cardinality $\ell = |P|$ defined according to the dataset's intrinsic dimensionality, typically estimated by the correlation fractal dimension D_2. Choosing $\ell \in [\lceil D_2 \rceil + 1; 2\lceil D_2 \rceil + 1]$ yields a practical balance between preprocessing cost and pruning effectiveness, improving query performance.

Pivot selection aims to maximize dispersion in the metric space by selecting well-separated elements from the dataset. To this end, the Omni-Technique employs the *Hull of Foci (HF)* algorithm, which iteratively selects pivots based on an error minimization criterion derived from their distances to the current pivot set. Given P, each candidate $s_i \in S \setminus P$ is assigned an error that quantifies how uniformly it is positioned relative to the existing pivots. The element minimizing this error is selected as the next pivot, and the process repeats until ℓ pivots are obtained. Consequently, pivots tend to lie near the dataset's boundary, enhancing the discriminative power of the resulting *Omni-coordinates.*

During query processing, distances from the query object to the pivots are combined with the triangle inequality to prune candidates that cannot satisfy the similarity predicate, substantially reducing distance computations. The procedure comprises two stages: (i) a filtering phase, which produces a superset of potential answers (allowing false positives); and (ii) a refinement phase, in which candidates are truly verified in the original space.

2.6 Related Work

Several approaches have been proposed to incorporate similarity queries into RDBMSs. The SimilarQL framework [17] extends PostgreSQL by allowing the specification of similarity queries directly in SQL via a set of PL/pgSQL functions. The MIGUE-Sim system [18] provides operators and functions for similarity query processing, exploiting native PostgreSQL resources, including a GiST index based on an R-tree to accelerate k-nearest neighbor queries.

In the context of result diversification, most existing approaches were originally developed outside an RDBMS environment. For instance, works such as *diversity browsing* [19] explore integrating diversification algorithms with specific indexing structures, such as the *VP-Tree*, combining distance- and coverage-based search strategies to reduce redundant regions in the search space. Another approach uses graph-based structures, such as the HNSW index, that incorporate diversity criteria during graph traversal, accounting for both high- and low-dimensional settings [20].

Conversely, the DiveScan module [21] integrates the diversification algorithms *BRID* and *FM*, originally proposed outside the RDBMS context, into the relational engine. It relies solely on native PostgreSQL features, combining sequential and R-tree–based indexed strategies to support diversified query processing without external components. Nevertheless, it still depends on iterative pairwise candidate comparisons, which constrains scalability in large-scale settings.

3 The PRIDE Method

Similarity search algorithms with diversification typically incur high computational cost, because, beyond evaluating candidates with respect to the query center, they require pairwise comparisons among candidates to enforce diversity constraints. This additional processing increases algorithmic complexity and hinders efficient integration into relational systems.

To enable efficient diversified similarity search within an RDBMS, we propose *PRIDE*, a method based on the observation that nearby elements tend to behave similarly with respect to a set of pivots. As illustrated in Fig. 1, each object is mapped to a combination of pivot-induced rings, producing a discrete representation called a *radical*. Rather than performing explicit pairwise diversification, PRIDE groups objects by radicals and selects a single representative per group, typically the element closest to the query center, thereby avoiding costly candidate-to-candidate comparisons and enabling efficient integration into relational systems.

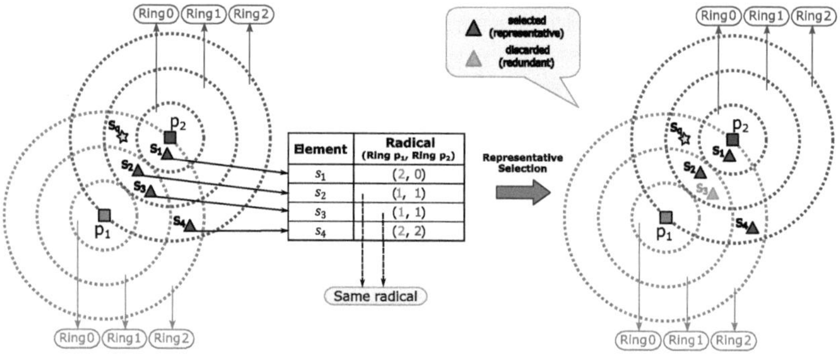

Fig. 1. Illustration of the PRIDE diversification strategy. Objects are grouped according to pivot-ring radicals and only one representative per radical is selected to reduce local redundancy.

3.1 Precomputed Structures

Let $S = \{s_1, s_2, \ldots, s_n\}$ be a dataset defined over a metric domain $\mathbb{S}$ with distance function d. Before query execution, PRIDE requires precomputing and storing auxiliary structures in the RDBMS. The primary structure is the *pivot set*, represented as an array $P = \{p_1, \ldots p_j, \ldots, p_\ell\} \subseteq S$, where $\ell = |P|$ denotes the number of pivots and $p_j \neq p_g$ for $j \neq g$. In the relational schema, each pivot is associated with its corresponding vector attribute S, stored as either a `CUBE` or a `DOUBLE PRECISION[]` data type. This representation supports flexible access strategies, enabling both sequential scans and index-based retrieval.

Additionally, for each pair $\langle S, P \rangle$, the scalar

$$max\_dist(S, P) = \max\{ ds_i, p_j \mid s_i \in S,\ p_j \in P \} \quad (1)$$

is maintained. It corresponds to the maximum observed distance between any data element and any pivot, and is used at query time to parameterize the width of the radial bands (*rings*) that define the radicals used for grouping elements.

Optionally, the method supports a global pruning phase inspired by the Omni technique to reduce the candidate set before the diversification. This requires a *coordinate base* that stores, for each element $s_i \in S$, its distances to all pivots in P. These distances can be stored either as individual `double precision` columns, which enables using a B$^+$-tree, or as a single vector attribute, representing the distances to all pivots in a single tuple.

3.2 Similarity Queries with Diversity

Given a query center $s_q \in \mathbb{S}$, an element $s_i \in \mathbb{S}$ and a distance function d, PRIDE supports the following diversified similarity operators:

- **Diversified range comparison operator** (*dRng*): given a radius $\xi > 0$, returns TRUE if the comparison $s_i\ dRng_{\mathsf{g}}[d, \xi]\ s_q$ indicates that $ds_i, s_q \leq \xi$ and that s_i was selected by a diversification algorithm g.
- **Diversified k-nearest neighbors comparison operator** (k-*NDN*): given $k > 0$, returns TRUE when, in the comparison $s_i\ k\text{-}NDN_{\mathsf{g}}[d, k]\ s_q$, the element s_i belongs to the set of the k diversified elements closest to s_q selected by a diversification algorithm g.

These operators enable PRIDE to express two classes of diversified similarity queries: the diversified range and the diversified k-nearest neighbors queries.

Diversified Range Query. A $\sigma_{(\mathsf{S}\ dRng_{\mathsf{g}}[d,\xi]\ s_q)}\mathsf{T}$ query retrieves tuples in which the value s_i of a complex attribute $\mathsf{S} \subset \mathbb{S}$ satisfies the similarity condition with respect to the query center s_q (i.e., $ds_i, s_q \leq \xi$) and is retained after applying the diversification algorithm g.

Diversified range queries are processed by instantiating g with the $PRIDE_r$ algorithm: the *Pivot-Ring Indexable Diversified Exploration for Range queries.* Figure 2 illustrates its main steps in a two-dimensional Euclidean space, considering a dataset $S = \{s_1, s_2, s_3, s_4, s_5, s_6\}$ and a pivot set $P = \{p_1, p_2\}$ (Fig. 2(a)).

PRIDE requires a prior structuring of the metric space through pivots, performed before query evaluation to collect information that accelerates subsequent queries. To this purpose, radial partitions are defined using the precomputed maximum distance between any dataset element to any pivot: $max\_dist(S, P)$

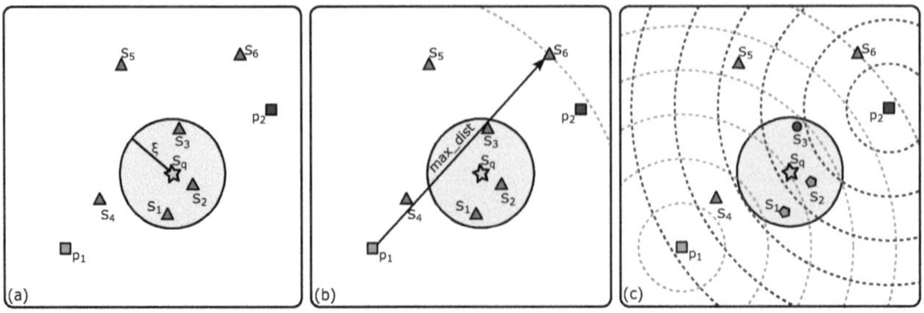

Fig. 2. Steps of the $PRIDE_r$ algorithm: (a) radius-based filter; (b) computation of $max\_dist(S, P)$; and (c) partition into $m + 1$ rings, grouping by radicals and selection of one representative per cell.

(Fig. 2(b)). Given an integer parameter $m \geq 0$, the interval $[0, max\_dist(S, P)]$ is uniformly divided into $m + 1$ rings of equal width, defined as:

$$thickness = \frac{max\_dist(S, P)}{m + 1}. \tag{2}$$

This discretization is applied to each pivot $p_j \in P$, inducing a radial partition of the metric space. The intersections of rings across pivots define disjoint regions, termed *Metric Intersection Parallelotopes (MIPs)*, each corresponding to a unique combination of distance bands (Fig. 2(c)). Accordingly, for each candidate $s_i \in S$ and pivot $p_j \in P$, the ring index is computed as:

$$ring(s_i, p_j) = \min\left\{m, \left\lfloor \frac{ds_i, p_j}{thickness} \right\rfloor\right\}. \tag{3}$$

From these values, the radical of element s_i is defined as:

$$\rho(s_i) = \big(ring(s_i, p_1), \ldots, ring(s_i, p_\ell)\big), \tag{4}$$

which uniquely identifies a MIP, that is, every element that shares the same radical belongs to the same region of the metric space. The elements s_i are then grouped according to their radicals.

A query execution constructs the candidate set $C = \{\, s_i \in S \backslash \{s_q\} \mid ds_q, s_i \leq \xi \,\}$, containing all elements within the query radius ξ (Fig. 2(a)). This step restricts the search space and can be implemented via sequential scan, spatial indexing, or pivot-based pruning. Thereafter, it selects the element closest to the query center s_q in each MIP, ensuring local relevance within each region. In the example of Fig. 2(c), elements s_1 and s_2 are selected, while s_3 is discarded because it shares the same radical as s_2. Thus, the final result set is defined as:

$$R = \bigcup_{\hat{r}} \{\, s^\star_{\hat{r}} \,\}, \tag{5}$$

where $s^\star_{\hat{r}}$ is the element closest to s_q among those in the same radical $\hat{r}$.

The algorithm ensures that each MIP contributes at most one element, promoting structural diversity and reducing local redundancies in the result set. Since selection is performed independently within each MIP, the method balances relevance and diversity without pairwise candidate comparisons, enabling efficient execution and fostering the use of indexes in relational environments.

Diversified k-Nearest Neighbors Query. The diversified k-nearest neighbors query, expressed as $\sigma_{(\mathsf{S}\ k\text{-}NDN_{\mathfrak{g}[d,k]}\ s_q)}\mathsf{T}$, returns the k elements closest to s_q while jointly enforcing relevance and diversity criteria. In this work, $\mathfrak{g}$ is instantiated as $PRIDE_k$ (*Pivot-Ring Indexable Diversified Exploration for k-nearest neighbors*), the PRIDE algorithm tailored to diversified k-NN queries.

Unlike the diversified range query, which is parameterized by a radius ξ, the k-nearest neighbors query is defined by an integer $k > 0$ that specifies the required number of diversified results. The diversification strategy remains unchanged: candidates are represented by their radicals, defined by the pivot-induced rings, and at most one is selected per MIP, prioritizing those closest to the query center s_q. The algorithm processes candidates in ascending order of distance to s_q, selecting representatives from previously uncovered parallelotopes until k elements are obtained, or the candidate set is exhausted.

Construction of the Candidate Set. The construction of the candidate set C affects the overall performance, as it determines which elements are evaluated against the pivots. In dense datasets, scanning all elements in S is often prohibitive, making pruning strategies essential to limit the candidate set. In this work, two primary strategies are employed for the efficient construction of C:

- **R-tree indexing:** In PostgreSQL, GiST-based R-tree indexes over attributes of type `CUBE` enable efficient spatial filtering of candidates.
- **Global pivot-based pruning:** Inspired by the Omni technique, this strategy leverages precomputed distances between elements and pivots to discard candidates that cannot satisfy the search predicate.

To enable these strategies in PostgreSQL, a radius ξ must be specified to bound the search region, as both R-tree indexing and pivot-based pruning depend on this parameter to filter candidates. However, for diversified k-nearest neighbors queries, an appropriate ξ is not known a priori. Thus, it is not possible to predefine a radius that simultaneously guarantees at least k diversified results and avoids an excessively large search region. To address this limitation, a progressive radius expansion strategy is adopted. An initial value for ξ is either provided as a parameter or derived from the ring width (i.e., $\xi = \mathit{thickness}$), constructing the candidate set C accordingly.

If the number of selected elements is less than k, the radius is expanded and a new iteration is executed. In this work, the expansion increases the radius by one ring width, i.e., $\xi \leftarrow \xi + \mathit{thickness}$. To avoid redundant processing, previously examined elements are stored in an auxiliary structure and excluded from subsequent iterations, even as the radius grows.

4 Experimental Evaluation

This section presents the experimental evaluation of the proposed method. We first analyze the impact of the parameter m, which controls the granularity of PRIDE's radial discretization. Next, we compare the algorithms $BRID_k$, $BRID_r$, *FM*, $PRIDE_r$, and $PRIDE_k$ in terms of performance and result quality. The algorithms were implemented in PostgreSQL 17.3[2], and the experiments were conducted on a computer running Windows 11, equipped with an Intel® Core™ i7-10750H processor and 32 GB of RAM.

4.1 Influence of the Parameter m

Parameter m is the number of rings used to partition the data space, controlling the granularity of PRIDE's radial discretization. Smaller values yield wider rings and greater candidate aggregation within each radial band, whereas larger values produce finer partitions, increasing the number of distinct radicals and the degree of structural fragmentation.

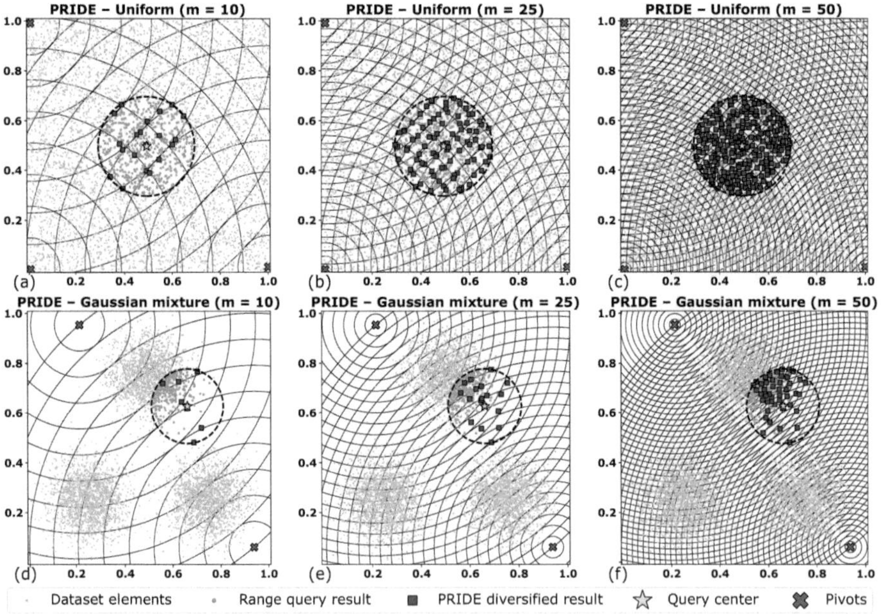

Fig. 3. Influence of parameter m on radial discretization and radical formation. The first row presents examples from a uniformly distributed dataset, and the second from a dataset generated by a mixture of three Gaussian distributions.

[2] https://github.com/AnnaLauton/PRIDE.git.

To illustrate this effect, two synthetic two-dimensional datasets (for ease of visualization) were used, each containing 5,000 elements: one uniformly distributed and another following a mixture of three Gaussian distributions (Fig. 3). The example shows the pivot-induced discretization for $m = \{10, 25, 50\}$ in both cases, highlighting how increasing m progressively refines the spatial partitioning.

In the uniform dataset (Fig. 3(a)–(c)), increasing m markedly raises the number of elements retained after diversification. For $m = 10$, only about 3% of the range-query results are preserved, indicating strong aggregation. For $m = 25$, this proportion increases to 14%, reflecting improved separation among radicals. For $m = 50$, about 41% of the elements are retained, evidencing a finer discretization and broader coverage of the space.

A similar trend is observed for the mixture of Gaussian distributions (Fig. 3(d)–(f)), although less pronounced due to data concentration and the locality of the query center. For $m = 10$, only about 2.6% of the elements are retained; this increases to 5.8% for $m = 25$ and to 15% for $m = 50$. This more gradual growth indicates that dense regions tend to keep multiple elements mapped to the same radical even as the granularity increases.

Table 1. Effect of parameter m on the structure of radicals.

m	Uniform			Gaussian		
	# *Radicals*	Occupancy	Singleton (%)	# *Radicals*	Occupancy	Singleton (%)
5	51	98.04	0.00	16	312.50	12.50
10	145	34.48	6.90	44	113.64	6.82
15	292	17.12	8.56	82	60.98	13.41
20	471	10.62	13.16	123	40.65	9.76
25	670	7.46	11.94	179	27.93	13.41
30	877	5.70	14.60	231	21.65	12.99
35	1159	4.31	19.59	300	16.67	17.67
40	1407	3.55	23.03	365	13.70	18.63
45	1654	3.02	27.45	434	11.52	21.89
50	1949	2.57	34.12	509	9.82	23.58

Table 1 presents a quantitative analysis of the impact of parameter m on the radical structure, for both distributions. For each value of m, it reports the number of distinct radicals, the average occupancy per radical, and the proportion of radicals containing a single element.

In the uniform dataset, increasing m from 5 to 50 raised the number of radicals from approximately 50 to 2,000, reduced the average occupancy from ≈ 100 to 2.6, and increased the proportion of singleton radicals from 0.00% to 34%. In the Gaussian dataset, the number of radicals grows from 16 to ≈ 500, with the average occupancy decreasing from 312 to 10 and the proportion of singleton radicals reaching 24%.

Comparatively, the uniform dataset exhibits larger fragmentation for the same m, whereas the Gaussian dataset retains higher aggregation due to spatial concentration. These results show that m is a control parameter for the radial discretization granularity: smaller values promote aggregation and more compact results, while larger values increase fragmentation and the ability to separate regions, directly influencing the level of diversification achieved by PRIDE.

4.2 Performance Evaluation

To evaluate performance, we compared the algorithms $BRID_k$, $BRID_r$, *FM*, $PRIDE_r$, and $PRIDE_k$ across three datasets with distinct characteristics: `Airbnb Paris`[3] comprising geographical coordinates of 81,853 listings from Paris (collected in September 2025), with a measured intrinsic dimensionality of 1.38; `Corel`[4] containing 68,040 image feature vectors with 32 dimensions and a measured intrinsic dimensionality of 2.67 and `Glove`[5] consisting of 400,000 word embeddings with 50 dimensions trained on Wikipedia 2014 and Gigaword 5, with a measured intrinsic dimensionality of 4.51.

The number of pivots and the pivot elements chosen for each dataset were defined following the Omni-technique strategy. Accordingly, we used 3 pivots for `Airbnb Paris`, 4 for `Corel`, and 6 for `Glove`. Additionally, the value of m in PRIDE and the Φ used by FM were defined based on the diversification behavior observed in the results produced by BRID, aiming at fair comparisons.

For all algorithms, we evaluated both sequential execution and GiST R-tree–based indexing for constructing the candidate set C. For PRIDE, we additionally considered global pivot-based pruning inspired by the Omni technique, with two variants: (i) storing pivot distances in a single vector attribute (*array*); and (ii) using one column per pivot, each indexed with a B^+-tree.

Figure 4 reports the average execution time (ms, log scale) for diversified k-NN queries with $k \in \{5, 25, 50, 100\}$ and diversified range queries, where the ξ values are defined from the average radius observed for diversified k-NN query execution. Each query is executed 20 times using randomly selected query centers.

For the `Airbnb Paris` dataset, $PRIDE_k$ indexed with the R-tree consistently outperformed the competing diversified k-NN methods. Taking $k = 50$ for example, the best result was achieved by $PRIDE_k$ with global *OMNI cols* pruning, attaining reductions of up to 99.76% and speed-ups of up to 410× over R-tree-indexed $BRID_K$. For diversified range queries, $PRIDE_r$ also delivered the best performance across all evaluated configurations, reaching reductions of up to 98.56% and speed-ups of up to 70× for $k = 50$ with global *OMNI cols* pruning. These results suggest that, in low-dimensional settings, combining pivots with

[3] Inside Airbnb: https://insideairbnb.com/get-the-data/.

[4] Corel Image Features: https://doi.org/10.24432/C5K599.

[5] Global Vectors for Word Representation: https://nlp.stanford.edu/projects/glove/.

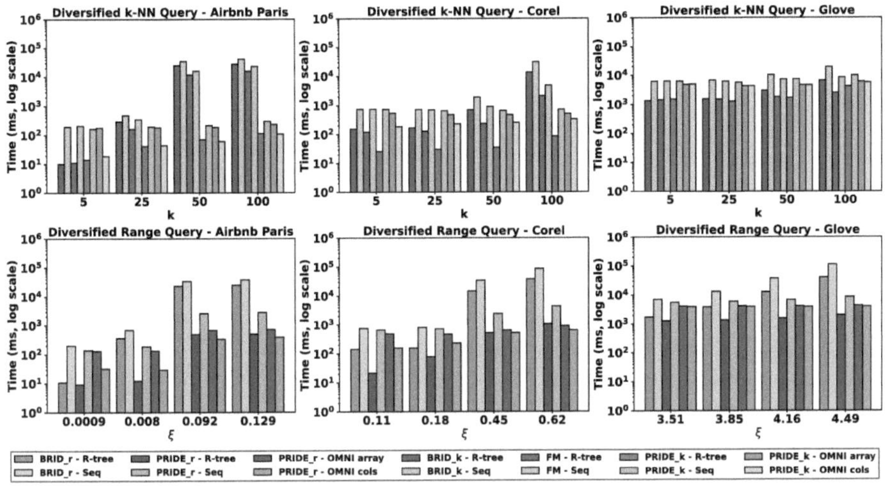

Fig. 4. Average execution time of the diversified k-NN and diversified range-query algorithms for different values of k and ξ in the evaluated datasets.

B^+-tree indexes over precomputed distances is highly effective, while *BRID* and *FM* incur higher costs due to iterative pairwise candidate comparisons.

For `Corel`, *PRIDE* also achieves the best performance across all evaluated configurations, with execution time reductions of up to 99.36% (speed-ups of up to 157×) when comparing the indexed methods $PRIDE_k$ and $BRID_K$, and up to 98.31% (speed-ups of up to 59×) when comparing $PRIDE_r$ and $BRID_R$, both for $k = 100$. These results show that combining spatial filtering with radical-based structural diversification substantially reduces execution time compared with iterative candidate-comparison approaches.

PRIDE remains competitive on the high-cardinality, high-dimensional `Glove` dataset. For diversified range queries, $PRIDE_r$ indexed with an R-tree achieves execution time reductions of up to 94.97% (up to 20× faster) compared with indexed $BRID_r$ for $k = 100$. For diversified k-NN queries, it achieves execution time reductions of up to 44% (up to 1.79× faster) when comparing the R-tree-indexed methods $PRIDE_k$ and $BRID_k$ for $k = 50$. However, for $k = 100$, *FM* with R-tree outperforms the other methods. This behavior reflects the higher overhead of pivot-based approaches in high-dimensional spaces, although *PRIDE* still remains competitive in both result quality and processing time, but it highlights that accurately capturing the data distribution requires additional pivots, increasing the number of distance computations and the maintenance cost of auxiliary structures. Thus, achieving high performance depends on careful parameter tuning, which is difficult to generalize across datasets with distinct characteristics and application requirements.

Overall, *BRID* and *FM* incur significantly higher execution costs because they enforce diversity via iterative comparisons among candidates and previously selected elements. In contrast, *PRIDE* shifts diversification to a pivot-induced structural organization of the space, substantially reducing the need for explicit pairwise comparisons. This advantage is particularly evident in the `Airbnb Paris` and `Corel` datasets, where $PRIDE_r$ and $PRIDE_k$ consistently achieve much lower execution times across most evaluated scenarios.

4.3 Quality Evaluation

We used the same datasets and parameters for the quality evaluation. The algorithms $BRID_k$, *FM*, and $PRIDE_k$ were evaluated, since all return the same number of elements, enabling direct comparison. The evaluation considered the ILD and harmonic quality metrics, as summarized in Table 2. For `Airbnb Paris`, $PRIDE_k$ achieved the best results for $k = \{5, 25, 100\}$ in both metrics, with gains of up to 330.70% in ILD and 313.2% in harmonic quality relative to *FM*, the second-best method. For `Corel`, $PRIDE_k$ consistently achieved the best performance across all values of k, reaching improvements of up to 76.98% in ILD and 41.26% in harmonic quality over *FM*. For `Glove`, $PRIDE_k$ obtained higher ILD values for $k = \{25, 50, 100\}$, with gains of up to 30.64% compared with *FM*. Regarding harmonic quality, it outperformed the competing methods for $k = \{5, 25\}$, achieving gains of up to 4.88%. For larger values of k, however, $BRID_k$ achieved better harmonic quality, with improvements of up to 19.1% over $PRIDE_k$. Overall, these results indicate that $PRIDE_k$ produces highly diversified result sets while preserving a strong balance between similarity and diversity in most scenarios, while consistently achieving significantly lower execution times.

Table 2. Quality evaluation using ILD and harmonic quality.

Dataset	k	ILD			Harmonic Quality		
		$BRID_k$	FM	$PRIDE_k$	$BRID_k$	FM	$PRIDE_k$
`Airbnb Paris`	5	0.000650	0.001527	**0.002628**	0.001297	0.003044	**0.005227**
	25	0.004100	0.003100	**0.011148**	0.008128	0.006162	**0.021807**
	50	**0.024812**	0.004375	0.017605	**0.047212**	0.008675	0.033993
	100	0.026036	0.006261	**0.026965**	0.049464	0.012366	**0.051112**
`Corel`	5	0.127626	0.131084	**0.142659**	0.201184	0.205440	**0.219183**
	25	0.170273	0.160759	**0.210508**	0.249731	0.239575	**0.288523**
	50	0.212086	0.174609	**0.267096**	0.289275	0.254213	**0.335346**
	100	0.298409	0.189363	**0.335125**	0.350094	0.268970	**0.379944**
`Glove`	5	3.014669	**3.484121**	3.015663	0.410926	0.398144	**0.411364**
	25	3.614712	3.747208	**3.866401**	0.382733	0.372025	**0.390187**
	50	3.903272	3.973681	**4.359455**	**0.371303**	0.363421	0.337037
	100	4.225522	4.153362	**5.425646**	**0.359029**	0.355723	0.301459

5 Conclusions

This work presented *PRIDE*, a technique for processing diversified similarity queries directly in RDBMSs. By leveraging pivots and radial discretization of the metric space, *PRIDE* organizes data into regions and enables efficient representative selection without iterative comparisons. Compared with methods such as *BRID* and *FM*, *PRIDE* substantially reduces the cost of diversification while maintaining a strong balance between similarity and diversity.

As future work, we intend to: (i) investigate adaptive strategies for defining the parameter m, considering the data distribution and the formation of MIPs induced by ring intersections with respect to the pivots; and (ii) explore non-uniform radial partitions of the metric space that adapt ring widths according to local data density.

Acknowledgments. This work was supported by the São Paulo Research Foundation (FAPESP) (Grants 23/18026-8 and 24/13328-9), the National Council for Scientific and Technological Development (CNPq), and the Brazilian Federal Agency for Support of Graduate Education (CAPES).

Disclosure of Interests. The authors have no competing interests relevant to the content of this article.

Use of Generative AI. Generative AI tools were used only for linguistic revision and textual reorganization. The responsibility for the scientific content and final manuscript remains with the authors.

References

1. Chandrasekaran, D., Mago, V.: Evolution of semantic similarity—a survey. ACM Comput. Surv. **54**(2) (2021). https://doi.org/10.1145/3440755. Article 41:1–41:37
2. Hambarde, K.A., Proença, H.: Information retrieval: recent advances and beyond. IEEE Access **11**, 76581–76604 (2023). https://doi.org/10.1109/ACCESS.2023.3295776
3. Yang, P., Wang, H., Yang, J., Qian, Z., Zhang, Y., Lin, X.: Deep learning approaches for similarity computation: a survey. IEEE Trans. Knowl. Data Eng. **36**(12), 7893–7912 (2024). https://doi.org/10.1109/TKDE.2024.3422484
4. Shu, X., Ye, Y.: Knowledge Discovery: methods from data mining and machine learning. Soc. Sci. Res. **110**, 102817 (2023). https://doi.org/10.1016/j.ssresearch.2022.102817
5. Gupta, S., Thakar, U., Tokekar, S.: A comprehensive survey on techniques for numerical similarity measurement. Expert Syst. Appl. **277**, 127235 (2025). https://doi.org/10.1016/j.eswa.2025.127235
6. Zezula, P., Amato, G., Dohnal, V., Batko, M.: Similarity search: the metric space approach. In: Advances in Database Systems, vol. 32. Kluwer, Boston (2006)
7. Lima, E.L.: Metric Spaces, 6th edn. IMPA, Rio de Janeiro (2020)

8. Vieira, M.R., et al.: On query result diversification. In: Proceedings of the 2011 IEEE 27th International Conference on Data Engineering (ICDE), Hannover, pp. 1163–1174. IEEE (2011). https://doi.org/10.1109/ICDE.2011.5767846
9. Skopal, T., Dohnal, V., Batko, M., Zezula, P.: Distinct nearest neighbors queries for similarity search in very large multimedia databases. In: Proceedings of the 11th ACM International Workshop on Web Information and Data Management (WIDM), Hong Kong, pp. 11–14. ACM (2009). https://doi.org/10.1145/1651587.1651592
10. Santos, L.F.D., Oliveira, W.D., Ferreira, M.R.P., Traina, A.J.M., Traina, C.: Parameter-free and domain-independent similarity search with diversity. In: Proceedings of the 25th International Conference on Scientific and Statistical Database Management (SSDBM), Baltimore. ACM (2013). https://doi.org/10.1145/2484838.2484854. Article No. 5
11. Zhang, M., Hurley, N.: Avoiding monotony: improving the diversity of recommendation lists. In: Proceedings of the 2008 ACM Conference on Recommender Systems (RecSys), Lausanne, pp. 123–130. ACM (2008). https://doi.org/10.1145/1454008.1454030
12. Smyth, B., McClave, P.: Similarity vs. diversity. In: Aha, D.W., Watson, I. (eds.) ICCBR 2001. LNCS (LNAI), vol. 2080, pp. 347–361. Springer, Heidelberg (2001). https://doi.org/10.1007/3-540-44593-5_25
13. Comer, D.: Ubiquitous B-Tree. ACM Comput. Surv. **11**(2), 121–137 (1979). https://doi.org/10.1145/356770.356776
14. Guttman, A.: R-trees: a dynamic index structure for spatial searching. In: Proceedings of the 1984 ACM SIGMOD International Conference on Management of Data, Boston, pp. 47–57. ACM (1984). https://doi.org/10.1145/602259.602266
15. Hellerstein, J.M., Naughton, J.F., Pfeffer, A.: Generalized search trees for database systems. In: Dayal, U., Gray, P.M.D., Nishio, S. (eds.) Proceedings of the International Conference on Very Large Databases (VLDB), Zurich, pp. 562–573. Morgan Kaufmann (1995)
16. Traina, C., Santos Filho, R.F., Traina, A.J.M., Vieira, M.R., Faloutsos, C.: The Omni-family of all-purpose access methods: a simple and effective way to make similarity search more efficient. VLDB J. **16**(4), 483–505 (2007). https://doi.org/10.1007/s00778-005-0178-0
17. Traina, C., Moriyama, A., Rocha, G., Cordeiro, R., Ciferri, C.D.A., Traina, A.: The SimilarQL framework: similarity queries in plain SQL. In: Proceedings of the 34th ACM/SIGAPP Symposium on Applied Computing (SAC), Limassol, pp. 468–471. ACM (2019). https://doi.org/10.1145/3297280.3299736
18. Eleuterio, I.A.R., Cazzolato, M.T., Teixeira, L.R., Gutierrez, M.A., Traina, A.J.M., Traina, C.: MIGUE-Sim: speeding up similarity queries with native RDBMS resources. In: Proceedings of the 39th ACM/SIGAPP Symposium on Applied Computing (SAC), Avila, pp. 321–328. ACM (2024). https://doi.org/10.1145/3605098.3636019
19. Jasbick, D., Santos, L., de Oliveira, D., Bedo, M.: Some branches may bear rotten fruits: diversity browsing VP-trees. In: Satoh, S. (ed.) SISAP 2020. LNCS, vol. 12440, pp. 140–154. Springer, Cham (2020). https://doi.org/10.1007/978-3-030-60936-8_11

20. Weber, M., Silva-Leite, J., Santos, L., de Oliveira, D., Bedo, M.: Adicionando suporte á diversificação de resultados em índices HNSW considerando espaços de baixa e alta dimensionalidade. In: Annals of the XXXIX Brazilian Symposium on Databases (SBBD), Florianópolis, pp. 14–26. SBC (2024). https://doi.org/10.5753/sbbd.2024.240618
21. Lauton, A.J.C., Traina, A.J.M., Traina Jr., C.: DiveScan: Um Módulo para Recuperação de Dados por Similaridade com Diversidade em Postgres. In: Annals of the XL Brazilian Symposium on Databases (SBBD), Fortaleza. SBC (2025). https://doi.org/10.5753/sbbd.2025.247779

Learning Joinable Column Representations via Set Encoding

Hyejin Hong[1,2], Kenji Hatano[1], and Kyoung-Sook Kim[2(✉)]

[1] Doshisha University, Kyoto, Japan
{hong,hatano}@mil.doshisha.ac.jp
[2] National Institute of Advanced Industrial Science and Technology, Tokyo, Japan
{hyejin.hon,ks.kim}@aist.go.jp

Abstract. Identifying joinable column pairs in large-scale table collections is fundamental to data integration and data lake exploration. Existing studies have proposed methods that encode columns as text using pre-trained language models and learn similarity between them. However, these approaches do not adequately capture the permutation invariance and distributional characteristics of the column values. This paper revisits the representation assumption underlying joinable column search and formulates column representation learning as a supervised set representation learning problem. By integrating value-level embeddings with permutation-invariant aggregation, our method captures both semantic and distributional characteristics of columns. Experiments on two benchmark datasets show that our method achieves competitive or better performance than existing approaches in most evaluation settings. Furthermore, in the value-shuffling experiment, our method maintains stable retrieval performance under variations in value ordering, supporting the effectiveness of set-based modeling for joinable column search.

Keywords: Joinable column search · Column representation learning · Set encoding · Data lake discovery

1 Introduction

The rapid growth of data lakes and open data repositories has led to the accumulation of millions of heterogeneous tables [3]. Table join discovery, which determines whether columns from different tables are semantically joinable, is a fundamental task in data integration, data analysis, and machine learning pipelines [20]. Traditional approaches rely on rule-based methods leveraging column names, data types, or statistical features, as well as similarity estimation based on hand-crafted features [12]. However, identifying joinable columns remains a major bottleneck due to schema heterogeneity, ambiguous and inconsistent value representations, and the combinatorial explosion of candidate column pairs in large-scale datasets. These challenges make semantic matching computationally expensive and error-prone, resulting in limited scalability and generalization in diverse data lake environments [4].

G. Vargas-Solar et al. (Eds.): ADBIS 2026, LNCS 16937, pp. 354–370, 2027.
https://doi.org/10.1007/978-3-032-39820-8_23

To address these limitations, recent studies have proposed learning-based approaches that encode columns or entire tables into distributed embedding representations and estimate joinability via similarity [8]. With the advancement of pre-trained language models (PLMs), several studies represent tables as text and derive embeddings for column names and cell values [25]. Although these methods achieve strong performance in effectively capturing semantic relationships, they overlook a fundamental structural property of tabular data: columns are inherently unordered. They typically model columns as sequences using order-sensitive encoders such as Transformers or RNNs [21].

In tabular data, the order of values within a column is typically arbitrary and semantically meaningless [1]. Thus, modeling columns as sequences introduces an unnecessary inductive bias that is inconsistent with the underlying data structure [27]. This mismatch can lead to unstable representations, where variations in record ordering or sampling affect the learned embeddings, thereby degrading the robustness and reproducibility of joinability prediction [16]. In contrast, a column is more naturally viewed as an unordered set of values, suggesting that order-invariant modeling is more appropriate for this task.

This paper revisits the representation assumption underlying joinable column search by explicitly treating columns as unordered sets of values. Based on this view, we formulate column representation learning as a supervised set representation learning problem and propose Supervised Joinable Set Encoding, which learns order-invariant representations optimized for joinability. Leveraging architectures such as Deep Sets and Set Transformer, our approach captures both semantic and distributional characteristics of column values through permutation-invariant aggregation. To scale to large data lake environments, we further adopt an offline-online framework. In the offline phase, the model learns a joinability-aware embedding space. In the online phase, efficient nearest-neighbor search enables scalable and accurate retrieval of joinable column candidates.

Our main contributions are summarized as follows:

- We reformulate column representation learning by modeling columns as unordered sets, addressing the mismatch between tabular data structure and sequence-based encoding.
- We propose a supervised set-based representation learning method for joinable column search using Set Encoders.
- We demonstrate improved accuracy and robustness to variations in value ordering through extensive experiments.

To evaluate the effectiveness of our method, we investigate the following research questions (RQs):

RQ1: Does the set-based representation assumption better fit joinable column search than the ordered-sequence assumption?
RQ2: How do permutation-invariant aggregation mechanisms and PLMs affect the retrieval effectiveness of joinable column search?
RQ3: How robust are the learned column representations to perturbations in the ordering of column values?

2 Related Work

This section introduces related studies on joinable column search in large-scale table collections.

2.1 Neural Approaches for Table Joinability

Identifying related tables in data lakes, such as unionable, joinable, or subset relationships, is a fundamental problem in data integration and data discovery [7,11]. Recent studies have explored neural approaches that learn representations of tabular data for these tasks. DeepJoin [6] is a representative method that leverages pre-trained language models to encode table columns as textual sequences and learns similarity between columns for joinability prediction. While it demonstrates strong performance by capturing semantic similarity between column values, it treats columns as ordered sequences, which may not fully reflect the order-invariant nature of tabular data and the distributional characteristics of value sets.

More recently, TabSketchFM [13] has been proposed as a neural tabular model for data discovery over data lakes. It introduces a sketch-based pre-training strategy to learn compact table representations and is fine-tuned for multiple tasks, including unionability, joinability, and subset detection [19,28]. Furthermore, it supports table-level retrieval, enabling efficient search for related tables given a query, and demonstrates strong generalization across datasets and tasks. However, both approaches have limitations in capturing fine-grained column-level characteristics. DeepJoin relies on sequence-based encoding of column values, while TabSketchFM focuses on table-level representations through sketch-based summarization. As a result, they do not explicitly model the order invariance and value distribution properties that are essential for accurately modeling joinable column relationships [24].

In contrast, our work revisits the representation assumption underlying joinable column search by modeling columns as unordered sets of value embeddings rather than ordered textual sequences. Set Encoders provide a natural mechanism for learning joinability-aware representations under this formulation.

2.2 Set Encoder

Set Encoder-based approaches such as Deep Sets [26] and Set Transformer [14] have been proposed for learning representations of unordered data. These methods are designed to be permutation-invariant, ensuring that the output representation does not depend on the order of input elements. Set Encoders have been successfully applied in various domains involving unordered data, including point cloud processing, multi-instance learning, and recommendation systems [9,22,23]. Deep Sets provides a simple and computationally efficient framework based on element-wise transformations and aggregation, while Set Transformer extends this idea by incorporating self-attention mechanisms to capture interactions among elements.

Despite their suitability for modeling unordered data, their application to table join discovery remains largely unexplored. In particular, existing studies on joinable column search have rarely adopted Set Encoders as the primary mechanism for modeling columns as sets of values. Instead, most approaches still rely on sequence-based encoders derived from natural language processing models. Moreover, the combination of Set Encoder-based representation learning with supervised joinability objectives has not been sufficiently explored. This gap motivates our work, where we explicitly model columns as sets and learn order-invariant representations under joinability supervision.

3 Proposed Method

In this study, we address the problem of determining joinable column pairs among columns contained in multiple tables. The set of values constituting each column (value set) is treated as an order-invariant input, and column representations are learned using Set Encoders (Deep Sets [26], Set Transformer [14]).

Unlike sequence-based approaches, our method explicitly models a column as a set of values and adopts a two-stage architecture consisting of value-level encoding and set-level aggregation. This design allows the model to capture semantic information at the value level while enforcing permutation invariance at the column level, which is essential for stable joinability estimation. This formulation enables more stable and robust column representations compared to sequence-based approaches.

The objective of this problem is to learn a score function that determines whether any two columns are semantically joinable. Therefore, columns are formulated not as sequential data but as unordered sets, and representation learning suitable for set structures is performed.

3.1 Overview of Our Method

The overall architecture of our method is shown in Fig. 1. The method consists of two stages: supervised column representation learning (offline) and joinability estimation using the trained model (online).

The overall processing steps are as follows.

1. Generation of column-value embeddings.
2. Column representation learning using Set Encoder (Deep Sets/Set Transformer).
3. Learning a joinability scoring model by supervised learning (offline).
4. Precomputation and indexing of column representations using the trained model.
5. Search for joinable columns given a query column (online).

This configuration enables learning column representations that do not depend on record order or sampling.

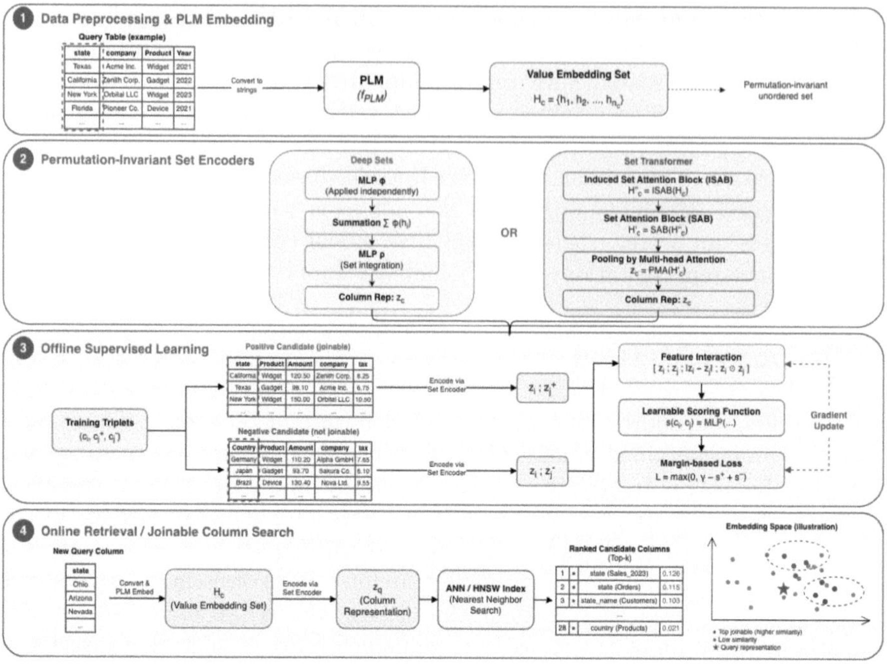

Fig. 1. Overview of the proposed set-based column encoding framework for joinable column search. Our method encodes each column using a set encoder, such as Deep Sets or Set Transformer. The learned column representations are used for supervised joinability learning and online nearest-neighbor retrieval.

3.2 Set Encoding

In our approach, column values are converted into embedding vectors by a PLM, and the resulting set of embeddings is given as input to a Set Encoder. Although multiple language models can be employed for vectorization, we adopt a lightweight yet efficient pre-trained language model to enable fast and effective exploration. Set Encoders based on Deep Sets [26] and Set Transformer [14] are then trained using joinability supervision. Because the Set Encoder is permutation-invariant, the resulting column representations are theoretically insensitive to the ordering of column values.

First, it is necessary to vectorize the column values. Each column consists of multiple values, and a column c is represented as a value set as in Eq. (1).

$$c = x_1,\ x_2,\ \ldots,\ x_{n_c} \tag{1}$$

Here, x_i is a value contained in column c, and n_c differs from column to column.

Each value x_i may include text or numeric data. In this work, numeric values are also converted into strings, and embeddings are generated uniformly using a PLM f_{PLM}.

$$\mathbf{h}_i = f_{\text{PLM}}(x_i), \quad \mathbf{h}_i \in \mathbb{R}^d \tag{2}$$

Here, d is the embedding dimension. Column c is represented as the following set of embeddings of values within the column (hereafter, value embedding set).

$$H_c = \{\mathbf{h}_1, \mathbf{h}_2, \dots, \mathbf{h}_{n_c}\} \tag{3}$$

At this stage, the order of column values is not considered.

We use two types of Set Encoders to aggregate the value embedding set into a column representation.

$$f(H_c) = f(\{\mathbf{h}_{\pi(1)}, \dots, \mathbf{h}_{\pi(n_c)}\}) \tag{4}$$

Here, π denotes an arbitrary permutation.

Column Representation Learning Based on Deep Sets. Deep Sets is a method based on the idea that a permutation-invariant function on a set can be represented in the following form.

$$\mathbf{z}_c = \rho\left(\sum_{\mathbf{h}_i \in H_c} \phi(\mathbf{h}_i)\right) \tag{5}$$

In Eq. (5), $\phi\cdot$ is a multilayer perceptron (MLP) applied to each value within a column, and $\rho\cdot$ is an MLP that integrates the entire set. This structure guarantees permutation invariance for any permutation π.

$$\rho\left(\sum_i \phi(\mathbf{h}_i)\right) = \rho\left(\sum_i \phi(\mathbf{h}_{\pi(i)})\right) \tag{6}$$

Due to the structure of Eq. (6), it is possible to obtain a column representation that does not depend on the order of column values and can handle a variable number of column values. Deep Sets has a simple structure and high computational efficiency, making it suitable for large-scale data.

Column Representation Learning Based on Set Transformer. Although Deep Sets provides a simple and efficient way to obtain permutation-invariant column representations, it processes each value independently before aggregation. Therefore, it does not explicitly model interactions among column values. To address this limitation, we also apply Set Transformer as another Set Encoder variant in the proposed framework.

The Set Transformer encoder in the proposed framework consists of an Induced Set Attention Block (ISAB), a Set Attention Block (SAB), and Pooling by Multihead Attention (PMA). First, ISAB is applied to the value embedding set H_c in order to efficiently model interactions among values using inducing points:

$$H_c'' = \mathrm{ISAB}(H_c). \tag{7}$$

ISAB reduces the computational cost of full self-attention by introducing a set of learnable inducing points. This makes ISAB suitable for encoding columns whose number of values varies across columns and can be large in real-world data lakes.

Next, SAB is applied to the output of ISAB to further refine the set representation by modeling interactions among the transformed value embeddings:

$$H'_c = \mathrm{SAB}(H''_c). \tag{8}$$

Through this process, the Set Transformer can capture relationships among column values while maintaining permutation invariance. After that, the whole set is aggregated by PMA to obtain a fixed-dimensional column representation:

$$\mathbf{z}_c = \mathrm{PMA}(H'_c). \tag{9}$$

Thus, the overall encoding process of the Set Transformer can be summarized as follows:

$$\mathbf{z}_c = \mathrm{PMA}\left(\mathrm{SAB}\left(\mathrm{ISAB}(H_c)\right)\right). \tag{10}$$

This structure enables column representation learning that considers not only the semantic characteristics of individual values but also the relationships among column values. In particular, ISAB provides an efficient attention-based approximation for scalable set encoding, SAB further captures value-level interactions, and PMA aggregates the resulting set representation into a fixed-dimensional column vector. As a result, the Set Transformer can produce an order-invariant column representation while considering representative and relational patterns in the value set.

3.3 Joinable Column Search

To balance efficiency and expressiveness, we adopt a two-stage retrieval framework. In the first stage, cosine similarity is used to retrieve a small set of candidate columns from the ANN index, because it can be computed efficiently at scale. In the second stage, the retrieved candidates are re-ranked using the learned MLP scorer, which captures non-linear interactions between column representations.

Candidate Retrieval. We first retrieve candidate columns using cosine similarity in the embedding space:

$$s_{\mathrm{retrieve}}(c_q, c_i) = \mathrm{sim}(\mathbf{z}_{c_q}, \mathbf{z}_{c_i}) \tag{11}$$

Cosine similarity is suitable for this stage because it can be efficiently combined with ANN indexing methods such as HNSW [15], enabling scalable retrieval over large collections.

Re-ranking. The retrieved candidates are then re-ranked using the learned MLP scoring function:

$$s_{\text{rank}}(c_q, c_i) = \text{MLP}([z_q; z_i; |z_q - z_i|; z_q \odot z_i]) \tag{12}$$

This second stage refines the ranking by capturing non-linear and feature-level interactions that cannot be fully represented by cosine similarity alone. By restricting the MLP computation to only a small candidate set, our method maintains scalability while improving ranking accuracy. The final output is obtained by selecting the top-ranked columns based on s_{rank}.

4 Experiments

This section describes the evaluation experiments conducted to verify the effectiveness of our method. The experiments were designed with reference to the environment of LakeBench [5], a benchmark specialized for the table join task, and evaluated joinable column search performance on large-scale tabular data. Specifically, we analyze (1) the validity of the set-based representation assumption for joinable column search (RQ1), (2) the impact of Set Encoder Architecture (RQ2), and (3) the robustness of our method to variations in value ordering within table data (RQ3).

4.1 Datasets

For evaluation, we used the following datasets provided by LakeBench [5]. These datasets are widely used benchmarks for table join tasks and contain large-scale and heterogeneous tabular data, making them suitable for evaluating both scalability and robustness.

The Open Data dataset is constructed from public open data, whereas the Web Table dataset is constructed from tables collected from the Web. They contain large-scale and diverse table structures. In each dataset, joinable column pairs are provided as positive examples and non-joinable column pairs as negative examples. In our experiments, we divided the labeled join query into three subsets in a 2:1:1 ratio for train, validation, and test.

- **Open Data**[1] **:** A dataset composed of publicly available open data, containing diverse table formats and column granularities [17]. The OpenData dataset contains 3,171 join queries.
- **Web Table**[2] **:** A dataset constructed based on tables collected from the Web, containing substantial noise and variations in notation. The Web Table dataset contains 5,824 join queries.

[1] Open Data, https://open.canada.ca/en, accessed on: September 21, 2026.
[2] Web Table, https://webdatacommons.org/WebTables/, accessed on: September 21, 2026.

4.2 Language Models

PLMs were used to generate embeddings of values within columns. In our experiments, two types of language models were used, and their performance when combined with Set Encoders was compared.

DistilBERT [18] is a model obtained by distilling BERT, combining fast inference performance with stable language understanding capability. It can generate effective embeddings even for short text such as values within Web table columns. CANINE [2] is a language model that processes inputs at the character level and does not depend on subword segmentation. It can learn robust representations even for values within columns that contain many numbers and symbols.

To ensure fairness of comparison, DistilBERT was fixed in the comparison with existing methods (RQ1). To analyze RQ2, we compare different combinations of Set Encoder architectures and PLMs by switching between DistilBERT and CANINE for value-level embedding generation. This setup allows us to analyze how the choice of language model interacts with Set Encoder-based representation learning.

4.3 Comparison Methods

To verify the effectiveness of our method, we evaluated it against representative existing methods for the table join task: DeepJoin [6] and TabSketchFM [13]. All of these methods were proposed for searching joinable columns in large-scale tabular data.

The methods used in the comparative experiments are as follows.

DeepJoin: A deep learning-based method that learns column representations using a PLM and estimates semantic joinability between columns in a regression manner without relying on lexical matching.

TabSketchFM: TabSketchFM is a neural tabular model that uses sketch-based pre-training and fine-tuning for data discovery tasks. Following its joinability setting, we use the sketch-based column representations produced by the model, including numerical and MinHash sketches, for column-level retrieval.

Proposed Method (Deep Sets): A supervised column representation learning method based on a Set Encoder that applies Deep Sets to value sets.

Proposed Method (Set Transformer): A method that applies Set Transformer to value sets and learns column representations while considering relationships among column values.

These methods were selected because they represent different approaches to joinable column search, including deep learning-based semantic matching (DeepJoin) and sketch-based pre-training (TabSketchFM).

4.4 Evaluation Metrics

For evaluation metrics, we used ranking metrics adopted in LakeBench. In addition, performance was measured using Precision, Recall, and NDCG for the top

$K \in \{5, 10, 20, 30, 40, 50\}$ search results. Each metric is reported as the average over all queries.

Precision ($P@K$)**:** The proportion of correct results among the top K predicted results

Recall ($R@K$)**:** The proportion of all existing correct answers that are included in the top K

NDCG [10] ($NDCG@k$)**:** A metric for evaluating ranking quality while taking rank positions into account

4.5 Environments

All models were implemented in PyTorch and trained using the Hugging Face Transformers library. Unless otherwise specified, we used a batch size of 64, a learning rate of 2×10^{-5}, and a weight decay of 0.01. All experiments were conducted on a single compute node equipped with two Intel Xeon Platinum 8558 CPUs, NVIDIA H200 SXM5 GPUs, 2 TB of main memory, and two 7.68 TB NVMe SSDs. The node was connected through InfiniBand NDR200 links, with InfiniBand HDR used for the storage interconnect.

5 Discussion

This section presents the results and discussion of the evaluation experiments for each RQ. Our method outperformed existing methods such as DeepJoin and TabSketchFM in many evaluation settings. In particular, regardless of the dataset, the proportion of joinable columns appearing at higher ranks was greatly improved, indicating that our method can learn an embedding space suitable for joinable column search.

5.1 Set-Based Representation Assumption for Joinable Column Search (RQ1)

RQ1 examines whether the set-based representation assumption is more appropriate for joinable column search than the ordered-sequence assumption. From the results shown in Figs. 2, 3 and 4, we observe that the proposed set-based column modeling approach achieves performance comparable to or better than other methods across Precision, Recall, and NDCG on both the Web Table and Open Data datasets.

Our method reduces the dependence on arbitrary value order by explicitly modeling a column as an unordered set of values. Each cell value is first encoded using a PLM, and the resulting value embeddings are then aggregated using a Set Encoder. This allows the model to capture the semantic and distributional characteristics of the column while reducing dependence on the arbitrary order of column values.

These results support the assumption that a column should be represented as an unordered set of values rather than as an ordered sequence. In joinable column search, the essential information lies in the semantic domain and value distribution of a column, not in the order in which its values appear. Therefore, imposing an ordered-sequence structure on column values introduces an unnecessary inductive bias, because the row order of a table can be changed by preprocessing, sorting, extraction, or storage procedures without changing the joinability of the column.

The improvements in Recall and NDCG further indicate that the proposed set-based representation is effective not only for retrieving joinable columns but also for ranking them appropriately. This suggests that the learned representation forms a meaningful semantic neighborhood in the embedding space, allowing multiple joinable candidates to be placed near the query column. Such behavior is difficult to achieve with approaches that rely mainly on lexical overlap, simple set similarity, or sequence-sensitive representations.

Overall, the results support the validity of the set-based representation assumption. By removing unnecessary order dependency, our method reduces the risk of learning spurious ordering patterns and provides a more suitable inductive bias for learning joinability-aware column representations (Fig. 3).

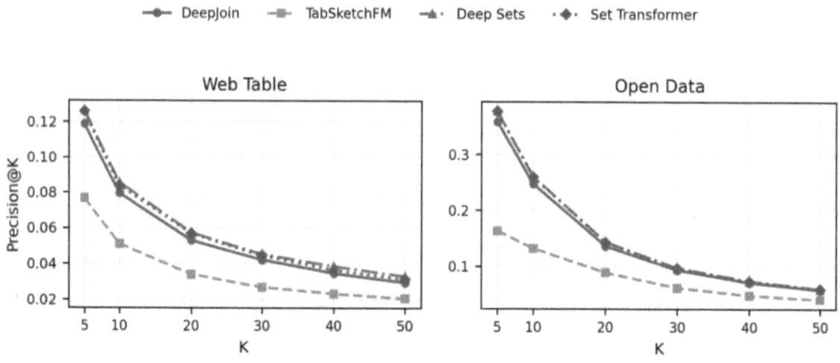

Fig. 2. Precision@K comparison across datasets

5.2 Effect of Permutation-Invariant Aggregation and PLMs (RQ2)

Next, we analyze how the choice of Set Encoder architecture affects the performance of joinable column search. In the proposed framework, we implement set-based column encoding using two representative Set Encoder variants: Deep Sets and Set Transformer. We further compare these Set Encoders using DistilBERT and CANINE, which were described in the experimental setup, to examine how the combination of aggregation architecture and value representation influences joinable column retrieval.

Figure 5 shows the retrieval effectiveness of different combinations of Set Encoders and PLMs. Focusing on the Set Encoder architecture, Deep Sets achieves stable and strong results across evaluation metrics, particularly when

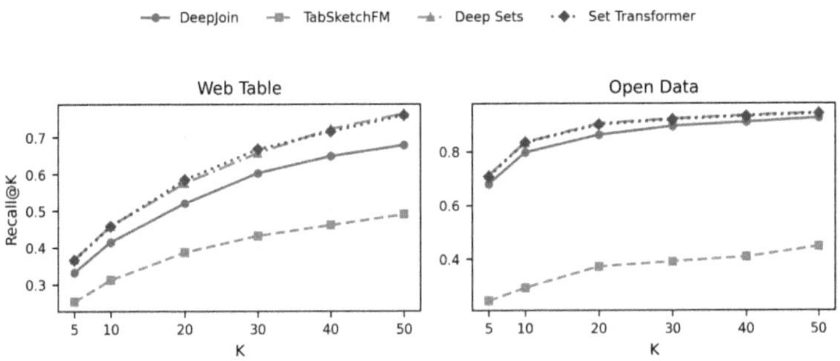

Fig. 3. Recall@K comparison across datasets

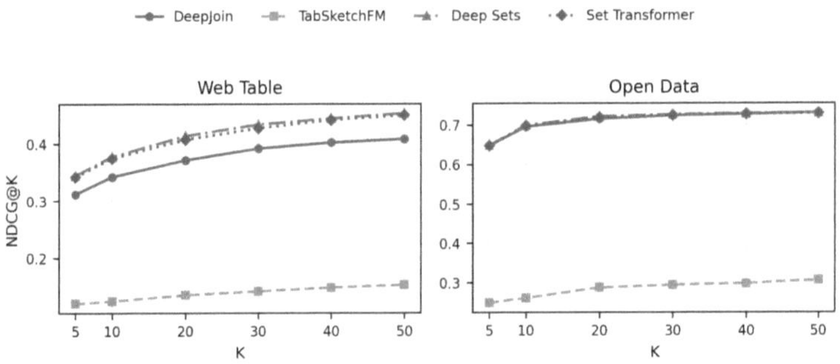

Fig. 4. NDCG@K comparison across datasets

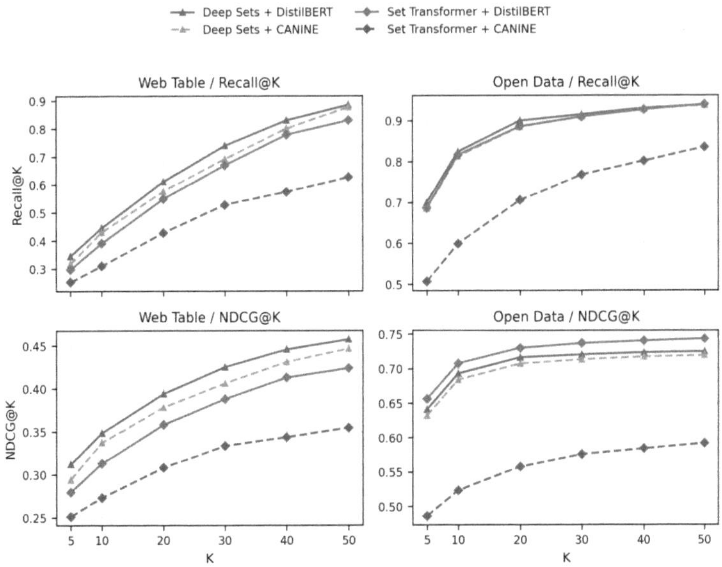

Fig. 5. Comparison of PLMs (DistilBERT vs CANINE)

combined with DistilBERT. This suggests that simple permutation-invariant aggregation is effective when the input value embeddings already capture meaningful semantic information.

Set Transformer, which models interactions among values through attention-based set modeling, also achieves competitive results in several settings. However, when combined with CANINE, its effectiveness tends to decrease in some cases. This may be due to the interaction between CANINE's character-level representations and the attention-based aggregation mechanism of Set Transformer. When value embeddings are generated by CANINE, the attention-based aggregation mechanism of Set Transformer may emphasize local or surface-level variations in character-level representations. Although this can be beneficial for tasks that rely on fine-grained relationships among set elements, it may be less suitable for joinable column search, where compatibility is mainly determined by shared semantic domains or overall value distributions.

These results indicate that, for joinable column search, capturing the global distribution of value representations is often sufficient for effective retrieval. Deep Sets offers high computational efficiency due to its element-wise transformation and aggregation approach. Set Transformer, on the other hand, provides a more expressive aggregation mechanism by modeling interactions among values through attention-based set modeling, although this expressiveness comes with additional computational cost. For the datasets considered here, this suggests that effective retrieval mainly requires column representations that reflect the overall semantic domain and value distribution.

5.3 Robustness to Order Variations in Table Data (RQ3)

To evaluate the robustness of joinability estimation with respect to input ordering, we conducted a query-side shuffle experiment. Since column values in relational tables do not have an intrinsic order, an appropriate column representation for joinable column search should be stable with respect to permutations of the input values. For a shuffle ratio $p \in \{30, 50, 100\}$, we randomly selected $p\%$ of the values within each query column and permuted only the selected values. We use these three shuffle ratios to examine different levels of order perturbation, because sequence-based methods may be affected differently depending on how much of the original value order is preserved. This setting allows us to isolate the effect of input-order perturbation at query time.

We define performance retention as the ratio between the performance under the shuffled setting and the performance under the original setting:

$$\text{Retention}_{m@k}(p) = \frac{m@k(\mathcal{Q}^{(p)}, \mathcal{D})}{m@k(\mathcal{Q}^{(0)}, \mathcal{D})} \times 100, \tag{13}$$

where $m@k$ denotes an evaluation metric such as Precision@k, Recall@k, or NDCG@k. $\mathcal{Q}^{(0)}$ denotes the original query columns, $\mathcal{Q}^{(p)}$ denotes the query columns after applying $p\%$ shuffle, and $\mathcal{D}$ denotes the unchanged database columns. A retention value close to 100% indicates that the model preserves its original performance even after the query column order is perturbed.

Figure 6 shows the performance under the shuffle setting and the corresponding performance retention. We mainly report the results under the 50% shuffle setting, because the 30% and 100% shuffle settings showed similar trends.

Our method uses two Set Encoder variants, Deep Sets and Set Transformer, both of which preserve retrieval effectiveness after shuffling at levels comparable to those obtained with the original query columns. This result indicates that the proposed set-based column encoding is robust to order variations in table data.

This robustness stems from the structure of our method. Deep Sets and Set Transformer differ in their aggregation mechanisms, but both are designed to construct column representations without depending on the input order. Thus, the resulting representations mainly encode order-independent information about the column values, rather than relying on their arrangement.

In contrast, the baseline method DeepJoin shows noticeable performance degradation after shuffling. Its average performance retention decreases to approximately 72.0% for Precision, 74.7% for Recall, and 57.2% for NDCG compared with the original results. This performance drop indicates that sequence-based representations are sensitive to perturbations in value ordering. TabSketchFM also shows sensitivity in terms of Recall, although its Precision and NDCG remain almost unchanged.

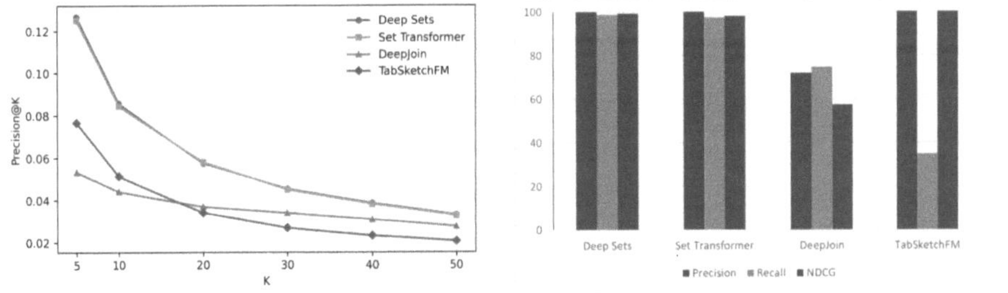

(a) Precision@K under shuffle (b) Performance retention after shuffle

Fig. 6. Robustness analysis under the 50% shuffle setting. The proposed Set Encoder variants, Deep Sets and Set Transformer, maintain stable performance after perturbing the order of values in query columns.

6 Conclusion

In this study, we revisited the fundamental assumption in table join discovery and argued that a column should be modeled as an unordered set rather than an ordered sequence. Based on this perspective, we proposed a supervised column representation learning method using Set Encoders, which enables order-invariant modeling of column values.

Experimental results on both Web Table and Open Data datasets showed that our method achieves competitive or better performance than existing methods across multiple evaluation metrics. These findings support the view that set-based modeling provides a more appropriate inductive bias than sequence-based approaches for capturing the intrinsic characteristics of tabular data.

Furthermore, the results revealed that explicitly modeling columns as sets leads to more stable and robust representations. In particular, our method maintained performance even under random shuffling of column values, highlighting its invariance to input ordering and its suitability for real-world tabular data. This property is particularly important in practical environments, where the order of data may be arbitrarily affected by preprocessing steps.

Overall, the results indicate that removing unnecessary order dependence is useful for learning reliable column representations for joinable column search. By removing unnecessary order dependency, our method achieves both improved performance and enhanced robustness.

As future work, reducing the computational cost of value-level embedding and extending the framework to incorporate table-level semantics remain important directions. Such extensions will further improve scalability and applicability in large-scale data lake environments.

Acknowledgments. This work was conducted with support from the policy budget project of the National Institute of Advanced Industrial Science and Technology, "Research and Development on Foundation Models of Generative AI for the Physical Domain," JSPS KAKENHI Number JP23H03694 and JP23H03401, and the JST Support for Pioneering Research Initiated by the Next Generation program JPMJSP2129.

References

1. Chen, J., Jiménez-Ruiz, E., Horrocks, I. and Sutton, C.: Learning semantic annotations for tabular data. In: Proceedings of the Twenty-Eighth International Joint Conference on Artificial Intelligence, pp. 2088–2094 (2019)
2. Jonathan, H., Clark, D., Garrette, I., Turc, J., Wieting: Pre-training an efficient tokenization-free encoder for language representation. Canine. Trans. Assoc. Comput. Linguist. **10**, 73–91 (2022)
3. Cong, T., Nargesian, F., Jagadish, H.V.: Pylon: Semantic table union search in data lakes. CoRR, abs/2301.04901 (2023)
4. Dargahi Nobari, A., Rafiei, D.: DTT: An example-driven tabular transformer for joinability by leveraging large language models. Proc. ACM Manage. Data **2**(1), (2024)
5. Deng, Y., et al.: Lakebench: a benchmark for discovering joinable and unionable tables in data lakes. Proc. VLDB Endowment **17**(8), 1925–1938 (2024)
6. Dong, Y., Xiao, C., Nozawa, T., Enomoto, M., Oyamada, M.: Deepjoin: joinable table discovery with pre-trained language models. Proc. VLDB Endowment **16**(10), 2458–2470 (2023)
7. Fan, G., Wang, J., Li, Y., Miller, R.J.: Table discovery in data lakes: State-of-the-art and future directions. In: Companion of the 2023 International Conference on Management of Data, pp. 69–75 (2023)

8. Fan, G., Wang, J., Li, Y., Zhang, D., Miller, R.: Semantics-aware dataset discovery from data lakes with contextualized column-based representation learning. Proc. VLDB Endowment **16**(7), 1726–1739 (2023)
9. Gim, M., Park, D., Spranger, M., Maruyama, K., Kang, J.: Recipebowl: a cooking recommender for ingredients and recipes using set transformer. IEEE Access **9**, 143623–143633 (2021)
10. Järvelin, K., Kekäläinen, J.: Cumulated gain-based evaluation of IR techniques. ACM Trans. Inform. Syst. **20**(4), 422–446 (2002)
11. Ji, D., Luo, H., Bao, Z., Culpepper, J.S.: Table integration in data lakes unleashed: Pairwise integrability judgment, integrable set discovery, and multi-tuple conflict resolution. VLDB J. **34**(3), 36 (2025)
12. Kang, J., Naughton, J.F.: On schema matching with opaque column names and data values. In: Proceedings of the 2003 ACM SIGMOD International Conference on Management of Data, pp. 205–216 (2003)
13. Khatiwada, A., et al. Tabsketchfm: Sketch-based tabular representation learning for data discovery over data lakes. In: 2025 IEEE 41st International Conference on Data Engineering (ICDE), pp. 1523–1536 (2025)
14. Lee, J., et al.: Set transformer: A framework for attention-based permutation-invariant neural networks. In: International Conference on Machine Learning, pp. 3744–3753. Proceedings of Machine Learning Research (2019)
15. Malkov, Y.A., Yashunin, D.A.: Efficient and robust approximate nearest neighbor search using hierarchical navigable small world graphs. IEEE Trans. Pattern Anal. Mach. Intell. **42**(04), 824–836 (2020)
16. Mouravieff, R., Piwowarski, B., Lamprier, S.: Structural deep encoding for table question answering. In: Findings of the Association for Computational Linguistics: ACL, pp. 2389–2402 (2025)
17. Nargesian, F., Zhu, E., Pu, K.Q., Miller, R.J.: Table union search on open data. Proc. VLDB Endowment **11**(7), 813–825 (2018)
18. Sanh, V., Debut, L., Chaumond, J., Wolf, T.: Distilbert, a distilled version of bert: smaller, faster, cheaper and lighter. arXiv preprint arXiv:1910.01108 (2019)
19. Santos, A., Bessa, A., Chirigati, F., Musco, C., Freire, J.: Correlation sketches for approximate join-correlation queries. In: Proceedings of the 2021 International Conference on Management of Data, pp. 1531–1544 (2021)
20. Subramaniam, P., Khurana, U., Srinivas, K., Samulowitz, H.: Numjoin: Discovering numeric joinable tables with semantically related columns. In: Proceedings of the 32nd ACM International Conference on Information and Knowledge Management, pp. 5096–5100 (2023)
21. Vaswani, A., et al. Attention is all you need. In: Advances in Neural Information Processing Systems, vol. 30 (2017)
22. Pengxiang, W., Chen, C., Yi, J., Metaxas, D.: Point cloud processing via recurrent set encoding. Proc. AAAI Conf. Artif. Intell. **33**(01), 5441–5449 (2019)
23. Xie, J., Tong, G.: Advances in set function learning: a survey of techniques and applications. ACM Comput. Surv. **57**(7), (2025)
24. Yang, J., et al.: TableFormer: robust transformer modeling for table-text encoding. In: Proceedings of the 60th Annual Meeting of the Association for Computational Linguistics (Volume 1: Long Papers), pp. 528–537 (2022)
25. Yin, P., Neubig, G., Yih, W.T., Riedel, S.: Tabert: Pretraining for joint understanding of textual and tabular data. arXiv preprint arXiv:2005.08314 (2020)
26. Zaheer, Z., et al:. Deep sets. In: Advances in Neural Information Processing Systems, vol. 30 (2017)

27. Zheng, Y., Tang, Z., Qiu, Y., Schölkopf, B., Zhang, K.: Detecting and identifying selection structure in sequential data. In: Proceedings of the 41st International Conference on Machine Learning (2024)
28. Zhu, E., Nargesian, F., Pu, K.Q. and Miller, R.J.: LSH ensemble: internet-scale domain search. Proc. VLDB Endowment **9**(12), 1185–1196 (2016)

Embedding Generation: *Gembed* an Open In-Database Extension to Use Them All

Joel Díaz(✉) and Alberto Abelló

Universitat Politècnica de Catalunya, 08034 Barcelona, Spain
joeldiazalvarez2@gmail.com, alberto.abello@upc.edu

Abstract. Deep-learning has become pervasive, finding new applications every day. One of these is the generation of *embeddings* (i.e., high-dimensional numerical vectors) capturing the semantics of different kinds of unstructured data (e.g., natural language, images). The relevance of embeddings in multiple domains has given rise to a plethora of libraries and models to generate them, but also different specialized storage systems to manage and compare such high-dimensional vectors. Instead, we present a portable, extensible, and interoperable software artifact that facilitates the encapsulation of any of those libraries and models in a general-purpose DBMS through its own extension mechanism. We demonstrate this by creating open-source extensions for PostgreSQL, MySQL and Redis, and experimentally showing the performance improvement of in-database embedding generation.

Keywords: Embedding generation · In-database processing · Portability · Extensibility · Interoperability

1 Introduction

The convergence of Artificial Intelligence (AI) and data management has fundamentally reshaped how information is stored, analyzed, and retrieved. Central to this shift is the concept of *embeddings*, which are numerical representations of data projected into a continuous high-dimensional vector space that capture semantic meaning and context. They have become the foundational layer for cutting-edge applications like semantic search, content recommendation, and, most notably, Retrieval-Augmented Generation (RAG) systems [16]. They can be generated by different specific embedding models. Although these can belong to different neural network (NN) architectures (e.g., BERT for text, ViT for images, or CLIP and SigLIP for both), the generation is always a computationally expensive task involving large amounts of matrix multiplications as the data passes through the multiple layers of the NN, which often requires specialized hardware like GPUs. Indeed, the cost grows with the size of both the input and the output vector. Moreover, using an external/remote inference service introduces significant latency (serialization and network overhead). Recognising this new challenge, modern RDBMSs have started to incorporate native support for

G. Vargas-Solar et al. (Eds.): ADBIS 2026, LNCS 16937, pp. 371–387, 2027.
https://doi.org/10.1007/978-3-032-39820-8_24

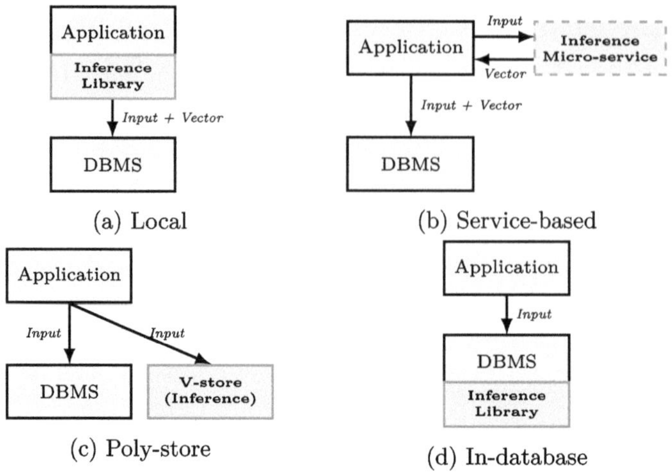

Fig. 1. Existing embedding generation architectures

vector data types, operators, and indexes [10]. However, most of them still do not support vector generation or do it in a limited and rigid way.

Thus, Fig. 1 illustrates the four basic architectural patterns of embedding generation (a.k.a. inference) and storage (combinations are possible). Figure 1a corresponds to the use of a library inside the same application (typically in Python). However, because of either using some external inference provider or due to the lack of mature native tools for embedding generation in languages like Go, Java or C#, developers can also be forced to separately handle vectorization tasks in the form of (Python-based) micro-services, as sketched in Fig. 1b, adding architectural complexity and especially network latency. These two patterns result in high-dimensional vectors being transferred to the DBMS for storage and indexing. Indeed, the size of these vectors depends on the model being used, but typically ranges from 128 to 4096 dimensions, which results in a significant size increment, compared to only inserting the corresponding data. Moreover, in the case of requiring an inference provider, remote access also adds an economic cost. Alternatively, Fig. 1c depicts the possibility of including a poly-store architecture using a generic DBMS for tabular/semi-structured data and a specialised store (V-store) for generating, storing, managing, and indexing high-dimensional vectors [8], which in turn complicates and penalizes the performance of typical RAG hybrid queries involving both kinds of data together. Finally, we have the option, as in Fig. 1d, of delegating the vectorization to the generic but enhanced DBMS [9,13].

Thus, we advocate for the latter, including the vector generation inside the DBMS. This is clearly, aligned with recent research efforts [4,5], but also with DBMS industry (see Sect. 2). However, existing in-database implementations are proprietary and tightly coupled to the engine, preventing portability across different systems. Also, they are frequently limited to text-based inputs, failing to flexibly accommodate the increasing need for multi-modal embedding. Furthermore, they often lack the flexibility to choose the most appropriate model (there are tens of thousands to choose in a public repository like HuggingFace), and support diverse execution strategies (such as leveraging GPUs), communication protocols (e.g., HTTP, gRPC), or simply choosing the most appropriate inference engine (e.g., LibTorch, ONNX Runtime, Candle, TensorRT). Indeed, having in-database vector generation should not mean we cannot plug the best and most recent contributions of the community.

Contributions. This paper addresses these limitations by proposing and evaluating *Gembed*, a unified novel extension for flexible in-database embedding generation. Its contributions are: (1) **Portability** to any DBMS (Relational or not) as soon as it supports C extensibility (demonstrated with PostgreSQL, MySQL, Redis, and in general any Java application[1]); (2) **Extensibility** by registering new inference engines (demonstrated with ONNX Runtime and Candle, through FastEmbed and EmbedAnything wrappers) and embedding models (demonstrated with five of them downloaded from HuggingFace); (3) **Interoperability** by implementing a single interface, ensuring it is agnostic of the of the information exchange mechanisms; this facilitates to (a) choose between local or remote embedding (demonstrated with HTTP and gRPC protocols); and (b) be ready for multi-modal workloads by just treating inputs as generic containers (demonstrated for text and image); (4) **Empirically demonstrate** that in-database embedding generation reduces both complexity and cost compared to the use of a library, a micro-service and a poly-store architecture.

The paper is organized as follows. Section 2 presents the related work. Section 3 details the proposed software architecture and Sect. 4 its implementation in PostgreSQL, whose performance is scrutinized in Sect. 5. Section 6 draws some important take-away messages and Sect. 7 concludes the paper.

2 Related Work

The primary functionality of V-stores is to perform efficient Approximate Nearest Neighbor (ANN) searches [14], which find the most similar vectors to a given (query) vector by implementing techniques like *Hierarchical Navigable Small World* (HNSW), *Inverted File Index* (IVF), or *DiskANN* [15]. Popular examples of V-stores (surveyed in [12]) are ChromaDB,[2] Qdrant,[3] or Hakes[4] [6]. These systems often operate as standalone services, but more often, because of lacking many of the features offered by a DBMS, they require data to be synchronized from the primary operational database (usually an RDBMS), leading to a polystore architecture as in Fig. 1c.

[1] https://github.com/JoelDiaz222/pg_gembed|mysql_gembed|redis_gembed|spring-gembed-demo.
[2] https://docs.trychroma.com/docs/overview/introduction.
[3] https://qdrant.tech.
[4] https://github.com/nusdbsystem/HAKES.

One could think of simplifying that architecture by just representing embeddings as regular arrays of floating point numbers, as any RDBMS supports. However, this creates an impedance mismatch, and the lack of specialized operators hinders distance calculations and complicates queries. Thus, most mainstream RDBMSs have also developed their native support for vector management, including specialized data types, optimized operators, and indexes: PostgreSQL (since 2021), SQLite (2024), Oracle Database (2024), MySQL (2024), MariaDB (2025), and Microsoft SQL Server (2025). An analysis of the performance of both V-stores and RDBMS (especially in RAG) can be found in [1,7,11].

V-stores like Chroma and Qdrant support not only vector management, but also vector generation. Nevertheless, this can hardly be considered "in-database" since they do not share the complexity of a true DBMS. Regarding other NOSQL systems, MongoDB recommends vectorizing in the application layer, but already has a functionality in preview to embed remotely using Voyager.[5] Others like Google Cloud Spanner and BigQuery as well as Snowflake also offer vectorization as a service through their API, always limited to their data types and models.

On the other hand, some RDBMS do support in-database embedding generation, either natively or through extensions. *Oracle for AI* includes text embedding generation locally via the ONNX Runtime, and remotely through REST providers; and multi-modal embedding, like images using CLIP.[6] *MySQL Community Edition* does not currently include this feature, but *MySQL AI* and *MySQL HeatWave GenAI* do include routines to generate embeddings in-database, either for individual texts or in batches.[7] Finally, in PostgreSQL, there are two main extensions: *PostgresML*[8] and *pgai*[9] to generate embeddings. The former takes full advantage of GPUs alongside the database engine to provide access to LLMs, RAG pipelines (including only embedding generation from text), vector search, ML algorithms and NLP tasks inside the database engine. In contrast, the latter relies on using inference providers (such as OpenAI or AWS Bedrock) for text embedding generation and calling LLMs via the SQL interface. A notable downside of this implementation is that it runs in a separate Python process.

Gembed is not a replacement for all those embedding possibilities, but an enhancement that allows to easily and flexibly generate vectors inside DBMSs with a single interface for any input and using the backend and model required by the user. Architecturally, it follows the well-established pattern of extending a DBMS via UDFs/UDTs to wrap external libraries, as pioneered by PostGIS[10] for geospatial data. However, embedding models add concerns central to *Gembed*

---

[5] https://www.voyageai.com.

[6] https://docs.oracle.com/en/database/oracle/oracle-database/26/vecse/generate-embeddings.html.

[7] https://dev.mysql.com/doc/mysql-ai/9.6/en.

[8] https://github.com/postgresml/postgresml.

[9] https://github.com/timescale/pgai.

[10] https://postgis.net.

that this pattern traditionally lacks: caching large model weights across calls, and routing across heterogeneous local (CPU/GPU) and remote inference backends.

3 Proposed Architecture

To address the limitations of existing embedding generation, specifically the data shipping overhead as well as architectural complexity and rigidity described in previous sections, we propose *Gembed*. The fundamental shift is moving the inference logic that is typically handled in the application directly into the DBMS, and further define three different components that separate concerns: The DBMS *Adapter* handles database-specific data marshaling and type conversion, the *Core* manages inference engine routing and memory ownership, and the *Backend* performs the actual mathematical operations for vectorization.

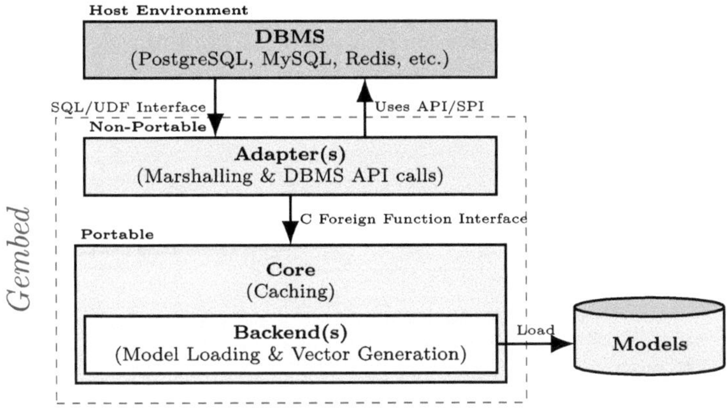

Fig. 2. Layered architecture

As stated in Sect. 1, the main contributions of this architecture are portability, extensibility and interoperability, decoupling the inference logic from the DBMS. Hence, the architecture is layered as shown in Fig. 2. Firstly, in order for the *Core* to be portable, it should not depend on specific characteristics of the DBMS it runs on. Indeed, we have a DBMS-specific *Adapter*, handling data formats transformations and communication with the corresponding host. Then, we use C Foreign Function Interface (C-FFI), which is a way of allowing interoperability between different programming languages. This ensures that the *Core* logic is shielded and remains independent of the DBMS, but at the same time provides high-performance embedding logic through a pluggable interface that allows being extended with new inference engines. Plugging *Backends*, each corresponding to a local or remote inference engine and the corresponding communication protocol, is done statically (i.e., recompiling the *Core*), which is more robust and faster. As a downside, in order to add a new one, the source code has to be modified and the *Core* recompiled. However, this is not a frequent task, and anyway could be automated. Alternatively, *Backends* could also be plugged dynamically, which would be more convenient for the user. Finally, embedding *Models* can be in either a local or remote repository, and loaded dynamically, though for robustness they can also be registered at compile time.

Adapter. This part of the architecture is a thin layer, necessary for decoupling the *Core* from the concrete DBMS. It has to be tailor-made for each DBMS (using its own extensibility mechanism). The layer's responsibilities are:

1. **Marshal the input:** It transforms DBMS-specific types into standard C-compatible types. An example of this, in Fig. 3, is converting a PostgreSQL array of texts into an array of string slices (i.e., pointers and lengths). Then, data must be transformed into native Rust strings encoded in UTF-8.
2. **Call the C-FFI exposed by the *Core*:** Once the input types are compatible with the API, it calls the *Core*. Functions must be declared either "`extern`" in C or "`native`" in Java.
3. **Marshal the output:** Once the call to the *Core* returns, the output has to be turned back into DBMS-specific types. Any memory allocated for the embedding generation should also be freed at this point.

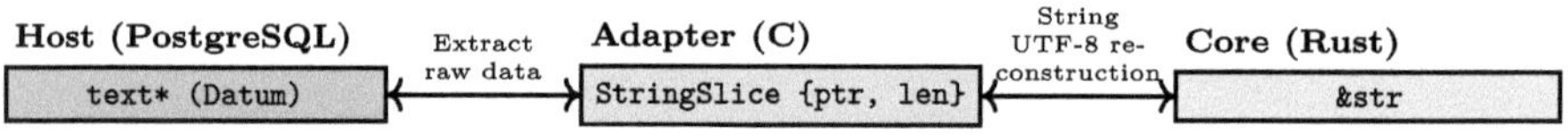

Fig. 3. Example of text marshaling

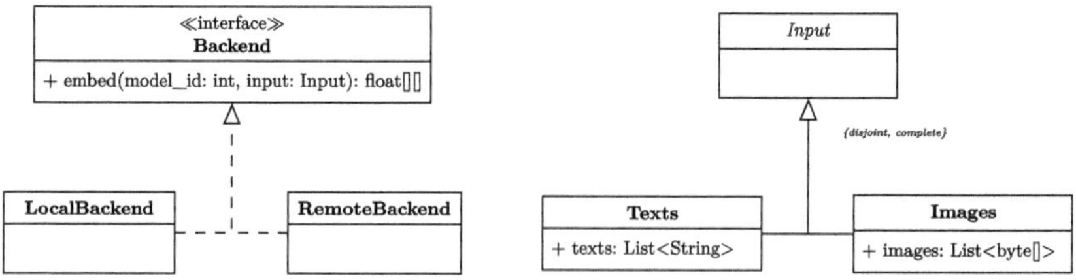

Fig. 4. Class diagram of the *strategy pattern*

Core. On the one hand, not all DBMS engines are written in the same programming language (e.g., PostgreSQL is written in C, MySQL in C++, and H2 and Neo4j in Java). To achieve cross-language portability in a performant way, the *Core* exposes a standard interface through C-FFI. On the other hand, another key aspect is offering an easy way to add inference engines to the *Core*, which is based on the software design *strategy pattern* that abstracts the logic of a set of algorithms into separate interchangeable classes [3] (see Fig. 4). Thus, adding a new engine is as easy as creating a class and implementing the common interface, which contains the necessary methods for embedding generation.

Backend. Finally, we can plug any local library or remote service to generate embeddings for any data type. Thus, the user can choose the most appropriate embedding engine (e.g., depending on the available hardware) and model (e.g., by domain or generated vector size) to be executed either locally or remotely, which are then fed from a common `Input` class, specialized according to the kind of input provided. Indeed, embeddings are model-specific, not input-specific (e.g., OpenCLIP[11] can embed texts, images, or both at the same time, since it is multi-modal).

4 Implementation

In the next subsections, we go into more depth on the implementation details of the *Core* and the corresponding PostgreSQL *Adapter* to explain how they help to achieve our goals.

4.1 Core

The first choice when implementing the *Core*[12] is the programming language. To consider portability, it must be callable from multiple programming languages, since not all DBMS engines are written in the same one. Embedding generation should be done as quickly as possible, so a compiled language (e.g., C) is preferred over an interpreted one (e.g., Python). Moreover, enforcing safety is a concern, as the *Core* has to run alongside the DBMS engine and it cannot cause it to crash. With all this in mind, the choice was *Rust*, which is also widely adopted in the AI community, having available high-performance libraries such as FastEmbed or EmbedAnything (wrapping ONNX and ONNX/Candle, respectively), which are used by *Gembed* as *Engines* for local vectorization capabilities.

On the other hand, the internal software architecture relies on three key design patterns (namely *Strategy Pattern*, *Registry Pattern*, and *Inversion of Control*) to decouple the *Core* logic from specific embedding implementations [3], as well as other mechanisms to improve performance (namely *Caching*).

Strategy pattern. The core is built around the `Backend` trait, which serves as the strategy interface and allows the *Core* to remain agnostic of whether vectorization happens locally (e.g., via FastEmbed) or remotely (e.g., via a gRPC client). Thus, the same *Backend* can run different embedding models (e.g., ONNX can use different architectures of embedding models) to vectorize different kinds of inputs (i.e., text, image, etc.).

Registry Pattern and Inversion of Control. The *registry pattern* allows one to manage and access shared objects or instances in a centralized way. In the context

[11] https://github.com/mlfoundations/open_clip.

[12] Made available in https://github.com/JoelDiaz222/gembed.

of the *Core*, we have a `BackendRegistry` that acts as a Service Locator helping manage inference engines. In a typical registration flow, a central registry is not only responsible for maintaining a list of implementations but also for orchestrating their initialization. This would result in a tightly coupled architecture where the *Core* would require explicit knowledge of the backend-specific requirements (e.g., configuration parameters, resource allocation). However, *Gembed* uses *inversion of control*. Instead of the registry explicitly initializing dependencies, individual *Backends* register themselves into a global list at link-time, which effectively decouples them from the *Core*.

Caching. At runtime, the DBMS *Adapter* specifies which data to embed, and the engine and model to do it. Then, the library or framework being used (e.g., SentenceTransformers, OpenCLIP) downloads the model, stores it locally and loads it. However, it still has to be cached to avoid unnecessary reloads. The strategy depends on whether the embedding backend is local or remote. For the former, the embedding model itself must be cached, but for the latter, we simply need the gRPC/HTTP client to be initialized once and then reused, because the actual model caching is handled by the service provider.

4.2 Adapter

This section exemplifies the implementation of an *Adapter* for PostgreSQL, linked to its *pgvector* extension.[13] The reason for choosing PostgreSQL is not only that it is one of the most used RDBMS, but also that it easily allows extensibility, making embedding generation accessible through the SQL interface. Three other implementations have also been done and made available to the community for MySQL, Redis and in general for any Java application,[1] though not detailed here due to lack of space.

```
CREATE FUNCTION embed(backend_name text, model_name text,
    input anynonarray, type input_type) RETURNS vector
AS '<module_pathname>', 'embed_dispatch' LANGUAGE C;
```

Listing 1.1. Signature of a PostgreSQL UDF to embed any non-array data

One of the most important decisions when developing user-defined functions is their signature. For example, we can define the main "embed" function as in Listing 1.1. The parameters that can vary between function invocations are: (1) BackendName (e.g., corresponding to local with the ONNX Runtime or Hugging Face's Candle, or external with a gRPC or HTTP micro-service); (2) ModelName; (3) Input data to vectorize, as well as (4) its type (namely text or image). The underlying implementation of this function is written in C.

The result of embedding generation is converted into a `Datum`, which is the implementation of `vector` data type in *pgvector*. This integration avoids having to cast the embeddings outside the C function to the `vector` data type, thus improving performance and directly allowing users to take advantage of *pgvector*'s operators and indexes.

[13] https://github.com/pgvector/pgvector.

5 Experiments

This section presents the experiments[14] performed to evaluate the implementation of *Gembed* for PostgreSQL (a.k.a. *pg_gembed*). First of all, we need to say that a direct comparison against other PostgreSQL extensions in Sect. 2 is not straightforward, because *pgai*, whose GitHub repository has been recently archived, only allows vectorization in the background, through HTTP calls either remotely or locally with Ollama, and *PostgresML* is also tightly coupled to its engine, uses slower Python bindings and is not integrated with *pgvector*.

Hardware. The hardware used is AMD Ryzen 7950X, with 16 cores and 32 threads, 64 GB, and an NVIDIA GeForce RTX 4090 GPU. All tests were conducted in Python v3.12.3, and the same inference engine, EmbedAnything,[15] was used in the *Gembed Core*, the application layer, and the HTTP and gRPC micro-services. It was chosen because it provides a Rust-based implementation accessible from both Python and Rust, so the performance differences are only attributable to architectural differences rather than the underlying calculations.

Systems. The DBMS was PostgreSQL v18.1, paired with the *pgvector*[13] v0.8.1 for vector operations, storage, and indexing. Regarding V-stores, the chosen alternatives were ChromaDB[2] v1.4.1, and Qdrant[3] v1.16.3, which was run as a Docker v27.3.1 image. The reason for configuring ChromaDB as in-process and Qdrant as a Docker image was to show two common alternatives of V-stores. Thus, some extra network latency when communicating with the Qdrant server is expected, which should not appear when using ChromaDB.

Metrics. Unless otherwise specified, the timing results are reported in seconds, and correspond to the average of ten executions (shown as markers in the charts), accompanied by the standard deviation ranges (represented with two error bars around each) to show statistical dispersion.

Models. The embedding models chosen to generate vectors from sentences are `sentence-transformers/all-MiniLM-L6-v2` (`MiniLM`) and `BAAI/bge-large-en-v1.5` (`bge-large`) with 384 and 1024 dimensions, respectively. For embedding images, the models were `openai/clip-vit-base-patch32`, `openai/clip-vit-large-patch14`, `google/siglip-large-patch16-384` (see Fig. 7a). All of them were downloaded from HuggingFace.

Datasets. The data to be embedded were randomly picked in each of the ten executions from a set of reviews and images generated by the Parallel Data Generation Framework (PDGF) included in the TPCx-AI [2].

The next sections contain experiments to demonstrate the interoperability, extensibility and portability of *Gembed*, as well as the benefit of having in-database embedding generation.

[14] https://github.com/JoelDiaz222/gembed-sandbox/tree/main/python-scripts.

[15] https://embed-anything.com.

5.1 Interoperability

The main purpose of this experiment is to analyze the performance of different interoperability mechanisms for in-database vectorization, in terms of throughput and system resources (namely CPU and memory use). The evaluation consists of embedding different numbers of texts (from 2^5 to 2^{13} in powers of two, which are inserted along with the text they correspond to into PostgreSQL (without any index). We embed text reviews using six different embedding generation configurations: (1) In-Database Local (PG Local), through *pg_gembed* locally; (2) In-Database Remote (PG gRPC), using *pg_gembed* gRPC client to call a micro-service; (3) In-Database Remote (PG HTTP), using *pg_gembed* HTTP client to call a micro-service; (4) Application Local (App. Local), directly within the Python application process before data is sent to the DBMS (used as baseline); (5) Application Remote (App. gRPC), calling an external gRPC microservice before insertion; (6) Application Remote (App. HTTP), calling an external HTTP (FastAPI) micro-service before insertion. However, in order to make this comparable, we use the same model as well as the same inference engine in all cases, at the same time that we change the communication protocol. Thus, with this experiment we also demonstrate *Gembed* interoperability by using it to smoothly implement all three in-database strategies of embedding generation.

Figure 5a compares the throughput as the number of embeddings grow, depending on how they are generated. To visually facilitate the comparison, we take "Python Direct" as a baseline and use it as denominator. Thus, we clearly see that all alternatives follow the same trend (i.e., flat lines) with decreasing standard deviation ranges. In all three cases, we can see that the in-database (i.e., "PG") embedding generation shows higher performance than the "External" counterpart, because when vectorization occurs outside the database, every embedding must be transferred to be inserted. For a batch of 32 vectors, each vector having 384 dimensions, and using 4-bytes floating-point precision, the resulting payload size is $32 \times 384 \times 4 = 49,152$ bytes.

On the other hand, despite the RDBMS as well as the HTTP and gRPC micro-services being executed in the same machine, resulting in negligible remote request latency and representing a best-case scenario for external methods, still *Gembed* versions using gRPC and HTTP are faster than the corresponding external counterpart. Indeed, apart from having to transfer a bigger payload to the database, the data has to be serialized by the Python process, deserialized by PostgreSQL and converted to *pgvector* types to be stored. All in all, the local *pg_gembed* option beats the others, since it completely removes the communication latency and does not require intermediate buffers in the application layer for embeddings.

From another perspective, we can see in Fig. 6 that system CPU and memory usage grows with the input size. However, the trend does not change for the different alternatives. Only if we drilled down, we would appreciate that resources are actually used either inside or outside PostgreSQL.

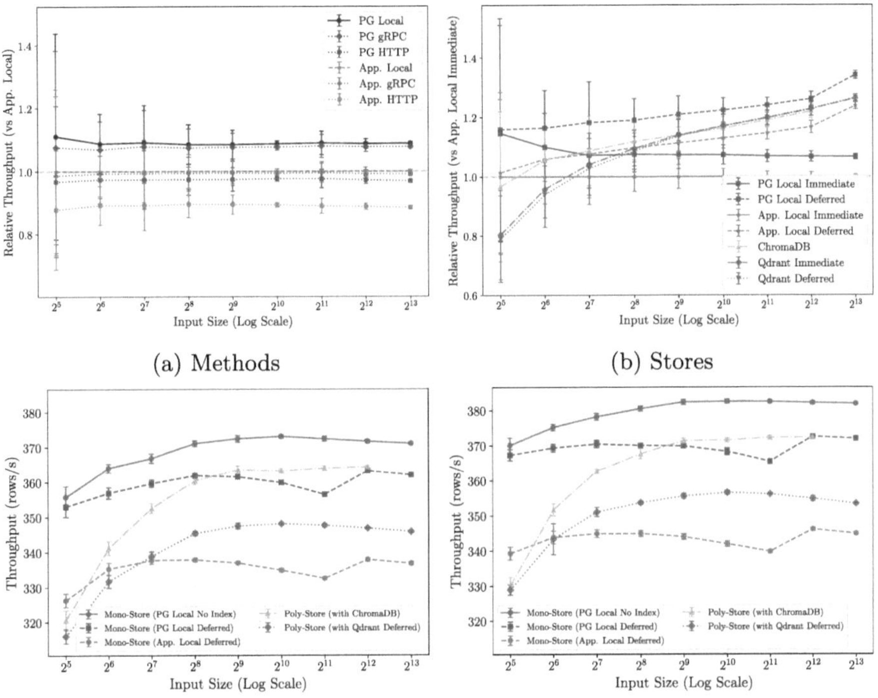

(a) Methods (b) Stores

(c) Cold Start (d) Pre-existing Data

Fig. 5. Throughput comparisons of vector generation

5.2 In-Database

The main purpose of this experiment is to compare the combination of *pgvector* and *pg_gembed* for in-database embedding generation and storage, against vectorizing in the application layer and storing the result in a specialized V-store (namely ChromaDB and Qdrant). Thus, the embedding alternatives being compared are: (1) PG In-Database Immediate Index (PG Local Immediate), generation with *pg_gembed* locally, and storage in PostgreSQL with the *pgvector* `vector` datatype and index; (2) Application Local Immediate Index (App. Local Immediate), generation directly within the Python application process, and storage in PostgreSQL with the *pgvector* `vector` datatype and index; (3) ChromaDB Immediate, generation within the Python application process, and storage in ChromaDB; (4) Qdrant Immediate, generation within the Python application process, together with storage and indexing in Qdrant. In a scenario like this, aiming at maximizing throughput of vectorization and storage, another option is deferring the index creation until the data ingestion has finalized. In PostgreSQL, this can be done by creating the *pgvector* index after the ingestion, and Qdrant offers specialized configuration for disabling indexes for bulk upload. However, ChromaDB does not offer a similar option, and we add three alterna-

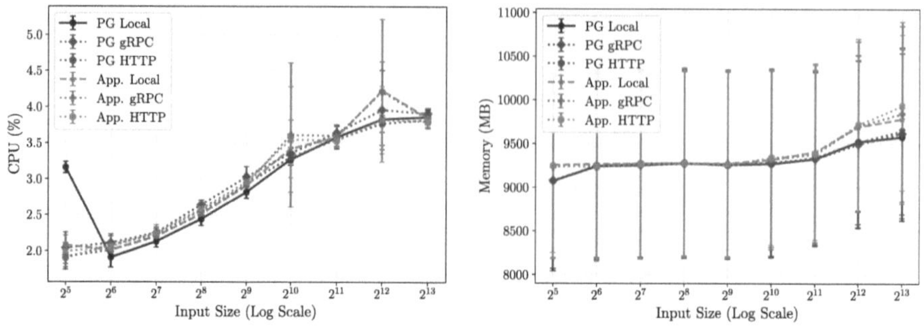

(a) CPU usage (b) Memory usage

Fig. 6. System resource usage during embedding generation.

tives: (5) PG Local Deferred; (6) App. Local Deferred; and (7) Qdrant Deferred. The input is the same as in Sect. 5.1. However, in PostgreSQL, we have now a table with a *pgvector* HNSW index. In ChromaDB and Qdrant collections the corresponding indexes are configured with the same parameters the PostgreSQL index has.

Figure 5b shows the throughput of each of the alternatives (again taking "PG External Immediate" as baseline in the denominator). Firstly, PostgreSQL with local in-database embedding generation and deferred index construction has the highest throughput. It is worth noting that deferring the index construction increases the throughput for PostgreSQL, but does not have a similar increase in the case of Qdrant. Also, the performance of Qdrant is greatly improved as the input size grows, which should be interpreted as a higher constant initial insertion cost that pays off in the long term. It is not until an input size of 2^9 that its throughput reaches that of ChromaDB. Also, we experienced that ChromaDB fails for an input size larger than 5461 vectors, so its line is discontinued beyond 2^{12} in this and all other experiments.

Vector generation is not always straightforward and often requires to query and operate embeddings in combination with Relational data. Indeed, instead of just vectorizing the review data, a contextual representation of each product (e.g., name, description and price, along with its categories and most recent reviews) can also be embedded, which corresponds to a typical RAG application. Thus, next conducted experiment compares a mono-store architecture (PostgreSQL plus *pgvector* and *pg_gembed*) against poly-store architectures that combine purely PostgreSQL for structured data and either ChromaDB or Qdrant for embeddings. The structured data consists of products, where each can have multiple categories (from 1–3) and multiple reviews (from 2–5). This is divided into two scenarios: (a) **Cold Start:** Both storage systems are initially empty. (b) **Pre-existing Data:** The RDBMS already has all the structured data, and only the embeddings have to be generated. Thus, the poly-stores first have to query PostgreSQL to obtain the data to be vectorized. The index construction is deferred in all cases.

Results can be seen in Figs. 5c and 5d, respectively. We can observe that the behaviour is basically the same in both cases, and in-database with indexing beats the poly-stores in smaller input sizes, due to avoiding the transfer of data and vectors. However, for larger input sizes, the mono-stores' throughput drops due to some anomaly in *pgvector* index implementation, and is smaller than the poly-store with ChromaDB. We include results for the mono-store with *pg_gembed* but no indexing, to isolate this effect and show that performance drop is due to a problem in *pgvector* indexing and not in-database vectorization, though its superior performance is not directly comparable against options including index. The main difference between the V-stores can be attributed to ChromaDB being configured as an embedded, in-process database, while Qdrant running as a Docker image, with extra communication overhead.

Model Identifier	Arch.	Dim.
`openai/clip-vit-base-patch32`	CLIP	512
`openai/clip-vit-large-patch14`	CLIP	768
`google/siglip-large-patch16-384`	SigLIP	1024

(a) Embedding model characteristics

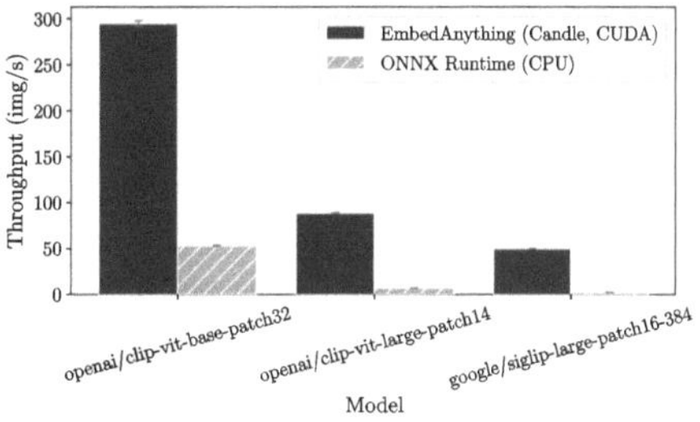

(b) Comparison of backends and models

Fig. 7. Examples of extensibility

5.3 Extensibility

In this experiment, we aim to show how *Gembed* seamlessly makes it possible to use different input types, embedding backends, model architectures, and acceleration hardware just with a simple parameter change to the in-database call. Thus, instead of text, we generate embeddings for 2^{10} images (generated with PDGF) using two different backends: (1) **EmbedAnything**, configured to use Candle and CUDA, so vectorization is performed on the GPU; and (2) **ONNX Runtime**, set up to vectorize on the CPU. Since in this case, we vectorize images instead of texts, we use the models in Fig. 7a, chosen because of their differences in architecture and vector size. It is worth noting that this experiment is not a comparison of the Candle framework against the ONNX Runtime. For this to be the case, the same acceleration hardware should be used, as well as ensuring both backend implementations use similar optimizations.

All the images are stored in a temporary directory, and its path is passed as a parameter to *Gembed*. This avoids the constant overhead of passing the images to PostgreSQL as BLOBs. For the same reason, the output vectors of the inference are ignored, and they are neither stored nor transferred back to the Python process. Figure 7b shows the throughput corresponding to each embedding backend and model used. As the model size increases, both backends decrease their throughput, which is expected due to the higher inference time. Also unsurprisingly, despite ONNX Runtime backend takes advantage of the 32 CPU threads when vectorizing, the GPU achieves a speed-up of 18.33 in the case of the SigLIP, showing the benefits of this type of accelerator for AI workloads.

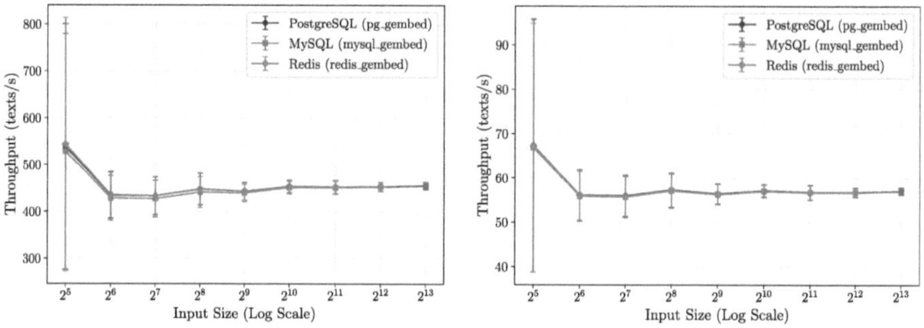

(a) MiniLM (b) bge-large

Fig. 8. Comparison of adapters and embedding models

5.4 Portability

Finally, we demonstrate how *Gembed* can be ported to different systems (two Relational and one NOSQL) through its adapters:[1] (1) pg_gembed (for **PostgreSQL** v18.1), (2) mysql_gembed (for **MySQL** v9.6.0), and (3) redis_gembed (for **Redis** v8.6.1). We embed the same text reviews (2^5–2^{13}) with the different DBMS adapters. Two different models are used (namely `MiniLM` and `bge-large`) to show that the performance differences are not due to this factor. As in Sect. 5.3, the generated vectors are not stored, only the corresponding adapter's function is invoked and its results discarded to avoid inflating query times with a constant value. Figure 8 illustrates the throughput relative to the adapter and model used.

Firstly, we can see that if we disregard the scale, the trend is similar for both models (with higher absolute throughput for the smaller model, and lower for the bigger one). In small batches, the initialization cost dominates, and then throughput grows linearly until the memory available is saturated (approximately for 2^8 reviews being embedded). In general, Redis and PostgreSQL offer similar performance and slightly better than MySQL. The reason behind this might be that loading the extension in the connection's backend can be more efficient than loading it on the server, as MySQL does. However, loading it only once in the server instead of once per connection would pay off in the long term, in case of using multiple connections. Also, Redis is discontinued beyond 2^{12} because of size limitations in the Lua wrapper used to invoke the vectorization function.

6 Discussion

Gembed facilitated multiple analyses, whose findings are summarized next.

Firstly, we should notice that improvement looks smaller than it actually is, because most of the time in all the experiments is taken by the initial Python call and embedding generation, regardless of where this happens. For example, there are tasks not affected by *Gembed* consuming $72.146ms$ across all alternatives to generate 2^5 vectors in Fig. 5a. Thus, PG Local consumes only $73.636ms - 72.146ms = 1.490ms$ for the data management affected by our contributions, while App. Local and App. HTTP use respectively $80.773ms - 72.146ms = 8.627ms$ (i.e., speedup seems $\frac{80.773ms}{73.636ms} = 1.10\times$, actually being $\frac{8.627ms}{1.490ms} = 5.79\times$) and $90.808ms - 72.146ms = 18.662ms$ (i.e., seems $1.23\times$ vs. actually $12.52\times$).

This said, we have seen that in-database vectorization consistently outperforms standard application-level approaches and questions the necessity of dedicated V-stores. In all experiments, its throughput is higher on average, while often having a lower CPU and memory usage. It is worth noting that even when using a gRPC client, its throughput is still higher than the counterpart at application-level (i.e., inference does not necessarily have to be performed locally to benefit from *Gembed*). When data to be vectorized is already in the database, the performance improvement is even higher (allowing for a much simpler mono-store software architecture, capable of providing ACID guarantees).

Finally mention that the *Core* is reused in all three implementations. Thus, such code reusability together with the mechanisms it contains to prevent erroneous user calls crashing the host makes vectorization intrinsically more robust (besides eliminating the "language tax" without implementing any wrapper). Hence, we can easily and safely offer all DBMSs multiple vectorization backends (e.g., local or remote; using CPU or GPU) for the user to choose the most appropriate one for their needs and overcome potential limitations in the extensibility mechanism of the host (e.g., PostgreSQL loading the embedding model once per connection if using a local backend). Moreover, the possibility of transparently using remote vectorization facilitates horizontal scalability and load balancing.

7 Conclusion

In this paper, we have presented *Gembed*, a portable, interoperable and extensible software artifact for in-database embedding generation. Its portability is exemplified through three different open-source implementations extending PostgreSQL, MySQL and Redis. Moreover, we also showed its interoperability with different inference libraries that can be called either locally or remotely. Finally, we experimentally demonstrated the performance improvement obtained by using in-database embedding generation with five of embedding models for both natural language and image processing, but *Gembed* could also be extended with any other pre-trained model to deal with any other kind of unstructured data. As future work, *Gembed* can be improved so that in the presence of different vectorization backends, it automatically chooses the optimal one (either performance- or cost-wise).

Acknowledgments. This work was supported by the project PID2024-156019OB-I00 under funding schema MICIU/AEI/10.13039/501100011033 and ERFD/EU.

References

1. Amanbayev, A., Tsan, B., Dang, T., Rusu, F.: Filtered approximate nearest neighbor search in vector databases: System design and performance analysis (2026). https://arxiv.org/abs/2602.11443
2. Brücke, C., Härtling, P., Palacios, R.E., Patel, H., Rabl, T.: TPCx-AI - an industry standard benchmark for artificial intelligence and machine learning systems. Proc. VLDB Endow. **16**(12) (2023). https://doi.org/10.14778/3611540.3611554
3. Gamma, E., Helm, R., Johnson, R.E., Vlissides, J.: Design patterns: elements of reusable object-oriented software, Addison-Wesley Professional (1995)
4. Guidotti, E., Shlyk, D., Montanelli, S., Ferrara, A.: In-database text classification with BornSQL. In: Proceedings of the 29th International Conference on Extending Database Technology, EDBT. OpenProceedings.org (2026). https://doi.org/10.48786/edbt.2026.19
5. Haque, R.R., Mai, A.L., Brucato, M., Abouzied, A., Haas, P.J., Meliou, A.: Stochastic sketchrefine: Scaling in-database decision-making under uncertainty to millions of tuples. Proc. VLDB Endow. **18**(9) (2025). https://doi.org/10.14778/3746405.3746431
6. Hu, G., et al.: HAKES: scalable vector database for embedding search service. Proc. VLDB Endow. **18**(9) (2025). https://doi.org/10.14778/3746405.3746427
7. Jing, Z., et al.: When large language models meet vector databases: a survey (2025). https://arxiv.org/abs/2402.01763
8. Johnson, J., Douze, M., Jégou, H.: Billion-scale similarity search with GPUs. IEEE Trans. Big Data **7**(3), (2021). https://doi.org/10.1109/TBDATA.2019.2921572
9. Kim, H., Lim, C., An, H., Sen, R., Park, K.: Exqutor: Extended query optimizer for vector-augmented analytical queries. CoRR **abs/2512.09695** (2025). https://doi.org/10.48550/ARXIV.2512.09695
10. Liu, J., Zhang, Y., Jin, C., Gupta, A., Liu, S., Wang, J.: Vector search in PostgreSQL: A decoupled approach. In: 16th Conference on Innovative Data Systems Research, CIDR. www.cidrdb.org (2026). https://www.vldb.org/cidrdb/papers/2026/p2-liu.pdf
11. Niinimaki, M., Shrestha, S.R., Udofia, A.: Comparison of vector database management systems for retrieval augmented generation. In: 29th Int. Computer Science and Engineering Conference, ICSEC. IEEE, (2025). https://doi.org/10.1109/ICSEC67360.2025.11298006
12. Pan, J.J., Wang, J., Li, G.: Survey of vector database management systems. VLDB J. **33**(5), (2024). https://doi.org/10.1007/S00778-024-00864-X
13. Sanca, V., Ailamaki, A.: Efficient model-relational data management: Challenges and opportunities. IEEE Trans. Knowl. Data Eng. **36**(12) (2024). https://doi.org/10.1109/TKDE.2024.3384276

14. Taipalus, T.: Vector database management systems: Fundamental concepts, use-cases, and current challenges. Cogn. Syst. Res. **85** (2024). https://doi.org/10.1016/J.COGSYS.2024.101216
15. Wang, Z., et al.: A comprehensive survey on data augmentation. IEEE Trans. Knowl. Data Eng. **38**(1) (2026). https://doi.org/10.1109/TKDE.2025.3622600
16. Wei, C., et al.: AnalyticDB-V: A hybrid analytical engine towards query fusion for structured and unstructured data. Proc. VLDB Endow. **13**(12) (2020). doi:https://doi.org/10.14778/3415478.3415541

Expert-Guided Counterfactual Explanations for Credit Risk

Riccardo Benassi[1], Matteo Paganelli[1(✉)], Gennaro Aloe[2], Enrico Bagli[2], Mario Calò Carducci[2], Pietro Giuffrida[2], Nicola Lavecchia[2], Matteo Squadrani[2], Elvira Maria Rosaria Oliva[2], Maurizio Vincini[1], and Francesco Guerra[1]

[1] University of Modena and Reggio Emilia, Modena, Italy
{riccardo.benassi,matteo.paganelli,maurizio.vincini, francesco.guerra}@unimore.it

[2] CRIF S.p.A., Bologna, Italy
{G.Aloe2,e.bagli,m.carducci,p.giuffrida,N.Lavecchia,m.squadrani, E.Oliva}@crif.com

Abstract. Counterfactual explanations provide actionable recourse by identifying changes that lead to a desired outcome. However, most methods rely on uniform feature costs or geometric proximity, assuming all feature changes are equally feasible and overlooking the heterogeneous effort required in practice. In financial settings, this often leads to explanations that are valid but impractical. We propose CREDIX, a model-agnostic framework for cost-aware counterfactual explanations in credit risk modeling. This method integrates heterogeneous feature costs and domain constraints into a multi-objective evolutionary optimization scheme, balancing validity, proximity, and intervention effort. Additionally, it includes an LLM-based cost-elicitation component, to reduce the effort for manual cost definition. Experiments on two benchmark credit datasets with linear and non-linear models show that incorporating feature-dependent costs improves the practical feasibility of counterfactual explanations while preserving competitive performance.

Keywords: Counterfactual Explanation · Explainable Artificial Intelligence (XAI) · Credit Risk

1 Introduction

The growing use of AI in high-stakes decision-making raises concerns about transparency, accountability, and fairness, particularly in regulated domains such as credit risk assessment, where automated decisions directly affect individuals' access to financial services. Recent regulations, including the European Union AI Act [9], explicitly require explainability and human oversight in such contexts, making explanations essential for both compliance and trust.

G. Vargas-Solar et al. (Eds.): ADBIS 2026, LNCS 16937, pp. 388–404, 2027.
https://doi.org/10.1007/978-3-032-39820-8_25

Among the various explanation paradigms, counterfactual explanations are especially appealing for their intuitive nature. Given an instance receiving an unfavorable outcome, a counterfactual explanation identifies the minimal changes required to obtain a desired outcome. For example, an applicant denied a loan might be informed that reducing existing debt or increasing income would have resulted in approval. A key property of such explanations is actionability: the suggested changes should correspond to interventions that the individual can realistically perform. In the example above, reducing debt or increasing income may be feasible, whereas modifying immutable attributes, such as place of birth, is not. Thus, counterfactual explanations are designed not only to justify a decision, but also to indicate actionable steps for reversing it.

However, actionability alone does not guarantee practical feasibility: the interventions required for each modifiable feature can vary significantly in effort, time, and uncertainty. For instance, increasing income, reducing debt, or changing employment status may all be actionable, but the associated adjustments have very different practical implications for the individual. This introduces a fundamental trade-off in counterfactual generation. A useful explanation should simultaneously satisfy multiple criteria: it must be valid (i.e., change the model prediction), remain close to the original instance, and require changes that are realistically affordable in terms of effort. These objectives are often conflicting. A small increase in income may minimally alter the original profile but be difficult to achieve in practice, whereas a larger reduction in debt may imply a greater shift in the feature space but be more attainable in the short term.

Several recent approaches have focused on improving feasibility by incorporating actionability constraints, structural dependencies, or causal relationships [4,15,16,21,22,24,26], while others [8] adopt multi-objective formulations to jointly optimize multiple competing criteria. However, most of these methods still assume uniform feature costs, effectively treating all modifications as equally feasible, or collapse heterogeneous criteria into a single scalar objective, making the weighting of objectives implicit and difficult to calibrate. This limits their ability to represent the inherent trade-offs among competing desiderata and may yield counterfactual explanations that are formally valid but impractical to implement. In particular, the estimation of feature modification costs remains largely underexplored and typically relies on manual specification by domain experts, which is expensive, subjective, and difficult to scale.

In this work, we propose CREDIX, a model-agnostic framework for generating cost-aware counterfactual explanations in credit scoring. The central idea is to incorporate heterogeneous feature modification costs within a multi-objective optimization process, preserving trade-offs among competing criteria and enabling the generation of diverse, non-dominated solutions. To explore this space, we adopt a Pareto-based evolutionary strategy [6], which maintains a set of candidate solutions such that no objective can be improved without worsening another, and then selects solutions that balance validity, plausibility, and intervention cost. Within this framework, a critical component is the estimation of feature modification costs, which directly shape the optimization landscape and the resulting trade-offs. To reduce the reliance on manual expert input, we introduce a novel component that leverages Large Language Models (LLMs) to estimate feature modification costs. Rather than directly predicting absolute cost values, the proposed approach formulates cost estimation as a set of pairwise comparisons, which are subsequently aggregated using a Bradley–Terry [3] model, a standard probabilistic approach for modeling pairwise comparisons, to derive a consistent global ranking.

We evaluate CREDIX on multiple benchmark credit datasets using both linear and non-linear classifiers and relying on standard quantitative metrics.

The main contributions of this work can be summarized as follows:

- We propose a model-agnostic, multi-objective framework for generating counterfactual explanations that explicitly incorporates heterogeneous feature modification costs and preserves trade-offs among competing objectives.
- We introduce an LLM-based approach for cost estimation based on pairwise comparisons and Bradley–Terry aggregation, enabling consistent integration of domain knowledge within the optimization process.
- We provide a comprehensive evaluation that exploits well-established quantitative metrics to verify the quality of the generated explanations.

2 Related Work

Counterfactual explanation methods can be broadly categorized into optimization-based, heuristic search, instance-based, and decision-tree-based approaches[10].

Optimization-based methods represent a central paradigm, typically formulating counterfactual generation as the minimization of multiple objectives. A closely related line of work is transformation-based approaches, which generate counterfactuals through learned feature transformations or masking models [2]. Early work such as WACH [27] does not explicitly model feasibility or structural constraints. Subsequent approaches improve realism through latent or manifold regularization, e.g., CEM [7], CEGP [13], and CCHVAE [20], which promote distributional plausibility via learned latent representations. Other methods explicitly target diversity or structured constraints: DICE [16] introduces diversity-promoting objectives, while AR [26] and LiCE [19] formulate counterfactuals as constrained or mixed-integer optimization problems. FOCUS [14] extends this line to tree ensembles via differentiable surrogates.

Heuristic and evolutionary methods provide model-agnostic alternatives better suited to complex constraint spaces. CERTIFAI [24] and MOC [5] use genetic search to optimize validity and proximity, with later extensions incorporating feasibility, robustness, and feature dependencies (e.g., GECO [23], GRACON [12], MCCE [22]). ProCE [8] further extends this family with a multi-objective evolutionary formulation supporting multiple constraints in a unified framework.

Instance-based methods emphasize realism by retrieving training data points. NICE [4] identifies nearby instances with opposite predictions, while FACE [21] formulates counterfactual search as a graph shortest-path problem. These methods naturally ensure plausibility but are limited by dataset coverage and provide limited flexibility for incorporating structured or domain-specific constraints.

Tree-based approaches are a further line of work that exploits the internal structure of decision trees or ensembles. FeatTweak [25] modifies minimally feature values to satisfy alternative decision paths across a majority of trees, while LORE [11] learns local surrogate trees to extract rule-based counterfactuals.

Table 1. Comparison of counterfactual explainers across key properties: model-agnostic applicability, actionability constraints, structured constraints (monotonicity and relational dependencies), dependency modeling (data and causal), and integration of expert knowledge for feature modification costs. ✓ indicates support; ✗ indicates no explicit support; ✓* indicates partial or limited support.

Method	Model-agnostic	Actionability	Constraints	Dependencies	Expert costs
NICE [4]	✓	✗	✗	✗	✗
FACE [21]	✓	✓	✓	✗	✗
DICE [16]	✓	✓	✓	✗	✗
AR [26]	✗	✓	✓*	✗	✗
FeasibleCF [15]	✗	✗	✓	✓	✗
MCCE [22]	✓	✓	✗	✓*	✗
CERTIFAI [24]	✓	✓	✗	✗	✗
ProCE [8]	✓	✓*	✓	✓	✗
CREDIX	✓	✓	✓	✓	✓

Overall, recent literature shows increasing attention toward feasibility, structural constraints, and even causal relationships, bringing several approaches closer to expert-aware settings. However, as summarized in Table 1, most approaches address only subsets of these factors and rarely incorporate domain expertise in the form of feature modification costs in a systematic way. CREDIX addresses this gap by integrating actionability and expert-informed cost modeling directly into a unified multi-objective optimization framework, aligning algorithmic trade-offs with practical feasibility in credit decision settings.

3 The CREDIX Approach

CREDIX is a model-agnostic framework for cost-aware counterfactual explanations in credit scoring. It formulates counterfactual generation as a constrained multi-objective optimization, balancing validity, plausibility, and heterogeneous intervention costs. Domain constraints, expert knowledge, and an LLM-based cost elicitation component jointly ensure feasible and realistic recourse actions.

3.1 Problem Formulation

Let $f : \mathcal{X} \to \{0, 1\}$ be a credit scoring classifier that either rejects (class 0) or approves (class 1) a loan application, and let $x \in \mathcal{X}$ denote an instance describing an applicant such that $f(x) = 0$. The goal of counterfactual explanation is to identify an alternative instance $x' \in \mathcal{X}$ such that $f(x') = 1$, while satisfying a set of desirable properties. While the problem is often formulated as finding the closest instance x' that flips the prediction, real-world credit scenarios require additional constraints. In particular, counterfactuals should be (i) actionable, i.e., modify only features that can realistically change; (ii) plausible, i.e., remain consistent with the data distribution; and (iii) cost-aware, i.e., account for the heterogeneous effort associated with different feature modifications. To model this aspect, each actionable feature is associated with a cost vector c, encoding the relative effort required for intervention. Since these criteria are heterogeneous and potentially conflicting, we formulate counterfactual generation as a constrained multi-objective optimization problem (as described in Sect. 3.4):

$$\mathbf{L}(x', x, f, c) = \left(L_{\text{valid}}(x', f),\ L_{\text{cost}}(x, x', c),\ L_{\text{plaus}}(x')\right)$$

where the objectives capture prediction validity, intervention cost, and statistical plausibility, respectively (Sect. 3.3). Additional constraints, such as feature immutability and monotonicity, further restrict the search space.

3.2 Data Representation and Distance Functions

Before defining the objective functions, we describe the data representation used for counterfactual search. In CREDIX, instances are discretized using supervised optimal binning [17], a standard preprocessing step in credit scoring applications, to partition features into risk-homogeneous intervals. Each feature value x_j is mapped to a discrete bin $b_j(x_j) \in \mathcal{B}_j$, learned to maximize class separation subject to constraints such as minimum support. Because perturbations occur at the bin level, regardless of the predictive model, the distance between the original instance x and the counterfactual instance x' is measured by comparing their corresponding feature values. For feature j, the distance is defined as the number of bin transitions between x_j and x'_j:

$$d_j(x_j, x'_j) = |b_j(x_j) - b_j(x'_j)|.$$

For linear models, the binned representation is further transformed through Weight of Evidence (WoE) encoding [28]. For each bin $B_{j,k}$, WoE is defined as

$$\text{WoE}_{j,k} = \log \frac{P(x_j \in B_{j,k} \mid y = 0)}{P(x_j \in B_{j,k} \mid y = 1)},$$

where $P(x_j \in B_{j,k} \mid y = 0 \text{ } or \text{ } 1)$ denotes the proportion of instances with negative/positive outcome whose feature value falls into bin $B_{j,k}$. For an instance x', we denote by $WoE(x') \in \mathbb{R}^d$ the vector that assigns to each feature j the

Algorithm 1. Feature cost estimation via LLM and Bradley–Terry

Input: Set of actionable features A, language model LLM, number of repetitions R
Output: Cost vector c

$P \leftarrow \emptyset$
for each pair (f_i, f_j) with $i < j$ **do**
  for $r = 1, \ldots, R$ **do**
    $(f_a, f_b) \leftarrow$ randomly permute (f_i, f_j)
    pref $\leftarrow \mathrm{LLM}(f_a, f_b)$
    $P \leftarrow P \cup \{(f_i, f_j, \text{pref})\}$
  end for
end for
$\beta \leftarrow \mathrm{FitBradleyTerry}(P)$
$c \leftarrow \mathrm{NormalizeOrDiscretize}(\beta)$
return c

WoE value of the bin containing x'_j, i.e., $WoE_j(x') = \mathrm{WoE}_{j,b_j(x'_j)}$. WoE provides a monotonic risk-oriented representation that improves coefficient interpretability in credit scoring. Non-linear models use the binned representation directly. Crucially, counterfactual distance is always computed in the discretized space to ensure that proximity reflects interpretable transitions across risk-related features rather than numerical distances in the encoded feature space.

3.3 Objective Functions

Counterfactual quality in CREDIX is defined through three complementary objectives: (i) decision boundary proximity, (ii) intervention cost, and (iii) statistical plausibility.

Validity Constraint and Boundary Proximity. A counterfactual must flip the model prediction from rejection to approval. Let $s(x')$ denote the predicted probability of the risky class and τ the decision threshold. Since an applicant is classified as risky when $s(x') > \tau$, validity is enforced as a strict constraint: $s(x') \leq \tau$. Subject to this condition, the objective is to favor candidates closest to the decision boundary, avoiding unnecessary shifts into the favorable region. We define the boundary proximity objective to be minimized as:

$$L_{\text{valid}}(x', f) = \tau - s(x'),$$

subject to the validity constraint $s(x') \leq \tau$.

Feature Modification Cost. In credit scoring, not all feature changes are equally feasible. To capture this aspect, we introduce a cost-sensitive objective:

$$L_{\text{cost}}(x, x', c) = \sum_{j \in a} c_j \, d_j(x_j, x'_j),$$

where A is the set of actionable features, c_j is the intervention cost of feature j, and d_j is the feature-wise bin distance (Sect. 3.2). This objective explicitly penalizes interventions on features that are harder, slower, or less realistic to modify, allowing the optimization process to distinguish between geometrically similar but practically different counterfactuals.

Although the cost vector c can be manually specified by domain experts, this process can be challenging and time-consuming. To address this, we introduce an LLM-based cost elicitation procedure (as detailed in Algorithm 1). Instead of assigning absolute scores, the LLM performs pairwise comparisons between feature modifications, determining which intervention is more costly under domain-specific conditions. Pairwise judgments are repeated under random prompt permutations to reduce positional bias and then aggregated through a Bradley–Terry model [3]:

$$P(f_i \succ f_j) = \frac{e^{\beta_i}}{e^{\beta_i} + e^{\beta_j}},$$

where β_i represents the latent cost associated with feature i. The resulting scores are normalized to obtain the cost vector used in optimization.

Statistical Plausibility. Validity and low cost alone do not guarantee that a counterfactual is realistic. To discourage solutions in implausible regions of the feature space, we introduce a plausibility objective acting as a regularization term. Plausibility is evaluated in the WoE space via a Mahalanobis distance [1]:

$$L_{\text{plaus}}(x') = (WoE(x') - \mu)^{\top} \Sigma^{-1} (WoE(x') - \mu),$$

where μ, Σ are the empirical mean and covariance estimated from the training data. This term encourages counterfactuals to remain in high-density regions and can be extended to account for causal dependencies when available.

Overall, the three objectives capture complementary and potentially conflicting aspects of counterfactual quality. Treating them separately allows CREDIX to preserve trade-offs instead of collapsing them through predefined weights.

3.4 Optimization via NSGA-II

CREDIX adopts a genetic optimization strategy based on NSGA-II [6], detailed in Algorithm 2. NSGA-II is a Pareto-based evolutionary algorithm that ranks solutions by non-dominance, preserving trade-offs among objectives.

Given an instance x and a model f, the algorithm initializes a population of size n by applying random perturbations to actionable features A (line 1). The population evolves over G generations (lines 2–10). In each iteration, candidates are evaluated against the objectives defined in Sect. 3.3 and ranked via non-dominated sorting, which partitions the solutions into Pareto fronts ordered by dominance level (line 3). To promote diversity, a crowding distance is computed within each front as the sum of normalized distances between neighboring solutions in the objective space (line 4), to quantify solution density. The algorithm performs tournament selection based on Pareto rank and crowding distance (line 5), followed by crossover and mutation to generate offspring (line 6).

Algorithm 2. Multi-objective counterfactual generation via NSGA-II

Input: Instance x, model f, set of actionable features a, cost vector c, generations G, population size n
Output: Counterfactual x'

1: $P_0 \leftarrow$ InitializePopulation(x, a, n)
2: **for** $g = 0, \ldots, G-1$ **do**
3: $\quad F_g \leftarrow$ BuildParetoFronts(P_g, x, f, c)
4: $\quad D_g \leftarrow$ ComputeCrowdingDistance(F_g)
5: $\quad M_g \leftarrow$ TournamentSelection(F_g, D_g)
6: $\quad Q_g \leftarrow$ CrossoverAndMutation(M_g, a)
7: $\quad R_g \leftarrow P_g \cup Q_g$
8: $\quad F_g^* \leftarrow$ BuildParetoFronts(R_g, x, f, c)
9: $\quad D_g^* \leftarrow$ ComputeCrowdingDistance(F_g^*)
10: $\quad P_{g+1} \leftarrow$ SelectNextPopulation(R_g, F_g^*, D_g^*, n)
11: **end for**
12: $F_F \leftarrow$ BuildParetoFronts(P_G, x, f, c)
13: $x' \leftarrow$ FinalSelection(FirstFront$(F_F), x)$
14: **return** x'

The parent and offspring populations are merged and re-ranked, and the best n candidates are selected for the next generation (lines 7–10). Upon convergence, the final solution is selected from the first Pareto front as the instance minimizing the representation-dependent distance to the original input x (Sect. 3.2). Crucially, this post-hoc selection ensures that minimality does not prematurely dominate the search; rather, it allows the algorithm to first explore a diverse set of high-quality trade-offs before choosing a minimal-distance explanation.

4 Experimental Evaluation

The experimental evaluation is designed to assess CREDIX along four complementary research questions. **RQ1 (Effectiveness)** evaluates the quality of the generated counterfactual explanations against state-of-the-art methods; **RQ2 (Efficiency)** analyzes the computational performance of CREDIX and the trade-off between solution quality and runtime; **RQ3 (LLM-based cost estimation)** studies the estimation of feature modification costs using LLMs with different models and prompts; and **RQ4 (Ablation study)** investigates the contribution of CREDIX's optimization objectives to its overall performance.

Datasets. The evaluation is conducted on two publicly available credit-risk datasets commonly used in the literature: *German Credit*[1] and *Lending Club*[2]. The *German Credit* dataset contains information about loan applicants evaluated by a financial institution. It includes 1K records describing demographic

[1] https://github.com/raam93/DiCE_evaluations/blob/master/datasets/german_credit.csv.
[2] https://github.com/raam93/DiCE_evaluations/blob/master/datasets/lending.csv.

Table 2. German Credit

Feature	Cost	Constraint
savings	1	↑
other_installments	3	bank/stores → none
age	5	↑

Table 3. Lending Club

Feature	Cost	Constraint
annual_inc	1	↑
emp_length	3	↑
credit_years	5	↑

characteristics, financial status, and credit history. The prediction task is a binary classification problem that determines whether an applicant is a good or bad credit risk. The *Lending Club* dataset comprises more than 40K loan records issued by a peer-to-peer lending platform between 2007 and 2011. Following preprocessing strategies adopted in prior studies [16], we retain eight relevant attributes: employment length, income, open credit accounts, credit history, loan grade, home ownership, loan purpose, and state of residence. The binary predictive task is to determine whether a borrower will repay the loan.

Baselines. We compare CREDIX against representative counterfactual generation approaches covering instance-based, optimization-based, and heuristic paradigms.

- **BF-expert** is a brute-force baseline that exhaustively explores the discretized search space to minimize the overall change effort, based on feature costs defined by domain experts. In the event of a tie, it selects the solution with the smallest change in predicted probability;
- **NICE** [4] is an instance method that generates counterfactuals by retrieving and adapting nearest training instances with opposite predictions;
- **FACE** [21] builds a graph over training instances, with edge weights combining feature-space distance and local data density, and derives counterfactuals via shortest-path search that favors transitions through high-density (plausible) regions;
- **DICE-R** [16] is one of the variants provided in the original DICE framework, formulating counterfactual generation as a randomized search procedure in input space, producing diverse candidate explanations through random sampling and selection over prediction and proximity objectives;
- **AR** [26] models recourse generation as an Integer Programming problem defined over a discretized action space, identifying minimal-cost feature changes that flip the prediction; its application is restricted to linear models;
- **OptBin** [18] is a scorecard-specific mixed-integer optimization approach that searches over binned variables to generate valid, close, sparse, and realistic counterfactuals under actionability constraints;
- **ProCE** [8] is an evolutionary multi-objective method, like CREDIX, that optimizes counterfactuals w.r.t. prediction change, autoencoder-based plausibility, and causal distance, but without feature-dependent cost modeling.

Setup. To evaluate counterfactual generation across both linear and non-linear decision boundaries, we use two predictive models: Logistic Regression (LR), a linear classifier, and CatBoost, a gradient boosting model designed for heterogeneous tabular data. The classification threshold is fixed at 0.5. For each dataset, actionability and monotonicity constraints are specified according to domain knowledge, considering only a small set of semantically meaningful variables that can realistically be modified in credit decision scenarios. Tables 2 and 3 report the actionable features together with their expert-defined costs and the corresponding monotonicity or value-transition constraints. The default configuration of CREDIX uses Mistral-3.2-24B as the LLM for feature cost estimation.

Metrics. Following the benchmarking framework of Guidotti et al. [10], we adopt standard counterfactual evaluation metrics, referring to the same paper for their formal definitions. We measure *coverage* as the fraction of generated counterfactuals, plus *actionability* and *constraint compliance* as the fraction of generated counterfactuals that respect mutability and monotonicity constraints, respectively. *Proximity* is defined as the distance between original instances and counterfactuals, while *sparsity* counts the number of modified features. *Plausibility* is computed as the distance to the nearest same-class data point, and *discriminative power* is measured as the accuracy of a 1-NN classifier trained on original and counterfactual instances. We further report *probability change* between original and counterfactual predictions, *recourse cost* based on expert-defined feature weights, and *efficiency* as average runtime per explanation (ms). Higher values are desirable for validity and discriminative power, while lower values indicate better performance for all other metrics.

4.1 Effectiveness

First, we assess the ability of each method to generate counterfactuals that are feasible, actionable and compliant with monotonicity constraints. While methods achieve near-perfect coverage (i.e., above 90%), FACE is a notable exception, exhibiting substantially lower coverage (35% and 22% on German Credit and 38%–34% on Lending Club, for LR and CatBoost respectively). This occurs because FACE searches for existing records in the dataset that simultaneously satisfy actionability and monotonicity constraints while flipping the prediction; if no such instance exists, it cannot generate a counterfactual. For actionability and monotonicity, methods that explicitly enforce these constraints achieve full compliance. NICE is the only method that does not support mutability constraints: despite high coverage, it exhibits low actionability compliance (18%–36% across datasets and models), rendering most of its recourse unsuitable for practical use. Furthermore, neither NICE nor OptBin support monotonicity constraints, meaning their reported compliance is purely empirical. NICE yields 100% and 86% for German Credit under LR and CatBoost, respectively, and 100% and 97% for Lending Club. In contrast, OptBin maintains 100% actionability but only 72% monotonicity compliance for German Credit, which means its suggested recourse could violate intuitive logic by recommending a borrower to reduce savings or increase debt exposure. In light of these findings, we exclude FACE and NICE from the subsequent comparative analysis.

Table 4. Overall performance across datasets and models. Column abbreviations denote Proximity (Prox), Plausibility (Plau), Discriminative Power (Disc), Delta probability (ΔP), Sparsity (Spar), and Recourse cost (Cost). Arrows indicate whether lower (↓) or higher (↑) values are preferred. The symbol "–" indicates that the corresponding method is not applicable to the considered model. **Bold** values indicate the best score within each dataset-model configuration, while underlined values denote the second-best result. The last row reports weighted averages across datasets, with weights proportional to the number of explanations for each dataset-model pair.

Data	Method	LR						CatBoost					
		Prox↓	Plau↓	Disc↑	ΔP↓	Spar↓	Cost↓	Prox↓	Plau↓	Disc↑	ΔP↓	Spar↓	Cost↓
German Credit	BF-exp	0.18	0.34	0.22	0.17	**1.01**	**1.51**	0.17	0.29	0.27	0.20	**1.02**	**1.53**
	Dice-R	0.30	0.37	0.38	0.23	1.60	6.88	0.29	0.37	0.35	0.24	1.64	6.21
	AR	0.28	0.42	0.35	0.21	**1.01**	7.28	–	–	–	–	–	–
	OptBin	0.22	0.24	**0.65**	0.14	1.60	6.20	–	–	–	–	–	–
	ProCE	0.20	0.24	0.48	0.21	1.09	3.19	0.18	0.22	0.45	0.23	1.04	2.53
	CREDIX	**0.15**	**0.22**	0.53	**0.13**	1.18	2.91	**0.15**	**0.21**	**0.46**	**0.18**	1.04	2.40
Lending Club	BF-exp	0.27	**0.23**	0.66	0.08	**1.04**	**2.26**	0.29	**0.26**	0.68	0.09	**1.13**	**2.88**
	Dice-R	0.71	0.54	0.58	0.12	1.77	12.15	0.65	0.51	0.61	0.14	1.76	11.71
	AR	0.35	0.27	0.62	0.09	**1.04**	3.01	–	–	–	–	–	–
	OptBin	0.34	0.26	0.64	0.09	1.07	2.90	–	–	–	–	–	–
	ProCE	0.32	0.27	0.64	0.08	1.15	3.48	0.28	0.28	**0.78**	0.09	1.24	4.65
	CREDIX	**0.26**	0.24	**0.70**	**0.07**	1.31	3.28	**0.22**	0.27	0.77	**0.08**	1.34	4.19
Avg	BF-exp	0.24	0.27	0.51	0.11	**1.03**	**2.00**	0.22	0.27	0.52	0.13	**1.09**	**2.36**
	Dice-R	0.57	0.48	0.51	0.16	1.71	10.32	0.51	0.46	0.51	0.18	1.71	9.61
	AR	0.33	0.32	0.53	0.13	**1.03**	4.49	–	–	–	–	–	–
	OptBin	0.30	0.25	**0.64**	0.11	1.25	4.04	–	–	–	–	–	–
	ProCE	0.28	0.26	0.58	0.13	1.13	3.38	0.24	0.26	**0.65**	0.14	1.16	3.84
	CREDIX	**0.22**	**0.23**	**0.64**	**0.09**	1.26	3.15	**0.19**	**0.25**	**0.65**	**0.12**	1.23	3.51

Table 4 reports the quality of the generated counterfactual explanations. Overall, the results highlight clear trade-offs between minimal perturbations, realism, and decision impact. First, we observe a strong alignment between proximity and plausibility across methods. This is particularly evident for BF-exp and CREDIX, with the latter achieving the best average scores (0.19–0.25 across models for both metrics), indicating highly localized and plausible counterfactuals. ProCE is slightly less local (0.24–0.28 on average), while Dice-R produces substantially more distant explanations (around 0.50 on average), reflecting less constrained perturbations. Regarding recourse cost, and sparsity, BF-exp achieves the lowest average recourse cost (2.00–2.36), as expected from its exhaustive search strategy. However, CREDIX remains consistently competitive, achieving costs of 3.15 (LR) and 3.51 (CatBoost), improving over ProCE (3.38 and 3.84, respectively) while maintaining comparable sparsity (around 1.25 vs. 1.15 on average). This confirms that CREDIX reduces intervention cost without increasing explanation complexity.

Regarding probability variation, BF-exp and CREDIX exhibit very similar behavior, with average ΔP values of approximately 0.10–0.12 across models. This indicates that both methods generate counterfactuals that are minimally sufficient to cross the decision boundary, without overshooting. In contrast, several baselines (e.g., Dice-R) tend to produce larger deviations from the decision boundary, indicating less controlled interventions. Finally, regarding discriminative power, OptBin achieves strong results under LR (0.64 on average), but it supports linear models only and does not enforce monotonicity. In contrast, CREDIX and ProCE remain stable across models, with an average discriminative power above 0.6.

Key Insight. CREDIX achieves the best trade-off between recourse cost and explanation quality, producing low-cost, realistic, and stable counterfactuals close to the decision boundary across datasets and models.

4.2 Efficiency Analysis

We analyze the computational efficiency of all methods using the Logistic Regression model; Catboost exhibits similar trends and is omitted for brevity.

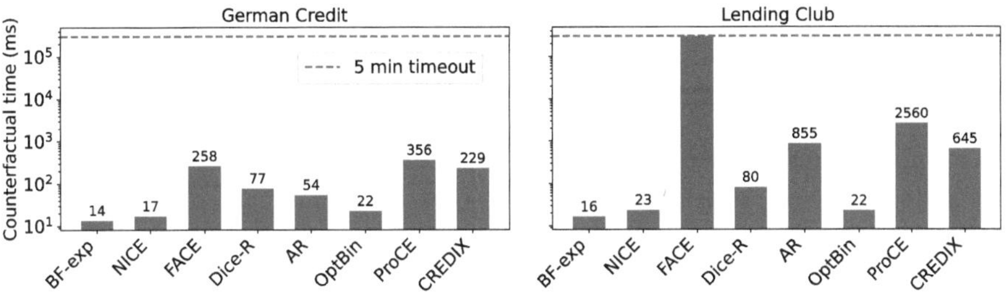

Fig. 1. Average time required to generate a single counterfactual explanation under Logistic Regression for German Credit and Lending Club (logarithmic scale, in ms).

As shown in Fig. 1, the average runtime per explanation closely reflects the underlying generation strategy for each method. BF-exp is consistently the fastest approach because it performs an exhaustive search over a small, discrete action space. NICE is similarly efficient, as it relies on nearest-neighbor retrieval rather than iterative optimization. A second group of methods, including DICE-R and AR, exhibits intermediate runtimes. While DICE-R runs a randomized search in the input space, which remains relatively contained, AR solves an optimization problem over a discretized action space, leading to moderately higher runtimes. In contrast, FACE is substantially slower and increasingly time-consuming as the dataset size grows: on Lending Club, it reaches the imposed 5-min timeout threshold. The highest computational cost is observed for evolutionary approaches, ProCE and CREDIX due to their population-based multi-objective optimization. However, CREDIX consistently outperforms ProCE, reducing runtime from 356.17 ms to 228.79 ms on German Credit and from 2559.93 ms to 644.9 ms on Lending Club. The main reason for this improvement is that CREDIX replaces the autoencoder-based plausibility component in ProCE with vectorized operations, thereby removing the need for repeated neural forward passes. Despite being the most time-consuming among practical methods, CREDIX remains within interactive limits (about 0.6 s per explanation on the most complex dataset), providing a favorable trade-off between efficiency and explanation quality.

Finally, we conduct a scalability stress test by increasing the number of actionable features in German Credit from 3 to 13. This configuration is typically unrealistic for credit-risk applications, where only a limited subset of variables is considered actionable; however, it exposes markedly different scaling behaviors across methods. BF-exp degrades dramatically from 13.5 ms to 34610.67 ms, confirming the expected combinatorial explosion induced by exhaustive search. ProCE experiences a similarly severe spike (356.17 ms to 61649.66 ms) due to the computational overhead of its autoencoder module. In contrast, CREDIX exhibits a more controlled increase, from 228.79 ms to 1068.14 ms, remaining within tractable computational limits even in higher-dimensional spaces.
Key Takeaway. CREDIX is more computationally demanding than instance- and optimization-based baselines, but remains feasible for interactive settings and scales better than competing optimization-based methods.

4.3 LLM-Based Cost Estimation

We study the problem of estimating feature modification costs using LLMs as preference oracles, with two objectives: (i) assessing the robustness of different LLM backbones in recovering an expert-provided ranking, and (ii) comparing pairwise preference elicitation with direct scoring strategies. We evaluate LLaMA-3.1-8B, Mistral-3.2-24B, and GPT-5.4-mini, representing different trade-offs between cost and reasoning capability. Two prompting strategies are considered: pairwise comparisons (as used in CREDIX) and direct scoring, where the LLM assigns absolute importance scores to each feature independently. We also vary the number of repetitions $R \in \{3, 5, 10\}$, where each repetition corresponds to an independent LLM query under temperature 0.2. In the direct setting, repetitions correspond to independent scoring runs, and final costs are obtained by averaging. Ranking quality is measured using Kendall's τ against an expert reference. The results of this analysis are reported in Table 5.

Overall, pairwise prompting consistently outperforms direct scoring across models and repetition settings, confirming that decomposing the task into pairwise comparisons yields more stable rankings. Smaller models also benefit significantly from this formulation, while Mistral-3.2-24B achieves the best overall trade-off between accuracy and cost, justifying its use in CREDIX. Direct scoring is generally less stable, particularly at low repetition regimes, indicating higher sensitivity to calibration and prompt ambiguity.

Despite the cost estimation is performed offline, only once per dataset, and is not a critical factor, we further complement the previous analysis by evaluating

Table 5. Ranking quality (Kendall's τ) in the LLM-based estimation of feature modification costs with respect to an expert-provided reference ranking, comparing different LLMs, repetition settings, and prompting strategies (pairwise vs direct).

Model	Prompt	German Credit			Lending Club		
		3	5	10	3	5	10
llama-3.1-8b	Pairwise	0.33	1.00	1.00	0.33	1.00	1.00
	Direct	0.33	0.82	0.82	0.33	0.33	1.00
mistral-3.2-24b	Pairwise	1.00	1.00	1.00	1.00	1.00	1.00
	Direct	0.33	0.33	0.33	1.00	1.00	1.00
gpt-5.4-mini	Pairwise	1.00	1.00	1.00	1.00	1.00	1.00
	Direct	1.00	1.00	1.00	1.00	1.00	1.00
Avg	Pairwise	0.78	1.00	1.00	0.78	1.00	1.00
	Direct	0.56	0.72	0.72	0.78	0.78	1.00

the computational cost in using different LLM models and prompting strategies. The results show that pairwise prompting is faster per query (1–4 s vs. 2–12 s for direct scoring), but requires a much larger number of queries due to pairwise combinations, making end-to-end runtime dependent on the comparison budget. As a result, direct scoring can be more efficient overall despite higher per-call latency. End-to-end execution instead highlights that the times for the default configuration (Mistral-3.2-24B, pairwise) range from 33.34 s ($R = 3$) to 88.72 s ($R = 10$) on average across the two datasets. GPT-5.4-mini is faster (11.15 s–41.46 s) with negligible loading overhead (0.04 s) since it is accessed through a remote API, while local models incur a one-time cost of 34.27 s (LLaMA) and 99.94 s (Mistral).
Key Takeaway. Pairwise prompting provides more reliable feature-cost rankings than direct scoring, especially for smaller LLMs, but incurs higher end-to-end execution times due to the combinatorial number of feature comparisons.

4.4 Ablation Study

This experiment evaluates the contribution of the main objectives in CREDIX by removing them from the optimization process. We consider two variants: $CREDIX\setminus plau$, which removes the plausibility objective, and $CREDIX\setminus exp$, which removes the feature modification cost objective. Results are reported in Table 6. Removing the plausibility objective generally degrades explanation quality. In particular, plausibility scores consistently increase across all settings (e.g., from 0.21 to 0.24 on German Credit), confirming that the WoE-based manifold regularization effectively steers the search toward more realistic regions of the feature space. This variant also reduces discriminative power (e.g., from 0.46 to 0.37 with LR, and from 0.77 to 0.73 with CatBoost on Lending Club), suggesting that plausibility plays a role in identifying more representative counterfactuals for the target class. The only improvement observed in this configuration is a

Table 6. Ablation study of CREDIX. *CREDIX\plau* removes the plausibility objective, while *CREDIX\exp* removes the feature modification cost objective. Column abbreviations denote Proximity (Prox), Plausibility (Plau), Discriminative Power (Disc), Delta probability (ΔP), Sparsity (Spar), and Recourse cost (Cost). Arrows indicate whether lower (↓) or higher (↑) values are preferred.

Data	Method	LR						CatBoost					
		Prox↓	Plau↓	Disc↑	ΔP↓	Spar↓	Cost↓	Prox↓	Plau↓	Disc↑	ΔP↓	Spar↓	Cost↓
German Credit	CREDIX	**0.15**	**0.22**	0.53	0.13	1.18	2.91	**0.15**	**0.21**	0.46	0.18	**1.04**	2.40
	\plau	**0.15**	0.24	0.46	**0.12**	**1.15**	**2.63**	**0.15**	0.24	0.37	**0.17**	**1.04**	**2.13**
	\exp	0.16	**0.22**	**0.54**	0.13	1.20	3.09	0.17	0.24	**0.48**	0.18	1.15	3.23
Lending Club	CREDIX	**0.26**	**0.24**	**0.70**	**0.07**	1.31	3.28	**0.22**	**0.27**	**0.77**	**0.08**	1.34	4.19
	\plau	**0.26**	**0.24**	0.69	**0.07**	**1.26**	**3.15**	0.26	0.28	0.73	**0.08**	**1.29**	**4.11**
	\exp	0.27	0.25	**0.70**	**0.07**	1.37	3.92	0.31	0.32	**0.77**	**0.08**	1.60	5.82

slight reduction in recourse cost across all settings (e.g., from 2.91 to 2.63 with LR, and from 2.40 to 2.13 with CatBoost on German Credit), indicating that enforcing realism may come at the expense of slightly more costly interventions. Removing the cost objective has the strongest impact on recourse cost, which consistently increases (e.g., from 2.40 to 3.23 and from 4.19 to 5.82 on German Credit and Lending Club with CatBoost), confirming that this component effectively guides the search toward less demanding recourse actions. This variant also tends to slightly degrade plausibility, suggesting that more costly interventions are often associated with less realistic modifications.

Key Takeaway. The full CREDIX formulation achieves the best trade-off: plausibility improves realism and discriminative power, while cost optimization reduces the effort required to achieve recourse.

5 Conclusion

We introduced CREDIX, a model-agnostic evolutionary framework for cost-aware counterfactual explanations that incorporates heterogeneous feature costs, domain constraints, and LLM-based cost estimation, addressing limitations of proximity-based methods in credit risk. Experiments across datasets and models show that CREDIX achieves the best trade-off, generating counterfactuals close to the decision boundary while reducing intervention cost and preserving plausibility. It is more computationally expensive than instance-based methods but remains suitable for interactive use and scales better than other optimization-based approaches with respect to dataset size and actionable features.

Acknowledgments. This work was supported by the AURORA research project (Prog. n. PG/2024/194752, CUP: E39J24001430009), funded under the Regione Emilia-Romagna call DGR 1985/23, Regional Law 14.

Declaration on Generative AI. During the preparation of this work, the authors used ChatGPT to improve the writing style and readability of manually drafted text. All suggestions were reviewed and validated by the authors.

References

1. Reprint of: Mahalanobis, p.c. (1936): on the generalised distance in statistics. Sankhya A **80** (2018). https://api.semanticscholar.org/CorpusID:239595337
2. Angiulli, F., Fassetti, F., Nisticò, S.: Finding local explanations through masking models. In: Yin, H. (ed.) IDEAL 2021. LNCS, vol. 13113, pp. 467–475. Springer, Cham (2021). https://doi.org/10.1007/978-3-030-91608-4_46
3. Bradley, R.A., Terry, M.E.: Rank analysis of incomplete block designs: I. The method of paired comparisons. Biometrika **39**, 324 (1952). https://api.semanticscholar.org/CorpusID:125209808
4. Brughmans, D., Leyman, P., Martens, D.: NICE: an algorithm for nearest instance counterfactual explanations. Data Min. Knowl. Discov. **38**(5), 2665–2703 (2024)
5. Dandl, S., Molnar, C., Binder, M., Bischl, B.: Multi-objective counterfactual explanations. In: Bäck, T., et al. (eds.) PPSN 2020. LNCS, vol. 12269, pp. 448–469. Springer, Cham (2020). https://doi.org/10.1007/978-3-030-58112-1_31
6. Deb, K., Agrawal, S., Pratap, A., Meyarivan, T.: A fast and elitist multiobjective genetic algorithm: NSGA-II. IEEE Trans. Evol. Comput. **6**(2), 182–197 (2002)
7. Dhurandhar, A., et al.: Explanations based on the missing: towards contrastive explanations with pertinent negatives. In: NeurIPS, pp. 590–601 (2018)
8. Duong, T.D., Li, Q., Xu, G.: Causality-based counterfactual explanation for classification models. Knowl.-Based Syst. **300**, 112200 (2024). https://doi.org/https://doi.org/10.1016/j.knosys.2024.112200
9. European Union: Artificial intelligence act (EU) 2024/1689 (2024). https://eur-lex.europa.eu/legal-content/EN/TXT/?uri=CELEX:32024R1689
10. Guidotti, R.: Counterfactual explanations and how to find them: literature review and benchmarking. Data Min. Knowl. Discov. **38**(5), 2770–2824 (2024)
11. Guidotti, R., Monreale, A., Giannotti, F., Pedreschi, D., Ruggieri, S., Turini, F.: Factual and counterfactual explanations for black box decision making. IEEE Intell. Syst. **34**(6), 14–23 (2019)
12. Jung, H., Kang, S., Kim, H., Won, D., Lee, S.: Counterfactual explanation based on gradual construction for deep networks. Pattern Recognit. **132**, 108958 (2022)
13. Van Looveren, A., Klaise, J.: Interpretable counterfactual explanations guided by prototypes. In: Oliver, N., Pérez-Cruz, F., Kramer, S., Read, J., Lozano, J.A. (eds.) ECML PKDD 2021. LNCS (LNAI), vol. 12976, pp. 650–665. Springer, Cham (2021). https://doi.org/10.1007/978-3-030-86520-7_40
14. Lucic, A., Oosterhuis, H., Haned, H., de Rijke, M.: FOCUS: flexible optimizable counterfactual explanations for tree ensembles. In: AAAI. AAAI Press (2022)
15. Mahajan, D., Tan, C., Sharma, A.: Preserving causal constraints in counterfactual explanations for machine learning classifiers. CoRR **abs/1912.03277** (2019)
16. Mothilal, R.K., Sharma, A., Tan, C.: Explaining machine learning classifiers through diverse counterfactual explanations. In: FAT*, pp. 607–617. ACM (2020)
17. Navas-Palencia, G.: Optimal binning: mathematical programming formulation (2020). https://doi.org/10.48550/arXiv.2001.08025
18. Navas-Palencia, G.: Optimal counterfactual explanations for scorecard modelling (2021). https://arxiv.org/abs/2104.08619

19. Nemecek, J., Pevný, T., Marecek, J.: Generating likely counterfactuals using sum-product networks. In: ICLR. OpenReview.net (2025)
20. Pawelczyk, M., Broelemann, K., Kasneci, G.: Learning model-agnostic counterfactual explanations for tabular data. In: WWW. ACM / IW3C2 (2020)
21. Poyiadzi, R., Sokol, K., Santos-Rodríguez, R., Bie, T.D., Flach, P.A.: FACE: feasible and actionable counterfactual explanations. In: AIES. ACM (2020)
22. Redelmeier, A., Jullum, M., Aas, K., Løland, A.: MCCE: Monte Carlo sampling of valid and realistic counterfactual explanations for tabular data. Data Min. Knowl. Discov. **38**(4), 1830–1861 (2024)
23. Schleich, M., Geng, Z., Zhang, Y., Suciu, D.: GeCo: quality counterfactual explanations in real time. Proc. VLDB Endow. **14**(9), 1681–1693 (2021)
24. Sharma, S., Henderson, J., Ghosh, J.: CERTIFAI: a common framework to provide explanations and analyse the fairness and robustness of black-box models. In: AIES, pp. 166–172. ACM (2020)
25. Tolomei, G., Silvestri, F., Haines, A., Lalmas, M.: Interpretable predictions of tree-based ensembles via actionable feature tweaking. In: KDD. ACM (2017)
26. Ustun, B., Spangher, A., Liu, Y.: Actionable recourse in linear classification. In: FAT, pp. 10–19. ACM (2019)
27. Wachter, S., Mittelstadt, B., Russell, C.: Counterfactual explanations without opening the black box: automated decisions and the GDPR. Harv. J. L. & Tech. **31**(2), 841–887 (2018). https://ssrn.com/abstract=3063289
28. Weed, D.L.: Weight of evidence: a review of concept and methods. Risk Anal. **25**(6), 1545–1557 (2005). https://doi.org/https://doi.org/10.1111/j.1539-6924.2005.00699.x

Tutorials

Deep Learning for Time Series Classification and Regression with aeon

Ali Ismail-Fawaz[1(✉)], Maxime Devanne[1], Antoine Guillaume[2], Anthony Bagnall[3], and Germain Forestier[1,4]

[1] IRIMAS, Université de Haute-Alsace, Mulhouse, France
ali.ismail-fawaz@uha.fr, maxime.devanne@uha.fr , germain.forestier@monash.edu
[2] Novahé, Saint-Cloud, France
antoine.guillaume@novahe.fr
[3] School of Electronics and Computer Science, University of Southampton, Southampton, UK
A.J.Bagnall@soton.ac.uk
[4] DSAI, Monash University, Melbourne, Australia

Abstract. We present a tutorial on deep learning for time series classification and regression with `aeon`, a Python library dedicated to time series machine learning. The tutorial first introduces the `aeon` toolkit and its unified interface, before focusing on neural architectures tailored to sequential data. We describe how participants will train and evaluate deep learning models for both classification and regression tasks using the `scikit-learn`-compatible API. In addition, we highlight a practical application in skeleton-based rehabilitation motion assessment, where deep models are applied to multivariate motion sequences from the Rehab-Pile archive. This application demonstrates how learned representations can support real-world healthcare scenarios involving movement analysis and assessment. More details about the tutorial schedule and materials are available on the tutorial webpage:
https://aeon-tutorials.github.io/ADBIS-2026/.

Keywords: Time series · Deep learning · Classification · Regression · Rehabilitation · aeon

1 Introduction

Time series data [15] appears in many scientific and industrial contexts, ranging from biomedical signals to sensor recordings and financial measurements. While traditional machine learning approaches [5] remain relevant, deep learning methods [12,16] have gained significant traction due to their ability to automatically learn hierarchical representations directly from raw sequences.

Time series classification (TSC) [15] assigns categorical labels to sequences, whereas time series regression (TSER) [7] predicts continuous outcomes. Both

G. Vargas-Solar et al. (Eds.): ADBIS 2026, LNCS 16937, pp. 407–414, 2027.
https://doi.org/10.1007/978-3-032-39820-8_26

tasks benefit from neural architectures such as convolutional neural networks (CNNs), residual networks, and hybrid approaches designed to capture temporal dependencies and spatial structure.

This tutorial focuses on deep learning models implemented in `aeon`, and concludes with a domain-specific application to human motion rehabilitation.

2 Related Work on Deep Learning for Time Series Classification and Regression

Several deep learning architectures have been successfully applied to both Time Series Classification (TSC) and Time Series Regression (TSER). Fully Convolutional Networks (FCN) employ stacked convolutional layers with global average pooling to learn discriminative temporal features [19]. ResNet introduces residual connections to facilitate the training of deeper convolutional networks [19]. InceptionTime and its hierarchical extension H-InceptionTime use multi-scale convolutional modules to capture temporal patterns at different receptive fields [11,13]. LITETime and LITEMVTime are lightweight Inception-based models designed for efficient univariate and multivariate time series learning [8,10]. ConvTran combines convolutional feature extraction with transformer-based self-attention [6], whereas VanTran relies solely on a vanilla transformer encoder to model long-range temporal dependencies [18]. These architectures have demonstrated strong performance across both TSC and TSER tasks.

3 Overview of the `aeon` Toolkit

`aeon` [14] is an open-source Python library designed for time series machine learning. It provides a unified interface for a wide range of learning tasks on sequential data, including classification, regression, clustering, forecasting, anomaly detection, segmentation, and similarity search. The toolkit follows the design principles of `scikit-learn` [17], exposing a consistent estimator API based on the `fit` and `predict` paradigm, which allows integration with existing machine learning workflows.

A key objective of `aeon` is to make state-of-the-art time series algorithms accessible through a common framework while supporting reproducibility and practical usability. The library supports both univariate and multivariate time series and includes utilities for data loading, preprocessing, evaluation, and experimentation. In this tutorial, we focus specifically on its deep learning functionality for classification and regression, showing how neural models can be used within the same interface as other `aeon` estimators.

4 Deep Learning in `aeon`

The `aeon` toolkit provides implementations of modern neural architectures for time series learning, following a consistent estimator interface compatible with `scikit-learn`. This design allows users to train deep models using familiar commands while retaining access to time series specific data handling and evaluation utilities.

The deep learning module includes several neural architectures that have been adapted for time series data. These include convolutional models such as Fully Convolutional Networks (FCN), which learn local temporal patterns, and Residual Networks (ResNet) [19], which enable the training of deeper models through skip connections. More recent architectures, such as Inception-based models [8,10,13], capture patterns at multiple temporal scales, while hybrid approaches [1,11] combine different architectural components to improve representation learning.

These models support multivariate sequences [2] and can leverage hardware acceleration when available. They are particularly useful when the goal is to learn representations directly from raw or lightly processed time series, reducing the need for handcrafted features.

5 Using Deep Learning Models

The practical part of the tutorial demonstrates how deep learning models can be trained using the same workflow as other estimators in `aeon`. Participants will see how to load benchmark datasets [4], instantiate a neural model, fit it to training data, and generate predictions on unseen cases.

5.1 Classification

For classification, the objective is to assign each input time series to one of a finite number of classes. The following example loads a classification dataset, trains a Fully Convolutional Network, and produces class probability estimates for the test set.

```
from aeon.datasets import load_classification
from aeon.classification.deep_learning import FCNClassifier

X, y = load_classification("ArrowHead", split="TRAIN")
X_test, _ = load_classification("ArrowHead", split="TEST")

clf = FCNClassifier(n_epochs=50, batch_size=16)
clf.fit(X, y)

probs = clf.predict_proba(X_test)
```

5.2 Regression

For regression, the target variable is continuous rather than categorical. The workflow remains similar, but the model outputs numerical predictions rather than class labels or class probabilities.

```python
from aeon.datasets import load_regression
from aeon.regression.deep_learning import ResNetRegressor

X, y = load_regression("BarCrawl6min", split="TRAIN")
X_test , _ = load_regression("BarCrawl6min", split="TEST")

reg = ResNetRegressor(n_epochs=50, batch_size=16)
reg.fit(X, y)

preds = reg.predict(X_test)
```

6 Tutorial Content Description

The tutorial is structured to guide participants progressively from general concepts to practical implementation. It begins with an introduction to time series machine learning and the role of deep learning methods in this context. We then present the aeon toolkit, highlighting its design principles and how it simplifies the use of advanced algorithms for sequential data.

The core of the tutorial focuses on deep learning models for time series classification and regression. We explain the intuition behind common neural architectures and discuss their strengths for modelling temporal data. Participants will learn how convolutional, residual, and multi-scale architectures can be used to learn discriminative representations from univariate and multivariate time series.

This is followed by a coding demonstration in which participants will learn how to load datasets, configure models, train estimators, and evaluate predictions using aeon. The tutorial will emphasize practical usage rather than implementation details of neural networks from scratch, making the session accessible to participants who want to apply these methods in their own work.

In the final part, we present a domain-specific application on skeleton-based human motion rehabilitation using the Rehab-Pile archive [9]. This example illustrates how the presented methods can be applied to real-world motion data and highlights the challenges and opportunities associated with rehabilitation-oriented time series analysis.

7 Tutorial Format and Schedule

The tutorial is designed as a 90-min session combining conceptual presentation and practical demonstration. The first part, lasting approximately one hour, introduces the fundamental concepts of time series deep learning and the aeon framework. This includes explanations of neural architectures and their application to classification and regression tasks.

The second part consists of a hands-on coding demonstration of around 20 min, where participants will follow the implementation of deep learning models using aeon. This segment focuses on practical usage, including data loading, model training, and prediction.

The session concludes with a 10-min question-and-answer segment, allowing participants to discuss specific use cases and clarify technical details.

8 Target Audience and Prerequisites

This tutorial is intended for researchers and practitioners working in data science and machine learning who are interested in temporal or sequential data. It is particularly relevant for those who wish to apply deep learning techniques to time series problems in domains such as healthcare, sensor analysis, or human motion understanding.

Participants are expected to have a basic understanding of machine learning concepts and familiarity with Python programming. Prior exposure to deep learning or time series analysis can be beneficial, but is not strictly required, as the tutorial will introduce the necessary concepts before moving to practical examples.

The proposed tutorial builds on a series of previous tutorials and demonstrations delivered by the authors on time series machine learning and deep learning methods:

- Tutorial on deep learning for time series classification with aeon at EGC 2024[1]
- Tutorial on time series machine learning with aeon at ECML 2024[2]
- Tutorial on time series classification and regression with aeon at KDD 2024 [3][3]
- Tutorial on imperfect data time series classification with aeon at DSAA 2025[4]
- Demonstration at ECML 2025 on time series classification and regression with aeon[5]

These previous events have allowed us to refine both the pedagogical structure and the practical content of the tutorial, ensuring a balanced combination of theoretical background and hands-on experience.

9 Application: Skeleton-Based Rehabilitation with Rehab-Pile

Beyond benchmark datasets, deep learning models for time series are particularly suited to structured motion data. One important application domain is rehabilitation, where patient movements are recorded as sequences of joint coordinates over time.

Skeleton-based motion data [9] can be represented as multivariate time series, with each dimension corresponding to joint positions or angles. These sequences

1 https://germain-forestier.info/e-egc.pdf.
2 https://aeon-tutorials.github.io/ECML-2024/.
3 https://aeon-tutorials.github.io/KDD-2024/.
4 https://aeon-tutorials.github.io/DSAA-2025/.
5 https://aeon-tutorials.github.io/ECML-Demo-2025/.

capture both spatial configuration and temporal evolution, making them well suited to deep neural models. In this setting, the objective may be to recognize exercise types, assess execution quality, detect compensatory movements, or predict continuous rehabilitation scores.

In this tutorial, we consider the Rehab-Pile archive, a collection of rehabilitation exercise recordings designed for movement assessment. The application will show how skeleton sequences can be formatted as time series data and used with deep learning models in `aeon`. This part of the tutorial connects the general methodology to a concrete healthcare scenario.

10 Tutors' Short Biographies

10.1 In-person Tutorial Presenters

Ali Ismail-Fawaz (AF) is an Associate Professor in Computer Science at the University of Haute-Alsace since 2025. He received his PhD in Computer Science from the University of Haute-Alsace in 2025. After completing his doctorate, he joined the University of Haute-Alsace in Mulhouse, France, as an Associate Professor, where he is part of the IRIMAS research institute. His main research topic is focused on time series machine learning, while addressing different applications mainly skeleton-based human motion and EEG signals. He is a core developer of the `aeon` toolkit and is leading the deep learning part of the package with a recent kick off for a deep forecasting module and is partner in the P16 Inria grant for the development of *aeon*, that is supporting this tutorial.[6]. His work has addressed different tasks such as classification, regression, generation, and clustering (https://hadifawaz1999.github.io/).

Germain Forestier (GF) is a university professor at the University of Haute-Alsace in Mulhouse France. He is part of the IRIMAS research institute, for which he is head of the computer science department. His research is mainly oriented around time series analysis, with a speciality in deep learning models (https://germain-forestier.info/). He is co-author of the deep learning review for time series classification for which the deep learning portions of the tutorial will be based on mostly, as well as new papers which he is co-authored as well. His contributions to the deep learning community in time series classification have been significant recently. He is also a core developer of the `aeon` toolkit and PI of the P16 Inria grant for the development of *aeon*.

Antoine Guillaume (AG) is an AI engineer at Novahé. He is currently working in the industry to create, maintain, and deploy software products focused on generative AI, agents, and time series. He is also engaged in the study of time series similarity search within the context of rare event prediction for critical industrial systems and shapelet-based methods. He is a core developer of the `aeon` toolkit. (https://baraline.github.io/).

[6] https://p16.inria.fr/fr/.

10.2 Tutorial Contributors

Anthony Bagnall (AB) is a Professor in Computer Science at the University of Southampton. His primary research interest is in developing algorithms for time series machine learning, including classification, regression and clustering, and finding novel areas of application. He has ongoing research collaborations with scientists on four continents and a track record of consultancy with industrial partners. He is an action editor for ECML 2026, is on the editorial board for the Data Mining and Knowledge Discovery journal and regularly reviews for data mining conferences such as KDD, ICDM and SDM. He helps maintain the time series classification archive (https://www.timeseriesclassification.com), including the UCR archive, that has been used in thousands of publications. More details are available at: https://www.southampton.ac.uk/people/62tpqc/professor-tony-bagnall.

Maxime Devanne (MD) is an Associate Professor in Computer Science at the University of Haute-Alsace since 2019. He received his PhD in Computer Science from both the University of Lille (France) and the Università di Firenze (Italy) in 2015. From 2016 to 2019, he was a postdoctoral researcher at IMT Atlantique and the Hospital of Brest. His main research interests are time series and human motion analysis with deep learning-based approaches (https://maxime-devanne.com).

11 Conclusion

We presented a tutorial on the deep learning capabilities of the `aeon` toolkit for time series classification and regression, along with an application to skeleton-based rehabilitation. By combining flexible neural architectures with a unified interface, `aeon` provides a practical framework for both research and real-world deployment. The Rehab-Pile example highlights the potential of deep time series models in healthcare settings, where accurate and automated analysis of movement data is increasingly important.

Acknowledgments. This work was supported by the P16 Inria grant, the ANR DELEGATION project (grant ANR-21-CE23-0014) and the ANR Terminus project (ANR-25-CE23-2879) of the French Agence Nationale de la Recherche.

References

1. Badi, O., et al.: COCALITE: a hybrid model COmbining CAtch22 and lite for time series classification. In: 2024 IEEE International Conference on Big Data (BigData), pp. 1229–1236. IEEE (2024)
2. Bagnall, A., et al.: The UEA multivariate time series classification archive. arXiv preprint arXiv:1811.00075 (2018)
3. Bagnall, A., et al.: A hands-on introduction to time series classification and regression. In: Proceedings of the 30th ACM SIGKDD Conference on Knowledge Discovery and Data Mining, pp. 6410–6411 (2024)

4. Dau, H.A., et al.: The UCR time series archive. IEEE/CAA J. Automatica Sinica **6**(6), 1293–1305 (2019)
5. Dempster, A., Petitjean, F., Webb, G.I.: Rocket: exceptionally fast and accurate time series classification using random convolutional kernels. arXiv preprint arXiv:1910.13051 (2019)
6. Foumani, N.M., Tan, C.W., Webb, G.I., Salehi, M.: Improving position encoding of transformers for multivariate time series classification. Data Min. Knowl. Disc. (2024)
7. Guijo-Rubio, D., Middlehurst, M., Arcencio, G., Silva, D.F., Bagnall, A.: Unsupervised feature based algorithms for time series extrinsic regression. Data Min. Knowl. Disc. (2023)
8. Ismail-Fawaz, A., Devanne, M., Berretti, S., Weber, J., Forestier, G.: LITE: light inception with boosting techniques for time series classification. In: 2023 IEEE 10th International Conference on Data Science and Advanced Analytics (DSAA), pp. 1–10. IEEE (2023)
9. Ismail-Fawaz, A., Devanne, M., Berretti, S., Weber, J., Forestier, G.: Deep learning for skeleton based human motion rehabilitation assessment: a benchmark. arXiv preprint arXiv:2507.21018 (2025)
10. Ismail-Fawaz, A., Devanne, M., Berretti, S., Weber, J., Forestier, G.: Look into the lite in deep learning for time series classification. Int. J. Data Sci. Anal. **20**(4), 4029–4049 (2025)
11. Ismail-Fawaz, A., Devanne, M., Weber, J., Forestier, G.: Deep learning for time series classification using new hand-crafted convolution filters. In: 2022 IEEE International Conference on Big Data (Big Data), pp. 972–981. IEEE (2022)
12. Ismail Fawaz, H., Forestier, G., Weber, J., Idoumghar, L., Muller, P.A.: Deep learning for time series classification: a review. Data Min. Knowl. Disc. **33**(4), 917–963 (2019)
13. Ismail Fawaz, H., et al.: InceptionTime: finding AlexNet for time series classification. Data Min. Knowl. Disc. **34**(6), 1936–1962 (2020)
14. Middlehurst, M., et al.: aeon: a python toolkit for learning from time series. J. Mach. Learn. Res. **25**(289), 1–10 (2024)
15. Middlehurst, M., Schäfer, P., Bagnall, A.: Bake off redux: a review and experimental evaluation of recent time series classification algorithms: M. middlehurst et al. Data Mining Knowl. Discov. **38**(4), 1958–2031 (2024)
16. Mohammadi Foumani, N., Miller, L., Tan, C.W., Webb, G.I., Forestier, G., Salehi, M.: Deep learning for time series classification and extrinsic regression: a current survey. ACM Comput. Surv. **56**(9), 1–45 (2024)
17. Pedregosa, F., et al.: Scikit-learn: machine learning in python. the. J. Mach. Learn. Res. **12**, 2825–2830 (2011)
18. Petrovich, M., Black, M.J., Varol, G.: Action-conditioned 3d human motion synthesis with transformer VAE. In: Proceedings of the IEEE/CVF International Conference on Computer Vision, pp. 10985–10995 (2021)
19. Wang, Z., Yan, W., Oates, T.: Time series classification from scratch with deep neural networks: a strong baseline. In: 2017 International Joint Conference on Neural Networks (IJCNN), pp. 1578–1585. IEEE (2017)

Navigating the Vector Search Landscape: ANN Indexes for Modern AI Systems

Ilias Azizi[1(✉)], Vassilis Christophides[2,3], and Themis Palpanas[1]

[1] LIPADE, Université Paris Cité, Paris, France
azizii.ilias@gmail.com, themis@mi.parisdescartes.fr
[2] ETIS, CNRS, ENSEA,Cedex, France
vassilis.christophides@ensea.fr
[3] IPAL, Singapore, Singapore

Abstract. Vector databases have become a cornerstone of modern data science and AI applications, enabling the retrieval of relevant data based on semantic meaning and context under strict latency, accuracy, and resource constraints. This demand has strongly shaped the development of approximate nearest neighbor (ANN) methods and accelerated the emergence of new approaches at an unprecedented pace. As a result, vector search is moving beyond static, vector-only indexing techniques toward dynamic, predicate-aware, and workload-aware designs that better reflect the requirements of real deployments. Recent systems increasingly account for updates, query diversity, structured filters, hardware constraints, and resource efficiency, shaping a new generation of vector search solutions for modern data management systems.

This tutorial provides a structured introduction to this evolving landscape from both algorithmic and systems perspectives. It first presents the foundations of vector search and the main ANN indexing families, including space-partitioning, hashing-based, quantization-based, and graph-based methods. It then discusses how these techniques are integrated into modern AI pipelines through hybrid and filtered search, query optimization, adaptive execution, benchmarking methodologies, and index maintenance. Finally, it highlights recent research directions driven by emerging applications, including retrieval-augmented generation, AI agents, memory infrastructure, and energy-aware vector search.

Keywords: Vector Indexing · Approximate Nearest Neighbor Search

1 Introduction

Vector data has become ubiquitous in modern information systems. While vectors have long been used in scientific computing, signal processing, multimedia retrieval, and data analytics, recent advances in machine learning have transformed them into a general-purpose representation for multimodal data [21,44]. Text documents, images, audio signals, videos, user profiles, products, source code, scientific observations, and even structured records can now be mapped

G. Vargas-Solar et al. (Eds.): ADBIS 2026, LNCS 16937, pp. 415–424, 2027.
https://doi.org/10.1007/978-3-032-39820-8_27

into high-dimensional embedding spaces, where semantic or functional similarity is reflected by geometric proximity. This shift is mainly driven by the widespread adoption of representation learning and foundation models [7,58].

Large language models, dense retrievers, vision-language models, and recommender systems increasingly generate embeddings for documents, queries, images, users, and items [17,34,35,49,51,58]. Learned representations are also widely used in scientific and industrial applications, including classification, clustering, anomaly detection, data discovery, and data attribution methods in explainable AI [42,43]. As a result, embedding vectors are now generated at massive scale and on a continuous basis, leading to collections that may contain millions or billions of high-dimensional vectors. Vector search has therefore become a core component of modern data systems, enabling efficient retrieval over these large collections of embeddings [21]. It supports a wide range of applications, including semantic search [34,35,58], recommendation [17,51], multimedia retrieval [49,58], or data attribution methods in explainable AI [43]. In these applications, data objects are represented as vectors, and queries require retrieving the most similar vectors according to a given similarity function.

Formally, given a dataset $\mathcal{X} = \{x_1, \ldots, x_n\} \subset \mathbb{R}^d$, a query vector $q \in \mathbb{R}^d$, and a similarity function, vector search aims to retrieve the k nearest neighbors of q in $\mathcal{X}$. A straightforward solution computes the similarity between q and every vector in the dataset and returns the top-k results. However, this exhaustive scan has time complexity $O(nd)$ and becomes impractical at large scale, especially when collections contain millions or billions (n) of high-dimensional (d) vectors [22]. To avoid this exhaustive scan at query time, nearest-neighbor indexes are built to organize the vector collection and accelerate search [19,47]. In many application settings, strict exactness is less important than meeting latency and throughput requirements; therefore, systems often trade a controlled amount of result accuracy for faster query processing [20,46].

Approximate Nearest Neighbor (ANN) search addresses this issue by trading a controlled amount of accuracy for substantial gains in latency, throughput, and memory efficiency [6,50]. This has led to a rich ecosystem of vector indexes. Space-partitioning methods, including tree-based and clustering-based approaches, organize the vector space into regions or subsets so that similar vectors are likely to reside in the same or nearby partitions [9,19,47]. Hash-based techniques map vectors into one or multiple hash tables, with the goal that similar vectors collide with high probability and can therefore be retrieved by probing only a small number of buckets [55,56]. Graph-based methods represent the dataset as a proximity graph, where vertices correspond to data vectors and edges connect vectors that are close according to the target similarity measure; at query time, search traverses the graph greedily or with beam search to progressively move toward the nearest neighbors [4,5,14,24,25,39–41,52]. Quantization-based approaches mainly reduce the cost of storage and distance computation by encoding vectors into compact representations, enabling faster approximate comparisons and lower memory footprint [1,26,27,30,33]. These techniques are not mutually exclusive and are often combined in practical systems: for example, quantization can be integrated with inverted files, clustering, or graph structures to reduce memory usage and accelerate distance computations [1,4,48,52,53,60].

Building an efficient vector search system should essentially balance diverse performance metrics such as accuracy, latency, and throughput. This requires careful choices about query execution, including parameter tuning, parallelism, and hardware utilization [1,37,48]. Beyond recall and latency, recent work increasingly considers memory footprint, indexing cost, distance computations, hardware utilization, and energy consumption [6,46,62]. As vector similarity is frequently combined with structured predicates or metadata constraints, filtered and hybrid vector search has become a core system challenge [2,36].

Vector search systems must also adapt to evolving workloads and dynamic data. This includes handling insertions, deletions, and updates, as well as improving performance for hard or out-of-distribution queries through workload-aware indexing and index maintenance [13,29,31,59]. At the same time, rigorous benchmarking is needed to evaluate performance across datasets, recall targets, hardware settings, and similarity measures [3,10,50]. These issues are becoming even more important with emerging workloads such as RAG, AI agents, long-term memory, and multimodal search, where retrieval quality, freshness, robustness, and energy efficiency directly affect the behavior of downstream AI systems [18,23,31,32,57].

This tutorial aims to provide a structured introduction to vector indexes from both algorithmic and system perspectives. It first presents the foundations of vector search and the main ANN indexing families, including space-partitioning, and graph-based methods. It then discusses how these techniques are integrated into modern AI pipelines through hybrid and filtered search, query optimization, adaptive execution, and benchmarking methodologies. Finally, it highlights recent research directions for emerging applications such as vector search for LLM-based applications and long-term memory.

Target Audience and Assumed Background. The tutorial targets researchers, graduate students, and practitioners interested in data management, information retrieval, machine learning systems, and vector databases. It is suitable both for newcomers who want a structured introduction to vector indexing and for experienced participants interested in system-level design choices and recent research directions. The assumed background is basic knowledge of algorithms, data structures, and machine learning representations. Familiarity with high-dimensional vectors, similarity measures, or database indexing is useful, but not required. The tutorial introduces the necessary fundamentals before discussing advanced ANN indexing techniques and system-design issues.

Relation to Previous Tutorials. Recent tutorials have addressed faster ANN execution [11], filtered vector search [16], and dense retrieval pipelines [8]. These works focus on specific aspects such as parallelism, streaming, early termination, constrained retrieval, or IR-oriented applications. Our tutorial is complementary: it provides a unified, system-oriented introduction to vector indexes, connecting

ANN indexing families with hybrid search, query optimization, benchmarking, energy footprint, and emerging AI-native workloads.

Table 1. Tutorial outline.

Time	Part	Content
10 min	Introduction and Motivation	Role of vector search in modern data systems; applications in semantic search, recommendation, RAG, multimedia, and scientific data; main challenges in scale, latency, accuracy, and energy consumption.
10 min	Problem Definition and Fundamentals	Exact and approximate vector similarity search; distance measures and embedding spaces; quality–efficiency trade-offs in recall, latency, and memory.
30 min	Families of ANN Indexing Techniques	Space-partitioning methods, including trees, hashing, and clustering; subspace-collision methods; graph-based proximity indexes; comparative overview and design trade-offs.
15 min	Hybrid and Filtered Search	Combination of multiple indexing strategies; filtered and constrained vector search; query-aware indexing and query optimization techniques.
10 min	Evaluation and Benchmarking	Measures such as recall, latency, throughput, and cost; benchmark datasets and methodologies; practical evaluation pitfalls.
10 min	Emerging Trends and Research Directions	Vector search for AI agents and large language models; adaptive and learned indexes; AI-native data systems.
5 min	Conclusion and Discussion	Key takeaways, open challenges, and Q&A.

2 Tutorial Scope

In this 1.5-hour tutorial, we cover the foundations, indexing techniques, system-level challenges, and emerging directions of vector search. The tutorial is organized into seven parts, summarized in Table 1.

2.1 Introduction and Motivation

We start by motivating vector search as a building block of modern AI systems. We discuss its role in semantic search [34], recommendation [17], multimedia retrieval [49], Machine Learning [43], and Retrieval-Augmented Generation (RAG) [35,58]. We formalize the nearest-neighbor search problem and explain why exact search becomes increasingly expensive as vector collections grow to millions or billions of objects. In this context, we introduce approximate nearest-neighbor (ANN) search, where systems trade a controlled loss in accuracy for lower latency, higher throughput, and reduced resource consumption. We highlight the main challenges that make indexing necessary: large-scale collections, strict latency requirements, accuracy constraints, dynamic workloads, and energy consumption.

2.2 Families of ANN Indexing Techniques

We then review the main families of ANN indexing methods and the principles behind their design. We cover space-partitioning methods, including trees [19, 45], hashing [28], and clustering-based approaches [33,38], followed by subspace-collision techniques that exploit lower-dimensional projections or partitions of the feature space [28,56]. We then focus on graph-based indexes [25,39,52], where proximity graphs support efficient navigation toward nearest neighbors. This part concludes with a comparative discussion of the design trade-offs across these families, including construction cost, memory footprint, search efficiency, update support, and robustness across datasets.

2.3 Hybrid and Filtered Search

This part discusses vector search in realistic data-system settings, where vector similarity is often combined with structured predicates and metadata filters. We cover filtered and constrained vector search [2,36], the combination of multiple indexing strategies [4,54,63], and query-aware indexing [13,29]. We also discuss query optimization techniques used to balance selectivity, recall, and execution cost [12,61]. The goal is to show how ANN search moves from a standalone similarity-search problem to an operator that must interact with predicates, cost models, and system-level constraints.

2.4 Evaluation and Benchmarking

We discuss how vector search systems should be evaluated. We present standard measures, and explain how benchmark datasets and workload choices affect conclusions [3,6,10,50]. Beyond recall and latency, we emphasize the need to report construction time, memory usage, update costs, throughput, tail latency, and energy consumption. We also highlight practical evaluation pitfalls [15], including unfair parameter tuning, ignoring construction and maintenance costs, reporting only average recall, overlooking energy consumption, and using workloads that do not reflect deployment constraints.

2.5 Emerging Trends and Research Directions

We conclude the technical part with emerging research directions. We discuss vector search for AI agents and large language models, where retrieval quality directly affects downstream reasoning and generation. We also cover adaptive and learned indexes, as well as AI-native data systems where vector search becomes a first-class component of the data management stack [18,23,31,32,57]. Finally, we discuss privacy-preserving and decentralized ANN search, including settings where vectors, queries, or index ownership are distributed across multiple parties and where retrieval must satisfy privacy, security, or data-sovereignty constraints.

2.6 Conclusion and Discussion

The tutorial ends with a summary of the main takeaways and a discussion of open challenges, including scalability, robustness, dynamic updates, evaluation methodology, privacy, and resource-efficient retrieval.

3 Presenters

Ilias Azizi. is a postdoctoral researcher at Université Paris Cité, LIPADE. His research focuses on scalable similarity search, vector databases, and graph-based approximate nearest neighbor search. He has worked on the design, optimization, and evaluation of efficient vector search methods, with publications in database venues including VLDB and SIGMOD.

Vassilis Christophides. is a Professor of Computer Science at ENSEA, Cergy. He has previously been a Full Professor at the University of Crete, an advanced research scientist at INRIA Paris, and a Distinguished Scientist at Technicolor. His research spans machine learning systems, data science, big data computing, databases, web information systems, and scientific data management. He has authored more than 160 articles in leading journals and conferences, received the 2004 SIGMOD Test of Time Award and several ISWC best paper awards, and has coordinated 22 research projects. He has served in major conference roles, including General Chair of EDBT/ICDT 2014 and Area Chair for ICDE 2016, and is an elected member of the Executive Board of the EDBT Association, as well as a member of ACM and IEEE.

Themis Palpanas. is an ACM Fellow, a Senior Fellow of the French University Institute (IUF), and a Distinguished Professor of Computer Science at Université Paris Cité. He has been the Founding Director of the Data Intelligence Institute of Paris (diiP). He has authored 15 patents, received 3 best paper awards and the IBM SUR award, served as Program Chair for VLDB 2025 and IEEE BigData 2023, General Chair for VLDB 2013, and Editor-in-Chief for BDR. He has been working on high-dimensional vector management and analytics for more than 15 years, has developed several state-of-the-art methods, and has delivered 20 tutorials on these subjects in top international conferences.

Acknowledgments. Supported by EU Horizon projects ARMADA (101168951) and DataGEMS (101188416), and by $Y\Pi AI\Theta A$ & NextGenerationEU project HARSH ($Y\Pi 3TA - 0560901$) that is carried out within the framework of the National Recovery and Resilience Plan "Greece 2.0" with funding from the European Union – NextGenerationEU. This work was granted access to the HPC resources of IDRIS under the allocation 2025-A0191012641 made by GENCI.

References

1. Aguerrebere, C., Bhati, I.S., Hildebrand, M., Tepper, M., Willke, T.: Similarity search in the blink of an eye with compressed indices. Proc. VLDB Endowment **16**(11), 3433–3446 (2023)
2. Ait Aomar, A., Echihabi, K., Arnaboldi, M., Alagiannis, I., Hilloulin, D., Cherkaoui, M.: RWalks: random walks as attribute diffusers for filtered vector search. Proc. ACM Manag. Data **3**(3), 1–26 (2025)
3. Aumüller, M., Bernhardsson, E., Faithfull, A.: Ann-benchmarks: a benchmarking tool for approximate nearest neighbor algorithms. In: Beecks, C., Borutta, F., Kröger, P., Seidl, T. (eds.) International Conference on Similarity Search and Applications, pp. 34–49. Springer, Cham (2017).https://doi.org/10.1007/978-3-319-68474-1_3
4. Azizi, I., Echihabi, K., Palpanas, T.: ELPIS: graph-based similarity search for scalable data science. Proc. VLDB Endowment **16**(6), 1548–1559 (2023)
5. Azizi, I., Echihabi, K., Palpanas, T.: Graph-based vector search: an experimental evaluation of the state-of-the-art. Proc. ACM Manag. Data **3**(1), 1–31 (2025)
6. Azizi, I., Echihabi, K., Palpanas, T., Christophides, V.: Toward efficient and scalable design of in-memory graph-based vector search. arXiv e-prints pp. arXiv–2509 (2025)
7. Bommasani, R., et al.: On the opportunities and risks of foundation models. arXiv preprint arXiv:2108.07258 (2021)
8. Bruch, S.: Advances in vector search. In: Proceedings of the Eighteenth ACM International Conference on Web Search and Data Mining, pp. 995–997 (2025)
9. Camerra, A., Shieh, J., Palpanas, T., Rakthanmanon, T., Keogh, E.: Beyond One Billion Time Series: indexing and Mining Very Large Time Series Collections With *i*SAX2+. Knowl. Inf. Syst. **39**(1), 123–151 (2014)
10. Ceccarello, M., Levchenko, A., Ileana, I., Palpanas, T.: Evaluating and generating query workloads for high dimensional vector similarity search. In: Proceedings of the 31st ACM SIGKDD Conference on Knowledge Discovery and Data Mining, V.2, KDD, pp. 5299–5310. ACM (2025). https://doi.org/10.1145/3711896.3737383, https://doi.org/10.1145/3711896.3737383
11. Chatzakis, M., Del Gaudio, F., Sideri, S., Palpanas, T.: The quest for faster ANN vector search. EDBT (2026)
12. Chatzakis, M., Papakonstantinou, Y., Palpanas, T.: DARTH: declarative recall through early termination for approximate nearest neighbor search. Proc. ACM Manag. Data **3**(4), 1–26 (2025)
13. Chen, M., Zhang, K., He, Z., Jing, Y., Wang, X.S.: RoarGraph: a projected bipartite graph for efficient cross-modal approximate nearest neighbor search. arXiv preprint arXiv:2408.08933 (2024)
14. Chen, Q., et al.: SPTAG: a library for fast approximate nearest neighbor search (2018). https://github.com/Microsoft/SPTAG
15. Chen, T., et al.: Reveal hidden pitfalls and navigate next generation of vector similarity search from task-centric views:[experiments & analysis]. Proceedings of the ACM on Management of Data **4**(1 (SIGMOD)), 1–25 (2026)

16. Chronis, Y., Caminal, H., Papakonstantinou, Y., Özcan, F., Ailamaki, A.: Filtered vector search: state-of-the-art and research opportunities. Proc. VLDB Endowment **18**(12), 5488–5492 (2025)
17. Covington, P., Adams, J., Sargin, E.: Deep neural networks for youtube recommendations. In: Proceedings of the 10th ACM Conference on Recommender Systems, pp. 191–198 (2016). https://doi.org/10.1145/2959100.2959190
18. Deng, Y., et al.: AlayaDB: the data foundation for efficient and effective long-context LLM inference. In: Companion of the 2025 International Conference on Management of Data, pp. 364–377 (2025)
19. Echihabi, K., Fatourou, P., Zoumpatianos, K., Palpanas, T., Benbrahim, H.: Hercules Against Data Series Similarity Search. PVLDB **15**(10) (2022)
20. Echihabi, K., Palpanas, T., Zoumpatianos, K.: New trends in high-D vector similarity search: AI-driven, progressive, and distributed. Proceedings VLDB Endow. **14**(12), 3198–3201 (2021). http://www.vldb.org/pvldb/vol14/p3198-echihabi.pdf
21. Echihabi, K., Zoumpatianos, K., Palpanas, T.: Scalable machine learning on high-dimensional vectors: from data series to deep network embeddings. In: WIMS 2020: The 10th International Conference on Web Intelligence, Mining and Semantics, pp. 1–6. ACM (2020)
22. Echihabi, K., Zoumpatianos, K., Palpanas, T., Benbrahim, H.: The Lernaean Hydra of Data Series Similarity Search: an Experimental Evaluation of the State of the Art. PVLDB **12**(2) (2018)
23. Fan, W., et al.: A survey on rag meeting LLMs: towards retrieval-augmented large language models. In: Proceedings of the 30th ACM SIGKDD Conference on Knowledge Discovery and Data Mining, pp. 6491–6501 (2024)
24. Fu, C., Wang, C., Cai, D.: High dimensional similarity search with satellite system graph: efficiency, scalability, and unindexed query compatibility. IEEE Trans. Pattern Anal. Mach. Intell. (2021)
25. Fu, C., Xiang, C., Wang, C., Cai, D.: Fast approximate nearest neighbor search with the navigating spreading-out graph. Proc. VLDB Endow. **12**(5), 461–474 (2019)
26. Gao, J., Long, C.: RaBitQ: quantizing high-dimensional vectors with a theoretical error bound for approximate nearest neighbor search. Proc. ACM Manag. Data **2**(3), 1–27 (2024)
27. Gou, Y., Gao, J., Xu, Y., Long, C.: SymphonyQG: towards symphonious integration of quantization and graph for approximate nearest neighbor search. Proc. ACM Manag. Data **3**(1), 1–26 (2025)
28. Jafari, O., Maurya, P., Nagarkar, P., Islam, K.M., Crushev, C.: A survey on locality sensitive hashing algorithms and their applications. arXiv preprint arXiv:2102.08942 (2021)
29. Jaiswal, S., Krishnaswamy, R., Garg, A., Simhadri, H.V., Agrawal, S.: OOD-Diskann: efficient and scalable graph ANNS for out-of-distribution queries. arXiv preprint arXiv:2211.12850 (2022)
30. Jégou, H., Douze, M., Schmid, C.: Product quantization for nearest neighbor search. IEEE Trans. Pattern Anal. Mach. Intell. **33**, 117–128 (2011)
31. Jiang, W., Subramanian, S., Graves, C., Alonso, G., Yazdanbakhsh, A., Dadu, V.: RAGO: systematic performance optimization for retrieval-augmented generation serving. In: Proceedings of the 52nd Annual International Symposium on Computer Architecture, pp. 974–989 (2025)
32. Jing, Z., Su, Y., Han, Y.: When large language models meet vector databases: a survey. In: 2025 Conference on Artificial Intelligence x Multimedia (AIxMM), pp. 7–13. IEEE (2025)

33. Johnson, J., Douze, M., Jégou, H.: Billion-scale similarity search with GPUs. IEEE Trans. Big Data **7**(3), 535–547 (2019)
34. Karpukhin, V., Oguz, B., Min, S., et al.: Dense passage retrieval for open-domain question answering. In: Proceedings of the 2020 Conference on Empirical Methods in Natural Language Processing (2020). https://aclanthology.org/2020.emnlp-main.550/
35. Lewis, P., Perez, E., Piktus, A., et al.: Retrieval-augmented generation for knowledge-intensive nlp tasks. In: Advances in Neural Information Processing Systems, vol. 33 (2020). https://arxiv.org/abs/2005.11401
36. Lu, D., Caminal, H., Chatzakis, M., Papakonstantinou, Y., Chronis, Y., Jain, V., Özcan, F.: An in-depth study of filter-agnostic vector search on a postgresql database system: [experiments and analysis]. Proceedings of the ACM on Management of Data (SIGMOD) (2026)
37. pgvector maintainers, P.G.D.G..: pgvector: vector search extension for postgresql with HNSW support (2023). https://github.com/pgvector/pgvector. supports HNSW indexing
38. Malinen, M.I., Fränti, P.: Balanced K-Means for Clustering. In: Fränti, P., Brown, G., Loog, M., Escolano, F., Pelillo, M. (eds.) S+SSPR 2014. LNCS, vol. 8621, pp. 32–41. Springer, Heidelberg (2014). https://doi.org/10.1007/978-3-662-44415-3_4
39. Malkov, Y.A., Yashunin, D.A.: Efficient and robust approximate nearest neighbor search using hierarchical navigable small world graphs. IEEE Trans. Pattern Anal. Mach. Intell. **42**(4), 824–836 (2020)
40. Manohar, M.D., et al.: ParlayANN: scalable and deterministic parallel graph-based approximate nearest neighbor search algorithms. In: Proceedings of the 29th ACM SIGPLAN Annual Symposium on Principles and Practice of Parallel Programming, pp. 270–285 (2024)
41. Munoz, J.V., Gonçalves, M.A., Dias, Z., Torres, R.D.S.: Hierarchical clustering-based graphs for large scale approximate nearest neighbor search. Pattern Recogn. **96**, 106970 (2019)
42. Myrtakis, N., Castellani, A., Tsamardinos, I.: EDDI: explainable data drift monitoring using influence. In: 42nd IEEE International Conference on Data Engineering (ICDE) Montreal (2026)
43. Myrtakis, N., Tsamardinos, I., Christophides, V.: Data glitches discovery using influence-based model explanations. In: Proceedings of the 31st ACM SIGKDD Conference on Knowledge Discovery and Data Mining V. 1, pp. 1068–1079 (2025)
44. Palpanas, T.: Data series management: the road to big sequence analytics. ACM SIGMOD Rec. **44**(2), 47–52 (2015)
45. Palpanas, T.: Evolution of a Data Series Index: the iSAX Family of Data Series Indexes. Commun. Comput. Inf. Sci. (CCIS), 1197 (2020)
46. Pan, J.J., Wang, J., Li, G.: Vector database management techniques and systems. In: Companion of the 2024 International Conference on Management of Data, pp. 597–604 (2024)
47. Peng, B., Fatourou, P., Palpanas, T.: MESSI: in-memory data series indexing. In: 2020 IEEE 36th International Conference on Data Engineering (ICDE), pp. 337–348. IEEE (2020)
48. Qdrant Team: Qdrant vector database (2022). https://qdrant.tech/. Accessed 01 Oct 2025
49. Radford, A., Kim, J.W., Hallacy, C., et al.: Learning transferable visual models from natural language supervision. In: Proceedings of the 38th International Conference on Machine Learning (2021). https://arxiv.org/abs/2103.00020

50. Simhadri, H.V., Aumuller, M., Douze, M., et al.: Results of the neurips'21 challenge on billion-scale approximate nearest neighbor search. In: Proceedings of Machine Learning Research, vol. 176 (2022). https://arxiv.org/abs/2205.03763
51. Song, L., et al.: Large-scale training system for 100-million classification at alibaba. In: Proceedings of the 26th ACM SIGKDD International Conference on Knowledge Discovery & Data Mining, pp. 2909–2930 (2020)
52. Subramanya, S.J., Kadekodi, R., Krishaswamy, R., Simhadri, H.V.: DiskANN: fast accurate billion-point nearest neighbor search on a single node. In: Proceedings of the 33rd International Conference on Neural Information Processing Systems, pp. 13766–13776 (2019)
53. Team, E.: Elasticsearch: distributed, restful search and analytics engine (2010). https://www.elastic.co/elasticsearch. Accessed 17 Oct 2025
54. Wang, J., et al.: Trinary-projection trees for approximate nearest neighbor search. IEEE Trans. Pattern Anal. Mach. Intell. **36**(2), 388–403 (2013)
55. Wei, J., Lee, X., Liao, Z., Palpanas, T., Peng, B.: Subspace collision: an efficient and accurate framework for high-dimensional approximate nearest neighbor search. Proc. ACM Manag. Data **3**(1), 1–29 (2025)
56. Wei, J., Peng, B., Lee, X., Palpanas, T.: DET-LSH: a locality-sensitive hashing scheme with dynamic encoding tree for approximate nearest neighbor search. Proc. VLDB Endow. **17**(9), 2241–2254 (2024)
57. Wei, J., Xu, Q., Yang, C.: The virtuous cycle: Ai-powered vector search and vector search-augmented AI. arXiv preprint arXiv:2603.09347 (2026)
58. Wu, Z., et al.: DeepSeek-vl2: mixture-of-experts vision-language models for advanced multimodal understanding. arXiv preprint arXiv:2412.10302 (2024)
59. Xu, Y., et al.: SPFresh: incremental in-place update for billion-scale vector search. In: Proceedings of the 29th Symposium on Operating Systems Principles, pp. 545–561 (2023)
60. Yahoo Japan Corporation: NGT: neighborhood graph and tree for high-dimensional data (2022). https://github.com/yahoojapan/NGT. Accessed 20 Oct 2024
61. Zhang, C., J. Miller, R.: Distribution-aware exploration for adaptive HNSW search. Proc. ACM Manag. Data **4**(1 (SIGMOD)), 1–27 (2026)
62. Zhang, Y., Liu, S., Wang, J.: Are there fundamental limitations in supporting vector data management in relational databases? a case study of postgresql. In: 2024 IEEE 40th International Conference on Data Engineering (ICDE), pp. 3640–3653. IEEE (2024)
63. Zhao, X., Tian, Y., Huang, K., Zheng, B., Zhou, X.: Towards efficient index construction and approximate nearest neighbor search in high-dimensional spaces. Proc. VLDB Endowment **16**(8), 1979–1991 (2023)

Towards Optimized Big Satellite Data Management in Agricultural Monitoring Through Causal-Based xAI: A Tutorial from the EDEM

Michele Linardi[1(✉)] and Claudia Paris[2]

[1] ETIS, UMR 8051, CYU, ENSEA, CNRS, Cergy, France
michele.linardi@cyu.fr
[2] University of Twente, ITC, 7522NH Enschede, The Netherlands
c.paris@utwente.nl

Abstract. The massive amount of Earth Observation (EO) data collected daily from spaceborne and airborne sensors, combined with recent advances in Earth Observation (AI4EO), provides new opportunities for accurate and continuous environmental monitoring. This is particularly relevant for agricultural applications: crop type mapping, yield estimation, and phenology monitoring, which are inherently dynamic and require within-season updates, driving the need to store and process large volumes of multi-temporal EO data. In this context, explainable Artificial Intelligence (xAI) is becoming an operational necessity: in government and policy settings, AI4EO outputs directly influence agricultural subsidies, insurance compensation, and compliance monitoring, making interpretability a legal and institutional requirement rather than a mere scientific desideratum. This tutorial provides a structured overview of the state of the art at the intersection of xAI, Deep Learning (DL), and EO-based agricultural monitoring, with emphasis on crop type mapping. We discuss the limits of off-the-shelf attribution methods on satellite image classifiers and show how xAI can be leveraged not only for transparency but also as an active lever for data selection and scalable large-scale EO processing. We further examine how agronomic domain knowledge: spectral indices, phenological calendars, crop-specific priors can constrain and enrich DL explanations. Finally, we outline future perspectives towards causal estimation and concept-based explainability, and discuss how these directions could reshape big satellite data management for the European Conference on Advances in Databases and Information Systems (ADBIS) and Data Management (DM) communities.

Keywords: xAI · Deep Learning · Crop Mapping · Big Satellite Data · AI4EO

G. Vargas-Solar et al. (Eds.): ADBIS 2026, LNCS 16937, pp. 425–434, 2027.
https://doi.org/10.1007/978-3-032-39820-8_28

1 Introduction

The volume of Earth Observation EO data collected daily from spaceborne and airborne sensors has grown to an unprecedented scale, offering continuous, global observations of the Earth's surface across a wide range of spatial, spectral, and temporal resolutions.

This wealth of data [2,7,11,15,39] represents an opportunity for environmental monitoring, enabling the systematic study of dynamic processes, from land cover change to agricultural dynamics.

Recent advances in AI4EO, and in DL enable multiple agricultural downstream tasks, including crop type mapping, crop boundary delineation, yield estimation, and phenology monitoring [41]. Croplands are inherently dynamic: seasonal phenological cycles, weather variability, and diverse management practices cause the spectral signature recorded by optical satellite sensors of a given parcel to evolve substantially within a single growing season. This temporal complexity drives the need for within-season updates and, in turn, for the storage and processing of large volumes of multi-temporal EO data [13,22,35,36,38]. At the same time, the spatial heterogeneity of agricultural landscapes where field sizes, crop mixes, and farming systems vary significantly across regions makes it difficult to build models that generalise from one area to another without substantial re-annotation effort.

Despite the abundance of satellite imagery, the scarcity of labeled training samples still hampers DL models, which have become the dominant paradigm for EO classification tasks, requiring large and representative annotated datasets to achieve good generalisation [41]. Collecting field data or producing manually annotated labels is, however, extremely time-consuming and expensive at scale.

A complementary and underexplored perspective concerns the role that *explainability* can play, not only as a post-hoc interpretability tool, but as an active mechanism for managing data at scale.

Beyond transparency, we argue that xAI constitutes a powerful lever for *satellite data wrangling*, especially for the extraction, filtering, and validation of EO data at scale. This argument is particularly salient in the context of the *patch-based paradigm* [5,17], a dominant design choice in modern DL-based crop classification, which enriches classification by capturing local spectral and spatial context. If, on one hand, it is a structural asset for explainability, it is prohibitively expensive at the scene level, becoming tractable at the patch level, allowing xAI methods to drive principled data selection and reduce the effective volume to be stored, labeled, and processed.

This tutorial surveys the intersection of xAI, DL, and EO-based crop mapping, covering the limits of off-the-shelf attribution methods on satellite data and the use of agronomic domain knowledge. We will discuss the role of xAI as an active lever for data selection and large-scale EO processing, providing an overview of causal estimation and concept-based explainability, and discuss how these directions could reshape big satellite data management, which is an unexplored class of use cases for the ADBIS and DM communities.

2 Background

Problem Statement. The growing availability of satellite imagery offers unprecedented opportunities for large-scale agricultural monitoring. In particular, multispectral (e.g. Sentinel-2) and hyperspectral platforms (e.g., DESIS and PRISMA), now provide continuous, global coverage at spatial resolutions suitable for field-level crop identification. The problem of translating such a large amount of raw spectral data into reliable, operationally useful crop maps remains a fundamentally difficult challenge at the intersection of machine learning, remote sensing, and data management.

We formally define the problem under the lens of our tutorial, namely Crop Mapping, as follows:

Definition 1. (Crop Mapping). Let $\mathcal{I} \in \mathbb{R}^{H \times W \times B \times T}$ denote a multi-temporal remote sensing image acquired over an agricultural region, where H and W are the spatial dimensions (in pixels), B is the number of spectral bands, and T is the number of acquisition dates (time steps).

Let $\mathcal{C} = \{c_1, c_2, \ldots, c_K\}$ be a finite set of K crop type labels (e.g., wheat, maize, sunflower, fallow).
Pixel-level formulation. For each pixel location $(i, j) \in \{1, \ldots, H\} \times \{1, \ldots, W\}$, let $\mathbf{x}_{ij} \in \mathbb{R}^{B \times T}$ denote the associated spectro-temporal feature vector. Crop mapping seeks to learn a classifier:

$$f : \mathbb{R}^{B \times T} \longrightarrow \mathcal{C} \tag{1}$$

such that $f(\mathbf{x}_{ij}) = c_k$ assigns the most probable crop type to each pixel, yielding the final map $\mathcal{M} \in \mathcal{C}^{H \times W}$.
Patch-level extension. Under the patch-based paradigm, the pixel-level vector $\mathbf{x}_{ij}$ is replaced by a spatial neighbourhood tensor. For a window of size $P \times P$ centred at (i, j), the patch is defined as:

$$\mathbf{p}_{ij} \in \mathbb{R}^{P \times P \times B \times T} \tag{2}$$

The classifier is then extended to:

$$f : \mathbb{R}^{P \times P \times B \times T} \longrightarrow \mathcal{C} \tag{3}$$

capturing local spatial context alongside spectral and temporal information.

The patch-based classification paradigm provides a model with local spatial context, namely, field boundaries, texture, and neighborhood crops that pixel-level approaches miss. If such a paradigm permits improving generalizability, on the other hand, it clearly triggers a space explosion. If we consider that the Sentinel-2 tile at 10 m resolution already contains millions of pixels, with a 32×32 patch and a stride of 1, the number of patches explodes combinatorially. If we consider multiplying by the number of spectral bands and time steps, the resulting dataset is in the terabyte-to-petabyte range.

In our context, we note that three compounding factors drive the data explosion:

- **Volume**: (up to) billions of candidate patches per acquisition date.
- **Dimensionality**: for satellite optical data, each patch is a 3D tensor (spatial × spectral × temporal).
- **Validation cost**: ground-truth crop labels are expensive to collect in the field, making supervised learning hard to scale.

Contemporary approaches to crop classification increasingly rely on the patch-based paradigm: a spatial window is convolved across the image, and the resulting overlapping patches encode local spectral and contextual information that are typically modelled by convolutional or transformer-based classifiers.

Such a design is well-motivated for at least two reasons [9]. First, crops are underrepresented by isolated pixels; their spectral signatures are shaped by surrounding land use, and phenological stage. Capturing the spatial context through patch extraction consistently improves classification accuracy. Second, the patch-based paradigm naturally enables local explainability by confining the model's receptive field to a bounded spatial neighbourhood; feature importance can be computed at the patch level rather than over the full image, dramatically reducing the complexity of attribution methods. Each patch constitutes an analysis unit, making it tractable to ask which spectral bands, spatial positions, or temporal observations influence a given prediction. A similar question would be computationally prohibitive at the scene level.

On the other hand, the patch-based paradigm suffers from global data volume, inflating the total number of data items:

Example 1. A single multispectral tile at 10-meter resolution [8] already contains tens of millions of pixels; Such a space can produce up to 12 billion spectral observations, depending on the time and bands considered.

Such data explosion constitutes a fundamental bottleneck that affects every downstream step: storage, retrieval, labelling, training, and validation. The patch-based paradigm thus presents a characteristic trade-off: it tames the complexity of local feature attribution while simultaneously amplifying the global data management burden.

xAI as a Data Wrangling Lever. The focus of our tutorial is on xAI methods applied to patch-based crop classifiers. We argue that they are not only a post-hoc interpretability tool that can *Control* (Detect spurious correlations, season/sensor biases), *Improve* (Rank bands and spatial scales by importance, prune redundant features), *Discover* (Reveal unexpected spectral signatures triggeringnew crop type hypotheses) and *Justify* (Produce saliency maps and attribution scores to provide explainable outputs for regulators and farmers). As a matter of fact, we argue that they constitute an active lever for managing satellite data at scale. In Fig. 1, we depict a complete Crop Mapping (classification framework) that adopts the patch-based paradigm. Classification on an entire scene (Remote sensing image) occurs at the patch level (Fig. 1(c)). In turn, a patch becomes the scope of explanations that are consumed to adapt the model and the data.

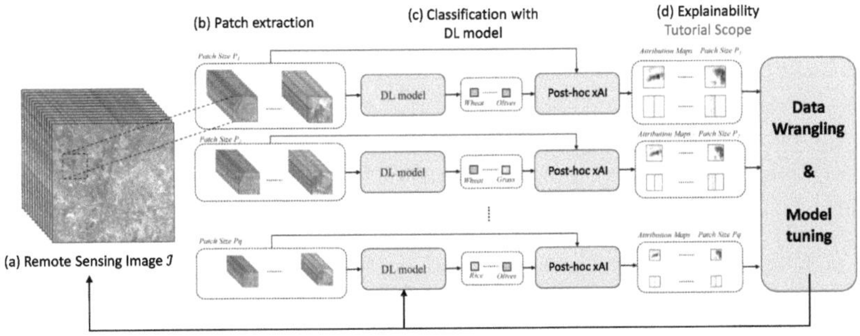

Fig. 1. *(a)* Input Remote sensing image $\mathcal{I}$, *(b)* patch extraction and *(c)* classification. *(d)* Post-hoc explainability (tutorial scope) and actions taken (data and model correction).

LNCSsubsubsectionTutorial Scope and Goal. In the next section, we will present the rationale and the opportunities of applying xAI methods in the remote sensing research, especially for the crop type mapping problem. Specifically, our tutorial aims to provide a solid overview of the current state-of-the-art techniques proposed in the ML/AI communities and applied to EO-based agricultural mapping. In this sense, we will discuss the main hurdles to applying xAI over satellite image DL models, showing why an out-of-the-box application of well-known techniques can be a limited solution. We will also address how AI can be leveraged not only for prediction but also for optimizing data wrangling and enabling scalable solutions for large-scale EO processing, by identifying the most informative observations across space and time.

3 Tutorial Content

In this section we outline the main elements we will present in our tutorial (1.5 hours in total).

Part I—Foundations (45 min)

1.1 Earth Observation Data for Agricultural Monitoring. In the first part, we introduce the main EO data sources for agricultural monitoring, covering multispectral sensors (Sentinel-2 [11], Landsat [39]) and hyperspectral platforms (DESIS [2], PRISMA [7], EnMAP [15]), their key spectral indices (Normalized Difference Vegetation Indice (NDVI) and Enhanced Vegetation Index (EVI) [18,29]) and agronomic interpretation, and the multi-temporal structure imposed by phenological cycles [42]. We also review access platforms and data formats, including Copernicus [4], Google Earth Engine [14], and Microsoft Planetary Computer [26], as well as standard benchmark datasets used in crop mapping research: TimeSen2Crop [38], Sen4AgriNet [35], PASTIS [13], and CropHarvest [36].

Part II—Deep Learning and xAI for Crop Maping (45 min)

2.1 Deep Learning Architectures for Crop Mapping. In the second part of the tutorial, we will introduce the main DL paradigms used in Remote Sensing, especially for crop mapping. This will allow us to introduce, in turn, the xAI methods and discuss current possibilities and challenges.

The main DL architectures used in crop mapping are:

- *Spatial models* CNNs, Fully Convolutional Networks, and Vision Transformers process patch-level spectral and contextual information for per-pixel or per-patch classification [10,21,23].
- *Temporal models* Recurrent networks (LSTM, GRU) and temporal attention encoders (TAE, LTAE) operate on multi-date time series, with a particular focus on early-season classification [12,16,30].
- *Spatio-temporal models* 3D-CNNs, ConvLSTM, and transformer-based architectures (U-TAE, Presto, SatMAE) jointly model spatial and temporal dependencies, culminating in geospatial foundation models and their fine-tuning strategies for downstream crop mapping tasks [13,27,37].

2.2 xAI and Data Management. The central thread of our tutorial focuses on explainability and its benefits for data management in large-scale EO processing. We first motivate the *patch as the natural explainability unit*: its bounded receptive field makes local attribution methods producing spatially coherent importance scores across spectral bands, spatial positions, and acquisition dates [24,28,34]. We then examine the *limits of off-the-shelf xAI* in this setting, where spatial autocorrelation, spectral collinearity, and temporal redundancy systematically destabilise standard attribution methods, and review proxy metrics used to evaluate explanation quality without ground-truth attributions [3,32,40].

To address these limits, we show how *agronomic domain knowledge* spectral indices and phenological calendars can constrain the attribution search space and align expert explanations [1,19,20,31].

We then demonstrate how xAI becomes an active *data management lever*: attribution-guided patch selection replaces exhaustive extraction, reducing the effective data volume while preserving the most informative observations. In this context, we move beyond associative attribution to *causal estimation*, discussing interventional framework capabilities [6,9].

4 Related Work

Two recent tutorials share thematic ground with the present work. Mayer et al. [25] provide a hands-on introduction to explainability methods at KDD 2023, covering the landscape of attribution techniques, the diversity of stakeholder needs, and common pitfalls in the practical deployment of xAI systems. While their treatment is thorough on the methodological side, it remains domain-agnostic and does not address the specific challenges posed by multi-temporal, multi-spectral EO data.

Schwalbe et al. [33] adopt a complementary perspective at ECAI 2025, focusing on concept-based explanations for vision and language models.

Our tutorial grounds explainability in EO use case; it frames xAI not only as an interpretability tool but as a data management lever for large-scale patch-based pipelines; and it bridges the xAI, EO, and DM communities.

5 Presenters Background

Dr. Claudia Paris is a Senior Assistant Professor (UD1) in the Faculty of Geoinformation and Earth Observation Sciences (ITC) at the University of Twente, Enschede, the Netherlands. She received the "Laurea" (B.S.), the "Laurea Specialistica" (M.S.) (summa cum laude) degrees in Telecommunication Engineering and the Ph.D. in Information and Communication Technology from the University of Trento, Italy, in 2010, 2012, 2016, respectively. Her research focuses on designing innovative and automated Geospatial Artificial Intelligence (GeoAI) methodologies for the analysis and classification of large-scale Earth Observation (EO) data for various applications (e.g., forest/agricultural mapping and monitoring) by leveraging high-performance computing (HPC) and cloud computing platforms (Google Earth Engine). She also investigates the integration of multitemporal and multimodal remote sensing data using Geospatial Foundation Models (Geo-FM) and Vision Language Models (VLM) to support precision farming applications, including crop type mapping, monitoring of heterogeneous and intercropped agricultural systems, and fine-scale crop boundary delineation. Dr. Paris was twice the recipient of the prestigious Symposium Prize Paper Award (exceptional paper in terms of content and impact on the Geoscience & Remote Sensing Society) at the 2016 IEEE IGARSS (Beijing, China, 2016) and at the 2017 IEEE IGARSS (Fort Worth, TX, USA, 2017). She also won the IEEE Geoscience and Remote Sensing Society 2022 Letters Prize Paper Award (exceptional paper in terms of content and impact on the GRS-Society).

Dr. Michele Linardi is an assistant professor with the CY Cergy Paris University since September 2021. He obtained a Master of Science in Computer Science in 2014 from the University of Trento and Scuola Superiore Sant'Anna, Italy. In 2019, he earned a Ph.D. in Computer Science from Paris Descartes University. His doctoral dissertation, entitled Variable-Length Similarity Search for Very Large Data Series: Subsequence Matching, Motif, and Discord Detection, focused on scalable methods for time series similarity search and analytics. The research interests of Dr. Linardi are time series analytics and databases, with a special focus on machine learning for temporal data. Dr. Linardi serves as a reviewer on EDBT, ICDE, ADBIS, VLDBJ, and others. He is the coordinator of the EDEM project (ANR-24-CE23-6449, https://anr.fr/Projet-ANR-24-CE23-6449), funded by the French National Research Agency (ANR). EDEM aims to develop novel xAI solutions that produce relevant and actionable explanations for DL models applied to big satellite data, with the goal of enabling scalable, transparent, and trustworthy agricultural mapping and monitoring.

Acknowledgments. This work is supported by the "EDEM: Explaining Deep Learning Models of Satellite Time Series for the Agritech domain" project funded by l'Agence Nationale de la Recherche (ANR), EDEM project ANR-24-CE23-6449.

References

1. Abbas, A., et al.: Towards explainable AI4EO: an explainable deep learning approach for crop type mapping using satellite images time series. In: IEEE International Geoscience and Remote Sensing Symposium, IGARSS 2023, Pasadena, CA, USA, pp. 1088–1091. IEEE (2023). https://doi.org/10.1109/IGARSS52108.2023.10283125. https://doi.org/10.1109/IGARSS52108.2023.10283125
2. Alonso, K., et al.: Data preprocessing toolboxes for the DESIS hyperspectral sensor. Sensors **19**(16) (2019). https://doi.org/10.3390/s19163483
3. Alvarez-Melis, D., et al.: On the robustness of interpretability methods. In: ICML Workshop on Human Interpretability in Machine Learning (2018). https://arxiv.org/abs/1806.08049
4. Aschbacher, J., et al.: The european earth monitoring (GMES/Copernicus) programme: status and perspectives. Remote Sens. Environ. **120**, 3–8 (2012). https://doi.org/10.1016/j.rse.2011.08.028
5. Chen, Y.: Deep learning-based classification of hyperspectral data. IEEE J. Sel. Top. Appl. Earth Observations Remote Sens. **7**, 2094–2107 (2014). https://doi.org/10.1109/JSTARS.2014.2329330
6. Cheng, D., et al.: Linking model intervention to causal interpretation in model explanation. Pattern Recogn. **173**, 112814 (2026)
7. Cogliati, S., et al.: The PRISMA imaging spectroscopy mission: overview and first performance analysis. Remote Sens. Environ. **262**, 112499 (2021). https://doi.org/10.1016/j.rse.2021.112499
8. Copernicus Data Space Ecosystem: Sentinel-2 mission documentation (2024). https://documentation.dataspace.copernicus.eu/Data/SentinelMissions/Sentinel2.html. Accessed Jun 2026
9. Dabo, S., et al.: Rethinking hyperspectral image classification (HSIC) benchmark with explainability (xAI) under a causal estimation perspective. In: Proceedings of the Workshops of the EDBT/ICDT 2026 Joint Conference co-located with the EDBT/ICDT 2025 Joint Conference, Tampere, Finland. CEUR Workshop Proceedings, vol. 4192. CEUR-WS.org (2026)
10. Dosovitskiy, A., et al.: An image is worth 16x16 words: transformers for image recognition at scale. In: International Conference on Learning Representations (ICLR) (2021). https://openreview.net/forum?id=YicbFdNTTy
11. Drusch, M., et al.: Sentinel-2: ESA's optical high-resolution mission for GMES operational services. Remote Sens. Environ. **120**, 25–36 (2012)
12. Garnot, V.S.F.: Satellite image time series classification with pixel-set encoders and temporal self-attention. In: Proceedings of the IEEE/CVF Conference on Computer Vision and Pattern Recognition (CVPR), pp. 12325–12334 (2020). https://doi.org/10.1109/CVPR42600.2020.01234
13. Garnot, V.S.F.: Panoptic segmentation of satellite image time series with convolutional temporal attention networks. In: Proceedings of the IEEE/CVF International Conference on Computer Vision (ICCV), pp. 4872–4881 (2021). https://doi.org/10.1109/ICCV48922.2021.00483

14. Gorelick, N., et al.: Google earth engine: planetary-scale geospatial analysis for everyone. Remote Sens. Environ. **202**, 18–27 (2017). https://doi.org/10.1016/j.rse.2017.06.031
15. Guanter, L., et al.: The EnMAP spaceborne imaging spectroscopy mission for earth observation. Remote Sens. **7**(7), 8830–8857 (2015). https://doi.org/10.3390/rs70708830
16. Hochreiter, S., et al.: Long short-term memory. Neural Comput. **9**(8), 1735–1780 (1997). https://doi.org/10.1162/neco.1997.9.8.1735
17. Hu, W., et al.: Deep convolutional neural networks for hyperspectral image classification. J. Sens., 258619 (2015). https://doi.org/10.1155/2015/258619
18. Huete, A., et al.: Overview of the radiometric and biophysical performance of the MODIS vegetation indices. Remote Sens. Environ. **83**(1–2), 195–213 (2002). https://doi.org/10.1016/S0034-4257(02)00096-2
19. Interdonato, R.: DuPLO: a dual view point deep learning architecture for time series classification, vol. 149, pp. 91–104 (2019). https://doi.org/10.1016/j.isprsjprs.2019.01.011
20. Kim, B., et al.: Interpretability beyond classification output: quantitative testing with concept activation vectors (TCAV). In: Proceedings of the 35th International Conference on Machine Learning (ICML), pp. 2668–2677 (2018). https://proceedings.mlr.press/v80/kim18d.html
21. LeCun, Y., et al.: Gradient-based learning applied to document recognition. Proc. IEEE **86**(11), 2278–2324 (1998). https://doi.org/10.1109/5.726791
22. Li, W., et al.: Fine-grained hierarchical crop type classification from integrated hyperspectral enmap data and multispectral sentinel-2 time series: a large-scale dataset and dual-stream transformer method. Remote Sens. Environ. **344**, 115525 (2026). https://www.sciencedirect.com/science/article/pii/S0034425726002956
23. Long, J.: Fully convolutional networks for semantic segmentation. In: Proceedings of the IEEE Conference on Computer Vision and Pattern Recognition (CVPR), pp. 3431–3440 (2015). https://doi.org/10.1109/CVPR.2015.7298965
24. Lundberg, S.M., et al.: A unified approach to interpreting model predictions. In: Advances in Neural Information Processing Systems (NeurIPS), vol. 30, pp. 4765–4774 (2017). https://proceedings.neurips.cc/paper/2017/hash/8a20a8621978632d76c43dfd28b67767-Abstract.html
25. Mayer, M.C., et al.: Hands-on tutorial: "explanations in AI: methods, stakeholders and pitfalls". In: Proceedings of the 29th ACM SIGKDD Conference on Knowledge Discovery and Data Mining (KDD '23), pp. 5783–5785. Association for Computing Machinery, New York, NY, USA (2023). https://doi.org/10.1145/3580305.3599181
26. Microsoft: Microsoft planetary computer (2022). https://planetarycomputer.microsoft.com. Accessed 2024
27. Reed, C.: Scale-MAE: a scale-aware masked autoencoder for multiscale geospatial representation learning. In: Proceedings of the IEEE/CVF International Conference on Computer Vision (ICCV), pp. 4088–4099 (2023). https://doi.org/10.1109/ICCV51070.2023.00378
28. Ribeiro, M.T., et al.: "Why Should I Trust You?": explaining the predictions of any classifier. In: Proceedings of the 22nd ACM SIGKDD International Conference on Knowledge Discovery and Data Mining, pp. 1135–1144 (2016). https://doi.org/10.1145/2939672.2939778
29. Rouse, J.W., et al.: Monitoring vegetation systems in the great plains with ERTS. NASA Spec. Publ. **351**, 309–317 (1974)
30. Rußwurm, M., et al.: Self-attention for raw optical satellite time series classification **169**, 421–435 (2020). https://doi.org/10.1016/j.isprsjprs.2020.06.006

31. Rußwurm, M., et al.: Semantic segmentation of satellite time series with temporal convolutional networks and domain adaptation. ISPRS J. Photogramm. Remote. Sens. **167**, 231–244 (2020). https://doi.org/10.1016/j.isprsjprs.2020.06.005
32. Samek, W., et al.: Evaluating the visualization of what a deep neural network has learned. IEEE Trans. Neural Netw. Learn. Syst. **28**(11), 2660–2673 (2017). https://doi.org/10.1109/TNNLS.2016.2599820
33. Schwalbe, G., et al.: Explaining vision and language models — a concept-based approach. In: Tutorial at the European Conference on Artificial Intelligence (ECAI) (2025)
34. Simonyan, K., et al.: Deep inside convolutional networks: visualising image classification models and saliency maps. arXiv preprint arXiv:1312.6034 (2014). https://arxiv.org/abs/1312.6034
35. Sykas, D.: A sentinel-2 multiyear, multicountry benchmark dataset for crop classification and segmentation with deep learning. IEEE J. Sel. Top. Appl. Earth Observations Remote Sens. **15**, 3323–3339 (2022). https://doi.org/10.1109/JSTARS.2022.3164771
36. Tseng, G., et al.: CropHarvest: a global dataset for crop-type classification. In: Thirty-fifth Conference on Neural Information Processing Systems Datasets and Benchmarks Track (2021). https://openreview.net/forum?id=JtjzUXPEaCu
37. Tseng, G., et al.: Lightweight, pre-trained transformers for remote sensing timeseries. In: arXiv preprint (2023). https://arxiv.org/abs/2304.14065
38. Weikmann, G., et al.: Timesen2crop: a million labeled samples dataset of sentinel 2 image time series for crop-type classification. IEEE J. Sel. Top. Appl. Earth Observations Remote Sens. **14**, 4699–4708 (2021). https://doi.org/10.1109/JSTARS.2021.3073965
39. Wulder, M.A., et al.: Fifty years of Landsat science and impacts. Remote Sens. Environ. **280**, 113195 (2022). https://doi.org/10.1016/j.rse.2022.113195
40. Yeh, C.K., et al.: On the (in)fidelity and sensitivity of explanations. In: Advances in Neural Information Processing Systems (NeurIPS), vol. 32 (2019). https://proceedings.neurips.cc/paper/2019/hash/a7471fdc77b3435276507cc8f2dc2569-Abstract.html
41. Yuan, Q., et al.: Deep learning in environmental remote sensing: achievements and challenges. Remote Sens. Environ. **241**, 111716 (2020)
42. Zhu, Z., et al.: Continuous monitoring of land disturbance based on Landsat time series. Remote Sens. Environ. **238**, 111116 (2020). https://doi.org/10.1016/j.rse.2019.111116

Digital Tourism From Tripadvisor Circulation Graphs to Behavior Extraction and Characterization

Nicolas Travers(✉)

De Vinci Higher Education, De Vinci Research Center, Paris, France
nicolas.travers@devinci.fr
http://www.devinci.fr/research-center/

Abstract. Digital Tourism has emerged as a powerful research field for understanding how tourists move, experience destinations, and shape urban dynamics through the massive digital traces they leave on online platforms such as TripAdvisor. This presentation summarizes a set of approaches that model tourist mobility using graph-based representations, particularly circulation graphs stored and analyzed in Neo4j. By building aggregating time series in a graph at multi-scale and various time frames, these methods enable both quantitative and qualitative analyses of mobility and provide key indicators based on graph advanced algorithms. Beyond mobility measurement, new approaches combining topology and geodesic measures help characterize propagation effects across territories while optimizing computations on large datasets. Advanced mining techniques—ranging from centrality normalization, sequential pattern extraction to frequent graph mining and distributing frameworks—allow the discovery of recurrent movement structures, seasonal trends, hidden patterns and early signals of latent overtourism. The talk also highlights briefly how sentiment analysis and graph models can capture evolving perceptions of authenticity in online reviews before, during, and after visiting a country of origin. Overall, the presented work demonstrates how scalable graph analytics and data mining can support decision-making in tourism marketing, urban planning, and policy design.

Keywords: Graph Databases · Graph Mining · Digital Tourism

1 Introduction

The increasing adoption of digital platforms such as TripAdvisor, GoogleMaps, Booking, Instagram and Airbnb has transformed tourism into a data-rich domain. Tourists continuously leave digital traces through reviews, ratings, photographs, and mobility footprints. These traces provide unprecedented opportunities to understand tourist behavior at multiple spatial and temporal scales [15].

G. Vargas-Solar et al. (Eds.): ADBIS 2026, LNCS 16937, pp. 435–445, 2027.
https://doi.org/10.1007/978-3-032-39820-8_29

Traditional tourism studies relied on surveys and observational methods. While valuable, they suffer from limited scalability and temporal coverage. Digital tourism complements these methods by enabling the analysis of millions of online reviews. The challenge is no longer collecting information but modeling and analyzing complex interactions among tourists, locations, and territories [25].

Graph theory provides a natural representation for these interactions. Locations can be represented as nodes, movements as edges, and tourist attributes as contextual information, called *Circulation Graphs* or in a more abstract way *MultiDiGraph* [11]. Graph databases such as Neo4j further facilitate the storage, querying, and analysis of large-scale tourism networks. The convergence of graph analytics, data mining, geospatial analysis, and artificial intelligence has enabled the emergence of a new generation of methods for understanding tourist mobility, destination attractiveness, territorial dynamics, and visitor perceptions.

This tutorial introduces the main concepts, models, and algorithms used in graph-based digital tourism. It presents a unified framework for researchers entering the field based on those previous works.

2 Related Work

This section reviews the main research dimensions covered in this tutorial: graph-based tourism modeling, structural analysis of circulation networks, graph mining and scalability, and sequential and trajectory pattern mining.

2.1 Graph Modeling and Topological Analysis of Tourism Mobility

The emergence of digital tourism has been largely driven by the availability of user-generated content on online platforms. Early studies relied on geotagged photographs, check-ins, GPS trajectories, and social media interactions to reconstruct tourist mobility networks and identify major tourism corridors, attraction hubs, and spatial interaction patterns [5,22,30,38]. These approaches demonstrated that tourist behavior can be represented as a network of movements between locations, enabling the application of graph theory concepts to tourism analysis. Graph-based representations rapidly became a natural framework for studying tourism flows since they simultaneously capture mobility topology, destination attractiveness, and interactions among Points of Interest (POIs).

To better characterize mobility dynamics, circulation graph models [3,12,28] were proposed to represent tourist movements extracted from reviews and digital traces. Instead of modeling isolated visits, circulation graphs reconstruct sequences of visited locations and transform them into directed mobility networks where nodes represent destinations and edges represent successive visits. Neo4Tourism [7] extended this idea by introducing a graph database framework implemented in Neo4j, capable of integrating tourist profiles, temporal dimensions, geographic hierarchies, and mobility relationships within a unified graph structure. Such representations support the generation of multi-scale aggregated graphs ranging from local districts to international destinations, enabling both local and global analyses of tourist behavior.

Beyond graph modeling, the state-of-the-art focuses on understanding the structure of tourism networks. Some works applied centrality measures [4,21] to characterize influential destinations, tourism hubs, or the role of specific attractions in the overall circulation process. Degree, betweenness, closeness, eigenvector centralities and PageRank have been employed to measure different aspects of destination importance, from local popularity to global influence. In parallel, community detection algorithms [36,41] have been used to uncover tourism regions or destination clusters, revealing groups of locations that are frequently visited together and therefore form coherent tourism systems.

Several studies also circulation graphs to analyze spatial interactions among destinations and understand tourist behavior at multiple geographic scales [13]. In particular, normalized PageRank approaches have been proposed to compare the influence of destinations across different circulation graphs, overcoming the limitations of traditional centrality measures whose scores are highly dependent on graph topology and cannot be compared with each other.

Other studies have investigated graph propagation processes. Tourism mobility often extends beyond simple origin-destination flows and exhibits diffusion phenomena where visitors progressively spread from major attractions toward secondary territories [10,33,34]. Understanding this territorial diffusion is particularly important for destination management and tourism planning. To address this issue, some works combine graph topology, geodesic distances, and spanning-tree approximations to characterize the depth and spatial extent of tourist propagation while reducing the computational complexity associated with large circulation graphs [32].

2.2 Graph Mining and Scalable Analytics

Graph mining techniques extend standard network analysis by discovering hidden structures, recurrent patterns, and emerging behaviors that are not directly observable through previously mentioned graph measures. These approaches aim to transform large tourism graphs into knowledge by identifying recurrent mobility structures, destination associations, and evolving tourism dynamics.

Frequent Itemset Mining (FIM) has long been recognized as a fundamental technique for discovering co-occurring entities. In tourism, itemsets correspond to groups of locations frequently visited together and therefore provide insights into destination complementarities and visitor preferences. Classical approaches such as Apriori and FP-Growth have been widely applied to trajectory analysis, recommendation systems, and tourism planning [6,17]. However, the increasing size of tourism datasets creates significant computational challenges. To address scalability issues, distributed SAT-based frameworks have recently been proposed, partitioning the mining process across distributed infrastructure while improving performance, scalability, and fault tolerance [26].

Frequent Subgraph Mining (FSM) represents another important graph mining technique. Instead of discovering recurring sets of locations, FSM identifies recurring graph structures and mobility topologies. Such structures often reveal stable tourism corridors, destination clusters, and recurrent structured behaviors [24,29,31]. Since graph patterns preserve topological information, they provide richer insights than traditional itemsets. Recent studies exploited frequent subgraph mining to identify latent overtourism signals by detecting recurring mobility structures associated with increasing territorial pressure and destination attractiveness [2].

Sequential Pattern Mining (SPM) aims to identify frequent ordered sequences of visited locations and therefore captures the temporal dimension of tourist mobility. Classical algorithms such as SPADE [39], PrefixSpan [30], or SPAM [5] have been applied to tourism datasets derived from GPS trajectories, mobile phone records, Flickr photographs, and social media platforms [9,27]. These approaches reveal common itineraries, preferred visitation orders, and recurrent behavioral routines that cannot be identified through static graph analysis alone.

Trajectory mining has also been combined with clustering [14,18], Markov models [40], association rule mining [22], and semantic trajectory analysis through graphlet decomposition [1]. By integrating spatial, temporal, and contextual dimensions, these complementary approaches provide a richer understanding of tourist mobility and destination exploration processes.

Last but not least, Graph Neural Networks (GNNs) constitute a promising research direction for tourism behavior extraction. Unlike traditional graph algorithms, GNNs learn latent representations directly from graph topology and node/edge properties. This ability allows them to model complex dependencies and non-linear interactions between destinations. Applications include mobility prediction, tourist recommendation, destination attractiveness estimation, crowd forecasting, and trends detection [23,35,37]. Although still relatively recent in tourism research, GNNs offer promising perspectives for integrating graph mining and predictive analytics within a unified learning framework.

2.3 Research Gaps and Tutorial Positioning

Although significant progress has been achieved, several challenges remain. First, many studies focus on a single analytical dimension such as mobility, recommendations, sentiment analysis, or prediction, making it difficult to obtain a holistic understanding of tourism dynamics. Second, comparisons across destinations, populations, and geographic scales remain difficult due to the lack of normalized indicators capable of producing comparable results across heterogeneous circulation graphs. Third, the scalability of graph analytics continues to be a challenge when dealing with national or international datasets containing millions of users, locations, and mobility relationships. Finally, while machine learning and graph neural networks provide promising predictive capabilities, their integration with explainable graph analytics remains limited.

This tutorial positions itself at the intersection of graph databases, network science, graph mining, and behavioral analytics. It proposes a unified overview of circulation graph construction, structural analysis, scalable mining techniques, and behavior-oriented applications. The tutorial aims to provide researchers and practitioners with the foundations required to develop the next generation of digital tourism analytics systems.

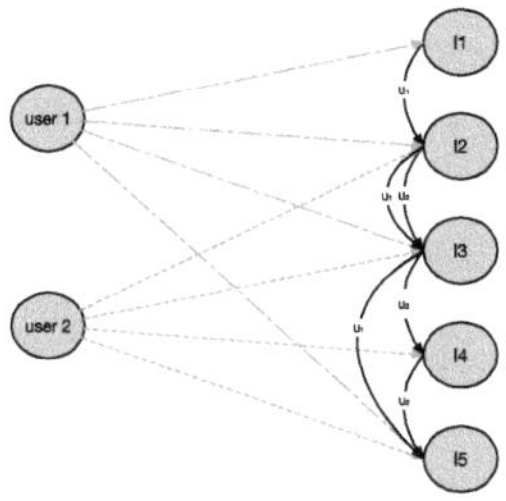

Fig. 1. Circulation Graph Modeling

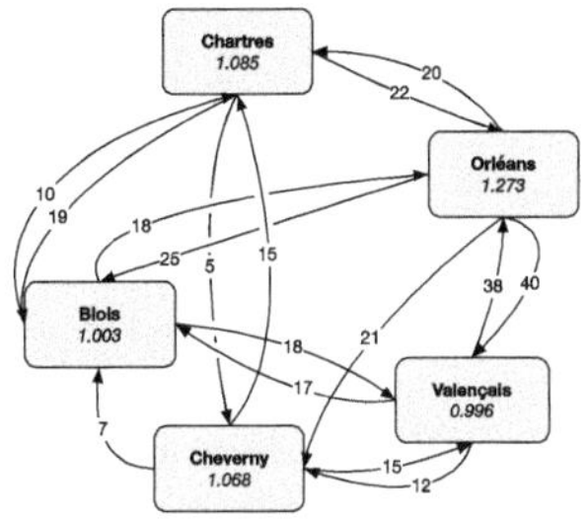

Fig. 2. Aggregated Circulation Graph

3 Building a Circulation Graph for Digital Tourism

To formalize and illustrate the tutorial, the so-called circulation graph is modeled as a directed multigraph or `multidigraph`, $\mathcal{G} = (\mathcal{V}, \mathcal{E})$, which consists of a non-empty finite set $\mathcal{V}$ of vertices and a set $\mathcal{E} \subseteq \mathcal{V} \times \mathcal{V}$ of directed edges. Each directed edge $(u, v) \in \mathcal{E}$ has a start (tail) vertex u and an end (head) vertex v. In a multidigraph, multiple edges with the same endpoints can be represented by multiple directed connections between the same pair of vertices. The out-degree of a vertex $v_i \in \mathcal{V}$ is denoted as $outdegree(v_i)$, the number of edges leaving v_i.

The set $L_\mathcal{E}$ represents the labels or attributes associated with the edges in the multidigraph $\mathcal{G}$. Each edge $e_i \in \mathcal{E}$ may have one or more labels from $L_\mathcal{E}$, representing properties linked to tourists' information such as weights, types, nationalities, or any other information.

Similarly, the set $L_\mathcal{V}$ represents the labels or attributes associated with the vertices in the multidigraph $\mathcal{G}$. Each vertex $v_i \in \mathcal{V}$ may have one or more labels from $L_\mathcal{V}$, representing properties linked to locations information such as names, identifiers, etc.

A multidigraph can be transformed into a simple directed graph $\mathcal{G}^* \in \mathcal{G}$ by removing duplicate edges and self-loops. This results in a graph where each pair of vertices is connected by, at most, one directed edge.

$$\mathcal{G}^* \subset \mathcal{G} | \mathcal{V}^* = \mathcal{V} \wedge \mathcal{E}^* \subset \mathcal{E} \wedge (\forall e = (u, v) \in \mathcal{E}^* | u \neq v \wedge \nexists e' \neq e \in \mathcal{E}^* \wedge e' = (u, v))$$

Figure 1 illustrate the construction of a circulation graph where an edge e exists when a user has posted two successive reviews between two locations v_1 & v_2. Edges' labels are inherited from users' properties and review time. Notice that, we consider that a trip is composed of reviews on v_1 and v_2 written at most at 7 days apart coming from tourism trip definition [16].

3.1 Circulation Graph Manipulation

Once the circulation graph has been constructed, the main objective is to manipulate it in order to extract interpretable indicators for tourism analysis.

First, centrality measures help identify the most influential locations in the network. Among them, PageRank is particularly suitable because it captures both the popularity of a destination $PR(v_i)$ and its role within tourist circulation flows. However, PageRank values are strongly dependent on graph size and topology. To enable comparisons across destinations and aggregation levels, normalized indicators such as the Tourist Circulation Factor (TCF) and the Global Circulation Factor (GCF) can be computed [13] using filter and aggregation queries in `Cypher`. These indicators provide a robust way to identify tourism hot spots and compare their importance across cities, regions, or countries.

Second, circulation graphs can be used to study how tourists propagate through a territory. While centrality focuses on individual locations, propagation analysis investigates how visitors spread from major attractions toward peripheral areas. To characterize this phenomenon, graph topology can be combined with geographical distances through the Remoteness Influence Factor (RIF) [32]. Since large circulation graphs may contain thousands of locations and relationships, minimum spanning-tree extraction is used to preserve the dominant mobility structure while reducing computational complexity.

Finally, these analyses are supported by the `Neo4Tourism` architecture [7], which stores circulation graphs in `Neo4j` and enables their manipulation through `Cypher` queries. Locations can be aggregated at multiple spatial scales (districts, cities, regions, countries as shown in Fig. 2) and filtered according to temporal periods or tourist profiles. This graph-based infrastructure facilitates the computation of mobility indicators, propagation measures, and graph mining algorithms on large tourism datasets.

3.2 Graph Mining

While structural indicators such as centralities and propagation measures provide a local or global views of tourist mobility, graph mining techniques aim at discovering recurrent patterns hidden within circulation graphs.

A first family of methods relies on Frequent Itemset Mining (FIM), where each tourist trip is represented as a set of visited locations $s = [v_i, v_{i+1}, ..., v_{i+k}]$. The objective is to identify groups of POIs that frequently appear together in tourists' itineraries. Such itemsets provide useful insights into destination complementarities, attraction bundles, and tourism recommendation systems. However, the combinatorial nature of FIM rapidly becomes a scalability challenge when dealing with millions of reviews and thousands of locations. To address this issue, distributed approaches based on SAT solving and parallel computation have been proposed, enabling the extraction of frequent itemsets on large tourism datasets while maintaining flexibility for integrating complex constraints [26].

Beyond co-occurrence analysis, circulation graphs preserve the temporal ordering of visits and therefore allow the discovery of sequential behaviors. Sequential Pattern Mining (SPM) techniques identify recurrent ordered sequences $s = (v_i, v_{i+1}, ..., v_{i+k})$ of visited locations and reveal typical tourist itineraries. Building upon this idea, the `SeqPatTour` framework [3] reduces the multidigraph complexity by resuming the structural information, then extraction path with temporal constraints, verifies the those patterns within the initial circulation graph (Fig. 3). The resulting patterns can be analyzed according to temporal periods, tourist profiles, or geographic scales.

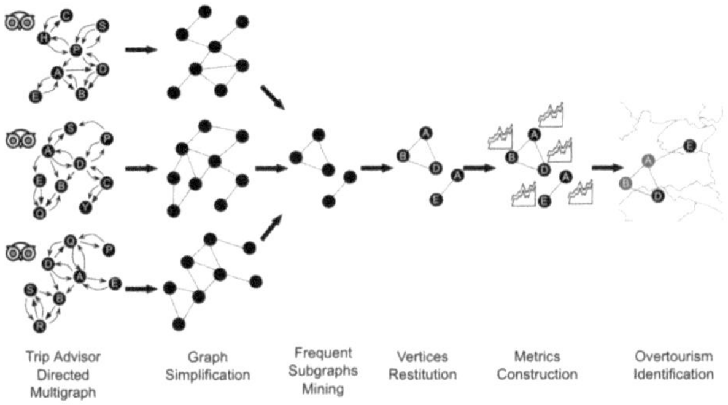

Fig. 3. SeqPatTour Framework & Overtourism

More recently, frequent subgraph mining approaches have been introduced to preserve not only the order of visits but also the topology of tourist movements. Instead of identifying sequences or sets of locations, these methods extract recurrent mobility sequences and focus on nodes attractiveness based on the Huff model [19]. This approach has been successfully applied to the detection of latent overtourism signals, where frequently occurring subgraphs reveal emerging hotspots and territorial pressure before visible overcrowding effects appear [2].

Current research investigates the scalability of frequent subgraph mining through distributed graph-processing frameworks such as Pregel. In this context, graph exploration is distributed across multiple computing nodes, allowing larger circulation graphs to be processed. However, several challenges remain. It requires the generation of graph signatures to identify isomorphic patterns, which may become computationally expensive. In addition, duplicate pattern generation, graph isomorphism verification, and memory consumption represent important bottlenecks when analyzing large-scale tourism datasets.

Another ongoing work focuses on Graph Neural Networks (GNNs) to learn latent representations of destinations and tourist behaviors. A major challenge lies in the construction of meaningful graph embeddings. Tourism data are inherently heterogeneous and involve numerous dimensions, including temporal information (seasonality, visit periods), mobility sequences, tourist profiles (nationality, age group, travel motivation), and destination attributes (categories, ratings, geographic context). Another important issue concerns spatial discretization, as destinations may be represented at different geographic resolutions ranging from individual POIs, boroughs to cities. Current research explores how these heterogeneous features can be integrated into GNN architectures to behavior prediction, recommendations, attractiveness estimation, and overtourism forecasting.

3.3 Behavior Analysis: An Interdisciplinary Research

Beyond graph analytics, understanding tourist behavior requires interdisciplinary collaborations combining computer science, geography, sociology, and marketing. A first research direction investigates tourist mobility from a geographer perspective. Circulation graphs provide a large-scale representation of tourist movements, but their interpretation benefits from confronting graph patterns with traditional mobility indicators such as transport usage. In collaboration with geographers, graph-derived mobility structures can therefore be compared with real transportation networks and observed travel practices, helping to better understand how tourists navigate within cities [20].

A second research direction focuses on tourist perceptions and authenticity. In collaboration with marketing and management researchers, digital traces can be used to analyze how perceptions evolve before, during, and after an experience. For instance, studies on Italian food authenticity investigated whether visiting Italy modifies tourists' perception of Italian restaurants abroad. Sequential patterns extracted from circulation graphs make it possible to identify tourists who experienced Italian food in this setting. By combining these sequences with sentiment analysis and rating evolution, researchers can study how authenticity perceptions change through direct experience and cultural heritage [8].

4 Conclusion and Perspectives

This tutorial presented a graph-based framework for analyzing digital tourism through the construction and exploitation of circulation graphs derived from online reviews. Starting from the modeling of tourist mobility as multidigraphs, we introduced methods for building, storing, and manipulating circulation graphs at multiple spatial and temporal scales using graph databases.

We then explored structural analysis techniques for identifying tourism hot spots through normalized PageRank indicators and understanding territorial diffusion through propagation measures. Building upon these graph representations, we reviewed graph mining approaches ranging from frequent itemset mining and sequential pattern extraction to frequent subgraph mining, highlighting mobility behaviors and latent overtourism signals. Finally, we illustrated how graph analytics can support interdisciplinary research by combining mobility analysis with geographers and perceptions of authenticity in Marketing Science.

Some promising research directions arise on scalable graph mining with Pregel, and also Graph Neural Networks to learn richer representations of destinations and tourist behaviors with heterogeneous features.

Acknowledgments. A great thanks to all collaborators on those works: EIREST Laboratory, Metropole Européenne de Lille and Bordeaux Métropole.

References

1. Ahmed, N.K., Neville, J., Rossi, R.A., Duffield, N.: Efficient Graphlet Counting for Large Networks. In: IEEE ICDM'15, pp. 1–10 (2015)
2. Alatrista-Salas, H., Chareyron, G., Djebali, S., Dlala, I.O., Travers, N.: From flows to graphs: data-driven insights on latent overtourism with frequent pattern mining. In: Chrysanthis, P.K., Nørvåg, K., Stefanidis, K., Zhang, Z., Quintarelli, E., Zumpano, E. (eds.) ADBIS 2025 DOING Workshop. LNCS, vol. 2676, pp. 327–342. Springer, Cham (2025). https://doi.org/10.1007/978-3-032-05727-3_28
3. Alatrista-Salas, H., Chareyron, G., Djebali, S., Ouled Dlala, I., Travers, N.: SeqPatTour: sequential patterns-based metrics for better understanding the tourism behaviour. Qual. Quant. **60**(2), 6157–6184 (2026)
4. Amen, M.A., Afara, A., Nia, H.A.: Exploring the link between street layout centrality and walkability for sustainable tourism in historical urban areas. Urban Sci. **7**(2) (2023)
5. Ayres, J., Flannick, J., Gehrke, J., Yiu, T.: Sequential pattern mining using a bitmap representation. In: ACM SIGKDD, pp. 429–435. KDD '02 (2002)
6. Cai, G., Hio, C., Bermingham, L., Lee, K., Lee, I.: Mining frequent trajectory patterns and regions-of-interest from flickr photos. In: HICS'14 (2014)
7. Chareyron, G., Quelhas, U., Travers, N.: Tourism analysis on graphs with neo4tourism, pp. 37–44 (2020). WISE'20
8. Chatzopoulou, E., Travers, N.: Authenticity goes digital: a big data analysis of the influence of the country of origin and authenticity perceptions on tripAdvisor ethnic restaurant reviews. (). from micro to macro: dealing with uncertainties in the global marketplace (2022)
9. Choe, Y., Lee, C.K., Choi, J., Kim, M., won Sim, K.: Identifying tourist spatial and temporal patterns using GPS and sequence alignment method. JTR **62**(6), 1181–1201 (2023)
10. Chua, A., Servillo, L., Marcheggiani, E., Moere, A.V.: Mapping cilento: using geotagged social media data to characterize tourist flows in southern italy. Tour. Manage. **57**, 295–310 (2016)
11. Diestel, R.: Graph Theory, Graduate Texts in Mathematics, vol. 173, 6 edn. Springer, Heidelberg (2025)
12. Ding, D., Zheng, Y., Zhang, Y., Liu, Y.: Understanding attractions'connection patterns based on intra-destination tourist mobility: a network motif approach. Humani. Soc. Sci. Commun. **11**(1), 636 (2024)
13. Djebali, S., Loas, N., Travers, N.: Indicators for Measuring Tourist Mobility. In: Huang, Z., Beek, W., Wang, H., Zhou, R., Zhang, Y. (eds.) WISE 2020. LNCS, vol. 12342, pp. 398–413. Springer, Cham (2020). https://doi.org/10.1007/978-3-030-62005-9_29
14. Farzanyar, X., Cercone, N.: Trip pattern mining using large scale geo-tagged photos. In: ICCSIT'15, pp. 113 (2015)
15. Fournier, C., Jacquot, S.: Les traces numériques des touristes: un renouvellement de l'observation touristique? Espaces Tourisme & Loisirs **316**, 66–72 (2014)
16. Gössling, S., Scott, D., Hall, C.M.: Global trends in length of stay: implications for destination management and climate change. J. Sustain. Tour. **26**(12), 2087–2101 (2018)
17. Harianja, A.P., Tampubolon, A.: Comparative analysis of apriori, FP-growth, and eclat algorithms in determining tourist visit patterns in simalungun regency. JAIEA **5**(2), 3436–3441 (2026)

18. Höpken, W., Müller, M., Fuchs, M., Lexhagen, M.: Flickr data for analysing tourists' spatial behaviour and movement patterns: a comparison of clustering techniques. J. Hospitality Tourism Technol. **11**(1), 69–82 (2020)
19. Huff, D.L.: Defining and estimating a trading area. J. Mark. **28**(3), 34–38 (1964)
20. Jacquot, S., Mondo, M., Travers, N., Chareyron, G.: La métropolisation touristique au prisme des traces numériques: la métropole européenne de lille entre enquêtes et observatoire. Bull. de l'Assoc. de Géographes Français 102(1) (2025)
21. Kanrak, M., Lean, H.H., Nonthapot, S.: Analysis of tourism destination centrality and structural properties of tourism system: complex network perspective. Uncertain Supply Chain Manag. **12**, 115–124 (2024)
22. Lee, I., Cai, G., Lee, K.: Exploration of geo-tagged photos through data mining approaches. Expert Syst. Appl. **41**(2), 397–405 (2014)
23. Liu, S., et al.: STGIN: spatial-temporal graph interaction network for large-scale POI recommendation. In: CIKM'23, pp. 4120–4124 (2023)
24. Liu, W., et al.: Cluster analysis of microscopic spatio-temporal patterns of tourists' movement behaviors in mountainous scenic areas using open GPS-trajectory data. Tourism Manag. **93**, 104614 (2022)
25. March, R., Woodside, A.G.: Tourism behaviour: travellers' decisions and actions. CABI Publishing (2005)
26. Martin-Prin, J., Ouled Dlala, I., Travers, N., Jabbour, S.: A distributed SAT-based framework for closed frequent itemset mining. In: ADMA'22 (2022)
27. Orellana, D., Bregt, A.K., Ligtenberg, A., Wachowicz, M.: Exploring visitor movement patterns in natural recreational areas. Tourism Manag. **33**(3) (2012)
28. Pan, X., Liu, T., Yan, L.: Exploring structural heterogeneity and organizational patterns of tourist flow networks among motivational subgroups. Plos One **20**(6), e0323558 (2025)
29. Park, S., Zhong, R.R.: Pattern recognition of travel mobility in a city destination: application of network motif analytics. JTR **61**(5), 1201–1216 (2022)
30. Pei, J., et al.: PrefixSpan: mining sequential patterns efficiently by prefix-projected pattern growth. In: ICDE'01, pp. 215–224 (2001)
31. Peng, S., Yamamoto, A.: Mining Disjoint Sequential Pattern Pairs from Tourist Trajectory Data. In: Appice, A., Tsoumakas, G., Manolopoulos, Y., Matwin, S. (eds.) DS 2020. LNCS (LNAI), vol. 12323, pp. 645–658. Springer, Cham (2020). https://doi.org/10.1007/978-3-030-61527-7_42
32. Prevoteau, H., Djebali, S., Laiping, Z., Travers, N.: Propagation measure on circulation graphs for tourism behavior analysis. In: SAC'22, pp. 556–563 (2022)
33. Sun, Y., Fan, H., Helbich, M., Zipf, A.: Analyzing human activities through volunteered geographic information: using flickr to analyze spatial and temporal patterns of tourist accommodation. In: Krisp, J.M. (ed.) Progress in Location-Based Services. LNCS, pp. 57–69. Springer, Berlin, Heidelberg (2013). https://doi.org/10.1007/978-3-642-34203-5_4
34. Vu, H.Q., Li, G., Law, R., Ye, B.H.: Exploring the travel behaviors of inbound tourists to Hong Kong using geotagged photos. Tour. Manage. **46** (2015)
35. Wang, L., et al.: Bi-Level Graph Structure Learning for Next POI Recommendation. TKDE **36**(11) (2024)
36. Xu, D., Zhang, J.H., Huang, Z., Zhou, Y., Fan, Q.: Tourism community detection: a space of flows perspective. Tourism Manag. **93**, 104577 (2022)
37. Yan, X., et al.: Spatio-temporal hypergraph learning for next POI recommendation. In: SIGIR'23 (2023)
38. Yang, L., Wu, L., Liu, Y., Kang, C.: Quantifying tourist behavior patterns by travel motifs and geo-tagged photos from flickr. Int. J. Geo-Info 6(11) (2017)

39. Zaki, M.J.: SPADE: an efficient algorithm for mining frequent sequences. Mach. Learn. **42**, 31–60 (2001)
40. Zheng, Y.T., Zha, Z.J., Chua, T.S.: Mining travel patterns from geotagged photos. ACM TIST **3**(3) (2012)
41. Zheng, Y., Zhang, Y., Makkonen, T., Li, M., Mou, N., Liu, Y.: Rethinking the community detection for tourist mobility networks: special structures and their implications for tourism. Inf. Technol. Tourism **28**(1), 12 (2025)

A Survey on Multisided Fairness in Recommender Systems

Reza Shafiloo(✉), Maria Stratigi, and Kostas Stefanidis

Data Science Research Centre, Tampere University, Tampere, Finland
{reza.shafiloo,maria.stratigi,konstantinos.stefanidis}@tuni.fi

Abstract. While traditional recommender systems primarily optimize recommendation accuracy, growing attention has been devoted to fairness, as decisions can create unequal outcomes for different affected parties. This challenge is particularly important in multisided recommender systems, where recommendations influence not only consumers but also providers, items, and platforms. In this survey, we review the literature on multisided fairness in recommender systems. We discuss key stakeholder groups, fairness objectives, and fairness-aware recommendation methods, including pre-processing, in-processing, and post-processing approaches. We further examine recommendation settings with limited item availability, where recommendation becomes an allocation problem and fairness must be considered across multiple interactions. Finally, we outline open challenges and future research directions.

Keywords: Multisided Fairness · Multi-Stakeholder Recommendations · Fairness-aware Recommendations

1 Introduction

Recommender systems increasingly mediate access to information, products, services, and opportunities across digital platforms, including e-commerce, news, health, education, tourism, and entertainment systems [9,28]. They typically learn from historical interactions, such as ratings, clicks, reviews, and purchases, and use these signals to predict which items are likely to match each user's interests. However, because recommendation models are trained on historical data, they may reproduce and amplify existing biases. For example, popular items may receive repeated exposure, while less popular items remain less visible [15]. Similarly, active users may receive higher-quality recommendations because they provide more interaction data, whereas less active users may receive lower-quality recommendations. Fairness in recommendation becomes particularly challenging in multisided environments, where recommendation decisions affect several stakeholders simultaneously. Consumers may expect accurate and useful recommendations, providers may seek fair visibility for their items, items may require balanced exposure, and platforms may need to balance engagement, revenue, and long-term ecosystem health. These objectives are not always aligned: improving

G. Vargas-Solar et al. (Eds.): ADBIS 2026, LNCS 16937, pp. 446–456, 2027.
https://doi.org/10.1007/978-3-032-39820-8_30

fairness or utility for one stakeholder may reduce the opportunities or benefits of another [21,28]. Therefore, fairness-aware recommendation should not be studied only from a single stakeholder perspective.

These challenges have motivated growing research on multisided fairness in recommender systems. Multisided fairness examines how recommendation decisions distribute utility, exposure, opportunities, and benefits across multiple affected parties, and how potentially competing fairness objectives can be balanced. A particularly underexplored setting arises when recommended items have limited availability, such as limited seats, tickets, appointments, or products. In such cases, recommendation is not only a ranking problem but also an allocation problem, because assigning a scarce item to one user can reduce the opportunity for other users to receive the same item. In this survey, we review the emerging literature on multisided fairness in recommender systems. We discuss key stakeholder groups, fairness objectives, and fairness-aware recommendation methods. We further examine recommendation settings with limited item availability, where fairness must be considered across multiple interactions and over time. Finally, we outline open challenges and future research directions.

2 Fairness in Recommender Systems

Bias and Fairness Concerns. Recommender systems learn from historical user interactions, such as ratings, clicks, purchases, and reviews. As a result, they can inherit and amplify biases present in the data or introduced by the recommendation process itself. One of the most widely studied examples is popularity bias, where popular items receive disproportionately high exposure while less popular items remain under-represented. Since popular items typically generate more interaction data, recommendation models can estimate their relevance more accurately, which further reinforces their visibility. This feedback loop can limit catalog coverage, reduce recommendation diversity, and hinder the discovery of niche or long-tail items [17]. Biases can also affect different entities involved in recommendation. Consumers with rich interaction histories often receive more accurate recommendations than consumers with limited historical data, creating disparities in recommendation quality [10]. Similarly, providers may experience unequal visibility when recommendation algorithms repeatedly favor well-established providers over smaller or less active ones. Such disparities illustrate that recommendation quality alone is insufficient for evaluating a recommender system. The distribution of opportunities, exposure, and benefits across affected entities must also be considered.

Fairness has therefore emerged as an important objective in recommender systems. It refers to the equitable treatment of entities affected by recommendation decisions [23]. Existing work studies fairness from different perspectives, including consumer fairness, provider fairness and item fairness [10]. Depending on the application, fairness may aim to ensure comparable recommendation quality across consumers, balanced exposure among providers, equitable visibility of items, or reduced disparities between protected and non-protected groups.

Since these objectives are often conflicting, fairness is typically formulated as a trade-off between recommendation utility and equitable outcomes.

Fairness-Aware Recommendation Methods. Existing fairness-aware recommendation methods are commonly grouped into pre-processing, in-processing, and post-processing approaches [23]. Pre-processing methods address unfairness before model training by modifying the input data. Their objective is to reduce biases embedded in historical interactions, ratings, or user behavior patterns. Representative approaches include data balancing, causal data repair, synthetic data generation, and bias mitigation techniques that alter the training distribution before learning takes place [5,7,13,26]. By improving the quality and representativeness of the input data, these methods aim to prevent unfair patterns from being learned by the recommendation model. In-processing methods incorporate fairness directly into the learning process. These approaches modify the recommendation algorithm by introducing fairness-aware objective functions, regularization terms, constraints, or optimization strategies [4,32,36,38]. The model is trained to jointly optimize recommendation quality and fairness objectives, allowing fairness considerations to become part of the model behavior itself. As a result, in-processing methods can provide stronger fairness guarantees, although they often require changes to the underlying recommendation architecture. Post-processing methods introduce fairness after recommendation scores or ranked lists have been produced. These methods adjust the output of an existing recommender through re-ranking, score modification, or allocation strategies [8,12,31]. Because they do not require retraining the recommendation model, post-processing approaches are particularly attractive in deployed systems where modifying the underlying algorithm may be costly or impractical. Existing work further distinguishes between non-parametric methods, which rely on heuristic or rule-based adjustments, and parametric methods, which learn parameters that guide the fairness-aware re-ranking process [18].

Overall, fairness-aware recommendation seeks to balance recommendation utility with equitable outcomes across affected entities. While early research primarily focused on consumer-side fairness, recent studies increasingly recognize that recommendation decisions affect multiple stakeholders simultaneously. This observation has motivated the development of multisided fairness approaches, which consider the interests and fairness objectives of several stakeholder groups within the same recommendation process.

3 Multisided Fairness in Recommender Systems

Motivation. Traditional fairness-aware recommender systems primarily focus on the fairness experienced by consumers. However, recommendation decisions often affect multiple entities simultaneously. In many application domains, recommendations influence not only the users who receive them, but also the providers that supply items, the items competing for visibility, and the platforms that mediate these interactions. Consequently, fairness cannot be viewed solely as a consumer-side objective. This observation has motivated the study of multisided fairness in recommender systems. A recommender system is considered multisided when recommendation outcomes affect the utility, opportunities, or benefits of multiple stakeholder groups. Typical examples include online marketplaces, media platforms, recruitment systems, and crowdsourcing platforms, where recommendations directly influence both demand-side and supply-side participants [16,19,22]. In these environments, recommendation decisions determine not only which items consumers discover, but also which providers gain visibility and which items receive exposure. The need for multisided fairness arises because recommendation objectives across stakeholders are often interdependent. Improving recommendation quality for consumers may concentrate exposure among a small number of providers, while increasing provider visibility may reduce consumer utility. Similarly, platform objectives such as revenue maximization or marketplace sustainability may not always align with the interests of consumers or providers [21,22,24]. As a result, recommendation decisions frequently involve trade-offs among competing fairness and utility objectives.

The literature increasingly recognizes that fairness should be evaluated beyond a single stakeholder perspective [6,34]. Existing studies have shown that recommendation algorithms can amplify popularity bias, interaction bias, and exposure inequalities, creating systematic advantages for active consumers, popular items, or dominant providers [29,30,32]. If such effects remain unaddressed, they can reduce marketplace diversity, discourage provider participation, and weaken user trust in the recommendation process [22,34]. Therefore, multisided fairness aims to balance the interests of multiple stakeholders while maintaining the overall effectiveness and sustainability of the recommender system.

Stakeholders. The literature identifies several recurring stakeholder categories in recommender systems. Although the exact stakeholders depend on the application domain, consumers, providers, items, and platforms constitute the most common stakeholder groups.

Consumers. Consumers are the recipients of recommendations and are traditionally the primary focus of recommender systems. Their objective is to receive relevant, useful, and personalized recommendations. Fairness at the consumer level typically concerns the equitable distribution of recommendation quality across users or user groups [21,22,35]. For example, in recruitment systems, consumers may correspond to job seekers or candidates [19,27].

Providers. Providers supply the items or services that are recommended. Their objective is to obtain visibility, engagement, and economic benefit through recommendation exposure. Provider fairness aims to prevent recommendation opportunities from being concentrated among a small subset of providers and seeks a more equitable distribution of exposure across the provider population [24,30,34,37]. Depending on the domain, providers may correspond to merchants, content creators, publishers, organizations, or employers.

Items. Items can also be treated as stakeholders when fairness concerns the allocation of recommendation exposure among individual items. This perspective is particularly relevant in the presence of popularity bias, where a small number of highly popular items dominate recommendation lists while many relevant items remain under-exposed [29]. Item-level fairness is also important in settings where providers maintain large inventories and fairness is desired both across and within provider catalogs.

Platforms. The platform acts as an intermediary between consumers and providers and controls the recommendation process. In addition to facilitating interactions, platforms often pursue objectives such as revenue generation, user retention, marketplace growth, and long-term sustainability [11,20,22,25]. For this reason, several studies explicitly treat the platform as a stakeholder whose objectives must be balanced against consumer and provider fairness.

Domain-Specific Stakeholders. Some application domains involve additional actors whose interests are influenced by recommendation decisions. For example, recruitment systems may include recruiters and hiring managers [19,27], while crowdsourcing platforms may involve workers, requesters, and workplaces [16]. These examples highlight that stakeholder definitions should be adapted to the characteristics of the application and the decision-making process supported by the recommender system.

Overall, multisided fairness requires considering how recommendation decisions affect multiple stakeholders simultaneously. Because stakeholder objectives are often competing, fairness is increasingly viewed as a problem of balancing utility, exposure, opportunities, and long-term benefits across all affected parties.

Methods. Similar to fairness-aware recommender systems, methods for multisided fairness can be categorized into pre-processing, in-processing, and post-processing approaches, while the specific techniques used in each category may differ according to the stakeholder, fairness goal, and system setting. In addition, many recent approaches formulate multisided fairness as a multi-objective optimization problem, where the utilities of different stakeholders are jointly considered during recommendation generation [11,33].

Pre-processing methods introduce fairness before model training by modifying the data used to learn recommendations. These methods are useful when unfairness comes from biased interaction data, popularity imbalance, or under-representation of some stakeholder groups. Different pre-processing strategies have been used in the literature. Some approaches inject synthetic ratings for tail items to reduce popularity bias and improve long-tail visibility [14]. Other methods balance the training data by changing the representation of protected groups, such as increasing the presence of women artists in music recommendation [2]. A further strategy uses upsampling to increase the influence of minority providers or under-represented provider groups during relevance learning [3]. In multi-stakeholder settings, these methods can support provider and item fairness by giving less visible providers, minority groups, or long-tail items more learning signals. However, pre-processing may be less effective when unfairness is mainly created during ranking, exposure allocation, or platform-level optimization.

In-processing methods integrate fairness directly into the learning or optimization process. These methods modify the objective function, representation learning, or training weights so that the model learns to balance recommendation quality with stakeholder fairness. Some approaches use adaptive weighting to increase the effect of disadvantaged users or under-exposed providers during training [35]. Others use adversarial learning, graph neural networks, robust optimization, or debiasing techniques to reduce provider bias, regional bias, or group-level performance gaps [24,27,32,36]. In this group, multi-objective optimization is often used as a learning strategy, because the model must jointly consider consumer utility, provider exposure, item visibility, and sometimes platform revenue [11,33]. Depending on the application, optimization objectives may combine consumer relevance, provider exposure fairness, item diversity, and platform utility, requiring the system to balance potentially conflicting goals. Thus, in-processing methods are suitable when fairness should be part of the model behavior itself, not only a correction applied after recommendations are produced.

Post-processing methods introduce fairness after a baseline recommender has produced relevance scores or ranked lists. These methods usually re-rank items, adjust scores, or allocate recommendation slots by combining relevance with fairness terms for consumers, providers, or items. They are common in multi-stakeholder recommendation because they can be applied to existing systems without retraining the base model. Some methods balance consumer and producer fairness through optimization-based re-ranking [21,25]. Others use fair allocation principles, max-min fairness, or exposure guarantees to improve provider visibility while preserving consumer utility. These approaches often view recommendation exposure as a resource that should be distributed across stakeholders according to fairness criteria, such as proportionality, equality of opportunity, or minimum exposure guarantees [22,34,37]. Post-processing can also support item and platform fairness through weighted re-ranking or profit-aware re-ranking [20,29]. In limited item settings, this group can become an allocation method, where scarce items are assigned by fairness-adjusted scores and delivery histories [30]. In such scenarios, fairness must be evaluated not only at the level of individual recommendations but also across repeated allocation decisions over time.

4 Evaluation Metrics

Evaluation in multi-stakeholder recommenders should measure how recommendation outcomes affect different stakeholders and how fairness interventions influence the trade-off between utility and equitable outcomes. It should not only report ranking quality for consumers but also show whether consumers, providers, items, and platforms receive balanced outcomes. Therefore, evaluation metrics can be organized into consumer-side, provider-side, item-side, platform-side.

Consumer-side metrics evaluate whether users receive fair and useful recommendations. Many works measure consumer fairness by comparing recommendation quality across user groups, such as active and inactive users, protected and unprotected groups, or mainstream and non-mainstream users [25,29,32,36]. Common metrics include performance gap, NDCG difference, prediction error gap, and deviation from consumer fairness. Some works also use individual-level metrics, such as the min-max ratio, to check whether some users receive much worse recommendation quality than others [37]. In hiring recommendation, fairness can also be measured through qualification-aware or opportunity-based metrics [19,27]. Also, entropy-based metrics can be used to evaluate how evenly consumers receive limited items from different provider categories over time [30].

Provider-side metrics evaluate whether providers receive fair visibility or exposure in recommendation lists. These metrics are important because exposure is linked to economic opportunity and long-term participation. Common metrics include exposure disparity, exposure ratio, disparate visibility, Gini index, entropy, max-min fairness, and variance or coefficient of variation of provider exposure [11,29,30,34,35,37]. Some works also use exposure guarantees, such as maximin share, or measure the fraction of providers that receive enough exposure [22]. **Item-side** metrics evaluate whether items receive balanced recommendation opportunities. This is needed because provider fairness does not always imply item fairness. A provider may receive enough exposure, while only a few popular items in its inventory are repeatedly recommended. Common item-side metrics include long-tail coverage, catalog coverage, novelty, entropy of item exposure, average percentage of long-tail items, and deviation from item fairness [14,29]. Some works also compare exposure across item groups, such as high-price and low-price items, or popular and less popular items [20,21].

Platform-side and system-level metrics evaluate whether fairness is achieved while preserving broader platform goals. These goals may include revenue, profit, engagement, or long-term sustainability. Some works report revenue-related metrics, such as gains, price, spending, or pay-per-click, together with consumer and provider fairness metrics [11,20]. In limited item recommendation, system-level fairness can also be measured through allocation-based metrics, such as cumulative delivery distribution [30]. This metric shows whether scarce items reach a broader set of consumers, which can increase the chance of purchase and support platform revenue over time. Overall, evaluating multisided fairness remains challenging because improvements for one stakeholder may come at the expense of another. As a result, recent studies increasingly report multiple fairness and utility metrics simultaneously, providing a more comprehensive view of recommendation quality across the entire recommendation ecosystem [6,29].

5 Multisided Fairness Under Limited Item Availability

Most fairness-aware recommender systems assume that recommended items are always available. However, many real-world applications involve limited resources, such as event tickets, hotel rooms, healthcare appointments, course seats, or limited-edition products. In these settings, recommendation is not only a ranking problem but also an allocation problem. Specifically, allocating a scarce item to one consumer may reduce or eliminate the opportunity for other consumers to receive the same item. Consequently, fairness depends not only on recommendation relevance but also on how opportunities are distributed among stakeholders over time. This setting introduces additional challenges for multisided fairness, as recommendation decisions affect both consumers competing for limited resources and providers whose inventories are allocated through the recommendation process. Recent work has begun to address fairness under limited availability. [1] studies recommendation loss in multi-session recommendation settings and propose compensation mechanisms that reduce disparities among consumers who miss access to preferred items. More recently, [30] introduces EQUALI, a framework that extends fairness considerations to both consumers and providers. The framework incorporates historical interactions and previous allocation outcomes into the recommendation process, aiming to distribute limited recommendation opportunities more fairly across multiple stakeholders.

6 Open Challenges and Future Directions

Despite significant progress, several challenges remain open for achieving fair recommendation outcomes across multiple stakeholders.

Balancing Multiple Fairness Objectives. Multisided recommender systems must often balance competing objectives across consumers, providers, items, and platforms. Improving fairness for one stakeholder may negatively affect another stakeholder's utility or exposure. Designing recommendation algorithms that effectively navigate these trade-offs while maintaining recommendation quality remains a fundamental challenge.

Evaluation Metrics for Multisided Fairness. Existing evaluation metrics primarily focus on individual stakeholders, such as recommendation accuracy for consumers or exposure fairness for providers. However, there is no widely accepted framework for jointly evaluating fairness across multiple stakeholders. Developing evaluation methodologies that capture the overall fairness of a recommendation ecosystem remains an important research direction.

Dynamic and Longitudinal Fairness. Fairness is often evaluated within a single recommendation session, whereas recommendation decisions frequently have long-term consequences. Historical interactions, accumulated exposure, and previous allocation decisions can influence future opportunities for both consumers and providers. This challenge becomes particularly important in settings with limited item availability, where fairness depends on how scarce opportunities are distributed over time.

Explainability and Transparency. As recommender systems increasingly incorporate fairness objectives, stakeholders may seek explanations for recommendation and allocation decisions. Providing transparent and understandable explanations can help users, providers, and platform operators understand potential fairness trade-offs and increase trust in the recommendation process. Integrating explainability with multisided fairness remains largely unexplored.

Real-World Deployment and User Studies. Most existing approaches are evaluated using offline experiments and benchmark datasets. However, the practical impact of multisided fairness interventions on consumer behavior, provider participation, and platform sustainability is still not well understood. More real-world deployments, online evaluations, and user studies are needed to assess the effectiveness of fairness-aware recommendation strategies in practice.

Disclosure of Interests. The authors have no competing interests to declare that are relevant to the content of this article.

References

1. Azzalini, D., Azzalini, F., Criscuolo, C., Dolci, T., Martinenghi, D., Amer-Yahia, S.: Loss compensation in multi-session recommendation under limited availability. In: EDBT, pp. 522–533 (2024)
2. Bauer, C., Ferraro, A.: Strategies for mitigating artist gender bias in music recommendation: a simulation study. In: Music Recommender Systems Workshop (2023)
3. Boratto, L., Fenu, G., Marras, M.: Interplay between upsampling and regularization for provider fairness in recommender systems. User Model. User-Adap. Inter. **31**(3), 421–455 (2021)
4. Borges, R., Stefanidis, K.: Feature-blind fairness in collaborative filtering recommender systems. Knowl. Inf. Syst. **64**(4), 943–962 (2022)
5. Brunet, M.E., Alkalay-Houlihan, C., Anderson, A., Zemel, R.: Understanding the origins of bias in word embeddings. In: Machine Learning, pp. 803–811 (2019)
6. Burke, R., et al.: De-centering the (Traditional) user: multistakeholder evaluation of recommender systems. Int. J. Hum. Comput. Stud. **203** (2025)
7. Calmon, F., Wei, D., Vinzamuri, B., Natesan Ramamurthy, K., Varshney, K.R.: Optimized pre-processing for discrimination prevention. Adv. Neural Inf. Process. Syst., 30 (2017)
8. Carraro, D., Bridge, D.: Enhancing recommendation diversity by re-ranking with large language models. ACM Trans. Recommender Syst. (2024)
9. Dalla Vecchia, A., Migliorini, S., Quintarelli, E., Stefanidis, K.: Multi-sided fairness in sequential task assignment. Inf. Syst. **139**(3), 102700 (7 2026)
10. Deldjoo, Y., Anelli, V.W., Zamani, H., Bellogin, A., Di Noia, T.: A flexible framework for evaluating user and item fairness in recommender systems. User Model. User-Adap. Inter., 1–55 (2021)
11. Gao, H., Lu, Y., Zhu, N.: A Fairness-Aware Recommender System Based on Genetic Algorithms for User. Provider and Platform Optimization, ICAACE (2025)
12. Gómez, E., Contreras, D., Boratto, L., Salamó, M.: Enhancing recommender systems with provider fairness through preference distribution-awareness. Inf. Manage. Data Insights **5**(1), 100311 (2025)

13. González-Sendino, R., Serrano, E., Bajo, J.: Mitigating bias in artificial intelligence: fair data generation via causal models for transparent and explainable decision-making. Futur. Gener. Comput. Syst. **155**, 384–401 (2024)
14. Gulsoy, M., Yalcin, E., Bilge, A.: EquiRate: balanced rating injection approach for popularity bias mitigation in recommender systems. PeerJ Comput. Sci. **11** (2025)
15. Hamedani, E.M., Kaedi, M.: Recommending the long tail items through personalized diversification. Knowl.-Based Syst. **164**, 348–357 (2019)
16. Huang, W., Li, P., Li, B., Liu, Q., Nie, L., Bao, H.: Three-sided online stable task assignment in spatial crowdsourcing. Inf. Sci. **654**, 119878 (1 2024)
17. Jain, A., Singh, P.K., Dhar, J.: Multi-objective item evaluation for diverse as well as novel item recommendations. Expert Syst. Appl. **139** (2020)
18. Jin, D., et al.: A survey on fairness-aware recommender systems. CoRR abs/2306.00403 (2023)
19. Kaya, M., Bogers, T.: Mapping stakeholder needs to multi-sided fairness in candidate recommendation for algorithmic hiring. RecSys., 257–267 (2025)
20. Liu, S., et al.: Towards platform profit-aware fairness in personalized recommendation. Int. J. Mach. Learn. Cybern. **15**(10), 4341–4356 (2024)
21. Naghiaei, M., Rahmani, H.A., Deldjoo, Y.: CPFair: personalized consumer and producer fairness re-ranking for recommender systems. In: ACM SIGIR (2022)
22. Patro, G.K., Biswas, A., Ganguly, N., Gummadi, K.P., Chakraborty, A.: FairRec: two-sided fairness for personalized recommendations in two-sided platforms. In: The Web Conference (2020)
23. Pitoura, E., Stefanidis, K., Koutrika, G.: Fairness in rankings and recommendations: an overview. VLDB J. **31**(3), 431–458 (2022)
24. Qi, T., et al.: ProFairRec: provider Fairness-aware News Recommendation. SIGIR, pp. 1164–1173 (2022)
25. Rahmani, H.A., Naghiaei, M., Deldjoo, Y.: A Personalized framework for consumer and producer group fairness optimization in recommender systems. ACM Trans. Recommender Syst. **2**(3), 1–24 (9 2024)
26. Salimi, B., Rodriguez, L., Howe, B., Suciu, D.: Interventional fairness: causal database repair for algorithmic fairness. In: SIGMOD, pp. 793–810 (2019)
27. Schellingerhout, R., Barile, F., Tintarev, N.: OKRA: an explainable, heterogeneous, multi-stakeholder job recommender system. In: Advances in IR (2025)
28. Shafiloo, R., Kaedi, M., Pourmiri, A.: Considering user dynamic preferences for mitigating negative effects of long-tail in recommender systems. Inf. Sci. **669**, 120558 (2024)
29. Shafiloo, R., Stratigi, M., Peltonen, J., Olsson, T., Stefanidis, K.: The many facets of fairness in recommender systems: consumers, providers and items. Inf. Syst. **137**, 102643 (2026)
30. Shafiloo, R., Stratigi, M., Peltonen, J., Stefanidis, K.: Multisided fairness under limited item availability in recommender systems. Inf. Sci. **731** (2026)
31. Stratigi, M., Nummenmaa, J., Pitoura, E., Stefanidis, K.: Fair sequential group recommendations. In: SAC, pp. 1443–1452 (2020)
32. Tang, J., Shen, S., Wang, Z., Gong, Z., Zhang, J., Chen, X.: When fairness meets bias: a debiased framework for fairness aware top-n recommendation, RecSys (2023)
33. Wu, H., Ma, C., Mitra, B., Diaz, F., Liu, X.: A Multi-Objective Optimization Framework for Multi-Stakeholder Fairness-Aware Recommendation. ACM Trans. Inf. Syst. **41**(2) (2022)
34. Xu, C., et al.: P-MMF: provider max-min fairness re-ranking in recommender system. In: The Web Conference (2023)

35. Xu, L., Lin, Z., Wang, J., Chen, S., Zhao, W.X., Wen, J.R.: Promoting two-sided fairness with adaptive weights for providers and customers in recommendation. RecSys (2024)
36. Yang, H., Liu, Z., Zhang, Z., Zhuang, C., Chen, X.: Towards robust fairness-aware recommendation, RecSys (2023)
37. Ye, X., et al.: Regret-aware Re-ranking for guaranteeing two-sided fairness and accuracy in recommender systems. ACM Trans. Inf. Syst. **1**(1) (2025)
38. Zehlike, M., Yang, K., Stoyanovich, J.: Fairness in ranking, part II: learning-to-rank and recommender systems. ACM Comput. Surv. **55**(6), 1–41 (2022)

Author Index

G. Vargas-Solar et al. (Eds.): ADBIS 2026, LNCS 16937, pp. 457–458, 2027.
https://doi.org/10.1007/978-3-032-39820-8

MIX
Papier aus verantwortungsvollen Quellen
Paper from responsible sources
FSC® C105338

If you have any concerns about our products,
you can contact us on
ProductSafety@springernature.com

In case Publisher is established outside the EU,
the EU authorized representative is:
Springer Nature Customer Service Center GmbH
Europaplatz 3, 69115 Heidelberg, Germany

Printed by Libri Plureos GmbH
in Hamburg, Germany